Basic Problems

of

Philosophy

PRENTICE-HALL PHILOSOPHY SERIES
Arthur E. Murphy, Ph.D., Editor

Basic Problems
of
Philosophy

Selected Readings with Introductions

---

edited by

DANIEL J. BRONSTEIN
YERVANT H. KRIKORIAN
PHILIP P. WIENER

Professors of Philosophy
The City College, New York

SECOND EDITION

Englewood Cliffs

PRENTICE-HALL, INC.

First printing .... June, 1955
Second printing .... January, 1956
Third printing .... June, 1957
Fourth printing .... March, 1959
Fifth printing .... June, 1960
Sixth printing .... June, 1961

PRINTED IN THE UNITED STATES OF AMERICA
06767—C

Preface to the Second Edition

TO MAKE THIS BOOK more readable and more useful for the teaching of philosophy, some of the selections from the first edition have been eliminated, and a number of new readings have been added. Many of the changes were suggested by teachers who used the first edition and were kind enough to give us the benefit of their experience and judgment. We wish to thank especially, among these, Professor Ellery B. Haskell, Professor Paul O. Kristeller, Professor Henry M. Magid, Professor Arthur E. Murphy, Professor Murray Stolnitz, Professor Harry Tarter, and Dr. Michael Wyschogrod for their criticisms and helpful ideas.

D. J. B.
Y. H. K.
P. P. W.

Preface to the First Edition

THIS VOLUME has been prepared to introduce the reader—layman or student—to the problems of philosophy through the writings of some of the outstanding philosophers. The selections have been grouped around the major philosophical problems. Since many of these are interconnected, any classification is bound to be somewhat arbitrary, and reading the selections in a different order will not impair their value. No attempt has been made to include all schools of thought or to discuss all the problems of philosophy; the guiding aim has been to present diverse views on the basic problems in order to encourage the reader to do his own thinking. It is hoped that he will soon discern the breadth of vision and consecutiveness of thought that characterize philosophy.

We have coöperated with one another on the selections and the introductions, but the responsibility for the chapters is as follows:

Chapters One, Five, and Nine	Daniel J. Bronstein
Chapters Two, Three, and Four	Philip P. Wiener
Chapters Six, Seven, and Eight	Yervant H. Krikorian

We gratefully acknowledge our indebtedness to Professor Milton K. Munitz of New York University for attending our conferences and for his many fruitful suggestions and valuable criticisms.

D. J. B.
Y. H. K.
P. P. W.

Contents

CHAPTER THREE
Philosophy of Politics and History

CHAPTER FOUR
Philosophy of Science

CHAPTER FIVE
Theory of Knowledge

CHAPTER SIX

Theories of Art and Aesthetic Experience

CHAPTER SEVEN

The Philosophy of Religion

CHAPTER EIGHT

Theories of Reality

CHAPTER NINE

What Is Philosophy?

Basic Problems

of

Philosophy

Chapter One

METHODOLOGY

INTRODUCTION

A N experienced mountain climber planning to ascend a difficult peak makes a survey of the existing trails before starting out. He may find that one trail goes only part of the way up, that another is dangerous in wet weather, or that a third requires special climbing equipment. After trying all the trails, he may blaze a new one better than the others.

A mouse in a maze doesn't pause to examine alternative routes to see which will lead most rapidly to his goal. Confronted by a problem beyond his capacity to solve except by the "method of trial and error," he enters and re-enters the same blind alleys until he finally "learns" the maze.

In our search for knowledge we try to emulate the mountain climber, but there are times when, because of a lack of systematic knowledge, we can do no better than to adopt the tactics of the mouse.

The selections that follow illustrate or describe some of the methods philosophers and scientists have developed to reach the goals they set themselves. It is important to be aware of these ends before evaluating the methods used in attaining them. Just as one mountain climber may prefer a winding scenic trail which does not reach the highest point, while another is intent on reaching the top by the shortest route, so one philosopher may devote his energies to the clarification of such fundamental common notions as virtue, knowledge, justice, and human happiness, as Socrates did, while another, Descartes, for example, is satisfied with nothing less than the reconstruction of the entire edifice of human knowledge on secure foundations. Others may be primarily interested in a correct understanding of natural phenomena, as Bacon was, or in the genesis and justification of human beliefs, like Peirce.

Amidst this diversity of subject matter it may be asked: What is the unifying feature of this chapter? It is the concern with those procedures and techniques which have been devised to aid us in extending our knowledge—that is to say, in clarifying and justifying what we already know, as well as in discovering what is still unknown. This is what we shall mean by *methodology*.

In this sense, methodological issues may arise not only in the context of philosophical discussion but in mathematics, natural science, law, economics, and so on.

They arise most conspicuously where two competing methodologies both claim dominion over an area of human experience. In such a case, a methodological conflict occurs, as, for example, the one between religion and science. Each of the sciences, for example, astronomy, geology, medicine, biology (the theory of evolution), has had to establish its claims and vindicate its methods against the opposition of an entrenched theology. The sciences were victorious, but the conflict continues today in such fields as ethics and social policy. Still unsettled is a question such as, "Is right conduct to be determined by standards laid down in sacred texts, or by the laws and customs of a particular community, or by the dictates of individual conscience, or by some other method?" Such a question shows the interrelations of methodology with other branches of philosophy treated in this book, for example, with the philosophy of religion, the philosophy of politics, and ethics. Perplexing questions like this should be clarified by a study of the methods developed by philosophers to help decrease the extent of human ignorance.

The Socratic method is frequently tagged as the "method of question and answer," implying that Socrates is a destructive critic who makes no positive contribution to the discussion. But let us see whether such a conception can be justified by Socrates' actual performance. What kind of question does he ask to open the discussion? How does he proceed when it is answered, as it usually is, in the conventional manner? We will find that he starts with some innocent sounding but difficult question such as, "What is knowledge?" or "Do you think that it is worse to commit, or to suffer, injustice?" The answer is likely to be an ill-considered generalization of ordinary experience. Socrates continues by asking leading questions about our ordinary experience, which, because they appear unrelated to the original hypothesis, catch his companion off guard; eventually the answers reveal an inconsistency between the generalization and the admitted facts of experience. This is likely to lead to a redefinition of the fundamental concept, whether it is knowledge, justice, courage, friendship, or pleasure. The new definition is then subjected to the same sort of critical examination as the old one. Often all proposed definitions are found wanting. Although the reader may be dissatisfied because of the negative character of the results, Socrates considers it no small achievement to produce an awareness of the inadequacy of commonly accepted notions, for such an awareness is a prerequisite to the search for satisfactory definitions. Perhaps Socrates' most notable contribution to logic and methodology was his emphasis on the importance of clearly defined concepts.

The attempt to clarify fundamental ideas is an arduous undertaking, and most people are not likely to engage in it voluntarily. As self-appointed gadfly, challenging the conventional but unexamined opinions held by his fellow Athenians, Socrates induced them to think about such things as the meaning of justice and the function of a state. The clarification of ethical and political concepts was the immediate goal of the Socratic inquiry. But in the broader context of enlightened action, the analysis served as a guide for personal and social conduct. Socrates, and his disciples too, did not hesitate to carry his principles into the political arena. For his interest was not primarily in the meaning of words, but rather in the creation of a just state and the realization of the good life.

The didactic function of the Socratic method, in aiding us to probe beneath clichés and conventional dogmas, has long been recognized. In the hands of a skillful teacher it can be of great assistance, enabling the student to cultivate a critical attitude towards generalizations and to discover for himself why his position is untenable and how to reformulate it more adequately. It can easily be abused, however, and often is by self-styled dialecticians who are able only to reproduce Socrates' irony without his wisdom and whose sole purpose is to create confusion and to heap ridicule on an opponent. If Socrates himself appears, on occasion, to be doing this (for example, when questioning Thrasymachus), it should be recalled that he was often arguing with clever Sophists whose bluster and cunning would otherwise have carried the audience, and that his main purpose, in such cases, was to help lift the fog which the Sophists had knowingly spread over fundamental ideas. When dealing with the Athenian youths who were interested in knowledge, his manner and method were noticeably mellower.

Descartes (1596–1650), like Socrates before him, felt the need of exposing the vain pretensions mistaken by his contemporaries for genuine knowledge. But for him no piecemeal reforms would suffice—only a general overhauling of all his beliefs "so that they might later on be replaced either by others which were better, or by the same, when I had made them conform to the uniformity of a rational scheme."

In describing his "method of arriving at a knowledge of all the things of which my mind was capable," Descartes says he saw no reason why the method of mathematics could not be applied to all the fields of human knowledge. This notion of a "Universal Mathematics" as the key to nature, which was suggested to Descartes by his invention of analytic geometry, did not seem extravagant in the 17th century. The discoveries of Kepler, Galileo, and Newton all seemed to substantiate it, and even in such fields as metaphysics, ethics, and jurisprudence writers attempted, following the pattern of Euclid's geometry, to derive a systematic body of truths from (so-called) self-evident axioms.

Descartes' universal doubt has been derided as both futile and disingenuous. Yet, if conscientiously carried out, a critical review of our opinions in the Cartesian fashion can have a healthy effect in unearthing prejudice and other ill-founded notions which we are all too prone to adopt without sufficient scrutiny. However, we must be courageous enough to be patient in the face of ignorance and not in too much of a hurry to substitute new dogmas for the old.

Another rebel against the teaching of the Schools, Francis Bacon (1561–1626), an older contemporary of Descartes, also proposed a program of intellectual reconstruction. Unlike the French philosopher, however, Bacon had no use for a method that starts with *a priori* principles [1] and attempts from them to deduce the nature of the world. His new method of investigation (the "inductive method"), which

---

[1] By an *a priori* principle is meant one which appears to be so clear and rational that no sense experience is needed to establish it. An example would be Aristotle's belief that *nature does nothing in vain*. Another would be that *every triangle has three sides*. A priori principles or propositions are contrasted with *a posteriori* propositions, which can only be discovered and verified by experience. Examples would be that *the earth is round*, or that *malaria is transmitted by a mosquito*. (See selection 26.) See footnotes on page 289.

stressed the importance of an observation of nature unfettered by preconceived notions, was developed in conscious opposition to the untested theorizing about nature so common among the ancients and scholastics. But in his anxiety to combat the tendency of the latter to discover natural laws by appealing to Aristotle instead of nature, he was led to undervalue the rôle of the mind in selecting and interpreting the raw data of experience. There are passages in Bacon's writings in which he pays his respects to the interpretation of the understanding (hypothesis), but he thinks of this as the last stage of the process of inquiry rather than its guiding principle. He insists on a careful tabulation of all observed data as a prerequisite to the discovery of correct laws and sound principles. And his descriptions of experiments would lead us to suppose that the method of scientific discovery is a laborious but uninspired digging for facts, from which true generalizations and laws of nature would flow as a matter of course, even as water does from the ground when we have done enough digging. If this were all there is to scientific method, we should not have had to wait for the scientific genius of a Galileo or a Newton to discover the laws of dynamics. Their fruitful hypotheses suggested experiments which would not otherwise have been performed; these led to new and improved hypotheses which were in turn verified by further observations and experiments. If their original hypotheses were not to be found in the works of Aristotle or his scholastic interpreters, neither were they gleaned from Bacon's tables of Inclusion and Exclusion. No neat formulae or shortcuts have ever been devised which can cause such hypotheses to arise in the mind. They are the product of a fertile mind that has proper regard for the facts, but that is also capable of reading a new meaning in them.

Bacon's chief contribution to philosophy was not his analysis of the method of science, which he oversimplified, but his acute dissection of the errors and fallacies of human reasoning (the famous Idols) and his recognition that the method of authority would have to be replaced by a new method before the scientific awakening which he correctly foresaw could become a reality.

Whereas Bacon was one of the most famous of the advocates of the method of science, Henri Bergson (1860–1941) was one of its most popular disparagers. To him it was a feeble instrument incapable of revealing what he considered the essence of reality, that is, change and continuity. Genuine knowledge, he held, is attainable only by a "kind of intellectual sympathy" called *intuition*. An illustration may serve to suggest what Bergson had in mind: a shipwrecked sailor writes a book describing his experiences. These may be vividly and dramatically portrayed; but printed words, though they make evoke vicarious emotions, cannot impart the sense of reality felt by the author. He first has to reconstruct a continuous series of events from memory and at a distance. Then he has to select and describe those portions which he considers worth reporting. The result is a number of fragmentary glimpses, a poor substitute for the immediate experience of a flux of events. If this is true of descriptions in our everyday language, Bergson believed it all the more true of scientific writing, where the scientist consciously abstracts from those features of experience which do not interest him. This conceptual analysis, according to Bergson, yields only static, quantitative, abstract symbols, which have merely practical value; whereas intuition can reveal the dynamic, qualitative, concrete reality. But it is difficult to gather from Bergson's writings the precise nature of this intuitive apprehension which he so exalted, calling it the ideal method of metaphysics; perhaps it is essentially indescribable. Although he thought of his philosophy as a purified empiricism, Bergson's attempt to grasp the essence of reality by immediate insight is regarded by many critics as belonging to the tradition of mysticism.

Bergson's glowing account of the virtues of the intuitive method of discerning the nature of the real is in sharp contrast to the sober, devastating analysis which Charles Peirce (1839–1914) gives of this method in his classic essay, "The Fixation of Belief," written in 1877. Peirce shows the advantages and disadvantages of the various methods practiced by men in "fixing" their beliefs—the methods of tenacity (not a method of reaching, but rather of retaining a belief), authority, intuition (which he calls the *a priori* method), and the method of science. As he points out, there is a fatal weakness in the first three methods, for whoever relies on them in forming his opinions cannot reasonably be surprised if those opinions turn out to be erroneous.

Moreover, there is nothing in these three methods which would lead anyone employing them to discover his error or even to suspect its presence. A glance at the conflicting faiths and ideologies in the world today shows that beliefs reached by appealing to authority (or to intuition) are at variance with the beliefs at which others have arrived by the same method. To resolve these differences, further reliance on the same method is futile, because in each case it will re-enforce the old opinion. Thus, discussion is at a standstill until a method is invoked which can distinguish the true from the false. The method of science can do this because it has been designed to produce beliefs which are in conformity with the facts. Not that it cannot lead to erroneous beliefs. It can. It is not unusual for two investigators, both using scientific method, to reach divergent conclusions, in which case at least one of them must be in error. But—and this is the point—the error can be discovered and the disagreement overcome by the continued use of scientific method, by which we mean constructing hypotheses, testing them by careful observations and controlled experiments, and employing all the other devices (such as analogy and sampling techniques) that have made scientific investigations so fruitful. Thus, what Peirce refers to briefly as the method of science, has one critical advantage over its rivals—it is *self-corrective*.

Does this mean that we have a ground for assurance that all differences of opinion can be resolved by the method of science? Peirce's answer would probably be: "Yes, ultimately"—since he defines the truth as that upon which all who investigate will ultimately agree.[2] But this answer, it should be noted, is compatible with the existence of unresolved differences at any specified time, so that it actually offers scant hope for the termination of philosophical and religious conflicts in the near future.

But can we resolve differences between those who do not acknowledge the author-

---

[2] There is something unsatisfactory, as Peirce realized, in his statement that "the sole object of inquiry is the settlement of opinion." Psychologically, this is correct, but it will not do as an account of the logic of inquiry. Since Peirce wants inquiry to serve a normative function, its goal must be not merely the settlement of opinion, but the attainment of true belief.

ity of the method of science and those who do? Is there any answer to the critic who claims that the very procedure we have instituted for investigating the methods of authority, intuition, revelation, and for comparing them with the method of science, commits us at the start to the method of science? Have we not decided that the methods of authority and intuition are inadequate because they violate certain conditions set up as necessary by the method of science? And if we thus assume that the method of science can be the arbiter of all methods including itself, are we not convicted of circular reasoning?

This is another way of asking how we *justify* our commitment to the method of science. The answer can only be in terms of what we hope to accomplish by using any of these methods. Do we want comfortable beliefs? Do we want beliefs that will stack up well with those of our social set? Do we want a method that will make it unnecessary for us ever to change our minds? Then one of the other methods would be preferable to the method of science. Or do we want a method which is most likely to lead to beliefs that are true? People tend to choose that method which they think can best accomplish the end they desire.[3] The methods of science, conceived broadly as the methods of rational inquiry, have been constructed, and are constantly being improved, for the precise purpose of leading men to those beliefs which are true—or most probable in the face of all the discoverable evidence. When scientific method is understood in this way, there can be no neutral canons of reasonableness to which we can appeal for adjudication of a contest between the advocates of faith or intuition and the defenders of scientific method. And the intuitionists might reject such canons if they did exist. Our choice of the method of science is a *decision* in terms of a goal, and it can only be sensibly challenged by showing that there are better ways of reaching *that goal*. Such challenges have been made, for example by Bergson, who would attribute Galileo's discoveries to an intuition of pure duration, which was not vouchsafed to Aristotle. This challenge can be met only by a careful study of Galileo's actual procedure and his analysis of his own experiments. It might also require a clearer statement of the process of intuition than is supplied by Bergson. Finally, if a critic should question our right to claim that the methods of science are most likely to lead to true beliefs, we could only refer him to the history of thought.

Many discussions among philosophers concerning the adequacy of scientific method bog down because there is no agreed interpretation of that phrase, *scientific method*. Critics are inclined to identify scientific method with some doctrinaire *philosophical* interpretation like behaviorism, pragmatism, positivism, physicalism, or one of the many types of naturalism. But one who chooses scientific method in preference to its alternatives is not *necessarily* committed to *any* of these philosophies. Nor can *scientific method* be identified with the various interpretations of their procedure which have been given by physicists, biologists, or other scientists. In the "Fixation of Belief" Peirce has done no more than contrast scientific method with some competing methods of stabilizing belief. A great deal needs to be said in explanation of such elements of scientific method as *observation, verification, prob-*

---

[3] Of course, none of these methods can tell us what end to desire.

ability, proof, hypothesis, induction, and *deduction.*[4] In the selection from Claude Bernard, a famous experimenter explains the relations between hypotheses, observations, and experiments, and then describes an actual experiment which shows the experimental method at work.

One of the perennial questions of scientific methodology concerns its applicability to the social sciences. This thorny question is tackled by Morris R. Cohen in our last selection.

If it is difficult to meet the demand of critics that we demonstrate the *adequacy* of scientific method in all domains of human interest, it is well to remember that a preference for scientific method need not rest on such a demonstration. It can be defended, as we have seen, on two grounds, one logical and one historical: namely, (1) scientific method, in contrast to its alternatives, is self-corrective, and (2) with many notable triumphs to its credit in the natural sciences, it now bids fair to extend and deepen man's knowledge in related fields.

Methodology is far from being a completed structure set forth satisfactorily in a number of canons or rules. A great deal of work needs to be done in clarifying the concepts and methods of science, and in applying them to fields in which more profound knowledge is of great urgency to the human race. This presents a challenge to any student interested in philosophy. D. J. B.

---

[4] For a discussion of these topics the student is referred to Chapter Four and to the bibliography at the end of this chapter.

*1. A Definition of Justice**

PLATO (B.C. 427–347)

All this time Thrasymachus had been trying more than once to break in upon our conversation; but his neighbours had restrained him, wishing to hear the argument to the end. In the pause after my last words he could keep quiet no longer; but gathering himself up like a wild beast he sprang at us as if he would tear us in pieces. Polemarchus and I were

* From Plato's *Republic*, Book I, translated by the late Francis Cornford. Permission to reprint has been granted by The Clarendon Press, Oxford.

frightened out of our wits, when he burst out to the whole company:

What is the matter with you two, Socrates? Why do you go on in this imbecile way, politely deferring to each other's nonsense? If you really want to know what justice means, stop asking questions and scoring off the answers you get. You know very well it is easier to ask questions than to answer them. Answer yourself, and tell us what you think justice means. I won't have you telling us it is the same as what is obligatory or useful or advantageous or profitable or expedient; I want a clear and precise statement; I won't put up with that sort of verbiage.

I was amazed by this onslaught and looked at him in terror. If I had not seen this wolf before he saw me, I really believe I should have been struck dumb; [1] but fortunately I had looked at him earlier, when he was beginning to get exasperated with our argument; so I was able to reply, though rather tremulously:

Don't be hard on us, Thrasymachus. If Polemarchus and I have gone astray in our search, you may be quite sure the mistake was not intentional. If we had been looking for a piece of gold, we should never have deliberately allowed politeness to spoil our chance of finding it; and now when we are looking for justice, a thing much more precious than gold, you cannot imagine we should defer to each other in that foolish way and not do our best to bring it to light. You must believe we are in earnest, my friend; but I am afraid the task is beyond our powers, and we might expect a man of your ability to pity us instead of being so severe.

Thrasymachus replied with a burst of sardonic laughter.

Good Lord, he said; Socrates at his old trick of shamming ignorance! I knew it; I told the others you would refuse to commit yourself and do anything sooner than answer a question.

Yes, Thrasymachus, I replied; because you are clever enough to know that if you asked someone what are the 'actors of the number twelve, and at the same time warned him: 'Look here, you are not to tell me that 12 is twice 6, or 3 times 4, or 6 times 2, or 4 times 3; I won't put up with any such nonsense' you must surely see that no one would answer a question put like that. He

would say: 'What do you mean, Thrasymachus? Am I forbidden to give any of these answers, even if one happens to be right? Do you want me to give a wrong one?' What would you say to that?

Humph! said he. As if that were a fair analogy!

I don't see why it is not, said I; but in any case, do you suppose our barring a certain answer would prevent the man from giving it, if he thought it was the truth?

Do you mean that you are going to give me one of those answers I barred?

I should not be surprised, if it seemed to me true, on reflection.

And what if I give you another definition of justice, better than any of those? What penalty are you prepared to pay? [2]

The penalty deserved by ignorance, which must surely be to receive instruction from the wise. So I would suggest that as a suitable punishment.

I like your notion of a penalty! he said; but you must pay the costs as well.

I will, when I have any money.

That will be all right, said Glaucon; we will all subscribe for Socrates. So let us have your definition, Thrasymachus.

Oh yes, he said; so that Socrates may play the old game of questioning and refuting someone else, instead of giving an answer himself!

But really, I protested, what can you expect from a man who does not know the answer or profess to know it, and, besides that, has been forbidden by no mean authority to put forward any notions he may have? Surely the definition should naturally come from you, who say you do know the answer and can tell it us. Please do not disappoint us. I

---

[1] A popular superstition, that if a wolf sees you first, you become dumb.

[2] In certain lawsuits the defendant, if found guilty, was allowed to propose a penalty alternative to that demanded by the prosecution. The judges then decided which should be inflicted. The 'costs' here means the fee which the sophist, unlike Socrates, expected from his pupils.

should take it as a kindness, and I hope you will not be chary of giving Glaucon and the rest of us the advantage of your instruction.

Glaucon and the others added their entreaties to mine. Thrasymachus was evidently longing to win credit, for he was sure he had an admirable answer ready, though he made a show of insisting that I should be the one to reply. In the end he gave way and exclaimed:

So this is what Socrates' wisdom comes to! He refuses to teach, and goes about learning from others without offering so much as thanks in return.

I do learn from others, Thrasymachus; that is quite true; but you are wrong to call me ungrateful. I give in return all I can—praise; for I have no money. And how ready I am to applaud any idea that seems to me sound, you will see in a moment, when you have stated your own; for I am sure that will be sound.

Listen then, Thrasymachus began. What I say is that 'just' or 'right' means nothing but what is to the interest of the stronger party. Well, where is your applause? You don't mean to give it me.

I will, as soon as I understand, I said. I don't see yet what you mean by right being the interest of the stronger party. For instance, Polydamas, the athlete, is stronger than we are, and it is to his interest to eat beef for the sake of his muscles; but surely you don't mean that the same diet would be good for weaker men and therefore be right for us?

You are trying to be funny, Socrates. It's a low trick to take my words in the sense you think will be most damaging.

No, no, I protested; but you must explain.

Don't you know, then, that a state may be ruled by a despot, or a democracy, or an aristocracy?

Of course.

And that the ruling element is always the strongest?

Yes.

Well then, in every case the laws are made by the ruling party in its own interest; a democracy makes democratic laws, a despot autocratic ones, and so on. By making these laws they define as 'right' for their subjects whatever is for their own interest, and they call anyone who breaks them a 'wrongdoer' and punish him accordingly. That is what I mean: in all states alike 'right' has the same meaning, namely what is for the interest of the party established in power, and that is the strongest. So the sound conclusion is that what is 'right' is the same everywhere: the interest of the stronger party.

Now I see what you mean, said I; whether it is true or not, I must try to make out. When you define right in terms of interest, you are yourself giving one of those answers you forbade to me; though, to be sure, you add 'to the stronger party.'

An insignificant addition, perhaps!

Its importance is not clear yet; what is clear is that we must find out whether your definition is true. I agree myself that right is in a sense a matter of interest; but when you add 'to the stronger party,' I don't know about that. I must consider.

Go ahead, then.

I will. Tell me this. No doubt you also think it is right to obey the men in power?

I do.

Are they infallible in every type of state, or can they sometimes make a mistake?

Of course they can make a mistake.

In framing laws, then, they may do their work well or badly?

No doubt.

Well, that is to say, when the laws they make are to their own interest; badly, when they are not?

Yes.

But the subjects are to obey any law

they lay down, and they will then be doing right?

Of course.

If so, by your account, it will be right to do what is not to the interest of the stronger party, as well as what is so.

What's that you are saying?

Just what you said, I believe; but let us look again. Haven't you admitted that the rulers, when they enjoin certain acts on their subjects, sometimes mistake their own best interests, and at the same time that it is right for the subjects to obey, whatever they may enjoin?

Yes, I suppose so.

Well, that amounts to admitting that it is right to do what is not to the interest of the rulers or the stronger party. They may unwittingly enjoin what is to their own disadvantage; and you say it is right for the others to do as they are told. In that case, their duty must be the opposite of what you said, because the weaker will have been ordered to do what is against the interest of the stronger. You with your intelligence must see how that follows.

Yes, Socrates, said Polemarchus, that is undeniable.

No doubt, Cleitophon broke in, if you are to be a witness on Socrates' side.

No witness is needed, replied Polemarchus; Thrasymachus himself admits that rulers sometimes ordain acts that are to their own disadvantage, and that it is the subjects' duty to do them.

That is because Thrasymachus said it was right to do what you are told by the men in power.

Yes, but he also said that what is to the interest of the stronger party is right; and, after making both these assertions, he admitted that the stronger sometimes command the weaker subjects to act against their interests. From all which it follows that what is in the stronger's interest is no more right than what is not.

No, said Cleitophon; he meant whatever the stronger *believes* to be in his own interest. That is what the subject must do, and what Thrasymachus meant to define as right.

That was not what he said, rejoined Polemarchus.

No matter, Polemarchus, said I; if Thrasymachus says so now, let us take him in that sense. Now, Thrasymachus, tell me, was that what you intended to say—that right means what the stronger thinks is to his interest, whether it really is so or not?

Most certainly not, he replied. Do you suppose I should speak of a man as 'stronger' or 'superior' at the very moment when he is making a mistake?

I did think you said as much when you admitted that rulers are not always infallible.

That is because you are a quibbler, Socrates. Would you say a man deserves to be called a physician at the moment when he makes a mistake in treating his patient and just in respect of that mistake; or a mathematician, when he does a sum wrong and just in so far as he gets a wrong result? Of course we do commonly speak of a physician or a mathematician or a scholar having made a mistake; but really none of these, I should say, is ever mistaken, in so far as he is worthy of the name we give him. So strictly speaking—and you are all for being precise—no one who practices a craft makes mistakes. A man is mistaken when his knowledge fails him; and at that moment he is no craftsman. And what is true of craftsmanship or any sort of skill is true of the ruler: he is never mistaken so long as he is acting as a ruler; though anyone might speak of a ruler making a mistake, just as he might of a physician. You must understand that I was talking in that loose way when I answered your question just now; but the precise statement is this. The ruler, in so far as he is acting as a ruler, makes no mistakes and consequently enjoins what is best for himself; and that is what the subject is to do. So, as I said at first, 'right' means doing what is to the interest of the stronger.

Very well, Thrasymachus, said I. So you think I am quibbling?

I am sure you are.

You believe my questions were maliciously designed to damage your position?

I know it. But you will gain nothing by that. You cannot outwit me by cunning, and you are not the man to crush me in the open.

Bless your soul, I answered, I should not think of trying. But, to prevent any more misunderstanding, when you speak of that ruler or stronger party whose interest the weaker ought to serve, please make it clear whether you are using the words in the ordinary way or in that strict sense you have just defined.

I mean a ruler in the strictest possible sense. Now quibble away and be as malicious as you can. I want no mercy. But you are no match for me.

Do you think me mad enough to beard a lion or try to outwit a Thrasymachus?

You did try just now, he retorted, but it wasn't a success.

Enough of this, said I. Now tell me about the physician in that strict sense you spoke of: is it his business to earn money or to treat his patients? Remember, I mean your physician who is worthy of the name.

To treat his patients.

And what of the ship's captain in the true sense? Is he a mere seaman or the commander of the crew?

The commander.

Yes, we shall not speak of him as a seaman just because he is on board a ship. That is not the point. He is called captain because of his skill and authority over the crew.

Quite true.

And each of these people has some special interest? [3]

No doubt.

And the craft in question exists for the very purpose of discovering that interest and providing for it?

Yes.

Can it equally be said of any craft that it has an interest, other than its own greatest possible perfection?

What do you mean by that?

Here is an illustration. If you ask me whether it is sufficient for the human body just to be itself, with no need of help from without, I should say, Certainly not; it has weaknesses and defects, and its condition is not all that it might be. That is precisely why the art of medicine was invented: it was designed to help the body and provide for its interests. Would not that be true?

It would.

But now take the art of medicine itself. Has that any defects or weaknesses? Does any art stand in need of some further perfection, as the eye would be imperfect without the power of vision or the ear without hearing, so that in their case an art is required that will study their interests and provide for their carrying out those functions? Has the art itself any corresponding need of some further art to remedy its defects and look after its interests; and will that further art require yet another, and so on for ever? Or will every art look after its own interests? Or, finally, is it not true that no art needs to have its weaknesses remedied or its interests studied either by another art or by itself, because no art has in itself any weakness or fault, and the only interest it is re-

---

[3] All the persons mentioned have some interest. The craftsman *qua* craftsman has an interest in doing his work as well as possible, which is the same thing as serving the interest of the subjects on whom his craft is exercised: and the subjects have their interest, which the craftsman is there to promote.

quired to serve is that of its subject-matter? In itself, an art is sound and flawless, so long as it is entirely true to its own nature as an art in the strictest sense—and it is the strict sense that I want you to keep in view. Is not that true?

So it appears.

Then, said I, the art of medicine does not study its own interest, but the needs of the body, just as a groom shows his skill by caring for horses, not for the art of grooming. And so every art seeks, not its own advantage—for it has no deficiencies—but the interest of the subject on which it is exercised.

It appears so.

But surely, Thrasymachus, every art has authority and superior power over its subject.

To this he agreed, though very reluctantly.

So far as arts are concerned, then, no art ever studies or enjoins the interest of the superior or stronger party, but always that of the weaker over which it has authority.

Thrasymachus assented to this at last, though he tried to put up a fight. I then went on:

So the physician, as such, studies only the patient's interest, not his own. For as we agreed, the business of the physician, in the strict sense, is not to make money for himself, but to exercise his power over the patient's body; and the ship's captain, again, considered strictly as no mere sailor, but in command of the crew, will study and enjoin the interest of his subordinates, not his own.

He agreed reluctantly.

And so with government of any kind: no ruler, in so far as he is acting as ruler, will study or enjoin what is for his own interest. All that he says and does will be said and done with a view to what is good and proper for the subject for whom he practises his art.

At this point, when everyone could see that Thrasymachus' definition of justice had been turned inside out, instead of making any reply, he said:

Socrates, have you a nurse?

Why do you ask such a question as that? I said. Wouldn't it be better to answer mine?

Because she lets you go about sniffling like a child whose nose wants wiping. She hasn't even taught you to know a shepherd when you see one, or his sheep either.

What makes you say that?

Why, you imagine that a herdsman studies the interests of his flocks or cattle, tending and fattening them up with some other end in view than his master's profit or his own; and so you don't see that, in politics, the genuine ruler regards his subjects exactly like sheep, and thinks of nothing else, night and day, but the good he can get out of them for himself. You are so far out in your notions of right and wrong, justice and injustice, as not to know that 'right' actually means what is good for someone else, and to be 'just' means serving the interest of the stronger who rules, at the cost of the subject who obeys; whereas injustice is just the reverse, asserting its authority over those innocents who are called just, so that they minister solely to their master's advantage and happiness, and not in the least degree to their own. Innocent as you are yourself, Socrates, you must see that a just man always has the worst of it. Take a private business: when a partnership is wound up, you will never find that the more honest of two partners comes off with the larger share; and in their relations to the state, when there are taxes to be paid, the honest man will pay more than the other on the same amount of property; or if there is money to be distributed, the dishonest will get it all. When either of them hold some public office, even if the just man loses in no other way, his private affairs at any rate will suffer from neglect, while his principles will not allow him to help himself from the public funds; not to mention the offence he will give to his friends and relations by refusing to sacrifice those principles to do them a good turn. Injustice has all the opposite advantages. I am speaking of the type I described just now, the man who can get the better of other people on a large scale: you must fix your eye on him, if you want to judge how much it is to one's own interest not to be just. You can see that best in the most consummate form of injustice, which rewards wrongdoing with supreme welfare and happiness and reduces its victims, if they won't retaliate in kind, to misery. That form is despotism, which uses force or fraud to plunder the goods of others, public or private, sacred or profane, and to do it in a wholesale way. If you are caught committing any one of these crimes on a small scale, you are punished and disgraced; they call it sacrilege, kidnapping, burglary, theft and brigandage. But if, besides taking their property, you turn all your countrymen into slaves, you will hear no more of those ugly names; your countrymen themselves will call you the happiest of men and bless your name, and so will everyone who hears of such a complete triumph of injustice; for when people denounce injustice, it is because they are afraid of suffering wrong, not of doing it. So true is it, Socrates, that injustice, on a grand enough scale, is superior to justice in strength and freedom and autocratic power; and 'right,' as I said at first, means simply what serves the interest of the stronger party; 'wrong' means what is for the interest and profit of oneself.

Having deluged our ears with this torrent of words, as the man at the baths might empty a bucket over one's head, Thrasymachus meant to take himself off; but the company obliged him to stay

and defend his position. I was specially urgent in my entreaties.

My good Thrasymachus, said I, do you propose to fling a doctrine like that at our heads and then go away without explaining it properly or letting us point out to you whether it is true or not? Is it so small a matter in your eyes to determine the whole course of conduct which every one of us must follow to get the best out of life?

Don't I realize it is a serious matter? he retorted.

Apparently not, said I; or else you have no consideration for us, and do not care whether we shall lead better or worse lives for being ignorant of this truth you profess to know. Do take the trouble to let us into your secret; if you treat us handsomely, you may be sure it will be a good investment; there are so many of us to show our gratitude. I will make no secret of my own conviction, which is that injustice is not more profitable than justice, even when left free to work its will unchecked. No; let your unjust man have full power to do wrong, whether by successful violence or by escaping detection; all the same he will not convince me that he will gain more than he would by being just. There may be others here who feel as I do, and set justice above injustice. It is for you to convince us that we are not well advised.

How can I? he replied. If you are not convinced by what I have just said, what more can I do for you? Do you want to be fed with my ideas out of a spoon?

God forbid! I exclaimed; not that. But I do want you to stand by your own words; or, if you shift your ground, shift it openly and stop trying to hoodwink us as you are doing now. You see, Thrasymachus, to go back to your earlier argument, in speaking of the shepherd you did not think it necessary to keep to that strict sense you laid down when you defined the genuine physician. You represent him, in his character of shepherd, as feeding up his flock, not for their own sake but for the table or the market, as if he were out to make money as caterer or a cattle-dealer, rather than a shepherd. Surely the sole concern of the shepherd's art is to do the best for the charges put under its care; its own best interest is sufficiently provided for, so long as it does not fall short of all that shepherding should imply. On that principle it followed, I thought, that any kind of authority, in the state or in private life, must, in its character of authority, consider solely what is best for those under its care. Now what is your opinion? Do you think that the men who govern states—I mean rulers in the strict sense—have no reluctance to hold office?

I don't think so, he replied; I know it.

Well, but haven't you noticed, Thrasymachus, that in other positions of authority no one is willing to act unless he is paid wages, which he demands on the assumption that all the benefit of his action will go to his charges? Tell me: Don't we always distinguish one form of skill from another by its power to effect some particular result? Do say what you really think, so that we may get on.

Yes, that is the distinction.

And also each brings us some benefit that is peculiar to it: medicine gives health, for example; the art of navigation, safety at sea; and so on.

Yes.

And wage-earning brings us wages; that is its distinctive product. Now, speaking with that precision which you proposed, you would not say that the art of navigation is the same as the art of medicine, merely on the ground that a ship's captain regained his health on a voyage, because the sea air was good for him. No more would you identify the practice of medicine with wage-earning because a man may keep his health while earning wages, or a physician attending a case may receive a fee.

No.

And, since we agreed that the benefit obtained by each form of skill is peculiar to it, any common benefit enjoyed alike by all these practitioners must come from some further practice common to them all?

It would seem so.

Yes, we must say that if they all earn wages, they get that benefit in so far as they are engaged in wage-earning as well as in practising their several arts.

He agreed reluctantly.

This benefit, then—the receipt of wages—does not come to a man from his special art. If we are to speak strictly, the physician, as such, produces health; the builder, a house; and then each, in his further capacity of wage-earner, gets his pay. Thus every art has its own function and benefits its proper subject. But suppose the practitioner is not paid; does he then get any benefit from his art?

Clearly not.

And is he doing no good to anyone either, when he works for nothing?

No, I suppose he does some good.

Well then, Thrasymachus, it is now clear that no form of skill or authority provides for its own benefit. As we were saying some time ago, it always studies and prescribes what is good for its subject—the interest of the weaker party, not of the stronger. And that, my friend, is why I said that no one is willing to be in a position of authority and undertake to set straight other men's troubles, without demanding to be paid; because, if he is to do his work well, he will never, in his capacity of ruler, do, or command others to do, what is best for himself, but only what is best for the subject. For that reason, if he is to consent, he must have his recompense, in the shape of money or honour, or of punishment in case of refusal.

What do you mean, Socrates? asked Glaucon. I recognize two of your three kinds of reward; but I don't understand what you mean by speaking of punishment as a recompense.

Then you don't understand the recompense required by the best type of men, or their motive for accepting authority when they do consent. You surely know that a passion for honours or for money is rightly regarded as something to be ashamed of.

Yes, I do.

For that reason, I said, good men are unwilling to rule, either for money's sake or for honour. They have no wish to be called mercenary for demanding to be paid, or thieves for making a secret profit out of their office; nor yet will honours tempt them, for they are not ambitious. So they must be forced to consent under threat of penalty; that may be why a readiness to accept power under no such constraint is thought discreditable. And the heaviest penalty for declining to rule is to be ruled by someone inferior to yourself. That is the fear, I believe, that makes decent people accept power; and when they do so, they face the prospect of authority with no idea that they are coming into the enjoyment of a comfortable berth; it is forced upon them because they can find no one better than themselves, or even as good, to be entrusted with power. If there could ever be a society of perfect men, there might well be as much competition to evade office as there now is to gain it; and it would then be clearly seen that the genuine ruler's nature is to seek only the advantage of the subject, with the consequence that any man of understanding would sooner have another to do the best for him than be at the pains to do the best for that other himself. On this point, then, I entirely disagree with Thrasymachus' doctrine that right means what is to the interest of the stronger.*

* [See Selection 8 for the continuation of this discussion.]

2. Novum Organum*

Francis Bacon (1561–1626)

Aphorisms

I

Man, being the servant and interpreter of Nature, can do and understand so much and so much only as he has observed in fact or in thought of the course of nature: beyond this he neither knows anything nor can do anything.

XXXVIII

The idols and false notions which are now in possession of the human understanding, and have taken deep root therein, not only so beset men's minds that truth can hardly find entrance, but even after entrance obtained, they will again in the very instauration of the

* The Preface and part of the *Aphorisms Concerning the Interpretation of Nature and the Kingdom of Man,* from the *Novum Organum,* first published 1620.

sciences meet and trouble us, unless men being forewarned of the danger fortify themselves as far as may be against their assaults.

XXXIX

There are four classes of Idols which beset men's minds. To these for distinction's sake I have assigned names,—calling the first class *Idols of the Tribe;* the second, *Idols of the Cave;* the third, *Idols of the Marketplace;* the fourth, *Idols of the Theatre.*

XL

The formation of ideas and axioms by true induction is no doubt the proper remedy to be applied for the keeping off and clearing away of idols. To point them out, however, is of great use; for the doctrine of Idols is to the Interpretation of Nature what the doctrine of the refutation of Sophisms is to common Logic.

XLI

The Idols of the Tribe have their foundation in human nature itself, and in the tribe or race of men. For it is a false assertion that the sense of man is the measure of things. On the contrary, all perceptions as well of the sense as of the mind are according to the measure of man and not according to the measure of the universe. And the human understanding is like a false mirror, which, receiving rays irregularly, distorts and discolours the nature of things by mingling its own nature with it.

XLII

The Idols of the Cave are the idols of the individual man. For every one (besides the errors common to human nature in general) has a cave or den of his own, which refracts and discolours the light of nature; owing either to his own proper and peculiar nature; or to his education and conversation with others; or to the reading of books, and the authority of those whom he esteems and admires; or to the differences of impressions, accordingly as they take place in a mind preoccupied and predisposed or in a mind indifferent and settled; or the like. So that the spirit of man (according as it is meted out to different individuals) is in fact a thing variable and full of perturbation, and governed as it were by chance. Whence it was well observed by Heraclitus that men look for sciences in their own lesser worlds, and not in the greater or common world.

XLIII

There are also Idols formed by the intercourse and association of men with each other, which I call Idols of the Market-place, on account of the commerce and consort of men there. For it is by discourse that men associate; and words are imposed according to the apprehension of the vulgar. And therefore the ill and unfit choice of words wonderfully obstructs the understanding. Nor do the definitions or explanations wherewith in some things learned men are wont to guard and defend themselves, by any means set the matter right. But words plainly force and overrule the understanding, and throw all into confusion, and lead men away into numberless empty controversies and idle fancies.

XLIV

Lastly, there are Idols which have immigrated into men's minds from the various dogmas of philosophies, and also from wrong laws of demonstration. These I call Idols of the Theatre; because in my judgment all the received systems are but so many stage-plays, representing worlds of their own creation after an unreal and scenic fashion. Nor is it only of the systems now in vogue, or only of the ancient sects and philosophies, that I speak; for many more plays of the same kind may yet be composed and in like artificial manner set forth; seeing that errors the most widely different have nevertheless causes for the most part alike. Neither again do I mean this only of entire systems, but also of many principles and axioms in science, which by tradition, credulity, and negligence have come to be received.

But of these several kinds of Idols I must speak more largely and exactly, that the understanding may be duly cautioned

XLV

The human understanding is of its own nature prone to suppose the existence of more order and regularity in the world than it finds. And though there be many things in nature which are singular and unmatched, yet it devises for them parallels and conjugates and relatives which do not exist. Hence the fiction that all celestial bodies move in perfect circles; spirals and dragons being (except in name) utterly rejected. Hence too the element of Fire with its orb is brought in, to make up the square with the other three which the sense perceives. Hence also the ratio of density of the so-called elements is arbitrarily fixed at ten to one. And so on of the other dreams. And these fancies affect not dogmas only, but simple notions also.

XLVI

The human understanding when it has once adopted an opinion (either as being the received opinion or as being agreeable to itself) draws all things else to support and agree with it. And though there be a greater number and weight of instances to be found on the other side, yet these it either neglects and despises, or else by some distinction sets aside and rejects; in order that by this great and pernicious predetermination the authority of its former conclusions may remain inviolate. And therefore it was a good answer that was made by one who when they showed him hanging in a temple a picture of those who had paid their vows as having escaped shipwreck, and would have him say whether he did not now acknowledge the power of the gods,—"Aye," asked he again, "but where are they painted that were drowned after their vows?" And such is the way of all superstition, whether in astrology, dreams, omens, divine judgments, or the like; wherein men, having a delight in such vanities, mark the events where they are fulfilled, but where they fail, though this happen much oftener, neglect and pass them by. But with far more subtlety does this mischief insinuate itself into philosophy and the sciences; in which the first conclusion colours and brings into conformity with itself all that come after, though far sounder and better. Besides, independently of that delight and vanity which I have described, it is the peculiar and perpetual error of the human intellect to be more moved and excited by affirmatives than by negatives; whereas it ought properly to hold itself indifferently disposed towards both alike. Indeed in the establishment of any true axiom, the negative instance is the more forcible of the two.

XLVII

The human understanding is moved by those things most which strike and enter the mind simultaneously and suddenly, and so fill the imagination; and then it feigns and supposes all other things to be somehow, though it cannot see how, similar to those few things by which it is surrounded. But for that going to and fro to remote and heterogeneous instances, by which axioms are tried as in the fire, the intellect is altogether slow and unfit, unless it be forced thereto by severe laws and overruling authority.

XLVIII

The human understanding is unquiet; it cannot stop or rest, and still presses onward, but in vain. Therefore it is that we cannot conceive of any end or limit to the world; but always as of necessity it occurs to us that there is something beyond. Neither again can it be conceived how eternity has flowed down to the present day; for that distinction which is commonly received on infinity in time past and in time to come can by no means hold; for it would thence follow that one infinity is greater than another, and that infinity is wasting away and tending to become finite. The like subtlety arises touching the infinite divisibility of lines, from the same inability of thought to stop. But this inability interferes more mischievously in the discovery of causes: for although the most general principles in nature ought to be held merely positive, as they are discovered, and cannot with truth be referred to a cause; nevertheless the human understanding being unable to rest still seeks something prior in the order of nature. And then it is that in struggling towards that which is further off it falls back upon that which is more nigh at hand; namely, on final causes: which have relation clearly to the nature of man rather than to the nature of the universe; and from this source have strangely defiled philosophy. But he is no less an unskilled and shallow philosopher who seeks causes of that which is most general, than he who in things subordinate and subaltern omits to do so.

XLIX

The human understanding is no dry light, but receives an infusion from the will and affections; whence proceed sciences which may be called "sciences as one would." For what a man had rather were true he more readily believes. Therefore he rejects difficult things from impatience of research; sober things, because they narrow hope; the deeper things of nature, from superstition; the light of experience, from arrogance and pride, lest his mind should seem to be occupied with things mean and transitory; things not commonly believed, out of deference to the opinion of the vulgar. Numberless in short are the ways, and sometimes imperceptible, in which the affections colour and infect the understanding.

L

But by far the greatest hindrance and aberration of the human understanding proceeds from the dulness, incompetency, and deceptions of the senses; in that things which strike the sense outweigh things which do not immediately strike it, though they be more important. Hence it is that speculation commonly ceases where sight ceases; insomuch that of things invisible there is little or no observation. Hence all the working of the spirits inclosed in tangible bodies lies hid and unobserved of men. So also all the more subtle changes of form in the parts of coarser substances (which they commonly call alteration, though it is in truth local motion through exceedingly small spaces) is in like manner unobserved. And yet unless these two things just mentioned be searched out and brought to light, nothing great can be achieved in nature, as far as the production of works is concerned. So again the essential nature of our common air, and of all bodies less dense than air (which are very many), is almost unknown. For the sense by itself is a thing infirm and erring; neither can instruments for enlarging or sharpening the senses do much; but all the truer kind of interpretation of nature is effected by instances and experiments fit and apposite; wherein the sense decides touching the experiment only, and the experiment touching the point in nature and the thing itself.

LI

The human understanding is of its own nature prone to abstractions and gives a constancy to things which are fleeting. But to resolve nature into abstractions is less to our purpose than to dissect her into parts; as did the school of Democritus, which went further into nature than the rest . . .

LII

Such then are the idols, which I call *Idols of the Tribe;* and which take their rise either from the homogeneity of the substance of the human spirit, or from its preoccupation, or from its narrowness, or from its restless motion, or from an infusion of the affections, or from the incompetency of the senses, or from the mode of impression.

LIII

The *Idols of the Cave* take their rise in the peculiar constitution, mental or bodily, of each individual; and also in education, habit, and accident. Of this kind there is a great number and variety; but I will instance those the pointing out of which contains the most important caution, and which have most effect in disturbing the clearness of the understanding.

LIV

Men become attached to certain particular sciences and speculations, either because they fancy themselves the authors and inventors thereof, or because they have bestowed the greatest pains upon them and become most

habituated to them. But men of this kind, if they betake themselves to philosophy and contemplations of a general character, distort and colour them in obedience to their former fancies; a thing especially to be noticed in Aristotle, who made his natural philosophy a mere bond-servant to his logic, thereby rendering it contentious and well nigh useless. The race of chemists again out of a few experiments of the furnace have built up a fantastic philosophy, framed with reference to a few things; and Gilbert also, after he had employed himself most laboriously in the study and observation of the loadstone, proceeded at once to construct an entire system in accordance with his favourite subject.

LV

There is one principal and as it were radical distinction between different minds, in respect of philosophy and the sciences; which is this: that some minds are stronger and apter to mark the differences of things, others to mark their resemblances. The steady and acute mind can fix its contemplations and dwell and fasten on the subtlest distinctions: the lofty and discursive mind recognises and puts together the finest and most general resemblances. Both kinds however easily err in excess, by catching the one at gradations, the other at shadows.

LVI

There are found some minds given to an extreme admiration of antiquity, others to an extreme love and appetite for novelty; but few so duly tempered that they can hold the mean, neither carping at what has been well laid down by the ancients, nor despising what is well introduced by the moderns. This however, turns to the great injury of the sciences and philosophy; since these affections of antiquity and novelty are the humours of partisans rather than judgments; and truth is to be sought for not in the felicity of any age, which is an unstable thing, but in the light of nature and experience, which is eternal. These factions therefore must be abjured, and care must be taken that the intellect be not hurried by them into assent.

LVII

Contemplations of nature and of bodies in their simple form break up and distract the understanding, while contemplations of nature and bodies in their composition and configuration overpower and dissolve the understanding: a distinction well seen in the school of Leucippus and Democritus as compared with the other philosophies. For that school is so busied with the particles that it hardly attends to the structure; while the others are so lost in admiration of the structure that they do not penetrate to the simplicity of nature. These kinds of contemplation should therefore be alternated and taken by turns; that so the understanding may be rendered at once penetrating and comprehensive, and the inconveniences above mentioned, with the idols which proceed from them, may be avoided.

LVIII

Let such then be our provision and contemplative prudence for keeping off and dislodging the *Idols of the Cave,* which grow for the most part either out of the predominance of a favourite subject, or out of an excessive tendency to compare or to distinguish, or out of partiality for particular ages, or out of the largeness or minuteness of the objects contemplated. And generally let every student of nature take this as a rule,— that whatever his mind seizes and dwells upon with peculiar satisfaction is to be held in suspicion, and that so much the

more care is to be taken in dealing with such questions to keep the understanding even and clear.

LIX

But the *Idols of the Marketplace* are the most troublesome of all: idols which have crept into the understanding through the alliances of words and names. For men believe that their reason governs words; but it is also true that words react on the understanding; and this it is that has rendered philosophy and the sciences sophistical and inactive. Now words, being commonly framed and applied according to the capacity of the vulgar, follow those lines of division which are most obvious to the vulgar understanding. And whenever an understanding of greater acuteness or a more diligent observation would alter those lines to suit the true divisions of nature, words stand in the way and resist the change. Whence it comes to pass that the high and formal discussions of learned men end oftentimes in disputes about words and names; with which (according to the use and wisdom of the mathematicians) it would be more prudent to begin, and so by means of definitions reduce them to order. Yet even definitions cannot cure this evil in dealing with natural and material things; since the definitions themselves consist of words, and those words beget others: so that it is necessary to recur to individual instances, and those in due series and order; as I shall say presently when I come to the method and scheme for the formation of notions and axioms.

LX

The idols imposed by words on the understanding are of two kinds. They are either names of things which do not exist (for as there are things left unnamed through lack of observation, so likewise are there names which result from fantastic suppositions and to which nothing in reality corresponds), or they are names of things which exist, but yet confused and ill-defined, and hastily and irregularly derived from realities. Of the former kind are Fortune, the Prime Mover, Planetary Orbits, Element of Fire, and like fictions which owe their origin to false and idle theories. And this class of idols is more easily expelled, because to get rid of them it is only necessary that all theories should be steadily rejected and dismissed as obsolete.

But the other class, which springs out of a faulty and unskillful abstraction, is intricate and deeply rooted. Let us take for example such a word as *humid;* and see how far the several things which the word is used to signify agree with each other; and we shall find the word *humid* to be nothing else than a mark loosely and confusedly applied to denote a variety of actions which will not bear to be reduced to any constant meaning. For it both signifies that which easily spreads itself round any other body; and that which in itself is indeterminate and cannot solidise; and that which readily yields in every direction; and that which easily divides and scatters itself; and that which easily unites and collects itself; and that which readily flows and is put in motion; and that which readily clings to another body and wets it; and that which is easily reduced to a liquid, or being solid easily melts. Accordingly when you come to apply the word,—if you take it in one sense, flame is humid; if in another, air is not humid; if in another, fine dust is humid; if in another, glass is humid. So that it is easy to see that the notion is taken by abstraction only from water and common and ordinary liquids, without any due verification.

There are however in words certain degrees of distortion and error. One of the least faulty kinds is that of names of substances, especially of lowest species

and well-deduced (for the notion of *chalk* and of *mud* is good, of *earth* bad); a more faulty kind is that of actions, as to *generate,* to *corrupt,* to *alter;* the most faulty is of qualities (except such as are the immediate objects of the sense) as *heavy, light, rare, dense,* and the like. Yet in all these cases some notions are of necessity a little better than others, in proportion to the greater variety of subjects that fall within the range of the human sense.

LXI

But the *Idols of the Theatre* are not innate, nor do they steal into the understanding secretly, but are plainly impressed and received into the mind from the play-books of philosophical systems and the perverted rules of demonstration. To attempt refutations in this case would be merely inconsistent with what I have already said: for since we agree neither upon principles nor upon demonstrations there is no place for argument. And this is so far well, inasmuch as it leaves the honour of the ancients untouched. For they are no wise disparaged —the question between them and me being only as to the way. For as the saying is, the lame man who keeps the right road outstrips the runner who takes a wrong one. Nay it is obvious that when a man runs the wrong way, the more active and swift he is the further he will go astray.

But the course I propose for the discovery of sciences is such as leaves but little to the acuteness and strength of wits, but places all wits and understandings nearly on a level. For as in the drawing of a straight line or a perfect circle, much depends on the steadiness and practice of the hand, if it be done by aim of hand only, but if with the aid of rule or compass, little or nothing; so is it exactly with my plan. But though particular confutations would be of no avail, yet touching the sects and general divisions of such systems I must say something; something also touching the external signs which show that they are unsound; and finally something touching the causes of such great infelicity and of such lasting and general agreement in error; that so the access to truth may be made less difficult, and the human understanding may the more willingly submit to its purgation and dismiss its idols.

LXII

Idols of the Theatre, or of Systems, are many, and there can be and perhaps will be yet many more. For were it not that now for many ages men's minds have been busied with religion and theology; and were it not that civil governments, especially monarchies, have been averse to such novelties, even in matters speculative; so that men labour therein to the peril and harming of their fortunes,—not only unrewarded, but exposed also to contempt and envy; doubtless there would have arisen many other philosophical sects like to those which in great variety flourished once among the Greeks. For as on the phenomena of the heavens many hypotheses may be constructed, so likewise (and more also) many various dogmas may be set up and established on the phenomena of philosophy. And in the plays of this philosophical theatre you may observe the same thing which is found in the theatre of the poets, that stories invented for the stage are more compact and elegant, and more as one would wish them to be, than true stories out of history.

In general however there is taken for the material of philosophy either a great deal out of a few things, or a very little out of many things; so that on both sides philosophy is based on too narrow a foundation of experiment and natural history, and decides on the authority of too few cases. For the Rational School of philosophers snatches from experience a variety of common instances, neither duly ascertained nor diligently examined and weighed, and leaves all the rest to meditation and agitation of wit.

There is also another class of philosophers, who having bestowed much diligent and careful labour on a few experiments, have thence made bold to educe and construct systems; wresting all other facts in a strange fashion to conformity therewith.

And there is yet a third class, consisting of those who out of faith and veneration mix their philosophy with theology and traditions; among whom the vanity of some has gone so far aside as to seek the origin of sciences among spirits and genii. So that this parent stock of errors —this false philosophy—is of three kinds; the Sophistical, the Empirical, and the Superstitious.

XCV

Those who have handled sciences have been either men of experiment or men of dogmas. The men of experiment are like the ant; they only collect and use: the reasoners resemble spiders, who make cobwebs out of their own substance. But the bee takes a middle course, it gathers its material from the flowers of the garden and of the field, but transforms and digests it by a power of its own. Not unlike this is the true business of philosophy; for it neither relies solely or chiefly on the powers of the mind, nor does it take the matter which it gathers from natural history and mechanical experiments and lay it up in the memory whole, as it finds it; but lays it up in the understanding altered and digested. Therefore from a closer and purer league between these two faculties, the experimental and the rational, (such as has never yet been made) much may be hoped.

3. *The Quest for Certainty** *

RENÉ DESCARTES (1596–1650)

MEDITATION I

Of the Things Which May Be Brought Within the Sphere of the Doubtful

It is now some years since I detected how many were the false beliefs that I had from my earliest youth admitted as true, and how doubtful was everything I had since constructed on this basis; and from that time I was convinced that I must once for all seriously undertake to rid myself of all the opinions which I had formerly accepted, and commence to build anew from the foundation, if I wanted to establish any firm and permanent structure in the sciences. But as this enterprise appeared to be a very great one, I waited until I had attained an age so mature that I could not hope that at any later date I should be better fitted to execute my design. This reason caused me to delay so long that I should feel that I was doing wrong were I to occupy in deliberation the time that yet remains to me for action. To-day, then, since very opportunely for the plan I have in view I have delivered my mind from every care [and am happily agitated by no passions] and since I have procured for myself an assured leisure in a peaceable retirement, I shall at last seriously and freely address myself to the general upheaval of all my former opinions.

Now for this object it is not necessary that I should show that all of these are false—I shall perhaps never arrive at this end. But inasmuch as reason already persuades me that I ought no less carefully to withhold my assent from matters which are not entirely certain and indubitable than from those which appear to me manifestly to be false, if I am able to find in each one some reason to doubt, this will suffice to justify my rejecting the whole. And for that end it will not be requisite that I should examine each in particular, which would be an endless undertaking; for owing to the fact that the destruction of the foundations of necessity brings with it the downfall of the rest of the edifice, I shall only in the first place attack those principles upon which all my former opinions rested.

All that up to the present time I have accepted as most true and certain I have learned either from the senses or through the senses; but it is sometimes proved to me that these senses are deceptive, and it is wiser not to trust entirely to any thing by which we have once been deceived.

But it may be that although the senses sometimes deceive us concerning things which are hardly perceptible, or very far away, there are yet many others to be

---

* The first two *Meditations on First Philosophy,* written in 1641 and translated from the Latin by E. S. Haldane and G. R. T. Ross in 1912. Published by the Cambridge University Press.

met with as to which we cannot reasonably have any doubt, although we recognise them by their means. For example, there is the fact that I am here, seated by the fire, attired in a dressing gown, having this paper in my hands and other similar matters. And how could I deny that these hands and this body are mine, were it not perhaps that I compare myself to certain persons, devoid of sense, whose cerebella are so troubled and clouded by the violent vapours of black bile, that they constantly assure us that they think they are kings when they are really quite poor, or that they are clothed in purple when they are really without covering, or who imagine that they have an earthenware head or are nothing but pumpkins or are made of glass. But they are mad, and I should not be any the less insane were I to follow examples so extravagant.

At the same time I must remember that I am a man, and that consequently I am in the habit of sleeping, and in my dreams representing to myself the same things or sometimes even less probable things, than do those who are insane in their waking moments. How often has it happened to me that in the night I dreamt that I found myself in this particular place, that I was dressed and seated near the fire, whilst in reality I was lying undressed in bed! At this moment it does indeed seem to me that it is with eyes awake that I am looking at this paper; that this head which I move is not asleep, that it is deliberately and of set purpose that I extend my hand and perceive it; what happens in sleep does not appear so clear nor so distinct as does all this. But in thinking over this I remind myself that on many occasions I have in sleep been deceived by similar illusions, and in dwelling carefully on this reflection I see so manifestly that there are no certain indications by which we may clearly distinguish wakefulness from sleep that I am lost in astonishment. And my astonishment is such that it is almost capable of persuading me that I now dream.

Now let us assume that we are asleep and that all these particulars, e.g. that we open our eyes, shake our head, extend our hands, and so on, are but false delusions; and let us reflect that possibly neither our hands nor our whole body are such as they appear to us to be. At the same time we must at least confess that the things which are represented to us in sleep are like painted representations which can only have been formed as the counterparts of something real and true, and that in this way those general things at least, i.e. eyes, a head, hands, and a whole body, are not imaginary things, but things really existent. For, as a matter of fact, painters, even when they study with the greatest skill to represent sirens and satyrs by forms the most strange and extraordinary, cannot give them natures which are entirely new, but merely make a certain medley of the members of different animals; or if their imagination is extravagant enough to invent something so novel that nothing similar has ever before been seen, and that then their work represents a thing purely fictitious and absolutely false, it is certain all the same that the colours of which this is composed are necessarily real. And for the same reason, although these general things, to wit, [a body], eyes, a head, and such like, may be imaginary, we are bound at the same time to confess that there are at least some other objects yet more simple and more universal, which are real and true; and of these just in the same way as with certain real colours, all these images of things which dwell in our thoughts, whether true and real or false and fantastic, are formed.

To such a class of things pertains corporeal nature in general, and its extension, the figure of extended things, their quantity or magnitude and number, as also the place in which they are, the time which measures their duration, and so on.

That is possibly why our reasoning is not unjust when we conclude from this that Physics, Astronomy, Medicine and all other sciences which have as their end the consideration of composite things, are very dubious and uncertain; but that Arithmetic, Geometry and other sciences of that kind which only treat of things that are very simple and very general, without taking great trouble to ascertain whether they are actually existent or not, contain some measure of certainty and an element of the indubitable. For whether I am awake or asleep, two and three together always form five, and the square can never have more than four sides, and it does not seem possible that truths so clear and apparent can be suspected of any falsity [or uncertainty].

Nevertheless I have long had fixed in my mind the belief that an all-powerful God existed by whom I have been created such as I am. But how do I know that He has not brought it to pass that there is no earth, no heaven, no extended body, no magnitude, no place, and that nevertheless [I possess the perceptions of all these things and that] they seem to me to exist just exactly as I now see them? And, besides, as I sometimes imagine that others deceive themselves in the things which they think they know best, how do I know that I am not deceived every time that I add two and three, or count the sides of a square, or judge of things yet simpler, if anything simpler can be imagined? But possibly God has not desired that I should be thus deceived, for He is said to be supremely good. If, however, it is contrary to His goodness to have made me such that I constantly deceive myself, it would also appear to be contrary to His goodness to permit me to be sometimes deceived, and never-

theless I cannot doubt that He does permit this.

There may indeed be those who would prefer to deny the existence of a God so powerful, rather than believe that all other things are uncertain. But let us not oppose them for the present, and grant that all that is said of a God is a fable; nevertheless in whatever way they suppose that I have arrived at the state of being that I have reached—whether they attribute it to fate or to accident, or make out that it is by a continual succession of antecedents, or by some other method—since to err and deceive oneself is a defect, it is clear that the greater will be the probability of my being so imperfect as to deceive myself ever, as is the Author to whom they assign my origin the less powerful. To these reasons I have certainly nothing to reply, but at the end I feel constrained to confess that there is nothing in all that I formerly believed to be true, of which I cannot in some measure doubt, and that not merely through want of thought or through levity, but for reasons which are very powerful and maturely considered; so that henceforth I ought not the less carefully to refrain from giving credence to these opinions than to that which is manifestly false, if I desire to arrive at any certainty [in the sciences].

But it is not sufficient to have made these remarks, we must also be careful to keep them in mind. For these ancient and commonly held opinions still revert frequently to my mind, long and familiar custom having given them the right to occupy my mind against my inclination and rendered them almost masters of my belief; nor will I ever lose the habit of deferring to them or of placing my confidence in them, so long as I consider them as they really are, i.e. opinions in some measure doubtful, as I have just shown, and at the same time highly probable, so that there is much more reason to believe than to deny them.

That is why I consider that I shall not be acting amiss, if, taking of set purpose a contrary belief, I allow myself to be deceived, and for a certain time pretend that all these opinions are entirely false and imaginary, until at last, having thus balanced my former prejudices with my latter [so that they cannot divert my opinions more to one side than to the other], my judgment will no longer be dominated by bad usage or turned away from the right knowledge of the truth. For I am assured that there can be neither peril nor error in this course, and that I cannot at present yield too much to distrust, since I am not considering the question of action, but only of knowledge.

I shall then suppose, not that God who is supremely good and the fountain of truth, but some evil genius not less powerful than deceitful, has employed his whole energies in deceiving me; I shall consider that the heavens, the earth, colours, figures, sound, and all other external things are nought but the illusions and dreams of which this genius has availed himself in order to lay traps for my credulity; I shall consider myself as having no hands, no eyes, no flesh, no blood, nor any senses, yet falsely believing myself to possess all these things; I shall remain obstinately attached to this idea, and if by this means it is not in my power to arrive at the knowledge of any truth, I may at least do what is in my power [i.e. suspend my judgment], and with firm purpose avoid giving credence to any false thing, or being imposed upon by this arch deceiver, however powerful and deceptive he may be. But this task is a laborious one, and insensibly a certain lassitude leads me into the course of my ordinary life. And just as a captive who in sleep enjoys imaginary liberty, when he begins to suspect that his liberty is but a dream, fears to awaken, and conspires with these agreeable illusions that the deception may be prolonged, so insensibly of my own accord I fall back into my former opinions, and I dread awakening from this slumber, lest the laborious wakefulness which would follow the tranquillity of this repose should have to be spent not in daylight, but in the excessive darkness of the difficulties which have just been discussed.

MEDITATION II

Of the Nature of the Human Mind; and That It Is More Easily Known Than the Body

The Meditation of yesterday filled my mind with so many doubts that it is no longer in my power to forget them. And yet I do not see in what manner I can resolve them; and, just as if I had all of a sudden fallen into very deep water, I am so disconcerted that I can neither make certain of setting my feet on the bottom, nor can I swim and so support myself on the surface. I shall nevertheless make an effort and follow anew the same path as that on which I yesterday entered, i.e. I shall proceed by setting aside all that in which the least doubt could be supposed to exist, just as if I had discovered that it was absolutely false; and I shall ever follow in this road until I have met with something which is certain, or at least, if I can do nothing else, until I have learned for certain that there is nothing in the world that is certain. Archimedes, in order that he might draw the terrestrial globe out of its place, and transport it elsewhere, demanded only that one point should be fixed and immoveable; in the same way I shall have the right to conceive high hopes if I am happy enough to discover one thing only which is certain and indubitable.

I suppose, then, that all the things that I see are false; I persuade myself that nothing has ever existed of all that my fallacious memory represents to me.

I consider that I possess no senses; I imagine that body, figure, extension, movement and place are but the fictions of my mind. What, then, can be esteemed as true? Perhaps nothing at all, unless that there is nothing in the world that is certain.

But how can I know there is not something different from those things that I have just considered, of which one cannot have the slightest doubt? Is there not some God, or some other being by whatever name we call it, who puts these reflections into my mind? That is not necessary, for is it not possible that I am capable of producing them myself? I myself, am I not at least something? But I have already denied that I had senses and body. Yet I hesitate, for what follows from that? Am I so dependent on body and senses that I cannot exist without these? But I was persuaded that there was nothing in all the world, that there was no heaven, no earth, that there were no minds, nor any bodies: was I not then likewise persuaded that I did not exist? Not at all; of a surety I myself did exist since I persuaded myself of something [or merely because I thought of something]. But there is some deceiver or other, very powerful and very cunning, who ever employs his ingenuity in deceiving me. Then without doubt I exist also if he deceives me, and let him deceive me as much as he will, he can never cause me to be nothing so long as I think that I am something. So that after having reflected well and carefully examined all things, we must come to the definite conclusion that this proposition: I am, I exist, is necessarily true each time that I pronounce it, or that I mentally conceive it.

But I do not yet know clearly enough what I am, I who am certain that I am; and hence I must be careful to see that I do not imprudently take some other object in place of myself, and thus that I do not go astray in respect of this knowledge that I hold to be the most certain and most evident of all that I have formerly learned. That is why I shall now consider anew what I believed myself to be before I embarked upon these last reflections; and of my former opinions I shall withdraw all that might even in a small degree be invalidated by the reasons which I have just brought forward, in order that there may be nothing at all left beyond what is absolutely certain and indubitable.

What then did I formerly believe myself to be? Undoubtedly I believed myself to be a man. But what is a man? Shall I say a reasonable animal? Certainly not; for then I should have to inquire what an animal is, and what is reasonable; and thus from a single question I should insensibly fall into an infinitude of others more difficult; and I should not wish to waste the little time and leisure remaining to me in trying to unravel subtleties like these. But I shall rather stop here to consider the thoughts which of themselves spring up in my mind, and which were not inspired by anything beyond my own nature alone when I applied myself to the consideration of my being. In the first place, then, I considered myself as having a face, hands, arms, and all that system of members composed of bones and flesh as seen in a corpse which I designated by the name of body. In addition to this I considered that I was nourished, that I walked, that I felt, and that I thought, and I referred all these actions to the soul: but I did not stop to consider what the soul was, or if I did stop, I imagined that it was something extremely rare and subtle like a wind, a flame, or an ether, which was spread throughout my grosser parts. As to body I had no manner of doubt about its nature, but thought I had a very clear knowledge of it; and if I had desired to explain it according to the notions that I had then formed of it, I should have described it thus: By the body I understand all that which can be defined by a certain figure: something which can be confined in a certain place, and which can fill a given space in such a way that every other body will be excluded from it; which can be perceived either by touch, or by sight, or by hearing, or by taste, or by smell: which can be moved in many ways not, in truth, by itself, but something which is foreign to it, by which it is touched [and from which it receives impressions]: for to have the power of self-movement, as also of feeling or of thinking, I did not consider to appertain to the nature of body: on the contrary, I was rather astonished to find that faculties similar to them existed in some bodies.

But what am I, now that I suppose that there is a certain genius which is extremely powerful, and, if I may say so, malicious, who employs all his powers in deceiving me? Can I affirm that I possess the least of all those things which I have just said pertain to the nature of body? I pause to consider, I resolve all these things in my mind, and find none of which I can say that it pertains to me. It would be tedious to stop to enumerate them. Let us pass to the attributes of soul and see if there is any one which is in me? What of nutrition or walking [the first mentioned]? But if it is so that I have no body it is also true that I can neither walk nor take nourishment. Another attribute is sensation. But one cannot feel without body, and besides I have thought I perceived many things during sleep that I recognised in my waking moments as not having been experienced at all. What of thinking? I find here that thought is an attribute that belongs to me; it alone cannot be separated from me. I am, I exist, that is certain. But how often? Just when I think; for it might possibly be the case if I ceased entirely to think, that I should likewise cease altogether

to exist. I do not now admit anything which is not necessarily true: to speak accurately I am not more than a thing which thinks, that is to say a mind or a soul, or an understanding, or a reason, which are terms whose significance was formerly unknown to me. I am, however, a real thing and really exist; but what thing? I have answered: a thing which thinks.

And what more? I shall exercise my imagination [in order to see if I am not something more]. I am not a collection of members which we call the human body: I am not a subtle air distributed through these members, I am not a wind, a fire, a vapour, a breath, nor anything at all which I can imagine or conceive; because I have assumed that all these were nothing. Without changing that supposition I find that I only leave myself certain of the fact that I am somewhat. But perhaps it is true that these same things which I supposed were nonexistent because they are unknown to me, are really not different from the self which I know. I am not sure about this, I shall not dispute about it now; I can only give judgment on things that are known to me. I know that I exist, and I inquire what I am, I whom I know to exist. But it is very certain that the knowledge of my existence taken in its precise significance does not depend on things whose existence is not yet known to me; consequently it does not depend on those which I can feign in imagination. And indeed the very term *feign* in imagination proves to me my error, for I really do this if I image myself a something, since to imagine is nothing else than to contemplate the figure or image of a corporeal thing. But I already know for certain that I am, and that it may be that all these images, and, speaking generally, all things that relate to the nature of body are nothing but dreams [and chimeras]. For this reason I see clearly that I have as little reason to say, "I shall stimulate my imagination in order to know more distinctly what I am," than if I were to say, "I am now awake, and I perceive somewhat that is real and true: but because I do not yet perceive it distinctly enough, I shall go to sleep of express purpose, so that my dreams may represent the perception with greatest truth and evidence." And, thus, I know for certain that nothing of all that I can understand by means of my imagination belongs to this knowledge which I have of myself, and that it is necessary to recall the mind from this mode of thought with the utmost diligence in order that it may be able to know its own nature with perfect distinctness.

But what then am I? A thing which thinks. What is a thing which thinks? It is a thing which doubts, understands, [conceives], affirms, denies, wills, refuses, which also imagines and feels.

Certainly it is no small matter if all these things pertain to my nature. But why should they not so pertain? Am I not that being who now doubts nearly everything, who nevertheless understands certain things, who affirms that one only is true, who denies all the others, who desires to know more, is averse from being deceived, who imagines many things, sometimes indeed despite his will, and who perceives many likewise, as by the intervention of the bodily organs? Is there nothing in all this which is as true as it is certain that I exist, even though I should always sleep and though he who has given me being employed all his ingenuity in deceiving me? Is there likewise any one of these attributes which can be distinguished from my thought, or which might be said to be separated from myself? For it is so evident of itself that it is I who doubts, who understands, and who desires, that there is no reason here to add anything to explain it. And I have certainly the power of imagining likewise; for although it may happen (as I formerly supposed) that none of the things which I imagine are true, nevertheless this power of imagining does not cease to be really in use, and it forms part of my thought. Finally, I am the same who feels, that is to say, who perceives certain things, as by the organs of sense, since in truth I see light, I hear noise, I feel heat. But it will be said that these phenomena are false and that I am dreaming. Let it be so; still it is at least quite certain that it seems to me that I see light, that I hear noise and that I feel heat. That cannot be false; properly speaking it is what is in me called feeling; and used in this precise sense that is no other thing than thinking.

From this time I begin to know what I am with a little more clearness and distinction than before; but nevertheless it still seems to me, and I cannot prevent myself from thinking, that corporeal things, whose images are framed by thought, which are tested by the senses, are much more distinctly known than that obscure part of me which does not come under the imagination. Although really it is very strange to say that I know and understand more distinctly these things whose existence seems to me dubious, which are unknown to me, and which do not belong to me, than others of the truth of which I am convinced, which are known to me and which pertain to my real nature, in a word, than myself. But I see clearly how the case stands: my mind loves to wander, and cannot yet suffer itself to be retained within the just limits of truth. Very good, let us once more give it the freest rein, so that, when afterwards we seize the proper occasion for pulling up, it may the more easily be regulated and controlled.

Let us begin by considering the commonest matters, those which we believe to be the most distinctly comprehended, to wit, the bodies which we touch and see; not indeed bodies in general, for these general ideas are usually a little more confused, but let us consider one body in particular. Let us take for example, this piece of wax: it has been taken quite freshly from the hive, and it has not yet lost the sweetness of the honey which it contains; it still retains somewhat of the odour of the flowers from which it has been culled; its colour, its figure, its size are apparent; it is hard, cold, easily handled, and if you strike it with the finger, it will emit a sound. Finally all the things which are requisite to cause us distinctly to recognise a body, are met within it. But notice that while I speak and approach the fire what remained of the taste is exhaled, the smell evaporates, the colour alters, the figure is destroyed, the size increases, it becomes liquid, it heats, scarcely can one handle it, and when one strikes it, no sound is emitted. Does the same wax remain after this change? We must confess that it remains; none would judge otherwise. What then did I know so distinctly in this piece of wax? It could certainly be nothing of all that the senses brought to my notice, since all these things which fall under taste, smell, sight, touch, and hearing, are found to be changed, and yet the same wax remains.

Perhaps it was what I now think, viz. that this wax was not that sweetness of honey, nor that agreeable scent of flowers, nor that particular whiteness, nor that figure, nor that sound, but simply a body which a little before appeared to me as perceptible under these forms, and which is now perceptible under others. But what, precisely, is it that I imagine when I form such conceptions? Let us attentively consider this, and, abstracting from all that does not belong to the wax, let us see what remains. Certainly nothing remains excepting a certain extended thing which is flexible and movable. But what is the

meaning of flexible and movable? Is it not that I imagine that this piece of wax being round is capable of becoming square and of passing from a square to a triangular figure? No, certainly it is not that, since I imagine it admits of an infinitude of similar changes, and I nevertheless do not know how to compass the infinitude by my imagination, and consequently this conception which I have of the wax is not brought about by the faculty of imagination. What now is this extension? Is it not also unknown? For it becomes greater when the wax is melted, greater when it is boiled, and greater still when the heat increases; and I should not conceive [clearly] according to truth what wax is, if I did not think that even this piece that we are considering is capable of receiving more variations in extension than I have ever imagined. We must then grant that I could not even understand through the imagination what this piece of wax is, and that it is my mind alone which perceives it. I say this piece of wax in particular, for as to wax in general it is yet clearer. But what is this piece of wax which cannot be understood excepting by the [understanding or] mind? It is certainly the same that I see, touch, imagine, and finally it is the same which I have always believed it to be from the beginning. But what must particularly be observed is that its perception is neither an act of vision, nor of touch, nor of imagination, and has never been such although it may have appeared formerly to be so, but only an intuition of the mind, which may be imperfect and confused as it was formerly, or clear and distinct as it is at present, according as my attention is more or less directed to the elements which are found in it, and of which it is composed.

Yet in the meantime I am greatly astonished when I consider [the great feebleness of mind] and its proneness to fall [insensibly] into error; for although without giving expression to my thoughts I consider all this in my own mind, words often impede me and I am almost deceived by the terms of ordinary language. For we say that we see the same wax, if it is present, and not that we simply judge that it is the same from its having the same colour and figure. From this I should conclude that I knew the wax by means of vision and not simply by the intuition of the mind; unless by chance I remember that, when looking from a window and saying I see men who pass in the street, I really do not see them, but infer that what I see is men, just as I say that I see wax. And yet what do I see from the window but hats and coats which may cover automatic machines? Yet I judge these to be men. And similarly solely by the faculty of judgment which rests in my mind, I comprehend that which I believed I saw with my eyes.

A man who makes it his aim to raise his knowledge above the common should be ashamed to derive the occasion for doubting from the forms of speech invented by the vulgar; I prefer to pass on and consider whether I had a more evident and perfect conception of what the wax was when I first perceived it, and when I believed I knew it by means of the external senses or at least by the common sense as it is called, that is to say by the imaginative faculty, or whether my present conception is clearer now that I have most carefully examined what it is, and in what way it can be known. It would certainly be absurd to doubt as to this. For what was there in this first perception which was distinct? What was there which might not as well have been perceived by any of the animals? But when I distinguish the wax from its external forms, and when, just as if I had taken from it its vestments, I consider it quite naked, it is certain that although some error may still be found in my judgment, I can neverthe-

less not perceive it thus without a human mind.

But finally what shall I say of this mind, that is, of myself, for up to this point I do not admit in myself anything but mind? What then, I who seem to perceive this piece of wax distinctly, do I not know myself, not only with much more truth and certainty, but also with much more distinctness and clearness? For if I judge that the wax is or exists from the fact that I see it, it certainly follows much more clearly that I am or that I exist myself from the fact that I see it. For it may be that what I see is not really wax, it may also be that I do not possess eyes with which to see anything; but it cannot be that when I see, or (for I no longer take account of the distinction) when I think I see, that I myself who think am nought. So if I judge that the wax exists from the fact that I touch it, the same thing will follow, to wit, that I am; and if I judge that my imagination, or some other cause, whatever it is, persuades me that the wax exists, I shall still conclude the same. And what I have here remarked of wax may be applied to all other things which are external to me [and which are met with outside of me]. And further, if the [notion or] perception of wax has seemed to me clearer and more distinct, not only after the sight or the touch, but also after many other causes have rendered it quite manifest to me, with how much more [evidence] and distinctness must it be said that I now know myself, since all the reasons which contribute to the knowledge of wax, or any other body whatever, are yet better proofs of the nature of my mind! And there are so many other things in the mind itself which may contribute to the elucidation of its nature, that those which depend on body such as these just mentioned, hardly merit being taken into account.

But finally here I am, having insensibly reverted to the point I desired, for, since it is now manifest to me that even bodies are not properly speaking known by the senses or by the faculty of imagination, but by the understanding only, and since they are not known from the fact that they are seen or touched, but only because they are understood, I see clearly that there is nothing which is easier for me to know than my mind. But because it is difficult to rid oneself so promptly of an opinion to which one was accustomed for so long, it will be well that I should halt a little at this point, so that by the length of my meditation I may more deeply imprint on my memory this new knowledge.

4. An Introduction to Metaphysics *

Henri Bergson (1860–1941)

A comparison of the definitions of metaphysics and the various conceptions of the absolute leads to the discovery that philosophers, in spite of their apparent divergencies, agree in distinguishing two profoundly different ways of knowing a thing. The first implies that we move round the object; the second that we enter into it. The first depends on the point of view at which we are placed and on the symbols by which we express ourselves. The second neither depends on a point of view nor relies on any symbol. The first kind of knowledge may be said to stop at the *relative;* the second, in those cases where it is possible, to attain the *absolute.*

Consider, for example, the movement of an object in space. My perception of the motion will vary with the point of view, moving or stationary, from which I observe it. My expression of it will vary with the systems of axes, or the points of reference, to which I relate it; that is, with the symbols by which I translate it. For this double reason I call such motion *relative:* in the one case, as in the other, I am placed outside the object itself. But when I speak of an *absolute* movement, I am attributing to the moving object an interior and, so to speak, states of mind; I also imply that I am in sympathy with those states, and that I insert myself in them by an effort of imagination. Then, according as the object is moving or stationary, according as it adopts one movement or another, what I experience will vary. And what I experience will depend neither on the point of view I may take up in regard to the object, since I am inside the object itself, nor on the symbols by which I may translate the motion, since I have rejected all translations in order to possess the original. In short, I shall no longer grasp the movement from without, remaining where I am, but from where it is, from within, as it is in itself. I shall possess an absolute.

Consider, again, a character whose adventures are related to me in a novel. The author may multiply the traits of his hero's character, may make him

---

* Pages 1-30 of *An Introduction to Metaphysics* by Henri Bergson, published 1912 by G. P. Putnam's Sons, and reprinted with their permission.

speak and act as much as he pleases, but all this can never be equivalent to the simple and indivisible feeling which I should experience if I were able for an instant to identify myself with the person of the hero himself. Out of that indivisible feeling, as from a spring, all the words, gestures, and actions of the man would appear to me to flow naturally. They would no longer be accidents which, added to the idea I had already formed of the character, continually enriched that idea, without ever completing it. The character would be given to me all at once, in its entirety, and the thousand incidents which manifest it, instead of adding themselves to the idea and so enriching it, would seem to me, on the contrary, to detach themselves from it, without, however, exhausting it or impoverishing its essence. All the things I am told about the man provide me with so many points of view from which I can observe him. All the traits which describe him, and which can make him known to me only by so many comparisons with persons or things I know already, are signs by which he is expressed more or less symbolically. Symbols and points of view, therefore, place me outside him; they give me only what he has in common with others, and not what belongs to him and to him alone. But that which is properly himself, that which constitutes his essence, cannot be perceived from without, being internal by definition, nor be expressed by symbols, being incommensurable with everything else. Description, history, and analysis leave me here in the relative. Coincidence with the person himself would alone give me the absolute.

It is in this sense, and in this sense only, that *absolute* is synonymous with *perfection*. Were all the photographs of a town, taken from all possible points of view, to go on indefinitely completing one another, they would never be equivalent to the solid town in which we walk about. Were all the translations of a poem into all possible languages to add together their various shades of meaning and, correcting each other by a kind of mutual retouching, to give a more and more faithful image of the poem they translate, they would yet never succeed in rendering the inner meaning of the original. A representation taken from a certain point of view, a translation made with certain symbols, will always remain imperfect in comparison with the object of which a view has been taken, or which the symbols seek to express. But the absolute, which is the object and not its representation, the original and not its translation, is perfect, by being perfectly what it is.

It is doubtless for this reason that the *absolute* has often been identified with the *infinite*. Suppose that I wished to communicate to some one who did not know Greek the extraordinarily simple impression that a passage in Homer makes upon me; I should first give a translation of the lines, I should then comment on my translation, and then develop the commentary; in this way, by piling up explanation on explanation, I might approach nearer and nearer to what I wanted to express; but I should never quite reach it. When you raise your arm, you accomplish a movement of which you have, from within, a simple perception; but for me, watching it from the outside, your arm passes through one point, then through another, and between these two there will be still other points; so that, if I began to count, the operation would go on for ever. Viewed from the inside, then, an absolute is a simple thing; but looked at from the outside, that is to say, relatively to other things, it becomes, in relation to these signs which express it, the gold coin for which we never seem able to finish giving small change. Now, that which lends itself at the same time both to an indivisible apprehension and to an inexhaustible enumeration is, by the very definition of the word, an infinite.

It follows from this that an absolute could only be given in an *intuition,* whilst everything else falls within the province of *analysis.* By intuition is meant the kind of *intellectual sympathy* by which one places oneself within an object in order to coincide with what is unique in it and consequently inexpressible. Analysis, on the contrary, is the operation which reduces the object to elements already known, that is, to elements common both to it and other objects. To analyze, therefore, is to express a thing as a function of something other than itself. All analysis is thus a translation, a development into symbols, a representation taken from successive points of view from which we note as many resemblances as possible between the new object which we are studying and others which we believe we know already. In its eternally unsatisfied desire to embrace the object around which it is compelled to turn, analysis multiplies without end the number of its points of view in order to complete its always incomplete representation, and ceaselessly varies its symbols that it may perfect the always imperfect translation. It goes on, therefore, to infinity. But intuition, if intuition is possible, is a simple act.

Now it is easy to see that the ordinary function of positive science is analysis. Positive science works, then, above all, with symbols. Even the most concrete of the natural sciences, those concerned with life, confine themselves to the visible form of living beings, their organs and anatomical elements. They make comparisons between these forms, they reduce the more complex to the more simple; in short, they study the workings of life in what is, so to speak, only its visual symbol. If there exists any means of possessing a reality absolutely instead of knowing it relatively, of plac-

ing oneself within it instead of looking at it from outside points of view, of having the intuition instead of making the analysis: in short, of seizing it without any expression, translation, or symbolic representation—metaphysics is that means. *Metaphysics, then, is the science which claims to dispense with symbols.*

There is one reality, at least, which we all seize from within, by intuition and not by simple analysis. It is our own personality in its flowing through time— our self which endures. We may sympathize intellectually with nothing else, but we certainly sympathize with our own selves.

When I direct my attention inward to contemplate my own self (supposed for the moment to be inactive), I perceive at first, as a crust solidified on the surface, all the perceptions which come to it from the material world. These perceptions are clear, distinct, juxtaposed, or juxtaposable one with another; they tend to group themselves into objects. Next, I notice the memories which more or less adhere to these perceptions and which serve to interpret them. These memories have been detached, as it were, from the depth of my personality, drawn to the surface by the perceptions which resemble them; they rest on the surface of my mind without being absolutely myself. Lastly, I feel the stir of tendencies and motor habits—a crowd of virtual actions, more or less firmly bound to these perceptions and memories. All these clearly defined elements appear more distinct from me, the more distinct they are from each other. Radiating, as they do, from within outwards, they form, collectively, the surface of a sphere which tends to grow larger and lose itself in the exterior world. But if I draw myself in from the periphery towards the centre, if I search in the depth of my being that which is most uniformly, most constantly, and most enduringly myself, I find an altogether different thing.

There is, beneath these sharply cut crystals and this frozen surface, a continuous flux which is not comparable to any flux I have ever seen. There is a succession of states, each of which announces that which follows and contains that which precedes it. They can, properly speaking, only be said to form multiple states when I have already passed them and turn back to observe their track. Whilst I was experiencing them they were so solidly organized, so profoundly animated with a common life, that I could not have said where any one of them finished or where another commenced. In reality no one of them begins or ends, but all extend into each other.

This inner life may be compared to the unrolling of a coil, for there is no living being who does not feel himself coming gradually to the end of his rôle; and to live is to grow old. But it may just as well be compared to a continual rolling up, like that of a thread on a ball, for our past follows us, it swells incessantly with the present that it picks up on its way; and consciousness means memory.

But actually it is neither an unrolling nor a rolling up, for these two similes evoke the idea of lines and surfaces whose parts are homogeneous and superposable on one another. Now, there are no two identical moments in the life of the same conscious being. Take the simplest sensation, suppose it constant, absorb in it the entire personality: the consciousness which will accompany this sensation cannot remain identical with itself for two consecutive moments, because the second moment always contains, over and above the first, the memory that the first has bequeathed to it. A consciousness which could experience two identical moments would be a consciousness without memory. It would die and be born again continually. In

what other way could one represent unconsciousness?

It would be better, then, to use as a comparison the myriad-tinted spectrum, with its insensible gradations leading from one shade to another. A current of feeling which passed along the spectrum, assuming in turn the tint of each of its shades, would experience a series of gradual changes, each of which would announce the one to follow and would sum up those which preceded it. Yet even here the successive shades of the spectrum always remain external one to another. They are juxtaposed; they occupy space. But pure duration, on the contrary, excludes all idea of juxtaposition, reciprocal externality, and extension.

Let us, then, rather, imagine an infinitely small elastic body, contracted, if it were possible, to a mathematical point. Let this be drawn out gradually in such a manner that from the point comes a constantly lengthening line. Let us fix our attention not on the line as a line, but on the action by which it is traced. Let us bear in mind that this action, in spite of its duration, is indivisible if accomplished without stopping, that if a stopping-point is inserted, we have two actions instead of one, that each of these separate actions is then the indivisible operation of which we speak, and that it is not the moving action itself which is divisible, but, rather, the stationary line it leaves behind it as its track in space. Finally, let us free ourselves from the space which underlies the movement in order to consider only the movement itself, the act of tension or extension; in short, pure mobility. We shall have this time a more faithful image of the development of our self in duration.

However, even this image is incomplete, and, indeed, every comparison will be insufficient, because the unrolling of our duration resembles in some of its aspects the unity of an advancing movement and in others the multiplicity of expanding states; and, clearly, no metaphor can express one of these two aspects without sacrificing the other. If I use the comparison of the spectrum with its thousand shades, I have before me a thing already made, whilst duration is continually in the making. If I think of an elastic which is being stretched, or of a spring which is extended or relaxed, I forget the richness of color, characteristic of duration that is lived, to see only the simple movement by which consciousness passes from one shade to another. The inner life is all this at once: variety of qualities, continuity of progress, and unity of direction. It cannot be represented by images.

But it is even less possible to represent it by *concepts,* that is by abstract, general, or simple ideas. It is true that no image can reproduce exactly the original feeling I have of the flow of my own conscious life. But it is not even necessary that I should attempt to render it. If a man is incapable of getting for himself the intuition of the constitutive duration of his own being, nothing will ever give it to him, concepts no more than images. Here the single aim of the philosopher should be to promote a certain effort, which in most men is usually fettered by habits of mind more useful to life. Now the image has at least this advantage, that it keeps us in the concrete. No image can replace the intuition of duration, but many diverse images, borrowed from very different orders of things, may, by the convergence of their action, direct consciousness to the precise point where there is a certain intuition to be seized. By choosing images as dissimilar as possible, we shall prevent any one of them from usurping the place of the intuition it is intended to call up, since it would then be driven away at once by its rivals. By providing that, in spite of their differences of aspect, they all require from the mind the same kind

of attention, and in some sort the same degree of tension, we shall gradually accustom consciousness to a particular and clearly-defined disposition—that precisely which it must adopt in order to appear to itself as it really is, without any veil. But, then, consciousness must at least consent to make the effort. For it will have been shown nothing: it will simply have been placed in the attitude it must take up in order to make the desired effort, and so come by itself to the intuition. Concepts on the contrary —especially if they are simple—have the disadvantage of being in reality symbols substituted for the object they symbolize, and demand no effort on our part. Examined closely, each of them, it would be seen, retains only that part of the object which is common to it and to others, and expresses, still more than the image does, a *comparison* between the object and others which resemble it. But as the comparison has made manifest a resemblance, as the resemblance is a property of the object, and as a property has every appearance of being a *part* of the object which possesses it, we easily persuade ourselves that by setting concept beside concept we are reconstructing the whole of the object with its parts, thus obtaining, so to speak, its intellectual equivalent. In this way we believe that we can form a faithful representation of duration by setting in line the concepts of unity, multiplicity, continuity, finite or infinite divisibility, etc. There precisely is the illusion. There also is the danger. Just in so far as abstract ideas can render service to analysis, that is, to the scientific study of the object in its relations to other objects, so far are they incapable of replacing intuition, that is, the metaphysical investigation of what is essential and unique in the object. For on the one hand these concepts, laid side by side, never actually give us more than an artificial reconstruction of the object, of which they can only symbolize certain general, and, in a way, impersonal aspects; it is therefore useless to believe that with them we can seize a reality of which they present to us the shadow alone. And, on the other hand, besides the illusion there is also a very serious danger. For the concept generalizes at the same time as it abstracts. The concept can only symbolize a particular property by making it common to an infinity of things. It therefore always more or less deforms the property by the extension it gives to it. Replaced in the metaphysical object to which it belongs, a property coincides with the object, or at least moulds itself on it, and adopts the same outline. Extracted from the metaphysical object, and presented in a concept, it grows indefinitely larger, and goes beyond the object itself, since henceforth it has to contain it, along with a number of other objects. Thus the different concepts that we form of the properties of a thing inscribe round it so many circles, each much too large and none of them fitting it exactly. And yet, in the thing itself the properties coincided with the thing, and coincided consequently with one another. So that if we are bent on reconstructing the object with concepts, some artifice must be sought whereby this coincidence of the object and its properties can be brought about. For example, we may choose one of the concepts and try, starting from it, to get round to the others. But we shall then soon discover that according as we start from one concept or another, the meeting and combination of the concepts will take place in an altogether different way. According as we start, for example, from unity or from multiplicity, we shall have to conceive differently the multiple unity of duration. Everything will depend on the weight we attribute to this or that concept, and this weight will always be arbitrary, since the concept extracted from the object has no weight, being only the shadow of a body. In this

way, as many different *systems* will spring up as there are external points of view from which the reality can be examined, or larger circles in which it can be enclosed. Simple concepts have, then, not only the inconvenience of dividing the concrete unity of the object into so many symbolical expressions; they also divide philosophy into distinct schools, each of which takes its seat, chooses its counters, and carries on with the others a game that will never end. Either metaphysics is only this play of ideas, or else, if it is a serious occupation of the mind, if it is a science and not simply an exercise, it must transcend concepts in order to reach intuition. Certainly, concepts are necessary to it, for all the other sciences work as a rule with concepts, and metaphysics cannot dispense with the other sciences. But it is only truly itself when it goes beyond the concept, or at least when it frees itself from rigid and ready-made concepts in order to create a kind very different from those which we habitually use; I mean supple, mobile, and almost fluid representations, always ready to mould themselves on the fleeting forms of intuition. We shall return later to this important point. Let it suffice us for the moment to have shown that our duration can be presented to us directly in an intuition, that it can be suggested to us indirectly by images, but that it can never—if we confine the word concept to its proper meaning—be enclosed in a conceptual representation.

Let us try for an instant to consider our duration as a multiplicity. It will then be necessary to add that the terms of this multiplicity, instead of being distinct, as they are in any other multiplicity, encroach on one another; and that while we can no doubt, by an effort of imagination, solidify duration once it has elapsed, divide it into juxtaposed portions and count all these portions, yet this operation is accomplished on the frozen memory of the duration, on the stationary trace which the mobility of duration leaves behind it, and not on the duration itself. We must admit, therefore, that if there is a multiplicity here, it bears no resemblance to any other multiplicity we know. Shall we say, then, that duration has unity? Doubtless, a continuity of elements which prolong themselves into one another participates in unity as much as in multiplicity; but this moving, changing, colored, living unity has hardly anything in common with the abstract, motionless, and empty unity which the concept of pure unity circumscribes. Shall we conclude from this that duration must be defined as unity and multiplicity at the same time? But singularly enough, however much I manipulate the two concepts, portion them out, combine them differently, practise on them the most subtle operations of mental chemistry, I never obtain anything which resembles the simple intuition that I have of duration; while, on the contrary, when I replace myself in duration by an effort of intuition, I immediately perceive how it is unity, multiplicity, and many other things besides. These different concepts, then, were only so many standpoints from which we could consider duration. Neither separated nor reunited have they made us penetrate into it.

We do penetrate into it, however, and that can only be by an effort of intuition. In this sense, an inner, absolute knowledge of the duration of the self by the self is possible. But if metaphysics here demands and can obtain an intuition, science has none the less need of an analysis. Now it is a confusion between the function of analysis and that of intuition which gives birth to the discussions between the schools and the conflicts between systems.

Psychology, in fact, proceeds like all the other sciences by analysis. It resolves the self, which has been given to it at first in a simple intuition, into sensations, feelings, ideas, etc., which it studies separately. It substitutes, then, for the self a series of elements which form the facts of psychology. But are these *elements* really *parts*? That is the whole question, and it is because it has been evaded that the problem of human personality has so often been stated in insoluble terms.

It is incontestable that every psychical state, simply because it belongs to a person, reflects the whole of a personality. Every feeling, however simple it may be, contains virtually within it the whole past and present of the being experiencing it, and, consequently, can only be separated and constituted into a "state" by an effort of abstraction or of analysis. But it is no less incontestable that without this effort of abstraction or analysis there would be no possible development of the science of psychology. What, then, exactly, is the operation by which a psychologist detaches a mental state in order to erect it into a more or less independent entity? He begins by neglecting that special coloring of the personality which cannot be expressed in known and common terms. Then he endeavors to isolate, in the person already thus simplified, some aspect which lends itself to an interesting inquiry. If he is considering inclination, for example, he will neglect the inexpressible shade which colors it, and which makes the inclination mine and not yours; he will fix his attention on the movement by which our personality *leans towards* a certain object: he will isolate this attitude, and it is this special aspect of the personality, this snapshot of the mobility of the inner life, this "diagram" of concrete inclination, that he will erect into an independent fact. There is in this something very like what an artist passing through Paris does when he makes, for example, a sketch of a tower of Notre Dame. The tower is inseparably united to the building, which is itself no less inseparably united to the ground, to its surroundings, to the whole of Paris, and so on. It is first necessary to detach it from all these; only one aspect of the whole is noted, that formed by the tower of Notre Dame. Moreover, the special form of this tower is due to the grouping of the stones of which it is composed; but the artist does not concern himself with these stones, he notes only the silhouette of the tower. For the real and internal organization of the thing he substitutes, then, an external and schematic representation. So that, on the whole, his sketch corresponds to an observation of the object from a certain point of view and to the choice of a certain means of representation. But exactly the same thing holds true of the operation by which the psychologist extracts a single mental state from the whole personality. This isolated psychical state is hardly anything but a sketch, the commencement of an artificial reconstruction; it is the whole considered under a certain elementary aspect in which we are specially interested and which we have carefully noted. It is not a part, but an element. It has not been obtained by a natural dismemberment, but by analysis.

Now beneath all the sketches he has made at Paris the visitor will probably, by way of memento, write the word "Paris." And as he has really seen Paris, he will be able, with the help of the original intuition he had of the whole, to place his sketches therein, and so join them up together. But there is no way of performing the inverse operation; it is impossible, even with an infinite number of accurate sketches, and even with the word "Paris" which indicates that they must be combined together, to get back to an intuition that one has never had, and to give oneself an impression of what Paris is like if one has never seen it. This is because we are not dealing here with real *parts,* but with mere *notes* of the total impression. To take a still more striking example, where the notation is more completely symbolic, suppose that I am shown, mixed together at random, the letters which make up a poem I am ignorant of. If the letters were *parts* of the poem, I could attempt to reconstitute the poem with them by trying the different possible arrangements, as a child does with the pieces of a Chinese puzzle. But I should never for a moment think of attempting such a thing in this case, because the letters are not *component parts,* but only *partial expressions,* which is quite a different thing. That is why, if I know the poem, I at once put each of the letters in its proper place and join them up without difficulty by a continuous connection, whilst the inverse operation is impossible. Even when I believe I am actually attempting this inverse operation, even when I put the letters end to end, I begin by thinking of some plausible meaning. I thereby give myself an intuition, and from this intuition I attempt to redescend to the elementary symbols which would reconstitute its expression. The very idea of reconstituting a thing by operations practised on symbolic elements alone implies such an absurdity that it would never occur to any one if they recollected that they were not dealing with fragments of the thing, but only, as it were, with fragments of its symbol.

Such is, however, the undertaking of the philosophers who try to reconstruct personality with psychical states, whether they confine themselves to those states alone, or whether they add a kind of thread for the purpose of joining the states together. Both empiricists and rationalists are victims of the same fallacy. Both of them mistake *partial notations* for *real parts,* thus confusing the point of view of analysis and of intuition, of science and of metaphysics.

5. *The Fixation of Belief* *

CHARLES S. PEIRCE (1839–1914)

Few persons care to study logic, because everybody conceives himself to be proficient enough in the art of reasoning already. But I observe that this satisfaction is limited to one's own ratiocination, and does not extend to that of other men.

We come to the full possession of our power of drawing inferences the last of all our faculties, for it is not so much a natural gift as a long and difficult art. The history of its practice would make a grand subject for a book. The medieval schoolman, following the Romans, made logic the earliest of a boy's studies after grammar, as being very easy. So it was as they understood it. Its fundamental principle, according to them, was, that all knowledge rests on either authority or reason; but that whatever is deduced by reason depends ultimately on a premise derived from authority. Accordingly, as soon as a boy was perfect in the syllogistic procedure, his intellectual kit of tools was held to be complete.

To Roger Bacon, that remarkable mind who in the middle of the thirteenth century was almost a scientific man, the schoolmen's conception of reasoning appeared only an obstacle to truth. He saw that experience alone teaches anything—a proposition which to us seems easy to understand, because a distinct conception of experience has been handed down to us from former generations; which to

him also seemed perfectly clear, because its difficulties had not yet unfolded themselves. Of all kinds of experience, the best, he thought, was interior illumination, which teaches many things about Nature which the external senses could never discover, such as the transubstantiation of bread.

Four centuries later, the more celebrated Bacon, in the first book of his "Novum Organum," gave his clear account of experience as something which must be opened to verification and re-examination.[1] But, superior as Lord Bacon's conception is to earlier notions, a modern reader who is not in awe of his grandiloquence is chiefly struck by the inadequacy of his view of scientific procedure. That we have only to make some crude experiments, to draw up briefs of the results in certain blank forms, to go through these by rule, checking off everything disproved and setting down the alternatives, and that thus in a few years physical science would be finished up—what an idea! "He wrote on science like a Lord Chancellor," indeed.

The early scientists, Copernicus, Tycho Brahe, Kepler, Galileo and Gilbert, had methods more like those of their modern brethren. Kepler undertook to draw a curve through the places of Mars; and his greatest service to science was in impressing on men's minds that this was the thing to be done if they

---

* Originally published in *Popular Science Monthly* (1877); a few minor omissions have been made.

[1] See page 15.

wished to improve astronomy; that they were not to content themselves with inquiring whether one system of epicycles was better than another but that they were to sit down by the figures and find out what the curve, in truth, was. He accomplished this by his incomparable energy and courage, blundering along in the most inconceivable way (to us), from one irrational hypothesis to another, until, after trying twenty-two of these, he fell, by the mere exhaustion of his invention, upon the orbit which a mind well furnished with the weapons of modern logic would have tried almost at the outset.[2]

In the same way, every work of science great enough to be remembered for a few generations affords some exemplification of the defective state of the art of reasoning of the time when it was written; and each chief step in science has been a lesson in logic. It was so when Lavoisier and his contemporaries took up the study of Chemistry. The old chemist's maxim had been, "Lege, lege, lege, labora, ora, et relege." Lavoisier's method was not to read and pray, not to dream that some long and complicated chemical process would have a certain effect, to put it into practice with dull patience, after its inevitable failure, to dream that with some modification it would have another result, and to end by publishing the last dream as a fact: his way was to carry his mind into his laboratory, and to make of his alembics and cucurbits instruments of thought, giving a new conception of reasoning as something which was to be done with one's eyes open, by manipulating real things instead of words and fancies . . .

---

[2] Twenty-one years after writing this comment on Kepler, that is, in 1893, Peirce retracted it, saying it was a "foolish remark" which he made because he had not then read the original work of Kepler. He now believed (in 1893) that it was a "marvelous piece of inductive reasoning." [D. J. B.]

The object of reasoning is to find out, from the consideration of what we already know, something else which we do not know. Consequently, reasoning is good if it be such as to give a true conclusion from true premises, and not otherwise. Thus, the question of validity is purely one of fact and not of thinking. A being the premises and B being the conclusion, the question is, whether these facts are really so related that if A is, B is. If so, the inference is valid; if not, not. It is not in the least the question whether, when the premises are accepted by the mind, we feel an impulse to accept the conclusion also. It is true that we do generally reason correctly by nature. But that is an accident; the true conclusion would remain true if we had no impulse to accept it; and the false one would remain false, though we could not resist the tendency to believe in it.

We are, doubtless, in the main logical animals, but we are not perfectly so. Most of us, for example, are naturally more sanguine and hopeful than logic would justify. We seem to be so constituted that in the absence of any facts to go upon we are happy and self-satisfied; so that the effect of experience is continually to counteract our hopes and aspirations. Yet a lifetime of the application of this corrective does not usually eradicate our sanguine disposition. Where hope is unchecked by any experience, it is likely that our optimism is extravagant. Logicality in regard to practical matters is the most useful quality an animal can possess, and might, therefore, result from the action of natural selection; but outside of these it is probably of more advantage to the animal to have his mind filled with pleasing and encouraging visions, independently of their truth; and thus, upon unpractical subjects, natural selection might occasion a fallacious tendency of thought.

That which determines us, from given premises, to draw one inference rather than another, is some habit of mind, whether it be constitutional or acquired. The habit is good or otherwise, according as it produces true conclusions from true premises or not; and an inference is regarded as valid or not, without reference to the truth or falsity of its conclusion specially, but according as the habit which determines it is such as to produce true conclusions in general or not. The particular habit of mind which governs this or that inference may be formulated in a proposition whose truth depends on the validity of the inferences which the habit determines; and such a formula is called a *guiding principle* of inference. Suppose, for example, that we observe that a rotating disk of copper quickly comes to rest when placed between the poles of a magnet, and we infer that this will happen with every disk of copper. The guiding principle is, that what is true of one piece of copper is true of another. Such a guiding principle with regard to copper would be much safer than with regard to many other substances—brass, for example.

A book might be written to signalize all the most important of these guiding principles of reasoning. It would probably be, we must confess, of no service to a person whose thought is directed wholly to practical subjects, and whose activity moves along thoroughly beaten paths. The problems which present themselves to such a mind are matters of routine which he has learned once for all to handle in learning his business. But let a man venture into an unfamiliar field, or where his results are not continually checked by experience, and all history shows that the most masculine intellect will ofttimes lose his orientation and waste his efforts in directions which bring him no nearer to his goal, or even carry him entirely astray. He is like a ship on the open sea, with no one on board who understands the rules of navigation. And in such a case some

general study of the guiding principles of reasoning would be sure to be found useful.

The subject could hardly be treated, however, without being first limited; since almost any fact may serve as a guiding principle. But it so happens that there exists a division among facts, such that in one class are all those which are absolutely essential as guiding principles, while in the other are all those which have any other interest as objects of research. This division is between those which are necessarily taken for granted in asking whether a certain conclusion follows from certain premises, and those which are not implied in that question. A moment's thought will show that a variety of facts are already assumed when the logical question is first asked. It is implied, for instance, that there are such states of mind as doubt and belief —that a passage from one to the other is possible, the object of thought remaining the same, and that this transition is subject to some rules which all minds are alike bound by. As these are facts which we must already know before we can have any clear conception of reasoning at all, it cannot be supposed to be any longer of much interest to inquire into their truth or falsity. On the other hand, it is easy to believe that those rules of reasoning which are deduced from the very idea of the process are the ones which are the most essential; and, indeed, that so long as it conforms to these it will, at least, not lead to false conclusions from true premises. In point of fact, the importance of what may be deduced from the assumptions involved in the logical question turns out to be greater than might be supposed, and this for reasons which it is difficult to exhibit at the outset. The only one which I shall here mention is, that conceptions which are really products of logical reflections, without being readily seen to be so, mingle with our ordinary thoughts, and are frequently the causes of great confusion. This is the case, for example, with the conception of quality. A quality as such is never an object of observation. We can see that a thing is blue or green, but the quality of being blue and the quality of being green are not things which we see; they are products of logical reflections. The truth is, that common-sense, or thought as it first emerges above the level of the narrowly practical, is deeply imbued with that bad logical quality to which the epithet *metaphysical* is commonly applied; and nothing can clear it up but a severe course of logic.

We generally know when we wish to ask a question and when we wish to pronounce a judgment, for there is a dissimilarity between the sensation of doubting and that of believing.

But this is not all which distinguishes doubt from belief. There is a practical difference. Our beliefs guide our desires and shape our actions. The Assassins, or followers of the Old Man of the Mountain, used to rush into death at his least command, because they believed that obedience to him would insure everlasting felicity. Had they doubted this, they would not have acted as they did. So it is with every belief, according to its degree. The feeling of believing is a more or less sure indication of there being established in our nature some habit which will determine our actions. Doubt never has such an effect.

Nor must we overlook a third point of difference. Doubt is an uneasy and dissatisfied state from which we struggle to free ourselves and pass into the state of belief; while the latter is a calm and satisfactory state which we do not wish to avoid, or to change to a belief in anything else. On the contrary, we cling tenaciously, not merely to believing, but to believing just what we do believe.

Thus, both doubt and belief have positive effects upon us, though very different ones. Belief does not make us act at once, but puts us into such a condition that we shall behave in a certain way, when the occasion arises. Doubt has not the least effect of this sort, but stimulates us to action until it is destroyed. This reminds us of the irritation of a nerve and the reflex action produced thereby; while for the analogue of belief, in the nervous system, we must look to what are called nervous associations— for example, to that habit of the nerves in consequence of which the smell of a peach will make the mouth water.

The irritation of doubt causes a struggle to attain a state of belief. I shall term this struggle *inquiry*, though it must be admitted that this is sometimes not a very apt designation.

The irritation of doubt is the only immediate motive for the struggle to attain belief. It is certainly best for us that our beliefs should be such as may truly guide our actions so as to satisfy our desires; and this reflection will make us reject any belief which does not seem to have been so formed as to insure this result. But it will only do so by creating a doubt in the place of that belief. With the doubt, therefore, the struggle begins, and with the cessation of doubt it ends. Hence, the sole object of inquiry is the settlement of opinion.[3] We may fancy that this is not enough for us, and that we seek not merely an opinion, but a true opinion. But put this fancy to the test, and it proves groundless; for as soon as a firm belief is reached we are entirely satisfied, whether the belief be false or true. And it is clear that nothing out of the sphere of our knowledge can be our object, for nothing which does not affect the mind can be a motive for a mental effort. The most that can be maintained is, that we seek for a belief that we shall *think* to be true. But we

---

[3] In later life Peirce changed his mind about this. See Charles Sanders Peirce, *Collected Papers,* Vol. 6, paragraph 485. [D. J. B.]

think each one of our beliefs to be true, and, indeed, it is mere tautology to say so.

That the settlement of opinion is the sole end of inquiry is a very important proposition. It sweeps away, at once, various vague and erroneous conceptions of proof. A few of these may be noticed here.

1. Some philosophers have imagined that to start an inquiry it was only necessary to utter a question or set it down on paper, and have even recommended us to begin our studies with questioning everything! But the mere putting of a proposition into the interrogative form does not stimulate the mind to any struggle after belief. There must be a real and living doubt, and without this all discussion is idle.

2. It is a very common idea that a demonstration must rest on some ultimate and absolutely indubitable propositions. These, according to one school, are first principles of a general nature; according to another, are first sensations. But, in point of fact, an inquiry, to have that completely satisfactory result called demonstration, has only to start with propositions perfectly free from all actual doubt. If the premises are not in fact doubted at all, they cannot be more satisfactory than they are.

3. Some people seem to love to argue a point after all the world is fully convinced of it. But no further advance can be made. When doubt ceases, mental action on the subject comes to an end; and, if it did go on, it would be without a purpose.

If the settlement of opinion is the sole object of inquiry, and if belief is of the nature of a habit, why should we not attain the desired end, by taking any answer to a question, which we may fancy, and constantly reiterating it to ourselves, dwelling on all which may conduce to that belief, and learning to turn with contempt and hatred from anything which might disturb it? This simple and direct method is really pursued by many men. I remember once being entreated not to read a certain newspaper lest it might change my opinion upon free-trade. "Lest I might be entrapped by its fallacies and misstatements," was the form of expression. "You are not," my friend said, "a special student of political economy. You might, therefore, easily be deceived by fallacious arguments upon the subject. You might, then, if you read this paper, be led to believe in protection. But you admit that free-trade is the true doctrine; and you do not wish to believe what is not true." I have often known this system to be deliberately adopted. Still oftener, the instinctive dislike of an undecided state of mind, exaggerated into a vague dread of doubt, makes men cling spasmodically to the views they already take. The man feels that, if he only holds to his belief without wavering, it will be entirely satisfactory. Nor can it be denied that a steady and immovable faith yields great peace of mind. It may, indeed, give rise to inconveniences, as if a man should resolutely continue to believe that fire would not burn him, or that he would be eternally damned if he received his *ingesta* otherwise than through a stomach-pump. But then the man who adopts this method will not allow that its inconveniences are greater than its advantages. He will say, "I hold steadfastly to the truth and the truth is always wholesome." And in many cases it may very well be that the pleasure he derives from his calm faith overbalances any inconveniences resulting from its deceptive character. Thus, if it be true that death is annihilation, then the man who believes that he will certainly go straight to heaven when he dies, provided he have fulfilled certain simple observances in this life, has a cheap pleasure which will not be followed by the least disappointment. A similar consideration seems to have weight with many persons in religious topics, for we frequently hear it said, "Oh, I could not believe so-and-so, because I should be wretched if I did." When an ostrich buries its head in the sand as danger approaches, it very likely takes the happiest course. It hides the danger, and then calmly says there is no danger; and, if it feels perfectly sure there is none, why should it raise its head to see? A man may go through life, systematically keeping out of view all that might cause a change in his opinions, and if he only succeeds—basing his method, as he does, on two fundamental psychological laws—I do not see what can be said against his doing so. It would be an egotistical impertinence to object that his procedure is irrational, for that only amounts to saying that his method of settling belief is not ours. He does not propose to himself to be rational, and indeed, will often talk with scorn of man's weak and illusive reason. So let him think as he pleases.

But this method of fixing belief, which may be called the method of tenacity, will be unable to hold its ground in practice. The social impulse is against it. The man who adopts it will find that other men think differently from him, and it will be apt to occur to him in some saner moment that their opinions are quite as good as his own, and this will shake his confidence in his belief. This conception, that another man's thought or sentiment may be equivalent to one's own, is a distinctly new step, and a highly important one. It arises from an impulse too strong in man to be suppressed, without danger of destroying the human species. Unless we make ourselves hermits, we shall necessarily influence each other's opinions; so that the problem becomes how to fix belief, not in the individual merely, but in the community.

Let the will of the state act, then, instead of that of the individual. Let an institution be created which shall have for its object to keep correct doctrines before the attention of the people, to reiterate them perpetually, and to teach them to the young; having at the same time power to prevent contrary doctrines from being taught, advocated, or expressed. Let all possible causes of a change of mind be removed from men's apprehensions. Let them be kept ignorant, lest they should learn of some reason to think otherwise than they do. Let their passions be enlisted, so that they may regard private and unusual opinions with hatred and horror. Then, let all men who reject the established belief be terrified into silence. Let the people turn out and tar-and-feather such men, or let inquisitions be made into the manner of thinking of suspected persons, and, when they are found guilty of forbidden beliefs, let them be subjected to some signal punishment. When complete agreement could not otherwise be reached, a general massacre of all who have not thought in a certain way has proved a very effective means of settling opinion in a country. If the power to do this be wanting, let a list of opinions be drawn up, to which no man of the least independence of thought can assent, and let the faithful be required to accept all these propositions, in order to segregate them as radically as possible from the influence of the rest of the world.

This method has, from the earliest times, been one of the chief means of upholding correct theological and political doctrines, and of preserving their universal or catholic character. In Rome, especially, it has been practised from the days of Numa Pompilius to those of Pius Nonus. This is the most perfect example in history; but wherever there is a priesthood—and no religion has been without one—this method has been more or less made use of. Wherever there is an aristocracy, or a guild, or any association of a class of men whose interests depend, or are supposed to depend, on certain propositions, there will be inevitably found some traces of this natural product of social feeling. Cruelties always accompany this system; and when it is consistently carried out, they become atrocities of the most horrible kind in the eyes of any rational man. Nor should this occasion surprise, for the officer of a society does not feel justified in surrendering the interests of that society for the sake of mercy, as he might his own private interests. It is natural, therefore, that sympathy and fellowship should thus produce a most ruthless power.

In judging this method of fixing belief, which may be called the method of authority, we must, in the first place, allow its immeasurable mental and moral superiority to the method of tenacity. Its success is proportionately greater; and, in fact, it has over and over again worked the most majestic results. The mere structures of stone which it has caused to be put together—in Siam, for example, in Egypt, and in Europe—have many of them a sublimity hardly more than rivalled by the greatest works of Nature. And, except the geological epochs, there are no periods of time so vast as those which are measured by some of these organized faiths. If we scrutinize the matter closely, we shall find that there has not been one of their creeds which has remained always the same; yet the change is so slow as to be imperceptible during one person's life, so that individual belief remains sensibly fixed. For the mass of mankind, then, there is perhaps no better method than this. If it is their highest impulse to be intellectual slaves, then slaves they ought to remain.

But no institution can undertake to regulate opinions upon every subject. Only the most important ones can be attended to, and on the rest men's minds must be left to the action of natural causes. This imperfection will be no source of weakness so long as men are in such a state of culture that one opinion does not influence another—that is, so long as they cannot put two and two together. But in the most priest-ridden states some individuals will be found who are raised above that condition. These men possess a wider sort of social feeling; they see that men in other countries and in other ages have held to very different doctrines from those which they themselves have been brought up to believe; and they cannot help seeing that it is the mere accident of their having been taught as they have, and of their having been surrounded with the manners and associations they have, that has caused them to believe as they do and not far differently. Nor can their candour resist the reflection that there is no reason to rate their own views at a higher value than those of other nations and other centuries; thus giving rise to doubts in their minds.

They will further perceive that such doubts as these must exist in their minds with reference to every belief which seems to be determined by the caprice either of themselves or of those who originated the popular opinions. The willful adherence to a belief, and the arbitrary forcing of it upon others, must, therefore, both be given up. A different new method of settling opinions must be adopted, that shall not only produce an impulse to believe, but shall also decide what proposition it is which is to be believed. Let the action of natural preferences be unimpeded, then, and under their influence let men, conversing together and regarding matters in different lights, gradually develop beliefs in harmony with natural causes. This method resembles that by which conceptions of art have been brought to maturity. The most perfect example of it is to be found in the history of metaphysical philosophy. Systems of this sort have not usually rested upon any observed facts, at least not in any great degree. They have been chiefly adopted because their fundamental propositions seemed "agreeable to reason." This is an apt expression; it does not mean that which agrees with experience, but that which we find ourselves inclined to believe. Plato, for example, finds it agreeable to reason that the distances of the celestial spheres from one another should be proportional to the different lengths of strings which produce harmonious chords. Many philosophers have been led to their main conclusions by considerations like this; but this is the lowest and least developed form which the method takes, for it is clear that another man might find Kepler's theory, that the celestial spheres are proportional to the inscribed and circumscribed spheres of the different regular solids, more agreeable to *his* reason. But the shock of opinions will soon lead men to rest on preferences of a far more universal nature. Take, for example, the doctrine that man only acts selfishly— that is, from the consideration that acting in one way will afford him more pleasure than acting in another. This rests on no fact in the world, but it has had a wide acceptance as being the only reasonable theory.

This method is far more intellectual and respectable from the point of view of reason than either of the others which we have noticed. But its failure has been the most manifest. It makes of inquiry something similar to the development of taste; but taste, unfortunately, is always more or less a matter of fashion, and accordingly metaphysicians have never come to any fixed agreement, but the pendulum has swung backward and forward between a more material and a more spiritual philosophy, from the earliest times to the latest. And so from this, which has been called the *a priori* method, we are driven, in Lord Bacon's phrase, to a true induction. We have

examined into this *a priori* method as something which promised to deliver our opinions from their accidental and capricious element. But development, while it is a process which eliminates the effect of some casual circumstances, only magnifies that of others. This method, therefore, does not differ in a very essential way from that of authority. The government may not have lifted its finger to influence my convictions; I may have been left outwardly quite free to choose, we will say, between monogamy and polygamy, and, appealing to my conscience only, I may have concluded that the latter practice is in itself licentious. But when I come to see that the chief obstacle to the spread of Christianity among a people of as high culture as the Hindoos has been a conviction of the immorality of our way of treating women, I cannot help seeing that, though governments do not interfere, sentiments in their development will be very greatly determined by accidental causes. Now, there are some people, among whom I must suppose that my reader is to be found, who, when they see that any belief of theirs is determined by any circumstance extraneous to the facts, will from that moment not merely admit in words that that belief is doubtful, but will experience a real doubt of it, so that it ceases in some degree to be a belief.

To satisfy our doubts, therefore, it is necessary that a method should be found by which our beliefs may be caused by nothing human, but by some external permanency—by something upon which our thinking has no effect. Some mystics imagine that they have such a method in a private inspiration from on high. But that is only a form of the method of tenacity, in which the conception of truth as something public is not yet developed. Our external permanency would not be external, in our sense, if it was restricted in its influence to one individual. It must be something which affects, or might affect, every man. And, though these affections are necessarily as various as are individual conditions, yet the method must be such that the ultimate conclusion of every man shall be the same. Such is the method of science. Its fundamental hypothesis, restated in more familiar language, is this: There are Real things, whose characters are entirely independent of our opinions about them; those realities affect our senses according to regular laws, and, though our sensations are as different as are our relations to the objects, yet, by taking advantage of the laws of perception, we can ascertain by reasoning how things really are; and any man, if he have sufficient experience and he reason enough about it, will be led to the one True conclusion. The new conception here involved is that of Reality. It may be asked how I know that there are any realities. If this hypothesis is the sole support of my method of inquiry, my method of inquiry must not be used to support my hypothesis. The reply is this: 1. If investigation cannot be regarded as proving that there are Real things, it at least does not lead to a contrary conclusion; but the method and the conception on which it is based remain ever in harmony. No doubts of the method, therefore, necessarily arise from its practice, as is the case with all the others. 2. The feeling which gives rise to any method of fixing belief is a dissatisfaction at two repugnant propositions. But here already is a vague concession that there is some *one* thing to which a proposition should conform. Nobody, therefore, can really doubt that there are realities, for, if he did, doubt would not be a source of dissatisfaction. The hypothesis, therefore, is one which every mind admits. So that the social impulse does not cause men to doubt it. 3. Everybody uses the scientific method about a great many things, and only ceases to use it when he does not know

how to apply it. 4. Experience of the method has not led us to doubt it, but, on the contrary, scientific investigation has had the most wonderful triumphs in the way of settling opinion. These afford the explanation of my not doubting the method or the hypothesis which it supposes; and not having any doubt, nor believing that anybody else whom I could influence has, it would be the merest babble for me to say more about it. If there be anybody with a living doubt upon the subject, let him consider it. . . .

This is the only one of the four methods which presents any distinction of a right and a wrong way. If I adopt the method of tenacity, and shut myself out from all influences, whatever I think necessary to doing this, is necessary according to that method. So with the method of authority: the state may try to put down heresy by means which, from a scientific point of view, seem very ill-calculated to accomplish its purposes; but the only test *on that method* is what the state thinks; so that it cannot pursue the method wrongly. So with the *a priori* method. The very essence of it is to think as one is inclined to think. All metaphysicians will be sure to do that, however they may be inclined to judge each other to be perversely wrong. The Hegelian system recognizes every natural tendency of thought as logical, although it is certain to be abolished by counter-tendencies. Hegel thinks there is a regular system in the succession of these tendencies, in consequence of which, after drifting one way and the other for a long time, opinion will at last go right. And it is true that metaphysicians get the right ideas at last; Hegel's system of Nature represents tolerably the science of that day; and one may be sure that whatever scientific investigation has put out of doubt will presently receive *a priori* demonstration on the part of the metaphysicians. But with the scientific method the case is different.

I may start with known and observed facts to proceed to the unknown; and yet the rules which I follow in doing so may not be such as investigation would approve. The test of whether I am truly following the method is not an immediate appeal to my feelings and purposes, but, on the contrary, itself involves the application of the method. Hence it is that bad reasoning as well as good reasoning is possible; and this fact is the foundation of the practical side of logic.

It is not to be supposed that the first three methods of settling opinion present no advantage whatever over the scientific method. On the contrary, each has some peculiar convenience of its own. The *a priori* method is distinguished for its comfortable conclusions. It is the nature of the process to adopt whatever belief we are inclined to, and there are certain flatteries to the vanity of man which we all believe by nature, until we are awakened from our pleasing dream by rough facts. The method of authority will always govern the mass of mankind; and those who wield the various forms of organized force in the state will never be convinced that dangerous reasoning ought not to be suppressed in some way. If liberty of speech is to be untrammelled from the grosser forms of constraint, then uniformity of opinion will be secured by a moral terrorism to which the respectability of society will give its thorough approval. Following the method of authority is the path of peace. Certain non-conformities are permitted; certain others (considered unsafe) are forbidden. These are different in different countries and in different ages; but, wherever you are, let it be known that you seriously hold a tabooed belief, and you may be perfectly sure of being treated with a cruelty less brutal but more refined than hunting you like a wolf. Thus, the greatest intellectual benefactors of mankind have never dared, and dare not now, to utter the whole of their thought; and thus a shade of *prima facie* doubt is cast upon every proposition which is considered essential to the security of society. Singularly enough, the persecution does not all come from without; but a man torments himself and is oftentimes most distressed at finding himself believing propositions which he has been brought up to regard with aversion. The peaceful and sympathetic man will, therefore, find it hard to resist the temptation to submit his opinions to authority. But most of all I admire the method of tenacity for its strength, simplicity, and directness. Men who pursue it are distinguished for their decision of character, which becomes very easy with such a mental rule. They do not waste time in trying to make up their minds what they want, but, fastening like lightning upon whatever alternative comes first, they hold it to the end, whatever happens, without an instant's irresolution. This is one of the splendid qualities which generally accompany brilliant, unlasting success. It is impossible not to envy the man who can dismiss reason, although we know how it must turn out at last.

Such are the advantages which the other methods of settling opinion have over scientific investigation. A man should consider well of them; and then he should consider that, after all, he wishes his opinions to coincide with the fact, and that there is no reason why the results of those three methods should do so. To bring about this effect is the prerogative of the method of science. Upon such considerations he has to make his choice—a choice which is far more than the adoption of any intellectual opinion, which is one of the ruling decisions of his life, to which, when once made, he is bound to adhere. The force of habit will sometimes cause a man to hold on to old beliefs, after he is in a condition to see that they have no sound basis. But reflection upon the state of the case will overcome these habits, and he ought to allow reflection its full weight. People sometimes shrink from doing this, having an idea that beliefs are wholesome which they cannot help feeling rest on nothing. But let such persons suppose an analogous though different case from their own. Let them ask themselves what they would say to a reformed Mussulman who should hesitate to give up his old notions in regard to the relations of the sexes; or to a reformed Catholic who should still shrink from reading the Bible. Would they not say that these persons ought to consider the matter fully, and clearly understand the new doctrine, and then ought to embrace it, in its entirety? But, above all, let it be considered that what is more wholesome than any particular belief is integrity of belief, and that to avoid looking into the support of any belief from a fear that it may turn out rotten is quite as immoral as it is disadvantageous. The person who confesses that there is such a thing as truth, which is distinguished from falsehood simply by this, that if

acted on it will carry us to the point we aim at and not astray, and then, though convinced of this, dares not know the truth and seeks to avoid it, is in a sorry state of mind indeed.

Yes, the other methods do have their merits: a clear logical conscience does cost something—just as any virtue, just as all that we cherish, costs us dear. But we should not desire it to be otherwise. The genius of a man's logical method should be loved and reverenced as his bride, whom he has chosen from all the world. He need not contemn the others; on the contrary, he may honour them deeply, and in doing so he only honours her the more. But she is the one that he has chosen, and he knows that he was right in making that choice. And having made it, he will work and fight for her, and will not complain that there are blows to take, hoping that there may be as many and as hard to give, and will strive to be the worthy knight and champion of her from the blaze of whose splendours he draws his inspiration and his courage.

6. *The Experimental Method* *

CLAUDE BERNARD (1813–1878)

To be true to the principles of the experimental method, a scientist must satisfy two sorts of conditions, and he must possess two qualities of mind which are indispensable for reaching his goal and discovering the truth.

* From Part I and Part III of *An Introduction to the Study of Experimental Medicine* first published in 1865. (Translated from the French by Daniel J. Bronstein.)

As an observer, he must describe simply. His only concern should be to avoid errors of observation. He must see what is there, no more and no less. For this purpose he may use any instruments which can help him make his observations more complete. The observer must be a photographer of phenomena: his observations must exactly represent nature. He must observe without preconceived ideas. His mind must be passive, that is to say, he should listen to nature and do her dictation, but not intrude himself. After the facts have been observed and recorded there will be need for ideas and for reasoning. The experimenter will then step in to interpret the phenomena.

He will make predictions and arrange experiential tests of his hypotheses or preconceived ideas. He will do this by reflection, trying out, groping, comparing, combining,—in order to find those experimental conditions best suited for attaining his goal. He must have a preconceived idea when experimenting. The mind of the experimenter must be active, that is to say, he must put questions to nature, questions which arise from the many hypotheses which suggest themselves to him.

But once the experimental conditions have been established, according to the preconceived idea, there will be a premeditated observation. Phenomena then appear which the experimenter has produced. He must first describe them; later he can decide whether the idea which gave rise to his experiment has been verified or not. Once the result of his experiment is clear, the experimenter is confronted by data which it is up to him to describe without being influenced by preconceived ideas. The experimenter must now disappear, or rather, all at once he must become an observer. And it is only after he has carefully noted the results of his experiment, just as he would do for any ordinary observations, that he may allow himself to reason, compare and try to reach a decision as to whether his experimental hypothesis has been verified or falsified by these results.

To return to the figure of speech used earlier, we could say that the experimenter puts questions to nature, but that as soon as she speaks, he must stop talking and take notes, listening until the very end, and submitting to her decisions. It has been said that the experimenter must force nature to reveal her secrets by plying her with all sorts of questions. But he must let her answer and never substitute his own answers. Nor must he choose that part only of the total answer which fits in with his own hypothesis. We will see later that this is one of the great pitfalls of the experimental method. An experimenter who cherishes his preconceived idea and reads his experimental findings in the light of his idea, becomes a victim of this pitfall. He only observes part of what is there since he fails to notice whatever he has not foreseen. An experimenter must cling to his idea only in order to elicit a response from nature. When nature answers, he must be submissive; he must be prepared to abandon his idea, to modify it or to replace it with another. He must allow himself to be taught by the facts which his experiment has uncovered for him.

In every experiment there are two phases to be considered. In the first phase we anticipate and also help to bring about the occurrence of the experimental conditions. In the second phase we note the results of the experiment. It is not possible to devise an experiment without having a preconceived idea. As we have said, to devise an experiment is to put a question to nature. We can't think of the question without also having the idea which brings about an answer. I therefore consider it an absolute principle that an experiment must always be constructed in the light of a preconceived idea. It doesn't even matter if this idea is vague or ill-defined. When it comes to recording the results of the experiment, I would insist on strict observation without any recourse to the preconceived idea which led to that observation.

In the first phase of the experimental process the mind of the scientist is active; in the second, his senses are active and he observes and records what there is to see. A striking proof of the point I've just made was furnished by François Huber.[1] Although he was blind, this great naturalist thought out and prepared some remarkable experiments. His man-servant, who didn't have a scientific idea in his head, observed the results of his experiments. Huber was the directing mind,—he devised the experiment. But this mind was forced to borrow someone else's senses. The assistant received sense-impressions and executed the orders of this directing mind which had planned the experiment in the light of a preconceived notion.

Those who object to the use of hypotheses and preconceived ideas in the experimental method make the mistake of confusing the planning of an experiment with the observation of its results. It is true that we must set aside hypotheses and preconceived ideas when we note the results of an experiment. But we must be careful not to proscribe hypotheses and ideas in the planning of an experiment or in imagining how we can observe what will happen. On the contrary, as we shall soon see, we must give free rein to our imagination. The source of all reasoning and invention is an idea. And all progress depends on that idea. We must never smother it or drive it away on the pretense that it may be harmful. It need only be subjected to certain rules and tests,—and this is an entirely different matter.

The genuine scientist is one who combines experimental theory and experimental practice. (1) He notes a fact. (2) In the light of this fact an idea occurs to him. (3) As a result of this idea, he reasons and sets up an experiment. He then figures out what its mate-

rial conditions shall be. (4) As a result of this experiment there occur certain new phenomena which must be observed, and so forth. The mind of the scientist is always working between two observations. The first observation is the initial step in the process of reasoning, while the second is its conclusion. To make matters clear I have forced myself to separate the diverse operations of experimental reasoning. But when all this occurs in the mind of the scientist, who abandons himself to investigation in a field as baffling as medicine still is, there is such an intermingling of the observed facts, some of which occurred during the experiment, while others were consequences of the experiment, that it is impossible and also useless to try to separate them. It will suffice if we remember that the *a priori* idea, or better, an hypothesis, is the starting point of an experiment and that we must let ourselves go with it freely, provided only that we observe carefully and fully the experimental results. If the hypothesis is not verified and must be abandoned, the facts which it will have helped us to discover will remain as undeniable results of our investigation.

The observer and the experimenter correspond to two different phases of experimental research. The observer does not reason, but merely takes note of the facts. The experimenter, on the other hand, does reason—he bases himself on the facts which have been discovered and tries to derive new facts by using his imagination and his powers of reasoning. But while in theory we can distinguish the experimenter from the observer, in practice it is impossible to separate them, since we see that one and the same investigator must be alternately observer and experimenter. This happens whenever a scientist discovers and develops by himself the whole of a scientific subject. It is more common, however, for the different parts of the experimental

[1] François Huber, *New Observations on the Abeilles,* 2nd ed., expanded by his son, Pierre Huber, Geneva, 1814.

process to be shared by several men. Whether in medicine or natural history, there are some who merely collect and bring together observations; others, basing themselves on these observations, may offer ingenious hypotheses which seem very promising; other suggested hypotheses will be less ingenious and also less promising. Scientists will attempt to realize experimentally the conditions which are needed to test these hypotheses. Finally, there are those who apply themselves especially to the task of generalizing and systematizing the results obtained by various observers and experimenters. This parceling out of the experimental domain is a good thing because in this way each of its diverse parts will be well taken care of. In fact, it is well known that in certain sciences the instruments of observation and experimentation may become quite specialized. Their management and use may require a certain manual dexterity or a sharpening of our senses. But while I admit the need for specialization in the practice of science, I unhesitatingly reject it for theoretical science. I believe that to make generalization one's specialty is unphilosophic and unscientific, even though such a notion has been advocated by a modern school of philosophy which prides itself on the fact that its doctrines are based on the sciences.

However, experimental science cannot make progress by being one-sided; it will go forward only by uniting all the strands of the experimental method so that they converge toward a common goal. Those who collect observations are performing a useful task only because these observations will ultimately become a part of experimental thought. Otherwise, the endless accumulation of observations would lead nowhere. Those who construct hypotheses to fit the observations which others have collected are making a useful contribution only

because someone else will conduct experiments with a view to verifying these hypotheses. Otherwise, these unverified or unverifiable hypotheses would only lead to systems of thought reminiscent of scholasticism. In spite of all their dexterity, experimenters cannot solve problems unless they are inspired by a fortunate hypothesis which is based on careful and precise observations. Finally, those who generalize can construct lasting theories only if they themselves are acquainted with the scientific details which these theories aim to set forth. Scientific generalization must proceed from particular facts to principles, and principles will be more stable when they are well supported by many detailed observations, just as a stake is more solid when it is deeply embedded in the ground.

Thus we see that the essential parts of the experimental method are interrelated. Facts are necessary materials; but they enrich science because of the role they play in experimental reasoning or theory. Ideas backed up by facts produce a science. An experimental hypothesis is nothing but a preconceived scientific idea. A theory is only a scientific idea tested by experiment. Reasoning only gives form to our ideas in such a way that everything is ultimately based on an idea. As I see it, the idea constitutes the starting point, or the prime mover, of all scientific thought. At the same time it is our goal as we try to conquer the unknown.

PART III

Applications of the Experimental Method to the Study of Living Things

The ideas which we have developed will be better understood if we apply them to investigations in physiology and experimental medicine. . . . I have chosen the following examples with this end in view. . . .

There are many different ways of starting a scientific investigation. I shall illustrate two of the most important: (1) Where an experimental investigation has an observation as its starting point, and (2) where the investigation begins with an hypothesis or theory.

I. An Experimental Investigation which Starts with an Observation

Experimental ideas are often born by chance, due to some lucky observation. Nothing is more common. In fact, it is the easiest way for scientific work to get started. We take a walk, so to speak, in the field of science, and look at what happens to be before our eyes. Bacon compares scientific investigation to a hunt. Observations are the game. Pressing the analogy further, we could add that if the game appears when we are looking for it, it also appears when we are not looking for it, or even when we are looking for game of another species. I will [now] give an example in which these two cases occur one after the other. At the same time, I shall take care to analyze every circumstance of this physiological investigation in order to point up the principles which we have developed in the first part of this study.

First example. Some rabbits were brought from the market to my laboratory one day. They were put on a table where they urinated; I happened to notice that their urine was clear and acid. This fact struck me because the urine of rabbits is ordinarily cloudy and alkaline, just like other herbivorous animals, while the urine of carnivorous animals, as we know, is clear and acid. This observation, that the rabbits had an acid urine, gave me the idea that nutritionally they were in the same state as carnivorous animals. I guessed that they had probably not eaten for a long time and that fasting had transformed

them into veritable carnivorous animals, —they were living on their own blood. Nothing was easier than to verify this preconceived idea or hypothesis by an experiment. I gave the rabbits grass to eat, and some hours later their urine became cloudy and alkaline. I then had them fast and after twenty four or thirty six hours at most, their urine became again clear and strongly acid. Then, after eating grass, their urine became alkaline again etc. I repeated this simple experiment on the rabbits a great many times, and always with the same result. I then repeated it with a horse, another herbivorous animal whose urine is normally cloudy and alkaline. I found that fasting led in a short time to an acid urine with such an increase in urea that it sometimes crystallized spontaneously in cooled urine. As a result of my experiments I reached the following general proposition which was not known at the time. It is this: all fasting animals are nourished by meat, so that, while fasting, the urine of herbivorous animals resembles that of carnivorous animals.

We have here a very simple particular fact, which enables us to see clearly how experimental thought develops. When we notice something that we are not accustomed to see, we must ask how it arose, or in other words, what is its proximate cause. An answer or an idea will then occur to the mind which will need to be tested by an experiment. When I noted that the rabbits had an acid urine, I instinctively looked for its cause. The experimental idea consisted in the connection, which occurred spontaneously to my mind, between acidity of the urine in rabbits and the state of fasting, which I considered to resemble the condition of a meat-eater. Implicitly, in the form of a syllogism, I constructed the following inductive argument. The urine of carnivorous animals is acid; now these rabbits have acid urine; hence they are carnivorous, that is they are fasting.

This remained to be established by experiment. But to prove that my fasting rabbits were, in fact, carnivorous, I had to give a counter-proof. I had to show experimentally that a rabbit fed on meat would have a clear, acid urine, just as it did when fasting. So I fed some rabbits on cold boiled beef, which they take very nicely when given nothing else. My prediction was verified again,—during this feeding period their urine was clear and acid.

To complete my experiment I made an autopsy on my animals to see if the digestion of meat took place similarly for a rabbit as for carnivorous animals. I found, in fact, all the evidences of a very fine digestion in the intestinal reactions; and I noted that all the chyliferous vessels were gorged with a very abundant chyle—white and milky as with carnivorous animals. . . .

II. An Experimental Investigation That Starts with an Hypothesis or Theory

We have already said, and we shall see later on, that in reporting an observation we must never go beyond the facts. But it is different when we are setting up an experiment. I would like to show that hypotheses are indispensable and useful precisely because they go beyond the facts and thus carry science forward. The function of hypotheses is not merely to make us try new experiments; often they help us discover new facts that we would not have discovered without them. In the preceding [example] we have seen that one can start from a particular fact and then proceed step by step to more general ideas, that is to say to a theory. But as we are about to see, it is also possible to start with a hypothesis deduced from a theory. In this case, although we are dealing with a proposition logically derived from a theory, it is nevertheless still a hypothesis requiring verification by experiment. In fact, the theory in such a case only represents previously discovered facts, which support the hypothesis but which cannot be used to demonstrate it experimentally. We have said that in such a case we should not become a slave to the theory. If we wish to promote scientific development and discover the truth, we must keep our intellectual independence. The following example will prove this point.

In 1843, in one of my first studies, I undertook to find out what happened to the various alimentary substances in nutrition. As I have already said, I began with sugar, a definite substance which is easier to recognize and trace inside the body than any other substance. I injected solutions of cane sugar into the blood of animals and I noted that even when injected in weak doses, the sugar was passed in the urine. Later I recognized that by modifying and transforming this cane sugar the gastric juice made it assimilable, that is to say, capable of destruction in the blood. Now, I wanted to know in what organ the nutritive sugar was disappearing, and I formed the hypothesis that sugar introduced into the blood by nutrition could be destroyed in the lungs or in the general capillaries. In fact, the prevailing theory at that time, which was naturally my starting point, assumed that in all animals, sugar came exclusively from foods and that this sugar was destroyed in animal organisms by combustion, that is, respiration. It was for this reason that sugar was called respiratory nutriment. But I immediately discovered that the theory as to the origin of sugar in animals was incorrect. In fact, by a series of experiments which I shall describe later, instead of discovering the organ which destroys sugar, I found one which makes sugar, and I found that the blood of all animals contains sugar, even when they don't eat any sugar. I thus discovered a new fact, unforeseen by cur-

rent theoretical knowledge and un-
noticed, doubtless because men were
laboring under the influence of contrary
views in which they had placed too much
confidence. Consequently, I immediately
abandoned my hypotheses concerning
the destruction of sugar, in order to
pursue this unexpected result which has
since become the fruitful beginning of a
new line of investigation, and a mine of
discoveries which is still not exhausted.

In these investigations I have adhered
to the principles of the experimental
method which we have established; that
is to say, when I have discovered, by
careful observation, some new fact which
is in contradiction to a theory, instead of
clinging to the theory and abandoning
the fact, I have kept the fact and studied
it, and I have hastened to give up the
theory. In this way, I have followed the
precept of our second chapter, which
was: *When we meet a fact which is in
opposition to a prevailing theory, we
must accept the fact and abandon the
theory even if the latter is generally
accepted, and supported by great names.*

As we have said, we must distinguish
between principles and theories, and we
must never regard theories as absolutes.
Here we had a theory according to which
only the vegetable kingdom can create
the essential materials which the animal
kingdom is supposed to destroy. According to this theory, which was established
and maintained by the most illustrious
chemists of our day, animals are not able
to produce sugar in their bodies. If I had
had absolute faith in this theory, I would
have concluded that my experiment was
infected with error; and experimenters
less bold than myself would have condemned it immediately, and would have
paid no attention to an observation,
which according to the accepted theory
was bound to be the result of an error,
since it showed sugar in the blood of an
animal which had not been fed any
starch, or sugary materials.

But instead of being preoccupied with
the validity of the theory, I was concerned only with the fact, whose reality
I was trying to establish. By new experiments and suitable counter-proofs I was
led to confirm my first observation and
to discover that the liver was the organ
where animal sugar was formed in certain given circumstances and later
spread throughout the blood and into
the tissues and fluids.

That glycogenesis (or the faculty of
producing sugar) is possessed by animals as well as vegetables, was one of
my discoveries and is to-day an acknowledged scientific fact. But we still have
no plausible account of this phenomenon.
The new facts which I have made known
have been the source of a great number
of studies and of many different theories.
Some of these theories appear to contradict others while some seem to contradict my own views. When entering on
new terrain we must not fear to express
dangerous views—for our goal is to
stimulate research in all directions. As
Priestley said, we must not remain silent
for fear of making a mistake. For this
would be false modesty. Therefore I
have constructed more or less hypothetical theories on glycogenesis; after me,
others have done likewise. All these
theories are incomplete and provisional
as are all theories at the frontiers of
science. They will only last for a while;
they are bound to be replaced by others
as science advances. Theories are like
the successive steps taken by science as
it advances and enlarges its horizon;
they necessarily represent and comprise
more facts as science advances. Genuine
progress is achieved when we replace
one theory by others which go further,
until we find one which is based on a
larger number of facts. In the case before us, the important thing is not to
condemn the old theory in order to support a more recent one, but rather to
open up a new path. For well observed

facts never die, even if the theories which led to their discovery become obsolete. Facts are the indispensable elements of scientific progress. Only when it has enough facts and has penetrated far enough in the analysis of phenomena to discover the law behind the facts, and also their causes—only then can science go forward.

To summarize, a theory is only an hypothesis which has been verified by some facts—sometimes the number of verifications is small, sometimes it is large. Those hypotheses which are verified by the largest number of facts are the best. But still, they are never final and we must not have absolute faith in them. We have just seen that if we had had absolute confidence in the prevailing theory of the destruction of sugar in ani-

mals, we would probably not have found the trail of new facts. The experiment, it is true, was suggested by an hypothesis which was itself based on a theory. But once the results of the experiment became apparent, the theory and the hypothesis had to disappear; for the experimental fact was now only an observation which had to be made without any preconceived idea.

In sciences as complex and new as physiology, the great principle is not to put much stock in hypotheses and theories, but to have an attentive eye always on what is revealed by experiment. Something apparently accidental and inexplicable can become the occasion for discovering an important new fact.

7. The Form or Method of Research in the Social and Natural Sciences*

Morris R. Cohen (1881–1947)

The great Poincaré once remarked that while physicists had a subject-matter, sociologists were engaged almost entirely in considering their methods. Allowing for the inevitable divergence between the sober facts and heightened Gallic wit, there is still in this remark a just rebuke (from one who had a right to deliver it) to those romantic souls who cherish the persistent illusion that

* From *Reason and Nature*, first published by Harcourt, Brace and Company, 1931, recently reissued by The Free Press. Permission to reprint was granted by Felix S. Cohen.

by some new trick of method the social sciences can readily be put on a par with the physical sciences with regard to definiteness and universal demonstrability. The maximum logical accuracy can be attained only by recognizing the exact degree of probability that our subject matter will allow.

From the fact that social questions are inherently more complicated than those of physics or biology—since the social involves the latter but not vice versa—certain observations as to methodologic possibilities follow at once.

(A) The Complexity and Variability of Social Phenomena

In the first place, agreement based on demonstration is less easy and actually less prevalent in the social than in the natural sciences, because the greater complexity of social facts makes it less easy to sharpen an issue to an isolable point and to settle it by direct observation of an indefinitely repeatable fact. The issue between the Copernican and the Ptolemaic astronomy in the days of Galileo was reduced to the question whether Venus does or does not show phases like the moon's, and this was settled by looking through a telescope. If Venus did not forever repeat her cycle, and if the difference between a full circle of light and one partly covered by a crescent shadow were not so readily perceived, the matter could not be so readily settled.

With the greater complexity of social facts are connected (1) their less repeatable character, (2) their less direct observability, (3) their greater variability and lesser uniformity, and (4) the greater difficulty of isolating one factor at a time. These phases are so dependent on one another that we shall not treat them separately.

The practical difficulties of repeating social facts for purposes of direct observation are too obvious to need detailed mention. What needs to be more often recognized is that social facts are essentially unrepeatable just to the extent that they are merely historical. The past fact cannot be directly observed. Its existence is established by reasoning upon assumed probabilities. In the case of physical history or geology, our proof rests on definitely established and verified laws of natural science. In the case of human history the principles assumed are neither so definite nor so readily verifiable.[1]

The greater variability of social **facts** may, if we wish, be viewed as another phase of their complexity. Any cubic centimeter of hydrogen will for most purposes of physics or biology be as good as another. But observation on one community will not generally be so applicable to another. Even purely biologic facts, e.g., the effects of diet, seem to be more variable in the human than in other species. Reasoning from examples in the social realm is intellectually a most hazardous venture. We seldom escape the fallacy of selection, of attributing to the whole class what is true only of our selected instances. To urge as some philosophers do that this is true only because physical knowledge is thinner and depends more upon the principle of indifference, is to urge an interpretation, not a denial, of the fact.

It is, of course, true that for certain social questions we can treat all individuals as alike. Thus, for vital statistics every birth or death counts the same, no matter who is involved. Likewise, in certain economic or juristic questions we ignore all individual differences. Yet there can be no doubt that the applicability of such rules in the social sciences is more limited and surrounded with greater difficulty than the application of the laws of the natural sciences to their wider material.

J. S. Mill in his *Logic* has raised the interesting question as to why it is that in certain inquiries one observation or experiment may be decisive while in other cases large numbers of observations bring no such certain results. In the main this difference holds between physical and social observation.

---

[1] Thus it is difficult to refute the assertion that race differences are constant and not changed in the course of time by direct or selective influence of the environment. For if history fails to record any extensive intermarriage of a race like the Hebrew with other peoples and yet shows marked changes in physiognomy as members of the race settle in different lands, it is still open to proponents of the theory to assert that they *must have* intermarried.

I venture to suggest a rather simple explanation of this fact—a fact that puzzled Mill because he did not fully grasp the logic of hypothesis. In any fairly uniform realm like that of physics, where we can vary one factor at a time, it is possible to have a crucial experiment, that is, it is possible to reduce an issue to a question of yes or no, so that the result refutes and eliminates one hypothesis and leaves the other in possession of the field. But where the number of possible causes is indefinitely large, and where we cannot always isolate a given factor, it is obviously difficult to eliminate an hypothesis; and the elimination of one hypothesis from a very large number does not produce the impression of progress in the establishment of a definite cause.

The last observation suggests that the greater complexity and variability of social fact also make its purely theoretical development more difficult. In general, social situations are networks in which one cannot change one factor without affecting a great many others. It is therefore, difficult to determine the specific effects of any one factor. Moreover, social elements seldom admit of simple addition. The behaviour of the same individuals in a large group will not in general be the same as their behaviour in a smaller group. This makes it difficult to apply the mathematical methods which have proved so fruitful in the natural sciences. For these mathematical methods depend upon our ability to pass from a small number of instances to an indefinitely large number by the process of summation or integration.

Where the number of units is indefinitely large we can assume continuity in variation. But the application of continuous curves to very limited groups of figures to which our social observation is usually restricted produces pseudo-science, for example, the assertion that if our distribution is skewed we have a proof of teleology.

The relatively small number of observations that we generally have to deal with in the social sciences makes the application of the probability curve a source of grave errors. For all the mathematical theorems of probability refer only to infinite series (for which we substitute as a practical equivalent "the long run"). Where the number is small there is no assurance that we have eliminated the fallacy of selection. The mathematical error of applying a continuous curve to a discrete number of observations produces ludicrous results. It is vain to expect that the crudeness of our observation and the vagueness of our fundamental categories will be cured by manipulation of the paraphernalia of statistical methods. The mathematical theory of probability enables us to manipulate complex probabilities when we have some determinate ratio to begin with, such as that American pennies fall heads as often as tails. But social scientists seldom take the trouble to formulate the material assumptions of probability (or "indifference") which underlie their conclusions as to the probability of a given event, e.g. a rise in the price of gold. They thus endow their reasoning with the magical appearance of bringing forth material propositions out of the forms of pure mathematics. Actually the material assumptions of statistical workers are often purely aesthetic in origin, being dictated by an unintelligent regard for smoothness and symmetry in graphs.

Physical categories have themselves been clarified by analysis. The dimensions of the different categories that we talk about—energy, action, force, momentum, etc.—are numerically determined in terms of m (mass), l (length), t (time). In the social sciences the very categories that we use are hazy, subject to variable usage and to confusing suggestion. Does law determine the state, or the state make the law? How many thousands of learned men have discussed this and similar questions without fixing the precise meaning of the terms "state" and "law." [2]

It is a familiar observation that the difficulty of framing exact concepts in the social realm causes much confusion through ambiguity. To this it should be added that vague concepts make possible the constant appeal to vague propositions as self-evidently true. Open any book on social science at random and you will find the author trying to settle issues by appealing to what seems self-evident. Yet most of such self-evident propositions are vague, and when we ask for their precise meaning and for the evidence in their favor, our progress stops. In the natural sciences the questioning of what seems self-evident is relatively simple because when we have a simple proposition we can more readily formulate a true or an exclusive alternative. In social matters where difference of opinion is greater and demonstration more difficult, we cling all the more tenaciously to our primary assumption, so that our assumptions largely mould what we shall accept as facts.

Any one who naively believes that social facts come to us all finished and that our theories or assumptions must simply fit them, is bound to be shocked in a court of law or elsewhere to find how many facts persons honestly see because they expected them rather than because they objectively happen. That psychoanalysts, economists, sociologists, and moralists labour more or less in the same situation, the tremendous diversity of opinion among them amply indicates.

[2] Before Fourier definitely established the exact "dimensions" of the various physical categories, physicists could dispute (as the Cartesians and the Leibnizians did) as to the proper measure of "living" forces. Social science likewise needs a system of categories the exact dimensions of which are so clear as to make impossible the many confusions of which the example in the text is only one illustration.

Will a classical anthropologist admit that some Indians had a patriarchal form of kinship before adopting the matriarchal type? Is it a *fact* that the suppression of certain desires, deliberately or as a result of imitation, necessarily produces pathologic states of mind? One has but to scrutinize the statement to see how much must be assumed before it can be shown that a fact is involved here.

Is corporal punishment in schools, or free divorce, an evil or not? Under the influence of general opinions one can readily maintain it as a fact that all the consequences of such practices are evil. But one who refuses to admit that these practices are evils can be equally consistent.

Is this true in the natural sciences? Certainly not to the same extent. Because theories do not to the same extent influence what we shall regard as physical or biologic fact, false theorems have never been such serious obstacles to the progress of natural science. The statements in popular histories that the Ptolemaic, the phlogiston, or the caloric hypothesis stopped the progress of science have no foundation. On the contrary, these and other false theories in physics were useful in suggesting new lines of research. It is this fact that led Darwin to remark that false observations (on which others rely) are much more dangerous to the progress of science than false theories. Now in the social sciences we certainly do not have the elaborate safeguards against false observation that the natural sciences with their simpler material and many instruments of precision find it necessary to cultivate. The very circumstance that social facts are apt to be more familiar makes it easier to be misled as to the amount of accurate knowledge that we have about them.

From another point of view we may

express this by saying that in the social sciences we are more at the mercy of our authorities with regard to what are the facts. The social worker or field anthropologist has less opportunity to preserve his specimens than the naturalist or laboratory worker. If a later social worker or field anthropologist finds the fact to be different from what was reported by his predecessor, there is the possibility not only that they have observed different things but also that the social facts have changed.

In this connection it is well to note that the invention of a technical term often creates facts for social science. Certain individuals become *introverts* when the term is invented, just as many people begin to suffer from a disease the moment they read about it. Psychiatry is full of such technical terms; and if a criminal is rich enough he generally finds experts to qualify his state of mind with a sufficient number of technical terms to overawe those not used to scrutinizing authorities. The technical terms of natural science are useful precisely because they carry no aroma of approval or disapproval with them.

(B) Are There Any Social Laws?

In view of the paucity of generally recognized laws in social science it is well to ask categorically if the search for them is fully justified. The existence of similarities in different societies at different times and places has been used as a proof of the existence of "a uniform law in the psychic and social development of mankind at all times and under all circumstances." [3] But *similarities* of customs and beliefs, even if they are not superficial or due to the prepossession of the observer, are not laws. As human

beings resemble one another in their physical, biologic, and psychologic traits, we naturally expect that their social expressions will have points of resemblance, especially when the outer material is similar. If the number of human traits were known and within manageable compass, the principle of limited possibilities (enunciated by Dr. Goldenweiser) might be a clue to the laws of social life. But even a finite or limited number of facts may be too large for our manipulation.

Physical laws are in fact all expressed in relatively simple analytic functions containing a small number of variables. If the number of these variables should become very large, or the functions too complicated, physical laws would cease to be readily manipulated or applicable. The science of physics would then be practically impossible. If, then, social phenomena depend upon more factors than we can readily manipulate, even the doctrine of universal determinism will not guarantee an attainable expression of laws governing the specific phenomena of social life. Social phenomena, though determined, might not to a finite mind in limited time display any laws at all.

Let us take a concrete example. A man says to a woman, "My dear!" The physical stimulus is here a very definite set of sound waves, and we have reason to believe that the physical effect of these waves is always determinate. But what the lady will in all cases say or do in response depends upon so many factors that only an astonishing complacency about our limited knowledge of human affairs would prompt a confident answer.

The *a priori* argument that there must be laws is based on the assumption that there are a finite number of elements or forms which must thus repeat themselves in an endless temporal series. But why

---

[3] Lester Ward, *Pure Sociology*, pp. 53, 54.

may not the repeatable forms and elements be only those which enter our physical laws? What guarantee is there that in the limited time open to us there must be a complete repetition of social patterns as well?

In any case, those who think that social science has been as successful as physical science in discovering and establishing laws may be invited to compile a list of such laws and to compare the list in respect to number, definiteness, and universal demonstrability, with a collection such as Northrup's *Laws of Physical Science*.

We may approach this issue more positively by considering three types of laws:

(1) Every general fact that can be authenticated can be regarded as a law. Thus, that gold is yellow is the assertion of a law, i.e. whenever you find a substance having a certain atomic weight, etc., it will also be yellow in colour. We do not generally call statements of this sort laws, because a long list of such statements would hardly constitute what is distinctive of advanced *science*. In the latter such statements are connected with others by logical principles. Nevertheless such laws or facts are basic to science, and in the social realm they do not seem so numerous or so readily authenticated. Is it a fact, for instance, that the negro race is not ambitious?

(2) The second type of law is that of empirical or statistical sequences, e.g. "Much sugar in a diet will be followed by decayed teeth." In natural science we regard these also as but the starting points of the scientific search for the third type of law. Why do such sequences hold? We answer this question if we find some more general connecting link, e.g. some chemical process connecting sugar with the tissue of the teeth.

The situation in the social sciences is logically similar. Empirical sequences are not scientifically satisfactory laws.

We are more apt, in the social realm, to find correlations that confirm our opinions and to neglect items that do not. If the graduates of a college get into *Who's Who* the college compiles such lists and claims credit. If they get into jail the college does not hold itself responsible.

(3) The third type of law is the statement of a universal abstract relation which can be connected systematically with other laws in the same field. Such laws we may indeed find in the social sciences, e.g. the laws governing the exchange of goods under free competition as worked out mathematically by Walras, Pareto, H. Schultz,[4] et al., but always these laws are on a plane of abstraction from which translation to actual experience is difficult and dangerous. The ideal entities represented by "free competition" and "economic man" are, to be sure, no more abstract than the ideal entities of physics, but nevertheless economics is a poorer basis for predicting actual events than is physics. For in physics the transition from laws governing rigid bodies to those applying to (say) lead bullets is made on the basis of new laws of compressibility or elasticity, while in economics the transition from our laws of supply and demand in an ideal market to those determining (say) New York Stock Exchange transactions is still largely a matter of guess-work.

On a similar plane is the law of social inertia, parallel in motive to Newton's first law of motion. If, following the suggestion of the law of inertia, we assume that all social phenomena persist unless something is brought into play to change them, we have a useful principle of methodic procedure. Similarly we may assume the law of social heredity—all social institutions will be transmitted by parents to children, or people will believe

---

[4] See *The Meaning of Statistical Demand Curves.*

and act as did their fathers before them except in so far as certain factors produce changes in our social arrangements and in our ideas and sentiments. Similar remarks may be made about the law of imitation or the law of differentiation in the division of labour, which certainly help to explain certain elementary aspects of most social phenomena.

The law of imitation has of course to take account of the impulse to do things differently in order to attract attention, and the law of social differentiation has to note the factors which make for uniformity, just as the biologic law of differentiation must be checked by noting the phenomena of convergent evolution. But until opposite tendencies or forces can be more precisely measured, these laws will not go very far to explain actual happenings.

All laws are abstract. They state what would be true of a given factor if all other things remained indifferent. In physics other things do remain in a measure indifferent. But in the social field the variation of one factor produces all sorts of disturbances in others.

Physical phenomena, in other words, do show certain abstract uniformities of repetition which enable us to predict what will happen with greater certainty than in the social realms.

These observations are reinforced by considering the precise meaning of social causation and social forces—terms borrowed by the social from the natural sciences, generally without regard for their precise meaning or their applicability to the questions of social science.

(C) Social and Natural Causation

The notion of cause originates in the field of legal procedure. A cause ($\alpha\iota\tau\iota\alpha$) is a case or ground for an action. The Stoics, basing themselves on certain notions of Heraclitus, brought the notion of law into the conception of natural happenings. Law to them meant not mere uniformity that just happens to exist, but something decreed by the World-Reason or $\lambda\delta\gamma\circ\varsigma$. Violations of it are possible but reprehensible. This is still the popular view, which speaks of certain acts as unnatural and of nature punishing all violations of her laws. The notion of a law of nature as a non-purposeful but absolute uniformity, so that a single exception would deny its validity, arises from the modern application of mathematics to physics. The proposition that all x's are y's is simply false if one x is not a y.

Modern physics seeks to attain such laws by the process of abstraction. Thus, the proposition that all bodies fall to the earth suggests itself as such a law. But if we remember the behaviour of smoke, of birds or balloons, some modification of this statement is necessary if universality is to be attained. This is achieved in the statement that all bodies attract one another. For in the case of bodies which do not fall we can show the presence of some force which counteracts the attraction of the earth so that the latter force is thus recognized. If the counteracting forces did not themselves operate according to a known law, the law of gravitation would be useless. We can predict phenomena only because the gravitational and the counteracting forces are independently measurable. Unless similarly social forces are measurable and there is some common unit or correlation of social forces, the whole notion of law as employed in the physical sciences may be unapplicable. When religious and economic interests pull individuals in different directions, which force will prevail? Such a question can certainly not be answered on any scientific basis. We do not know how many units of one social force will counteract another. All we can say is that in some cases religious motives prevail over economic ones, in some cases the reverse is true, and in most cases we cannot separate the motives at all.

The difference between social and natural causation is confused by the doctrine that social "forces" are psychic, and that at least one of them, desire, acts like a physical force—indeed, that it obeys the Newtonian laws of motion.[5] Obviously if social phenomena are not merely physical, the term "social force" can at best be only a metaphor and we should be careful to note its real difference from physical force.

This difference is ignored when a popular sociologist speaks of social motion as following the line of least resistance even more closely than does nature herself.[6] In natural science we know what a straight line is before considering any given physical process. But what is denoted by the metaphor, the "straight line" or the "line of least resistance" in any given social process, is something that we arbitrarily tell only after the event. Psychic forces are not physical forces.

If purely psychic forces operate at all, it is in the way of desire as an actually felt state of mind. But as we have seen before in our discussion of psychic causality, desire can be said to bring about results only if there happens to be also some adequate physical or physiological mechanism at hand, so that the relation between the desire and what follows does not replace the physical causation but is an entirely different type of relation.

Similarly, social forces are not merely psychological. What is called social causation may be regarded as a teleologic relation. But the fact that in social relations we deal with large groups enables us to depart from individual psychology. We can thus say with greater certainty

that an economic opportunity will be utilized, or that the religion of their fathers will be followed by a large group of persons, than that it will be utilized or followed by a single individual whose specific disposition we do not know. We cannot tell what a given individual will think of the next war, but we can be fairly certain that every nation will, like Rome, manage to be convinced that its side is the just one.

Social causation, then, need not be like that of individual purposes. The overcrowding in cities does not intentionally bring about certain social diseases, any more than the invention of the cotton-gin was intended to bring about the economic changes which led to the fall of the older southern aristocracy and the political changes which led to the Civil War. It is of greater importance to recognize that social science is for the most part concerned not like physics with laws expressing the invariant repetition of elements, nor with laws of individual psychic events, but with laws about the relation of very complex patterns to one another.

Consider a number of examples of social causations. It is surely significant to inquire as to the effects of density of population. Is feminism a cause or an effect of the greater economic opportunity open to women? Is poverty the cause or the effect of a higher birth rate? In all such cases a causal relation means some connection not between individual events, or mere sums of such events, but between diverse patterns of distribution, sometimes of the same group of events. If social institutions as specific groups of events are themselves called events, we must distinguish the different levels of the term *events*. It will, however, prevent confusion if we remember that a social institution is a mode of viewing or grouping a number of events and is, therefore, strictly speaking, not a datable event, although the constituent

[5] Lester F. Ward, *Psychic Factors in Civilization,* pp. 94, 123.

[6] Ross, E. A., *Foundations of Sociology,* p. 43.

events may occur between two dates.

Thus it is that in social causation the cause does not disappear when it produces an effect, but can be said to continue and to be modified by its effects. A system of education may affect the commerce of a people and that in turn may modify the system of education. That is possible because "system of education" is not a single temporal event but a pattern of events actually coeval with the pattern of events called "the commerce of a people." The causal relation or the interaction between them is predominantly a matter of logical analysis of groups of phenomena.

The purely scientific interest is thus best served by isolating some one aspect of social phenomena—e.g. the economic, the political, the religious—and tracing the effect of changes in that aspect. Even the historian must select and restrict himself to certain phases of social events. But the practical interest in social outcome is not immediately satisfied by uniform sequences nor by the merely necessary conditions of social happenings which are too numerous to be very interesting. It needs, rather, a knowledge of the quantitative adjustments of *all* the factors necessary to produce a desired effect. This is seldom attainable. We can under certain conditions tell, for example, that a reduction of price or certain forms of advertising will increase sales. But the variation of any one factor due to local conditions is very large, and our concrete practical knowledge always involves guesswork. Hence, it can never guarantee us against fatal errors.

(D) Tendencies as Laws

One of the most usual ways of generalizing from insufficient instances and ignoring or lightly disposing of contrary facts is to call our generalization a tendency. There is an apparent analogy to this situation in the popular formulation of the laws of physics, e.g., when the law of gravitation is stated as a tendency of two bodies to move toward each other. The word *tendency,* however, can always be eliminated from physics if we remember the law of composition of forces. As the force of gravity and the resistance of a table to a falling body can both be independently measured, there is no logical difficulty in saying that the law or force of gravity is operative even when the body is brought to rest on the table.

But in the social sciences, where single factors cannot be easily isolated and independently measured, an essential indeterminateness in discussion is inevitably produced by reliance on the notion of "tendency." For conflicting schools or parties can begin with the assertion of opposite tendencies and never really join in a definite issue. Thus one party may base its political theory on the assertion that all men love or tend to love liberty, and dismiss contrary facts as sacrifices which men make in the interest of peace, etc. The opposing party can base itself on the opposite assertion that men inherently tend to love order and to fear or hate the burden of responsibility so much that they prefer to obey even insane tyrants; and the facts which cannot be so described can be attributed to exceptionally unbearable conditions etc. Obviously if the strength of these opposing tendencies were measurable and determined, the seemingly opposite assertions might be seen to be theoretically equivalent, that is to say, they would lead to the same predictions as to whether people will or will not obey under given conditions. Of course, the emotional bias in favour of one set of words over the other will, so long as words have emotional associations, make people of different experience or temperament cling to different formulae. But the outstanding fact of methodologic importance is the indetermination involved in the use of the notion of tendency, and the vain and interminable disputes that it makes possible.

It is of course scientifically useful to resist the suggestion of proposed plausible generalization by discovering contrary "tendencies." Also the existence of opposite "tendencies" must be considered before we can proceed to measure them. But the temptation to set up tendencies as laws makes social science essentially indeterminate in the sense that diverse schools set up diverse principles all with the same show of truth. Thus when the Durkheim school of anthropology says all religion is totemic in origin, or that all magic is simply an illegitimate use of the supernatural, many phenomena are aptly described, but others are ignored. Rival schools start with these other facts and deny Durkheim's theory in toto. Both sides are right if they admit that they are describing some facts, and both are wrong if they pretend to describe all the facts of religion or magic. The way out of such typical sloughs of social science is to recognize that while full description of some of the facts may be needed in the beginning of social science, the ideal end is to attain universal statements about partial aspects of all the phenomena in a given class.[7]

---

[7] To call a correlation a tendency is to admit that we have not yet purified the concepts correlated of the foreign ingredients which block the regular manifestation of some causal relationship.

If what the grocer sells as sugar is in fact not uniformly sweet, we may say that grains of the stuff *have a tendency to be* sweet. It will require the careful work of a chemist to distinguish the $C_{12} H_{22} O_{11}$ that *is* sweet from the other substances that *are not* sweet. It is just this work of analysis and refining, a hundred times more difficult with social institutions than with sugar, that a complacent reliance upon "tendencies" as the substance of social science discourages. Like fictions, meta-

(E) Type Analysis

Various philosophers, Dilthey, Spranger, Rickert, Troeltsch, and other opponents of the interpretation of history on the basis of natural laws, have urged that it is individual concepts like humanity, Christianity, the Renaissance, etc., that enable us to organize history and the cultural sciences. It does seem, at first blush, that concepts of this kind do enable us to build up science, in the sense of a significant synthesis of facts; and yet they seem to have nothing to do with laws of repetition but denote unique and essentially unrepeatable objects. But critical reflection will, I think, show that here as elsewhere there is no extension of definite systematic knowledge except in terms of abstract universals which deal with repeatable elements. Historical concepts like *the Renaissance* are convenient symbols to sum up a group of facts. But to understand the meaning of these facts and what determined their interconnection we must resort to assumptions of psychology, economics, politics, and other social sciences. If you ask why is one who has caught the spirit of the Renaissance able to appreciate facts which others would not notice or understand, the answer is not found in the magical potency of the individual concept, but in the fact that familiarity with any field of human experience develops many definite habits of expectation, i.e. implicit assumptions as to laws which bind phenomena together. This is also true in other fields, e.g., physiography and field biology. Such knowledge becomes more and more reliable to the extent that these implicit assumptions are made explicit and critically tested.

The theory of type analysis does, however, call our attention to a signifi-

---

phors, and false theories, "tendencies" are valuable stimulants for scientific thought, but they will not take the place of food.

cant phase of social inquiry. To the extent that social science is descriptive or follows the method of natural history, it must begin with actual wholes or complexes rather than with clearly defined elements. If we begin some social study, e.g., of panics, slavery, totemism, or the different moral codes in different classes of a community, we necessarily begin with vague terms such as "forced labour," "the average man," "the prosperous classes," etc. These are not finished geometric diagrams, but hints of meaning pointing in a general direction. It is the task of the inquiry itself to make these vague concepts more definite by applying them to the concrete material. The greater complexity, however, of social facts makes it more difficult to apply our concepts directly to any given social fact or situation. We therefore take many facts or situations and make a sort of composite photograph in which individual variations fade out. We let memory select the significant features. There can be little doubt that this ability to see the type in phenomena is characteristic of social insight. This is particularly true in historical and anthropological studies, which lose all scientific value when they sink into anecdotal or merely factual description.

However, in social science as in natural sciences like mineralogy, chemistry, and biology, the study of types, if it leads anywhere, only makes explicit fundamental laws.

A type is an ideal configuration of distinguishable but not always separable features. It has a scientific value in that it enables us to look for and identify certain characters after we have recognized others that co-exist with them in a given type. (When the type includes rhythms or patterns of successive events we obtain laws of succession of events analogous to those of natural science.)

The advantage of operating with types is that while laws deal with highly abstract elements which become more and more insufficient as our phenomena become more complicated, types are more definite combinations or patterns which become familiar to us through continual reference. They are, in Santayana's phrase, concretions in discourse and thought. The procedure which begins with a study of types thus follows the order of learning in daily life, where we do not begin with sensations or other hypothetical elements but with complexes involving both sense-perception and conceptual thought, which are progressively refined in the growth of knowledge.

It is well also in view of the complexity of social inquiry always to keep in mind the picture of the totality denoted by the type. For in isolating abstract elements we are apt to forget how they function in the actual totality from which they are abstracted. This is illustrated in legal theories of free contract that ignore the fact that in actual life the labourer is not free to bargain as to terms, or in economic theories which ignore the fact that the desire to buy in the cheapest market may not operate in actual instances owing to sentiment, prejudice, unintelligence, etc.

In general we may say that it is not science which initiates the general belief in universal laws. Science finds such beliefs and tries to test and refine them. In practical life we all seek to justify our beliefs or acts by very wide general propositions or premises. It is only when the *result* of such premises appears distasteful that people resist their plausibility, and then the very contrary propositions are likely to be asserted, though the latter also lead to difficulties. The intellectually timid who refuse to give justifying reasons may frequently escape the embarrassment of inconsistency and acquire a reputation for sobriety of judgment. But if rational scientific knowledge has greater potency in preparing us

to meet a changing world (not immediately but in the long run), it is precisely because it depends upon our
isolating or abstracting the relevant and
recurrent elements and studying their
temporal succession. An intelligent use
of type analysis therefore depends upon
this very ability of neglecting in the
phenomena before us all that is irrelevant and non-typical. The essence of
scientific genius (whether in the natural
or the social sciences) is just this ability
to discover points of view from which
new arrangements of facts are visible
and under which order and system can
be introduced into what has hitherto
appeared as hopeless chaos. The weakness of the ordinary account of induction
is that it minimizes this inventive genius.
It talks of the facts suggesting their explanation as if all one has to do is to
look at the facts, whereupon the true
explanation is automatically precipitated
from their sensible traits. A more adequate view of the learning process,
which, by allowing for its a priori element, can explain how this scientific
insight is both possible and rare, is held
today by the Gestalt psychologists. We
see the world not in terms of pure sensa
—yellowness, bigness, roundness, etc.—
but in terms of organized configurations,
e.g. bananas, baseball games, beautiful
women, and bunches of grapes. How such
configurations are organized depends not
only upon the objective character of our
environment but as well upon the observer's intellectual and emotional make-
up. Such a view can account for the fact
that Wordsworth, looking at a daffodil,
sees more than Peter Bell, and that
Roentgen, looking at a spoiled camera
plate, sees something that no other
observer ever saw.

On this analysis, the fundamental
unity of common sense, social science,
and natural science is apparent. But it
will not do to dismiss the differences in
certainty, accuracy, universality, and

coherency that actually distinguish these
fields as "mere matters of degree." The
word "mere" is itself not only a term of
degree but the one quantitative word in
the English language that has a superlative without a comparative (i.e. without
any ordering relation which could give
its degrees a meaning). Thus it is a
dangerous invitation to slipshod thinking. Not only are differences of degree as
important as any other differences, but
the similarity of different things which
leads the superficial to renounce further
thought is the necessary basis for significant distinctions. The differences in
approximation to the ideals of science
between common opinion and the professional thought of men like Boas, Pound,
and Maitland, or between such thought
and that of Einstein, Mendeléyev, and
Loeb, demand our appreciation and reflection. What we have called type
analysis, involving as it does a certain
lack of explicitness in its assumptions,
of definiteness in its terms, of coherency
and accuracy in its conclusions, may not
be the ultimate ideal of social science,
but it is all we can expect in the foreseeable future. Though it is proper to
distinguish this level of thought from
the plane attained in the natural sciences
we should not deny it the adjective
scientific unless we are ready to eliminate such names as Galen, Leeuwenhoek,
Pasteur, and Darwin from the rosters of
science.

§ IV. THE FACULTY OR TYPE OF MENTALITY INVOLVED

The foregoing considerations suggest
the element of truth in the Aristotelian
view that while physical science depends
on theoretical reason ($\gamma o \tilde{v} \varsigma$), practical
social science involves more sound judg-
ment ($\phi\rho\acute{o}\nu\eta\sigma\iota\varsigma$). Sound judgment
means ability to guess (or intuit) what
is relevant and decisive, and to make a
rapid estimate of the sum of a large

number of factors that have not been accurately determined. In practice the statesman, the business man, and even the physician may often find the suggestive remark of a novelist like Balzac of greater help than long chapters from the most scientific psychology, since the latter deals with elements, whereas in conduct we deal with whole situations. This frequently gives rise to a philistine anti-rationalism. What is the use of speculating about the ultimate good? Why not, rather, use our intelligence to increase the sum of justice and happiness in actual cases? But *can* decision be intelligent if inquiries as to the ultimate meaning of justice and happiness are prohibited? How will the restricted use of intelligence in that case be different from the uncritical acceptance of traditional judgments as to what is good and what is bad in specific cases?

The efforts of the human intellect may be viewed as a tension between two poles —one to do justice to the fullness of the concrete case before us, the other to grasp an underlying abstract universal principle that controls much more than the one case before us.

None of our works shows these forces in perfectly stable equilibrium. The problems of engineering, medication, administration, and statesmanship generally depend more upon not overlooking any of the relevant factors. But in pure science as in personal religion and poetry intense concentration on one phase rather than justice to many is the dominant trait. To the extent that the social sciences aim at the adjustment of human difficulties, they involve more judgment and circumspection. To the extent that they aim at insight or θεωρία, they are at one with pure science and with religion and poetry.

SUGGESTED FURTHER READINGS FOR CHAPTER ONE

* Aristotle, *Works,* Oxford ed., especially Vol. I.

Blanshard, Brand, *The Nature of Thought,* Vol. II.

Bridgman, P. W., *The Logic of Modern Physics,* especially Ch. I.

Broad, C. D., *Scientific Thought.*

Campbell, Norman, *What is Science?*

* ———, *Physics, the Elements.*

Carnap, Rudolf, *The Unity of Science.*

———, *Foundations of Logic and Mathematics,* in *International Encyclopedia of Unified Science,* Vol. I, No. 3.

Cohen, M. R., *Reason and Nature,* Bk. I, Ch. III.

Dewey, John, *How We Think,* 2nd ed.

* Galileo, Galilei, *Two New Sciences.* The Macmillan Co., 1914; originally appeared in 1638.

Jevons, W. S., *Principles of Science,* Ch. XXI, XXIII.

Lenzen, Victor, *Procedures of Empirical Science,* in *International Encyclopedia of Unified Science,* Vol. I, No. 5.

Mach, Ernst, *Science of Mechanics.*

Mill, John Stuart, *Logic,* Bk. III, VI.

* More difficult or advanced.

Murphy, A. E., *The Uses of Reason.*

Nagel, Ernest, *Principles of the Theory of Probability,* in *International Encyclopedia of Unified Science,* Vol. I, No. 6; for further references on *Probability* see the bibliography in this pamphlet.

Peirce, Charles S., *Collected Papers,* especially Vol. I and Vol. V.

Poincaré, Henri, *Foundations of Science.*

Reichenbach, Hans, *Experience and Prediction.*

* Russell, Bertrand, *Principles of Mathematics,* 2nd ed. (first ed., 1903).

Schiller, F. C. S., "Hypothesis," in *Studies in the History and Methods of Science,* Vol. II, ed. by Charles Singer.

Veblen, Thorstein, *The Place of Science in Modern Civilization.*

Chapter Two

PROBLEMS OF ETHICS

INTRODUCTION

I. Illustrations and Definition of Ethical Problems

THE various professions of law, medicine, teaching, and so on have certain "codes of ethics." A lawyer should not accept bribes to conceal or distort evidence; a physician should treat his patients with equal care regardless of their economic status; a teacher should not simply impose his personal opinions on his students; a minister should practice what he preaches. Every religion has ethical commandments: "Thou shalt not kill"; "Do unto others as you would have them do unto you." Ethical notions are implicit even in everyday phrases: "The end justifies the means," "Might makes right," "Every man for himself," "My country, right or wrong," "Good neighbor policy," "Fair play," and so on.

Consider an ethical problem that has affected the lives of many thinking persons who regard themselves as pacifists on religious or other grounds. They are, during wartime, faced with the choice of declaring themselves conscientious objectors or participating in a "justifiable" war. There are different kinds of pacifists, and some governments permit religious pacifists exemption from military conscription. But for all people, the fundamental question is the justification for war. In thinking through such a momentous question, we make certain assumptions about what is "justifiable" in general; for example, we may believe that taking arms against an aggressor is always the "right" course of action. But consider an extreme pacifist who clings to the principle of passive resistance on the ground that it is always wrong to kill a human being, even in self-defense. As moral philosophers, we ask if this view would make it wrong for anybody to kill a ruthless murderer in self-defense or to save innocent persons, for the state to inflict capital punishment, for a physician to put to death mercifully an incurable patient suffering great pain, or for a person facing excruciating torture to commit suicide.

In any case, the general principles which are assumed in coming to a decision as to what choice among alternative courses of conduct one *ought* to make are the subject matter of ethics or moral philosophy. This branch of philosophy is concerned with the understanding of what is meant by such terms as "good," "right," "justifiable," "duty," "responsibility," and so on, in judgments about how persons *ought* to conduct themselves when confronted with a choice of alternatives. Such "value-judgments" are implicit in praising or blaming others or ourselves. Though we are usually quick to blame others for not choosing what we consider right, we are rarely clear about the reasons for our own assurance that we know what is "right." It is not an easy matter to make explicit the meaning of ethical terms so that even all intelligent persons will agree, especially when their own interests and beliefs are at stake. Our understanding of what is good or bad, right or wrong, is entangled by conflicting ideas derived from diverse sources that influence us: parents, teachers, ministers, friends, favorite authors, movie stars. A young person's choice of a life career will often depend on whose ideals of living he holds highest in esteem. It has taken a lifetime of experience and reflection for the great moral teachers of mankind to come to certain conclusions about the good life in their search for a "way of life." Such was the case with Confucius, Laotze, Buddha, Zoroaster, Socrates, Epicurus, Epictetus, Jesus, Spinoza, Kant, Dewey, and other moral philosophers who sought answers to ethical problems.

In Western civilization we find contrasting ways of life and conflicting ethical ideals: the this-worldliness of classical and Renaissance culture opposed to the other-worldliness of medieval and mystic renunciation of all earthly desires, the Catholic ethic of Aquinas and the Protestant ethic of Kant, the evolutionary ethics of social reform, and the revolutionary ethics of violent seizure of power. Conflicts between established traditions and changing social conditions are one of the chief sources of ethical reflection over the meaning of accepted or socially sanctioned standards of good and bad. Coming in contact with other cultures different from our own, we are likely to wonder whether there is any common morality, but the problems of future international relations lead us to seek a just "bill of rights" for all peoples.

Ethical principles are assumed in making a choice between alternative possibilities in terms of better or worse. It is the aim of moral philosophy to clarify ethical choice by bringing to light the ethical principles assumed in any decision or proposed action and by examining them critically for their consistency and satisfactoriness.

It may be objected that reflection over abstract ethical principles such as are discussed in the selections below does not make one "a good person," that good character is a product of good breeding, good habits, good education, and good religious training (whereas ethics is just a verbal and intellectual exercise) and that what can be said about good in general is good for nothing in particular. There are certain confusions in this objection. In the first place, it assumes that we already know what good character, good breeding, good habits, good education, and good religious training are. This assumption is doubtful, since there are so many different opinions about what is good in regard to character, breeding, habits, education, and religion. In the second place, ethical theory does not claim to be a *sufficient* basis for molding character. Aristotle, in fact, in the first chapter of his *Ethics*, notes the importance of a stable set of habits for the formation of character and even regards young persons ruled by uncontrolled impulses as not yet ready for the study of ethics. Of course, Aristotle means by "young" not simply youthful in years, but in maturity of habits of self-control and of reflection over one's experiences.

Professional codes of ethics, religious commandments, and other practical precepts of conduct belong to the study of applied ethics or homiletics. The latter presupposes some ethical theory, as engineering presupposes physical theory or medicine, biology, though we are far from having reached the same degree of agreement and exactness in ethics as in physics and biology. Furthermore, the problems of ethics do not generally call for the precise quantitative laws of physical science. Aristotle makes it clear that each discipline has its own problems and degree of exactness relevant to those problems. It was a great enough step forward in the progress of ethics as a rational discipline for Socrates to have asked people to define the meanings of their ideas about justice, courage, friendship, and to show the need for greater clarity concerning these ideas.

Socrates' claim that "Virtue is Knowledge" may seem to some to stress unduly the power of clear ideas in guiding conduct, but it has appealed to thinking persons as much sounder than the romantic slogan "Ignorance is Bliss." It has been observed that if the latter were true, many people would be happier than they are.

II.   Greek Rationalism and Naturalism

Nearly all ethical systems aim at an ordering of the goods of life in accordance with some notion of what "good" means. If we take stock of the things we call good, we find, among the diverse assortment, the music we enjoy in relaxation, the view from a mountain top, the laughter of children at play—these are examples of simple enjoyments or harmless pleasures which would be classified by Socrates, in our first selection, as things good in themselves. Let us call them *intrinsic* goods and note their esthetic character.

There is another kind of good which is the opposite of being enjoyable in itself but is often regarded as a necessary means to the enjoyment of other things; for example, a severe course of physical training and dietary regimen is a means of restoring bodily health. Socrates placed such means in the class of irksome but needed activities. Let us call this class *instrumental* goods. The highest goods are those which are good both intrinsically and instrumentally. For examples, Socrates mentions intelligence, sight, and health, for these are enjoyed in themselves and also as means for securing other goods. The aim of Plato's *Republic* was to prove that justice belonged to this highest class of goods, contrary to the common opinion that it belongs to the lowest class of painful, but apparently necessary, instrumental means of preserving order. Would anybody really care for law or justice if he could get away with murder, rapine, and theft by the possession of the mythical ring of Gyges that makes its wearer invisible at will? The sceptical Glaucon thus challenges Socrates to prove that justice is more than an instrumental good to further the interests of those who seek to acquire the benefits of fame, wealth, and power "by hook or crook." A similar problem is raised by Plato when he asks whether it is better to do an injustice than to suffer one. It is obvious that such problems are social as well as individual. That is why Plato went on to answer the sceptical query of Glaucon, "Why is justice better than injustice?" by drawing up an ideal state in the *Republic,* for "the state is the individual writ in large characters." That is to say, Plato's problem of proving that the just man's life was more harmonious and happier than the unjust man's life was translated into the larger political problem of justice as the basis of social harmony. Likewise, Aristotle regarded man as a "political animal" and ethics as a preface to politics. But let us return to our problem of the meaning of good by consulting the opening chapter of Aristotle's *Nicomachean Ethics*.

Here we find Aristotle accepting the distinction between instrumental and intrinsic goods and associating them with the specific purposes or ends of human activities in society. These are as diverse as the occupations, arts, and sciences of men in any society. Within and among them there is a subordination of means and ends; for example, bricklaying is instrumental in building a house, and a house is a means to the end of family living. The latter is a means to maintaining a community. There must be some end, however, which is not regarded as a means to anything else, but is the common end of all human activities. That supreme end is called by Aristotle happiness or well-being, and whoever enjoys it for the greater part of his life is said to have a good life or to live well.

The meaning of good is then the same as that of happiness, and if Aristotle were merely looking for a verbal solution to the problem, there would have been no need for his writing ten chapters analyzing moral and intellectual virtues, pleasure, types of friendship, and the relation of the practical to the theoretical uses of the mind. The fact is, Aristotle recognizes, that there is little agreement about what constitutes happiness.

Various opinions identify happiness with the enjoyment of sensory pleasures, of public honor or fame, of wealth, of intellectual excellence. Is pleasure or the balance of pleasure over pain the only meaning of what is good? If so, how can we compare or measure pleasures and pains either in ourselves or in others without some definable unit or standard of comparison or measurement? How can one choose between the pleasure of games and that of serious study? Are there not some unpleasant tasks that *ought* to be done? These are crucial questions for the hedonist, and we are all hedonists whenever we regard only the pleasure of an activity as the sign of its moral value.

It is not pleasure in the abstract that people desire, but pleasurable activities or objects. Such objects seem to fall into three classes: objects that afford sensory excitation (food, drink, sex), the accumulation of wealth and the power that goes with it, and, thirdly, the social fame, public prestige, and praise that are often sought by persons who will sacrifice everything else for their sake. Most people desire all three of these kinds of "goods," but some regard one as more important to them than the others. Aristotle thought that a rational and moderate enjoyment of all of these goods entered into that harmonious realization of a person's desires during the whole course of his life which is called happiness (contrasted with momentary pleasure). Though the specific forms of happiness will vary with each person, the meaning of "the good life" is none other than the life which contains such pervasive happiness. Three kinds of lives—the sensual, the political, and the speculative—show how varied the problem is.

It is well to examine people's lives to test these opinions, Aristotle believes, rather than to try to discover what happiness is in some purely abstract way by establishing an absolute cause of all goodness, as Plato tried to do. Aristotle thus adopts an empirical approach to ethical problems. This becomes clear in his criticism of Plato's theory that there is a single Form of the Good which is the absolute source of all earthly goods. How can knowledge of such a transcendent Good make a man a better carpenter or physician, asks Aristotle. It is the *practicable* or realizable good that makes for happiness and not some purely theoretical possibility, humanly unattainable.

A good knife is one that cuts well, for the function of a knife is to cut. Aristotle generalizes this functional sense of goodness and arrives at the notion that the good of man, his happiness, must be inseparable from the function or activity peculiar to his nature. Now what distinguishes man (*homo sapiens*) from all other creatures is his reason or intelligence. Hence, the good man is one whose activity is guided by reason. It is only by making the most of his rational powers that man can live well. Aristotle, in fact, went as far at the end of his *Ethics* as to make philosophical contemplation the highest good.

The use of reason in ethical problems is not that of the mathematician or pure theoretician who seeks to demonstrate his conclusions with logical certainty. Each subject requires its own degree of certainty, and, considering the variability, diversity, and complexity of human nature and its activities, Aristotle repeatedly reminds us that we can indicate only approximately what it means to be reasonable in human affairs and that we must be guided by careful observation and practical experience. The reasonable course, he observes, is not simply an arithmetic mean, but falls somewhere between the extremes of too much and too little; temperance is found empirically to be an avoidance of the ill effects of over-indulgence and those of complete abstinence; courage is a mean between foolhardy exposure to danger and timid fear of all risks. There is historical evidence that Aristotle's ethical rule of the mean was suggested to him by the dietary rules of Greek physicians. The moral philosopher in this naturalistic type of ethics is "the physician of the soul."

But every honest physician knows how complex and varied are the causes of the derangements of human life. Besides physiological injuries, there are psychological and social maladjustments. Plato sought to put man's house in order by reference to an absolute Form of the Good. Aristotle and other naturalists, like Dewey, regard the good as relative to man's native endowments, interests, and abilities. They also emphasize the importance of habits in steadying the emotions and ordering the desires that motivate human conduct. And all of them realize that the social aspects of man's life bring ethics and politics together, so that a further discussion of the merits of their ethical systems would lead us into their theories of human nature, social classes, and the functions of the state. We shall have to postpone the political aspects of ethics to the next chapter and now go on to consider other approaches to ethical problems tied up with different conceptions of human nature and its possibilities for good.

These approaches are exemplified in the selections from the ethical writings of Spinoza, Kant, Bentham, Mill, Dewey, and Bradley, and some indications of how differently they regarded human nature may help explain their differences in ethical theory.

III. Spinoza's Rationalism

Spinoza's main work on *Ethics*, to which the selection from the *Improvement of the Understanding* may be read as a prelude, was written in the deductive form of Euclid's *Elements*. The idea was to treat human nature and ethical problems as calmly and thoughtfully as we consider a geometrical figure or problem, the elements being man's emotions, interests, and ideas instead of points, lines, and planes. Thus Spinoza hoped to introduce scientific objectivity and rational methods of proof into a subject ridden with prejudice, partiality, and rhetoric.

Spinoza explained in Book III of his *Ethics* why he chose the geometric method:

"The majority of those who have discussed the emotions and men's way of living seem to treat them not as things following the ordinary laws of nature but as things outside of nature. They even conceive man in nature as a sort of empire within an empire, for they believe that man disturbs the order of nature rather than obeys it, that man has absolute power over his actions determined by himself alone. . . . It will no doubt appear strange to them that I undertake to treat some errors and absurdities of men in a geometrical fashion. . . . But there is nothing erroneous in whatever happens in nature, for nature is always the same, its properties and its power of action are one and the same thing, in other words the laws according to which everything is produced and is transformed are everywhere and always the same. Consequently, there has to be a single and fixed method for understanding the nature of things of any kind, viz., the universal laws and rules of nature."

This "geometric method" of Spinoza's, common to science and philosophy in the seventeenth century, is an *a priori* method of deducing conclusions from definitions and axioms. Applied to ethics, it presupposes fixed, universal traits in all human beings and simple uniform laws governing their behavior under the influence of emotions. Emotions are regarded as confused ideas, and so long as they remain confused, human nature is slave to their strength, subject to the vicissitudes of external forces and compelled to suffer accordingly. The only salvation lies in the use of Reason, embodied in Euclid's geometric method. Reason can clarify the direction and end of each emotion and its relation to other emotions. Reason can discover the way to guide the expression of these emotions so as to avoid painful conflicts and mutual frustration. In Spinoza, Reason includes knowledge of the human mind and its relation to the whole of nature. Such knowledge is not only useful to man, but also constitutes his freedom from the bondage of blind passions and his highest good. In fact, such knowledge, for Spinoza, is divine. We must omit discussion of the metaphysics that goes with Spinoza's ethics and simply note the question: To what extent is ethics dependent on metaphysics?

IV. Kant's Ethics of Formal Duty

Kant maintained that morality was impossible without freedom of will or choice since we do not condemn a person's action as immoral if he could not have considered acting otherwise; for examples, consider the destructive acts of an infant, of a mentally sick person, or of someone drugged. An intoxicated driver, however, is held responsible for his recklessness since he was free not to become intoxicated before driving.

Now Kant believed on metaphysical grounds that physical nature was completely determined by universal and necessary laws, so that freedom of the will had to be grounded in another realm, in a higher moral world not limited by space or time as the natural world is. We know the laws governing that moral world through what Kant called the "faculty of practical reason." This faculty prescribes formal rules to a dutiful will whose universal aim is to respect persons as ends in themselves. Kant formulated this rule in a "categorical imperative": Act so that the principle of your action can be generalized by practical reason. A soldier's guerrilla tactics are not acceptable after his return to civilian life in a peaceful, rational society.

Kant rejected the condoning of "white lies" or the breaking of a promise by appealing to empirical consequences or social inclination because he regarded such consequences as not totally foreseeable and inclinations as transitory whereas the moral law should be certain and eternally binding. That is why he attacked social utility and pleasure as inadequate ethical standards or guides to the individual's sense of duty.

The good, then, for Kant is absolutely independent of the empirical facts or laws which the scientist reports in his accounts of nature, and proceeds categorically only from "the good will" or sense of duty. Kant insists that nothing in the laws of natural sciences tells us that we ought to treat human beings as moral ends in themselves and not merely as a means for the gratification of our personal desires. "Good will" is the sterling quality of all ethical character, and "good faith" the moral basis of legal contracts.

Now, we often do have to depend on people as necessary means; for example, if X wants to apply for a position requiring references, then X must use persons Y and Z, who know his qualifications, as means for securing the desired position. Kant calls such means-ends propositions "hypothetical imperatives" and distinguishes them sharply from what he considers to be the essentially ethical rule or "categorical imperative." Kant would say: X ought to apply for the position because X is one of the most qualified persons and because it is universally good for such persons to make themselves available to fill a vacancy; it is the duty of X to apply for the position, and of Y and Z to recommend him, regardless of what happens to other applicants.

One may question this Kantian cleavage between formal ethical rules and factual, scientific considerations. The empiricist would point out that the only reason for accepting any *application* of the categorical imperative lies in the empirical fact that violations of such maxims of conduct too often lead to disastrous social consequences. The empiricist, however, assumes that the formal ethical law has no meaning apart from its applications, which is tantamount to denying that ethical rules are purely formal. But the great contribution of Kant's ethics is its emphasis on the intrinsic value of individuals as ends in themselves and on the idea that being *worthy of* social approval is higher than merely selfish pleasure.

V. Bentham's Calculus of Happiness and Utilitarian Ethics

Bentham's hedonistic ethics is based on a calculus of pleasures and pains which teaches us what to seek and what to avoid in our private and public lives. The good is whatever promotes the happiness (measured by the predominance of pleasures over pains) of an individual or of the community (never more for Bentham than a sum of its individual members). There are physical, legal, social, and religious sanctions for pleasure and pain, the physical (including the physiological) being the basic cause or "groundwork of the political and the moral." An attempt is made by Bentham to measure pleasures and pains by considering their various aspects or dimensions, e.g. intensity, duration, and so forth.

Apart from the psychological difficulties of measuring pleasures and pains, there are other problems for this bold attempt to reduce ethics to a calculus. How can we foresee all the pleasurable and painful consequences of our actions or decisions which need to be guided by principles while we are not fully certain of the future? Are not pleasure and pain *too* variable and lacking in any verifiable common denominator to provide general rules of conduct or units of measurement of values? Can we dissociate our individual preferences from our relations to our fellow beings, and how can we calculate their pleasures as well as ours in arriving at a social policy? Some recent mathematical methods of considering a rational basis for justifying value judgments or social policies raise similar problems:

If a person (or a group) prefers A to B and B to C, shall we say it is irrational for him (or the group) to judge B or C *better than* A? And even if it were decided by logical agreement that such a judgment were irrational, would that decide the ethical problem: *ought* one prefer A to C? The logic of the social sciences is thus related to ethical problems, and if one seeks to free social sciences from such value judgments, the scope of these sciences becomes delimited to factual matters of no relevance to practical policy-making decisions. Bentham at least aimed to apply his ethical analysis to problems of legislation and penology.

John Stuart Mill was raised in the tenets of Bentham, but introduced the important point of distinguishing *qualities* of higher and lower among the desires that enter into moral choice. The "higher" discontent of a Socrates was for Mill an integral part of the greater freedom enjoyed by a mind not content with merely a quantity of pleasures of any kind.

The utilitarians rejected the two worlds of Kant, the natural and the moral, the physical and the spiritual, the temporal and the eternal, to which body and soul belong separately. They wished to bring ethics closer to the natural and social sciences. All ethical problems for them are natural and social problems, and the same intelligence that is used in the latter can be and should be used in the former. We have no higher faculties of moral intuition or infallible guides to conduct. The experimental reasoning of natural science and the trial-and-error habits of practical experience constitute the sole reliable means of resolving human problems. These problems occur in and because of changing social conditions. Accordingly, our moral conceptions and standards must be continually subject to revision. The aristocratic ethics of Plato and Aristotle, the *a priori* ethics of Spinoza, the supernatural revelations of medieval moralists, the intuitions of Protestant ethics, the two-worldly system of Kant—these all belong to past or passing cultures and require drastic modification in the scientific and technological era through which we are now living. The difference between the fact that we like or desire something and the value-judgment that we *ought* to desire it or that it is desir*able* goes to the heart of the ethical problem. That is, the judgment "I like driving at very high speed" expresses a particular fact, but most pedestrians would not like the generalization "I *ought to* drive at very high speed." Is it necessary to invoke Kant's transcendental "good-will" in order to justify moral intelligence? The utilitarians believe that the same intelligence that enables us in common sense and science to act in accordance with the connections and consequences of our decisions suffices for moral problems. It does not require more than ordinary intelligence to realize that driving at very high speeds is dangerous and therefore should not be permitted by law. Traffic laws are good because they are socially useful.

The distinctive feature of pragmatic or utilitarian ethics is that goods are not absolute, self-sufficient, and final termini of moral action. They depend always on psychological, social, and historical circumstances, in which reflection over what is desirable in terms of social consequences plays a decisive role.

Why should an individual citizen not accept a bribe to vote in a certain way? Others have done it and escaped detection and in some cases have made themselves prosperous that way. What Mill and Dewey would indicate is the effect of such bribe-taking on both the individual's character and on the society led by a government that gets into power by such means. The means used become incorporated in the character of the people who use the means, and when problems arise, as they will, which require persevering honesty, the bribe-takers and bribers will fail to meet the situation. We cannot be too sure what the consequences of our actions are, but we can be sure that there will be consequences and that we shall be affected by them. Reason is the instrumentality for considering all the consequences we can discover. It is "the slave of the passions," as Hume put it, but for Dewey the passions are subject to modification by intelligently formed and socially useful habits. Reason should cooperate with our needs rather than dictate to them or permit blind passion to do so. For Dewey, means and ends form a continuous series of habit-forming and socially consequential activities. What is sought and attained in one situation may serve as a means for the pursuit of further ends in subsequent situations. Against the static classical conception of a realm of fixed ends, Dewey introduces a dynamic experimental view of our moral life in which ends in view are not isolated from the means employed. For some means may defeat one's purposes; hence, the end does not justify the use of any means. The compatibility of our desires and the dependence of each person on his relations to other persons makes it of paramount importance to consider whether the means employed in the pursuit of a particular object of desire will not lead to the frustration of other desires. In its social orientation Dewey's ethics is in line with the utilitarian formula of the "greatest good for the greatest number."

The pragmatic, utilitarian ethics is to be contrasted with the formal ethics of duties as well as with the restricted hedonism of momentary pleasure. Those who hold to the absolute rule of duty or to the pleasure of the moment deny in principle that the natural and social consequences of their actions are pertinent to the good. The rational test of their position is whether we can consistently act in disregard of natural inclinations and social consequences.

VI. Bradley's Idealistic Critique of Hedonism

F. H. Bradley was a British idealist (along Hegelian lines) who criticized Bentham's hedonism and Mill's utilitarianism, and defended self-realization as a more concrete goal of moral activity than evanescent pleasures or happiness in the abstract. Reverting to Aristotle's functional idea of virtue as a kind of activity of the self, Bradley sharply takes to task the hedonist who confuses the pleasure that accompanies such activity with the end that truly guides it. He also indicts Mill for having set up a vague and unattainable ideal in the principle of the greatest happiness for the greatest number. Bradley's arguments are dialectical in the sense that they seek to expose formal contradictions and the incomplete character of empiricism in ethics.

*   *   *   *   *

The criticism of ethical generalizations depends on the method of valuation. Some philosophers reject empirical or scientific verification in ethics because in their opinion ethics is a "normative" discipline whose problems of what *ought* to be cannot be resolved by the methods of dealing with factual or scientific problems. Such philosophers resort to intuitions of eternal moral laws or to an autonomous moral sense or to revelations of a higher or supernatural world not open to scientific methods of inquiry. Among them is the ethical absolutist who maintains that if good is relative to human needs and desires, then all moral claims and obligations disappear. Dewey, on the other hand, proposes to treat ethical valuations as hypotheses that arise out of cultural conflicts and have to be tested experimentally by their instrumental value in resolving such conflicts in our human relations.

Many aspects of the ethical problem are intertwined with political, religious, legal, educational,[1] and other philosophical problems. For if the good man is one who lives in accordance with the rational laws of a stable society, as Plato and Aristotle taught; or in accordance with divine decrees, as religious systems preach; or in accordance with the economic interests of his class, as Marx says; then ethics becomes an integral part of a political, religious, or social philosophy. Even an iconoclast like Nietzsche, whose ethics aims to go beyond all good and evil by breaking with Philistine notions and the "slave morality of Christianity," envisages an ideal society of emancipated supermen.

Whether or not there are ethical goals inherent in politics, history, or the world order itself, as diverse philosophers have maintained, are questions which take us into philosophical topics to be discussed in other chapters of this book.

P. P. W.

---

[1] Consider the problems of church and state in education, divorce laws, child labor legislation, and so on.

8. *The Republic**

PLATO (B.C. 427–347)

Book II

When I had made these remarks I thought we had done with discussing: whereas it seems it was only a prelude. For Glaucon, with that eminent courage which he displays on all occasions, would not acquiesce in the retreat of Thrasymachus, and began thus: Socrates, do you wish really to convince us that it is on every account better to be just than to be unjust, or only to seem to have convinced us?

If it were in my power, I replied, I should prefer convincing you really.

Then, he proceeded, you are not doing what you wish. Let me ask you: Is there, in your opinion, a class of good things of such a kind that we are glad to possess them, not because we desire their consequences, but simply welcoming them for their own sake? Take, for example, the feelings of enjoyment and all those pleasures that are harmless, and that are followed by no result in the after time, beyond simple enjoyment in their possession.

Yes, I certainly think there is a class of this description.

Well, is there another class, do you think, of those which we value, both for their own sake and for their results? Such as intelligence, and sight, and health; all of which are welcome, I apprehend, on both accounts.

Yes.

And do you further recognize a third class of good things, which would include gymnastic training, and submission to medical treatment in illness, as well as the practice of medicine, and all other means of making money? Things like these we should describe as irksome, and yet beneficial to us; and while we should reject them viewed simply in themselves, we accept them for the sake of the emoluments, and of the other consequences which result from them.

Yes, undoubtedly there is such a third class also; but what then?

In which of these classes do you place justice?

I should say in the highest; that is, among the good things which will be valued by one who is in the pursuit of true happiness, alike for their own sake and for their consequences.

Then your opinion is not that of the many, by whom justice is ranked in the irksome class, as a thing which in itself, and for its own sake, is disagreeable and repulsive, but which it is well to practise for the credit of it, with an eye to emolument and a good name.

I know it is so: and under this idea Thrasymachus has been for a long time disparaging justice and praising injustice. But apparently I am a dull scholar.

* *The Republic of Plato,* translated into English by John L. Davies and David M. Vaughan, pp. 39-44 (London, 3d ed., 1866), by permission of The Macmillan Co., publishers. This is a continuation of the discussion in Selection 1 of Chapter One.

Pray then listen to my proposal, and tell me whether you agree to it. Thrasymachus appears to me to have yielded like a snake to your fascination sooner than he need have done; but for my part I am not satisfied as yet with the exposition that has been given of justice and injustice; for I long to be told what they respectively are, and what force they exert, taken simply by themselves, when residing in the soul, dismissing the consideration of their rewards and other consequences. This shall be my plan then, if you do not object: I will revive Thrasymachus' argument, and will first state the common view respecting the nature and origin of justice; in the second place, I will maintain that all who practise it do so against their will, because it is indispensable, not because it is a good thing; and thirdly, that they act reasonably in so doing, because the life of the unjust man is, as men say, far better than that of the just. Not that I think so myself, Socrates: only my ears are so dinned with what I hear from Thrasymachus and a thousand others, that I am puzzled. Now I have never heard the argument for the superiority of justice over injustice maintained to my satisfaction; for I should like to hear a panegyric upon it, considered simply in itself: and from you if from any one, I should expect such a treatment of the subject. Therefore I will speak as forcibly as I can in praise of an unjust life, and I shall thus give you a specimen of the manner in which I wish to hear you afterwards censure injustice and commend justice. See whether you approve of my plan.

Indeed I do; for on what other subject could a sensible man like better to talk and to hear others talk, again and again?

Admirably spoken! So now listen to me while I speak on my first theme, the nature and the origin of justice.

To commit injustice is, they say, in its nature, a good thing, and to suffer it an evil thing; but the evil of the latter exceeds the good of the former; and so, after the twofold experience of both doing and suffering injustice, those who cannot avoid the latter and compass the former find it expedient to make a compact of mutual abstinence from injustice. Hence arose legislation and contracts between man and man, and hence it became the custom to call that which the law enjoined just, as well as lawful. Such, they tell us, is justice, and so it came into being; and it stands midway between that which is best, to commit injustice with impunity, and that which is worst, to suffer injustice without any power of retaliating. And being a mean between these two extremes, the principle of justice is regarded with satisfaction, not as a positive good, but because the inability to commit injustice has rendered it valuable; for they say that one who had it in his power to be unjust, and who deserved the name of a man, would never be so weak as to contract with any one that both the parties should abstain from injustice. Such is the current account, Socrates, of the nature of justice, and of the circumstances in which it originated.

The truth of my second statement— that men practise justice unwillingly, and because they lack the power to violate it, will be most readily perceived, if we make a supposition like the following. Let us give full liberty to the just man and to the unjust alike, to do whatever they please, and then let us follow them, and see whither the inclination of each will lead him. In that case we shall surprise the just man in the act of travelling in the same direction as the unjust, owing to that covetous desire, the gratification of which every creature naturally pursues as a good, only that it is forced out of its path by law, and constrained to respect the principle of equality. That full liberty of action would, perhaps, be most effectually realized if they were invested with a power which they say was in old time possessed by the ancestor of Gyges the Lydian. He was a shepherd, so the story runs, in the service of the reigning sovereign of Lydia, when one day a violent storm of rain fell, the ground was rent asunder by an earthquake, and a yawning gulf appeared on the spot where he was feeding his flocks. Seeing what had happened, and wondering at it, he went down into the gulf, and among other marvellous objects he saw, as the legend relates, a hollow brazen horse, with windows in its sides, through which he looked, and beheld in the interior a corpse, apparently of superhuman size; from which he took nothing but a golden ring off the hand, and therewith made his way out. Now when the usual meeting of the shepherds occurred, for the purpose of sending to the king their monthly report of the state of his flocks, this shepherd came with the rest, wearing the ring. And, as he was seated with the company, he happened to turn the hoop of the ring round towards himself, till it came to the inside of his hand. Whereupon he became invisible to his neighbours, who fell to talking about him as if he were gone away. While he was marvelling at this, he again began playing with the ring, and turned the hoop to the outside, upon which he became once more visible. Having noticed this effect, he made experiments with the ring, to see whether it possessed this virtue; and so it was, that when he turned the hoop inwards he became invisible, and when he turned it outwards he was again visible. After this discovery, he immediately contrived to be appointed one of the messengers to carry the report to the king; and upon his arrival he seduced the queen, and, conspiring with her, slew the king, and took possession of the throne.

If then there were two such rings in existence, and if the just and the unjust man were each to put on one, it is to be thought that no one would be so steeled against temptation as to abide in the practice of justice, and resolutely to abstain from touching the property of his neighbours, when he had it in his power to help himself without fear to any thing he pleased in the market, or to go into private houses and have intercourse with whom he would, or to kill and release from prison according to his own pleasure, and in every thing else to act among men with the power of a god. And in thus following out his desires the just man will be doing precisely what the unjust man would do; and so they would both be pursuing the same path. Surely this will be allowed to be strong evidence that none are just willingly, but only by compulsion, because to be just is not a good to the individual; for all violate justice whenever they imagine that there is nothing to hinder them. And they do so because every one thinks that, in the individual case, injustice is much more profitable than justice; and they are right in so thinking, as the advocate of this doctrine will maintain. For if any one having this licence within his grasp were to refuse to do any injustice, or to touch the property of others, all who were aware of it would think him a most pitiful and irrational creature, though they would praise him before each other's faces, to impose on one another, through their fear of being treated with injustice. And so much for this topic.

[Thus ends Glaucon's case *vs.* Socrates.]

9. *The Nicomachean Ethics**

ARISTOTLE (B.C. 384–322)

Book I

Every art and every scientific inquiry, and similarly every action and purpose, may be said to aim at some good. Hence the good has been well defined as that at which all things aim. But it is clear that there is a difference in the ends; for the ends are sometimes activities, and sometimes results beyond the mere activities. Also, where there are certain ends beyond the actions, the results are naturally superior to the activities.

As there are various actions, arts, and sciences, it follows that the ends are also various. Thus health is the end of medicine, a vessel of shipbuilding, victory of strategy, and wealth of domestic economy. It often happens that there are a number of such arts or sciences which fall under a single faculty, as the art of making bridles, and all such other arts as make the instruments of horsemanship, under horsemanship, and this again as well as every military action under strategy, and in the same way other arts or sciences under other faculties. But in all these cases the ends of the architectonic arts or sciences, whatever they may be, are more desirable than those of the subordinate arts or sciences, as it is for the sake of the former that the latter are themselves sought after. It makes no difference to the argument whether the activities themselves are the ends of

---

* Translated by J. E. C. Welldon, with permission of Macmillan and Co., London.

the actions, or something else beyond the activities as in the above mentioned sciences.

If it is true that in the sphere of action there is an end which we wish for its own sake, and for the sake of which we wish everything else, and that we do not desire all things for the sake of something else (for, if that is so, the process will go on *ad infinitum,* and our desire will be idle and futile) it is clear that this will be the good or the supreme good. Does it not follow then that the knowledge of this supreme good is of great importance for the conduct of life, and that, *if we know it,* we shall be like archers who have a mark at which to aim, we shall have a better chance of attaining what we want? But, if this is the case, we must endeavour to comprehend, at least in outline, its nature, and the science or faculty to which it belongs.

It would seem that this is the most authoritative or architectonic science or faculty, and such is evidently the political; for it is the political science or faculty which determines what sciences are necessary in states, and what kind of sciences should be learnt, and how far they should be learnt by particular people. We perceive too that the faculties which are held in the highest esteem, e.g. strategy, domestic economy, and rhetoric, are subordinate to it. But as it makes use of the other practical sciences, and also legislates upon the things to be done and the things to be left undone, it follows that its end will comprehend the ends of all the other sciences, and will therefore be the true good of mankind. For although the good of an individual is identical with the good of a state, yet the good of the state, whether in attainment or in preservation, is evidently greater and more perfect. For while in an individual by himself it is something to be thankful for, it is nobler and more divine in a nation or state.

These then are the objects at which the present inquiry aims, and it is in a sense a political inquiry. But our statement of the case will be adequate, if it be made with all such clearness as the subject-matter admits; for it would be as wrong to expect the same degree of accuracy in all reasonings as in all manufactures. Things noble and just, which are the subjects of investigation in political science, exhibit so great a diversity and uncertainty that they are sometimes thought to have only a conventional, and not a natural, existence. There is the same sort of uncertainty in regard to good things, as it often happens that injuries result from them; thus there have been cases in which people were ruined by wealth, or again by courage. As our subjects then and our premises are of this nature, we must be content to indicate the truth roughly and in outline; and as our subjects and premises are true generally *but not universally,* we must be content to arrive at conclusions which are only generally true. It is right to receive the particular statements which are made in the same spirit; for an educated person will expect accuracy in each subject only so far as the nature of the subject allows; he might as well accept probable reasoning from a mathematician as require demonstrative proofs from a rhetorician. But everybody is competent to judge the subjects which he understands, and is a good judge of them. It follows that in particular subjects it is a person of *special* education, and in general a person of universal education, who is a good judge. Hence the young are not proper students of political science, as they have no experience of the actions of life which form the premises and subjects of the reasonings. Also it may be added that from their tendency to follow their emotions they will not study the subject to any purpose or profit, as its end is not knowledge but action. It makes no difference whether a person is young in years or youthful in character; for the defect *of which I speak* is not one of time but is due to the emotional character of his life and pursuits. Knowledge is as useless to such a person as it is to an intemperate person. But where the desires and actions of people are regulated by reason the knowledge of these subjects will be extremely valuable.

But having said so much by way of preface as to the students of political science, the spirit in which it should be studied, and the object which we set before ourselves, let us resume our argument as follows:

As every knowledge and moral purpose aspires to some good, what is in our view the good at which the political science aims, and what is the highest of all practical goods? As to its name there is, I may say, a general agreement. The masses and the cultured classes agree in calling it happiness, and conceive that "to live well" or "to do well" is the same thing as "to be happy." But as to the nature of happiness they do not agree, nor do the masses give the same account of it as the philosophers. The former define it as something visible and palpable, e.g. pleasure, wealth, or honour; different people give different definitions of it, and often the same person gives different definitions at different times; for when a person has been ill, it is health, when he is poor, it is wealth, and, if he is conscious of his own ignorance, he envies people who use grand language above his own comprehension. Some philosophers on the other hand have held that, besides these various goods, there is an absolute good which is the cause of goodness in them all. It would perhaps be a waste of time to examine all these opinions, it will be enough to examine such as are most popular or as seem to be more or less reasonable.

... It seems not unreasonable that people should derive their conception of the good or of happiness from men's lives. Thus ordinary or vulgar people conceive it to be pleasure, and accordingly approve a life of enjoyment. For there are practically three prominent lives, the sensual, the political, and, thirdly, the speculative. Now the mass of men present an absolutely slavish appearance, as choosing the life of brute beasts, but they meet with consideration because so many persons in authority share the tastes of Sardanapalus. Cultivated and practical people, on the other hand, identify happiness with honour, as honour is the general end of political life. But this appears too superficial for our present purpose; for honour seems to depend more upon the people who pay it than upon the person to whom it is paid, and we have an intuitive feeling that the good is something which is proper to a man himself and cannot easily be taken away from him. It seems too that the reason why men seek honour is that they may be confident of their own goodness. Accordingly they seek it at the hands of the wise and of those who know them well, and they seek it on the ground of virtue; hence it is clear that in their judgment at any rate virtue is superior to honour. It would perhaps be right then to look upon virtue rather than honour as being the end of the political life. Yet virtue again, it appears, lacks completeness; for it seems that a man may possess virtue and yet be asleep or inactive throughout life, and, not only so but he

may experience the greatest calamities and misfortunes. But nobody would call such a life a life of happiness, unless he were maintaining a paradox. It is not necessary to dwell further on this subject, as it is sufficiently discussed in the popular philosophical treatises. The third life is the speculative which we will investigate hereafter.

The life of money-making is in a sense of life of constraint, and it is clear that wealth is not the good of which we are in quest; for it is useful in part as a means to something else. It would be a more reasonable view therefore that the things mentioned before, viz. *sensual pleasure, honour and virtue,* are ends than that wealth is, as they are things which are desired on their own account. Yet these too are apparently not ends, although much argument has been employed to show that they are.

We may now dismiss this subject; but it will perhaps be best to consider the universal *good,* and to discuss the meaning in which the phrase is used, although there is this difficulty in such an inquiry, that the *doctrine of* ideas has been introduced by our friends.[1] Yet it will perhaps seem the best, and indeed the right course, at least when the truth is at stake, to go so far as to sacrifice what is near and dear to us, especially as we are philosophers. For friends and truth are both dear to us, but it is a sacred duty to prefer the truth.

Now the authors of this theory did not make ideas of things in which they predicated priority and posteriority. Hence they did not constitute an idea of numbers. But good is predicated equally of substance, quality and relation, and the absolute or essential, *i.e. substance,* is in its nature prior to the relative, as

---

[1] Aristotle is referring to Plato and his school (the Academy) in which he had been a student for nearly twenty years. What follows is Aristotle's criticism of the Platonic theory that there is only one *Form* of *Good.*—P.P.W.

relativity is like an offshoot or accident of existence; hence there cannot be an idea which is common to them both. Again, there are as many ways of predicating good as of predicating existence; for it is predicated of substance as e.g. of God or the mind, or of quality as of the virtues, or of quantity as of the mean, or of relativity as of the useful, or of time as of opportunity, or of place as of a habitation, and so on. It is clear then that it cannot be a common universal idea or a unity; otherwise it would not be predicated in all the categories but only in one. Thirdly, as there is a single science of all such things as fall under a single idea, there would have been a single science of all good things, *if the idea of "good" were single;* but in fact there are many sciences even of such good things as fall under a single category, strategy, e.g. being the science of opportunity in war, and medicine the science of opportunity in disease, medicine again being the science of the mean in respect of food, and gymnastic the science of the mean in respect of exercise. It would be difficult, too, to say what is meant by the "absolute" in anything, if in "absolute man" and in "man" there is one and the same conception of man. For there will be no difference between them in respect of manhood, and, if so, neither will there be any difference between "absolute good" and "good" in respect of goodness. Nor again will good be more good if it is eternal, since a white thing which lasts for a long time is not whiter than that which lasts for a single day.... However these are questions which may be deferred to another occasion; but there is an objection to my arguments which suggests itself, viz. that the *Platonic* theory does not apply to every good, that the things which in themselves are sought after and welcomed are reckoned as one species and the things which tend to produce or in any sense preserve these or to prevent their opposites are reckoned as goods in a secondary sense as being means to these. It is clear then that there will be two kinds of goods, some being absolute goods, and others secondary. Let us then separate goods which are merely serviceable from absolute goods and consider if they are conceived as falling under a single idea. But what kind of things is it that may be defined as absolute goods? Will it be all such as are sought after independently of their consequences, e.g. wisdom, sight, and certain pleasures and honours? For granting that we seek after these sometimes as means to something else, still we may define them as absolute goods. Or is none of these things an absolute good, nor anything else except the idea? But then the type *or idea* will be purposeless, *i.e. it will not comprise any particulars.* If, on the other hand, these things too are absolute goods, the conception of the good will necessarily appear the same in them all, as the conception of whiteness appears the same in snow and in white lead. But the conceptions of honour, wisdom and pleasure, are distinct and different in respect of goodness. "Good" then is not a common term falling under one idea. But in what sense is the term used? For it does not seem to be an accidental homonymy. Is it because all goods issue from one source or all tend to one end; or is it rather a case of analogy? for as the sight is to the body, so is the mind to the soul, *i.e. the mind may be called the eye of the soul, and so on.* But it will perhaps be well to leave this subject for the present, as an exact discussion of it would belong rather to a different branch of philosophy. But the same is true of the idea; for even if there is some one good which is predicated of all these things, or some abstract and absolute good, it will plainly not be such as a man finds practicable and attainable, and therefore will not be such a good as we are in search of. It will possibly be held, however, that it is worth while to apprehend this *universal good*, as having a relation to the goods which are attainable and practicable; for if we have this as a model, we shall be better able to know the things which are good relatively to ourselves, and, knowing them, to acquire them. Now although there is a certain plausibility in this theory, it seems not to harmonize with scientific experience; for while all sciences aim at a certain good and seek to supply a deficiency, they omit the knowledge of the universal good. Yet it is not reasonable to suppose that what would be so extremely helpful is ignored, and not sought at all by artists generally. But it is difficult to see what benefit a cobbler or carpenter will get in reference to his art by knowing the absolute good, or how the contemplation of the absolute idea will make a person a better physician or general. For it appears that a physician does not regard health abstractedly, but regards the health of man or rather perhaps of a particular man, as he gives his medicine to individuals.

But leaving this subject for the present let us revert to the good of which we are in quest and consider what its nature may be. For it is clearly different in different actions or arts; it is one thing in medicine, another in strategy, and so on. What then is the good in each of these instances? It is presumably that for the sake of which all else is done. This in medicine is health, in strategy, victory, in domestic architecture, a house, and so on. But in every action and purpose it is the end, as it is for the sake of the end that people all do everything else. If then there is a certain end of all action, it will be this which is the practicable good, and if there are several such ends it will be these.

Our argument has arrived by a different path at the same conclusion as before; but we must endeavour to elucidate it still further. As it appears that there are more ends than one and some of these, e.g. wealth, flutes, and instruments generally we desire as means to something else, it is evident that they are not all final ends. But the highest good is clearly something final. Hence if there is only one final end, this will be the object of which we are in search, and if there are more than one, it will be the most final of them. We speak of that which is sought after for its own sake as more final than that which is sought after as a means to something else; we speak of that which is never desired as a means to something else as more final than the things which are desired both in themselves and as means to something else; and we speak of a thing as absolutely final, if it is always desired in itself and never as a means to something else.

It seems that happiness preeminently answers to this description, as we always desire happiness for its own sake and never as a means to something else, whereas we desire honour, pleasure, intellect, and every virtue, partly for their own sakes (for we should desire them independently of what might result from them) but partly also as being means to happiness, because we suppose they will prove the instruments of happiness. Happiness, on the other hand, nobody desires for the sake of these things, nor indeed as a means to anything else at all.

We come to the same conclusion if we start from the consideration of self-sufficiency, if it may be assumed that the final good is self-sufficient. But when we speak of self-sufficiency, we do not mean that a person leads a solitary life all by himself, but that he has parents, children, wife, and friends, and fellow-citizens in general, as man is naturally a social being. But here it is necessary to prescribe some limit; for if the circle be extended so as to include parents, descendants, and friends' friends, it will go on indefinitely. Leaving this point, however, for future investigation, we define the self-sufficient as that which, taken by itself, makes life desirable, and wholly free from want, and this is our conception of happiness.

Again, we conceive happiness to be the most desirable of all things, and that not merely as one among other good things. If it were one among other good things, the addition of the smallest good would increase its desirableness; for the accession makes a superiority of goods, and the greater of two goods is always the more desirable. It appears then that happiness is something final and self-sufficient, being the end of all action.

Perhaps, however, it seems a truth which is generally admitted, that happiness is the supreme good; what is wanted is to define its nature a little more clearly. The best way of arriving at such a definition will probably be to ascertain the function of Man. For, as with a flute-player, a statuary, or any artisan, or in fact anybody who has a definite function and action, his goodness, or excellence seems to lie in his function, so it would seem to be with Man, if indeed he has a definite function. Can it be said then that, while a carpenter and a cobbler have definite functions and actions, Man, unlike them, is naturally functionless? The reasonable view is that, as the eye, the hand, the foot, and similarly each several part of the body has a definite function, so Man may be regarded as having a definite function apart from all these. What then, can this function be? It is not life; for life is apparently something which man shares with the plants; and it is something peculiar to him that we are looking for. We must exclude therefore the life of nutrition and increase. There is next what may be called the life of sensation. But this too, is apparently shared by Man with horses, cattle, and all other animals. There remains what I may call the practical life of the rational part of *Man's being*. But the rational part is twofold; it is rational partly in the sense of being obedient to reason, and partly in the sense of possessing reason and intelligence. The practical life too may be conceived of in two ways, viz., *either as a moral state, or as a moral activity:* but we must understand by it the life of activity, as this seems to be the truer form of the conception.

The function of Man then is an activity of soul in accordance with reason, or not independently of reason. Again the functions of a person of a certain kind, and of such a person who is good of his kind, e.g. of a harpist and a good harpist, are in our view generically the same, and this view is true of people of all kinds without exception, the superior excellence being only an addition to the function; for it is the function of a harpist to play the harp, and of a good harpist to play the harp well. This being so, if we define the function of Man as a kind of life, and this life as an activity of soul, or a course of action in conformity with reason, if the function of a good man is such activity or action of a good and noble kind, and if everything is successfully performed when it is performed in accordance with its proper excellence, it follows that the good of Man is an activity of soul in accordance with virtue or, if there are more virtues than one, in accordance with the best and most complete virtue. But it is necessary to add the words "in a complete life." For as one swallow or one day does not make a spring, so one day or a short time does not make a fortunate or happy man.

This may be taken as a sufficiently accurate sketch of the good; for it is right, I think, to draw the outlines first and afterwards to fill in the details. It would seem that anybody can carry on and complete what has been satisfactorily sketched in outline, and that time is a good inventor or cooperator in so doing. This is the way in which the arts have made their advances, as anybody can supply a deficiency.

But bearing in mind what has been already said, we must not look for the same degree of accuracy in all subjects; we must be content in each class of subjects with accuracy of such a kind as the subject-matter allows, and to such an extent as is proper to the inquiry.

10. *On the Improvement of the Understanding**

BENEDICT DE SPINOZA (1632–1677)

After experience has taught me that all the usual surroundings of social life are vain and futile; seeing that none of the objects of my fears contained in themselves anything either good or bad, except in so far as the mind is affected by them, I finally resolved to inquire whether there might be some real good having power to communicate itself, which would affect the mind singly, to the exclusion of all else; whether, in fact, there might be anything of which the discovery and attainment would enable me to enjoy continuous, supreme, and unending happiness. I say "I FINALLY resolved," for at first sight it seemed unwise willingly to lose hold on what was sure for the sake of something then uncertain. I could see the benefits which are acquired through fame and riches, and that I should be obliged to abandon the quest of such objects, if I seriously devoted myself to the search for something different and new. I perceived that if true happiness chanced to be placed in the former I should necessarily miss it; while if, on the other hand, it were not so placed, and I gave them my whole attention, I should equally fail.

I therefore debated whether it would not be possible to arrive at the new principle, or at any rate at a certainty concerning its existence, without changing the conduct and usual plan of my life; with this end in view I made many efforts, but in vain. For the ordinary surroundings of life which are esteemed by men (as their actions testify) to be the highest good, may be classed under the three heads—Riches, Fame, and the Pleasures of Sense: with these three the mind is so absorbed that it has little power to reflect on any different good. By sensual pleasure the mind is enthralled to the extent of quiescence, as if the supreme good were actually attained, so that it is quite incapable of thinking of any other object; when such pleasure has been gratified it is followed by extreme melancholy, whereby the mind, though not enthralled, is disturbed and dulled.

The pursuit of honors and riches is likewise very absorbing, especially if

* *The Chief Works of Benedict de Spinoza,* trans. from the Latin by R. H. M. Elwes (London, 1887), II, 1 ff. *Ethics* IV, without the geometric form.

such objects be sought simply for their own sake, inasmuch as they are then supposed to constitute the highest good. In the case of fame the mind is still more absorbed, for fame is conceived as always good for its own sake, and as the ultimate end to which all actions are directed. Further, the attainment of riches and fame is not followed as in the case of sensual pleasures by repentance, but, the more we acquire, the greater is our delight, and, consequently, the more we are incited to increase both the one and the other; on the other hand, if our hopes happen to be frustrated we are plunged into the deepest sadness. Fame has the further drawback that it compels its votaries to order their lives according to the opinions of their fellow-men, shunning what they usually shun, and seeking what they usually seek.

When I saw that all these ordinary objects of desire would be obstacles in the way of a search for something different and new—nay, that they were so opposed thereto, that either they or it would have to be abandoned, I was forced to inquire which would prove the most useful to me: for, as I say, I seemed to be willingly losing hold on a sure good for the sake of something uncertain. However, after I had reflected on the matter, I came in the first place to the conclusion that by abandoning the ordinary objects of pursuit, and betaking myself to a new quest, I should be leaving a good, uncertain by reason of its own nature, as may be gathered from what has been said, for the sake of a good not uncertain in its nature (for I sought for a fixed good), but only in the possibility of its attainment.

Further reflection convinced me, that if I could really get to the root of the matter, I should be leaving certain evils for a certain good. I thus perceived that I was in a state of great peril, and I compelled myself to seek with all my strength for a remedy, however uncer-tain it might be; as a sick man strug-gling with a deadly disease, when he sees that death will surely be upon him unless a remedy be found, is compelled to seek such a remedy although it may be uncer-tain with all his strength, inasmuch as his whole hope lies therein. All the ob-jects pursued by the multitude, not only bring no remedy that tends to preserve our being, but even act as hindrances, causing the death not seldom of those who possess them, and always of those who are possessed by them. There are many examples of men who have suffered persecution even to death for the sake of their riches, and of men who in pursuit of wealth have exposed themselves to so many dangers, that they have paid away their life as a penalty for their folly. Ex-amples are no less numerous of men, who have endured the utmost wretched-ness for the sake of gaining or preserv-ing their reputation. Lastly, there are innumerable cases of men, who have hastened their death through over-indul-gences in sensual pleasure. All these evils seem to have arisen from the fact, that happiness or unhappiness is made wholly to depend on the quality of the object which we love. When a thing is not loved, no quarrels will arise concerning it—no sadness will be felt if it perishes—no envy if it is possessed by another—no fear, no hatred, in short no disturbances of the mind. All these arise from the love of what is perishable, such as the objects already mentioned. But love toward a thing eternal and infinite feeds the mind wholly with joy, and is itself unmingled with any sadness, wherefore it is greatly to be desired and sought for with all our strength. Yet it was not at random that I used the words, "If I could go to the root of the matter," for, though what I have urged was perfectly clear to my mind, I could not forthwith lay aside all love of riches, sensual en-joyment, and fame. One thing was evident, namely, that while my mind was employed with these thoughts it turned away from its former objects of desire, and seriously considered the search for a new principle; this state of things was a great comfort to me, for I perceived that the evils were not such as to resist all remedies. Although these intervals were at first rare, and of very short duration, yet afterward, as the true good became more and more discernible to me, they became more frequent and more lasting; especially after I had recognized that the acquisition of wealth, sensual pleasure, or fame, is only a hindrance, so long as they are sought as ends not as means; if they be sought as means they will be under restraint, and, far from being hindrances, will further not a little the end for which they are sought, as I will show in due time.

I will here only briefly state what I mean by true good, and also what is the nature of the highest good. In order that this may be rightly understood, we must bear in mind that the terms good and evil are only applied relatively, so that the same thing may be called both good and bad, according to the relations in view, in the same way as it may be called perfect or imperfect. Nothing regarded in its own nature can be called perfect or imperfect; especially when we are aware that all things which come to pass, come to pass according to the eternal order and fixed laws of nature. However, human weakness cannot attain to this order in its own thoughts, but meanwhile man conceives a human character much more stable than his own, and sees that there is no reason why he should not himself acquire such a character. Thus he is led to seek for means which will bring him to this pitch of perfection, and calls everything which will serve as such means a true good. The chief good is that he should arrive, together with other individuals if possible, at the possession of the aforesaid

character. What that character is we shall show in due time, namely, that it is the knowledge of the union existing between the mind and the whole of nature. This, then, is the end for which I strive, to attain to such a character myself, and to endeavor that many should attain to it with me. In other words, it is part of my happiness to lend a helping hand, that many others may understand even as I do, so that their understanding and desire may entirely agree with my own. In order to bring this about, it is necessary to understand as much of nature as will enable us to attain to the aforesaid character, and also to form a social order such as is most conducive to the attainment of this character by the greatest number with the least difficulty and danger. We must seek the assistance of Moral Philosophy [1] and the Theory of Education; further, as health is no insignificant means for attaining our end, we must also include the whole science of Medicine, and, as many difficult things are by contrivance rendered easy, and we can in this way gain much time and convenience, the science of Mechanics must in no way be despised. But, before all things, a means must be devised for improving the understanding and purifying it, as far as may be at the outset, so that it may apprehend things without error, and in the best possible way.

Thus it is apparent to every one that I wish to direct all sciences to one end and aim, so that we may attain to the supreme human perfection which we have named; and, therefore, whatsoever in the sciences does not serve to promote our object will have to be rejected as useless. To sum up the matter in a word, all our actions and thoughts must be directed to this one end. Yet, as it is necessary that while we are endeavoring to

---

[1] I do no more here than enumerate the sciences necessary for our purpose; I lay no stress on their order.

attain our purpose, and bring the understanding into the right path, we should carry on our life, we are compelled first of all to lay down certain rules of life as provisionally good, to wit, the following:

I. To speak in a manner intelligible to the multitude, and to do all those things that do not hinder the attainment of our purpose. For we can gain from the multitude no small advantages, provided that we strive to accommodate ourselves to its understanding as far as possible: moreover, we shall in this way gain a friendly audience for the reception of the truth.

II. To indulge ourselves with pleasures only in so far as they are necessary for preserving health.

III. Lastly, to endeavor to obtain only sufficient money or other commodities to enable us to preserve our life and health, and to follow such general customs as are consistent with our purpose.

Having laid down these preliminary rules, I will betake myself to the first and most important task, namely, the amendment of the understanding, and the rendering it capable of understanding things in the manner necessary for attaining our end.

Of Human Bondage, or The Strength of the Emotions*

The impotence of man to govern or restrain the emotions I call bondage, for a man who is under their control is not his own master, but is mastered by fortune, in whose power he is, so that he is often forced to follow the worse, although he sees the better before him. I propose in this part to demonstrate why this is, and also to show what of good and evil the emotions possess.

But before I begin I should like to say a few words about perfection and imperfection, and about good and evil. If a man has proposed to do a thing and has accomplished it, he calls it perfect, and not only he, but every one else who has really known or has believed that he has known the mind and intention of the author of that work will call it perfect too. For example, having seen some work (which I suppose to be as yet not

finished), if we know that the intention of the author of that work is to build a house, we shall call the house imperfect; while, on the other hand, we shall call it perfect as soon as we see the work has been brought to the end which the author had determined for it. But if we see any work such as we have never seen before, and if we do not know the mind of the workman, we shall then not be able to say whether the work is perfect or imperfect.

This seems to have been the first signification of these words; but afterwards men began to form universal ideas, to think out for themselves types of houses, buildings, castles, and to prefer some types of things to others; and so it happened that each person called a thing perfect which seemed to agree with the universal idea which he had formed of that thing, and, on the other hand, he called a thing imperfect which seemed to

* From Spinoza's *Ethics,* Bk. IV.

agree less with his typal conception, although, according to the intention of the workman, it had been entirely completed. This appears to be the only reason why the words *perfect* and *imperfect* are commonly applied to natural objects which are not made with human hands; for men are in the habit of forming, both of natural as well as of artificial objects, universal ideas which they regard as types of things, and which they think Nature has in view, setting them before herself as types too; it being the common opinion that she does nothing except for the sake of some end. When, therefore, men see something done by Nature which does not altogether answer to that typal conception which they have of the thing, they think that Nature herself has failed or committed an error, and that she has left the thing imperfect.

Thus we see that the custom of applying the words *perfect* and *imperfect* to natural objects has arisen rather from prejudice than from true knowledge of them. For we have shown that Nature does nothing for the sake of an end, for that eternal and infinite Being whom we call God or Nature acts by the same necessity by which He exists; for we have shown that He acts by the same necessity of nature as that by which He exists. The reason or cause, therefore, why God or Nature acts and the reason why He exists are one and the same. Since, therefore, He exists for no end, He acts for no end; and since He has no principle or end of existence, He has no principle or end of action. A final cause, as it is called, is nothing, therefore, but human desire, in so far as this is considered as the principle or primary cause of anything. For example, when we say that the having a house to live in was the final cause of this or that house, we merely mean that a man, because he imagined the advantages of a domestic life, desired to build a house. Therefore,

having a house to live in, in so far as it is considered as a final cause, is merely this particular desire, which is really an efficient cause, and is considered as primary, because men are usually ignorant of the causes of their desires; for, as I have often said, we are conscious of our actions and desires, but ignorant of the causes by which we are determined to desire anything. As for the vulgar opinion that Nature sometimes fails or commits an error, or produces imperfect things, I class it amongst those fictions mentioned above.

Perfection, therefore, and imperfection are really only modes of thought; that is to say, notions which we are in the habit of forming from the comparison with one another of individuals of the same species or genus, and this is the reason why I have said that by reality and perfection I understand the same thing; for we are in the habit of referring all individuals in Nature to one genus, which is called the most general; that is to say, to the notion of being, which embraces absolutely all the individual objects in Nature. In so far, therefore, as we refer the individual objects in Nature to this genus, and compare them one with another, and discover that some possess more being or reality than others, in so far do we call some more perfect than others; and in so far as we assign to the latter anything which, like limitation, termination, impotence, etc., involves negation, shall we call them imperfect, because they do not affect our minds so strongly as those we call perfect, but not because anything which really belongs to them is wanting, or because Nature has committed an error. For nothing belongs to the nature of anything excepting that which follows from the necessity of the nature of the efficient cause, and whatever follows from the necessity of the nature of the efficient cause necessarily happens.

With regard to good and evil, these

terms indicate nothing positive in things considered in themselves, nor are they anything else than modes of thought, or notions which we form from the comparison of one thing with another. For one and the same thing may at the same time be both good and evil or indifferent. Music, for example, is good to a melancholy person, bad to one mourning, while to a deaf man it is neither good nor bad. But although things are so, we must retain these words. For since we desire to form for ourselves an idea of man upon which we may look as a model of human nature, it will be of service to us to retain these expressions in the sense I have mentioned.

By *good,* therefore, I understand in the following pages everything which we are certain is a means by which we may approach nearer and nearer to the model of human nature we set before us. By *evil,* on the contrary, I understand everything which we are certain hinders us from reaching that model. Again, I shall call men more or less perfect or imperfect in so far as they approach more or less nearly to this same model. For it is to be carefully observed, that when I say that an individual passes from a less to a greater perfection and *vice versâ,* I do not understand that from one essence or form he is changed into another (for a horse, for instance, would be as much destroyed if it were changed into a man as if it were changed into an insect), but rather we conceive that his power of action, in so far as it is understood by his own nature, is increased or diminished. Finally, by perfection generally, I understand, as I have said, reality; that is to say, the essence of any object in so far as it exists and acts in a certain manner, no regard being paid to its duration. For no individual thing can be said to be more perfect because for a longer time it has persevered in existence; inasmuch as the duration of things cannot be determined by their essence, the essence of things involving no fixed or determined period of existence; any object, whether it be more or less perfect, always being able to persevere in existence with the same force as that with which it commenced existence. All things, therefore, are equal in this respect.

Definitions

I.—By good, I understand that which we certainly know is useful to us.

II. By evil, on the contrary, I understand that which we certainly know hinders us from possessing anything that is good.

With regard to these two definitions, see the close of the preceding.

III. I call individual things contingent in so far as we discover nothing, whilst we attend to their essence alone, which necessarily posits their existence or which necessarily excludes it.

IV. I call these individual things possible, in so far as we are ignorant, whilst we attend to the cause from which they must be produced, whether these causes are determined to the production of these things.

V. By contrary emotions, I understand in the following pages those which, although they may be of the same kind, draw a man in different directions; such as voluptuousness and avarice, which are both a species of love, and are not contrary to one another by nature, but only by accident.

VI. I here call a thing past or future in so far as we have been or shall be affected by it; for example, in so far as we have seen a thing or are about to see it, in so far as it has strengthened us or will strengthen us, has injured or will injure us. For in so far as we thus imagine it do we affirm its existence; that is to say, the body is affected by no mode which excludes the existence of the thing, and therefore the body is affected by the image of the thing in the same way as if the thing itself were present. But because it generally happens that those who possess much experience hesitate when they think of a thing as past or future, and doubt greatly concerning its issue, therefore the emotions which spring from such images of things are not so constant, but are generally disturbed by the images of other things, until men become more sure of the issue.

However, it is to be observed that it is the same with time as it is with place; for as beyond a certain limit we can form no distinct imagination of distance —that is to say, as we usually imagine all objects to be equally distant from us, and as if they were on the same plane, if their distance from us exceeds 200 feet, or if their distance from the position we occupy is greater than we can distinctly imagine—so we imagine all objects to be equally distant from the present time, and refer them as if to one moment, if the period to which their existence belongs is separated from the present by a longer interval than we can usually imagine distinctly.

VII. By end for the sake of which we do anything, I understand appetite.

VIII. By virtue and power, I understand the same thing; that is to say, virtue, in so far as it is related to man, is the essence itself or nature of the man in so far as it has the power of effecting certain things which can be understood through the laws of its nature alone.

Axiom

There is no individual thing in Nature which is not surpassed in strength and power by some other thing; but any individual thing being given, another and a stronger is also given, by which the former can be destroyed.

The power by which individual things and, consequently, man preserve their being is the actual power of God or Na-

ture, not in so far as it is infinite, but in so far as it can be manifested by the actual essence of man. The power therefore of man, in so far as it is manifested by his actual essence is part of the infinite power of God or Nature, that is to say, part of His essence. Again, if it were possible that man could suffer no changes but those which can be understood through his nature alone, it would follow that he could not perish, but that he would exist forever necessarily; and this necessary existence must result from a cause whose power is either finite or infinite, that is to say, either from the power of man alone, which would be able to place at a distance from himself all other changes which could take their origin from external causes, or it must result from the infinite power of Nature by which all individual things would be so directed that man could suffer no changes but those tending to his preservation.

But the first case is absurd. The force by which man perseveres in existence is limited, and infinitely surpassed by the power of external causes. This is evident from the Axiom. Therefore if it were possible for a man to suffer no changes but those which could be understood through his own nature alone, and consequently (as we have shown) that he should always necessarily exist, this must follow from the infinite power of God; and therefore from the necessity of the divine nature, in so far as it is considered as affected by the idea of any one man, the whole order of Nature, in so far as it is conceived under the attributes of thought and extension, would have to be deduced. From this it would follow that man would be infinite, which (by the first part of this demonstration) is an absurdity. It is impossible, therefore, that a man can suffer no changes but those of which he is the adequate cause.

Hence it follows that a man is necessarily always subject to passions, and that he follows and obeys the common order of Nature, accommodating himself to it as far as the nature of things requires. The force and increase of any passion and its perseverance in existence are not limited by the power by which we endeavor to persevere in existence, but by the power of an external cause compared with our own power.

We call a thing good which contributes to the preservation of our being, and we call a thing evil if it is an obstacle to the preservation of our being; that is to say, a thing is called by us good or evil as it increases or diminishes, helps or restrains, our power of action. In so far, therefore, as we perceive that any object affects us with joy or sorrow do we call it good or evil, and therefore the knowledge of good or evil is nothing but an idea of joy or sorrow which necessarily follows from the emotion itself of joy or sorrow. But this idea is united to the emotion in the same way as the mind is united to the body, or, in other words, this idea is not actually distinguished from the emotion itself; that is to say, it is not actually distinguished from the idea of the modification of the body, unless in conception alone. This knowledge, therefore, of good and evil is nothing but the emotion itself of joy and sorrow in so far as we are conscious of it.

An emotion, in so far as it is related to the mind, is an idea by which the mind affirms a greater or less power of existence for its body than the body possessed before. Whenever, therefore, the mind is agitated by any emotion, the body is at the same time affected with a modification by which its power of action is increased or diminished. Again, this modification of the body receives from its own cause a power to persevere in its own being, a power, therefore, which cannot be restrained nor removed unless by a bodily cause affecting the body with a modification contrary to the first, and stronger than it. Thus the mind is affected by the idea of a modification stronger than the former and contrary to it; that is to say, it will be affected with an emotion stronger than the former and contrary to it, and this stronger emotion will exclude the existence of the other or remove it. Thus an emotion cannot be restrained nor removed unless by an opposed and stronger emotion.

An emotion, in so far as it is related to the mind, cannot be restrained nor removed unless by the idea of a bodily modification opposed to that which we suffer and stronger than it. For the emotion which we suffer cannot be restrained nor removed unless by an opposed and stronger emotion; that is to say, it cannot be removed unless by the idea of a bodily modification stronger than that which affects us, and opposed to it.

The force and increase of any passion and its perseverance in existence are limited by the power of an external cause compared with our own power and therefore the other actions or power of a man may be so far surpassed by force of some passion or emotion, that the emotion may obstinately cling to him.

An emotion is an idea by which the mind affirms a greater or less power of existence for the body than it possessed before, and therefore this idea has nothing positive which can be removed by the presence of the truth, and consequently the true knowledge of good and evil, in so far as it is true, can restrain no emotion. But in so far as it is an emotion will it restrain any other emotion, provided that the latter be the weaker of the two.

From the true knowledge of good and evil, in so far as this is an emotion, necessarily arises desire, which is greater in proportion as the emotion from which it springs is greater. But this desire (by hypothesis), because it springs from our understanding, something truly follows therefore in us in so far as we act, and therefore must be understood through our essence alone, and consequently its strength and increase must be limited by human power alone. But the desires which spring from the emotions by which we are agitated are greater as the emotions themselves are greater, and therefore their strength and increase must be limited by the power of external causes, a power which, if it be compared with our own, indefinitely surpasses it. The desires, therefore, which take their origin from such emotions as these may be much stronger than that which takes its origin from a true knowledge of good and evil, and the former may be able to restrain and extinguish the latter.

Desire is the very essence of man, that is to say, the effort by which a man strives to persevere in his being. The desire, therefore, which springs from joy, by that very emotion of joy is assisted or increased, while that which springs from sorrow, by that very emotion of sorrow is lessened or restrained, and so the force of the desire which springs from joy must be limited by human power, together with the power of an external cause, while that which springs from sorrow must be limited by human power alone. The latter is, therefore, weaker than the former.

I

The imagination is an idea by which the mind contemplates an object as present, an idea which nevertheless indicates the constitution of the human body rather than the nature of the external object. Imagination, therefore, is an emotion in so far as it indicates the constitution of the body. But the imagination increases in intensity in proportion as we imagine nothing which excludes the present existence of the external object. If, therefore, we imagine the cause of an emotion to be actually present with us, that emotion will be intenser or stronger than if we imagined the cause not to be present.

When I said that we are affected by the image of an object in the future or the past with the same emotion with which we should be affected if the object we imagined were actually present, I was careful to warn the reader that this was true in so far only as we attend to the image alone of the object itself, for the image is of the same nature whether we have imagined the object or not; but I have not denied that the image becomes weaker when we contemplate as present other objects which exclude the present existence of the future object.

The image of a past or future object, that is to say, of an object which we contemplate in relation to the past or future to the exclusion of the present, other things being equal, is weaker than the image of a present object, and consequently the emotion towards a future or past object, other things being equal, is weaker then than the emotion towards a present object.

The desire which springs from a knowledge of good and evil can be easily extinguished or restrained, in so far as this knowledge is connected with the future, by the desire of things which in the present are sweet.

II

In so far as we imagine any object to be necessary do we affirm its existence, and, on the other hand, we deny its existence in so far as we imagine it to be not necessary and therefore the emotion towards an object which we imagine as necessary, other things being equal, is stronger than that towards an object that is possible, contingent, or not necessary.

In so far as we imagine an object as contingent, we are not affected by the image of any other object which posits the existence of the first, but, on the contrary (by hypothesis), we imagine some things which exclude its present existence. But in so far as we imagine any object in the future to be possible do we imagine some things which posit its existence, that is to say, things which foster hope or fear, and therefore the emotion towards an object which we know does not exist in the present, and which we imagine as possible, other things being equal, is stronger than the emotion towards a contingent object.

The emotion towards an object which we imagine to exist in the present is stronger than if we imagined it as future, and is much stronger if we imagine the future to be at a great distance from the present time. The emotion, therefore, towards an object which we imagine will not exist for a long time is so much feebler than if we imagined it as present, and nevertheless is stronger than if we imagined it as contingent; and therefore the emotion towards a contingent object is much feebler than if we imagined the object to be present to us.

In so far as we imagine an object as contingent, we are affected with no image of any other object which posits the existence of the first. On the contrary, we imagine (by hypothesis) certain things which exclude its present existence. But in so far as we imagine it in relationship to past time are we sup-posed to imagine something which brings it back to the memory or which excites its image and therefore so far causes us to contemplate it as present. Therefore, the emotion towards a contingent object which we know does not exist in the present, other things being equal, will be weaker than the emotion towards a past object.

In these propositions I consider that I have explained why men are more strongly influenced by an opinion than by true reason, and why the true knowledge of good and evil causes disturbance in the mind, and often gives way to every kind of lust, whence the saying of the poet, *"Video meliora proboque, deteriora sequor."* [1] The same thought appears to have been in the mind of the Preacher when he said, *"He that increaseth knowledge increaseth sorrow."* I say these things not because I would be understood to conclude, therefore, that it is better to be ignorant than to be wise, or that the wise man in governing his passions is nothing better than the fool, but I say them because it is necessary for us to know both the strength and weakness of our nature, so that we may determine what reason can do and what it cannot do in governing our emotions.

---

[1] "Though I see the better, I follow the worse."

11. *The Metaphysic of Morals**

IMMANUEL KANT (1724–1804)

Nothing can possibly be conceived in the world, or even out of it, which can be called good without qualification, except a Good Will. Intelligence, wit, judgment, and the other *talents* of the mind, however they may be named, or courage, resolution, perseverance, as qualities of temperament, are undoubtedly good and desirable in many respects; but these gifts of nature may also become extremely bad and mischievous if the will which is to make use of them, and which, therefore, constitutes what is called *character,* is not good. It is the same with the *gifts of fortune.* Power, riches, honour, even health, and the general well-being and contentment with one's condition which is called *happiness,* inspire pride, and often presumption, if there is not a good will to correct the influence of these on the mind, and with this also to rectify the whole principle of acting, and adapt it to its end. The sight of a being who is not adorned with a single feature of a pure and good will, enjoying unbroken prosperity, can never give pleasure to an impartial rational spectator. Thus a good will appears to constitute the indispensable condition even of being worthy of happiness.

There are even some qualities which are of service to this good will itself, and may facilitate its action, yet which have no intrinsic unconditional value, but

always presuppose a good will, and this qualifies the esteem that we justly have for them, and does not permit us to regard them as absolutely good. Moderation in the affections and passions, self-control and calm deliberation are not only good in many respects, but even seem to constitute part of the intrinsic worth of the person; but they are far from deserving to be called good without qualification, although they have been so unconditionally praised by the ancients. For without the principles of a good will, they may become extremely bad, and the coolness of a villain not only makes him far more dangerous, but also directly makes him more abominable in our eyes than he would have been without it.

A good will is good not because of what it performs or effects, not by its aptness for the attainment of some proposed end, but simply by virtue of the volition, that is, it is good in itself, and considered by itself is to be esteemed much higher than all that can be brought about by it in favour of any inclination, nay, even of the sum total of all inclinations. Even if it should happen that, owing to special disfavour of fortune, or the niggardly provision of a stepmotherly nature, this will should wholly lack power to accomplish its purpose, if with its greatest efforts it should yet achieve nothing, and there should remain only the good will (not, to be sure, a mere wish, but the summoning of all

* Translated by T. K. Abbott, reproduced by permission of Longmans, Green and Co.

means in our power), then, like a jewel, it would still shine by its own light, as a thing which has its whole value in itself. Its usefulness or fruitlessness can neither add to nor take away anything from this value. It would be, as it were, only the setting to enable us to handle it the more conveniently in common commerce or to attract to it the attention of those who are not yet connoisseurs, but not to recommend it to true connoisseurs, or to determine its value.

There is, however, something so strange in this idea of the absolute value of the mere will, in which no account is taken of its utility, that notwithstanding the thorough assent of even common reason to the idea, yet a suspicion must arise that it may perhaps really be the product of mere high-flown fancy, and that we may have misunderstood the purpose of nature in assigning reason as the governor of our will. Therefore we will examine this idea from this point of view.

In the physical constitution of an organized being, that is, a being adapted suitably to the purposes of life, we assume it as a fundamental principle that no organ for any purpose will be found but what is also the fittest and best adapted for that purpose. Now in a being which has reason and a will, if the proper object of nature were its *conservation*, its *welfare*, in a word, its *happiness*, then nature would have hit upon a very bad arrangement in selecting the reason of the creature to carry out this purpose. For all the actions which the creature has to perform with a view to this purpose, and the whole rule of its conduct, would be far more surely prescribed to it by instinct, and that end would have been attained thereby much more certainly than it ever can be by reason. Should reason have been communicated to this favoured creature over and above, it must only

have served it to contemplate the happy constitution of its nature, to admire it, to congratulate itself thereon, and to feel thankful for it to the beneficent cause, but not that it should subject its desires to that weak and delusive guidance, and meddle bunglingly with the purpose of nature. In a word, nature would have taken care that reason should not break forth into *practical exercise*, nor have the presumption, with its weak insight, to think out for itself the plan of happiness, and of the means of attaining it. Nature would not only have taken on herself the choice of the ends, but also of the means, and with wise foresight would have entrusted both to instinct.

And, in fact, we find that the more a cultivated reason applies itself with deliberate purpose to the enjoyment of life and happiness, so much the more does the man fail of true satisfaction. And from this circumstance there arises in many, if they are candid enough to confess it, a certain degree of *misology*, that is, hatred of reason, especially in the case of those who are most experienced in the use of it, because after calculating all the advantages they derive, I do not say from the invention of all the arts of common luxury, but even from the sciences (which seem to them to be after all only a luxury of the understanding), they find that they have, in fact, only brought more trouble on their shoulders, rather than gained in happiness; and they end by envying, rather than despising, the more common stamp of men who keep closer to the guidance of mere instinct, and do not allow their reason much influence on their conduct. And this we must admit, that the judgment of those who would very much lower the lofty eulogies of the advantages which reason gives us in regard to the happiness and satisfaction of life, or who would even reduce them below zero, is by no means morose or ungrateful to the goodness with which the world is governed, but that there lies at the root of these judgments the idea that our existence has a different and far nobler end, for which, and not for happiness, reason is properly intended, and which must, therefore, be regarded as the supreme condition to which the private ends of man must, for the most part, be postponed.

For as reason is not competent to guide the will with certainty in regard to its objects and the satisfaction of all our wants (which it to some extent even multiplies), this being an end to which an implanted instinct would have led with much greater certainty; and since, nevertheless, reason is imparted to us as a practical faculty, *i.e.* as one which is to have influence on the *will*, therefore, admitting that nature generally in the distribution of her capacities has adapted the means to the end, its true destination must be to produce a *will*, not merely good as a *means* to something else, but *good in itself*, for which reason was absolutely necessary. This will then, though not indeed the sole and complete good, must be the supreme good and the condition of every other, even of the desire of happiness. Under these circumstances, there is nothing inconsistent with the wisdom of nature in the fact that the cultivation of the reason, which is requisite for the first and unconditional purpose, does in many ways interfere, at least in this life, with the attainment of the second, which is always conditional, namely, happiness. Nay, it may even reduce it to nothing, without nature thereby failing of her purpose. For reason recognises the establishment of a good will as its highest practical destination, and in attaining this purpose is capable only of a satisfaction of its own proper kind, namely, that from the attainment of an end, which end again is determined by reason only, notwithstanding that this may involve many a disappointment to the ends of inclination.

We have then to develop the notion of a will which deserves to be highly esteemed for itself, and is good without a view to anything further, a notion which exists already in the sound natural understanding, requiring rather to be cleared up than to be taught, and which in estimating the value of our actions always takes the first place, and constitutes the condition of all the rest. In order to do this we will take the notion of duty, which includes that of a good will, although implying certain subjective restrictions and hindrances. These, however, far from concealing it, or rendering it unrecognisable, rather bring it out by contrast, and make it shine forth so much the brighter.

I omit here all actions which are already recognised as inconsistent with duty, although they may be useful for this or that purpose, for with these the question whether they are done *from duty* cannot arise at all, since they even conflict with it. I also set aside those actions which really conform to duty, but to which men have *no* direct *inclination*, performing them because they are impelled thereto by some other inclination. For in this case we can readily distinguish whether the action which agrees with duty is done *from duty,* or from a selfish view. It is much harder to make this distinction when the action accords with duty, and the subject has besides a *direct* inclination to it. For example, it is always a matter of duty that a dealer should not overcharge an inexperienced purchaser, and wherever there is much commerce the prudent tradesman does not overcharge, but keeps a fixed price for everyone, so that a child buys of him as well as any other. Men are thus *honestly* served; but this is not enough to make us believe that the tradesman has so acted from duty and from principles of honesty: his own advantage required it; it is out of the question in this case to suppose that he might besides have a direct inclination in favour of the buyers, so that, as it were, from love he should give no advantage to one over another. Accordingly the action was done neither from duty nor from direct inclination, but merely with a selfish view.

On the other hand, it is a duty to maintain one's life; and, in addition, every one has also a direct inclination to do so. But on this account the often anxious care which most men take for it has no intrinsic worth, and their maxim has no moral import. They preserve their life *as duty requires,* no doubt, but not *because duty requires.* On the other hand, if adversity and hopeless sorrow have completely taken away the relish for life, if the unfortunate one, strong in mind, indignant at his fate rather than desponding or dejected, wishes for death, and yet preserves his life without loving it—not from inclination or fear, but from duty—then his maxim has a moral worth.

To be beneficent when we can is a duty; and besides this, there are many minds so sympathetically constituted that, without any other motive of vanity or self-interest, they find a pleasure in spreading joy around them, and can take delight in the satisfaction of others so far as it is their own work. But I maintain that in such a case an action of this kind, however proper, however amiable it may be, has nevertheless no true moral worth, but is on a level with other inclinations, *e.g.* the inclination to honour, which, if it is happily directed to that which is in fact of public utility and accordant with duty, and consequently honourable, deserves praise and encouragement, but not esteem. For the maxim lacks the moral import, namely, that such actions be done *from duty,* not from inclination. Put the case that the mind of that philanthropist were

clouded by sorrow of his own extinguishing all sympathy with the lot of others, and that while he still has the power to benefit others in distress, he is not touched by their trouble because he is absorbed with his own; and now suppose that he tears himself out of this dead insensibility, and performs the action without any inclination to it, but simply from duty, then first has his action its genuine moral worth. Further still; if nature has put little sympathy in the heart of this or that man; if he, supposed to be an upright man, is by temperament cold and indifferent to the sufferings of others, perhaps because in respect of his own he is provided with the special gift of patience and fortitude, and supposes, or even requires, that others should have the same—and such a man would certainly not be the meanest product of nature—but if nature had not specially framed him for a philanthropist, would he not still find in himself a source from whence to give himself a far higher worth than that of a good-natured temperament could be? Unquestionably. It is just in this that the moral worth of the character is brought out which is incomparably the highest of all, namely, that he is beneficent, not from inclination, but from duty.

To secure one's own happiness is a duty, at least indirectly; for discontent with one's condition, under a pressure of many anxieties and amidst unsatisfied wants, might easily become a great *temptation to transgression of duty.* But here again, without looking to duty, all men have already the strongest and most intimate inclination to happiness, because it is just in this idea that all inclinations are combined in one total. But the precept of happiness is often of such a sort that it greatly interferes with some inclinations, and yet a man cannot form any definite and certain conception of the sum of satisfaction of all of them which is called happiness. It is not then to be wondered at that a single inclination, definite both as to what it promises and as to the time within which it can be gratified, is often able to overcome such a fluctuating idea, and that a gouty patient, for instance, can choose to enjoy what he likes, and to suffer what he may, since, according to his calculation, on this occasion at least, he has [only] not sacrificed the enjoyment of the present moment to a possibly mistaken expectation of a happiness which is supposed to be found in health. But even in this case, if the general desire for happiness did not influence his will, and supposing that in his particular case health was not a necessary element in this calculation, there yet remains in this, as in all other cases, this law, namely, that he should promote his happiness not from inclination but from duty, and by this would his conduct first acquire true moral worth.

It is in this manner, undoubtedly, that we are to understand those passages of Scripture also in which we are commanded to love our neighbour, even our enemy. For love, as an affection, cannot be commanded, but beneficence for duty's sake may; even though we are not impelled to it by any inclination—nay, are even repelled by a natural and unconquerable aversion. This is *practical* love, and not *pathological*—a love which is seated in the will, and not in the propensions of sense—in principles of action and not of tender sympathy; and it is this love alone which can be commanded.

The second [1] proposition is: That an action done from duty derives its moral worth, *not from the purpose* which is to be attained by it, but from the maxim by which it is determined, and therefore does not depend on the realization of

the object of the action, but merely on the *principle of volition* by which the action has taken place, without regard to any object of desire. It is clear from what precedes that the purposes which we may have in view in our actions, or their effects regarded as ends and springs of the will, cannot give to actions any unconditional or moral worth. In what, then, can their worth lie, if it is not to consist in the will and in reference to its expected effect? It cannot lie anywhere but in the *principle of the will* without regard to the ends which can be attained by the action. For the will stands between its *à priori* principle, which is formal, and its *à posteriori* spring, which is material, as between two roads, and as it must be determined by something, it follows that it must be determined by the formal principle of volition when an action is done from duty, in which case every material principle has been withdrawn from it.

The third proposition, which is a consequence of the two preceding, I would express thus: *Duty is the necessity of acting from respect for the law.* I may have *inclination* for an object as the effect of my proposed action, but I cannot have *respect* for it, just for this reason, that it is an effect and not an energy of will. Similarly, I cannot have respect for inclination, whether my own or another's; I can at most, if my own, approve it; if another's, sometimes even love it; *i.e.* look on it as favourable to my own interest. It is only what is connected with my will as a principle, by no means as an effect—what does not subserve my inclination, but overpowers it, or at least in case of choice excludes it from its calculation—in other words, simply the law of itself which can be an object of respect, and hence a command. Now an action done from duty must wholly exclude the influence of inclination, and with it every object of the will, so that nothing remains which can deter-

---

[1] The first proposition was the law that conduct acquires true moral worth not from inclination or pleasure but from duty, as discussed above.—P.P.W.

mine the will except objectively the *law,* and subjectively *pure respect* for this practical law, and consequently the maxim [2] that I should follow this law even to the thwarting of all my inclinations.

Thus the moral worth of an action does not lie in the effect expected from it, nor in any principle of action which requires to borrow its motive from this expected effect. For all these effects—agreeableness of one's condition, and even the promotion of the happiness of others—could have been also brought about by other causes, so that for this there would have been no need of the will of a rational being; whereas it is in this alone that the supreme and unconditional good can be found. The pre-eminent good which we call moral can therefore consist in nothing else than *the conception of law* in itself, *which certainly is only possible in a rational being,* in so far as this conception, and not the expected effect, determines the will. This is a good which is already present in the person who acts accordingly, and we have not to wait for it to appear first in the result.[3]

---

[2] A *maxim* is the subjective principle of volition. The objective principle (*i.e.* that which would also serve subjectively as a practical principle to all rational beings if reason had full power over the faculty of desire) is the practical *law.*

[3] It might be here objected to me that I take refuge behind the word *respect* in an obscure feeling, instead of giving a distinct solution of the question by a concept of the reason. But although respect is a feeling, it is not a feeling *received* through influence, but is *self-wrought* by a rational concept, and, therefore, is specifically distinct from all feelings of the former kind, which may be referred either to inclination or fear. What I recognise immediately as a law for me, I recognise with respect. This merely signifies the consciousness that my will is *subordinate* to a law, without the intervention of other influences on my sense. The immediate determination of the will by the law, and the consciousness of this is called *respect,* so that this is regarded as an *effect* of the law on the subject, and not as the *cause* of it. Respect is properly the conception of a worth

But what sort of law can that be, the conception of which must determine the will, even without paying any regard to the effect expected from it, in order that this will may be called good absolutely and without qualification? As I have deprived the will of every impulse which could arise to it from obedience to any law, there remains nothing but the universal conformity of its actions to law in general, which alone is to serve the will as a principle, *i.e.,* I am never to act otherwise than so *that I could also will that my maxim should become a universal law.* Here now, it is the simple conformity to law in general, without assuming any particular law applicable to certain actions, that serves the will as its principle, and must so serve it, if duty is not to be a vain delusion and a chimerical notion. The common reason of men in its practical judgments perfectly coincides with this, and always has in view the principle here suggested. Let the question be, for example: May I when in distress make a promise with the intention not to keep it? I readily distinguish here between the two significations which the question may have: Whether it is prudent, or whether it is right, to make a false promise. The former may undoubtedly often be the

---

which thwarts my self-love. Accordingly it is something which is considered neither as an object of inclination nor of fear, although it has something analogous to both. The *object* of respect is the *law* only, and that, the law which we impose on *ourselves,* and yet recognise as necessary in itself. As a law, we are subjected to it without consulting self-love; as imposed by us on ourselves, it is a result of our will. In the former aspect it has an analogy to fear, in the latter to inclination. Respect for a person is properly only respect for the law (of honesty, &c.), of which he gives us an example. Since we also look on the improvement of our talents as a duty, we consider that we see in a person of talents, as it were, the *example of a law* (viz. to become like him in this by exercise), and this constitutes our respect. All so-called moral *interest* consists simply in *respect* for the law.

case. I see clearly indeed that it is not enough to extricate myself from a present difficulty by means of this subterfuge, but it must be well considered whether there may not hereafter spring from this lie much greater inconvenience than that from which I now free myself, and as, with all my supposed *cunning*, the consequences cannot be so easily foreseen but that credit once lost may be much more injurious to me than any mischief which I seek to avoid at present, it should be considered whether it would not be more *prudent* to act herein according to a universal maxim, and to make it a habit to promise nothing except with the intention of keeping it. But it is soon clear to me that such a maxim will still only be based on the fear of consequences. Now it is a wholly different thing to be truthful from duty, and to be so from apprehension of injurious consequences. In the first case, the very notion of the action already implies a law for me; in the second case, I must first look about elsewhere to see what results may be combined with it which would affect myself. For to deviate from the principle of duty is beyond all doubt wicked; but to be unfaithful to my maxim of prudence may often be very advantageous to me, although to abide by it is certainly safer. The shortest way, however, and an unerring one, to discover the answer to this question whether a lying promise is consistent with duty, is to ask myself, Should I be content that my maxim (to extricate myself from difficulty by a false promise) should hold good as a universal law, for myself as well as for others? and should I be able to say to myself, "Every one may make a deceitful promise when he finds himself in a difficulty from which he cannot otherwise extricate himself"? Then I presently become aware that while I can will the lie, I can by no means will that lying should be a universal law. For with such

a law there would be no promises at all, since it would be in vain to allege my intention in regard to my future actions to those who would not believe this allegation, or if they overhastily did so would pay me back in my own coin. Hence my maxim, as soon as it should be made a universal law, would necessarily destroy itself.

I do not, therefore, need any far-reaching penetration to discern what I have to do in order that my will may be morally good. Inexperienced in the course of the world, incapable of being prepared for all its contingencies, I only ask myself: Canst thou also will that thy maxim should be a universal law? If not, then it must be rejected, and that not because of a disadvantage accruing from it to myself or even to others, but because it cannot enter as a principle into a possible universal legislation, and reason extorts from me immediate respect for such legislation. I do not indeed as yet *discern* on what this respect is based (this the philosopher may inquire), but at least I understand this, that it is an estimation of the worth which far outweighs all worth of what is recommended by inclination, and that the necessity of acting from *pure* respect for the practical law is what constitutes duty, to which every other motive must give place, because it is the condition of a will being good *in itself*, and the worth of such a will is above everything.

Thus, then, without quitting the moral knowledge of common human reason, we have arrived at its principle. And although, no doubt, common men do not conceive it in such an abstract and universal form, yet they always have it really before their eyes, and use it as the standard of their decision. Here it would be easy to show how, with this compass in hand, men are well able to distinguish, in every case that occurs, what is good, what bad, conformably to duty or inconsistent with it, if, without in the least teaching them anything new, we only, like Socrates, direct their attention to the principle they themselves employ; and that therefore we do not need science and philosophy to know what we should do to be honest and good, yea, even wise and virtuous. Indeed we might well have conjectured beforehand that the knowledge of what every man is bound to do, and therefore also to know, would be within the reach of every man, even the commonest. Here we cannot forbear admiration when we see how great an advantage the practical judgment has over the theoretical in the common understanding of men. In the latter, if common reason ventures to depart from the laws of experience and from the perceptions of the senses it falls into mere inconceivabilities and self-contradictions, at least into a chaos of uncertainty, obscurity, and instability. But in the practical sphere it is just when the common understanding excludes all sensible springs from practical laws that its power of judgment begins to show itself to advantage. It then becomes even subtle, whether it be that it chicanes with its own conscience or with other claims respecting what is to be called right, or whether it desires for its own instruction to determine honestly the worth of actions; and, in the latter case, it may even have as good a hope of hitting the mark as any philosopher whatever can promise himself. Nay, it is almost more sure of doing so, because the philosopher cannot have any other principle, while he may easily perplex his judgment by a multitude of considerations foreign to the matter, and so turn aside from the right way. Would it not therefore be wiser in moral concerns to acquiesce in the judgment of common reason, or at most only to call in philosophy for the purpose of rendering the system of morals more complete and intelligible, and its rules more convenient for use (especially for disputation), but

not so as to draw off the common understanding from its happy simplicity, or to bring it by means of philosophy into a new path of inquiry and instruction?

Innocence is indeed a glorious thing, only, on the other hand, it is very sad that it cannot well maintain itself, and is easily seduced. On this account even wisdom—which otherwise consists more in conduct than in knowledge—yet has need of science, not in order to learn from it, but to secure for its precepts admission and permanence. Against all the commands of duty which reason represents to man as so deserving of respect, he feels in himself a powerful counterpoise in his wants and inclinations, the entire satisfaction of which he sums up under the name of happiness. Now reason issues its commands unyieldingly, without promising anything to the inclinations, and, as it were, with disregard and contempt for these claims, which are so impetuous, and at the same time so plausible, and which will not allow themselves to be suppressed by any command. Hence there arises a natural *dialectic*, i.e., a disposition to argue against these strict laws of duty and to question their validity, or at least their purity and strictness; and, if possible, to make them more accordant with our wishes and inclinations, that is to say, to corrupt them at their very source, and entirely to destroy their worth—a thing which even common practical reason cannot ultimately call good.

Thus is the *common reason of man* compelled to go out of its sphere, and to take a step into the field of a *practical philosophy*, not to satisfy any speculative want (which never occurs to it as long as it is content to be mere sound reason), but even on practical grounds, in order to attain in it information and clear instruction respecting the source of its principle, and the correct determination of it in opposition to the maxims which are based on wants and inclinations, so that it may escape from the perplexity of opposite claims, and not run the risk of losing all genuine moral principles through the equivocation into which it easily falls. Thus, when practical reason cultivates itself, there insensibly arises in it a dialectic which forces it to seek aid in philosophy, just as happens to it in its theoretic use; and in this case, therefore, as well as in the other, it will find rest nowhere but in a thorough critical examination of our reason.

12. *An Introduction to the Principles of Morals and Legislation*

JEREMY BENTHAM (1748–1832)

CHAPTER I

Of the Principle of Utility

I. Nature has placed mankind under the governance of two sovereign masters, *pain* and *pleasure*. It is for them alone to point out what we ought to do, as well as to determine what we shall do. On the one hand the standard of right and wrong, on the other the chain of causes and effects, are fastened to their throne. They govern us in all we do, in all we say, in all we think: every effort we can make to throw off our subjection, will serve but to demonstrate and confirm it. In words a man may pretend to abjure their empire: but in reality he will remain subject to it all the while. The *principle of utility* [1] recognises the subjection, and assumes it for the foundation of that system, the object of which is to rear the fabric of felicity by the hands of reason and of law. Systems which attempt to question it, deal in sounds instead of sense, in caprice instead of reason, in darkness instead of light.

But enough of metaphor and declamation: it is not by such means that moral science is to be improved.

II. The principle of utility is the foundation of the present work: it will

---

[1] Note by the Author, July 1822:

To this denomination has of late been added, or substituted, the *greatest happiness* or *greatest felicity* principle: this for shortness, instead of saying at length *that principle* which states the greatest happiness of all those whose interest is in question, as being the right and proper, and only right and proper and universally desirable, end of human action: of human action in every situation, and in particular in that of a functionary or set of functionaries exercising the powers of Government. The word *utility* does not so clearly point to the ideas of *pleasure* and *pain* as the words *happiness* and *felicity* do: nor does it lead us to the consideration of the *number,* of the interests affected; to the *number,* as being the circumstance, which contributes, in the largest proportion, to the formation of the standard here in question; the *standard of right and wrong,* by which alone the propriety of human conduct, in every situation, can with propriety be tried. This want of a sufficiently manifest connexion between the ideas of *happiness* and *pleasure* on the one hand, and the idea of *utility* on the other, I have every now and then found operating, and with but too much efficiency, as a bar to the acceptance, that might otherwise have been given, to this principle.—BENTHAM be proper therefore at the outset to give an explicit and determinate account of what is meant by it. By the principle [2] of utility is meant that principle which approves or disapproves of every action whatsoever, according to the tendency which it appears to have to augment or diminish the happiness of the party whose interest is in question: or, what is the same thing in other words, to promote or to oppose that happiness. I say of every action whatsoever; and therefore not only of every action of a private individual, but of every measure of government.

III. By utility is meant that property in any object, whereby it tends to produce benefit, advantage, pleasure, good, or happiness, (all this in the present case comes to the same thing) or (what comes again to the same thing) to prevent the happening of mischief, pain, evil, or unhappiness to the party whose interest is considered: if that party be the community in general, then the happiness of the community: if a particular individual, then the happiness of that individual.

IV. The interest of the community is one of the most general expressions that can occur in the phraseology of morals: no wonder that the meaning of it is often lost. When it has a meaning, it is this. The community is a fictitious *body,* composed of the individual persons who are considered as constituting as it were its *members.* The interest of the community then is, what?—the sum of the interests of the several members who compose it.

V. It is in vain to talk of the interest of the community, without understanding what is the interest of the individual.[3] A thing is said to promote the interest, or to be *for* the interest, of an individual, when it tends to add to the sum total of his pleasures: or, what comes to the same thing, to diminish the sum total of his pains.

VI. An action then may be said to be conformable to the principle of utility, or, for shortness sake, to utility, (meaning with respect to the community at large) when the tendency it has to augment the happiness of the community is greater than any it has to diminish it.

VII. A measure of government (which is but a particular kind of action, performed by a particular person or persons) may be said to be conformable to or dictated by the principle of utility, when in like manner the tendency which it has to augment the happiness of the community is greater than any which it has to diminish it.

VIII. When an action, or in particular a measure of government, is supposed by a man to be conformable to the principle of utility, it may be convenient, for the purposes of discourse, to imagine a kind of law or dictate, called a law or dictate of utility: and to speak of the action in question, as being conformable to such law or dictate.

IX. A man may be said to be a partisan of the principle of utility, when the approbation or disapprobation he annexes to any action, or to any meas-

[2] The word principle is derived from the Latin principium: which seems to be compounded of the two words *primus,* first, or chief, and *cipium,* a termination which seems to be derived from *capio,* to take, as in *mancipium, municipium;* to which are analogous, *auceps, forceps,* and others. It is a term of very vague and very extensive signification: it is applied to any thing which is conceived to serve as a foundation or beginning to any series of operations: in some cases, of physical operations; but of mental operations in the present case.

The principle here in question may be taken for an act of the mind; a sentiment; a sentiment of approbation; a sentiment which, when applied to an action, approves of its utility, as that quality of it by which the measure of approbation or disapprobation bestowed upon it ought to be governed.

[3] Interest is one of those words, which not having any superior *genus,* cannot in the ordinary way be defined.

ure, is determined by and proportioned to the tendency which he conceives it to have to augment or to diminish the happiness of the community: or in other words, to its conformity or unconformity to the laws or dictates of utility.

X. Of an action that is conformable to the principle of utility one may always say either that it is one that ought to be done, or at least that it is not one that ought not to be done. One may say also, that it is right it should be done; at least that it is not wrong it should be done: that it is a right action; at least that it is not a wrong action. When thus interpreted, the words *ought*, and *right* and *wrong*, and others of that stamp, have a meaning: when otherwise, they have none.

XI. Has the rectitude of this principle been ever formally contested? It should seem that it had, by those who have not known what they have been meaning. Is it susceptible of any direct proof? it should seem not: for that which is used to prove every thing else, cannot itself be proved: a chain of proofs must have their commencement somewhere. To give such proof is as impossible as it is needless.

XII. Not that there is or ever has been that human creature breathing, however stupid or perverse, who has not on many, perhaps on most occasions of his life, deferred to it. By the natural constitution of the human frame, on most occasions of their lives men in general embrace this principle, without thinking of it: if not for the ordering of their own actions, yet for the trying of their own actions, as well as of those of other men. There have been, at the same time, not many, perhaps, even of the most intelligent, who have been disposed to embrace it purely and without reserve. There are even few who have not taken some occasion or other to quarrel with it, either on account of their not understanding always how to apply it, or on

account of some prejudice or other which they were afraid to examine into, or could not bear to part with. For such is the stuff that man is made of: in principle and in practice, in a right track and in a wrong one, the rarest of all human qualities is consistency.

XIII. When a man attempts to combat the principle of utility, it is with reasons drawn, without his being aware of it, from that very principle itself.[4] His arguments, if they prove any thing, prove not that the principle is *wrong*, but that, according to the applications he supposes to be made of it, it is *misapplied*. Is it possible for a man to move the earth? Yes; but he must first find out another earth to stand upon.

XIV. To disprove the propriety of it by arguments is impossible; but, from the causes that have been mentioned, or from some confused or partial view of it, a man may happen to be disposed not to relish it. Where this is the case, if he thinks the settling of his opinions on such a subject worth the trouble, let him take the following steps, and at length, perhaps, he may come to reconcile himself to it.

1. Let him settle with himself, whether he would wish to discard this principle altogether; if so, let him consider what it is that all his reasonings (in matters of politics especially) can amount to?

2. If he would, let him settle with himself, whether he would judge and act without any principle, or whether there is any other he would judge and act by?

3. If there be, let him examine and satisfy himself whether the principle he thinks he has found is really any separate intelligible principle; or whether it

---

4 'The principle of utility, (I have heard it said) is a dangerous principle: it is dangerous on certain occasions to consult it.' This is as much as to say, what? that it is not consonant to utility, to consult utility: in short, that it is *not* consulting it, to consult it.

be not a mere principle in words, a kind of phrase, which at bottom expresses neither more nor less than the mere averment of his own unfounded sentiments; that is, what in another person he might be apt to call caprice?

4. If he is inclined to think that his own approbation or disapprobation, annexed to the idea of an act, without any regard to its consequences, is a sufficient foundation for him to judge and act upon, let him ask himself whether his sentiment is to be a standard of right and wrong, with respect to every other man, or whether every man's sentiment has the same privilege of being a standard to itself?

5. In the first case, let him ask himself whether his principle is not despotical, and hostile to all the rest of human race?

6. In the second case, whether it is not an anarchial, and whether at this rate there are not as many different standards of right and wrong as there are men? and whether even to the same man, the same thing, which is right today, may not (without the least change in its nature) be wrong to-morrow? and whether the same thing is not right and wrong in the same place at the same time? and in either case, whether all argument is not at an end? and whether, when two men have said, 'I like this,' and 'I don't like it,' they can (upon such a principle) have any thing more to say?

7. If he should have said to himself, No: for that the sentiment which he proposes as a standard must be grounded on reflection, let him say on what particulars the reflection is to turn? if on particulars having relation to the utility of the act, then let him say whether this is not deserting his own principle, and borrowing assistance from that very one in opposition to which he sets it up: or if not on those particulars, on what other particulars?

8. If he should be for compounding the matter, and adopting his own principle in part, and the principle of utility in part, let him say how far he will adopt it?

9. When he has settled with himself where he will stop, then let him ask himself how he justifies to himself the adopting it so far? and why he will not adopt it any farther?

10. Admitting any other principle than the principle of utility to be a right principle, a principle that it is right for a man to pursue; admitting (what is not true) that the word *right* can have a meaning without reference to utility, let him say whether there is any such thing as a *motive* that a man can have to pursue the dictates of it: if there is, let him say what the motive is, and how it is to be distinguished from those which enforce the dictates of utility: if not, then lastly let him say what it is this other principle can be good for?

.   .   .   .

CHAPTER III

Of the Four Sanctions or Sources of Pain and Pleasure

I. It has been shown that the happiness of the individuals, of whom a community is composed, that is their pleasures and their security, is the end and the sole end which the legislator ought to have in view: the sole standard, in conformity to which each individual ought, as far as depends upon the legislator, to be *made* to fashion his behaviour. But whether it be this or any thing else that is to be *done*, there is nothing by which a man can ultimately be *made* to do it, but either pain or pleasure. Having taken a general view of these two grand objects (*viz.* pleasure, and what comes to the same thing, immunity from pain) in the character of *final* causes; it will be necessary to take a view of pleasure and pain itself, in the character of *efficient* causes or means.

II. There are four distinguishable sources from which pleasure and pain are in use to flow: considered separately, they may be termed the *physical,* the *political,* the *moral,* and the *religious:* and inasmuch as the pleasures and pains belonging to each of them are capable of giving a binding force to any law or rule of conduct, they may all of them be termed *sanctions.*[5]

III. If it be in the present life, and from the ordinary course of nature, not purposely modified by the interposition of the will of any human being, nor by any extraordinary interposition of any superior invisible being, that the pleasure or the pain takes place or is expected, it may be said to issue from or to belong to the *physical sanction.*

IV. If at the hands of a *particular* person or set of persons in the community, who under names correspondent to that of *judge,* are chosen for the particular purpose of dispensing it, according to the will of the sovereign or supreme ruling power in the state, it may be said to issue from the *political sanction.*

V. If at the hands of such *chance* persons in the community, as the party in question may happen in the course of his life to have concerns with, according to each man's spontaneous disposition, and not according to any settled or concerted rule, it may be said to issue from the *moral* or *popular sanction.*[6]

VI. If from the immediate hand of a superior invisible being, either in the present life, or in a future, it may be said to issue from the *religious sanction.*

VII. Pleasures or pains which may be expected to issue from the *physical, political,* or *moral* sanctions, must all of them be expected to be experienced, if ever, in the *present* life: those which may be expected to issue from the *religious* sanction, may be expected to be experienced either in the *present* life or in a *future.*

VIII. Those which can be experienced in the present life, can of course be no others than such as human nature in the course of the present life is susceptible of: and from each of these sources may flow all the pleasures or pains of which, in the course of the present life, human nature is susceptible. With regard to these then (with which alone we have in this place any concern) those of them which belong to any one of those sanctions, differ not ultimately in kind from those which belong to any one of the other three: the only difference there is among them lies in the circumstances that accompany their production. A suffering which befalls a man in the natural and spontaneous course of things, shall be styled, for instance, a *calamity;* in which case, if it

---

[5] Sanctio, in Latin, was used to signify the *act of binding,* and, by a common grammatical transition, *any thing which serves to bind a man:* to wit, to the observance of such or such a mode of conduct. According to a Latin grammarian, the import of tne word is derived by rather a far-fetched process (such as those commonly are, and in a great measure indeed must be, by which intellectual ideas are derived from sensible ones) from the word *sanguis,* blood: because, among the Romans, with a view to inculcate into the people a persuasion that such or such a mode of conduct would be rendered obligatory upon a man by the force of what I call the religious sanction (that is, that he would be made to suffer by the extraordinary interposition of some superior being, if he failed to observe the mode of conduct in question) certain ceremonies were contrived by the priests: in the course of which ceremonies the blood of victims was made use of.

A Sanction then is a source of obligatory powers or *motives:* that is, of *pains* and *pleasures;* which, according as they are connected with such or such modes of conduct, operate, and are indeed the only things which can operate, as *motives.*

---

[6] Better termed *popular,* as more directly indicative of its constituent cause; as likewise of its relation to the more common phrase *public opinion . . .*

be supposed to befall him through any imprudence of his, it may be styled a punishment issuing from the physical sanction. Now this same suffering, if inflicted by the law, will be what is commonly called a *punishment;* if incurred for want of any friendly assistance, which the misconduct, or supposed misconduct, of the sufferer has occasioned to be withholden, a punishment issuing from the *moral* sanction; if through the immediate interposition of a particular providence, a punishment issuing from the religious sanction.

IX. A man's goods, or his person, are consumed by fire. If this happened to him by what is called an accident, it was a calamity: if by reason of his own imprudence (for instance, from his neglecting to put his candle out) it may be styled a punishment of the physical sanction: if it happened to him by the sentence of the political magistrate, a punishment belonging to the political sanction; that is, what is commonly called a punishment: if for want of any assistance which his *neighbour* withheld from him out of some dislike to his *moral* character, a punishment of the *moral* sanction: if by an immediate act of *God's* displeasure, manifested on account of some *sin* committed by him, or through any distraction of mind, occasioned by the dread of such displeasure, a punishment of the *religious* sanction.[7]

X. As to such of the pleasures and pains belonging to the religious sanction, as regard a future life, of what kind these may be we cannot know. These lie not open to our observation. During the present life they are matter only of expectation: and, whether that expectation be derived from natural or revealed religion, the particular kind of pleasure or pain, if it be different from all those which lie open to our observation, is what we can have no idea of. The best ideas we can obtain of such pains and pleasures are altogether unliquidated in point of quality. In what other respects our ideas of them *may* be liquidated will be considered in another place.

XI. Of these four sanctions the physical is altogether, we may observe, the ground-work of the political and the moral: so is it also of the religious, in as far as the latter bears relation to the present life. It is included in each of those other three. This may operate in any case, (that is, any of the pains or pleasures belônging to it may operate) independently of *them:* none of *them* can operate but by means of this. In a word, the powers of nature may operate of themselves; but neither the magistrate, nor men at large, *can* operate, nor is God in the case in question *supposed* to operate, but through the powers of nature.

XII. For these four objects, which in their nature have so much in common, it seemed of use to find a common name. It seemed of use, in the first place, for the convenience of giving a name to certain pleasures and pains, for which a name equally characteristic could hardly otherwise have been found: in the second place, for the sake of holding up the efficacy of certain moral forces, the influence of which is apt not to be sufficiently attended to. Does the political sanction exert an influence over the conduct of mankind? The moral, the religious sanctions do so too. In every inch of his career are the operations of the political magistrate liable to be aided or impeded by these two foreign powers: who, one or other of them, or both, are sure to be either his rivals or his allies. Does it happen to him to leave them out in his calculations? he will be sure almost to find himself mistaken in the result. Of

---

[7] A suffering conceived to befall a man by the immediate act of God, as above, is often, for shortness' sake, called a *judgment:* instead of saying, a suffering inflicted on him in consequence of a special judgment formed, and resolution thereupon taken, by the Deity.

all this we shall find abundant proofs in the sequel of this work. It behoves him, therefore, to have them continually before his eyes; and that under such a name as exhibits the relation they bear to his own purposes and designs.

CHAPTER IV

Value of a Lot of Pleasure or Pain, How to Be Measured

I. Pleasures then, and the avoidance of pains, are the *ends* which the legislator has in view: it behoves him therefore to understand their *value*. Pleasures and pains are the *instruments* he has to work with: it behoves him therefore to understand their force, which is again, in other words, their value.

II. To a person considered *by himself*, the value of a pleasure or pain considered *by itself*, will be greater or less, according to the four following circumstances [8]:

1. Its *intensity.*
2. Its *duration.*
3. Its *certainty* or *uncertainty.*
4. Its *propinquity* or *remoteness.*

III. These are the circumstances which are to be considered in estimating a pleasure or a pain considered each of them by itself. But when the value of any pleasure or pain is considered for the purpose of estimating the tendency of any *act* by which it is produced, there are two other circumstances to be taken into the account; these are,

5. Its *fecundity,* or the chance it has of being followed by sensations of the *same* kind: that is, pleasures, if it be a pleasure: pains, if it be a pain.

6. Its *purity,* or the chance it has of *not* being followed by sensations of the *opposite* kind: that is, pains, if it be a pleasure: pleasures, if it be a pain.

These two last, however, are in strictness scarcely to be deemed properties of the pleasure or the pain itself; they are not, therefore, in strictness to be taken into the account of the value of that pleasure or that pain. They are in strictness to be deemed properties only of the act, or other event, by which such pleasure or pain has been produced; and accordingly are only to be taken into the account of the tendency of such act or such event.

IV. To a *number* of persons, with reference to each of whom the value of a pleasure or a pain is considered, it will be greater or less, according to seven circumstances: to wit, the six preceding ones; *viz.*

1. Its *intensity.*
2. Its *duration.*
3. Its *certainty* or *uncer- tainty.*
4. Its *propinquity* or *remoteness.*
5. Its *fecundity.*
6. Its *purity.*

And one other; to wit:

7. Its *extent;* that is, the number of persons to whom it *extends;* or (in other words) who are affected by it.

V. To take an exact account then of the general tendency of any act, by which the interests of a community are affected, proceed as follows. Begin with any one person of those whose interests seem most immediately to be affected by it: and take an account,

1. Of the value of each distinguishable *pleasure* which appears to be produced by it in the *first* instance.

---

[8] These circumstances have since been denominated *elements* or *dimensions* of *value* in a pleasure or a pain.

Not long after the publication of the first edition, the following memoriter verses were framed, in the view of lodging more effectually, in the memory, these points, on which the whole fabric of morals and legislation may be seen to rest.

Intense, long, certain, speedy, fruitful, pure—
Such marks in *pleasures* and in *pains* endure.
Such pleasures seek if *private* be thy end:
If it be *public,* wide let them *extend.*
Such *pains* avoid, whichever be thy view:
If pains *must* come, let them *extend* to few.

2. Of the value of each *pain* which appears to be produced by it in the *first* instance.

3. Of the value of each pleasure which appears to be produced by it *after* the first. This constitutes the *fecundity* of the first *pleasure* and the *impurity* of the first *pain*.

4. Of the value of each *pain* which appears to be produced by it after the first. This constitutes the *fecundity* of the first *pain,* and the *impurity* of the first pleasure.

5. Sum up all the values of all the *pleasures* on the one side, and those of all the pains on the other. The balance, if it be on the side of pleasure, will give the *good* tendency of the act upon the whole, with respect to the interests of that *individual* person; if on the side of pain, the *bad* tendency of it upon the whole.

6. Take an account of the *number* of persons whose interests appear to be concerned; and repeat the above process with respect to each. *Sum up* the numbers expressive of the degrees of *good* tendency, which the act has, with respect to each individual, in regard to whom the tendency of it is *good* upon the whole: do this again with respect to each individual, in regard to whom the tendency of it is *good* upon the whole: do this again with respect to each individual, in regard to whom the tendency of it is *bad* upon the whole. Take the *balance;* which, if on the side of *pleasure,* will give the general *good tendency* of the act, with respect to the total number or community of individuals concerned; if on the side of pain, the general *evil tendency,* with respect to the same community.

VI. It is not to be expected that this process should be strictly pursued previously to every moral judgment, or to every legislative or judicial operation. It may, however, be always kept in view: and as near as the process actually pursued on these occasions approaches to it, so near will such process approach to the character of an exact one.

VII. The same process is alike applicable to pleasure and pain, in whatever shape they appear: and by whatever denomination they are distinguished: to pleasure, whether it be called *good* (which is properly the cause or instrument of pleasure) or *profit* (which is distant pleasure, or the cause or instrument of distant pleasure,) or *convenience,* or *advantage, benefit, emolument, happiness,* and so forth: to pain, whether it be called *evil,* (which corresponds to *good*) or *mischief,* or *inconvenience,* or *disadvantage,* or *loss,* or *unhappiness,* and so forth.

VIII. Nor is this a novel and unwarranted, any more than it is a useless theory. In all this there is nothing but what the practice of mankind, wheresoever they have a clear view of their own interest, is perfectly conformable to. An article of property, an estate in land, for instance, is valuable, on what account? On account of the pleasures of all kinds which it enables a man to produce, and what comes to the same thing the pains of all kinds which it enables him to avert. But the value of such an article of property is universally understood to rise or fall according to the length or shortness of the time which a man has in it: the certainty or uncertainty of its coming into possession: and the nearness or remoteness of the time at which, if at all, it is to come into possession. As to the *intensity* of the pleasures which a man may derive from it, this is never thought of, because it depends upon the use which each particular person may come to make of it; which cannot be estimated till the particular pleasures he may come to derive from it, or the particular pains he may come to exclude by means of it, are brought to view. For the same reason, neither does he think of the *fecundity* or *purity* of those pleasures.

Thus much for pleasure and pain, happiness and unhappiness, in *general*.

We come now to consider the several particular kinds of pain and pleasure.

13. *Utilitarianism**

JOHN STUART MILL (1806–1873)

There are few circumstances among those which make up the present condition of human knowledge more unlike what might have been expected, or more significant of the backward state in which speculation on the most important subjects still lingers, than the little progress which has been made in the decision of the controversy respecting the criterion of right and wrong. From the dawn of philosophy, the question concerning the *summum bonum*, or, what is the same thing, concerning the foundation of morality, has been accounted the main problem in speculative thought, has occupied the most gifted intellects and divided them into sects and schools, carrying on a vigorous warfare against one another. And after more than two thousand years the same discussions continue, philosophers are still ranged under the same contending banners, and neither thinkers nor mankind at large seem nearer to being unanimous on the subject than when the youth Socrates listened to the old Protagoras, and asserted (if Plato's dialogue be grounded on a real conversation) the theory of utilitarianism against the popular morality of the so-called sophist.

It is true that similar confusion and uncertainty and, in some cases, similar discordance exist respecting the first

principles of all the sciences, not excepting that which is deemed the most certain of them—mathematics, without much impairing, generally indeed without impairing at all, the trustworthiness of the conclusions of those sciences. An apparent anomaly, the explanation of which is that the detailed doctrines of a science are not usually deduced from, nor depend for their evidence upon, what are called its first principles. Were it not so, there would be no science more precarious, or whose conclusions were more insufficiently made out, than algebra, which derives none of its certainty from what are commonly taught to learners as its elements, since these, as laid down by some of its most eminent teachers, are as full of fictions as English law, and of mysteries as theology. The truths which are ultimately accepted as the first principles of a science are really the last results of metaphysical analysis, practised on the elementary notions with which the science is conversant; and their relation to the science is not that of foundations to an edifice, but of roots to a tree, which may perform their office equally well though they be never dug down to and exposed to light. But though in science the particular truths precede the general theory, the contrary might be expected to be the case with a practical art, such as morals or legislation. All action is for the sake of some

* London, 1863. From Chapters I and II.

end, and rules of action, it seems natural to suppose, must take their whole character and color from the end to which they are subservient. When we engage in a pursuit, a clear and precise conception of what we are pursuing would seem to be the first thing we need, instead of the last we are to look forward to. A test of right and wrong must be the means, one would think, of ascertaining what is right or wrong, and not a consequence of having already ascertained it.

The difficulty is not avoided by having recourse to the popular theory of a natural faculty, a sense or instinct, informing us of right and wrong. For—besides that the existence of such a moral instinct is itself one of the matters in dispute—those believers in it who have any pretensions to philosophy have been obliged to abandon the idea that it discerns what is right or wrong in the particular case in hand, as our other senses discern the sight or sound actually present. Our moral faculty, according to all those of its interpreters who are entitled to the name of thinkers, supplies us only with the general principles of moral judgments; it is a branch of our reason, not of our sensitive faculty; and must be looked to for the abstract doctrines of morality, not for perception of it in the concrete. The intuitive, no less than what may be termed the inductive, school of ethics insists on the necessity of general laws. They both agree that the morality of an individual action is not a question of direct perception, but of the application of a law to an individual case. They recognize also, to a great extent, the same moral laws, but differ as to their evidence and the source from which they derive their authority. According to the one opinion, the principles of morals are evident *a priori*, requiring nothing to command assent except that the meaning of the terms be understood. According to the other doctrine, right and wrong, as well as truth and falsehood, are questions of observation and

experience. But both hold equally that morality must be deduced from principles; and the intuitive school affirm as strongly as the inductive that there is a science of morals. Yet they seldom attempt to make out a list of the *a priori* principles which are to serve as the premises of the science; still more rarely do they make any effort to reduce those various principles to one first principle, or common ground of obligation. They either assume the ordinary precepts of morals as of *a priori* authority, or they lay down as the common groundwork of those maxims some generalities much less obviously authoritative than the maxims themselves, and which has never succeeded in gaining popular acceptance. Yet to support their pretensions there ought either to be some one fundamental principle or law at the root of all morality, or, if there be several, there should be a determinate order of precedence among them; and the one principle, or the rule for deciding between the various principles when they conflict, ought to be self-evident.

To inquire how far the bad effects of this deficiency have been mitigated in practice, or to what extent the moral beliefs of mankind have been vitiated or made uncertain by the absence of any distinct recognition of an ultimate standard, would imply a complete survey and criticism of past and present ethical doctrine. It would, however, be easy to show that whatever steadiness or consistency these moral beliefs have attained has been mainly due to the tacit influence of a standard not recognized. Although the non-existence of an acknowledged first principle has made ethics not so much a guide as a consecration of men's actual sentiments, still, as men's sentiments, both in favor and of aversion, are greatly influenced by what they suppose to be the effect of things upon their happiness, the principle of utility, or, as Bentham latterly called it, the greatest happiness principle, has had a large share in forming the moral doctrines even of those who most scornfully reject its authority. Nor is there any school of thought which refuses to admit that the influence of actions on happiness is a most material and even predominant consideration in many of the details of morals, however unwilling to acknowledge it as the fundamental principle of morality and the source of moral obligation. I might go much further and say that to all those *a priori* moralists who deem it necessary to argue at all, utilitarian arguments are indispensable. It is not my present purpose to criticize these thinkers; but I cannot help referring, for illustration, to a systematic treatise by one of the most illustrious of them, the *Metaphysics of Ethics* by Kant. This remarkable man, whose system of thought will long remain one of the landmarks in the history of philosophical speculation, does, in the treatise in question, lay down a universal first principle as the origin and ground of moral obligation; it is this: "So act that the rule on which thou actest would admit of being adopted as a law by all rational beings." But when he begins to deduce from this precept any of the actual duties of morality, he fails, almost grotesquely, to show that there would be any contradiction, any logical (not to say physical) impossibility, in the adoption by all rational beings of the most outrageously immoral rules of conduct. All he knows is that the *consequences* of their universal adoption would be such as no one would choose to incur.

On the present occasion, I shall, without further discussion of the other theories, attempt to contribute something towards the understanding and appreciation of the "utilitarian" or "happiness" theory, and towards such proof as it is susceptible of. It is evident that this cannot be proof in the ordinary and popular meaning of the term. Questions of ultimate ends are not amenable to direct proof. Whatever can be proved to be good must be so by being shown to be a means to something admitted to be good without proof. The medical art is proved to be good by its conducing to health; but how is it possible to prove that health is good? The art of music is good, for the reason, among others, that it produces pleasure; but what proof is it possible to give that pleasure is good? If, then, it is asserted that there is a comprehensive formula, including all things which are in themselves good, and that whatever else is good is not so as an end but as a means, the formula may be accepted or rejected, but is not a subject of what is commonly understood by proof. We are not, however, to infer that its acceptance or rejection must depend on blind impulse, or arbitrary choice. There is a larger meaning of the word "proof," in which this question is as amenable to it as any other of the disputed questions of philosophy. The subject is within the cognizance of the rational faculty; and neither does that faculty deal with it solely in the way of intuition. Considerations may be presented capable of determining the intellect either to give or withhold its assent to the doctrine; and this is equivalent to proof. . . .

The creed which accepts as the foundation of morals "utility" or the "greatest happiness principle" holds that actions are right in proportion as they tend to promote happiness, wrong as they tend to produce the reverse of happiness. By happiness is intended pleasure, and the absence of pain; by unhappiness, pain, and the privation of pleasure. To give a clear view of the moral standard set up by the theory, much more requires to be said; in particular, what things it includes in the ideas of pain and pleasure; and to what extent this is left an open question. But these supplementary explanations do not affect the theory of life on which this theory of morality is grounded—namely, that pleasure and freedom from pain are the only things desirable as ends; and that all desirable things (which are as numerous in the utilitarian as in any other scheme) are desirable either for the pleasure inherent in themselves, or as means to the promotion of pleasure and the prevention of pain.

Now such a theory of life excites in many minds, and among them in some of the most estimable in feeling and purpose, inveterate dislike. To suppose that life has (as they express it) no higher end than pleasure—no better and nobler object of desire and pursuit—they designate as utterly mean and groveling; as a doctrine worthy only of swine, to whom the followers of Epicurus were, at a very early period, contemptuously likened; and modern holders of the doctrine are occasionally made the subject of equally polite comparisons by its German, French, and English assailants.

When thus attacked, the Epicureans have always answered that it is not they, but their accusers, who represent human nature in a degrading light, since the accusation supposes human beings to be capable of no pleasures except those of which swine are capable. If this supposition were true, the charge could not be gainsaid, but would then be no longer an imputation; for if the sources of pleasure were precisely the same to human beings and to swine, the rule of life which is good enough for the one would be good enough for the other. The comparison of the Epicurean life to that of beasts is felt as degrading, precisely because a beast's pleasures do not satisfy a human being's conceptions of happiness. Human beings have faculties more elevated than the animal appetites and, when once made conscious of them, do not regard anything as happiness which does not include their gratification. I do not, indeed, consider the Epicureans to have been by any means

faultless in drawing out their scheme of consequences from the utilitarian principle. To do this in any sufficient manner, many Stoic, as well as Christian, elements require to be included. But there is no known Epicurean theory of life which does not assign to the pleasures of the intellect, of the feelings and imagination, and of the moral sentiments, a much higher value of pleasures than to those of mere sensation. It must be admitted, however, that utilitarian writers in general have placed the superiority of mental over bodily pleasures chiefly in the greater permanency, safety, uncostliness, etc., of the former—that is, in their circumstantial advantages rather than in their intrinsic nature. And on all these points utilitarians have fully proved their case; but they might have taken the other and, as it may be called, higher ground with entire consistency. It is quite compatible with the principle of utility to recognize the fact that some kinds of pleasure are more desirable and more valuable than others. It would be absurd that, while, in estimating all other things, quality is considered as well as quantity, the estimation of pleasures should be supposed to depend on quantity alone.

If I am asked what I mean by difference of quality in pleasures, or what makes one pleasure more valuable than another merely as a pleasure, except its being greater in amount, there is but one possible answer. Of two pleasures, if there be one to which all or almost all who have experience of both give a decided preference, irrespective of a feeling of moral obligation to prefer it, that is the more desirable pleasure. If one of the two is, by those who are competently acquainted with both, placed so far above the other that they prefer it, even though knowing it to be attended with a greater amount of discontent, and would not resign it for any quantity of the other pleasure which their nature is capable of, we are justified in ascribing to the preferred enjoyment a superiority in quality so far outweighing quantity as to render it, in comparison, of small account.

Now it is an unquestionable fact that those who are equally acquainted with and equally capable of appreciating and enjoying both, do give a most marked preference to the manner of existence which employs their higher faculties. Few human creatures would consent to be changed into any of the lower animals for a promise of the fullest allowance of a beast's pleasures; no intelligent human being would consent to be a fool, no instructed person would be an ignoramus, no person of feeling and conscience would be selfish and base, even though they should be persuaded that the fool, the dunce, or the rascal is better satisfied with his lot than they are with theirs. They would not resign what they possess more than he for the most complete satisfaction of all the desires which they have in common with him. If they ever fancy they would, it is only in cases of unhappiness so extreme that to escape from it they would exchange their lot for almost any other, however undesirable in their own eyes. A being of higher faculties requires more to make him happy, is capable probably of more acute suffering, and certainly accessible to it at more points, than one of an inferior type; but in spite of these liabilities, he can never really wish to sink into what he feels to be a lower grade of existence. We may give what explanation we please of this unwillingness; we may attribute it to pride, a name which is given indiscriminately to some of the most and to some of the least estimable feelings of which mankind are capable: we may refer it to the love of liberty and personal independence, an appeal to which was with the Stoics one of the most effective means for the inculcation of it; to the love of power or to the love of excitement, both of which do really enter into and contribute to it; but its most appropriate appellation is a sense of dignity, which all human beings possess in one form or other, and in some, though by no means in exact, proportion to their higher faculties, and which is so essential a part of the happiness of those in whom it is strong that nothing which conflicts with it could be otherwise than momentarily an object of desire to them. Whoever supposes that this preference takes place at a sacrifice of happiness— that the superior being, in anything like equal circumstances, is not happier than the inferior—confounds the two very different ideas of happiness and content. It is indisputable that the being whose capacities of enjoyment are low has the greatest chance of having them fully satisfied; and a highly endowed being will always feel that any happiness which he can look for, as the world is constituted, is imperfect. But he can learn to bear its imperfections, if they are at all bearable; and they will not make him envy the being who is indeed unconscious of the imperfections, but only because he feels not at all the good which those imperfections qualify. It is better to be a human being dissatisfied than a pig satisfied; better to be Socrates dissatisfied than a fool satisfied. And if the fool, or the pig, are of a different opinion, it is because they only know their own side of the question. The other party to the comparison knows both sides. . . .

According to the greatest happiness principle, as above explained, the ultimate end, with reference to and for the sake of which all other things are desirable—whether we are considering our own good or that of other people—is an existence exempt as far as possible from pain, and as rich as possible in enjoyments, both in point of quantity and quality; the test of quality and the rule for measuring it against quantity being the preference felt by those who, in their opportunities of experience, to which must be added their habits of self-consciousness and self-observation, are best furnished with the means of comparison. This, being, according to the utilitarian opinion, the end of human action, is necessarily also the standard of morality, which may accordingly be defined "the rules and precepts for human conduct," by the observance of which an existence such as has been described might be, to the greatest extent possible, secured to all mankind; and not to them only, but, so far as the nature of things admits, to the whole sentient creation.

Against this doctrine, however, arises another class of objectors who say that happiness, in any form, cannot be the rational purpose of human life and action; because, in the first place, it is unattainable; and they contemptuously ask, What right hast thou to be happy? —a question which Mr. Carlyle clinches by the addition, What right, a short time ago, hadst thou even *to be?* Next they say the men can do *without* happiness; that all noble human beings have felt this, and could not have become noble but by learning the lesson of *Entsagen,* or renunciation; which lesson, thoroughly learnt and submitted to, they affirm to be the beginning and necessary condition of all virtue.

The first of these objections would go to the root of the matter were it well founded; for if no happiness is to be had at all by human beings, the attainment of it cannot be the end of morality or of any rational conduct. Though, even in that case, something might still be said for the utilitarian theory, since utility includes not solely the pursuit of happiness, but the prevention or mitigation of unhappiness; and if the former aim be chimerical, there will be all the greater scope and more imperative need for the latter, so long at least as mankind think fit to live, and do not take refuge in the simultaneous act of suicide recommended under certain conditions by Novalis. When, however, it is thus positively asserted to be impossible that human life should be happy, the assertion, if not something like a verbal quibble, is at least an exaggeration. If by happiness be meant a continuity of highly pleasurable excitement, it is evident enough that this is impossible. A state of exalted pleasure lasts only moments or in some cases, and with some intermissions, hours, or days, and is the occasional brilliant flash of enjoyment, not its permanent and steady flame. Of this the philosophers who have taught that happiness is the end of life were as fully aware as those who taunt them. The happiness which they meant was not a life of rapture; but moments of such, in an existence made up of few and transitory pains, many and various pleasures, with a decided predominance of the active over the passive, and having as the foundation of the whole not to expect more from life than it is capable of bestowing. A life thus composed, to those who have been fortunate enough to obtain it, has always appeared worthy of the name of happiness. And such an existence is even now the lot of many, during some considerable portion of their lives. The present wretched education and wretched social arrangements are the only real hindrance to its being attainable by almost all.

The objectors perhaps may doubt whether human beings, if taught to consider happiness as the end of life, would be satisfied with such a moderate share of it. But great numbers of mankind have been satisfied with much less. The main constituents of a satisfied life appear to be two, either of which by itself is often found sufficient for the purpose: tranquility and excitement. With much tranquility, many find that they can be content with very little pleasure; with much excitement, many can reconcile themselves to a considerable quantity of pain. There is assuredly no inherent impossibility of enabling even the mass of mankind to unite both, since the two are so far from being incompatible that they are in natural alliance, the prolongation of either being a preparation for, and exciting a wish for, the other. It is only those in whom indolence amounts to a vice that do not desire excitement after an interval of repose; it is only those in whom the need of excitement is a disease that feel the tranquility which follows excitement dull and insipid, instead of pleasurable in direct proportion to the excitement which preceded it. When people who are tolerably fortunate in their outward lot do not find in life sufficient enjoyment to make it valuable to them, the cause generally is caring for nobody but themselves. To those who have neither public nor private affections, the excitements of life are much curtailed, and in any case dwindle in value as the time approaches when all selfish interests must be terminated by death; while those who leave after them objects of personal affection, and especially those who have also cultivated a fellow-feeling with the collective interests of mankind, retain as lively an interest in life on the eve of death as in the vigor of youth and health. Next to selfishness, the principal cause which makes life unsatisfactory is want of mental cultivation. A cultivated mind— I do not mean that of a philosopher, but any mind to which the fountains of knowledge have been opened, and which has been taught, in any tolerable degree, to exercise its faculties—finds sources of inexhaustible interest in all that surrounds it: in the objects of nature, the achievements of art, the imaginations of poetry, the incidents of history, the ways of mankind, past and present, and their prospects in the future. It is possible, indeed, to become indifferent to all this. and that too without having

exhausted a thousandth part of it, but only when one has had from the beginning no moral or human interest in these things, and has sought in them only the gratification of curiosity.

Now there is absolutely no reason in the nature of things why an amount of mental culture sufficient to give an intelligent interest in these objects of contemplation should not be the inheritance of every one born in a civilized country. As little is there an inherent necessity that any human being should be a selfish egotist, devoid of every feeling or care but those which center in his own miserable individuality. Something far superior to this is sufficiently common even now, to give ample earnest of what the human species may be made. Genuine private affections and a sincere interest in the public good are possible, though in unequal degrees, to every rightly brought up human being. In a world in which there is so much to interest, so much to enjoy, and so much also to correct and improve, every one who has this moderate amount of moral and intellectual requisites is capable of an existence which may be called enviable; and unless such a person, through bad laws or subjection to the will of others, is denied the liberty to use the sources of happiness within his reach, he will not fail to find this enviable existence, if he escape the positive evils of life, the great sources of physical and mental suffering —such as indigence, disease, and the unkindness, worthlessness, or premature loss of objects of affection. The main stress of the problem lies, therefore, in the contest with these calamities from which it is a rare good fortune entirely to escape; which, as things now are, cannot be obviated, and often cannot be in any material degree mitigated. Yet no one whose opinion deserves a moment's consideration can doubt that most of the great positive evils of the world are in themselves removable, and will, if human affairs continue to improve, be in the end reduced within narrow limits. Poverty, in any sense implying suffering, may be completely extinguished by the wisdom of society combined with the good sense and providence of individuals. Even that most intractable of enemies, disease, may be indefinitely reduced in dimensions by good physical and moral education and proper control of noxious influences, while the progress of science holds out a promise for the future of still more direct conquests over this detestable foe. And every advance in that direction relieves us from some, not only of the chances which cut short our own lives, but, what concerns us still more, which deprive us of those in whom our happiness is wrapt up. As for vicissitudes of fortune and other disappointments connected with worldly circumstances, these are principally the effect either of gross imprudence, of ill-regulated desires, or of bad or imperfect social institutions. All the grand sources, in short, of human suffering are in a great degree, many of them almost entirely, conquerable by human care and effort; and though their removal is grievously slow—though a long succession of generations will perish in the breach before the conquest is completed, and this world becomes all that, if will and knowledge were not wanting, it might easily be made—yet every mind sufficiently intelligent and generous to bear a part, however small and inconspicuous, in the endeavour will draw a noble enjoyment from the contest itself, which he would not for any bribe in the form of selfish indulgence consent to be without.

And this leads to the true estimation of what is said by the objectors concerning the possibility and the obligation of learning to do without happiness. Unquestionably it is possible to do without happiness; it is done involuntarily by nineteen-twentieths of mankind, even in those parts of our present world which are least deep in barbarism; and it often has to be done voluntarily by the hero or the martyr, for the sake of something which he prizes more than his individual happiness. But this something, what is it, unless the happiness of others or some of the requisites of happiness? It is noble to be capable of resigning entirely one's own portion of happiness, or chances of it; but, after all, this self-sacrifice must be for some end; it is not its own end; and if we are told that its end is not happiness but virtue, which is better than happiness, I ask, would the sacrifice be made if the hero or martyr did not believe that it would earn for others immunity from similar sacrifices? Would it be made if he thought that his renunciation of happiness for himself would produce no fruit for any of his fellow creatures, but to make their lot like his, and place them also in the condition of persons who have renounced happiness? All honor to those who can abnegate for themselves the personal enjoyment of life when by such renunciation they contribute worthily to increase the amount of happiness in the world; but he who does it or professes to do it for any other purpose is no more deserving of admiration than the ascetic mounted on his pillar. He may be an inspiriting proof of what men *can* do, but assuredly not an example of what they *should*.

Though it is only in a very imperfect state of the world's arrangements that any one can best serve the happiness of others by the absolute sacrifice of his own, yet, so long as the world is in that imperfect state, I fully acknowledge that the readiness to make such a sacrifice is the highest virtue which can be found in man. I will add that in this condition of the world, paradoxical as the assertion may be, the conscious ability to do without happiness gives the best prospect of realizing such happiness as is attainable.

For nothing except that consciousness can raise a person above the chances of life, by making him feel that, let fate and fortune do their worst, they have not power to subdue him; which, once felt, frees him from excess of anxiety concerning the evils of life, and enables him, like many a Stoic in the worst times of the Roman Empire, to cultivate in tranquility the sources of satisfaction accessible to him, without concerning himself about the uncertainty of their duration any more than about their inevitable end.

Meanwhile, let utilitarians never cease to claim the morality of self-devotion as a possession which belongs by as good a right to them as either to the Stoic or to the Transcendentalist. The utilitarian mortality does recognize in human beings the power of sacrificing their own greatest good for the good of others. It only refuses to admit that the sacrifice is itself a good. A sacrifice which does not increase or tend to increase the sum total of happiness, it considers as wasted. The only self-renunciation which it applauds is devotion to the happiness, or to some of the means of happiness, of others, either of mankind collectively or of individuals within the limits imposed by the collective interests of mankind.

I must again repeat what the assailants of utilitarianism seldom have the justice to acknowledge, that the happiness which forms the utilitarian standard of what is right in conduct is not the agent's own happiness but that of all concerned. As between his own happiness and that of others, utilitarianism requires him to be as strictly impartial as a disinterested and benevolent spectator. In the golden rule of Jesus of Nazareth, we read the complete spirit of the ethics of utility. "To do as you would be done by," and "to love your neighbor as yourself," constitute the ideal perfection of utilitarian morality. As the means of making the nearest approach to this ideal, utility would enjoin, first, that laws and social arrangements should place the happiness or (as, speaking practically, it may be called) the interest of every individual as nearly as possible in harmony with the interest of the whole; and, secondly, that education and opinion, which have so vast a power over human character, should so use that power as to establish in the mind of every individual an indissoluble association between his own happiness and the good of the whole, especially between his own happiness and the practice of such modes of conduct, negative and positive, as regard for the universal happiness prescribes; so that not only he may be unable to conceive the possibility of happiness to himself, consistently with conduct opposed to the general good, but also that a direct impulse to promote the general good may be in every individual one of the habitual motives of action, and the sentiments connected therewith may fill a large and prominent place in every human being's sentient existence. If the impugners of the utilitarian morality represented it to their own minds in this its true character, I know not what recommendation possessed by any other morality they could possibly affirm to be wanting to it; what more beautiful or more exalted developments of human nature any other ethical system can be supposed to foster, or what springs of action, not accessible to the utilitarian, such systems rely on for giving effect to their mandates. . . .

*14. Pleasure for Pleasure's Sake**

F. H. BRADLEY (1846–1924)

It is an old story, a theme too worn for the turning of sentences, and yet too living a moral not to find every day a new point and to break a fresh heart, that our lives are wasted in the pursuit of the impalpable, the search for the impossible and the unmeaning. Neither today nor yesterday, but throughout the whole life of the race, the complaint has gone forth that all is vanity; that the ends for which we live and we die are "mere ideas," illusions begotten on the brain by the wish of the heart—poor phrases that stir the blood, until experience or reflection for a little, and death for all time, bring with it disenchantment and quiet. Duty for duty's sake, life for an end beyond sense, honor, and beauty, and love for the invisible—all these are first felt, and then seen to be dream and shadow and unreal vision. And our cry and our desire is for something that will satisfy us, something that we know and do not only think, something that is real and solid, that we can lay hold of and be sure of and that will not change in our hands. We have said good-by to our transcendent longings, we have hidden a sad but an eternal farewell to the hopes of our own and of the world's too credulous youth; we have parted forever from our early loves, from our fancies and aspirations beyond the human. We seek for the tangible and we find it in this world; for the knowl-

edge which can never deceive, and that is the certainty of our own well-being; we seek for the palpable, and we feel it; for the end which will satisfy us as men, and we find it, in a word, in happiness.

Happiness! Is that climax, or pathos, or cruel irony? Happiness is the end? Yes, happiness is the end which indeed we all reach after; for what more can we wish than that all should be well with us—that our wants should be filled and the desire of our hearts be gratified? And happiness cannot escape us, we must know it when we find it? Oh yes, it would be strange indeed to come to such a consummation and never to know it. And happiness is real and palpable, and we can find it by seeking it? Alas! the one question which no one can answer is, What is happiness?—which everyone in the end can answer is, what happiness is not. It has been called by every name among men, and has been sought on the heights and in the depths; it has been wooed in all the shapes on earth and in heaven, and what man has won it? Its name is a proverb for the visionary object of a universal and a fruitless search; of all the delusions which make a sport of our lives it is not one, but is one common title which covers and includes them all, which shows behind each in turn, but to vanish and appear behind another. The man who says that happiness is his mark, aims at nothing apart from the ends of others. He seeks the illusory goal of all men; and he differs

* From F. H. Bradley, *Ethical Studies* (1876).

from the rest that are and have been not at all, or only in his assertion that happiness is to be found by seeking it.

"But happiness," will be the reply, "is vague because it has been made so—is impalpable because projected beyond the solid world into the region of cloud and fiction—is visionary because diverted from its object, and used as a name for visions. Such ends are not happiness. But there is an end which men can seek and do find, which never deceives, which is real and tangible and felt to be happiness—and that end is pleasure. Pleasure is something we can be sure of, for it dwells not we know not where, but here in ourselves. It is found, and it can be found; it is the end for man and for beast, the one thing worth living for, the one thing they do live for and do really desire, and the only thing they ought to set before them. This is real, because we feel and know it to be real; and solely by partaking, or seeming to partake, in its reality do other ends pass for, and impose on the world as happiness."

We said that to answer the question, what happiness is, has been thought impossible; that there are few who, in the end, are unable to say what happiness is not. And if there be any one thing which well-nigh the whole voice of the world, from all ages, nations, and sorts of men, has agreed to declare is *not* happiness, that thing is pleasure and the search for it. Not in the school alone but round us in life, we see that to identify in the beginning pleasure and happiness leads in the end to the confession that there "is nothing in it," εὐδαιμονίαν ὅλως ἀδύνατον εἶναι. The "pursuit of pleasure" is a phrase which calls for a smile or a sigh, since the world has learned that, if pleasure is the end, it is an end which must not be made one, and is found there most where it is not sought. If to find pleasure is the end and science is the means, then indeed we must say

Die hohe Kraft
Der Wissenschaft,
Der ganzen Welt verborgen!
Und wer nicht denkt,
Dem wird sie geschenkt,
Er hat sie ohne Sorgen.[1]

Common opinion repeats its old song that the search for pleasure is the coarsest form of vulgar delusion, that if you want to be happy in the sense of pleased you must not think of pleasure, but, taking up some accredited form of living, must make that your end, and in that case, with moderately good fortune, you will be happy; if you are not, then it must be your own fault; but that, if you go further, you are like to fare worse. You had better *not* try elsewhere, or, at least, not for pleasure elsewhere.

So far the weight of popular experience bears heavily against the practicability of Hedonism. But Hedonism, we shall be told, does not of necessity mean the search by the individual for the pleasure of the individual. It is to such selfish pleasure-seeking alone that the proverbial condemnation of Hedonism applies. The end for modern Utilitarianism is not the pleasure of one, but the pleasure of all, the maximum of pleasurable, and minimum of painful, feeling in all sentient organisms, and not in my sentient organism; and against the possibility of realizing such an end common opinion has nothing to say. This we admit to be true, but in this shape the question has never fairly come before the popular mind; and it would be well to remember that if the individual, when he seeks pleasure, fails in his individual

---

[1] Thus rendered in Mr. C. Kegan Paul's version of *Faust:*

The highest might
Of science quite
    Is from the world concealed!

But whosoe'er
Expends no care,
    To him it is revealed.

aim, such a fact ought at least to inspire us with some doubt whether, when mankind seek the pleasure of the sentient world, that end be so much more real and tangible.

Opinion, then, as the result of popular experience so far as it has touched on the question, would appear to be against the practicability of Hedonism. Still vulgar opinion must not count against philosophical theory, though it certainly may against the still more vulgar preconception as to the reality and palpable character of pleasure.

But Hedonism, we must remember, does not assert itself simply as a theory which can be worked. It puts itself forward as moral, as the one and only possible account of morality. The fact is the moral world, Hedonism is the supposed explanation; and if we find that non-theoretical persons, who have direct cognizance of the fact, with but few exceptions reject the explanation, that ought to have great weight with us. And the case stands thus undeniably. When moral persons without a theory on the matter are told that the moral end for the individual and the race is the getting a maximum surplusage of pleasurable feeling, and that there is nothing in the whole world which has the smallest moral value except this end and the means to it, there is no gainsaying that they repudiate such a result. They feel that there are things "we should choose even if no pleasure came from them"; and that if we choose these things, being good, for ourselves, then we must choose them also for the race, if we care for the race as we do for ourselves. We may be told, indeed, that a vulgar objection of this sort is founded on a misunderstanding, and to this we shall have to recur; but for the present we prefer to believe that never, except on a misunderstanding, has the moral consciousness in any case acquiesced in Hedonism. And we must say, I think, that supposing it pos-

sible that Hedonism could be worked, yet common moral opinion is decided against its being, what it professes to be, a sufficient account of morals.

For morality and religion believe in some end for the man and for the race to be worked out; some idea to be realized in mankind and in the individual, and to be realized even though it should not be compatible with the minimum of pain and maximum of pleasure in human souls and bodies, to say nothing at all about other sentient organisms. The end for our morality and our religion is an idea (or call it what you will), which is thought of both as the moving principle and final aim of human progress, and that idea (whatever else it may be, or may not be) most certainly is not the mere idea of an increase of pleasure and a diminution of pain. What we represent to ourselves as the goal of our being we must take as a law for the guidance alike both of this and that man, and of the race as a whole; and if you do not use the vague phrase "happiness," but say fairly and nakedly that you mean "feeling pleased as much as possible and as long as possible," then you cannot, I think, bring the Hedonistic end before the moral consciousness without a sharp collision.

Now I am not saying that what is commonly believed must be true. I am perfectly ready to consider the possibility of the ordinary moral creed being a mistaken one; but the point which I wish to emphasize is this: The fact is the moral world, both on its external side of the family, society, and the State, and the work of the individual in them, and again, on its internal side of moral feeling and belief. The theory which will account for and justify these facts as a whole is the true moral theory; and any theory which cannot account for these facts may in some other way, perhaps, be a very good and correct theory, but it is *not* a *moral* theory. Supposing every other ethical theory to be false, it does not follow that therefore Hedonism is a true ethical theory. It does not follow because it has refuted its "intuitive moralists" (or what not?) that therefore it accounts for the facts of the moral consciousness. Admitted that it is workable, it has still to be proved moral—moral in the sense of explaining, not explaining away morality. And it can be proved moral by the refuting of some other theory, only on the strength of two assumptions. The first is that there must be some existing theory which is a sufficient account of morals, and that is an unproved assumption; the second is that the disjunction, that the "either—or" of "intuitive" and "utilitarian" is complete and exhaustive, and that is a false assumption.[2]

At the cost of repetition, and perhaps of wearisomeness, I must dwell a little longer on the ordinary consciousness. There are times indeed when we feel that increase of progress means increase of pleasure and that it is hard to consider them apart. I do not mean those moments (if there are such) when the music-hall theory of life seems real to us, but the hours (and there must be such) when advance in goodness and knowledge, and in the pleasure of them, have been so intermingled together, and brought home as one to our minds (in our own case or in that of others), that we feel it impossible to choose one and not also choose the other. And there doubtless are hours again, when all that is called progress seems so futile and disappointing that we bitterly feel "increase of knowledge" is indeed "increase of sorrow," and that he who thinks least is happiest; when we envy the beasts their lives without a past or a future, their heedless joys and easily forgotten griefs; and when for ourselves, and if for ourselves then for others, we could wish to cease or be as they are *"von allem Wissensqualm entladen."* These are the extremes; but when in the season neither of our exaltation nor of our depression we soberly consider the matter, then we choose most certainly for ourselves (and so also for others) what we think the highest life, *i. e.*, the life with the highest functions; and in that life we certainly include the feeling of pleasure; but if the alternative is presented to us of lower functions with less pains and greater pleasures, or higher functions with greater pains and less pleasures, then we must choose the latter.

And the alternative is conceivable. If it is impossible in fact that a stage of progress could come where by advancing further in the direction of what seems to it highest, humanity would decrease its surplus of pleasure (and I do not see how it is to be proved impossible)[3]—

---

[2] "Whoever would disprove the theory which makes utility our guide must produce another principle that were a surer and better guide.

"Now if we reject *utility* as the index to God's commands, we must assent to the theory of hypothesis which supposes a *moral sense*. One of the adverse theories which regard the nature of that index is certainly true."—AUSTIN's *Jurisprudence*, I, 79. [Austin was a Benthamite.—P. P. W.]

If we wished to cross an unknown bog, and two men came to us, of whom the one said, "Some one must know the way over this bog, for there must be a way, and you see there is no one here beside us two, and therefore one of us two must be able to guide you. And the other man does not know the way, as you can soon see; therefore I must"—should we answer, "Lead on, I follow"? Philosophy would indeed be the easiest of studies if we might arrive at truth by assuming that one of two accounts must be true, and prove the one by disproving the other; but in philosophy this is just what cannot be done.

---

[3] Mr. Mill's assertion that "most of the great positive evils of the world are in themselves removable" (*Utilitarianism*, p. 21), calls for no remark; but the reader may perhaps think that Mr. Spencer's doctrine of the Evanescence of Evil (*Social Statics*, p. 73, ff.) should be noticed. His proof seems (so far as I understand it) to rest on the following assumptions:

yet, at all events, the alternative can be brought directly before the mind. Advance in this direction (the higher) at the cost of pleasure, on the whole, after the pleasure of advance is counted in; advance in that direction (the lower) with the gain of pleasure, on the whole, even after the regrets of the nonadvance have been subtracted. The necessity for choice can be imagined; and there is no doubt, on the one side, what the choice of the moral man would be; there is no doubt, on the other side, what, if pleasure were the end, it ought to be. In such a case, what we think the most moral man and people would be therefore the most certain to act immorally, if Hedonism is morality.

But these consequences, it will be urged, do not apply to modern Utilitarianism. That creed, we shall be told, whether for the man or the race is high and self-sacrificing. For not only does it place the end in the pleasure of all, not the pleasure of one; but in addition it distinguishes pleasures according to their quality. The greatest quantity of pleasure is not the end; there are pleasures we desire in preference to others

(1) The natural environment of mankind is stationary. Can this be proved?

(2) The spiritual environment of mankind is stationary. Not only can this not be proved, but the opposite is, or ought to be, supposed by the doctrine of evolution. Progress must alter the environment.

(3) Apparently children are to be born in harmony with their surroundings and remain so till death.

(4) Moral evil in the sense of moral badness, is to disappear. It will be impossible to oppose one's private good to the general good, and act according to the former. Self-will will cease and with it the pain it brings.

All these assumptions, I think, are wanted. Nos. 3 and 4 represent absolute impossibilities, so far as I understand the matter. No. 2 is impossible on the supposition of continual progress. No other supposition can be proved to be true; and No. 1 cannot, I believe, be proved. How far Mr. Spencer's own teaching contradicts these assumptions is of no importance here.

even at the cost of discontent and dissatisfaction. These pleasures, then, are to be preferred, and these are the higher pleasures. Such a doctrine, it will be added, is surely moral.

The doctrine, we admit, has done homage to popular opinion, so far as, for the sake of it, to sacrifice its own consistency and desert its principle. This we shall have to prove later on. But yet we cannot for a moment think that it has succeeded in satisfying the demands of morality. Virtue is still a mere means to pleasure in ourselves or others and, as anything beyond, is worthless, if not immoral; is not virtue at all. What is right is determined by that which is most "grateful to the feelings" of connoisseurs in pleasures, who have tried them all. No compromise is possible on this point. Ordinary morality is clear that when it aims at virtue for itself and others, it has not got its eye on wages or perquisites; its motive, in the sense of the object of its conscious desire, is not the anticipated feeling of pleasure. What it has before its mind is an object, an act or an event, which is not (for itself at least) a state of the feeling self, in itself or others. To say that, in desiring the right, it proposes to itself a pleasure to be got by the right is to assert in the face of facts. To the moral mind that feeling is an accompaniment or a consequent and it may be thought of as such. But to think of it as more, to propose it as the end to which the act or objective event are the means, and nothing but the means, is simply to turn the moral point of view upside down. You may argue psychologically, if you will, and say that what is desired *is* pleasure (this is false, as we shall show in another Essay), and we are ready for argument's sake to admit it here; for here it makes not the smallest difference. The moral consciousness does not *think* it acts to get pleasure, and the point here at issue is not whether what it believes, and must believe, is or is not a psychological illusion, but whether Utilitarianism is in harmony therewith.

Hedonism in any form must teach "morality is a means to pleasure"; and whether that pleasure is to be got *in* morality or merely *by* morality, yet the getting of the pleasure is the ultimate aim. Pleasure for pleasure's sake is the end and nothing else is an end in any sense except so far as it is a means to pleasure. This, we repeat once more, is absolutely irreconcilable with ordinary moral beliefs. And not only is Hedonism repudiated by those beliefs as immoral, but as we saw, so far as the popular mind has pronounced upon it, it is also declared to be impracticable. These two points we wished to make clear, and with this result we have finished the first or introductory part of our undertaking.

It remains to ask in the second place, Why is it that pleasure-seeking as the search for my pleasure is declared vain, and pleasure itself impalpable and misleading, a something which gives us no standard to work by and no end to aim at, no system to realize in our lives? We must look for an answer to the nature of pleasure.

Pleasure and pain are feelings and they are nothing but feelings. It would perhaps be right to call them the two simple modes of *self*-feeling; but we are not here concerned with psychological accuracy. The point which we wish to emphasize and which we think is not doubtful is that, considered psychically, they are nothing whatever but states of the feeling self. This means that they exist in me only as long as I feel them, and only as I feel them, that beyond this they have no reference to anything else, no validity and no meaning whatever. They are "subjective" because they neither have, nor pretend to, reality beyond this or that subject. They are as they are felt to be, but they tell us nothing. In one word. they have no content; they

are as states of us, but they have nothing for us.

I do not think it is necessary to dwell on this matter. Let us proceed to the application. The practical end, if it is to be a practical goal and standard, must present itself to us as some definite unity, some concrete whole that we can realize in our acts, and carry out in our life. And pleasure (as pain) we find to be nothing but a name which stands for a series of this, that, and the other feelings, which are not except in the moment or moments that they are felt, which have as a series neither limitation of number, beginning nor end, nor in themselves any reference at all, any of them, beyond themselves. To realize, as such, the self which feels pleasure and pain means to realize this infinite perishing series.[4] And it is clear at once that this is not what is required for a practical end. Let us see the problem a little closer.

On the one side our Hedonist is aware, however dimly, of himself not as this, nor that, nor the other particular feeling or satisfaction, but as something which is not this, that, or the other, and yet is real, and is to be realized. Self-realization, as we saw, was the object of desire; and so, as above, on the one hand is the self, which we are forced to look on as a whole which is in its parts, as a living totality, as a universal present throughout, and constituted by its particulars; and this self is setting out, however unaware, to find itself as such and to satisfy itself as such, or not to find itself

---

[4] It is an abstraction, no doubt, to consider pleasurable feelings as mere pleasures, but it is not our abstraction but the Hedonist's. It is an abstraction, again, to consider feelings as merely particular. They cannot be that if they are *our* feelings, if they are the feelings of a self. But we can make our mere feeling self, as the self which feels mere pleasure and pain an object only in the series of its feelings, and these (as such a series) have no relations, each either within itself or beyond itself.

and not to satisfy itself at all. On the other side is the mere feeling self, the series of particular satisfactions, which the self has come (how, we need not here inquire) to take as its reality and as the sole possible field for its self-realization.

The point to observe is the heterogeneous nature of the self to be satisfied, and of the proposed satisfaction, and the consequent impossibility of a solution for the problem. The practical difficulty is soon forced on the seeker after pleasure.

Pleasures, we saw, were a perishing series. This one comes and the intense self-feeling proclaims satisfaction. It is gone and *we* are not satisfied. It was not that one, then, but this one now; and this one now is gone. It was not that one, then, but another and another; but another and another do not give us what we want; we are still left eager and confident till the flush of feeling dies down, and when that is gone there is nothing left. We are where we began, so far as the getting happiness goes, and we have not found ourselves, and we are not satisfied.

This is common experience and it is the practical refutation of Hedonism or of the seeking happiness in pleasure. Happiness for the ordinary man neither means a pleasure nor a number of pleasures. It means in general the finding of himself or the satisfaction of himself as a whole, and in particular it means the realization of his concrete ideal of life. "*This* is happiness," he says, not identifying happiness with one pleasure or a number of them, but understanding by it, "*in* this is become fact what I have at heart." But the Hedonist has said, Happiness is pleasure, and the Hedonist knows that happiness is a whole.[5] How,

then, if pleasures make no system, if they are a number of perishing particulars, can the whole that is sought be found in them? It is the old question, how find the universal in mere particulars? And the answer is the old answer, In their sum. The self is to be found, happiness is to be realized, in the sum of the moments of the feeling self. The practical direction is get *all* pleasures and you will have got happiness; and we saw above its well-known practical issue in weariness and dissatisfaction.

The theoretical reason is simple. The sum or the All of pleasures is a self-contradiction, and therefore the search for it is futile. A series which has no beginning, or, if a beginning yet no end, cannot be summed; there *is* no All, and yet the All is postulated, and the series is to be summed. But it cannot be summed till we are dead, and then, if we have realized it, we, I suppose, do not know it, and we are not happy; and before death we cannot have realized it, because there is always more to come, the series is always incomplete. What is the sum of pleasures and how many go to the sum? All of how many is it, and when are we at the end? After death or in life? Do you mean a finite number? Then more is beyond. Do you mean an infinite number? Then we never reach

<hr/>

[5] I am quite aware that with *some* Hedonistic writers "happiness" is not distinguished from "pleasure." They are said to be simply the same. This is an outrage on language, which avenges itself in the confusion described

below, footnote, p. 132. But the argument of the text is not affected by it. If happiness = pleasure, then "get happiness" = "get pleasure." What is pleasure? It is a general name, and "get happiness" will mean "get a general name." But a general name is not a reality, and cannot be got. The reality is the particular. "Get happiness" will mean then, "get some one pleasure." Is that it? No, we are to get all the happiness we can. And so, after all our quibbling, "get happiness" *does* mean "get the largest possible sum or collection of pleasures." Mr. Green, in his Introduction to Hume's *Treatise* (II, 7), has made this so clear that one might have hoped it could not have been misunderstood. On the whole subject of this Essay let me recommend the student to consult him.

it; for a further pleasure is conceivable, and nothing is infinite which has something still left outside of it. We must say, then, that no one ever reaches happiness. Or do you mean as much pleasure as a man can get? Then every one at every point is happy and happiness is always complete, for, by the Hedonistic theory, we all of us get as much as we can.[6]

The Hedonist has taken the universal

in the sense of all the particulars, and in this sense, here as everywhere, since the particulars are arising and perishing, the universal has no truth nor reality. The true universal, which unconsciously he seeks, is infinite, for it is a concrete whole concluded within itself, and complete; but the false universal is infinite in the sense of a process *ad indefinitum*. It is a demand for, a would-be, completeness, with everlasting present incompleteness. It is always finite, and so

---

[6] I am anxious that the reader should not pass by this argument as a verbal puzzle. Beside it there is certainly much more to be said against Hedonism; but the root of Hedonism is not understood, until it is seen (1) that pleasure, as such, is an abstraction (cf. Essay VII); (2) that the sum of pleasures is a fiction. On this latter head I fear that I must further enlarge.

"Get all you can" is a familiar phrase, and is very good sense. I say to a boy, "Go into that room and fetch out all the apples you can carry"; and there is no nonsense in that. There is a given finite sum of apples, which I do not know, but which, under all the conditions, is the maximum. This is got and brought, and the task is accomplished. Why then not say, "Get all the pleasures you can"? For these reasons. (a) Let it be granted that there is a given finite sum of pleasures for the man to get; yet *he* never *has* got it. Only death puts an end to the work; and after death nothing, or the same unfinished task. (b) There is really no such sum. A pleasure *is* only in the time during which I feel it. A past pleasure means either an idea, or *another* (secondary) impression. *Itself* is nothing at all; I did get it, I have not got it; and the "did get" is not the pleasure. In order to have the sum of pleasures, I must have them all *now,* which is impossible. Thus you cannot reach the end, and the effort to reach it is not in itself desirable. You may say, if you please, The end is an illusion, and the effort worthless in itself, but this particular effort gives a specific pleasure, which is the end. But if you do this, then you either (i) sink considerations of quantity, and the *greatest* happiness principle is given up; or (ii) the same problem as above breaks out with respect to the sum of specific pleasures.

If you admit that to get the greatest sum in life is unmeaning, then arises the question, Can you approximate, and make approximation the end? I will not raise the question, Can you approximate to a confessed fiction? and to avoid that, let us say, The end is for

me, at any given moment of life, to be having then the greatest possible number of units of pleasure. Here we fall into the dilemma given in the text. Either happiness is never reached, or there is no one who does not reach the most perfect happiness imaginable.

(1) *If* happiness means the greatest possible number of units then I *never* reach it. Whatever I have is finite, and beyond every finite sum another unit is conceivable.

(2) *If* happiness means having all I can get, no matter how much or how little, then, given the truth of the common Hedonistic psychology, every man at every moment has absolute happiness. This is very obvious. "Why so?" comes the objection, "if Mr. A. had done otherwise he would have had more pleasure." "You mean," I answer, "*If* he had been Mr. B." When, in ordinary language, we say, "He did not do what he could, or what was possible," we mean, "His energy did expend itself in this direction, failed to do so in that," and we impute inability as a fault, where it is the result of previous misdirection. But the common Hedonist cannot say this, because, according to him, there is only one possible direction of expenditure, *i. e.,* the greatest seeming pleasure. You have no choice between pleasure and something else, you can do nothing but gravitate to what seems most pleasant, and you cannot alter what seems except by your will, *i. e.,* by gravitation to what seems most pleasant. Every one has done his conceivable utmost to approximate and therefore is absolutely happy.

I think the better plan for the Hedonist would be to make happiness a fixed finite sum, which can be got, and beyond which nothing counts; and similarly to fix an unhappiness point on the scale; but we have pursued the subject far enough.

The question of the approximate character of all morality will be discussed in another place.

never is realized. The sum is never finished; when the last pleasure is reached we stand no nearer our end than at the first. It would be so, even if the pleasures did not die; but in addition the past pleasures have died; and we stand with heart unsatisfied and hands empty, driven on and beyond forever in pursuit of a delusion, through a weary round which never advances. . . .

Hedonism *is* bankrupt. With weariness we have pursued it, so far as was necessary, through its various shapes—from the selfish doctrine of the individual to the self-sacrificing spirit of modern Utilitarianism. We have seen that in every form it gives an end which is illusory and impalpable. We have seen that its efforts to compromise with the moral consciousness are useless; that in no shape will it give us a creed that holds water, and that will justify to the inquiring mind those moral beliefs which it is not prepared for the sake of any theory to relinquish. Whatever we may think of those who embrace the doctrine, whatever may be its practical results, yet, theoretically considered, we have seen, I trust, that it is immoral and false, and are ready to endorse the saying, 'Ηδονὴ τέλος, πόρνης δόγμα.' [7]

Modern Utilitarianism has a good object in view. Though we understand it differently, we have the same object in view, and that is why we are at issue with Utilitarianism.

We agree that it is desirable to have a standard of virtue which is palpable and "objective"; and therefore we refuse to place the end in what is most impalpable, what is absolutely and entirely "subjective."

We agree that the end is not the realization of an abstract idea; and therefore we refuse to take as our end the greatest amount of pleasure, for that is an abstract idea, and it is altogether unrealizable.

We agree that the end is not a "thing-in-itself," is not Heaven knows what or where, but is the end for us as men, τἀνθρώπινον ἀγαθόν; and therefore we refuse to find it in that element of the mind which is *least* distinctively human, and shared with us by the beasts that perish.

We agree that it must be κτητὸν ἀνθρώπῳ [a human possession]; and therefore we refuse to seek for it in that which has become a proverb for its fallaciousness.

We agree in the refusal to separate actions and consequences; and therefore we refuse to abstract from action one moment, viz., the accompanying or the consequent feeling, and put our test in the more or less of that.

We agree that happiness is the end; and therefore we say pleasure is not the end.

We agree that pleasure is *a* good; we say it is not *the* good.

We agree (strange fellowship!) with the author of the *Essay on Liberty* in affirming the ὃ πᾶσι δοκεῖ τουτ' εἶναι φαμέν; and therefore we dissent from a theory which gives the lie to the moral consciousness and whose psychological basis destroys and makes unmeaning the maxim.

We agree to make the self-evolution of ourselves and of humanity the end. We refuse to place progress in the greater or less amount of "grateful feeling." We repeat the good old doctrine that the test of higher and lower cannot lie in a feeling which accompanies the exercise of every function, but is to be found in the quality of the function itself. To measure that, we are to go to our idea of man and to his place in creation and his evolution in history.

In one single word, the end and the standard is self-realization, and is not the feeling of self-realizedness.

May we suggest, in conclusion, that of all our Utilitarians there is perhaps not one who has not still a great deal to learn from Aristotle's *Ethics?* . . .

---

[7] "Pleasure as the end is a pernicious doctrine."—Translated by P. P. W.

15. *Does Human Nature Change?* *

JOHN DEWEY

I have come to the conclusion that those who give different answers to the question I have asked in the title of this article are talking about different things. This statement in itself, however, is too easy a way out of the problem to be satisfactory. For there is a real problem, and so far as the question is a practical one instead of an academic one, I think the proper answer is that human nature *does* change.

By the practical side of the question, I mean the question whether or not important, almost fundamental, changes in the ways of human belief and action have taken place and are capable of still taking place. But to put this question in its proper perspective, we have first to recognize the sense in which human nature does not change. I do not think it can be shown that the innate needs of men have changed since man became man or that there is any evidence that they will change as long as man is on the earth.

By "needs" I mean the inherent demands that men make because of their constitution. Needs for food and drink and for moving about, for example, are so much a part of our being that we cannot imagine any condition under which they would cease to be. There are other things not so directly physical that seem to me equally engrained in human nature. I would mention as examples the

need for some kind of companionship; the need for exhibiting energy, for bringing one's powers to bear upon surrounding conditions; the need for both coöperation with and emulation of one's fellows for mutual aid and combat alike; the need for some sort of aesthetic expression and satisfaction; the need to lead and to follow; etc.

Whether my particular examples are well chosen or not does not matter so much as does recognition of the fact that there are some tendencies so integral a part of human nature that the latter would not be human nature if they changed. These tendencies used to be called instincts. Psychologists are now more chary of using that word than they used to be. But the word by which the tendencies are called does not matter much in comparison to the fact that human nature has its own constitution.

Where we are likely to go wrong after the fact is recognized that there is something unchangeable in the structure of human nature is the inference we draw from it. We suppose that the manifestation of these needs is also unalterable. We suppose that the manifestations we have got used to are as natural and as unalterable as are the needs from which they spring.

The need for food is so imperative that we call the persons insane who persistently refuse to take nourishment. But what kinds of food are wanted and used is a matter of acquired habit in-

* From *The Rotarian* (Feb. 1938), with the kind permission of the editor.

fluenced by both physical environment and social custom. To civilized people today, eating human flesh is an entirely unnatural thing. Yet there have been peoples to whom it seemed natural because it was socially authorized and even highly esteemed. There are well-accredited stories of persons, needing support from others, who have refused palatable and nourishing foods because they were not accustomed to them; the alien foods were so "unnatural" they preferred to starve rather than eat them.

Aristotle spoke for an entire social order as well as for himself when he said that slavery existed by nature. He would have regarded efforts to abolish slavery from society as an idle and utopian effort to change human nature where it was unchangeable. For according to him it was not simply the desire to be a master that was engrained in human nature. There were persons who were born with such an inherently slavish nature that it did violence to human nature to set them free.

The assertion that human nature cannot be changed is heard when social changes are urged as reforms and improvements of existing conditions. It is always heard when the proposed changes in institutions or conditions stand in sharp opposition to what exists. If the conservative were wiser, he would rest his objections in most cases, not upon the unchangeability of human nature, but upon the inertia of custom; upon the resistance that acquired habits offer to change after they are once acquired. It is hard to teach an old dog new tricks and it is harder yet to teach society to adopt customs which are contrary to those which have long prevailed. Conservatism of this type would be intelligent and it would compel those wanting change not only to moderate their pace, but also to ask how the changes they desire could be introduced with a minimum of shock and dislocation.

Nevertheless, there are few social changes that can be opposed on the ground that they are contrary to human nature itself. A proposal to have a society get along without food and drink is one of the few that are of this kind. Proposals to form communities in which there is no cohabitation have been made and the communities have endured for a time. But they are so nearly contrary to human nature that they have not endured long. These cases are almost the only ones in which social change can be opposed simply on the ground that human nature cannot be changed.

Take the institution of war, one of the oldest, most socially reputable of all human institutions. Efforts for stable peace are often opposed on the ground that man is by nature a fighting animal and that this phase of his nature is unalterable. The failure of peace movements in the past can be cited in support of this view. In fact, however, war is as much a social pattern as is the domestic slavery which the ancients thought to be an immutable fact.

I have already said that, in my opinion, combativeness is a constituent part of human nature. But I have also said that the manifestations of these native elements are subject to change because they are affected by custom and tradition. War does not exist because man has combative instincts, but because social conditions and forces have led, almost forced, these "instincts" into this channel.

There are a large number of other channels in which the need for combat has been satisfied, and there are other channels not yet discovered or explored into which it could be led with equal satisfaction. There is war against disease, against poverty, against insecurity, against injustice, in which multitudes of persons have found full opportunity for the exercise of their combative tendencies.

The time may be far off when men will cease to fulfill their need for combat by destroying each other and when they will manifest it in common and combined efforts against the forces that are enemies of all men equally. But the difficulties in the way are found in the persistence of certain acquired social customs and not in the unchangeability of the demand for combat.

Pugnacity and fear are native elements of human nature. But so are pity and sympathy. We send nurses and physicians to the battlefield and provide hospital facilities as "naturally" as we change bayonets and discharge machine guns. In early times there was a close connection between pugnacity and fighting, for the latter was done largely with the fists. Pugnacity plays a small part in generating wars today. Citizens of one country do not hate those of another nation by instinct. When they attack or are attacked, they do not use their fists in close combat, but throw shells from a great distance at persons whom they have never seen. In modern wars, anger and hatred come after the war has started; they are effects of war, not the cause of it.

It is a tough job sustaining a modern war; all the emotional reactions have to be excited. Propaganda and atrocity stories are enlisted. Aside from such extreme measures there has to be definite organization, as we saw in the World War, to keep up the morale of even noncombatants. And morale is largely a matter of keeping emotions at a certain pitch; and unfortunately fear, hatred, suspicion, are among the emotions most easily aroused.

I shall not attempt to dogmatize about the causes of modern wars. But I do not think that anyone will deny that they are social rather than psychological, though psychological appeal is highly important in working up a people to the point where they want to fight and in keeping them at it. I do not think, moreover, that anyone will deny that economic conditions are powerful among the social causes of war. The main point, however, is that whatever the sociological causes, they are affairs of tradition, custom, and institutional organization, and these factors belong among the changeable manifestations of human nature, not among the unchangeable elements.

I have used the case of war as a typical instance of what is changeable and what is unchangeable in human nature, in their relation to schemes of social change. I have selected the case because it is an extremely difficult one in which to effect durable changes, not because it is an easy one. The point is that the obstacles in the way are put there by social forces which do change from time to time, not by fixed elements of human nature. This fact is also illustrated in the failures of pacifists to achieve their ends by appeal simply to sympathy and pity. For while, as I have said, the kindly emotions are also a fixed constituent of human nature, the channel they take is dependent upon social conditions.

There is always a great outburst of these kindly emotions in time of war. Fellow feeling and the desire to help those in need are intense during war, as they are at every period of great disaster that comes home to observation or imagination. But they are canalized in their expression; they are confined to those upon our side. They occur simultaneously with manifestation of rage and fear against the other side, if not always in the same person, at least in the community generally. Hence the ultimate failure of pacifist appeals to the kindly elements of native human nature when they are separated from intelligent consideration of the social and economic forces at work.

William James made a great contribution in the title of one of his essays, *The Moral Equivalents of War*. The very title conveys the point I am making. Certain basic needs and emotions are permanent. But they are capable of finding expression in ways that are radically different from the ways in which they now currently operate.

An even more burning issue emerges when there is proposed any fundamental change in economic institutions and relations. Proposals for such sweeping change are among the commonplaces of our time. On the other hand, the proposals are met by the statement that the changes are impossible because they involve an impossible change in human nature. To this statement, advocates of the desired changes are only too likely to reply that the present system or some phase of it is contrary to human nature. The argument *pro* and *con* then gets put on the wrong ground.

As a matter of fact, economic institutions and relations are among the manifestations of human nature that are most susceptible of change. History is living evidence of the scope of these changes. Aristotle, for example, held that paying interest is unnatural, and the Middle Ages reëchoed the doctrine. All interest was usury, and it was only after economic conditions had so changed that payment of interest was a customary and in that sense a "natural" thing, that usury got its present meaning.

There have been times and places in which land was held in common and in which private ownership of land would have been regarded as the most monstrous of unnatural things. There have been other times and places when all wealth was possessed by an overlord and his subjects held wealth, if any, subject to his pleasure. The entire system of credit so fundamental in contemporary financial and industrial life is a modern invention. The invention of the joint stock company with limited liability of individuals has brought about a great change from earlier facts and conceptions of property. I think the need of owning something is one of the native elements of human nature. But it takes either ignorance or a very lively fancy to suppose that the system of ownership that exists in the United States in 1938, with all its complex relations and its interweaving with legal and political supports, is a necessary and unchangeable product of an inherent tendency to appropriate and possess.

Law is one of the most conservative of human institutions; yet through the cumulative effect of legislation and judicial decisions it changes, sometimes at a slow rate, sometimes rapidly. The changes in human relations that are brought about by changes in industrial and legal institutions then react to modify the ways in which human nature manifests itself, and this brings about still further changes in institutions, and so on indefinitely.

It is for these reasons that I say that those who hold that proposals for social change, even of rather a profound character, are impossible and utopian because of the fixity of human nature, confuse the resistance to change that comes from acquired habits with that which comes from original human nature. The savage, living in a primitive society, comes nearer to being a purely "natural" human being than does civilized man. Civilization itself is the product of altered human nature. But even the savage is bound by a mass of tribal customs and transmitted beliefs that modify his original nature, and it is these acquired habits that make it so difficult to transform him into a civilized human being.

The revolutionary radical, on the other hand, overlooks the force of engrained habits. He is right, in my opinion, about the indefinite plasticity of human nature. But he is wrong in thinking that patterns of desire, belief, and purpose do not have a force comparable to the momentum of physical objects once they are set in motion, and comparable to the inertia, the resistance to movement, possessed by these same objects when they are at rest. Habit, not original human nature, keeps things moving most of the time, about as they have moved in the past.

If human nature is unchangeable, then there is no such thing as education and all our efforts to educate are doomed to failure. For the very meaning of education is modification of native human nature in formation of those new ways of thinking, of feeling, of desiring, and of believing that are foreign to raw human nature. If the latter were unalterable, we might have training but not education. For training, as distinct from education, means simply the acquisition of certain skills. Native gifts can be trained to a point of higher efficiency without that development of new attitudes and dispositions which is the goal of education. But the result is mechanical. It is like supposing that while a musician may acquire by practice greater technical ability, he cannot rise from one plane of musical appreciation and creation to another.

The theory that human nature is unchangeable is thus the most depressing and pessimistic of all possible doctrines. If it were carried out logically, it would mean a doctrine of predestination from birth that would outdo the most rigid of theological doctrines. For according to it, persons are what they are at birth and nothing can be done about it, beyond the kind of training that an acrobat might give to the muscular system with which he is originally endowed. If a person is born with criminal tendencies, a criminal he will become and remain. If a person is born with an excessive amount of greed, he will become a person living by predatory activities at the expense of others; and so

on. I do not doubt at all the existence of differences in natural endowment. But what I am questioning is the notion that they doom individuals to a fixed channel of expression. It is difficult indeed to make a silk purse out of a sow's ear. But the particular form which, say, a natural musical endowment will take depends upon the social influences to which he is subjected. Beethoven in a savage tribe would doubtless have been outstanding as a musician, but he would not have been the Beethoven who composed symphonies.

The existence of almost every conceivable kind of social institution at some time and place in the history of the world is evidence of the plasticity of human nature. This fact does not prove that all these different social systems are of equal value, materially, morally, and culturally. The slightest observation shows that such is not the case. But the fact in proving the changeability of human nature indicates the attitude that should be taken toward proposals for social changes. The question is primarily whether they, in special cases, are desirable or not. And the way to answer that question is to try to discover what their consequences would be if they were adopted. Then if the conclusion is that they are desirable, the further question is how they can be accomplished with a minimum of waste, destruction, and needless dislocation.

In finding the answer to this question, we have to take into account the force of existing traditions and customs; of the patterns of action and belief that already exist. We have to find out what forces already at work can be reinforced so that they move toward the desired change and how the conditions that oppose change can be gradually weakened. Such questions as these can be considered on the basis of fact and reason.

The assertion that a proposed change is impossible because of the fixed constitution of human nature diverts attention from the question of whether or not a change is desirable and from the other question of how it shall be brought about. It throws the question into the arena of blind emotion and brute force. In the end, it encourages those who think that great changes can be produced offhand and by the use of sheer violence.

When our sciences of human nature and human relations are anything like as developed as are our sciences of physical nature, their chief concern will be with the problem of how human nature is most effectively modified. The question will not be whether it is capable of change, but of how it is to be changed under given conditions. This problem is ultimately that of education in its widest sense. Consequently, whatever represses and distorts the processes of education that might bring about a change in human dispositions with the minimum of waste puts a premium upon the forces that bring society to a state of deadlock, and thereby encourages the use of violence as a means of social change.

SUGGESTED FURTHER READINGS
FOR CHAPTER TWO

Bible: Book of Job, Isaiah, Gospel of St. Matthew (Sermon on the Mount).
Hippocratic Oath.
Letters of Abélard and Héloïse.
Aristotle, *Nicomachean Ethics.*
Augustine, *Confessions.*
Bentham, J., *Principles of Morals.*
Bergson, H., *Two Sources of Morality and Religion.*
Cohen, F. S., *Ethical Systems and Legal Ideals.*
Darwin, C., *Descent of Man,* ch. 3, "The Moral Sense."
Dewey, J., *Human Nature and Conduct.*
Edel, A., *Ethical Judgment.*
Epictetus, *Discourses* (Stoicism).
Epicurus, *Principal Doctrines* (transl. by C. Bailey).
Hume, D., *Treatise on Morals.*
Huxley, T., *Evolution and Ethics.*
Kropotkin, P., *Memoirs; Mutual Aid.*
Leibniz, G., *Theodicy* ("On the problem of evil").
Melden, A. I., *Ethical Theories: A Book of Readings.*
Mill, J. S., *Utilitarianism.*
Moore, G. E., *Ethics* (Home University Library); *Principia Ethica.*
Nietzsche, F., *Beyond Good and Evil.*
Pascal, B., *Thoughts.*
Plato, *Apology* ("Trial of Socrates"), *Lysis* ("On Friendship"), *Gorgias, Philebus* ("On Pleasure and the Good"); *The Republic.*
Santayana, G., *The Life of Reason.*
Sidgwick, H., *Methods of Ethics.*

Chapter Three

PHILOSOPHY OF POLITICS AND HISTORY

INTRODUCTION

THE trial of Socrates, made immortal by his pupil Plato in the *Apology*, shows how a philosopher courageously faced his enemies' political accusations that he was a speculative atheist, a Sophist who twisted the meanings of good and bad, and thus a corrupter of the youth who were charmed by his clever dialectic. Socrates' method of defense is to question his accuser (Meletus) and bring out contradictions, for example, why would any sensible citizen wish to corrupt and thus weaken the characters of the youth who are soon to be his fellow-citizens, with whom he must cooperate in order to achieve their common-welfare? The good of one is the good of all in an organic society. Self-knowledge also led Socrates to reject the possibility of going into exile among strangers whom he could not question philosophically. Hence, when he was convicted by the majority vote of a jury influenced by demagoguery or ignorance rather than by logic or an understanding of the value of freedom of discussion in a democratic state, Socrates calmly accepted the death penalty. He thus ironically proposed to teach his fellow Athenians for the last time that "an unexamined life is not worth living."

Just how far government may reasonably control the lives of individuals in their various associations with one another is one of the basic problems of all political theory. Political philosophy is concerned with the principles we assume or adopt in order to justify the political controls or laws regulating the lives of members of a state. What are the functions of the state in relation to the ends it serves? The political scientist or sociologist undertakes to answer this question by describing the machinery and operations of government and related institutions as he finds them in different states under different social and historical circumstances. But when he judges their adequacy in relation to the needs and possibilities of enriching the lives of the individuals who constitute society, he is said to be concerned with the philosophical side of politics. It is doubtful whether a political philosophy that disregarded the concrete historical and social circumstances which serve as a testing ground for the desirability of preserving or modifying existing political ideas would be more than an academic enterprise. Both Hobbes and Hegel aimed to *justify* a highly powerful and centralized state. Neither was content with a mere description of forms of government. Marx's revolutionary politics and Dewey's faith in democratic liberalism are both far from being merely descriptions of social and political institutions. They are bold and epochal hypotheses of what man's political life *ought* to be in the light of profound insights into the historical development of man's social existence and the possibilities of transforming it into a richer and fuller life for all. This problem was strikingly expressed in Rousseau's opening statement of his *Social Contract:* "Man is born free, but everywhere he is in chains." What is the social need or justification of the restraints of government on men who desire freedom?

Classical moral philosophers, though mindful of the value of personal freedom, were aware of its natural, social, and political conditions. Plato in his *Republic* pictured the ideal state as "the individual writ large" in order to analyze the conflicting desires and interests within and among men. Plato's ideal state was a perfect system of eternally fixed classes of men. It was intended to serve as the standard for judging existing states. His fixed social classes consisted of an élite ruling group of philosophers guided by pure reason, a soldiery of strength and courage to defend the state, and workers (figuratively representative of man's unruly passions) held in temperate check by obedience to the laws imposed on them. In this scheme, justice was conceived as emerging from the stable and harmonious relations among the three classes, each attending to its own business. Aristotle, judging the practical futility of this perfect state which abolished such age-old institutions as the family and private property among the rulers, constructed his political philosophy with more empirical notions of man's political problems, derived from his study of the different types of political constitutions adopted in the Greek city-states. But both Plato and Aristotle were agreed that some persons are by nature born to be rulers or masters and others to be ruled. If such an anti-democratic assumption is eternally grounded "in the nature of things," it would be foolish (as Hegel later insisted) to ask whether it ought to be so. But those who hold this view that political justice and class distinctions are predetermined once and for all time by "nature" have been challenged on the ground that social and political systems are products of customs, institutions, and conventions which are man-made. Since Plato and Aristotle believed in fixed natures, they were inclined to subordinate the man-made elements of law and politics to the inherent natures of different classes of people.

The metaphysical assumption of "inherent natures" has been used to justify slavery, original sin, the divine right of kings, and the nationalistic notion of a chosen people with a historic mission to perform. We find a much more empirical approach in Machiavelli, the first important modern political philosopher to analyze the state and political history in terms of how rulers and their subjects actually behave in diverse historical circumstances, rather than in terms of how they might or should behave under ideal conditions.

I. Hobbes on Human Nature and the "Social Contract"

Hobbes followed the lead of Machiavelli by attempting to deduce political principles from the actual manifestations of human nature in political relations. He believed that men could not lead a peaceful, civilized life together in society unless they submitted their natural "nasty, brutish and selfish" impulses to man-made laws and government. These man-made laws are not arbitrary but are determined by the immutable constitution of nature and human nature of which we have some knowledge in physics, psychology, and social science ("natural philosophy," "ethics," and "politics" in Hobbes's seventeenth-century language). The two parts of Hobbes's philosophy, "natural" and "civil," correspond approximately to what we call the natural and social sciences.

"The desires and passions of men are in themselves no sin," declares Hobbes. But, as a matter of objective social fact, men are unable to secure freedom to realize their needs without the restraints of law and a government powerful enough to keep the peace. In the absence of such restraining laws and government, men fall into the insecure and war-like "state of nature" where no man's life or possessions enjoy any protection from the brutish impulses and selfishness of human nature. "Enlightened self-interest" in Hobbes's political philosophy means that it is reasonable for men to submit willingly to the sovereign power of the state to punish anyone who breaks the laws, for the latter are made by men for the purpose of protecting one another. To say that government is necessary simply means that we cannot reasonably find a way of living freely in society without accepting the restraints of government through laws of our own making accompanied by penalties severe enough to instill fear in those who are impulsively inclined to disregard the laws.

Hobbes's problem is to show how individual freedom and legal necessity are not only consistent but also inseparable. He tried to incorporate his demonstration in a materialistic and mechanistic system of physical bodies, the human mind, and the state.[1] That was his way of being scientific about politics. In fact, however, his political sagacity owed much more to his psychological observations and long experience with statesmen and political situations in the turbulent civil wars of seventeenth-century England than to his philosophy of physics as a geometric science of matter in motion and of thinking as a form of such motion.

Hobbes's pessimistic view that human nature is essentially anti-social is often contrasted with Rousseau's belief in the innate or primitive goodness and strength of man's inherently social nature. These two opposing views of the characteristics of the state of nature rest on hypotheses about how men would act if they were removed from the restraining influences of social institutions, and customs, and laws. Some empirical idea of what this state of nature would be can be gained by considering a shipwrecked crew on an isolated island. How the starving group would behave would depend on the previous habits as well as on the impulses of each person to look out for himself or for his neighbor. As the natural resources of the island became cultivated, there would be further need for some sort of social organization arising from a mutual understanding of the practical advantages of securing mutual protection through law and government. This mutual and, most often, tacit understanding of the need for political and legal organization is what is meant by "the

---

[1] A materialistic system of philosophy is one which explains everything in terms of the laws of matter and motion. Hobbes believed, as most thinkers in the seventeenth century, that the physical world was a mechanism of geometric structure. However, the axioms of all deductive systems (mechanics or politics) were for Hobbes man-made conventions; hence, he regarded them as binding on our thoughts only because we have agreed to make them so.

social contract" as the basis of the state. Different theories exist among political philosophers as to the nature of this contract. That it is not simply a deliberate agreement of individuals to come together to form a state is obvious enough from man's social history. But certain elements of the theory persist in the doctrine that government is dependent on the consent of the governed and that every man has a natural right to life, liberty, and the pursuit of happiness.

The critical questions here are: What is the extent to which states depend for their existence on coercion and armed force, on the one hand, and the consent of its members, on the other hand? Is government by consent a fact or an ideal? What rôle do propaganda and state-controlled education play in securing consent to government by a particular group? What rôle do the diverse historical traditions, cultural customs, and institutional developments of different peoples in different parts of the world play in molding the character of the state or "the spirit of the laws," as Montesquieu called it?

Hobbes paid insufficient attention to the historical and economic factors that preserve and modify the forms of the state. Hegel stressed the historical force of custom and organized authority by attempting to prove an inner necessity controlling the march of history and the state. Marx regarded the state primarily as the weapon of the ruling class. Dewey regards the state as an instrument for social reform. Thus, the differences among the political philosophies of Plato, Hobbes, Hegel, Marx, and Dewey are intimately related to their theories of history and of human nature. We turn to a brief consideration and comparison of these very influential philosophies of history and of the state.

The significance of most "philosophies of history" lies in what they reveal of tacit ethical or political purposes. If you wish to know, for example, the political attitudes of a nation, read its approved history books or the official pronouncements of its leading statesmen and philosophers concerning the historic mission of their nation and its culture in relation to the rest of the world.

II.   Hegel's Idealistic Theory of History and of the State

Hegel's philosophy of the state is an outcome of a political conservatism supported by a spiritualistic philosophy of history. His idealism assimilates the nature of the world to the nature of man and interprets human nature in terms of its psychical and cultural manifestations. The physical world becomes merely a means for the realization of ideals of an ethical, political, or religious character. Hegel unifies the purposes or values of the human spirit under a single, rational, universal purpose, as absolute and necessary as God is traditionally supposed to be. Instead of a transcendent Being operating from another world of his own, Hegel's God or Absolute Spirit is present or immanent in all the cultural epochs of history as well as in the "lower order" of inanimate nature. Hegel's philosophy of history is a "higher" science of the manifestations of the human spirit in diverse cultural epochs, in the rise and fall of peoples, nations, and empires, in the succession of different types of art, religion, and philosophy. The history of civilization becomes the actual realization of an infinite, eternal, objective Mind as contrasted with the finite, temporal, subjective passions and interests which empiricists like Hobbes took to be the foundations of human history and society. The state becomes in Hegel's philosophy of history the most concrete embodiment of the objective purpose or meaning of the world, for the state exists by rational necessity and makes freedom possible for man by overcoming one-sided "natural" passions and individual or group interests. Individuals whose personal ideals are doomed to frustration do not realize, insists Hegel, what the mature philosophy of Hegel teaches, namely, that whatever is, is right. History teaches us what at once is, must, and ought to be the necessary plan of divine and absolute purpose. "The state is the divine idea on earth" means that there are no accidents, no arbitrary or capricious events, although there are disappointed individuals who in their ignorance may imagine otherwise. Hegel's philosophy teaches acceptance of the *status quo,* for what folly it would be to defy the Absolute!

Beside the logical problem of disentangling the *is,* the *must,* and the *ought,* which Hegel so ingeniously contrives to make identical, there are many other problems raised by Hegel's bold analysis of history as the basis for his justification of the state which he claimed came to perfection in the Prussian monarchy of his own day. The student should examine critically Hegel's answers to the following questions:

Does cultural history fall into the peculiar triadic pattern of the Thesis-Antithesis-Synthesis of Hegel's dialectic? Are the conflicts of vested interests merely logical contradictions? How does each stage of history negate the previous stage and yet salvage the cultural continuity ascribed to world history? How can we reconcile the national spirit of a people with the international spirit of the world-mind? What kinds of freedom do different types of state actually give men? How consistent is Hegel's view of the rôle of great men in history with his subordination of the individual to the inexorable march of the logic of the Absolute? Can there be any genuine temporal development in history if the Absolute has an eternally immutable and predetermined nature? Why must philosophy culminate in Hegel's system? In dealing with social sciences, must we abandon the empirical logic of the natural sciences with their pluralistic and tentative concepts and probabilities, for the dialectic of Hegel with its monistic and absolute conclusions?

In the field of cultural history, Hegel and the German romantic philosophers have made generalizations about the inevitable course of civilization which are no more or less reliable than their knowledge of the various phases of cultural development, the study of whose history they did so much to stimulate: the history of the arts, of literature, of religion, of law, of politics, and of philosophy. The remarkable organic correlations the Hegelians make among the art, philosophy, religion, and politics of any one culture rest on a great deal of cumulative historical evidence, regardless of whether we accept or reject Hegel's *a priori* development of his eternal categories. Bereft of its obscure Hegelianism, the Marxian insight into the close connection between economic and political change rests on *historical* studies of agricultural and industrial capitalism, the industrial revolution, the factory system, and political revolutions, regardless of the laws of dialectics. The further claims of Hegelians and Marxians concerning the cultural developments of history, for example, the cultural superiority of the Prussian military class and the advent of socialism in England or its status in the U.S.S.R., can and should be tested by a critical examination of the alleged philosophical necessity of their historical hypotheses. The nineteenth-century logic of science in Hegel's and Marx's time was intimately fused with the rationalistic assumption that some sort of *necessity* holds for material, empirical, or historical phenomena. But what was meant by historical or empirical necessity? This is a historical and philosophical question of utmost significance, for the answers of both Hegel and Marx and their followers today are assumed by many to be a sufficient ground for drawing what they hold to be inevitable political conclusions concerning the necessity for a concentration of political power in the hands of an organized minority.

One of the principal differences between the philosophies of Marx and Dewey is that Marx retained more of the Hegelian dialectical pattern of historical necessity than does Dewey. This is undoubtedly due to the difference between the nineteenth- and twentieth-century conceptions of scientific law. Though Dewey started his philosophic career as a Hegelian, he soon found Hegel's logic incompatible with that of the experimental methods of the natural sciences which Dewey wished to extend to the social sciences.

III. *Marxian Theory of History and of the State*

Whereas Hegel regarded philosophic reflection as supervening upon historical movements of spiritual forces, Marx claimed he was turning Hegel upside down by giving reflection a more active rôle in the making of history by revolutionary manipulation of class-struggle. This struggle is due to the relations of production inherent in capitalistic economy, namely, the exploitation of the working class by the ruling class. The exploitation of one class by another is explained as a necessary dialectic relation of the changing mode of production. The historical progress of society is towards a workers' democracy. The revolutionary leader's job is to help the exploited working class to become conscious of its true interests and to overthrow the political power of the exploiting class which makes use of the state as a weapon for the subjugation of the masses. Though Marx agrees with Hegel that the state has served certain social ends, like education and protection of life and property, he believes the capitalist state cannot continue to make for progress and has become, in truth, the armed force of the ruling class. The problem here is to distinguish different functions of the state and their relation to one another in different stages of history; e.g., capitalism today is not what it was in Marx's time.

Marx's chief contribution to the philosophy of politics and of history was in showing by concrete historical studies, for example, of agricultural capitalism and the effects of the British factory system, how specific social and political changes were correlated with the changing means of production, for example, the change from an agricultural, rural economy to an industrial, urban one. As a major result, his analysis showed there were no eternal laws of economics or politics as the classical school of Adam Smith and his followers assumed. Though Locke and Ricardo had pointed out how the exchange value of commodities and land was dependent on the labor that went into production and cultivation, they did not develop the consequences of the labor theory of value as Marx did. Marx and Engels, his life-long collaborator, saw in the exploitation of labor the source of the accrual of surplus-value for the capitalist *entrepreneur* with an increasing concentration of wealth in their hands and the intensification of class-struggle as a result of unemployment. The internal collapse of capitalism was predicted on the basis of crises precipitated by increasing lack of purchasing power on the part of the working population and concentration of wealth by the exploiting class. The middle class, on this theory, was to disappear gradually and take its place on one or another side of the barricades that would inevitably be thrown up by a revolutionary uprising of the oppressed class of industrial workers led by the class-conscious leaders of a revolutionary party. The manifesto of this party is printed below. It emphasizes the inevitability of the collapse of capitalism as a result of the intensified class-struggle, to be succeeded by a revolutionary seizure of political power and a dictatorship by the proletariat. Finally, this dictatorship, after liquidating the exploiting capitalist class, would itself "wither away" into a classless society.

Marx's ambiguous term "materialistic dialectics" was meant to be more empirical and scientific in its connotation than Hegel's idealistic dialectic. But another meaning to Marx's materialism lies in his view that history and politics depend on man's economic struggles and class conflicts. The term "economic" is crucial to the Marxist philosophy of history and politics. It ought to be noted that the term covers a broad variety of meanings in Marx's use of it, notably technological means of production, legal relations of private property or ownership of means of production, natural resources, labor, exchange of goods and services, the struggle for existence in human society. Insofar as technology depends on scientific research, law on social custom, natural resources on geography and climate, labor on reproduction, exchange on supply and demand, and the struggle for existence on social, biological, and physical conditions, we see that "economics" designates a very broad area. Hence, it is not surprising that so much can be claimed for the "economic factor" when so broadly and loosely applied to social and cultural history.

IV. Democratic Liberalism

It is not difficult for Dewey to criticize this Hegelian and Marxian doctrine of historical inevitability in the light of the logic of empirical science. It scarcely follows from an historical approach based on empirical method that the state must wither away and a classless society ensue inevitably. The state, for Dewey, can and should be democratically converted into an instrument for the social improvement of the living conditions of the masses. The cardinal hypothesis of political liberalism is that the social functions of the state can be democratically developed through experimental and educational agencies. We have already mentioned Dewey's abandonment of Hegel's strait-jacket of dialectics in favor of the extension of the experimental methods of the natural sciences to the social sciences. Against the view of both Hegelians and Marxists that imposes a pattern of certainty and monism on politics and history, Dewey insists that "probability and pluralism are the characteristics of the present state of science."

The theoreticians of the Communist Party in their unquestioning support of every policy of the U.S.S.R. are far from realizing the socialist democracy at which Marx aims. As harbingers of a new type of political authoritarianism, their subordination of individual freedom to the demands of a totalitarian state appears in the one-party system guaranteed by the so-called democratic constitution of the U.S.S.R. Liberals like Dewey point out the dangers of a one-party control of the newspapers, radio, schools, the arts and sciences, which are the principal agencies for the formation of public opinion. To the extent that ideas are used as instruments of political control, to that extent we cannot universally subordinate psychological factors to economic ones in history. Marx himself regarded a highly industrialized country like England a much more probable place for a successful socialistic revolution than an agricultural country like Russia, because industrial workers are much more likely to be conscious of their class status and their need for organization than farm workers or peasants, who see no need for collectivistic enterprises. The important point is that full-fledged social and economic democracy is not guaranteed by a merely formal political democracy which does not provide equality of economic opportunities for all groups, whether in the United States, England, or the U.S.S.R. In any case, the problem of all those who aim at spreading democracy is to provide both the economic and political opportunities that will yield the maximum participation of all in realizing the welfare of all.

The political philosophies outlined above differ not only in the particular political forms favored by each (absolute monarchy by Hobbes, constitutional monarchy by Hegel, dictatorship of the proletariat by Marx, and democracy by Dewey), but in their more general conceptions of human nature, history, and science: mechanistic materialism (Hobbes), objective idealism (Hegel), historical materialism (Marx), scientific naturalism (Dewey). It is logically possible to accept some parts of these political philosophies without accepting all of the more general theories that they advocate. To discriminate the wheat from the chaff requires a fuller understanding of the assumptions of each type of philosophy than can be given here. That such questions are not merely academic exercises is evident from the rôle that ideological indoctrination and education play in both war and peace.

Would we not in our present international dealings with the rival world powers, England and Russia, proceed more intelligently if everybody including the Americans, the British, and the Russians were enlightened on the crucial question: To what extent have the governments of the United States, Great Britain, and Russia been really working for or towards economic and social democracy in their own and less powerful countries?

It is a fact that in every existing state—no matter how democratic its pretensions are—individuals are penalized for expressing certain thoughts in public assemblies or in print, thoughts that are critical of existing governmental policy or of an institution backed by those powerful enough to use the machinery of the law-courts and law-enforcing agencies to suppress opposition or criticism. The penalties imposed on the critic need not be direct incarceration or death or deportation—witness Socrates who was given his choice between the latter two and chose death in order to teach the future citizenry of Athens and, we may add, of the world, a lesson in the political value of free thought and discussion. There are other more indirect forms of political tyranny: social ostracism, deprivation of economic opportunities in private or public employment, character assassination, and threats against the family and friends of the persecuted opposition. The extent to which suppression of such civil and political liberties as free discussion, the right of assembly, freedom of the press, the right of minority groups to organize for their own protection is practised under different forms of government is part of the subject-matter of social science. One of the chief obstacles in the slow progress of the social sciences is the difficulty of getting at the facts of secret inquisitions and star-chamber proceedings aimed at suppressing the opposition of individuals or minority groups. There is, however, the fact that certain methods of violence, like outright seizure of power by a dictatorial minority strong enough to suppress all opposition, are incompatible with the methods and aims of democratic liberalism.

The problem of political philosophy is to find the broad social principles which will guide us in deciding, after we have all the facts, to what extent any individual or group *ought to* be prevented from or penalized for exercising the civil liberties normally guaranteed by a democratic and liberal state. John Stuart Mill's essay *On Liberty* (1859), was published in the heyday of nineteenth-century *laissez-faire* political economy which promised indefinite prosperity and "the greatest good for the greatest number" on the basis of unrestricted individual enterprise. Mill feared that too much emphasis on economic self-advancement and freedom would lead to the neglect of moral progress, which to his mind was essentially a matter of individual freedom. However, in his later writings, Mill's democratic liberalism became more socialistic and he may be regarded as one of the forerunners of moderate British socialism which uses the methods of reform legislation rather than revolution. Political programs are generally linked with changing economic developments, but there are certain continuities in political history which are fundamental for any political philosophy. Of these continuities the civil liberties of freedom of thought, discussion, assembly, press, religious worship, and scientific inquiry are paramount rights of individuals which no system of political authority can ignore without endangering the very aim of social existence—human welfare. Mill's classic presentation of the arguments for unrestrained freedom for all individual thought and discussion, no matter how completely false or true or partially false and true the opinions in question are, is especially relevant today when authoritarian elements abroad and in our own midst threaten to stifle any hope of realizing a democratic and liberal civilization for mankind.

Mill's essay does, however, also raise further problems for our own age. Is "the tyranny of the majority" an inseparable evil of democracy? Should a minority group that would, in gaining control of a government, refuse democratic liberties to others, be free to gain such control under the protection of these civil liberties at present?

There are also problems connected with the theory of punishment (penology): Is legal punishment justified if it merely satisfies the revenge impulses of the offended or damaged persons? Or does the state merely have to punish criminals in order to deter them and others from violating the law? Or should the state readjust criminals to learning more useful forms of occupation? Or should we not seek also to eliminate the economic and social causes of crime—e.g., illiteracy, poverty, poor housing, racial, religious, and nationalistic hatreds?

In any case, whether our political problem is to justify the very existence of the state on a materialistic (Hobbes) or idealistic (Hegel) basis, or its overthrow by a dictatorship of the proletariat towards a classless society (Marx), or its gradual reform by an enlightened and free citizenry under a liberal democratic state, there is no easy or final settlement of the problem by philosophical principles that provide an absolute mechanical, historical, dialectical, or psychological necessity as a basis on which to meet the complex and variable needs of human beings. This is not a merely negative result, for it should turn our attention to the specific needs of mankind, to the elimination of economic and social inequities, and to the integrity of our own thoughts and lives in sharing the responsibility for the failure to advance human welfare by a more truly democratic way of living.

At this juncture of the world's seething politics, the tremendous and horrible cost of a second world war has led the frightened peoples of the world to realize the value of what some philosophers long ago envisaged: the establishment of an equitable system of law and order among nations. As Spinoza and Hegel recognized, Hobbes's war-like, predatory "state of nature" is not far from the actual relations of states that refuse to allow their absolute sovereignty to be limited by any international laws when dealing with other states. The stronger states dominate the weaker ones and have often enabled the greedy to thrive on the backs of the others without restraint. Resentment at such injustice, if it does not lead to war eventually, certainly saps all desire for human co-operation on a world-wide scale.

In the political writings of Immanuel Kant, the great eighteenth-century German enlightener, we find a prophetic, cosmopolitan plan for perpetual world peace. Nations, according to Kant, will sooner or later be driven to their senses by their awareness of the futility and waste of wars arising from the clash of powers each seeking its own interests. But a world federation of nations will not serve the ends of world peace unless it operates democratically to protect weaker nations from stronger ones. Furthermore, only when every nation has achieved democratic controls over any ruthless, war-bent group within its own borders will it be possible to nip war in the bud and to realize perpetual peace. Kant did not specify the economic roots of war so vividly and did not insist on an industrial democracy as Marx and Dewey did. But he believed that if nations can reach agreements in international trade, they ought also to co-operate on world peace, and he tried to show the rationale of world unity without resorting to the highly abstract metaphysics of history which Hegel used to defend Prussian nationalism.

Grotius, in the seventeenth century, wrote a treatise on international law which was based on eternal and natural law understood in theological terms. It remains to be seen whether a more empirical scrutiny of the possibilities of world organization can lead to a feasible solution of the immensely important problem of avoiding future wars which may destroy civilization entirely. There are common enemies against which all nations and peoples may unitedly devote their greatest energies: famine, poverty, disease, ignorance, and injustice.

P. P. W.

16. The Apology*
The Trial of Socrates (B.C. 399)

PLATO (B.C. 427–347)

CHARACTERS

Socrates

Meletus

Scene—The Court of Justice

Socrates. I cannot tell what impression my accusers have made upon you, Athenians. For my own part, I know that they nearly made me forget who I was, so persuasive were they; and yet they have scarcely uttered one single word of truth. But of all their many falsehoods, the one which astonished me most was when they said that I was a clever speaker, and that you must be careful not to let me deceive you. I thought that it was most shameless of them not to be ashamed to talk in that way; for as soon as I open my mouth they will be refuted, and I shall prove that I am not a clever speaker in any way at all—unless, indeed, by a clever speaker they mean a man who speaks the truth. If that is

their meaning, I agree with them that I am an orator not to be compared with them. My accusers, then I repeat, have said little or nothing that is true; but from me you shall hear the whole truth. Certainly you will not hear an elaborate speech, Athenians, dressed up, like theirs, with words and phrases. I will say to you what I have to say, without preparation, and in the words which come first, for I believe that my cause is just; so let none of you expect anything else. Indeed, my friends, it would hardly be seemly for me, at my age, to come before you like a young man with his specious phrases. But there is one thing, Athenians, which I do most earnestly beg and entreat of you. Do not be surprised and do not interrupt with shouts if in my defense I speak in the same way that I am accustomed to speak in the market-place, at the tables of the money-changers, where many of you have heard me, and elsewhere. The truth is this. I am more than seventy years old, and this is the first time that I have ever come before a law-court; so your manner of speech here is quite strange

* Translation of F. J. Church.

to me. If I had been really a stranger, you would have forgiven me for speaking in the language and the manner of my native country; and so now I ask you to grant me what I think I have a right to claim. Never mind the manner of my speech—it may be better or it may be worse—give your whole attention to the question, Is what I say just, or is it not? That is what makes a good judge, as speaking the truth makes a good orator.

I have to defend myself, Athenians, first against the old false accusations of my old accusers, and then against the later ones of my present accusers. For many men have been accusing me to you, and for very many years, who have not uttered a word of truth; and I fear them more than I fear Anytus and his associates, formidable as they are. But, my friends, those others are still more formidable; for they got hold of most of you when you were children, and they have been more persistent in accusing me untruthfully and have persuaded you that there is a certain Socrates, a wise man, who speculates about the heavens, and who investigates things that are beneath the earth, and who can make the worse argument appear the stronger. These men, Athenians, who spread abroad this report are the accusers whom I fear; for their hearers think that persons who pursue such inquiries never believe in the gods. Then they are many, and their attacks have been going on for a long time, and they spoke to you when you were at the age most readily to believe them, for you were all young, and many of you were children, and there was no one to answer them when they attacked me. And the most unreasonable thing of all is that I do not even know their names: I cannot tell you who they are except when one happens to be a comic poet. But all the rest who have persuaded you, from motives of resentment and prejudice, and sometimes, it may be, from conviction, are hardest to

cope with. For I cannot call any one of them forward in court to cross-examine him. I have, as it were, simply to spar with shadows in my defense, and to put questions which there is no one to answer. I ask you, therefore, to believe that, as I say, I have been attacked by two kinds of accusers—first, by Meletus and his associates, and, then, by those older ones of whom I have spoken. And, with your leave, I will defend myself first against my old accusers; for you heard their accusations first, and they were much more forceful than my present accusers are.

Well, I must make my defense, Athenians, and try in the short time allowed me to remove the prejudice which you have been so long a time acquiring. I hope that I may manage to do this, if it be good for you and for me, and that my defense may be successful; but I am quite aware of the nature of my task, and I know that it is a difficult one. Be the outcome, however, as is pleasing to God, I must obey the law and make my defense.

Let us begin from the beginning, then, and ask what is the accusation which has given rise to the prejudice against me, which was what Meletus relied on when he brought his indictment. What is the prejudice which my enemies have been spreading about me? I must assume that they are formally accusing me, and read their indictment. It would run somewhat in this fashion: "Socrates is a wrongdoer, who meddles with inquiries into things beneath the earth and in the heavens, and who makes the worse argument appear the stronger, and who teaches others these same things." That is what they say; and in the comedy of Aristophanes [Clouds] you yourselves saw a man called Socrates swinging round in a basket and saying that he walked the air, and sputtering a great deal of nonsense about matters of which I understand nothing, either more or less. I do not mean to disparage that kind of knowledge if there is any one who is wise about these matters. I trust Meletus may never be able to prosecute me for that. But the truth is, Athenians, I have nothing to do with these matters, and almost all of you are yourselves my witnesses of this. I beg all of you who have heard me discussing, and they are many, to inform your neighbors and tell them if any of you have ever heard me discussing such matters, either more or less. That will show you that the other common statements about me are as false as this one.

But the fact is that not one of these is true. And if you have heard that I undertake to educate men, and make money by so doing, that is not true either, though I think that it would be a fine thing to be able to educate men, as Gorgias of Leontini, and Prodicus of Ceos, and Hippias of Elis do. For each of them, my friends, can go into any city, and persuade the young men to leave the society of their fellow citizens, with any of whom they might associate for nothing, and to be only too glad to be allowed to pay money for the privilege of associating with themselves. And I believe that there is another wise man from Paros residing in Athens at this moment. I happened to meet Callias, the son of Hipponicus, a man who has spent more money on sophists than every one else put together. So I said to him (he has two sons), Callias, if your two sons had been foals or calves, we could have hired a trainer for them who would have made them perfect in the virtue which belongs to their nature. He would have been either a groom or a farmer. But whom do you intend to take to train them, seeing that they are men? Who understands the virtue which belongs to men and to citizens? I suppose that you must have thought of this, because of your sons. Is there such a person, said I, or not? Certainly there is, he replied.

Who is he, said I, and where does he come from, and what is his fee? Evenus, Socrates, he replied, from Paros, five minae. Then I thought that Evenus was a fortunate person if he really understood this art and could teach so cleverly. If I had possessed knowledge of that kind, I should have been conceited and disdainful. But, Athenians, the truth is that I do not possess it.

Perhaps some of you may reply: But, Socrates, what is the trouble with you? What has given rise to these prejudices against you? You must have been doing something out of the ordinary. All these rumors and reports of you would never have arisen if you had not been doing something different from other men. So tell us what it is, that we may not give our verdict in the dark. I think that that is a fair question, and I will try to explain to you what it is that has raised these prejudices against me and given me this reputation. Listen, then. Some of you, perhaps, will think that I am joking, but I assure you that I will tell you the whole truth. I have gained this reputation, Athenians, simply by reason of a certain wisdom. But by what kind of wisdom? It is by just that wisdom which is perhaps human wisdom. In that, it may be, I am really wise. But the men of whom I was speaking just now must be wise in a wisdom which is greater than human wisdom, or else I cannot describe it, for certainly I know nothing of it myself, and if any man says that I do, he lies and speaks to arouse prejudice against me. Do not interrupt me with shouts, Athenians, even if you think that I am boasting. What I am going to say is not my own. I will tell you who says it, and he is worthy of your respect. I will bring the god of Delphi to be the witness of my wisdom, if it is wisdom at all, and of its nature. You remember Chaerephon. From youth upwards he was my comrade; and also a partisan of your democracy, sharing your recent exile [1] and returning with you. You remember, too, Chaerephon's character—how impulsive he was in carrying through whatever he took in hand. Once he went to Delphi and ventured to put this question to the oracle—I entreat you again, my friends, not to interrupt me with your shouts—he asked if there was any one who was wiser than I. The priestess answered that there was no one. Chaerephon himself is dead, but his brother here will witness to what I say.

Now see why I tell you this. I am going to explain to you how the prejudice against me has arisen. When I heard of the oracle I began to reflect: What can the god mean by this riddle? I know very well that I am not wise, even in the smallest degree. Then what can he mean by saying that I am the wisest of men? It cannot be that he is speaking falsely, for he is a god and cannot lie. For a long time I was at a loss to understand his meaning. Then, very reluctantly, I turned to investigate it in this manner: I went to a man who was reputed to be wise, thinking that there, if anywhere, I should prove the answer wrong, and meaning to point out to the oracle its mistake, and to say, "You said that I was the wisest of men, but this man is wiser than I am." So I examined the man—I need not tell you his name, he was a politician—but this was the result, Athenians. When I conversed with him I came to see that, though a great many persons, and most of all he himself, thought that he was wise, yet he was not wise. Then I tried to prove to him that he was not wise, though he fancied that he was; and by so doing I made him indignant, and many of the bystanders. So when I went away, I thought to myself, "I am wiser than this man: neither of us knows anything that is really

worthwhile, but he thinks that he has knowledge when he has not, while I, having no knowledge, do not think that I have. I seem, at any rate, to be a little wiser than he is on this point: I do not think that I know what I do not know." Next I went to another man who was reputed to be still wiser than the last, with exactly the same result. And there again I made him, and many other men, indignant.

Then I went on to one man after another, seeing that I was arousing indignation every day, which caused me much grief and anxiety. Still I thought that I must set the god's command above everything. So I had to go to every man who seemed to possess any knowledge, and investigate the meaning of the oracle. Athenians, I must tell you the truth; by the dog, this was the result of the investigation which I made at the god's bidding: I found that the men whose reputation for wisdom stood highest were nearly the most lacking in it, while others who were looked down on as common people were much more intelligent. Now I must describe to you the wanderings which I undertook, like Heraclean labors, to prove the oracle irrefutable. After the politicians, I went to the poets, tragic, dithyrambic, and others, thinking that there I should find myself manifestly more ignorant than they. So I took up the poems on which I thought that they had spent most pains, and asked them what they meant, hoping at the same time to learn something from them. I am ashamed to tell you the truth, my friends, but I must say it. Almost any one of the bystanders could have talked about the works of these poets better than the poets themselves. So I soon found that it is not by wisdom that the poets create their works, but by a certain natural power and by inspiration, like soothsayers and prophets, who say many fine things, but who understand nothing of what they

[1] When *The Thirty* ruled Athens despotically in 404 B.C., five years before the trial of Socrates.—P. P. W.

say. The poets seemed to me to be in a similar situation. And at the same time I perceived that, because of their poetry, they thought that they were the wisest of men in other matters, too, which they were not. So I went away again, thinking that I had the same advantage over the poets that I had over the politicians.

Finally, I went to the artisans, for I knew very well that I possessed no knowledge at all worth speaking of, and I was sure that I should find that they knew many fine things. And in that I was not mistaken. They knew what I did not know, and so far they were wiser than I. But, Athenians, it seemed to me that the skilled artisans had the same failing as the poets. Each of them believed himself to be extremely wise in matters of the greatest importance because he was skilful in his own art: and this presumption of theirs obscured their real wisdom. So I asked myself, on behalf of the oracle, whether I would choose to remain as I was, without either their wisdom or their ignorance, or to possess both, as they did. And I answered to myself and to the oracle that it was better for me to remain as I was.

From this examination, Athenians, has arisen much fierce and bitter indignation, and from this a great many prejudices about me, and people say that I am "a wise man." For the bystanders always think that I am wise myself in any matter wherein I refute another. But, gentlemen, I believe that the god is really wise, and that by this oracle he meant that human wisdom is worth little or nothing. I do not think that he meant that Socrates was wise. He only made use of my name, and took me as an example, as though he would say to men, "He among you is the wisest who, like Socrates, knows that in truth his wisdom is worth nothing at all." Therefore I still go about testing and examining every man whom I think wise, whether

he be a citizen or a stranger, as the god has commanded me; and whenever I find that he is not wise, I point out to him, on the god's behalf, that he is not wise. I am so busy in this pursuit that I have never had leisure to take any part worth mentioning in public matters or to look after my private affairs. I am in great poverty as the result of my service to the god.

Besides this, the young men who follow me about, who are the sons of wealthy persons and have the most leisure, take pleasure in hearing men cross-examined. They often imitate me among themselves; then they try their hands at cross-examining other people. And, I imagine, they find plenty of men who think that they know a great deal when in fact they know little or nothing. Then the persons who are cross-examined get angry with me instead of with themselves, and say that Socrates is an abomination and corrupts the young. When they are asked, "Why, what does he do? what does he teach?" they do not know what to say; but, not to seem at a loss, they repeat the stock charges against all philosophers, and allege that he investigates things in the air and under the earth, and that he teaches people to disbelieve in the gods, and to make the worse argument appear the stronger. For, I suppose, they would not like to confess the truth, which is that they are shown up as ignorant pretenders to knowledge that they do not possess. So they have been filling your ears with their bitter prejudices for a long time, for they are ambitious, energetic, and numerous; and they speak vigorously and persuasively against me. Relying on this, Meletus, Anytus, and Lycon have attacked me. Meletus is indignant with me on the part of the poets, Anytus on the part of the artisans and politicians, and Lycon on the part of the orators. And so, as I said at the beginning, I shall be surprised if I am able, in the short time allowed me for my defense, to remove from your minds this prejudice which has grown so strong. What I have told you, Athenians, is the truth: I neither conceal nor do I suppress anything, small or great. Yet I know that it is just this plainness of speech which rouses indignation. But that is only a proof that my words are true, and that the prejudice against me, and the causes of it, are what I have said. And whether you investigate them now or hereafter, you will find that they are so.

What I have said must suffice as my defense against the charges of my first accusers. I will try next to defend myself against Meletus, that "good patriot," as he calls himself, and my later accusers. Let us assume that they are a new set of accusers, and read their indictment, as we did in the case of the others. It runs thus. He says that Socrates is a wrongdoer who corrupts the youth, and who does not believe in the gods whom the state believes in, but in other new divinities. Such is the accusation. Let us examine each point in it separately. Meletus says that I do wrong by corrupting the youth. But I say, Athenians, that he is doing wrong, for he is playing a solemn joke by casually bringing men to trial, and pretending to have a solemn interest in matters to which he has never given a moment's thought. Now I will try to prove to you that it is so.

Come here, Meletus. Is it not a fact that you think it very important that the young should be as good as possible?

Meletus. It is.

Socrates. Come then, tell the judges who is it who improves them? You care so much, you must know. You are accusing me, and bringing me to trial, because, as you say, you have discovered that I am the corrupter of the youth. Come now, reveal to the gentlemen who improves them. You see, Meletus, you

have nothing to say; you are silent. But don't you think that this is shameful? Is not your silence a conclusive proof of what I say—that you have never cared? Come, tell us, my good man, who makes the young better?

Mel. The laws.

Socr. That, my friend, is not my question. What man improves the young, who starts with the knowledge of the laws?

Mel. The judges here, Socrates.

Socr. What do you mean, Meletus? Can they educate the young and improve them?

Mel. Certainly.

Socr. All of them? or only some of them?

Mel. All of them.

Socr. By Hera, that is good news! Such a large supply of benefactors! And do the listeners here improve them, or not?

Mel. They do.

Socr. And do the senators?

Mel. Yes.

Socr. Well then, Meletus, do the members of the assembly corrupt the young or do they again all improve them?

Mel. They, too, improve them.

Socr. Then all the Athenians, apparently, make the young into good men except me, and I alone corrupt them. Is that your meaning?

Mel. Most certainly; that is my meaning.

Socr. You have discovered me to be most unfortunate. Now tell me: do you think that the same holds good in the case of horses? Does one man do them harm and every one else improve them? On the contrary, is it not one man only, or a very few—namely, those who are skilled with horses—who can improve them, while the majority of men harm them if they use them and have anything to do with them? Is it not so, Meletus, both with horses and with every other animal? Of course it is, whether you and Anytus say yes or no. The young would certainly be very fortunate if only one man corrupted them, and every one else did them good. The truth is, Meletus, you prove conclusively that you have never thought about the youth in your life. You exhibit your carelessness in not caring for the very matters about which you are prosecuting me.

Now be so good as to tell us, Meletus, is it better to live among good citizens or bad ones? Answer, my friend. I am not asking you at all a difficult question. Do not the bad harm their associates and the good, good?

Mel. Yes.

Socr. Is there any one who would rather be injured than benefited by his companions? Answer, my good sir; you are obliged by the law to answer. Does any one like to be injured?

Mel. Certainly not.

Socr. Well then, are you prosecuting me for corrupting the young and making them worse, voluntarily or involuntarily?

Mel. For doing it voluntarily.

Socr. What, Meletus? Do you mean to say that you, who are so much younger than I, are yet so much wiser than I that you know that bad citizens always do evil, and that good citizens do good, to those with whom they come in contact, while I am so extraordinarily ignorant as not to know that, if I make any of my companions evil, he will probably injure me in some way, and as to commit this great evil, as you allege, voluntarily? You will not make me believe that, nor anyone else either, I should think. Either I do not corrupt the young at all or if I do I do so involuntarily: so that you are lying in either case. And if I corrupt them involuntarily, the law does not call upon you to prosecute me for an error which is involuntary, but to take me aside privately and reprove and educate me. For,

of course, I shall cease from doing wrong involuntarily, as soon as I know that I have been doing wrong. But you avoided associating with me and educating me; instead you bring me up before the court, where the law sends persons, not for education, but for punishment.

The truth is, Athenians, as I said, it is quite clear that Meletus has never cared at all about these matters. However, now tell us, Meletus, how do you say that I corrupt the young? Clearly, according to your indictment, by teaching them not to believe in the gods the state believes in, but other new divinities instead. You mean that I corrupt the young by that teaching, do you not?

Mel. Yes, most certainly I mean that.

Socr. Then in the name of these gods of whom we are speaking, explain yourself a little more clearly to me and to these gentlemen here. I cannot understand what you mean. Do you mean that I teach the young to believe in some gods, but not in the gods of the state? Do you accuse me of teaching them to believe in strange gods? If that is your meaning, I myself believe in some gods, and my crime is not that of complete atheism. Or do you mean that I do not believe in the gods at all myself, and that I teach other people not to believe in them either?

Mel. I mean that you do not believe in the gods in any way whatever.

Socr. You amaze me, Meletus! Why do you say that? Do you mean that I believe neither the sun nor the moon to be gods, like other men?

Mel. I swear he does not, judges; he says that the sun is a stone, and the moon earth.

Socr. My dear Meletus, do you think that you are prosecuting Anaxagoras? You must have a very poor opinion of these men, and think them illiterate, if you imagine that they do not know that the works of Anaxagoras of Clazomenae are full of these doctrines. And so young men learn these things from me, when they can often buy them in the theatre for a drachma at most, and laugh at Socrates were he to pretend that these doctrines, which are very peculiar doctrines, too, were his own. But please tell me, do you really think that I do not believe in the gods at all?

Mel. Most certainly I do. You are a complete atheist.

Socr. No one believes that, Meletus, not even you yourself. It seems to me, Athenians, that Meletus is very insolent and reckless, and that he is prosecuting me simply out of insolence, recklessness and youthful bravado. For he seems to be testing me, by asking me a riddle that has no answer. "Will this wise Socrates," he says to himself, "see that I am joking and contradicting myself? or shall I deceive him and every one else who hears me?" Meletus seems to me to contradict himself in his indictment: it is as if he were to say, "Socrates is a wrongdoer who does not believe in the gods, but who believes in the gods." But this is joking.

Now, my friends, let us see why I think that this is his meaning. Do you answer me, Meletus; and do you, Athenians, remember the request which I made to you at the start, and do not interrupt me with shouts if I talk in my customary manner.

Is there any man, Meletus, who believes in the existence of things pertaining to men and not in the existence of men? Make him answer the question, gentlemen, without these interruptions. Is there any man who believes in the existence of horsemanship and not in the existence of horses? or in flute-playing and not in flute-players? There is not, my friend. If you will not answer, I will tell both you and the judges. But you must answer my next question. Is there any man who believes in the existence of divine things and not in the existence of divinities?

Mel. There is not.

Socr. I am very glad that these gentlemen have managed to extract an answer from you. Well then, you say that I believe in divine things, whether they be old or new ones, and that I teach others to believe in them; at any rate, according to your statement, I believe in divine things. That you have sworn in your indictment. But if I believe in divine things, I suppose it follows necessarily that I believe in divinities. Is it not so? It is. I assume that you grant that, as you do not answer. But do we not believe that divinities are either gods themselves or the children of the gods? Do you admit that?

Mel. I do.

Socr. Then you admit that I believe in divinities. Now, if these divinities are gods, then, as I say, you are joking and asking a riddle, and asserting that I do not believe in the gods, and at the same time that I do, since I believe in divinities. But if these divinities are the illegitimate children of the gods, either by the nymphs or by other mothers, as they are said to be, then, I ask, what man could believe in the existence of the children of the gods, and not in the existence of the gods? That would be as absurd as believing in the existence of the offspring of horses and asses, and not in the existence of horses and asses. You must have indicted me in this manner, Meletus, either to test me or because you could not find any crime that you could accuse me of with truth. But you will never contrive to persuade any man with any sense at all that a belief in divine things and things of the gods does not necessarily involve a belief in divinities, and in the gods, and in heroes.

But in truth, Athenians, I do not think that I need say very much to prove that I have not committed the crime for which Meletus is prosecuting me. What I have said is enough to prove that. But I repeat it is certainly true, as

I have already told you, that I have aroused much indignation. That is what will cause my condemnation if I am condemned; not Meletus nor Anytus either, but that prejudice and resentment of the multitude which have been the destruction of many good men before me, and I think will be so again. There is no fear that I shall be the last victim.

Perhaps some one will say: "Are you not ashamed, Socrates, of leading a life which is very likely now to cause your death?" I should answer him with justice, and say: My friend, if you think that a man of any worth at all ought to reckon the chances of life and death when he acts, or that he ought to think of anything but whether he is acting rightly or wrongly, and as a good or a bad man would act, you are mistaken. According to you, the demigods who died at Troy would be foolish, and among them the son of Thetis, who thought nothing of danger when the alternative was disgrace. For when his mother—and she was a goddess—addressed him, when he was resolved to slay Hector, in this fashion, "My son, if you avenge the death of your comrade Patroclus and slay Hector, you will die yourself, for 'fate awaits you straightway after Hector's death' "; when he heard this, he scorned danger and death; he feared much more to live a coward and not to avenge his friend. "Let me punish the evildoer and straightway die," he said, "that I may not remain here by the beaked ships jeered at, encumbering the earth." Do you suppose that he thought of danger or of death? For this, Athenians, I believe to be the truth. Wherever a man's station is, whether he has chosen it of his own will, or whether he has been placed at it by his commander, there it is his duty to remain and face the danger without thinking of death or of any other thing except disgrace.

When the generals whom you choose to command me, Athenians, assigned me my station at Potidaea and at Amphipolis and at Delium, I remained where they stationed me and ran the risk of death, like other men. It would be very strange conduct on my part if I were to desert my station now from fear of death or of any other thing when God has commanded me—as I am persuaded that he has done—to spend my life in searching for wisdom, and in examining myself and others. That would indeed be a very strange thing. Then certainly I might with justice be brought to trial for not believing in the gods, for I should be disobeying the oracle, and fearing death and thinking myself wise when I was not wise. For to fear death, my friends, is only to think ourselves wise without really being wise, for it is to think that we know what we do not know. For no one knows whether death may not be the greatest good that can happen to man. But men fear it as if they knew quite well that it was the greatest of evils. And what is this but that shameful ignorance of thinking that we know what we do not know? In this matter, too, my friends, perhaps I am different from the multitude; and if I were to claim to be at all wiser than others, it would be because, not knowing very much about the other world, I do not think I know. But I do know very well that it is evil and disgraceful to do wrong, and not to be persuaded by my superior, whether man or god. I will never do what I know to be evil, and shrink in fear from what I do not know to be good or evil. Even if you acquit me now, and do not listen to Anytus' argument that, if I am to be acquitted, I ought never to have been brought to trial at all, and that, as it is, you are bound to put me to death because, as he said, if I escape, all your sons will be utterly corrupted by practising what Socrates teaches. If you were therefore to say to me, "Socrates, this time we will not listen to Anytus; we will let you go, but on this condition that you give up this investigation of yours, and philosophy; if you are found following those pursuits again, you shall die." I say, if you offered to let me go on these terms, I should reply: Athenians, I hold you in the highest regard and affection, but I will be persuaded by the god rather than you; and as long as I have breath and strength I will not give up philosophy and exhorting you and declaring the truth to every one of you whom I meet, saying, as I am accustomed, "My good friend, you are a citizen of Athens, a city which is very great and very famous for its wisdom and power—are you not ashamed of caring so much for the making of money and for fame and prestige, when you neither think nor care about wisdom and truth and the improvement of your soul?" And if he disputes my words and says that he does care about these things, I shall not at once release him and go away: I shall question him and cross-examine him and test him. If I think that he does not possess virtue, though he says that he does, I shall reproach him for under-valuing the most valuable things, and over-valuing those that are less valuable. This I shall do to every one whom I meet, young or old, citizen or stranger, but especially to citizens, for they are more closely related to me. For know that the god has commanded me to do so. And I think that no greater good has ever befallen you in the state than my service to the god. For I spend my whole life in going about and persuading you all to give your first and greatest care to the improvement of your souls, and not till you have done that to think of your bodies or your wealth; and telling you that virtue does not come from wealth, but that wealth, and every other good thing which men have, whether in public or in private, comes from virtue. If then I corrupt the youth by this teaching, these things must be

harmful; but if any man says that I teach anything else, there is nothing in what he says. And therefore, Athenians, I say, whether you are persuaded by Anytus or not, whether you acquit me or not, I shall not change my way of life; no, not if I have to die for it many times.

Do not interrupt me, Athenians, with your shouts. Remember the request which I made to you, and do not interrupt my words. I think that it will profit you to hear them. I am going to say something more to you, at which you may be inclined to protest, but do not do that. Be sure that if you put me to death, who am what I have told you that I am, you will do yourselves more harm than me. Meletus and Anytus can do me no harm: that is impossible, for I am sure it is not allowed that a good man be injured by a worse. He may indeed kill me, or drive me into exile, or deprive me of my civil rights; and perhaps Meletus and others think those things great evils. But I do not think so: I think it is a much greater evil to do what he is doing now, and to try to put a man to death unjustly. And now, Athenians, I am not arguing in my own defense at all, as you might expect me to do, but rather in yours in order you may not make a mistake about the gift of the god to you by condemning me. For if you put me to death, you will not easily find another who, if I may use a ludicrous comparison, clings to the state as a sort of gadfly to a horse that is large and well-bred but rather sluggish from its size, and needing to be aroused. It seems to me that the god has attached me like that to the state, for I am constantly alighting upon you at every point to rouse, persuade, and reproach each of you all day long. You will not easily find anyone else, my friends, to fill my place; and if you are persuaded by me, you will spare my life. You are indignant, as drowsy persons are, when they are awakened, and, of course, if you are persuaded by Anytus, you could easily kill me with a single blow, and then sleep on undisturbed for the rest of your lives unless the god in his care for you sends another to arouse you. And you may easily see that it is the god who has given me to your city; for it is not human the way in which I have neglected all my own interests and endured seeing my private affairs neglected now for so many years, while occupying myself unceasingly in your interests, going to each of you privately, like a father or an elder brother, trying to persuade him to care for virtue. There would have been a reason for it, if I had gained any advantage by this, or if I had been paid for my exhortations; but you see yourselves that my accusers, though they accuse me of everything else without shame, have not had the shamelessness to say that I ever either exacted or demanded payment. To that they have no witness. And I think that I have sufficient witness to the truth of what I say —my poverty.

Perhaps it may seem strange to you that, though I go about giving this advice privately and meddling in others' affairs, yet I do not venture to come forward in the assembly and advise the state. You have often heard me speak of my reason for this, and in many places: it is that I have a certain divine sign, which is what Meletus has caricatured in his indictment. I have had it from childhood. It is a kind of voice which, whenever I hear it, always turns me back from something which I was going to do, but never urges me to act. It is this which forbids me to take part in politics. And I think it does well to forbid me. For, Athenians, it is quite certain that, if I had attempted to take part in politics, I should have perished at once and long ago without doing any good either to you or to myself. And do not be indignant with me for telling the

truth. There is no man who will preserve his life for long, either in Athens or elsewhere, if he firmly opposes the multitude, and tries to prevent the commission of much injustice and illegality in the state. He who would really fight for justice must do so as a private citizen, not as an office-holder, if he is to preserve his life, even for a short time.

I will prove to you that this is so by very strong evidence, not by mere words, but by what you value more—actions. Listen then to what has happened to me, that you may know that there is no man who could make me consent to do wrong from the fear of death, but that I would perish at once rather than give way. What I am going to tell you may be a commonplace in the law-court; nevertheless it is true. The only office that I ever held in the state, Athenians, was that of Senator. When you wished to try the ten generals who did not rescue their men after the battle of Arginusae, as a group, which was illegal, as you all came to think afterwards, the tribe Antiochis, to which I belong, held the presidency. On that occasion I alone of all the presidents opposed your illegal action and gave my vote against you. The orators were ready to impeach me and arrest me; and you were clamoring against me, and crying out to me to submit. But I thought that I ought to face the danger, with law and justice on my side, rather than join with you in your unjust proposal, from fear of imprisonment or death. That was when the state was democratic. When the oligarchy came in, the Thirty sent for me, with four others, to the council-chamber, and ordered us to bring Leon the Salaminian from Salamis, that they might put him to death. They were in the habit of frequently giving similar orders to many others, wishing to implicate as many as possible in their crimes. But, then, I again proved, not by mere words, but by my actions, that, if I may speak bluntly, I do not care a straw for death; but that I do care very much indeed about not doing anything unjust or impious. That government with all its power did not terrify me into doing anything unjust; but when we left the council-chamber, the other four went over to Salamis and brought Leon across to Athens; and I went home. And if the rule of the Thirty had not been overthrown soon afterwards, I should very likely have been put to death for what I did then. Many of you will be my witnesses in this matter.

Now do you think that I could have remained alive all these years if I had taken part in public affairs, and had always maintained the cause of justice like a good man, and had held it a paramount duty, as it is, to do so? Certainly not, Athenians, nor could any other man. But throughout my whole life, both in private and in public, whenever I have had to take part in public affairs, you will find I have always been the same and have never yielded unjustly to anyone; no, not to those whom my enemies falsely assert to have been my pupils. But I was never anyone's teacher. I have never withheld myself from anyone, young or old, who was anxious to hear me discuss while I was making my investigation; neither do I discuss for payment, and refuse to discuss without payment. I am ready to ask questions of rich and poor alike, and if any man wishes to answer me, and then listen to what I have to say, he may. And I cannot justly be charged with causing these men to turn out good or bad, for I never either taught or professed to teach any of them any knowledge whatever. And if any man asserts that he ever learned or heard anything from me in private which everyone else did not hear as well as he, be sure that he does not speak the truth.

Why is it, then, that people delight in spending so much time in my company?

You have heard why, Athenians. I told you the whole truth when I said that they delight in hearing me examine persons who think that they are wise when they are not wise. It is certainly very amusing to listen to that. And, I say, the god has commanded me to examine men, in oracles and in dreams and in every way in which the divine will was ever declared to man. This is the truth, Athenians, and if it were not the truth, it would be easily refuted. For if it were really the case that I have already corrupted some of the young men, and am now corrupting others, surely some of them, finding as they grew older that I had given them bad advice in their youth, would have come forward today to accuse me and take their revenge. Or if they were unwilling to do so themselves, surely their relatives, their fathers or brothers, or others, would, if I had done them any harm, have remembered it and taken their revenge. Certainly I see many of them in Court. Here is Crito, of my own deme and of my own age, the father of Critobulus; here is Lysanias of Sphettus, the father of Aeschines; here is also Antiphon of Cephisus, the father of Epigenes. Then here are others whose brothers have spent their time in my company—Nicostratus, the son of Theozotides and brother of Theodotus—and Theodotus is dead, so he at least cannot entreat his brother to be silent; here is Paralus, the son of Demodocus and the brother of Theages, here is Adeimantus, the son of Ariston, whose brother is Plato here; and Aeantodorus, whose brother is Aristodorus. And I can name many others to you, some of whom Meletus ought to have called as witnesses in the course of his own speech; but if he forgot to call them then, let him call them now—I will yield the floor to him—and tell us if he has any such evidence. No, on the contrary, my friends, you will find all these men ready to support me, the corrupter, the injurer, of their relatives, as Meletus and Anytus call me. Those of them who have been already corrupted might perhaps have some reason for supporting me, but what reason can their relatives have who are grown up, and who are uncorrupted, except the reason of truth and justice—that they know very well that Meletus is lying, and that I am speaking the truth?

Well, my friends, this, and perhaps more like this, is pretty much all I have to offer in my defense. There may be some one among you who will be indignant when he remembers how, even in a less important trial than this, he begged and entreated the judges, with many tears, to acquit him, and brought forward his children and many of his friends and relatives in Court in order to appeal to your feelings; and then finds that I shall do none of these things, though I am in what he would think the supreme danger. Perhaps he will harden himself against me when he notices this: it may make him angry, and he may cast his vote in anger. If it is so with any of you—I do not suppose that it is, but in case it should be so—I think that I should answer him reasonably if I said: "My friend, I have relatives, too, for, in the words of Homer, 'I am not born of an oak or a rock but of flesh and blood' "; and so, Athenians, I have relatives, and I have three sons, one of them a lad, and the other two still children. Yet I will not bring any of them forward before you and implore you to acquit me. And why will I do none of these things? It is not from arrogance, Athenians, nor because I lack respect for you—whether or not I can face death bravely is another question—but for my own good name, and for your good name, and for the good name of the whole state. I do not think it right, at my age and with my reputation, to do anything of that kind. Rightly or wrongly, men have made up their minds

that in some way Socrates is different from the multitude of men. And it will be shameful if those of you who are thought to excel in wisdom, or in bravery, or in any other virtue, are going to act in this fashion. I have often seen men of reputation behaving in an extraordinary way at their trial, as if they thought it a terrible fate to be killed, and as though they expected to live for ever if you did not put them to death. Such men seem to me to bring shame upon the state, for any stranger would suppose that the best and most eminent Athenians, who are selected by their fellow citizens to hold office, and for other honors, are no better than women. Those of you, Athenians, who have any reputation at all ought not to do these things, and you ought not to allow us to do them; you should show that you will be much more ready to condemn men who make the state ridiculous by these pitiful pieces of acting, than to men who remain quiet.

But apart from the question of reputation, my friends, I do not think that it is right to entreat the judge to acquit us, or to escape condemnation in that way. It is our duty to teach and persuade him. He does not sit to give away justice as a favor, but to pronounce judgment; and he has sworn, not to favor any man whom he would like to favor, but to judge according to law. And, therefore, we ought not to encourage you in the habits of breaking your oaths; and you ought not to allow yourselves to fall into this habit, for then neither you nor we would be acting piously. Therefore, Athenians, do not require me to do these things, for I believe them to be neither good nor just nor pious; and, more especially, do not ask me to do them today when Meletus is prosecuting me for impiety. For were I to be successful and persuade you by my entreaties to break your oaths, I should be clearly teaching you to believe that there are no gods, and I should be simply accusing myself by my defense of not believing in them. But, Athenians, that is very far from the truth. I do believe in the gods as no one of my accusers believes in them: and to you and to god I commit my cause to be decided as is best for you and for me.

(*He is found guilty by 281 votes to 220.*)

I am not indignant at the verdict which you have given, Athenians, for many reasons. I expected that you would find me guilty; and I am not so much surprised at that as at the numbers of the votes. I certainly never thought that the majority against me would have been so narrow. But now it seems that if only thirty votes had changed sides, I should have escaped. So I think that I have escaped Meletus, as it is; and not only have I escaped him, for it is perfectly clear that if Anytus and Lycon had not come forward to accuse me, too, he would not have obtained the fifth part of the votes, and would have had to pay a fine of a thousand drachmae.

So he proposes death as the penalty. Be it so. And what alternative penalty shall I propose to you, Athenians? What I deserve, of course, must I not? What then do I deserve to pay or to suffer for having determined not to spend my life in ease? I neglected the things which most men value, such as wealth, and family interests, and military commands, and popular oratory, and all the political appointments, and clubs, and factions, that there are in Athens; for I thought that I was really too honest a man to preserve my life if I engaged in these matters. So I did not go where I should have done no good either to you or to myself. I went, instead, to each one of you privately to do him, as I say, the greatest of benefits, and tried to persuade him not to think of his affairs until he had thought of himself and tried to make himself as good and wise as

possible, nor to think of the affairs of Athens until he had thought of Athens herself; and to care for other things in the same manner. Then what do I deserve for such a life? Something good, Athenians, if I am really to propose what I deserve; and something good which it would be suitable to me to receive. Then what is a suitable reward to be given to a poor benefactor who requires leisure to exhort you? There is no reward, Athenians, so suitable for him as a public maintenance in the prytaneum. It is a much more suitable reward for him than for any of you who has won a victory at the Olympic games with his horse or his chariots. Such a man only makes you seem happy, but I make you really happy; and he is not in want, and I am. So if I am to propose the penalty which I really deserve, I propose this—a public maintenance in the prytaneum.

Perhaps you think me stubborn and arrogant in what I am saying now, as in what I said about the entreaties and tears. It is not so, Athenians; it is rather that I am convinced that I never wronged any man voluntarily, though I cannot persuade you of that, for we have discussed together only a little time. If there were a law at Athens, as there is elsewhere, not to finish a trial of life and death in a single day, I think that I could have persuaded you; but now it is not easy in so short a time to clear myself of great prejudices. But when I am persuaded that I have never wronged any man, I shall certainly not wrong myself, or admit that I deserve to suffer any evil, or propose any evil for myself as a penalty. Why should I? Lest I should suffer the penalty which Meletus proposes when I say that I do not know whether it is a good or an evil? Shall I choose instead of it something which I know to be an evil, and propose that as a penalty? Shall I propose imprisonment? And why should I pass the rest of my days in prison, the slave of successive officials? Or shall I propose a fine, with imprisonment until it is paid? I have told you why I will not do that. I should have to remain in prison, for I have no money to pay a fine with. Shall I then propose exile? Perhaps you would agree to that. Life would indeed be very dear to me if I were unreasonable enough to expect that strangers would cheerfully tolerate my discussions and arguments when you who are my fellow citizens cannot endure them, and have found them so irksome and odious to you that you are seeking now to be relieved of them. No, indeed, Athenians, that is not likely. A fine life I should lead for an old man if I were to withdraw from Athens and pass the rest of my days in wandering from city to city, and continually being expelled. For I know very well that the young men will listen to me wherever I go, as they do here; and if I drive them away, they will persuade their elders to expel me; and if I do not drive them away, their fathers and kinsmen will expel me for their sakes.

Perhaps some one will say, "Why cannot you withdraw from Athens, Socrates, and hold your peace?" It is the most difficult thing in the world to make you understand why I cannot do that. If I say that I cannot hold my peace because that would be to disobey the god, you will think that I am not in earnest and will not believe me. And if I tell you that no greater good can happen to a man than to discuss virtue every day and the other matters about which you have heard me arguing and examining myself and others, and that an unexamined life is not worth living, then you will believe me still less. But that is so, my friends, though it is not easy to persuade you. And, what is more, I am not accustomed to think that I deserve anything evil. If I had been rich, I would have proposed as large a fine as I could pay: that would have done me no harm. But I am not rich enough to pay a fine unless you are willing to fix it at a sum within my means. Perhaps I could pay you a mina, so I propose that. Plato here, Athenians, and Crito, and Critobulus, and Apollodorus bid me propose thirty minae, and they will be sureties for me. So I propose thirty minae. They will be sufficient sureties to you for the money.

(He is condemned to death.)

You have not gained very much time, Athenians, and, as the price of it, you will have an evil name for all who wish to revile the state, and they will say that you put Socrates, a wise man, to death. For they will certainly call me wise, whether I am wise or not, when they want to reproach you. If you would have waited for a little while, your wishes would have been fulfilled in the course of nature; for you see that I am an old man, far advanced in years, and near to death. I am saying this not to all of you, only to those who have voted for my death. And to them I have something else to say. Perhaps, my friends, you think that I have been convicted because I was wanting in the arguments by which I could have persuaded you to acquit me, if, that is, I had thought it right to do or to say anything to escape punishment. It is not so. I have been convicted because I was wanting, not in arguments, but in impudence and shamelessness—because I would not plead before you as you would have liked to hear me plead, or appeal to you with weeping and wailing, or say and do many other things which I maintain are unworthy of me, but which you have been accustomed to from other men. But when I was defending myself, I thought that I ought not to do anything unworthy of a free man because of the danger which I ran, and I have not changed my mind now. I would very much rather defend myself as I did, and die, than as you would have had me do, and live. Both in a lawsuit and in war, there are some things which neither I nor any other man may do in order to escape from death. In battle, a man often sees that he may at least escape from death by throwing down his arms and falling on his knees before the pursuer to beg for his life. And there are many other ways of avoiding death in every danger if a man is willing to say and to do anything. But, my friends, I think that it is a much harder thing to escape from wickedness than from death, for wickedness is swifter than death. And now I, who am old and slow, have been overtaken by the slower pursuer: and my accusers, who are clever and swift, have been overtaken by the swifter pursuer—wickedness. And now I shall go away, sentenced by you to death; and they will go away, sentenced by truth to wickedness and injustice. And I abide by this award as well as they. Perhaps it was right for these things to be so; and I think that they are fairly balanced.

And now I wish to prophesy to you, Athenians, who have condemned me. For I am going to die, and that is the time when men have most prophetic power. And I prophesy to you who have sentenced me to death that a far more severe punishment than you have inflicted on me will surely overtake you as soon as I am dead. You have done this thing, thinking that you will be relieved from having to give an account of your lives. But I say that the result will be very different. There will be more men who will call you to account, whom I have held back, though you did not recognize it. And they will be harsher toward you than I have been, for they will be younger, and you will be more indignant with them. For if you think that you will restrain men from reproaching you for not living as you should, by putting them to death, you are very much mistaken. That way of escape is neither possible nor honorable. It is much more honorable and much easier not to suppress others, but to make yourselves as good as you can. This is my parting prophecy to you who have condemned me.

With you who have acquitted me I should like to discuss this thing that has happened, while the authorities are busy, and before I go to the place where I have to die. So, remain with me until I go: there is no reason why we should not talk with each other while it is possible. I wish to explain to you, as my friends, the meaning of what has happened to me. An amazing thing has happened to me, judges—for you I am right in calling judges. The prophetic sign has been constantly with me all through my life till now, opposing me in quite small matters if I were not going to act rightly. And now you yourselves see what has happened to me—a thing which might be thought, and which is sometimes actually reckoned, the supreme evil. But the divine sign did not oppose me when I was leaving my house in the morning, nor when I was coming up here to the court, nor at any point in my speech when I was going to say anything; though at other times it has often stopped me in the very act of speaking. But now, in this matter, it has never once opposed me, either in my words or my actions. I will tell you what I believe to be the reason. This thing that has come upon me must be a good; and those of us who think that death is an evil must needs be mistaken. I have a clear proof that that is so; for my accustomed sign would certainly have opposed me if I had not been going to meet with something good.

And if we reflect in another way, we shall see that we may well hope that death is a good. For the state of death is one of two things: either the dead man wholly ceases to be and loses all consciousness or, as we are told, it is a change and a migration of the soul to another place. And if death is the absence of all consciousness, and like the sleep of one whose slumbers are unbroken by any dreams, it will be a wonderful gain. For if a man had to select that night in which he slept so soundly that he did not even dream, and had to compare with it all the other nights and days of his life, and then had to say how many days and nights in his life he had spent better and more pleasantly than this night, I think that a private person, nay, even the great King himself, would find them easy to count, compared with the others. If that is the nature of death, I for one count it a gain. For then it appears that all time is nothing more than a single night. But if death is a journey to another place, and what we are told is true—that there are all who have died—what good could be greater than this, my judges? Would a journey not be worth taking, at the end of which, in the other world, we should be delivered from the pretended judges here and should find the true judges who are said to sit in judgment below, such as Minos and Rhadamanthus and Aeacus and Triptolemus, and the other demigods who were just in their own lives? Or what would you not give to discuss with Orpheus and Musaeus and Hesiod and Homer? I am willing to die many times if this be true. And for my own part I should find it wonderful to meet there Palamedes, and Ajax, the son of Telamon, and the other men of old who have died through an unjust judgment, and in comparing my experiences with theirs. That I think would be no small pleasure. And, above all, I could spend my time in examining those who are there, as I examine men here, and in finding out which of them is wise, and which of them thinks himself wise when

he is not wise. What would we not give, my judges, to be able to examine the leader of the great expedition against Troy, or Odysseus, or Sisyphus, or countless other men and women whom we could name? It would be an infinite happiness to discuss with them and to live with them and to examine them. Assuredly there they do not put men to death for doing that. For besides the other ways in which they are happier than we are, they are immortal, at least if what we are told is true.

And you, too, judges, must face death hopefully, and believe this as a truth that no evil can happen to a good man, either in life or after death. His fortunes are not neglected by the gods; and what has happened to me today has not happened by chance. I am persuaded that it was better for me to die now, and to be released from trouble; and that was the reason why the sign never turned me back. And so I am not at all angry with my accusers or with those who have condemned me to die. Yet it was not with this in mind that they accused me and condemned me, but meaning to do me an injury. So far I may blame them.

Yet I have one request to make of them. When my sons grow up, punish them, my friends, and harass them in the same way that I have harassed you, if they seem to you to care for riches or for any other thing more than virtue; and if they think that they are something when they are really nothing, reproach them, as I have reproached you, for not caring for what they should, and for thinking that they are something when really they are nothing. And if you will do this, I myself and my sons will have received justice from you.

But now the time has come, and we must go away—I to die, and you to live. Which is better is known to god alone.

*17. Leviathan**

THOMAS HOBBES (1588–1679)

The principal parts of philosophy are two. For two chief kinds of bodies, and very different from one another, offer themselves to such as search after their generation and properties; one whereof being the work of nature, is called a *natural body,* the other is called a *commonwealth,* and is made by the wills and agreement of men. And from these spring the two parts of philosophy, called *natural* and *civil.* But seeing that, for the knowledge of the properties of a commonwealth, it is necessary first to know the dispositions, affections, and manners of men, civil philosophy is again commonly divided into two parts, whereof one, which treats of men's dispositions and manners, is called *ethics;* and the other, which takes cognizance of their civil duties, is called *politics,* or simply *civil philosophy.* In the first place, therefore (after I have set down such premises as appertain to the nature of philosophy in general), I will discourse of *bodies natural;* in the second, of the *dispositions and manners of men;* and in the third, of the *civil duties of subjects....*

So that in the nature of man, we find three principal causes of quarrel. First, competition; second, diffidence; thirdly, glory.

The first, maketh men invade for gain; the second, for safety; and the third, for reputation. The first use violence, to make themselves masters of other men's persons, wives, children, and cattle; the second, to defend them; the third, for trifles, as a word, a smile, a different opinion, and any other sign of undervalue, either direct in their persons, or by reflection in their kindred, their friends, their nation, their profession, or their name.

Hereby it is manifest, that during the time men live without a common power to keep them all in awe, they are in that condition which is called war; and such a war, as is of every man, against every man. For WAR, consisteth not in battle only, or the act of fighting; but in a tract of time, wherein the will to contend by battle is sufficiently known: and therefore the notion of *time,* is to be considered in the nature of war; as it is in the nature of weather. For as the nature of foul weather, lieth not in a shower or two of rain; but in an inclination thereto of many days together: so the nature of war, consisteth not in actual fighting; but in the known disposition thereto, during all the time there is no assurance to the contrary. All other time is PEACE.

Whatsoever therefore is consequent to a time of war, where every man is enemy to every man; the same is consequent to the time, wherein men live without other security, than what their own strength, and their own invention shall furnish them withal. In such condition, there is no place for industry; because the fruit

---

* Selections from the *Elements of Philosophy.*

thereof is uncertain: and consequently no culture of the earth; no navigation, nor use of the commodities that may be imported by sea; no commodious building; no instruments of moving, and removing, such things as require much force; no knowledge of the face of the earth; no account of time; no arts; no letters; no society; and which is worst of all, continual fear, and danger of violent death; and the life of man, solitary, poor, nasty, brutish, and short.

It may seem strange to some man, that has not well weighed these things; that nature should thus dissociate, and render men apt to invade, and destroy one another: and he may therefore, not trusting to this inference, made from the passions, desire perhaps to have the same confirmed by experience. Let him therefore consider with himself, when taking a journey, he arms himself, and seeks to go well accompanied; when going to sleep, he locks his doors; when even in his house he locks his chests; and this when he knows there be laws, and public officers, armed, to revenge all injuries shall be done him; what opinion he has of his fellow-subjects, when he rides armed; of his fellow citizens, when he locks his doors; and of his children, and servants, when he locks his chests. Does he not there as much accuse mankind by his actions, as I do by my words? But neither of us accuse man's nature in it. The desires, and other passions of man, are in themselves no sin. No more are the actions, that proceed from those passions, till they know a law that forbids them: which till laws be made they cannot know: nor can any law be made, till they have agreed upon the person that shall make it.

It may peradventure be thought, there was never such a time, nor condition of war as this; and I believe it was never generally so, over all the world: but there are many places, where they live so now. But the savage people in many places of America, except the government of small families, the concord whereof dependeth on natural lust, have no government at all; and live at this day in that brutish manner, as I said before. Howsoever, it may be perceived what manner of life there would be, where there were no common power to fear, by the manner of life, which men that have formerly lived under a peaceful government, use to degenerate into, in a civil war.

But though there had never been any time, wherein particular men were in a condition of war one against another; yet in all times, kings, and persons of sovereign authority, because of their independency, are in continual jealousies, and in the state and posture of gladiators; having their weapons pointing, and their eyes fixed on one another; that is, their forts, garrisons, and guns upon the frontiers of their kingdoms; and continual spies upon their neighbours; which is a posture of war. But because they uphold thereby, the industry of their subjects; there does not follow from it, that misery, which accompanies the liberty of particular men.

To this war of every man, against every man, this also is consequent; that nothing can be unjust. The notions of right and wrong, justice and injustice have there no place. Where there is no common power, there is no law: where no law, no injustice. Force, and fraud, are in war the two cardinal virtues. Justice, and injustice are none of the faculties neither of the body, nor mind. If they were, they might be in a man that were alone in the world, as well as his senses, and passions. They are qualities, that relate to men in society, not in solitude. It is consequent also to the same condition, that there be no propriety, no dominion, no *mine* and *thine* distinct; but only that to be every man's, that he can get; and for so long, as he can keep it. And thus much for the ill condition, which man by mere nature is actually placed in; though with a possibility to come out of it, consisting partly in the passions, partly in his reason.

The passions that incline men to peace, are fear of death; desire of such things as are necessary to commodious living; and a hope by their industry to obtain them. And reason suggesteth convenient articles of peace, upon which men may be drawn to agreement. . . .

The final cause, end, or design of men, who naturally love liberty, and dominion over others, in the introduction of that restraint upon themselves, in which we see them live in commonwealths, is the foresight of their own preservation, and of a more contented life thereby; that is to say, of getting themselves out from that miserable condition of war, which is necessarily consequent, as hath been shown in chapter xiii, to the natural passions of men, when there is no visible power to keep them in awe, and tie them by fear of punishment to the performance of their covenants, and observation of those laws of nature set down. . . .

It is true, that certain living creatures, as bees, and ants, live sociably one with another, which are therefore by Aristotle numbered amongst political creatures; and yet have no other direction, than their particular judgments and appetites; nor speech, whereby one of them can signify to another, what he thinks expedient for the common benefit: and therefore some man may perhaps desire to know, why mankind cannot do the same. To which I answer,

First, that men are continually in competition for honour and dignity, which these creatures are not; and consequently amongst men there ariseth on that ground, envy and hatred, and finally war; but amongst these not so.

Secondly, that amongst these creatures, the common good differeth not from the private; and being by nature inclined to their private, they procure thereby the common benefit. But man, whose joy consisteth in comparing himself with other men, can relish nothing but what is eminent.

Thirdly, that these creatures, having not, as man, the use of reason, do not see, nor think they see any fault, in the administration of their common business; whereas amongst men, there are very many, that think themselves wiser, and able to govern the public, better than the rest; and these strive to reform and innovate, one this way, another that way; and thereby bring it into distraction and civil war.

Fourthly, that these creatures, though they have some use of voice, in making known to one another their desires, and other affections; yet they want that art of words, by which some men can represent to others, that which is good, in the likeness of evil; and evil, in the likeness of good; and augment, or diminish the apparent greatness of good and evil; discontenting men, and troubling their peace at their pleasure.

Fifthly, irrational creatures cannot distinguish between *injury* and *damage;* and therefore as long as they be at ease, they are not offended with their fellows: whereas man is then most troublesome, when he is most at ease: for then it is that he loves to shew his wisdom, and control the actions of them that govern the commonwealth.

Lastly, the agreement of these creatures is natural; that of men, is by covenant only, which is artificial: and therefore it is no wonder if there be somewhat else required, besides covenant, to make their agreement constant and lasting; which is a common power, to keep them in awe, and to direct their actions to the common benefit.

The only way to erect such a common power, as may be able to defend them from the invasion of foreigners, and the injuries of one another, and thereby to secure them in such sort, as that by their own industry, and by the fruits of the earth, they may nourish themselves and live contentedly; is, to confer all their power and strength upon one man, or upon one assembly of men, that may reduce all their wills, by plurality of voices, unto one will: which is as much as to say, to appoint one man, or assembly of men, to bear their person; and every one to own, and acknowledge himself to be author of whatsoever he that so beareth their person, shall act, or cause to be acted, in those things which concern the common peace and safety; and therein to submit their wills, every one to his will, and their judgments, to his judgment. This is more than consent, or concord; it is a real unity of them all, in one and the same person, made by covenant of every man with every man, in such manner, as if every man should say to every man, *I authorize and give up my right of governing myself, to this man, or to this assembly of men, on this condition, that thou give up thy right to him, and authorize all his actions in like manner.* This done, the multitude so united in one person, is called a COM-MONWEALTH, in Latin CIVITAS. This is the generation of that great LEVIATHAN, or rather, to speak more reverently, of that *mortal god,* to which we owe under the *immortal God,* our peace and defence. For by this authority, given him by every particular man in the commonwealth, he hath the use of so much power and strength conferred on him, that by terror thereof, he is enabled to perform the wills of them all, to peace at home, and mutual aid against their enemies abroad. And in him consisteth the essence of the commonwealth; which, to define it, is *one person, of whose acts as a great multitude, by mutual covenants one with another, have made themselves every one the author, to the end he may use the strength and means of them all, as he*

shall think expedient, for their peace and common defence.

And he that carrieth this person, is called SOVEREIGN, and said to have *sovereign power;* and every one besides, his SUBJECT.

The attaining to this sovereign power, is by two ways. One, by natural force; as when a man maketh his children, to submit themselves, and their children, to his government, as being able to destroy them if they refuse; or by war subdueth his enemies to his will, giving them their lives on that condition. The other, is when men agree amongst themselves, to submit to some man, or assembly of men, voluntarily, on confidence to be protected by him against all others. This latter, may be called a political commonwealth, or commonwealth by *institution;* and the former, a commonwealth by *acquisition....*

Liberty, or Freedom, signifieth, properly, the absence of opposition; by opposition, I mean external impediments of motion; and may be applied no less to irrational, and inanimate creatures, than to rational. For whatsoever is so tied, or environed, as it cannot move but within a certain space, which space is determined by the opposition of some external body, we say it hath not liberty to go further. And so of all living creatures, whilst they are imprisoned, or restrained, with walls, or chains; and of the water whilst it is kept in by banks, or vessels, that otherwise would spread itself into a larger space, we use to say, they are not at liberty, to move in such manner, as without those external impediments they would. But when the impediment of motion, is in the constitution of the thing itself, we use not to say: it wants the liberty, but the power to move; as when a stone lieth still, or a man is fastened to his bed by sickness.

And according to this proper, and generally received meaning of the word, a FREEMAN, *is he, that in those things, which by his strength and wit he is able to do, is not hindered to do what he has a will to.* But when the words *free,* and *liberty,* are applied to any thing but bodies, they are abused; for that which is not subject to motion is not subject to impediment: and therefore, when it is said, for example, the way is free, no liberty of the way is signified, but of those that walk in it without stop. And when we say a gift is free, there is not meant any liberty of the gift, but of the giver, that was not bound by any law or covenant to give it. So when we *speak freely,* it is not the liberty of voice, or pronunciation, but of the man, whom no law hath obliged to speak otherwise than he did. Lastly, from the use of the word *free-will,* no liberty can be inferred of the will, desire, or inclination, but the liberty of the man; which consisteth in this, that he finds no stop, in doing what he has the will, desire, or inclination to do.

Fear and liberty are consistent; as when a man throweth his goods into the sea for *fear* the ship should sink, he doth it nevertheless very willingly, and may refuse to do it if he will; it is therefore the action of one that was *free:* so a man sometimes pays his debt, only for *fear* of imprisonment, which because nobody hindered him from detaining, was the action of a man at *liberty.* And generally all actions which men do in commonwealths, for *fear* of the law, are actions, which the doers had *liberty* to omit.

Liberty, and *necessity* are consistent: as in the water, that hath not only *liberty,* but a *necessity* of descending by the channel; so likewise in the actions which men voluntarily do: which, because they proceed from their will, proceed from *liberty;* and yet, because every act of man's will, and every desire, and inclination proceedeth from some cause, and that from another cause, in a continual chain, whose first link is in the hand of God the first of all causes, proceed from *necessity.* So that to him that could see the connexion of those causes, the *necessity* of all men's voluntary actions, would appear manifest. And therefore God, that seeth, and disposeth all things, seeth also that the liberty of man in doing what he will, is accompanied with the *necessity* of doing that which God will, and no more, nor less. For though men may do many things, which God does not command, nor is therefore author of them; yet they can have no passion, nor appetite to any thing, of which appetite God's will is not the cause. And did not his will assure the *necessity* of man's will, and consequently of all that on man's will dependeth, the *liberty* of men would be a contradiction, and impediment to the omnipotence and *liberty* of God. And this shall suffice, as to the matter in hand, of that natural *liberty,* which only is properly called *liberty.*

But as men, for the attaining of peace, and conservation of themselves thereby, have made an artificial man, which we call a commonwealth; so also have they made artificial chains, called *civil laws,* which they themselves, by mutual covenants, have fastened at one end, to the lips of that man, or assembly, to whom they have given the sovereign power; and at the other end to their own ears. These bonds, in their own nature but weak, may nevertheless be made to hold, by the danger, though not by the difficulty of breaking them.

In relation to these bonds only it is, that I am to speak now, of the *liberty* of *subjects.* For seeing there is no commonwealth in the world, wherein there be rules enough set down, for the regulating of all the actions, and words of men; as being a thing impossible: it followeth necessarily, that in all kinds of actions by the laws praetermitted, men have the liberty, of doing what their own reasons shall suggest, for the most profitable to themselves. For if we take liberty in the proper sense, for corporal liberty; that is to say, freedom from chains and prison; it were very absurd for men to clamour as they do, for the liberty they so manifestly enjoy. Again, if we take liberty, for an exemption from laws, it is no less absurd, for men to demand as they do, that liberty, by which all other men may be masters of their lives. And yet, as absurd as it is, this is it they demand; not knowing that the laws are of no power to protect them, without a sword in the hands of a man, or men, to cause those laws to be put in execution. The liberty of a subject, lieth therefore only in those things, which in regulating their actions, the sovereign hath praetermitted: such as is the liberty to buy, and sell, and otherwise contract with one another; to choose their own abode, their own diet, their own trade of life, and institute their children as they themselves think fit; and the like.

Nevertheless we are not to understand, that by such liberty, the sovereign power of life and death, is either abolished, or limited. For it has been already shown, that nothing the sovereign representative can do to a subject, on what pretence soever, can properly be called injustice, or injury; because every subject is author of every act the sovereign doth; so that he never wanteth right to anything, otherwise, than as he himself is the subject of God, and bound thereby to observe the laws of nature. And therefore it may, and doth often happen in commonwealths, that a subject may be put to death, by the command of the sovereign power; and yet neither do the other wrong; as when Jephtha caused his daughter to be sacrificed: in which, and the like cases, he that so dieth, had liberty to do the action, for which he is nevertheless, without injury put to death. And the same holdeth also in a sovereign prince, that putteth to death an innocent sub-

ject. For though the action be against the law of nature, as being contrary to equity, as was the killing of Uriah, by David; yet it was not an injury to Uriah, but to God. Not to Uriah, because the right to do what he pleased was given him by Uriah himself: and yet to God, because David was God's subject, and prohibited all iniquity by the law of nature: which distinction, David himself, when he repented the fact, evidently confirmed, saying, *To thee only have I sinned*. In the same manner, the people of Athens, when they banished the most potent of their commonwealth for ten years, thought they committed no injustice; and yet they never questioned what crime he had done; but what hurt he would do: nay they commanded the banishment of they knew not whom; and every citizen bringing his oystershell into the market place, written with the name of him he desired should be banished, without actually accusing him, sometimes banished an Aristides, for his reputation of justice; and sometimes a scurrilous jester, as Hyperbolus, to make a jest of it. And yet a man cannot say, the sovereign people of Athens wanted right to banish them; or an Athenian the liberty to jest, or to be just.

The liberty, whereof there is so frequent and honourable mention, in the histories, and philosophy of the ancient Greeks, and Romans, and in the writings, and discourse of those that from them have received all their learning in the politics, is not the liberty of particular men; but the liberty of the commonwealth: which is the same with that which every man then should have, if there were no civil laws, nor commonwealth at all. And the effects of it also be the same. For as amongst masterless men, there is perpetual war, of every man against his neighbour; no inheritance, to transmit to the son, nor to expect from the father; no propriety of goods, or lands; no security; but a full and absolute liberty in every particular man; so in states, and commonwealth not dependent on one another, every commonwealth, not every man, has an absolute liberty, to do what it shall judge, that is to say, what that man, or assembly that representeth it, shall judge most conducing to their benefit. But withal, they live in the condition of a perpetual war, and upon the confines of battle, with their frontiers armed, and cannons planted against their neighbours round about. The Athenians, and Romans were free; that is, free commonwealth: not that any particular men had the liberty to resist their own representative; but that their representative had the liberty to resist, or invade other people. There is written on the turrets of the city of Lucca in great characters at this day, the word LIBERTAS; yet no man can thence infer, that a particular man has more liberty, or immunity from the service of the commonwealth there, than in Constantinople. Whether a commonwealth be monarchical, or popular, the freedom is still the same.

But it is an easy thing, for men to be deceived, by the specious name of liberty; and for want of judgment to distinguish, mistake that for their private inheritance, and birth-right, which is the right of the public only. And when the same error is confirmed by the authority of men in reputation for their writings on this subject, it is no wonder if it produce sedition, and change of government. In these western parts of the world, we are made to receive our opinions concerning the institution, and rights of commonwealths, from Aristotle, Cicero, and other men, Greeks and Romans, that living under popular states, derived those rights, not from the principles of nature, but transcribed them into their books, out of the practice of their own commonwealths, which were popular; as the grammarians describe the rules of language, out of the practice of the time; or the rules of poetry, out of the poems of Homer and Virgil. And because the Athenians were taught, to keep them from desire of changing their government, that they were freemen, and all that lived under monarchy were slaves; therefore Aristotle puts it down in his *Politics*, (*lib. 6 cap. ii.*) *In democracy,* LIBERTY *is to be supposed: for it is commonly held, that no man is* FREE *in any other government.* And as Aristotle; so Cicero, and other writers have grounded their civil doctrine, on the opinions of the Romans, who were taught to hate monarchy, at first, by them that having deposed their sovereign, shared amongst them the sovereignty of Rome; and afterwards by their successors. And by reading of these Greek, and Latin authors, men from their childhood have gotten a habit, under a false show of liberty, of favouring tumults, and of licentious controlling the actions of their sovereigns, and again of controlling those controllers; with the effusion of so much blood, as I think I may truly say, there was never any thing so dearly bought, as these western parts have bought the learning of the Greek and Latin tongues.

To come now to the particulars of the true liberty of a subject; that is to say, what are the things, which though commanded by the sovereign, he may nevertheless, without injustice, refuse to do; we are to consider, what rights we pass away, when we make a commonwealth; or, which is all one, what liberty we deny ourselves, by owning all the actions, without exception, of the man, or assembly, we make our sovereign. For in the act of our *submission,* consisteth both our *obligation,* and our *liberty;* which must therefore be inferred by arguments taken from thence; there being no obligation on any man, which ariseth not from some act of his own; for all men equally, are by nature free.

And because such arguments, must either be drawn from the express words, *I authorize all his actions,* or from the intention of him that submitteth himself to his power, which intention is to be understood by the end for which he so submitteth; the obligation, and liberty of the subject, is to be derived, either from those words, or others equivalent; or else from the end of the institution of sovereignty, namely, the peace of the subjects within themselves, and their defence against a common enemy.

First therefore, seeing sovereignty by institution, is by covenant of every one to every one; and sovereignty by acquisition, by covenants of the vanquished to the victor, or child to the parent; it is manifest, that every subject has liberty in all those things, the right whereof cannot by covenant be transferred. I have shewn before in the 14th chapter, that covenants, not to defend a man's own body, are void. Therefore,

If the sovereign command a man, though justly condemned, to kill, wound, or maim himself; or not to resist those that assault him; or to abstain from the use of food, air, medicine, or any other thing, without which he cannot live; yet hath that man the liberty to disobey.

If a man be interrogated by the sovereign, or his authority, concerning a crime done by himself, he is not bound, without assurance of pardon, to confess it; because no man, as I have shown in the same chapter, can be obliged by covenant to accuse himself.

Again, the consent of a subject to sovereign power, is contained in these words, *I authorize, or take upon me, all his actions;* in which there is no restriction at all, of his own former natural liberty: for by allowing him to *kill me,* I am not bound to kill myself when he commands me. It is one thing to say, *kill me, or my fellow, if you please;* another thing to say, *I will kill myself, or my fellow.* It followeth therefore, that

No man is bound by the words themselves, either to kill himself, or any other man; and consequently, that the obligation a man may sometimes have, upon the command of the sovereign to execute any dangerous, or dishonourable office, dependeth not on the words of our submission; but on the intention, which is to be understood by the end thereof. When therefore our refusal to obey, frustrates the end for which the sovereignty was ordained; then there is no liberty to refuse: otherwise there is.

Upon this ground, a man that is commanded as a soldier to fight against the enemy, though his sovereign have right enough to punish his refusal with death, may nevertheless in many cases refuse, without injustice; as when he substituteth a sufficient soldier in his place: for in this case he deserteth not the service of the commonwealth. And there is allowance to be made for natural timorousness; not only to women, of whom no such dangerous duty is expected, but also to men of feminine courage. When armies fight, there is on one side, or both, a running away; yet when they do it not out of treachery, but fear, they are not esteemed to do it unjustly, but dishonourably. For the same reason, to avoid battle, is not injustice, but cowardice. But he that inrolleth himself a soldier, or taketh imprest money, taketh away the excuse of a timorous nature; and is obliged, not only to go to the battle, but also not to run from it, without his captain's leave. And when the defence of the commonwealth, requireth at once the help of all that are able to bear arms, every one is obliged; because otherwise the institution of the commonwealth, which they have not the purpose, or courage to preserve, was in vain.

To resist the sword of the commonwealth, in defence of another man, guilty, or innocent, no man hath liberty; because such liberty, takes away from the sovereign, the means of protecting us; and is therefore destructive of the very essence of government. But in case a great many men together, have already resisted the sovereign power unjustly, or committed some capital crime, for which every one of them expecteth death, whether have they not the liberty then to join together, and assist, and defend one another? Certainly they have: for they but defend their lives, which the guilty man may as well do, as the innocent. There was indeed injustice in the first breach of their duty; their bearing of arms subsequent to it, though it be to maintain what they have done, is no new unjust act. And if it be only to defend their persons, it is not unjust at all. But the offer of pardon taketh from them, to whom it is offered, the plea of self-defence, and maketh their perseverance in assisting, or defending, the rest, unlawful.

As for other liberties, they depend on the silence of the law. In cases where the sovereign has prescribed no rule, there the subject hath the liberty to do, or forbear, according to his own discretion. And therefore such liberty is in some places more, and in some less; and in some times more, in other times less, according as they that have the sovereignty shall think most convenient. As for example, there was a time, when in England a man might enter into his own land, and dispossess such as wrongfully possessed it, by force. But in after times, that liberty of forcible entry, was taken away by a statute made, by the king, in parliament. And in some places of the world, men have the liberty of many wives: in other places, such liberty is not allowed.

If a subject have a controversy with his sovereign of debt, or of right of possession of lands or goods, or concerning any service required at his hands, or concerning any penalty, corporal, or pecuniary, grounded on a precedent law; he hath the same liberty to sue for his right, as if it were against a subject; and before such judges, as are appointed by the sovereign. For seeing the sovereign demandeth by force of a former law, and not by virtue of his power; he declareth thereby, that he requireth no more, than shall appear to be due by that law. The suit therefore is not contrary to the will of the sovereign; and consequently the subject hath the liberty to demand the hearing of his cause; and sentence, according to that law. But if he demand, or take anything by pretence of his power; there lieth, in that case, no action of law; for all that is done by him in virtue of his power, is done by the authority of every subject, and consequently he that brings an action against the sovereign, brings it against himself.

If a monarch, or sovereign assembly, grant a liberty to all, or any of his subjects, which grant standing, he is disabled to provide for their safety, the grant is void; unless he directly renounce, or transfer the sovereignty to another. For in that he might openly, if it had been his will, and in plain terms, have renounced, or transferred it, and did not; it is to be understood it was not his will, but that the grant proceeded from ignorance of the repugnancy between such a liberty and the sovereign power; and therefore the sovereignty is still retained; and consequently all those powers, which are necessary to the exercising thereof; such as are the power of war, and peace, of judicature, of appointing officers, and councillors, of levying money, and the rest named in the 18th chapter.

The obligation of subjects to the sovereign, is understood to last as long, and no longer, than the power lasteth, by which he is able to protect them. For the right men have by nature to protect themselves, when none else can protect them, can by no covenant be relinquished. The sovereignty is the soul of the commonwealth; which once departed from the body, the members do no more receive their motion from it. The end of obedience is protection; which, wheresoever a man seeth it, either in his own, or in another's sword, nature applieth his obedience to it, and his endeavour to maintain it. And though sovereignty, in the intention of them that make it, be immortal; yet it is in its own nature, not only subject to violent death, by foreign war; but also through the ignorance, and passions of men, it hath in it, from the very institution, many seeds of a natural mortality, by intestine discord.

If a subject be taken prisoner in war; or his person or his means of life be within the guards of the enemy, and hath his life and corporal liberty given him, on condition to be subject to the victor, he hath liberty to accept the condition; and having accepted it, is the subject of him that took him; because he had no other way to preserve himself. The case is the same, if he be detained on the same terms, in a foreign country. But if a man be held in prison, or bonds, or is not trusted with the liberty of his body; he cannot be understood to be bound by covenant to subjection; and therefore may, if he can, make his escape by any means whatsoever.

If a monarch shall relinquish the sovereignty, both for himself, and his heirs; his subjects return to the absolute liberty of nature; because, though nature may declare who are his sons, and who are the nearest of his kin; yet it dependeth on his own will, as hath been said in the precedent chapter, who shall be his heir. If therefore he will have no heir, there is no sovereignty, nor subjection. The case is the same, if he die without known kindred, and without declaration of his heir. For then there can no heir be known, and consequently no subjection be due.

If the sovereign banish his subject; during the banishment, he is not subject.

But he that is sent on a message, or hath leave to travel, is still subject; but it is, by contract between sovereigns, not by virtue of the covenant of subjection. For whosoever entereth into another's dominion, is subject to all the laws thereof; unless he have a privilege of the amity of the sovereigns, or by special licence.

If a monarch subdued by war, render himself subject to the victor; his subjects are delivered from their former obligation, and become obliged to the victor. If he be held prisoner, or have not the liberty of his own body; he is not understood to have given away the right of sovereignty; and therefore his subjects are obliged to yield obedience to the magistrates formerly placed, governing not in their own name, but in his. For, his right remaining, the question is only of the administration; that is to say, of the magistrates and officers; which, if he have not means to name, he is supposed to approve those, which he himself had formerly appointed. . . .

The law of nature, and the civil law, contain each other, and are of equal extent. For the laws of nature, which consist in equity, justice, gratitude, and other moral virtues on these depending, in the condition of mere nature (as I have said before in the end of the 15th chapter,) are not properly laws, but qualities that dispose men to peace, and to obedience. When a common-wealth is once settled, then are they actually laws, and not before; as being then the commands of the common-wealth; and therefore also civil laws: for it is the sovereign power that obliges men to obey them. For in the differences of private men, to declare, what is equity, what is justice, and what is moral virtue, and to make them binding, there is need of the ordinances of sovereign power, and punishments to be ordained for such as shall break them; which ordinances are therefore part of the civil law. The law of nature therefore is a part of the civil law in all common-wealths of the world. Reciprocally also, the civil law is a part of the dictates of nature. For justice, that is to say, performance of covenant, and giving to every man his own, is a dictate of the law of nature. But every subject in a common-wealth, hath covenanted to obey the civil law, (either one with another, as when they assemble to make a common representative, or with the representative itself one by one, when subdued by the sword they promise obedience, that they may receive life;) And therefore obedience to the civil law is part also of the law of nature. Civil, and natural law are not different kinds, but different parts of law; whereof one part being written, is called civil, the other unwritten, natural. But the right of nature, that is, the natural liberty of man, may by the civil law be abridged, and restrained: nay, the end of making laws, is no other, but such restraint; without the which there cannot possibly be any peace. And law was brought into the world for nothing else, but to limit the natural liberty of particular men, in such manner, as they might not hurt, but assist one another, and join together against a common enemy.

18. Introduction to the Philosophy of History

Georg Hegel (1770–1831)

The enquiry into the *essential destiny* of Reason—as far as it is considered in reference to the world—is identical with the question, *what is the ultimate purpose of the world?* And the expression implies that that purpose is to be realised. Two points of consideration suggest themselves: first, the *import* of this design—its abstract definition; and secondly, its *realisation*.

It must be observed at the outset, that the object we investigate—universal history—belongs to the realm of *Spirit*. The term "world" includes both physical and psychical nature. Physical nature also plays its part in the world's history, and from the very beginning attention will have to be paid to the fundamental natural relations thus involved. But Spirit, and the course of its development, is our substantial object. Our task does not require us to contemplate nature as a rational system in itself—though in its own proper domain it proves itself such —but simply in its relation to *Spirit*. On the stage on which we are observing it, —universal history—Spirit displays itself in its most concrete actuality. Notwithstanding this (or rather for the very purpose of comprehending the *general* principles which this, its form of *concrete actuality*, embodies) we must premise some abstract characteristics of the *nature of Spirit*. Such an explanation, however, cannot be given here under any other form than that of bare assertion. The present is not the occasion for unfolding the idea of Spirit speculatively; for whatever has a place in an introduction, must, as already observed, be taken as simply historical; something assumed as having been explained and proved elsewhere; or whose demonstration awaits the sequel of the Science of History itself.

We have therefore to mention here:

1. The abstract characteristics of the nature of Spirit.

2. What means Spirit uses in order to realise its Idea.

3. Lastly, we must consider the shape which the perfect embodiment of Spirit assumes—the state.

The nature of Spirit may be understood by a glance at its direct opposite—*Matter*. As the essence of matter is gravity, so, on the other hand, we may affirm that the substance, the essence of Spirit is freedom. All will readily assent to the doctrine that Spirit, among other properties, is also endowed with freedom; but philosophy teaches that all the qualities of Spirit exist only through freedom; that all are but means for attaining freedom; that all seek and produce this and this alone. It is a preception of speculative philosophy, that freedom is the sole truth of Spirit. Matter possesses gravity in virtue of its tendency towards a central point. It is essentially composite; consisting of parts that *exclude* each other. It seeks its unity; and therefore exhibits the tendency towards self-destruction, towards its opposite [an indivisible point]. If it could attain this, it would be matter no longer, it would have perished. It strives after the realisation of its Idea; for in unity it exists *ideally*. Spirit, on the contrary, may be defined as that which has its centre in itself. It has not a unity beyond itself, but has already found it; it exists *in* and *with itself*. Matter has its essence out of itself; Spirit is *self-contained existence* (Bei-sich-selbst-seyn). Now this is freedom, exactly. For if I am dependent, my being is referred to something else which I am not; I cannot exist independently of something external. I am free, on the contrary, when my existence depends upon myself. This self-contained existence of Spirit is none other than self-consciousness—consciousness of one's own being. Two things must be distinguished in consciousness; first, the fact *that I know;* secondly, *what I know.* In *self* consciousness these are merged in one; for Spirit *knows itself.* It involves an appreciation of its own nature, as also an energy enabling it to realise itself; to make itself *actually* that which it is *potentially.* According to this abstract definition it may be said of universal history, that it is the exhibition of Spirit in the process of working out the knowledge of that which it is potentially. And as the germ bears in itself the whole nature of the tree, and the taste and form of its fruits, so do the first traces of Spirit virtually contain the whole of that history. The Orientals have not attained the knowledge that Spirit—Man *as such*—is free; and because they do not know this they are not free. They only know that *one is free.* But on this very account, the freedom of that one is only caprice; ferocity—brutal recklessness or passion, or a mildness and tameness of the desires, which is itself only an accident of nature or mere caprice like the former.—That *one* is therefore only a despot; not a *free man.* The consciousness of freedom first arose among the Greeks, and therefore they were free; but they, and the Romans likewise, knew only that *some* are free,—not man as such. Even Plato and Aristotle did not know this. The Greeks, therefore, had slaves; and their whole life and the maintenance of their splendid liberty, was implicated with the institution of slavery: a fact moreover, which made that liberty on the one hand only an accidental, transient and limited growth; on the other hand, constituted it a rigorous thraldom of our common nature—of the human. The German nations, under the influence of Christianity, were the first to attain the consciousness, that man, as man, is free: that it is the *freedom* of Spirit which constitutes its essence. This consciousness arose first in religion, the inmost region of Spirit; but to introduce the principle into the various relations of the actual world, involves a more extensive problem than its simple implantation; a problem whose solution and application require a severe and lengthened process of culture. As an example of this, we may note that slavery did not cease immediately on the reception of Christianity. Still less did liberty predominate in states; or governments and constitutions adopt a rational organization, or recognise freedom as their basis. That application of the principle to political relations; the thorough moulding and interpenetration of the constitution of society by it, is a process identical with history itself. I have already directed attention to the distinction here involved, between a principle as such, and its *application;* i.e. its introduction and carrying out in the actuality of Spirit and life. This is a point of fundamental importance in our science, and one which must be constantly respected as essential. And in the same way as this distinction has attracted attention in view of the *Christian* principle of self-consciousness—freedom; it also shews itself as an essential one, in view of the principle of freedom *generally*. The history of the world is none other than the progress in the consciousness of freedom; a progress whose development according to the necessity of its nature, it is our business to investigate.

The general statement given above, of the various grades in the consciousness of freedom—and which we applied in the first instance to the fact that the Eastern nations knew only that *one* is

free; the Greek and Roman world only that *some* are free; whilst *we* know that all men absolutely (man *as man*) are free,—supplies us with the natural division of universal history, and suggests the mode of its discussion. This is remarked, however, only incidentally and anticipatively; some other ideas must be first explained.

The destiny of the spiritual world, and,—since this is the *substantial world*, while the physical remains subordinate to it, or, in the language of speculation, has no truth *as against* the spiritual,—the *final cause of the world at large,* we allege to be the *consciousness* of its own freedom on the part of Spirit, and *ipso facto,* the *reality* of that freedom. But that this term "freedom," without further qualification, is an indefinite, and incalculable ambiguous term; and that while that which it represents is the *ne plus ultra* of attainment, it is liable to an infinity of misunderstandings, confusions and errors, and to become the occasion for all imaginable excesses,—has never been more clearly known and felt than in modern times. Yet, for the present, we must content ourselves with the term itself without farther definition. Attention was also directed to the importance of the infinite difference between a principle in the abstract, and its actualization in the concrete. In the process before us, the essential nature of freedom—which involves in it absolute necessity,—is to be displayed as coming to a consciousness of itself (for it is in its very nature, self-consciousness) and thereby actualizing its existence. Itself is its own object of attainment, and the sole aim of Spirit. This result it is, at which the process of the world's history has been continually aiming; and to which the sacrifices that have ever and anon been laid on the vast altar of the earth, through the long lapse of ages, have been offered. This is the only aim that sees itself realised and fulfilled; the only pole of repose amid the ceaseless change of events and conditions, and the truly efficient principle that pervades them. This final aim is God's purpose with the world; but God is the absolutely perfect being, and can, therefore, will nothing other than himself—his own will. The nature of His will—that is, His nature itself—is what we here call the idea of freedom; translating the language of religion into that of thought. The question, then, which we may next put, is: What means does this principle of freedom use for its realisation? This is the second point we have to consider.

The question of the *means* by which freedom develops itself to a world, conducts us to the phenomenon of history itself. Although freedom is, primarily, an undeveloped idea, the means it uses are external and phenomenal; presenting themselves in history to our sensuous vision. The first glance at history convinces us that the actions of men proceed from their needs, their passions, their interests, their characters and talents; and impresses us with the belief that such needs, passions and interest are the sole springs of action—the efficient agents in this scene of activity. Among these may, perhaps, be found aims of a liberal or universal kind—benevolence it may be, or noble patriotism; but such virtues and general views are but insignificant as compared with the world and its doings. We may perhaps see the ideal of Reason actualized in those who adopt such aims, and within the spheres of their influence; but they bear only a trifling proportion to the mass of the human race; and the extent of that influence is limited accordingly. Passions, private aims, and the satisfaction of selfish desires, are on the other hand, most effective springs of action. Their power lies in the fact that they respect none of the limitations

which justice and morality would impose on them; and that these natural impulses have a more direct influence over man than the artificial and tedious discipline that tends to order and self-restraint, law and morality. When we look at this display of passions, and the consequences of their violence; the unreason which is associated not only with them, but even (rather we might say *especially*) with *good* designs and righteous aims; when we see the evil, the vice, the ruin that has befallen the most flourishing kingdoms which the mind of man ever created, we can scarce avoid being filled with sorrow at this universal taint of corruption: and, since this decay is not the work of mere nature, but of the human will—a moral embitterment—a revolt of the good spirit (if it have a place within us) may well be the result of our reflections. Without rhetorical exaggeration, a simply truthful combination of the miseries that have overwhelmed the noblest of nations and polities, and the finest exemplars of private virtue,—forms a picture of most fearful aspect, and excites emotions of the profoundest and most hopeless sadness, counter-balanced by no consolatory result. We endure in beholding it a mental torture, allowing no defence or escape but the consideration that what has happened could not be otherwise; that it is a fatality which no intervention could alter. And at last we draw back from the intolerable disgust with which these sorrowful reflections threaten us, into the more agreeable environment of our individual life—the present formed by our private aims and interests. In short we retreat into the selfishness that stands on the quiet shore, and thence enjoy in safety the distant spectacle of "wrecks confusedly hurled." But even regarding history as the slaughter-bench at which the happiness of peoples, the wisdom of states, and the virtue of individuals have been victimised—the question involuntarily arises—to what principle, to what final aim these enormous sacrifices have been offered. From this point the investigation usually proceeds to that which we have made the general commencement of our enquiry. Starting from this we pointed out those events which made up a picture so suggestive of gloomy emotions and thoughtful reflections—as *the very field* which we, for our part, regard as exhibiting only the means for realizing what we assert to be the essential destiny—the absolute aim, or—which comes to the same thing—the true *result* of the world's history. We have all along purposely eschewed "moral reflections" as a method of rising from the scene of particular historical events to the general principles which they embody. Besides, it is not the interest of such sentimentalities, really to rise above those depressing emotions; and to solve the enigmas of providence which the considerations that occasioned them, present. It is essential to their character to find a gloomy satisfaction in the empty and fruitless sublimities of that negative result. We return then to the point of view which we have adopted; observing that the successive steps (Momente) of the analysis to which it will lead us, will also evolve the conditions requisite for answering the enquiries suggested by the panorama of sin and suffering that history unfolds.

The *first* remark we have to make, and which—though already presented more than once—cannot be too often repeated when the occasion seems to call for it,—is that what we call *principle, aim, destiny,* or the nature and idea of Spirit, is something merely general and abstract. Principle—plant of existence—law—is an undeveloped essence, which *as such*—however true in itself—is not completely actual. Aims, principles, &c., have a place in our thoughts, in our subjective design only; but not yet in the sphere of actuality. That which exists for itself only, is a possibility, a potentiality; but has not yet emerged into existence. A *second* element must be introduced in order to produce actuality—viz. actuation, realization; and whose principle is the will—the activity of man in the widest sense. It is only by this activity that that Idea as well as abstract characteristics generally, are realized, actualized; for of themselves they are powerless. The motive power that puts them in operation, and gives them determinate existence, is the need, instinct, inclination, and passion of man. That some conception of mine should be developed into act and existence, is my earnest desire: I wish to assert my personality in connection with it: I wish to be satisfied by its execution. If I am to exert myself for any object, it must in some way or other be *my* object. In the accomplishment of such or such designs I must at the same time find *my* satisfaction; although the purpose for which I exert myself includes a complication of results, many of which have no interest for me. This is the absolute right of personal existence—to find *itself* satisfied in its activity and labour. If men are to interest themselves for anything, they must (so to speak) have part of their existence involved in it; find their individuality gratified by its attainment. Here a mistake must be avoided. We intend blame, and justly impute it as a fault, when we say of an individual, that he is "interested" (in taking part in such or such transactions) that is, seeks only his private advantage. In reprehending this we find fault with him for furthering his personal aims without any regard to a more comprehensive design; of which he takes advantage to promote his own interest, or which he even sacrifices with this view. But he who is active in *promoting an object,* is not simply "interested," but interested in that object itself. Language faithfully expresses this distinction.—Nothing therefore happens, nothing is accomplished, unless the individuals concerned, seek their own satisfaction in the issue. They are particular units of society; *i.e.* they have special needs, instincts, and interests generally, peculiar to themselves. Among these needs are not only such as we usually call necessities—the stimuli of individual desire and volition—but also those connected with individual views and convictions; or—to use a term expressing less decision—leanings of opinion; supposing the impulses of reflection, understanding, and reason, to have been awakened. In these cases people demand, if they are to exert themselves in any direction, that the object should commend itself to them; that in point of opinion,—whether as to its goodness, justice, advantage, profit, —they should be able to "enter into it" (dabei seyn). This is a consideration of especial importance in our age, when people are less than formerly influenced by reliance on others, and by authority; when, on the contrary, they devote their activities to a cause on the ground of their own understanding, their independent conviction and opinion.

We assert then that nothing has been accomplished without interest on the part of the actors; and—if interest be called passion, inasmuch as the whole individuality, to the neglect of all other actual or possible interests and aims, is devoted to an object with every fibre of volition, concentrating all its desires and powers upon it—we may affirm absolutely that *nothing great in the world* has been accomplished without *passion.* Two elements, therefore enter into the object of our investigation; the first the Idea, the second the complex of human passions; the one the warp, the other the woof of the vast tapestry of universal history. The concrete mean and union of the two is liberty, under the conditions of morality in a state. We

have spoken of the idea of freedom as the nature of Spirit, and the absolute goal of history. Passion is regarded as a thing of sinister aspect, as more or less immoral. Man is required to have no passions. Passion, it is true, is not quite the suitable word for what I wish to express. I mean here nothing more than human activity as resulting from private interests—special, or if you will, self-seeking designs—with this qualification, that the whole energy of will and character is devoted to their attainment; that other interests (which would in themselves constitute attractive aims), or rather all things else, are sacrificed to them. The object in question is so bound up with the man's will, that it entirely and alone determines the "hue of resolution," and is inseparable from it. It has become the very essence of his volition. For a person is a specific existence; not man in general (a term to which no real existence corresponds), but a particular human being. The term "character" likewise expresses this idiosyncrasy of will and intelligence. But *character* comprehends all peculiarities whatever; the way in which a person conducts himself in private relations, &c., and is not limited to his idiosyncrasy in its practical and active phase. I shall, therefore, use the term "passion"; understanding thereby the particular bent of character, as far as the peculiarities of volition are not limited to private interest, but supply the impelling and actuating force for accomplishing deeds shared in by the community at large. Passion is in the first instance the *subjective,* and therefore the *formal* side of energy, will, and activity—leaving the object or aim still undetermined. And there is a similar relation of formality to reality in merely individual conviction, individual views, individual conscience. It is always a question, of essential importance, what is the purport of my conviction, what the object of my passion, in deciding whether the one or the other is of a true and substantial nature. Conversely, if it is so, it will inevitably attain actual existence—be actualized.

From this comment on the second essential element in the historical embodiment of an aim, we infer—glancing at the institution of the state in passing —that a state is then well constituted and internally powerful, when the private interest of its citizens is one with the common interest of the state; when the one finds its gratification and realization in the other,—a proposition in itself very important. But in a state many institutions must be adopted, much political machinery invented, accompanied by appropriate political arrangements,—necessitating long struggles of the understanding before what is really appropriate can be discovered,— involving, moreover, contentions with private interest and passions, and a tedious discipline of these latter, in order to bring about the desired harmony. The epoch when a state attains this harmonious condition, marks the period of its bloom, its virtue, its vigour, and its prosperity. But the history of mankind does not begin with a *conscious* aim of any kind, as it is the case with the particular circles into which men form themselves of set purpose. The mere social instinct implies a conscious purpose of security for life and property; and when society has been constituted, this purpose becomes more comprehensive. The history of the world begins with its general aim—the realization of the idea of Spirit—only in an *implicit* form (*an sich*) that is, as nature; an inmost, unconscious instinct; and the whole process of history (as already observed), is directed to rendering this unconscious impulse a conscious one. Thus appearing in the form of merely natural existence, natural will— that which has been called the subjective side,—physical craving, instinct, pas-

sion, private interest, as also opinion and subjective conception,—spontaneously present themselves at the very commencement. This vast congeries of volitions, interests and activities, constitute the instruments and means of the world-spirit for attaining its object; bringing it to consciousness, and realizing it. And this aim is none other than finding itself —coming to itself—and contemplating itself in concrete actuality. But that those manifestations of vitality on the part of individuals and peoples, in which they seek and satisfy their own purposes, are, at the same time, the means and instruments of a higher and broader purpose of which they know nothing,— which they realise unconsciously,— might be made a matter of question; rather has been questioned, and in every variety of form negatived, decried and contemned as mere dreaming and "philosophy." But on this point I announced my view at the very outset, and asserted our hypothesis,—which, however, will appear in the sequel, in the form of a legitimate inference,—and our belief, that Reason governs the world, and has consequently governed its history. In relation to this independently universal and substantial existence—all else is subordinate, subservient to it, and the means for its development. But moreover this Reason is immanent in historical existence and attains to its own perfection in and through that existence. The union of universal abstract existence generally with the individual,—the subjective—that is this alone is truth, belongs to the department of speculation, and is treated in this general form in logic.—But in the process of the world's history itself,—as still incomplete,—the abstract final aim of history is not yet made the distinct object of desire and interest. While these limited sentiments are still unconscious of the purpose they are fulfilling, the universal principle is implicit in them, and is realizing itself through them. The question also assumes the form of the union of *freedom and necessity;* the latent abstract process of Spirit being regarded as *necessity,* while that which exhibits itself in the conscious will of men, as their interest, belongs to the domain of *freedom.* As the metaphysical connection (*i.e.* the connection in the Idea) of these forms of thought, belongs to logic, it would be out of place to analyse it here.

It is quite otherwise with the comprehensive relations that history has to do with. In this sphere are presented those momentous collisions between existing, acknowledged duties, laws, and rights, and those contingencies which are adverse to this fixed system; which assail and even destroy its foundations and existence; whose tenor may nevertheless seem good,—on the large scale advantageous,—yes, even indispensable and necessary. These contingencies realise themselves in history: they involve a general principle of a different order from that on which depends the *permanence* of a people or a state. This principle is an essential phase in the development of the *creating* Idea, of truth striving and urging towards [consciousness of] itself. Historical men—*world-historical individuals*—are those in whose aims such a general principle lies.

Caesar, in danger of losing a position, not perhaps at that time of superiority, yet at least of equality with the others who were at the head of the state, and of succumbing to those who were just on the point of becoming his enemies,—belongs essentially to this category. These enemies—who were at the same time pursuing *their* personal aims—had the form of the constitution, and the power conferred by an appearance of justice, on their side. Caesar was contending for the maintenance of his position, honour, and safety; and, since the power of his opponents included the sovereignty over the provinces of the Roman Empire, his victory secured for him the conquest of that entire empire; and he thus became—though leaving the form of the constitution—the autocrat of the state. That which secured for him the execution of a design, which in the first instance was of negative import—the autocracy of Rome,—was, however, at the same time an independently necessary feature in the history of Rome and of the world. It was not, then, his private gain merely, but an unconscious impulse that occasioned the accomplishment of that for which the time was ripe. Such are all great historical men,—whose own particular aims involve those large issues which are the will of the world-spirit. They may be called heroes, inasmuch as they have derived their purposes and their vocation, not from the calm, regular course of things, sanctioned by the existing order; but from a concealed fount—one which has not attained to phenomenal, present existence,—from that inner Spirit, still hidden beneath the surface, which, impinging on the outer world as on a shell, bursts it in pieces, because it is another kernel than that which belonged to the shell in question. They are men, therefore, who appear to draw the impulse of their life from themselves; and whose deeds have produced a condition of things and a complex of historical relations which appear to be only *their* interest, and *their* work.

Such individuals had no consciousness of the general Idea they were unfolding, while prosecuting those aims of theirs; on the contrary, they were practical, political men. But at the same time they were thinking men, who had an insight into the requirements of the time—*what was ripe for development*. This was the very truth for their age, for their world; the species next in order, so to speak, and which was already formed in the womb of time. It was theirs to know this nascent principle; the necessary, directly sequent step in progress, which their world was to take; to make this their aim, and to expend their energy in promoting it. World-historical men—the heroes of an epoch—must, therefore, be recognised as its clear-sighted ones; *their* deeds, *their* words are the best of that time. Great men have formed purposes to satisfy themselves, not others. Whatever prudent designs and counsels they might have learned from others, would be the more limited and inconsistent features in their career; for it was they who best understood affairs; from whom *others* learned, and approved, or at least acquiesced in—their policy. For that Spirit which had taken this fresh step in history is the inmost soul of all individuals; but in a state of unconsciousness which the great men in question aroused. Their fellows, therefore, follow these soul-leaders; for they feel the irresistible power of their own inner spirit thus embodied. If we go on to cast a look at the fate of these world-historical persons, whose vocation it was to be the agents of the world-spirit,—we shall find it to have been no happy one. They attained no calm enjoyment; their whole life was labour and trouble; their whole nature was nought else but their master-passion. When their object is attained they fall off like empty hulls from the kernel. They die early, iike Alexander; they are murdered, like Caesar; transported to St. Helena, like Napoleon. This fearful consolation—that historical men have not enjoyed what is called happiness, and of which only private life (and this may be passed under very various external circumstances) is capable,—this consolation those may draw from history, who stand in need of it; and it is craved by envy—vexed at what is great and transcendant,—striving, therefore, to depreciate it, and to find some flaw in it. Thus in modern times it has been demonstrated *ad nauseam*

that princes are generally unhappy on their thrones; in consideration of which the possession of a throne is tolerated, and men acquiesce in the fact that not themselves but the personages in question are its occupants. The free man, we may observe, is not envious, but gladly recognises what is great and exalted, and rejoices that it exists.

It is in the light of those common elements which constitute the interest and therefore the passions of individuals, that these historical men are to be regarded. They are *great* men, because they willed and accomplished something great; not a mere fancy, a mere intention, but that which met the case and fell in with the needs of the age. This mode of considering them also excludes the so-called "psychological" view, which—serving the purpose of envy most effectually—contrives so to refer all actions to the heart,—to bring them under such a subjective aspect—as that their authors appear to have done everything under the impulse of some passion, mean or grand,—some *morbid craving,*—and on account of these passions and cravings to have been not moral men. Alexander of Macedon partly subdued Greece, and then Asia; therefore he was possessed by a *morbid craving* for conquest. He is alleged to have acted from a craving for fame, for conquest; and the proof that these were the impelling motives is that he did that which resulted in fame. What pedagogue has not demonstrated of Alexander the Great—of Julius Caesar—that they were instigated by such passions, and were consequently immoral men?— whence the conclusion immediately follows that he, the pedagogue, is a better man than they, because he has not such passions; a proof of which lies in the fact that he does not conquer Asia,— vanquish Darius and Porus,—but while he enjoys life himself lets others enjoy it too. These psychologists are particu-

larly fond of contemplating those peculiarities of great historical figures which
appertain to them as private persons.
Man must eat and drink; he sustains
relations to friends and acquaintances;
he has passing impulses and ebullitions
of temper. "No man is a hero to his
valet-de-chambre," is a well-known
proverb; I have added—and Goethe repeated it ten years later—"but not because the former is no hero, but because
the latter is a valet." He takes off the
hero's boots, assists him to bed, knows
that he prefers champagne, &c. Historical personages waited upon in historical
literature by such psychological valets,
come poorly off; they are brought down
by these their attendants to a level with
—or rather a few degrees below the level
of—the morality of such exquisite dis-
cerners of spirits. The Thersites of
Homer who abuses the kings is a standing figure for all times. Blows—that is
beating with a solid cudgel—he does not
get in every age, as in the Homeric one;
but his envy, his egotism, is the thorn
which he has to carry in his flesh; and
the undying worm that gnaws him is the
tormenting consideration that his excellent views and vituperations remain absolutely without result in the world. But
our satisfaction at the fate of thersitism
also, may have its sinister side.

A world-historical individual is not so
unwise as to indulge a variety of wishes
to divide his regards. He is devoted to
the one aim, regardless of all else. It is
even possible that such men may treat
other great, even sacred interests, incon-
siderately; conduct which is indeed ob-
noxious to moral reprehension. But so
mighty a form must trample down many
an innocent flower—crush to pieces
many an object in its path.

The special interest of passion is thus
inseparable from the active development
of a general principle: for it is from the
special and determinate and from its
negation, that the universal results. Par-

ticularity contends with its like, and
some loss is involved in the issue. *It* is
not the general idea that is implicated in
opposition and combat, and that is exposed to danger. It remains in the background, untouched and uninjured. This
may be called the *cunning of reason,*—
that it sets the passions to work for itself, while that which develops its existence through such impulsion pays the
penalty, and suffers loss. For it is *phenomenal* being that is so treated, and of
this, part is of no value, part is positive
and real. The particular is for the most
part of too trifling value as compared
with the general: individuals are sacrificed and abandoned. The Idea pays the
penalty of determinate existence and of
corruptibility, not from itself, but from
the passions of individuals.

But though we might tolerate the idea
that individuals, their desires and the
gratification of them, are thus sacrificed,
and their happiness given up to the empire of chance, to which it belongs; and
that as a general rule, individuals come
under the category of means to an ulterior end,—there is one aspect of human individuality which we should
hesitate to regard in that subordinate
light, even in relation to the highest;
since it is absolutely no subordinate element, but exists in those individuals as
inherently eternal and divine. I mean
morality, ethics, religion. Even when
speaking of the realization of the great
ideal aim by means of individuals, the
subjective element in them—their interest and that of their cravings and impulses, their views and judgments,
though exhibited as the merely formal
side of their existence,—was spoken of
as having an infinite right to be con-
sulted. The first idea that presents itself
in speaking of *means* is that of something external to the object, and having
no share in the object itself. But merely
natural things—even the commonest
lifeless objects—used as means, must be

of such a kind as adapts them to their purpose; they must possess something in common with it. Human beings least of all, sustain the bare external relation of mere means to the great ideal aim. Not only do they in the very act of realising it, make it the occasion of satisfying personal desires, whose purport is diverse from that aim—but they share in that ideal aim itself; and are for that very reason objects of their own existence; not *formally* merely, as the world of living beings generally is—whose individual life is essentially subordinate to that of man, and is properly used *up* as an instrument. Men, on the contrary, are objects of existence to themselves, as regards the intrinsic import of the aim in question. To this order belongs that in them which we would exclude from the category of mere means,—morality, ethics, religion. That is to say, man is an object of existence in himself only in virtue of the divine that is in him,—that which was designated at the outset as *Reason;* which, in view of its activity and power of self-determination, was called *freedom.* And we affirm—without entering at present on the proof of the assertion—that religion, morality, &c. have their foundation and source in that principle, and so are essentially elevated above all alien necessity and chance. And here we must remark that individuals, to the extent of their freedom, are responsible for the depravation and enfeeblement of morals and religion. This is the seal of the absolute and sublime destiny of man—that he knows what is good and what is evil; that his destiny *is* his very ability to will either good or evil,—in one word, that he is the subject of moral imputation, imputation not only of evil, but of good; and not only concerning this or that particular matter, and all that happens *ab extrâ,* but *also* the good and evil attaching to his individual freedom. The brute alone is simply innocent. It would, however, demand an extensive explanation—as extensive as the analysis of moral freedom itself—to preclude or obviate all the misunderstandings which the statement that what is called innocent imports the entire unconsciousness of evil—is wont to occasion.

In contemplating the fate which virtue, morality, even piety experience in history, we must not fall into the litany of lamentations, that the good and pious often—or for the most part—fare ill in the world, while the evil-disposed and wicked prosper. The term *prosperity* is used in a variety of meanings—riches, outward honour, and the like. But in speaking of something which in and for itself constitutes an aim of existence, that so-called well or ill-faring of these or those isolated individuals cannot be regarded as an essential element in the rational order of the universal. With more justice than happiness,—or a fortunate environment for individuals,—it is demanded of the grand aim of the world's existence, that it should foster, nay involve the execution and ratification of good, moral, righteous purposes. What makes men morally discontented (a discontent, by the by, on which they somewhat pride themselves), is that they do not find the present adapted to the realization of aims which they hold to be right and just (more especially in modern times, ideals of political constitutions); they contrast unfavourably things as they *are,* with their idea of things as they *ought* to be. In this case it is not private interest nor passion that desires gratification, but reason, justice, liberty; and equipped with this title, the demand in question assumes a lofty bearing, and readily adopts a position not merely of discontent, but of open revolt against the actual condition of the world. To estimate such a feeling and such views aright, the demands insisted upon, and the very dogmatic opinions asserted, must be examined. At no time so much as in our own, have such general principles and notions been advanced, or with greater assurance. If in days gone by, history seems to present itself as a struggle of passions; in our time—though displays of passion are not wanting—it exhibits partly a predominance of the struggle of notions assuming the authority of principles; partly that of passions and interests essentially subjective, but under the mask of such higher sanctions. The pretensions thus contended for as legitimate in the name of that which has been stated as the ultimate aim of Reason, pass accordingly, for absolute aims,—to the same extent as religion, morals, ethics. Nothing, as before remarked, is now more common than the complaint that the *ideals* which imagination sets up are not realised—that these glorious dreams are destroyed by cold actuality. These ideals—which in the voyage of life founder on the rocks of hard reality —may be in the first instance only subjective, and belong to the idiosyncrasy of the individual, imagining himself the highest and wisest. Such do not properly belong to this category. For the fancies which the individual in his isolation indulges, cannot be the model for universal reality; just as *universal* law is not designed for the units of the mass. These as such may, in fact, find their interests decidedly thrust into the background. But by the term "Ideal," we also understand the ideal of reason, of the good, of the true. Poets, as *e.g.* Schiller, have painted such ideals touchingly and with strong emotion, and with the deeply melancholy conviction that they could not be realised. In affirming, on the contrary that the universal Reason *does* realise itself, we have indeed nothing to do with the individual empirically regarded. That admits of degrees of better and worse, since here chance and particularity have received authority from the Idea to exercise their monstrous power.

Much, therefore, in particular aspects of the grand phenomenon might be found fault with. This subjective fault-finding, —which, however, only keeps in view the individual and its deficiency, without taking notice of Reason pervading the whole,—is easy; and inasmuch as it asserts an excellent intention with regard to the good of the whole, and seems to result from a kindly heart, it feels authorized to give itself airs and assume great consequence. It is easier to discover a deficiency in individuals, in states, and in providence, than to see their real import and value. For in this merely negative fault-finding a proud position is taken,—one which overlooks the object, without having entered into it,—without having comprehended its positive aspect. Age generally makes men more tolerant; youth is always discontented. The tolerance of age is the result of the ripeness of a judgment which, not merely as the result of indifference, is satisfied even with what is inferior; but, more deeply taught by the grave experience of life, has been led to perceive the substantial, solid worth of the object in question. The insight then to which—in contradistinction from those ideals—philosophy is to lead us, is, that the actual world is as it ought to be—that the truly good—the universal divine reason—is not a mere abstraction, but a vital principle capable of realising itself. This *good,* this *Reason,* in its most concrete form, is God. God governs the world; the actual working of his government—the carrying out of his plan—is the history of the world. This plan philosophy strives to comprehend; for only that which has been developed as the result of it, possesses *bonâ fide* reality. That which does not accord with it, is negative, worthless existence. Before the pure light of this divine Idea—which is no mere ideal— the phantom of a world whose events are an incoherent concourse of fortuitous circumstances, utterly vanishes. Philosophy wishes to discover the substantial purport, the actual side of the divine idea, and to justify the so much despised actuality of things; for Reason is the comprehension of the divine work. But as to what concerns the perversion, corruption, and ruin of religious, ethical and moral purposes, and states of society generally, it must be affirmed, that in their *essence* these are infinite and eternal; but that the forms they assume may be of a limited order, and consequently belong to the domain of mere nature, and be subject to the sway of chance. They are therefore perishable, and exposed to decay and corruption. Religion and morality—in the same way as inherently universal essences—have the peculiarity of being present in the individual soul, in the full extent of their Idea, and therefore truly and really; although they may not manifest themselves in it *in extenso,* and are not applied to fully developed relations. The religion, the morality of a limited sphere of life—that of a shepherd or a peasant, *e.g.*—in its intensive concentration and limitation to a few perfectly simple relations of life,—has infinite worth; the same worth as the religion and morality of extensive knowledge, and of an existence rich in the compass of its relations and actions. This inner focus—this simple region of the claims of subjective freedom,—the home of volition, resolution, and action,—the abstract sphere of conscience,—that which comprises the responsibility and moral value of the individual, remains untouched; and is quite shut out from the noisy din of the world's history—including not merely external and temporal changes, but also those entailed by the absolute necessity inseparable from the realization of the Idea of freedom itself. But as a general truth this must be regarded as settled, that whatever in the world possesses claims as noble and glorious, has never-

theless a higher existence above it. The claim of the world-spirit rises above all special claims.

These observations may suffice in reference to the means which the world-spirit uses for realising its Idea. Stated simply and abstractly, this mediation involves the activity of personal existences in whom Reason is present as their absolute, substantial being; but a basis, in the first instance, still obscure and unknown to them. But the subject becomes more complicated and difficult when we regard individuals not merely in their aspect of activity, but more concretely, in conjunction with a particular manifestation of that activity in their religion and morality,—forms of existence which are intimately connected with Reason, and share in its absolute claims. Here the relation of mere means of an end disappears, and the chief bearings of this seeming difficulty in reference to the absolute aim of Spirit, have been briefly considered.

The third point to be analysed is, therefore—what is the object to be realised by these means; *i.e.* what is the form it assumes in the realm of the actual. We have spoken of *means;* but in the carrying out of a subjective, limited aim, we have also to take into consideration the element of a *material,* either already present or which has to be procured. Thus the question would arise: What is the material in which the ideal of Reason is wrought out? The primary answer would be,—personality itself—human desires—subjective generally. In human knowledge and volition, as its material element, Reason attains positive existence. We have considered subjective volition where it has an object which is the truth and essence of a reality, viz. where it constitutes a great world-historical passion. As a subjective will, occupied with limited passions, it is dependent, and can gratify its desires only within the limits of this dependence. But the subjective will has also a substantial life—a reality,—in which it moves in the region of *essential* being and has the essential itself as the object of its existence. This essential being is the union of the *subjective* with the *rational* will: it is the moral whole, the state, which is that form of actuality in which the individual has and enjoys his freedom; but on the condition of his recognition, believing in and willing that which is common to the whole. And this must not be understood as if the subjective will of the social unit attained its gratification and enjoyment through that common Will; as if this were a means provided for its benefit; as if the individual, in his relations to other individuals, thus limited his freedom, in order that this universal limitation—the mutual constraint of all—might secure a small space of liberty for each. Rather, we affirm, are law, morality, government, and they alone, the positive fact and completion of freedom. Freedom of a low and limited order, is mere caprice; which finds its exercise in the sphere of particular and limited desires.

Subjective volition—passion—is that which sets men in activity, that which effects "practical" actualization. The Idea is the inner spring of action; the state is the actually existing, realised moral life. For it is the unity of the universal, essential will, with that of the individual; and this is "morality." The individual living in this unity has a moral life; possesses a value that consists in this substantiality alone. Sophocles in his Antigone, says, "The divine commands are not of yesterday, nor of today; no, they have an infinite existence, and no one could say whence they came." The laws of morality are not accidental, but are the essentially rational. It is the very object of the state that what is essential in the practical activity of men, and in their disposi-

tions, should be duly recognised; that it should have a manifest existence, and maintain its position. It is the absolute interest of Reason that this moral whole should exist; and herein lies the justification and merit of heroes who have founded states,—however rude these may have been. In the history of the world, only those peoples can come under our notice which form a state. For it must be understood that this latter is the realization of freedom, *i.e.* of the absolute final aim, and that it exists for its own sake. It must further be understood that all the worth which the human being possesses—all spiritual actuality, he possesses only through the state. For his spiritual actuality consists in this, that his own essence—Reason—is objectively present to him, that it possesses objective immediate existence for him. Thus only is he fully conscious; thus only is he a partaker of morality—of a just and moral social and political life. For truth is the unity of the universal and subjective will; and the universal is to be found in the state, in its laws, its universal and rational arrangements. The state is the divine Idea as it exists on earth. We have in it, therefore, the object of history in a more definite shape than before; that in which freedom obtains objectivity, and lives in the enjoyment of this objectivity. For law is the objectivity of spirit; volition in its true form. Only that will which obeys law, is free; for it obeys itself—it is independent and so free. When the state or our country constitutes a community of existence; when the subjective will of man submits to laws,—the contradiction between liberty and necessity vanishes. The rational has necessary existence, as being the reality and substance of things, and we are free in recognising it as law, and following it as the substance of our own being. The objective and the subjective will are then reconciled, and present one identical homogeneous whole. For the morality (Sittlichkeit) of the state is not of that ethical (moralische) reflective kind, in which one's own conviction bears sway; this latter is rather the peculiarity of the modern time, while the true antique morality is based on the principle of abiding by one's duty [to the state at large]. An Athenian citizen did what was required of him, as it were from instinct; but if I reflect on the object of my activity, I must have the consciousness that my will has been called into exercise. But morality is duty—substantial right—a "*second* nature" as it has been justly called; for the *first* nature of man is his primary merely animal existence.

The development *in extenso* of the Idea of the state belongs to the philosophy of jurisprudence; but it must be observed that in the theories of our time various errors are current respecting it, which pass for established truths, and have become fixed prejudices. We will mention only a few of them, giving prominence to such as have a reference to the object of our history.

The error which first meets us is the direct contradictory of our principle that the state presents the realization of freedom; the opinion, viz., that man is free by *nature*, but that in *society*, in the state—to which nevertheless he is irresistibly impelled—he must limit this natural freedom. That man is free by nature is quite correct in one sense; viz., that he is so according to the idea of humanity; but we imply thereby that he is such only in virtue of his destiny—that he has an undeveloped power to become such; for the "nature" of an object is exactly synonymous with its "Idea." But the view in question imports more than this. When man is spoken of as "free by nature," the mode of his existence as well as his destiny is implied. His merely natural and primary condition is intended. In this sense a "state of nature" is assumed in which mankind at large are in the possession of their natural rights with the unconstrained exercise and enjoyment of their freedom. This assumption is not indeed raised to the dignity of the historical fact; it would indeed be difficult, were the attempt seriously made, to point out any such condition as actually existing, or as having ever occurred. Examples of a savage state of life can be pointed out, but they are marked by brutal passions and deeds of violence; while, however rude and simple their conditions, they involve social arrangements which (to use the common phrase) *restrain* freedom. That assumption is one of those nebulous images which theory produces; an idea which it cannot avoid originating, but which it fathers upon real existence, without sufficient historical justification.

What we find such a state of nature to be in actual experience, answers exactly to the idea of a *merely* natural condition. Freedom as the *ideal* of that which is original and natural, does not exist *as original and natural*. Rather must it be first sought out and won; and that by an incalculable medial discipline of the intellectual and moral powers. The state of nature is, therefore, predominantly that of injustice and violence, of untamed natural impulses, of inhuman deeds and feelings. Limitation is certainly produced by society and the state, but it is a limitation of the mere brute emotions and rude instincts; as also, in a more advanced stage of culture, of the premeditated self-will of caprice and passion. This kind of constraint is part of the instrumentality by which only, the consciousness of freedom and the desire for its attainment, in its true—that is rational and ideal form—can be obtained. To the notion of freedom, law and morality are indispensably requisite; and they are in and for themselves, universal existences, objects and aims; which are discovered only by the activity of thought, separating itself from the merely sensuous, and developing itself, in opposition thereto; and which must on the other hand, be introduced into and incorporated with the originally sensuous will, and that contrarily to its natural inclination. The perpetually recurring misapprehension of freedom consists in regarding that term only in its *formal*, subjective sense, abstracted from its essential objects and aims; thus a constraint put upon impulse, desire, passion—pertaining to the particular individual as such—a limitation of caprice and self-will is regarded as a fettering of freedom. We should on the contrary look upon such limitation as the indispensable proviso of emancipation. Society and the state are the very conditions in which freedom is realized.

19. The Communist Manifesto *

KARL MARX (1818–1883)

A specter is haunting Europe—the specter of Communism. All the powers of old Europe have entered into a holy alliance to exorcise this specter; Pope and Czar, Metternich and Guizot, French radicals and German police spies.

Where is the party in opposition that has not been decried as Communistic by its opponents in power? Where the opposition that has not hurled back the branding reproach of Communism, against the more advanced opposition parties, as well as against its reactionary adversaries?

Two things result from this fact.

I. Communism is already acknowledged by all European powers to be in itself a power.

II. It is high time that Communists should openly, in the face of the whole world, publish their views, their aims, their tendencies, and meet this nursery tale of the Specter of Communism with a Manifesto of the party itself.

To this end the Communists of various nationalities have assembled in London, and sketched the following manifesto to be published in the English, French, German, Italian, Flemish and Danish languages.

I

Bourgeois and Proletarians [1]

The history of all hitherto existing society [2] is the history of class struggles.

* First published in 1848. From the authorized English translation of 1888 edited by Engels. In part.

[1] By bourgeoisie is meant the class of modern Capitalists, owners of the means of social production and employers of wage-labor. By proletariat, the class of modern wage-laborers who, having no means of production of their own, are reduced to selling their labor-power in order to live.

[2] That is, all *written* history. In 1847, the pre-history of society, the social organization existing previous to recorded history, was all but unknown. Since then, Haxthausen discovered common ownership of land in Russia, Maurer proved it to be the social foundation from which all Teutonic races started in his-

Freeman and slave, patrician and plebeian, lord and serf, guild master [3] and journeyman, in a word, oppressor and oppressed, stood in constant opposition to one another, carried on an uninterrupted, now hidden, now open fight, that each time ended, either in the revolutionary reconstitution of society at large, or in the common ruin of the contending classes.

In the earlier epochs of history we find almost everywhere a complicated arrangement of society into various orders, a manifold gradation of social rank. In ancient Rome we have patricians, knights, plebeians, slaves; in the middle ages, feudal lords, vassals, guild masters, journeymen, apprentices, serfs; in almost all of these classes, again, subordinate gradations.

The modern bourgeois society that has sprouted from the ruins of feudal society, has not done away with class antagonisms. It has but established new classes, new conditions of oppression, new forms of struggle in place of the old ones.

Our epoch, the epoch of the bourgeois, possesses, however, this distinctive feature: it has simplified the class antagonisms. Society as a whole is more and more splitting up into two great hostile camps, into two great classes directly facing each other: Bourgeoisie and Proletariat.

tory, and by and by village communities were found to be, or to have been the primitive form of society everywhere from India to Ireland. The inner organization of this primitive Communistic society was laid bare, in its typical form, by Morgan's crowning discovery of the true nature of the *Gens* and its relation to the *Tribe*. With the dissolution of these primæval communities society begins to be differentiated into separate and finally antagonistic classes. I have attempted to retrace this process of dissolution in: "Der Ursprung der Familie, des Privateigenthums und des Staats," 2nd edit., Stuttgart, 1886. (English tr., "Origin of the Family, Property, and the State.")

[3] Guild master, that is a full member of a guild, a master within, not a head of a guild.

From the serfs of the middle ages sprang the chartered burghers of the earliest towns. From these burgesses the first elements of the bourgeoisie were developed.

The discovery of America, the rounding of the Cape, opened up fresh ground for the rising bourgeoisie. The East Indian and Chinese markets, the colonization of America, trade with the colonies, the increase in the means of exchange and in commodities generally, gave to commerce, to navigation, to industry, an impulse never before known, and thereby, to the revolutionary element in the tottering feudal society, a rapid development.

The feudal system of industry, under which industrial production was monopolized by close guilds, now no longer sufficed for the growing wants of the new markets. The manufacturing system took its place. The guild masters were pushed on one side by the manufacturing middle class; division of labor between the different corporate guilds vanished in the face of division of labor in each single workshop.

Meantime the markets kept ever growing, the demand ever rising. Even manufacture no longer sufficed. Thereupon steam and machinery revolutionized industrial production. The place of manufacture was taken by the giant, Modern Industry, the place of the industrial middle class, by industrial millionaires, the leaders of whole industrial armies, the modern bourgeois.

Modern industry has established the world's market, for which the discovery of America paved the way. The market has given an immense development to commerce, to navigation, to communication by land. This development has, in its turn, reacted on the extension of industry; and in proportion as industry, commerce, navigation and railways extended, in the same proportion the bourgeoisie developed, increased its capital, and pushed into the background every class handed down from the middle ages.

We see, therefore, how the modern bourgeoisie is itself the product of a long course of development, of a series of revolutions in the modes of production and of exchange.

Each step in the development of the bourgeoisie was accompanied by a corresponding political advance of that class. An oppressed class under the sway of the feudal nobility, an armed and self-governing association in the mediæval commune,[4] here independent urban republic (as in Italy and Germany), there taxable "third estate" of the monarchy (as in France), afterwards, in the period of manufacture proper, serving either the semi-feudal or the absolute monarchy as a counterpoise against the nobility, and, in fact, corner-stone of the great monarchies in general, the bourgeoisie has at last, since the establishment of Modern Industry and of the world's market, conquered for itself, in the modern representative State, exclusive political sway. The executive of the modern State is but a committee for managing the common affairs of the whole bourgeoisie.

The bourgeoisie, historically, has played a most revolutionary part.

The bourgeoisie, wherever it has got the upper hand, has put an end to all feudal, patriarchal, idyllic relations. It has pitilessly torn asunder the motley feudal ties that bound man to his "natural superiors," and has left remaining no other nexus between man and man than naked self-interest, callous "cash payment." It has drowned the most heavenly ecstasies of religious fervor, of

chivalrous enthusiasm, of philistine sentimentalism, in the icy water of egotistical calculation. It has resolved personal worth into exchange value, and in place of the numberless indefeasible chartered freedoms, has set up that single, unconscionable freedom—Free Trade. In one word, for exploitation, veiled by religious and political illusions, it has substituted naked, shameless, direct, brutal exploitation.

The bourgeoisie has stripped of its halo every occupation hitherto honored and looked up to with reverent awe. It has converted the physician, the lawyer, the priest, the poet, the man of science, into its paid wage laborers.

The bourgeoisie has torn away from the family its sentimental veil, and has reduced the family relation to a mere money relation.

The bourgeoisie has disclosed how it came to pass that the brutal display of vigor in the middle ages, which Reactionists so much admire, found its fitting complement in the most slothful indolence. It has been the first to show what man's activity can bring about. It has accomplished wonders far surpassing Egyptian pyramids, Roman aqueducts, and Gothic cathedrals; it has conducted expeditions that put in the shade all former Exoduses of nations and crusades.

The bourgeoisie cannot exist without constantly revolutionizing the instruments of production, and thereby the relations of production, and with them the whole relations of society. Conservation of the old modes of production in unaltered forms, was, on the contrary, the first condition of existence for all earlier industrial classes. Constant revolutionizing of production, uninterrupted disturbance of all social conditions, everlasting uncertainty and agitation, distinguish the bourgeois epoch from all earlier ones. All fixed, fast-frozen relations, with their train of ancient and venerable prejudices and opinions, are swept away;

---

[4] "Commune" was the name taken, in France, by the nascent towns even before they had conquered, from their feudal lords and masters, local self-government and political rights as the "Third Estate." Generally speaking, for the economical development of the bourgeoisie, England is here taken as the typical country; for its political development, France.

all new-formed ones become antiquated before they can ossify. All that is solid melts into air, all that is holy is profaned, and man is at last compelled to face with sober senses his real conditions of life and his relations with his kind.

The need of a constantly expanding market for its products chases the bourgeoisie over the whole surface of the globe. It must nestle everywhere, settle everywhere, establish connections everywhere.

The bourgeoisie has through its exploitation of the world's market given a cosmopolitan character to production and consumption in every country. To the great chagrin of Reactionists, it has drawn from under the feet of industry the national ground on which it stood. All old-established national industries have been destroyed or are daily being destroyed. They are dislodged by new industries, whose introduction becomes a life and death question for all civilized nations, by industries that no longer work up indigenous raw material, but raw material drawn from the remotest zones, industries whose products are consumed, not only at home, but in every quarter of the globe. In place of the old wants, satisfied by the productions of the country, we find new wants, requiring for their satisfaction the products of distant lands and climes. In place of the old local and national seclusion and self-sufficiency, we have intercourse in every direction, universal inter-dependence of nations. And as in material, so also in intellectual production. The intellectual creations of individual nations become common property. National one-sidedness and narrow-mindedness become more and more impossible, and from the numerous national and local literatures, there arises a world literature.

The bourgeoisie, by the rapid improvement of all instruments of production, by the immensely facilitated means of communication, draws all, even the most barbarian, nations into civilization. The cheap prices of its commodities are the heavy artillery with which it batters down all Chinese walls, with which it forces the barbarians' intensely obstinate hatred of foreigners to capitulate. It compels all nations, on pain of extinction, to adopt the bourgeois mode of production; it compels them to introduce what it calls civilization into their midst, i.e., to become bourgeois themselves. In one word, it creates a world after its own image.

The bourgeoisie has subjected the country to the rule of the towns. It has created enormous cities, has greatly increased the urban population as compared with the rural, and has thus rescued a considerable part of the population from the idiocy of rural life. Just as it has made the country dependent on the towns, so it has made barbarian and semi-barbarian countries dependent on the civilized ones, nations of peasants on nations of bourgeois, the East on the West.

The bourgeoisie keeps more and more doing away with the scattered state of the population, of the means of production, and of property. It has agglomerated population, centralized means of production, and has concentrated property in a few hands. The necessary consequence of this was political centralization. Independent, or but loosely connected provinces, with separate interests, laws, governments and systems of taxation, became lumped together into one nation, with one government, one code of laws, one national class interest, one frontier, and one customs tariff.

The bourgeoisie, during its rule of scarce one hundred years, has created more massive and more colossal productive forces than have all preceding generations together. Subjection of Nature's forces to man, machinery, application of chemistry to industry and agriculture, steam navigation, railways, electric telegraphs, clearing of whole continents for cultivation, canalization of rivers, whole populations conjured out of the ground —what earlier century had even a presentiment that such productive forces slumbered in the lap of social labor?

We see then: the means of production and of exchange on whose foundation the bourgeoisie built itself up, were generated in feudal society. At a certain stage in the development of these means of production and of exchange, the conditions under which feudal society produced and exchanged, the feudal organization of agriculture and manufacturing industry, in one word, the feudal relations of property, became no longer compatible with the already developed productive forces; they became so many fetters. They had to be burst asunder.

Into their place stepped free competition, accompanied by a social and political constitution adapted to it, and by the economical and political sway of the bourgeois class.

A similar movement is going on before our own eyes. Modern bourgeois society with its relations of production, of exchange, and of property, a society that has conjured up such gigantic means of production and of exchange, is like the sorcerer, who is no longer able to control the powers of the nether world whom he has called up by his spells. For many a decade past the history of industry and commerce is but the history of the revolt of modern productive forces against modern conditions of production, against the property relations that are the conditions for the existence of the bourgeoisie and of its rule. It is enough to mention the commercial crises that by their periodical return put on its trial, each time more threateningly, the existence of the bourgeois society. In these crises a great part not only of the existing products, but also of the previously created productive forces, is periodically destroyed.

In these crises there breaks out an epidemic that, in all earlier epochs, would have seemed an absurdity—the epidemic of overproduction. Society suddenly finds itself put back into a state of momentary barbarism; it appears as if a famine, a universal war of devastation had cut off the supply of every means of subsistence; industry and commerce seem to be destroyed; and why? because there is too much civilization, too much means of subsistence, too much industry, too much commerce. The productive forces at the disposal of society no longer tend to further the development of the conditions of bourgeois property; on the contrary, they have become too powerful for these conditions, by which they are fettered, and so soon as they overcome these fetters, they bring disorder into the whole of bourgeois society, endanger the existence of bourgeois property. The conditions of bourgeois society are too narrow to comprise the wealth created by them. And how does the bourgeoisie get over these crises? On the one hand by enforced destruction of a mass of productive forces; on the other, by the conquest of new markets, and by the more thorough exploitation of the old ones. That is to say, by paving the way for more extensive and more destructive crises, and by diminishing the means whereby crises are prevented.

The weapons with which the bourgeoisie felled feudalism to the ground are now turned against the bourgeoisie itself.

But not only has the bourgeoisie forged the weapons that bring death to itself; it has also called into existence the men who are to wield those weapons —the modern working class—the proletarians.

In proportion as the bourgeoisie, i. e., capital, is developed, in the same proportion is the proletariat, the modern working class, developed; a class of laborers, who live only so long as they find work, and who find work only so long as their labor increases capital. These laborers, who must sell themselves piecemeal, are a commodity, like every other article of commerce, and are consequently exposed to all the vicissitudes of competition, to all the fluctuations of the market.

Owing to the extensive use of machinery and to division of labor, the work of the proletarians has lost all individual character, and, consequently, all charm for the workman. He becomes an appendage of the machine, and it is only the most simple, most monotonous, and most easily acquired knack, that is required of him. Hence, the cost of production of a workman is restricted almost entirely to the means of subsistence that he requires for his maintenance, and for the propagation of his race. But the price of a commodity, and therefore also of labor, is equal, in the long run, to its cost of production. In proportion, therefore, as the repulsiveness of the work increases, the wage decreases. Nay, more, in proportion as the use of machinery and division of labor increase, in the same proportion the burden of toil also increases, whether by prolongation of the working hours, by increase of the work exacted in a given time, or by increased speed of the machinery, etc.

Modern industry has converted the little workshop of the patriarchal master into the great factory of the industry capitalist. Masses of laborers, crowded into the factory, are organized like soldiers. As privates of the industrial army they are placed under the command of a perfect hierarchy of officers and sergeants. Not only are they slaves of the bourgeois class, and of the bourgeois State, they are daily and hourly enslaved by the machine, by the over-seer, and, above all, by the individual bourgeois manufacturer himself. The more openly this despotism proclaims gain to be its end and aim, the more petty, the more hateful and the more embittering it is.

The less skill and exertion of strength is implied in manual labor, in other words, the more modern industry becomes developed, the more is the labor of men superseded by that of women. Differences of age and sex have no longer any distinctive social validity for the working class. All are instruments of labor, more or less expensive to use, according to age and sex.

No sooner is the exploitation of the laborer by the manufacturer so far at an end that he receives his wages in cash, than he is set upon by the other portions of the bourgeoisie, the landlord, the shopkeeper, the pawnbroker, etc.

The lower strata of the middle class— the small tradespeople, shopkeepers, and retired tradesmen generally, the handicraftsmen and peasants—all these sink gradually into the proletariat, partly because their diminutive capital does not suffice for the scale on which modern industry is carried on, and is swamped in the competition with the large capitalists, partly because their specialized skill is rendered worthless by new methods of production. Thus the proletariat is recruited from all classes of the population.

The proletariat goes through various stages of development. With its birth begins its struggle with the bourgeoisie. At first the contest is carried on by individual laborers, then by the work-people of a factory, then by the operatives of one trade, in one locality, against the individual bourgeois who directly exploits them. They direct their attacks not against the bourgeois conditions of production, but against the instruments of production themselves; they destroy imported wares that compete with their labor, they smash to pieces machinery, they set factories ablaze, they seek to restore by force the vanished status of the workman of the middle ages.

At this stage the laborers still form an incoherent mass scattered over the whole country, and broken up by their mutual competition. If anywhere they unite to form more compact bodies, this is not yet the consequence of their own active union, but of the union of the bourgeoisie, which class, in order to attain its own political ends, is compelled to set the whole proletariat in motion, and is moreover yet, for a time, able to do so. At this stage, therefore, the proletarians do not fight their enemies, but the enemies of their enemies, the remnants of absolute monarchy, and land owners, the non-industrial bourgeois, the petty bourgeoisie. Thus the whole historical movement is concentrated in the hands of the bourgeoisie; every victory so obtained is a victory for the bourgeoisie.

But with the development of industry the proletariat not only increases in number; it becomes concentrated in greater masses, its strength grows and it feels that strength more. The various interests and conditions of life within the ranks of the proletariat are more and more equalized, in proportion as machinery obliterates all distinctions of labor, and nearly everywhere reduces wages to the same low level. The growing competition among the bourgeois, and the resulting commercial crises, make the wages of the workers ever more fluctuating. The unceasing improvement of machinery, ever more rapidly developing, makes their livelihood more and more precarious; the collisions between individual workman and individual bourgeois take more and more the character of collisions between two classes. Thereupon the workers begin to form combinations (Trades' Unions) against the bourgeois; they club together in order to keep up the rate of wages; they found permanent associations in order to make provision beforehand for these occasional revolts. Here and there the contest breaks out into riots.

Now and then the workers are victorious, but only for a time. The real fruit of their battles lies not in the immediate result but in the ever improved means of communication that are created in modern industry and that place the workers of different localities in contact with one another. It was just this contact that was needed to centralize the numerous local struggles, all of the same character, into one national struggle between classes. But every class struggle is a political struggle. And that union, to attain which the burghers of the middle ages, with their miserable highways, required centuries, the modern proletarians, thanks to railways, achieve in a few years.

This organization of the proletarians into a class and consequently into a political party, is continually being upset again by the competition between the workers themselves. But it ever rises up again; stronger, firmer, mightier. It compels legislative recognition of particular interests of the workers, by taking advantage of the divisions among the bourgeoisie itself. Thus the ten-hours bill in England was carried.

Altogether collisions between the classes of the old society further, in many ways, the course of the development of the proletariat. The bourgeoisie finds itself involved in a constant battle. At first with the aristocracy; later on, with those portions of the bourgeoisie itself whose interests have become antagonistic to the progress of industry; at all times with the bourgeoisie of foreign countries. In all these countries it sees itself compelled to appeal to the proletariat, to ask for its help, and thus to drag it into the political arena. The bourgeoisie itself, therefore, supplies the proletariat with weapons for fighting the bourgeoisie.

Further, as we have already seen, entire sections of the ruling classes are, by the advance of industry, precipitated into the proletariat, or are at least threatened in their conditions of existence. These also supply the proletariat with fresh elements of enlightenment and progress.

Finally, in times when the class struggle nears the decisive hour, the process of dissolution going on within the ruling class, in fact within the whole range of old society, assumes such a violent, glaring character, that a small section of the ruling class cuts itself adrift, and joins the revolutionary class, the class that holds the future in its hands. Just as, therefore, at an earlier period, a section of the nobility went over to the bourgeoisie, so now a portion of the bourgeoisie goes over to the proletariat, and in particular, a portion of the bourgeois ideologists, who have raised themselves to the level of comprehending theoretically the historical movement as a whole.

Of all the classes that stand face to face with the bourgeoisie today, the proletariat alone is a really revolutionary class. The other classes decay and finally disappear in the face of modern industry; the proletariat is its special and essential product.

The lower middle class, the small manufacturer, the shopkeeper, the artisan, the peasant, all these fight against the bourgeoisie to save from extinction their existence as fractions of the middle class. They are therefore not revolutionary, but conservative. Nay, more, they are reactionary, for they try to roll back the wheel of history. If by chance they are revolutionary, they are so only in view of their impending transfer into the proletariat; they thus defend not their present, but their future interests, they desert their own standpoint to place themselves at that of the proletariat.

The "dangerous class," the social scum, that passively rotting class thrown off by the lowest layers of old society, may, here and there, be swept into the movement by a proletarian revolution; its conditions of life, however, prepare it far more for the part of a bribed tool of reactionary intrigue.

In the conditions of the proletariat, those of old society at large are already virtually swamped. The proletarian is without property; his relation to his wife and children has no longer anything in common with the bourgeois family relations; modern industrial labor, modern subjection to capital, the same in England as in France, in America as in Germany, has stripped him of every trace of national character. Law, morality, religion, are to him so many bourgeois prejudices, behind which lurk in ambush just as many bourgeois interests.

All the preceding classes that got the upper hand sought to fortify their already acquired status by subjecting society at large to their conditions of appropriation. The proletarians cannot become masters of the productive forces of society, except by abolishing their own previous mode of appropriation, and thereby also every other previous mode of appropriation. They have nothing of their own to secure and to fortify; their mission is to destroy all previous securities for, and insurances of, individual property.

All previous historical movements were movements of minorities, or in the interest of minorities. The proletarian movement is the self-conscious, independent movement of the immense majority, in the interest of the immense majority. The proletariat, the lowest stratum of our present society, cannot stir, cannot raise itself up, without the whole superincumbent strata of official society being sprung into the air.

Though not in substance, yet in form, the struggle of the proletariat with the bourgeoisie is at first a national struggle. The proletariat of each country must, of course, first of all settle matters with its own bourgeoisie.

In depicting the most general phases

of the development of the proletariat, we traced the more or less veiled civil war, raging within existing society, up to the point where that war breaks out into open revolution, and where the violent overthrow of the bourgeoisie lays the foundation for the sway of the proletariat.

Hitherto every form of society has been based, as we have already seen, on the antagonism of oppressing and oppressed classes. But in order to oppress a class certain conditions must be assured to it under which it can, at least, continue its slavish existence. The serf, in the period of serfdom, raised himself to membership in the commune, just as the petty bourgeois, under the yoke of feudal absolutism, managed to develop into a bourgeois. The modern laborer, on the contrary, instead of rising with the progress of industry, sinks deeper and deeper below the conditions of existence of his own class. He becomes a pauper, and pauperism develops more rapidly than population and wealth. And here it becomes evident that the bourgeoisie is unfit any longer to be the ruling class in society and to impose its conditions of existence upon society as an over-riding law. It is unfit to rule because it is incompetent to assure an existence to its slave within his slavery, because it cannot help letting him sink into such a state that it has to feed him instead of being fed by him. Society can no longer live under this bourgeoisie; in other words, its existence is no longer compatible with society.

The essential condition for the existence, and for the sway of the bourgeois class, is the formation and augmentation of capital; the condition for capital is wage-labor. Wage-labor rests exclusively on competition between the laborers. The advance of industry, whose involuntary promoter is the bourgeoisie, replaces the isolation of the laborers, due to competition, by their revolutionary combination, due to association. The development of modern industry, therefore, cuts from under its feet the very foundation on which the bourgeoisie produces and appropriates products. What the bourgeoisie therefore produces, above all, are its own grave diggers. Its fall and the victory of the proletariat are equally inevitable.

20. *The State and Revolution**

Nicolai Lenin (1870–1924)

In capitalist society, under the conditions most favorable to its development, we have a more or less complete democracy in the form of a democratic repub-

* From N. Lenin, *The State and Revolution*, New York, The Vanguard Press, 1926, pp. 191-206; written in Switzerland shortly before the Revolution of 1917, and first published in 1918.

lic. But this democracy is always bound by the narrow framework of capitalist exploitation, and consequently always remains, in reality, a democracy only for the minority, only for the possessing classes, only for the rich. Freedom in capitalist society always remains more or less the same as it was in the ancient

Greek republics, that is, freedom for the slave owners. The modern wage-slaves, in virtue of the conditions of capitalist exploitation, remain to such an extent crushed by want and poverty that they "cannot be bothered with democracy," have "no time for politics"; that, in the ordinary peaceful course of events, the majority of the population is debarred from participating in public political life.

The accuracy of this statement is perhaps most clearly proved by Germany, just because in this State constitutional legality has lasted and remained stable for a remarkably long time—for nearly half a century (1871–1914); and the Social-Democracy during this time has been able, far better than has been the case in other countries, to make use of "legality" in order to organize into a political party a larger proportion of the working class than has occurred anywhere else in the world.

What, then, is this highest proportion of politically conscious and active wage-slaves that has so far been observed in capitalist society? One million members of the Social-Democratic Party out of fifteen millions of wage-workers! Three millions industrially organized out of fifteen millions!

Democracy for an insignificant minority, democracy for the rich—that is the democracy of capitalist society. If we look more closely into the mechanism of capitalist democracy, everywhere—in the so-called "petty" details of the suffrage (the residential qualification, the exclusion of women, etc.), in the technique of the representative institutions, in the actual obstacles to the right of meeting (public buildings are not for the "poor"), in the purely capitalist organization of the daily press, etc., etc.—on all sides we shall see restrictions upon restrictions of democracy. These restrictions, exceptions, exclusions, obstacles for the poor, seem slight—especially in

the eyes of one who has himself never known want, and has never lived in close contact with the oppressed classes in their hard life, and nine-tenths, if not ninety-nine hundredths, of the bourgeois publicists and politicians are of this class! But in their sum these restrictions exclude and thrust out the poor from politics and from an active share in democracy. Marx splendidly grasped the *essence* of capitalist democracy, when, in his analysis of the experience of the Commune, he said that the oppressed are allowed, once every few years to decide which particular representatives of the oppressing class are to represent and repress them in Parliament!

But from this capitalist democracy—inevitably narrow, stealthily thrusting aside the poor, and therefore, to its core, hypocritical and treacherous—progress does not march along a simple, smooth and direct path to "greater and greater democracy," as the Liberal professors and the lower middle class opportunists would have us believe. No, progressive development—that is, towards Communism—marches through the dictatorship of the proletariat; and cannot do otherwise, for there is no one else who can *break the resistance* of the exploiting capitalists, and no other way of doing it.

And the dictatorship of the proletariat—that is, the organization of the advance-guard of the oppressed as the ruling class, for the purpose of crushing the oppressors—cannot produce merely an expansion of democracy. *Together* with an immense expansion of democracy—for the first time becoming democracy for the poor, democracy for the people, and not democracy for the rich folk—the dictatorship of the proletariat will produce a series of restrictions of liberty in the case of the oppressors, exploiters and capitalists. We must crush them in order to free humanity from wage-slavery; their resistance must be broken by force. It is clear that where there is suppression there must also be violence, and there cannot be liberty or democracy.

Engels expressed this splendidly in his letter to Bebel when he said, as the reader will remember, that "the proletariat needs the State, not in the interests of liberty, but for the purpose of crushing its opponents; and, when one will be able to speak of freedom, the State will have ceased to exist."

Democracy for the vast majority of the nation, and the suppression by force —that is, the exclusion from democracy —of the exploiters and oppressors of the nation; this is the modification of democracy which we shall see during the *transition* from capitalism to Communism.

Only in Communist society, when the resistance of the capitalists has finally been broken, when the capitalists have disappeared, when there are no longer any classes (that is, when there is no difference between the members of society in respect of their social means of production) *only then* "does the State disappear *and one can speak of freedom.*" Only then will be possible and will be realized a really full democracy, a democracy without any exceptions. And only then will democracy itself begin to wither away in virtue of the simple fact that, free from capitalist slavery, from the innumerable horrors, savagery, absurdities and infamies of capitalist exploitation, people will gradually *become accustomed* to the observation of the elementary rules of social life, known for centuries, repeated for thousands of years in all sermons. They will become accustomed to their observance without force, without constraint, without subjection, without the *special apparatus* for compulsion which is called the State.

The expression "the State withers away," is very well chosen, for it indicates the gradual and elemental nature of the process. Only habit can, and undoubtedly will, have such an effect: for we see around us millions of times how readily people get accustomed to observe the necessary rules of life in common, if there is no exploitation, if there is nothing that causes indignation, that calls forth protest and revolt and has to be suppressed.

Thus, in capitalist society, we have a democracy that is curtailed, wretched, false; a democracy only for the rich, for the minority. The dictatorship of the proletariat, the period of transition to Communism, will, for the first time, produce a democracy for the people, for the majority, side by side with the necessary suppression of the minority constituted by the exploiters. Communism alone is capable of giving a really complete democracy, and the fuller it is the more quickly will it become unnecessary and wither away of itself. In other words, under capitalism we have a State in the proper sense of the word: that is, a special instrument for the suppression of one class by another, and of the majority by the minority at that. Naturally, for the successful discharge of such a task as the systematic suppression by the minority of exploiters of the majority of exploited, the greatest ferocity and savagery of suppression is required, and seas of blood are needed, through which humanity has to direct its path, in a condition of slavery, serfdom and wage labor.

Again, during the *transition* from capitalism to Communism, suppression is *still* necessary; but in this case it is suppression of the minority of exploiters by the majority of exploited. A special instrument, a special machine for suppression—that is, the "State"—is necessary, but this is now a transitional State, no longer a State in the ordinary sense of the term. For the suppression of the minority of exploiters, by the majority of those who were *but yesterday* wage-slaves, is a matter comparatively so easy, simple and natural that it will cost far less bloodshed than the suppression of the risings of the slaves, serfs or wage laborers, and will cost the human race far less. And it is compatible with the diffusion of democracy over such an overwhelming majority of the nation that the need for any *special machinery* for *suppression* will gradually cease to exist. The exploiters are unable, of course, to suppress the people without a most complex machine for performing this duty; but *the people* can suppress the exploiters even with a very simple "machine"—almost without any "machine" at all, without any special apparatus—by the simple *organization of the armed masses* (such as the Councils of Workers' and Soldiers' Deputies, we may remark, anticipating a little).

Finally, only under Communism will the State become quite unnecessary, for there will be *no one* to suppress—"no one" in the sense of a *class*, in the sense of a systematic struggle with a definite section of the population. We are not utopians, and we do not in the least deny the possibility and inevitability of excesses by *individual persons*, and equally the need to suppress such excesses. But, in the first place, for this no special machine, no special instrument of repression is needed. This will be done by the armed nation itself, as simply and as readily as any crowd of civilized people, even in modern society, parts a pair of combatants or does not allow a woman to be outraged. And, secondly, we know that the fundamental social cause of excesses which violate the rules of social life is the exploitation of the masses, their want and their poverty. With the removal of this chief cause, excesses will inevitably begin to "wither away." We do not know how quickly and in what stages, but we know that they will be withering away. With their withering away, the State will also wither away. Marx, without plunging into Utopia, defined more fully what can *now* be defined regarding this future epoch: namely, the difference between the higher and lower phases (degrees, stages) of Communist society.

21. *Freedom and Culture**

JOHN DEWEY (1859–1951)

Important social movements develop some sort of philosophy by which to guide, nominally, at least, their practical efforts and also to justify them *ex post facto*. German culture has been especially ardent and prolific in this direc-

* *Freedom and Culture*, by John Dewey. Pages 80–99. Courtesy of G. P. Putnam's Sons, 1939.

tion, all attempts to deal with actual conditions on any other basis being regarded as proof that those engaged in them are mere "empiricists," a term of condemnation about equivalent to calling them quacks. In Marxism those who accepted any law except one having exclusively material support were utopian dreamers. The fact then that the dialectical formula was borrowed from the most metaphysical, in a non-scientific sense, of all modern philosophers was no deterrent to the vogue of the Marxist synthesis, since its practical character seemed to be vouched for not only by actual economic conditions and by Marx's predictions, but in particular by the increase in class conflict that was taking place.

The idea of class war took on a peculiarly timely quality because of its teaching that the then existing class struggle was that of bourgeoisie capitalists with the proletariat, the class of factory wage-workers having neither land nor any form of reserve capital. Moreover, Marx's study of the concrete facts of the factory system in Great Britain backed up his general theory with a considerable number of economic generalizations which proved sound on any theory:—such as the existence of economic cycles with crises of increasing severity, a tendency toward combination and concentration, etc. The simplified Romanticism of the principle of a negation of negations taught that class war would, through the mediation of a temporary dictatorship of the proletariat, finally usher in a classless society. In the latter the state as a political coercive power would wither away, all political agencies becoming organs of democratic administration of affairs of common interest. Even the anarchist with his opposition to all coercive power could find satisfaction in contemplation of this ultimate outcome.

Marxists object vigorously and naturally to any suggestion of an identification of their creed with theological systems of the past. But all absolutisms tend to assume a theological form and to arouse the kind of emotional ardor that has accompanied crusading religions in the past. The theological concerns and conflicts of the earlier centuries of our era involved, moreover,

contemporary interests not now recoverable in imagination. That is, they were more "practical" in fact than they now appear in retrospect. Similarly the monolithic and in itself speculative Marxist doctrine took on immediate practical coloring in connection with existing economic conditions and new forms of oppressions they had produced. There is nothing novel or peculiar in a combination of theory and practice in which practical events give definite color to an abstract theory, while the theory serves as a fountainhead of inspiration to action, providing also rallying cries and slogans. Exegesis can always serve to bridge gaps and inconsistencies; and every absolutistic creed demonstrates that no limits can be put to exegetical ingenuity. What actually happens can, accordingly, be brought into harmony with dogma while the latter is covertly accommodated to events.

There is no need to go into the full scope of Marxist philosophy upon its theoretical side. What is of concern here is the support alleged to be given by it to a strictly *scientific* form of social development, one which is inevitable *because* scientific. As is said of literary products, Marxism is "dated" in the matter of its claims to be peculiarly scientific. For just as *necessity* and search for a *single* all-comprehensive law was typical of the intellectual atmosphere of the forties of the last century, so *probability* and *pluralism* are the characteristics of the present state of science. That the older interpretation of the idea of causal necessity has undergone a shock does not need to be told to those acquainted with recent developments. It is not necessary, however, to go to the point of throwing the idea entirely overboard to make the point which is significant for the present topic.

There is a worldwide difference between the idea that causal sequences will be found in any given set of events taken for investigation, and the idea that *all* sets of events are linked together into a *single* whole by *one* causal law. Even if it be admitted that the former principle is a necessary postulate of scientific inquiry, the latter notion is metaphysical and *extra*-scientific. When natural science was first struggling to achieve its independence, and later when an attempt was made to take social phenomena out of the domain of arbitrary free-will, those who wanted to promote the new struggles borrowed from dominant theology the idea which the latter had made familiar, that of a single all-embracing causal force. The nature of the force and the way it worked were radically altered in the new apologetics for science. But the requirements of habit were satisfied in maintaining the old forms of thought—just as the first "horseless carriages" kept the shape of the carriages they displaced. The void left by surrender first of a supernatural force, and then of Nature (which had replaced Deity during the periods of deistic rationalism) is thus made good. Only gradually did the work of science and the specific conclusions it reached make it clear that science was not a competitor with theology for a single ultimate explanation, so that the justification was no longer resorted to.

The surrender does not mean that search for broad generalizations has been given up. It means that the nature and function of these generalizations have changed. They are now, in effect and function, formulae for effecting transformations from one field to another, the qualitative difference of the fields being maintained. The doctrine of the conservation of energy represents, for example, an exceedingly comprehensive generalization. In terms of the now discarded philosophy of science, it would be said to set up a force which is at once electrical, mechanical, thermal,

etc., and yet none of them, but a kind of nondescript Thing-in-itself back of all of them. In actual scientific procedure, it is a formula for converting any one of these forms of energy into any other, provided certain conditions are satisfied.

The same principle holds good of the recently discovered transmutation of chemical elements. It does not wipe out the differences of quality that mark off phenomena from one another but sets forth the conditions under which one kind is changed into another kind. Differences in the practical operations that are based upon science correspond with the change that has come about in theory—as the techniques of modern chemical industry are different from the dreams of the alchemists. No one today would think of undertaking a definite invention, the heavier-than-air flying boat, the internal combustion engine, and so on, by setting out from an alleged universal law of the working of some single ultimate force. The inventor who translates an idea into a working technological device starts from examination of special materials and tries special methods for combining them.

The practical techniques derived from the Marxist single all-embracing law of a single causative force follow the pattern discarded in scientific inquiry and in scientific engineering. What is necessary according to it is to promote class war in as great a variety of ways and on as many occasions as possible. For the essence of the theory, according to the dialectical method, is not recognition of class conflicts as *facts*—in which respect it provided a needed correction of the early nineteenth century notion of universal harmony and universal interdependence. Its distinguishing trait is that social progress is made by intensifying the conflict between the capitalistic employing classes and the proletarian employed class, so that the supreme principle of morals is to strengthen the power of the latter class.

The physical analogy is about like this: suppose that there had once been a theory that "nature abhors friction." It is then discovered that no mechanical work is done without resistance, and that there is no resistance without friction. It is then concluded that by abolishing lubrication and magnifying friction, a state of universal friction will by its own inner dialectic result in an adjustment of energies to one another which will provide the best possible conditions for doing useful work. Society *is* marked by conflict and friction of interests; interests may by some stretching and more consolidation be used to define classes. It may also be admitted that the conflict between them has under certain conditions served as a stimulus to social progress; it might even be admitted that a society in which there was no opposition of interests would be sunk in a condition of hopeless lethargy. But the idea of obtaining universal harmony by the greatest possible intensification of conflicts would remain analogous to the physical illustration given. Persons who are not Marxists often identify the proposition that serious strife of economic interests exists with the genuine Marxist thesis that it is the sole agency by which social change is effected in the desirable direction of a classless society.

The criticism made is not directed then to any generalization made by Marx on the basis of observation of actual conditions. On the contrary, the implication of the criticism is the necessity for *continued* observation of actual conditions, with testing and revision of all earlier generalization on the basis of what is now observed. The inherent theoretical weakness of Marxism is that it supposed a generalization that was made at a particular date and place (and made even then only by bringing observed facts under a premise drawn from a metaphysical source) can obviate the need for continued resort to observation, and to continual revision of generalizations in their office of working hypotheses. In the name of science, a thoroughly anti-scientific procedure was formulated, in accord with which a generalization is made having the nature of ultimate "truth," and hence holding good at all times and places.

Laissez-faire individualism indulged in the same kind of sweeping generalization but in the opposite direction. Doubtless, in accordance with the law of the union of opposites, this background played its part in creating a cultural atmosphere favorable to Marxism. But two opposite errors do not constitute one truth, especially when both errors have the same root. With some disregard for historic facts, the Marxist doctrine might even be regarded as a generalized version of that aspect of classic economic theory which held that completely free competition in the open market would automatically produce universal harmony of persons and nations, Marx converting competition of individuals into war of classes.

Marxism has, then, been selected as an illustration of the monistic block-universe theory of social causation. A few years ago the laissez-faire view, developed out of ideas of Adam Smith when they were wedded to ideas of utilitarian morals and psychology, would have been appropriately taken. The Russian Revolution is chiefly accountable for having brought Marxism to the foreground. Being conducted in the name of Marx, it claimed to be a large scale demonstration of the validity of the Marxist theory. The Union of Socialist Soviet Republics has fastened attention upon the theory as no idea ever succeeds on its own account in obtaining notice. It caused Marxism to be a terrifying menace in some quarters while giving it enormous prestige in other quarters. It led to a disruption of old socialist parties, as the Russian Revolution was held up in other countries as proof of the Marxist theory of class war and the dictatorship of the proletariat. The issue raised by events in Russia gave actuality to Marxist doctrine in every country of the globe.

An event of this sort cannot occur without arousing intense feeling, and corresponding conflicts of interpretation. In the present case, the division extends not only to the theory but to the facts of the situation. One can find data, real or alleged, to support almost any view as to the actual situation in the U.S.S.R., according to the source one takes to be authoritative. Facts, including statistics, are cited to show that extraordinary progress has been made in industrialization of the country and mechanization of agricultural pursuits, with an immense gain in productivity, and, what is more important, in creation of a genuine workers' republic, attended with striking rise in the material and cultural standards of living of the great mass of the population. But one may also find evidence to support the view that the dictatorship of the proletariat became first that of a party over the proletariat and then the dictatorship of a small band of bureaucrats over the party, until the latter, to maintain power, has adopted, with greatly improved technical skill in execution, all the repressive measures of the overthrown Czarist despotism. One can find evidence that, under a regime of governmental, instead of social, control, economic classes marked by great inequality of income are growing up. Such questions of fact are not settled by argument. Hence though there is no doubt in my own mind as to the conclusion available evidence points to, I shall not here attempt to take a stand on the particular issues of fact which are involved.

Certain facts that are not denied suffice as far as the present topic and problem are concerned. A monistic theory is accompanied in its practical execution by one-party control of press, schools, radio, the theater and every means of communication, even to effective restrictions imposed on private gatherings and private conversations. One of the reasons for the great difference in opinion about the state of facts—the point just mentioned—is the fact that effective dictatorship (and an ineffective dictatorship is not a dictatorship at all) exercises complete command over the press, over travel, over letters and personal communications. In consequence, only a few have access to the sources of information about political methods, and that few is just the group with the greatest interest in preventing free inquiry and report.

This suppression of freedom of belief and of speech, press and assembly is not among the facts in dispute for it is of the essence of the dictatorship, which in turn is of the essence of the doctrine the Revolution claims to have put in force. Nor is ruthless persecution and punishment of all dissenters one of the disputed facts. A succession of trials has eliminated from life (as well as from political action) every one of the men and women who brought on the Revolution, save a few relatively minor characters. The *justification* of the action is one of the things in controversy, but not the fact of the exile, imprisonment or execution of every important earlier leader. As a criterion for judging the theory back of revolutionary method of class war, it would not seem to make a great deal of difference whether we decide these men were traitors to their own cause of the liberation of humanity, or are victims of the desire of a clique to keep in their hands a monopoly of all power—great as will be the difference in our judgment about the character of the persons involved.

Events not in dispute confirm the

conclusion drawn from other historical instances that absolute principles are intolerant of dissent, for dissent from "The Truth" is more than an intellectual error. It is proof of an evil and dangerous will. When the dominant dogma is definitely theological, the evil will is described in one set of terms; when it is political, the phraseology is different, "counter-revolution" taking the place of "heresy."

The psychological and moral dispositions stimulated and the kind of activities in which they are expressed are extraordinarily similar. No general theory, moreover, is self-translating in application to particular events. Some body of persons must exist to state just what its significance is in its bearing upon this and that situation, and a body that merely interprets is impotent unless it has power to enforce decisions. The extreme danger of giving any body of persons power for whose exercise they are not accountable is a commonplace in a democracy. Arbitrary irresponsibility varies in direct ratio to the claim for absoluteness on the part of the principle in behalf of which power is exercised. To sustain the principle against heresy, or counter-revolutionary action, it finally becomes necessary to clothe the human officials that are supposed to represent the principle with the finality of the professed end. Divinity once hedged about kings. An earlier repudiation in Russia of glorification of individual persons, because of the immensely superior importance of collective action, gives way to Byzantine adulation of the Leader.

*   *   *

The experimental method of science is the exemplification of empirical method when experience has reached maturity. It is opposed equally to "vulgar" empiricism which recognizes only rule-of-thumb action, depending upon a succession of trial-and-error acts that are unregulated by connection with an idea which is both expressed and tested, and to that absolutism which insists there is but one Truth and that truth one already revealed and possessed by some group or party.

To repeat a statement already made in another connection, no generalization which, like Marxism, claims to state the final truth about changes (whether physical or social), can set forth the significance of the general idea that is accepted in connection with actual events as they happen. For the purpose of day by day *action,* the sole value of a theory is the significance given to concrete events, when they are viewed in the light of the theory, in the concrete relations they sustain to one another. It is no accident that the final effect of uniformity of ideas is to set up some selected body of persons above the theoretical generalization. Those who determine what the theory signifies in terms of the one important thing—namely, *what should be done*—are supreme over the theory even when they claim to act in subjection to it. The demand for uniformity of opinion, "the refusal to tolerate the existence of incompatible opinions," demands first that there be a party and then a select council of persons within the party, to decide just what after all is The Truth with respect to events as they arise—together with a truly theological technique of exegesis to explain the perfect consistency existing among a succession of inconsistent policies. Thus there has been the change from the earlier denunciation of democracy as identical with middle class capitalism and the labeling of all other socialists as Social-Fascists, to the present policy of a Popular Front, and to the presentation of Bolshevism as twentieth century democracy. And, again, change from denunciation of Nazi Germany to the beginnings of a virtual alliance with it, but now in the wholly praiseworthy interest of world peace, following upon the former orthodox doctrine that only communism can institute peace after a succession of wars international and civil. Scientific method in operating with working hypotheses instead of with fixed and final Truth is not forced to have an Inner Council to declare just what is the Truth nor to develop a system of exegesis which rivals the ancient theological way of explaining away apparent inconsistencies. It welcomes a clash of "incompatible opinions" as long as they can produce observed facts in their support.

Since Marxism has been taken as the example of a uniformitarian theory, basing itself upon "objective" factors of the environment in separation from their interaction with the factors of human nature, something will be said in closing about the ignoring of human qualities. For it contradicts the statement sometimes made that the essence of Marxism, at least as a practical doctrine, is appeal to the motive of self-interest. This statement is made as an accusation by non-Marxists, while it sometimes appears in what profess to be Marxist documents. But actually it comes close to reversing actual Marxist doctrine—the doctrine that the state of the forces of production is the sole causal force. For according to this view, all the factors of human nature are shaped from without by "materialistic," that is economic, forces. To give independent validity to any component of human nature would be, from the Marxist standpoint, a relapse into the "idealistic" type of theory that Marxism came to destroy.

A much juster criticism would be that Marxism systematically neglects everything on the side of human nature with respect to its being a factor having efficacy, save as it is previously determined by the state of the forces of production.

In claiming to replace "Utopian" socialisms, Marxism throws out psychological as well as moral considerations. Whether the theory is in fact able to live up to this claim—without which its "materialism" is meaningless—is another matter. For it would seem as if certain organic needs and appetites at least were required to set the "forces of production" moving. But if this bio-psychological factor is admitted, then it must *interact* with "external" factors, and there is no particular point at which its operation can be said to cease.

The point involved has a practical as well as theoretical force. Take for example the matter of classes and of class-*consciousness*, the latter being an imperatively required condition in the Marxist theory. According to orthodox Marxism, the class consciousness of the proletariat is generated by the fact that the state of economic forces represented by large-scale factory production throws wage-workers closely together with little or no direct intercourse with employers —such as existed, for example, in shops where hand tools were used. Physical conditions thus demarcate economic classes, and throw into relief the conflict of interests between employers and employees, together with the community of interests, if only in misery, that bind together the latter. Now as an observation there is an undeniable element of truth in this position—especially in contrast with the favorite editorial exhortation that there can be no conflict between "Capital" and "Labor" since each depends on the other. But the facts involved in the observation are not compatible with the ultimate theory. The formation of a class, especially of class consciousness, depends upon the operation of psychological factors which are not mentioned—and which the theory rules out.

22. *On Liberty**

JOHN STUART MILL (1806-1873)

The subject of this Essay is not the so-called Liberty of the Will, so unfortunately opposed to the misnamed doctrine of Philosophical Necessity; but Civil, or Social Liberty: the nature and limits of the power which can be legitimately exercised by society over the individual. A question seldom stated, and hardly ever discussed, in general terms, but which profoundly influences the practical controversies of the age by its latent presence, and is likely soon to make itself recognised as the vital question of the future. It is so far from being new, that, in a certain sense, it has divided mankind, almost from the remotest ages; but in the stage of progress into which the more civilised portions of the species have now entered, it presents itself under new conditions, and requires a different and more fundamental treatment.

The struggle between Liberty and Authority is the most conspicuous feature in the portions of history with which we are earliest familiar, particular in that of Greece, Rome, and England. But in old times this contest was between subjects, or some classes of subjects, and the Government. By liberty, was meant protection against the tyranny of the political rulers. The rulers were conceived (except in some of the popular governments of Greece) as in a necessarily antagonistic position to the people whom they ruled. They consisted of a governing One, or a governing tribe or caste, who derived their authority from inheritance or conquest, who, at all events, did not hold it at the pleasure of the governed, and whose supremacy men did not venture, perhaps did not desire, to contest, whatever precautions might be taken against its oppressive exercise. Their power was regarded as necessary, but also as highly dangerous; as a weapon which they would attempt to use against their subjects, no less than against external enemies. To prevent the weaker members of the community from being preyed upon by innumerable vultures, it was needful that there should be an animal of prey stronger than the rest, commissioned to keep them down. But as the king of the vultures would be no less bent upon preying on the flock than any of the minor harpies, it was indispensable to be in a perpetual attitude of defence against his beak and claws. The aim, therefore, of patriots was to set limits to the power which the ruler should be suffered to exercise over the community; and this limitation was what they meant by liberty. It was attempted in two ways. First, by obtaining a recognition of certain immunities, called political

---

* First published in England in 1859. This selection includes nearly all of the first chapter; the other two chapters are (II) "Thought and Discussion" and (III) "Of Individuality, as One of the Elements of Well-Being." Mill's summary of his second chapter is quoted at the end.

liberties or rights, which it was to be regarded as a breach of duty in the ruler to infringe, and which if he did infringe, specific resistance, or general rebellion, was held to be justifiable. A second, and generally a later expedient, was the establishment of constitutional checks, by which the consent of the community, or of a body of some sort, supposed to represent its interests, was made a necessary condition to some of the more important acts of the governing power. To the first of these modes of limitation, the ruling power, in most European countries, was compelled, more or less, to submit. It was not so with the second; and, to attain this, or when already in some degree possessed, to attain it more completely, became everywhere the principal object of the lovers of liberty. And so long as mankind were content to combat one enemy by another, and to be ruled by a master, on condition of being guaranteed more or less efficaciously against his tyranny, they did not carry their aspirations beyond this point.

A time, however, came, in the progress of human affairs, when men ceased to think it a necessity of nature that their governors should be an independent power, opposed in interest to themselves. It appeared to them much better that the various magistrates of the State should be their tenants or delegates, revocable at their pleasure. In that way alone, it seemed, could they have complete security that the powers of government would never be abused to their disadvantage. By degrees this new demand for elective and temporary rulers became the prominent object of the exertions of the popular party, wherever any such party existed; and superseded, to a considerable extent, the previous efforts to limit the power of rulers. As the struggle proceeded for making the ruling power emanate from the periodical choice of the ruled, some persons

began to think that too much importance had been attached to the limitation of the power itself. *That* (it might seem) was a resource against rulers whose interests were habitually opposed to those of the people. What was now wanted was, that the rulers should be identified with the people; that their interest and will should be the interest and will of the nation. The nation did not need to be protected against its own will. There was no fear of its tyrannising over itself. Let the rulers be effectually responsible to it, promptly removable by it, and it could afford to trust them with power of which it could itself dictate the use to be made. Their power was but the nation's own power, concentrated, and in a form convenient for exercise. This mode of thought, or rather perhaps of feeling, was common among the last generation of European liberalism, in the Continental section of which it still apparently predominates. Those who admit any limit to what a government may do, except in the case of such governments as they think ought not to exist, stand out as brilliant exceptions among the political thinkers of the Continent. A similar tone of sentiment might by this time have been prevalent in our own country, if the circumstances which for a time encouraged it, had continued unaltered.

But, in political and philosophical theories, as well as in persons, success discloses faults and infirmities which failure might have concealed from observation. The notion, that the people have no need to limit their power over themselves, might seem axiomatic, when popular government was a thing only dreamed about, or read of as having existed at some distant period of the past. Neither was that notion necessarily disturbed by such temporary aberrations as those of the French Revolution, the worst of which were the work of a usurping few, and which, in any case, belonged, not to the permanent working of popular institutions, but to a sudden and convulsive outbreak against monarchical and aristocratic despotism. In time, however, a democratic republic came to occupy a large portion of the earth's surface, and made itself felt as one of the most powerful members of the community of nations; and elective and responsible government became subject to the observations and criticisms which wait upon a great existing fact. It was now perceived that such phrases as "self-government," and "the power of the people over themselves," do not express the true state of the case. The "people" who exercise the power are not always the same people with those over whom it is exercised; and the "self-government" spoken of is not the government of each by himself, but of each by all the rest. The will of the people, moreover, practically means the will of the most numerous or the most active *part* of the people; the majority, or those who succeed in making themselves accepted as the majority; the people, consequently *may* desire to oppress a part of their number; and precautions are as much needed against this as against any other abuse of power. The limitation, therefore, of the power of government over individuals loses none of its importance when the holders of power are regularly accountable to the community, that is, to the strongest party therein. This view of things, recommending itself equally to the intelligence of thinkers and to the inclination of those important classes in European society to whose real or supposed interests democracy is adverse, has had no difficulty in establishing itself; and in political speculations "the tyranny of the majority" is now generally included among the evils against which society requires to be on its guard.

Like other tyrannies, the tyranny of the majority was at first, and is still

vulgarly, held in dread, chiefly as operating through the acts of the public authorities. But reflecting persons perceived that when society is itself the tyrant—society collectively over the separate individuals who compose it—its means of tyrannising are not restricted to the acts which it may do by the hands of its political functionaries. Society can and does execute its own mandates: and if it issues wrong mandates instead of right, or any mandates at all in things with which it ought not to meddle, it practises a social tyranny more formidable than many kinds of political oppression, since, though not usually upheld by such extreme penalties, it leaves fewer means of escape, penetrating much more deeply into the details of life, and enslaving the soul itself. Protection, therefore, against the tyranny of the magistrate is not enough: there needs protection also against the tyranny of the prevailing opinion and feeling; against the tendency of society to impose, by other means than civil penalties, its own ideas and practices as rules of conduct on those who dissent from them; to fetter the development, and, if possible, prevent the formation, of any individuality not in harmony with its ways, and compels all characters to fashion themselves upon the model of its own. There is a limit to the legitimate interference of collective opinion with individual independence: and to find that limit, and maintain it against encroachment, is as indispensable to a good condition of human affairs, as protection against political despotism.

But though this proposition is not likely to be contested in general terms, the practical question, where to place the limit—how to make the fitting adjustment between individual independence and social control—is a subject on which nearly everything remains to be done. All that makes existence valuable to any one, depends on the enforcement of restraints upon the actions of other people. Some rules of conduct, therefore, must be imposed, by law in the first place, and by opinion on many things which are not fit subjects for the operation of law. What these rules should be is the principal question in human affairs; but if we except a few of the most obvious cases, it is one of those which least progress has been made in resolving. No two ages, and scarcely any two countries, have decided it alike; and the decision of one age or country is a wonder to another. Yet the people of any given age and country no more suspect any difficulty in it, than if it were a subject on which mankind had always been agreed. The rules which obtain among themselves appear to them self-evident and self-justifying. This all but universal illusion is one of the examples of the magical influence of custom, which is not only, as the proverb says, a second nature, but is continually mistaken for the first. The effect of custom, in preventing any misgiving respecting the rules of conduct which mankind impose on one another, is all the more complete because the subject is one on which it is not generally considered necessary that reasons should be given, either by one person to others or by each to himself. People are accustomed to believe, and have been encouraged in the belief by some who aspire to the character of philosophers, that their feelings, on subjects of this nature, are better than reasons, and render reasons unnecessary. The practical principle which guides them to their opinions on the regulation of human conduct, is the feeling in each person's mind that everybody should be required to act as he, and those with whom he sympathises, would like them to act. No one, indeed, acknowledges to himself that his standard of judgment is his own liking; but an opinion on a point of conduct, not supported by reasons, can only count as one person's

preference; and if the reasons, when given, are a mere appeal to a similar preference felt by other people, it is still only many people's liking instead of one. To an ordinary man, however, his own preference, thus supported, is not only a perfectly satisfactory reason, but the only one he generally has for any of his notions of morality, taste, or propriety, which are not expressly written in his religious creed; and his chief guide in the interpretation even of that. Men's opinions, accordingly, on what is laudable or blamable, are affected by all the multifarious causes which influence their wishes in regard to the conduct of others, and which are as numerous as those which determine their wishes on any other subject. Sometimes their reason—at other times their prejudices or superstitions: often their social affections, not seldom their anti-social ones, their envy or jealousy, their arrogance or contemptuousness: but most commonly their desires or fears for themselves—their legitimate or illegitimate self-interest. Wherever there is an ascendant class, a large portion of the morality of the country emanates from its class interests, and its feelings of class superiority. The morality between Spartans and Helots, between planters and negroes, between princes and subjects, between nobles and roturiers, between men and women, has been for the most part the creation of these class interests and feelings: and the sentiments thus generated react in turn upon the moral feelings of the members of the ascendant class, in their relations among themselves. Where, on the other hand, a class, formerly ascendant, has lost its ascendancy, or where its ascendancy is unpopular, the prevailing moral sentiments frequently bear the impress of an impatient dislike of superiority. Another grand determining principle of the rules of conduct, both in act and forbearance, which have been enforced by law or opinion, has been the servility of mankind towards the supposed preferences or aversions of their temporal masters or of their gods. This servility, though essentially selfish, is not hypocrisy; it gives rise to perfectly genuine sentiments of abhorrence; it made men burn magicians and heretics. Among so many baser influences, the general and obvious interests of society have of course had a share, and a large one, in the direction of the moral sentiments: less, however, as a matter of reason, and on their own account, than as a consequence of the sympathies and antipathies which grew out of them: and sympathies and antipathies which had little or nothing to do with the interests of society, have made themselves felt in the establishment of moralities with quite as great force.

The likings and dislikings of society, or of some powerful portion of it, are thus the main thing which has practically determined the rules laid down for general observance, under the penalties of law or opinion. And in general, those who have been in advance of society in thought and feeling, have left this condition of things unassailed in principle, however they may have come into conflict with it in some of its details. They have occupied themselves rather in inquiring what things society ought to like or dislike, than in questioning whether its likings or dislikings should be a law to individuals. They preferred endeavouring to alter the feelings of mankind on the particular points on which they were themselves heretical, rather than make common cause in defence of freedom, with heretics generally. The only case in which the higher ground has been taken on principle and maintained with consistency, by any but an individual here and there, is that of religious belief: a case instructive in many ways, and not least so as forming a most striking instance of the fallibility of

what is called the moral sense: for the *odium theologicum,* in a sincere bigot, is one of the most unequivocal cases of moral feeling. Those who first broke the yoke of what called itself the Universal Church, were in general as little willing to permit difference of religious opinion as that church itself. But when the heat of the conflict was over, without giving a complete victory to any party, and each church or sect was reduced to limit its hopes to retaining possession of the ground it already occupied; minorities, seeing that they had no chance of becoming majorities, were under the necessity of pleading to those whom they could not convert, for permission to differ. It is accordingly on this battle field, almost solely, that the rights of the individual against society have been asserted on broad grounds of principle, and the claim of society to exercise authority over dissentients openly controverted. The great writers to whom the world owes what religious liberty it possesses, have mostly asserted freedom of conscience as an indefeasible right, and denied absolutely that a human being is accountable to others for his religious belief. Yet so natural to mankind is intolerance in whatever they really care about, that religious freedom has hardly anywhere been practically realised, except where religious indifference, which dislikes to have its peace disturbed by theological quarrels, has added its weight to the scale. In the minds of almost all religious persons, even in the most tolerant countries, the duty of toleration is admitted with tacit reserves. One person will bear with dissent in matters of church government, but not of dogma; another can tolerate everybody, short of a Papist or a Unitarian; another every one who believes in revealed religion; a few extend their charity a little further, but stop at the belief in a God and in a future state. Wherever the sentiment of the majority is still genuine and intense, it is found to have abated little of its claim to be obeyed.

In England, from the peculiar circumstances of our political history, though the yoke of opinion is perhaps heavier, that of law is lighter, than in most other countries of Europe; and there is considerable jealousy of direct interference, by the legislative or the executive power, with private conduct; not so much from any just regard for the independence of the individual, as from the still subsisting habit of looking on the government as representing an opposite interest to the public. The majority have not yet learnt to feel the power of the government their power, or its opinions their opinions. When they do so, individual liberty will probably be as much exposed to invasion from the government, as it already is from public opinion. But, as yet, there is a considerable amount of feeling ready to be called forth against any attempt of the law to control individuals in things in which they have not hitherto been accustomed to be controlled by it; and this with very little discrimination as to whether the matter is, or is not, within the legitimate sphere of legal control; insomuch that the feeling, highly salutary on the whole, is perhaps quite as often misplaced as well grounded in the particular instances of its application. There is, in fact, no recognised principle by which the propriety or impropriety of government interference is customarily tested. People decide according to their personal preferences. Some, whenever they see any good to be done, or evil to be remedied, would willingly instigate the government to undertake the business; while others prefer to bear almost any amount of social evil, rather than add one to the departments of human interests amenable to governmental control. And men range themselves on one or the other side in any particular case, according to this general direction of their sentiments; or

according to the degree of interest which they feel in the particular thing which it is proposed that the government should do, or according to the belief they entertain that the government would, or would not, do it in the manner they prefer; but very rarely on account of any opinion to which they consistently adhere, as to what things are fit to be done by a government. And it seems to me that in consequence of this absence of rule or principle, one side is at present as often wrong as the other; the interference of government is, with about equal frequency, improperly invoked and improperly condemned.

The object of this Essay is to assert one very simple principle, as entitled to govern absolutely the dealings of society with the individual in the way of compulsion and control, whether the means used be physical force in the form of legal penalties, or the moral coercion of public opinion. That principle is, that the sole end for which mankind are warranted, individually or collectively, in interfering with the liberty of action of any of their number, is self-protection. That the only purpose for which power can be rightfully exercised over any member of a civilised community, against his will, is to prevent harm to others. His own good, either physical or moral, is not a sufficient warrant. He cannot rightfully be compelled to do or forbear because it will be better for him to do so, because it will make him happier, because, in the opinions of others, to do so would be wise, or even right. These are good reasons for remonstrating with him, or reasoning with him, or persuading him, or entreating him, but not for compelling him, or visiting him with any evil in case he do otherwise. To justify that, the conduct from which it is desired to deter him must be calculated to produce evil to some one else. The only part of the conduct of any one, for which he is amenable to society, is that which concerns others. In the part which merely concerns himself, his independence is, of right, absolute. Over himself, over his own body and mind, the individual is sovereign.

It is, perhaps, hardly necessary to say that this doctrine is meant to apply only to human beings in the maturity of their faculties. We are not speaking of children, or of young persons below the age which the law may fix as that of manhood or womanhood. Those who are still in a state to require being taken care of by others, must be protected against their own actions as well as against external injury. For the same reason, we may leave out of consideration those backward states of society in which the race itself may be considered as in its nonage. The early difficulties in the way of spontaneous progress are so great, that there is seldom any choice of means for overcoming them; and a ruler full of the spirit of improvement is warranted in the use of any expedients that will attain an end, perhaps otherwise unattainable. Despotism is a legitimate mode of government in dealing with barbarians, provided the end be their improvement, and the means justified by actually effecting that end. Liberty, as a principle, has no application to any state of things anterior to the time when mankind have become capable of being improved by free and equal discussion. Until then, there is nothing for them but implicit obedience to an Akbar or a Charlemagne, if they are so fortunate as to find one. But as soon as mankind have attained the capacity of being guided to their own improvement by conviction or persuasion (a period long since reached in all nations with whom we need here concern ourselves), compulsion, either in the direct form or in that of pains and penalties for non-compliance, is no longer admissible as a means to their own good, and justifiable only for the security of others.

It is proper to state that I forego any advantage which could be derived to my argument from the idea of abstract right, as a thing independent of utility. I regard utility as the ultimate appeal on all ethical questions; but it must be utility in the largest sense, grounded on the permanent interests of a man as a progressive being. Those interests, I contend, authorise the subjection of individual spontaneity to external control, only in respect to those actions of each, which concern the interest of other people. If any one does an act hurtful to others, there is a *prima facie* case for punishing him, by law, or, where legal penalties are not safely applicable, by general disapprobation. There are also many positive acts for the benefit of others, which he may rightfully be compelled to perform; such as to give evidence in a court of justice; to bear his fair share in the common defence, or in any other joint work necessary to the interest of the society of which he enjoys the protection; and to perform certain acts of individual beneficence, such as saving a fellow-creature's life, or interposing to protect the defenceless against ill-usage, things which whenever it is obviously a man's duty to do, he may rightfully be made responsible to society for not doing. A person may cause evil to others not only by his actions but by his inaction, and in either case he is justly accountable to them for the injury. The latter case, it is true, requires a much more cautious exercise of compulsion than the former. To make any one answerable for doing evil to others is the rule; to make him answerable for not preventing evil is, comparatively speaking, the exception. Yet there are many cases clear enough and grave enough to justify that exception. In all things which regard the external relations of the individual, he is *de jure* amenable to those whose interests are concerned, and, if need be, to society as their protector. There are often good reasons for not holding him to the responsibility; but these reasons must arise from the special expediences of the case: either because it is a kind of case in which he is on the whole likely to act better, when left to his own discretion, than when controlled in any way in which society have it in their power to control him; or because the attempt to exercise control would produce other evils, greater than those which it would prevent. When such reasons as these preclude the enforcement of responsibility, the conscience of the agent himself should step into the vacant judgment seat, and protect those interests of others which have no external protection; judging himself all the more rigidly, because the case does not admit of his being made accountable to the judgment of his fellow-creatures.

But there is a sphere of action in which society, as distinguished from the individual, has, if any, only an indirect interest; comprehending all that portion of a person's life and conduct which affects only himself, or if it also affects others, only with their free, voluntary, and undeceived consent and participation. When I say only himself, I mean directly, and in the first instance; for whatever affects himself, may affect others through himself; and the objection which may be grounded on this contingency, will receive consideration in the sequel. This, then, is the appropriate region of human liberty. It comprises, first, the inward domain of consciousness; demanding liberty of conscience in the most comprehensive sense; liberty of thought and feeling; absolute freedom of opinion and sentiment on all subjects, practical or speculative, scientific, moral, or theological. The liberty of expressing and publishing opinions may seem to fall under a different principle, since it belongs to that part of the conduct of an individual which concerns other people; but, being almost of as much importance as the liberty of thought itself, and resting in great part on the same reasons, is practically inseparable from it. Secondly, the principle requires liberty of tastes and pursuits; of framing the plan of our life to suit our own character; of doing as we like, subject to such consequences as may follow: without impediment from our fellow-creatures, so long as what we do does not harm them, even though they should think our conduct foolish, perverse, or wrong. Thirdly, from this liberty of each individual, follows the liberty, within the same limits, of combination among individuals; freedom to unite, for any purpose not involving harm to others: the persons combining being supposed to be of full age, and not forced or deceived.

No society in which these liberties are not, on the whole, respected, is free, whatever may be its form of government; and none is completely free in which they do not exist absolute and unqualified. The only freedom which deserves the name, is that of pursuing our own good in our own way, so long as we do not attempt to deprive others of theirs, or impede their efforts to obtain it. Each is the proper guardian of his own health, whether bodily, *or* mental and spiritual. Mankind are greater gainers by suffering each other to live as seems good to themselves, than by compelling each to live as seems good to the rest.

Though this doctrine is anything but new, and, to some persons, may have the air of a truism, there is no doctrine which stands more directly opposed to the general tendency of existing opinion and practice. Society has expended fully as much effort in the attempt (according to its lights) to compel people to conform to its notions of personal as of social excellence. The ancient commonwealths thought themselves entitled to practise, and the ancient philosophers countenanced, the regulation of every part of private conduct by public authority, on the ground that the State had a deep interest in the whole bodily and mental discipline of every one of its citizens; a mode of thinking which may have been admissible in small republics surrounded by powerful enemies, in constant peril of being subverted by foreign attack or internal commotion, and to which even a short interval of relaxed energy and self-command might so easily be fatal that they could not afford to wait for the salutary permanent effects of freedom. In the modern world, the greater size of political communities, and, above all, the separation betwen spiritual and temporal authority (which placed the direction of men's consciences in other hands than those which controlled their worldly affairs), prevented so great an interference by law in the details of private life; but the engines of moral repression have been wielded more strenuously against divergence from the reigning opinion in self-regarding, than even in social matters; religion, the most powerful of the elements which have entered into the formation of moral feeling, having almost always been governed either by the ambition of a hierarchy, seeking control over every department of human conduct, or by the spirit of Puritanism. And some of those modern reformers who have placed themselves in strongest opposition to the religions of the past, have been noway behind either churches or sects in their assertion of the right of spiritual domination: M. Comte, in particular, whose social system, as unfolded in his *Système de Politique Positive,* aims at establishing (though by moral more than by legal appliances) a despotism of society over the individual, surpassing anything contemplated in the political ideal of the most rigid disciplinarian among the ancient philosophers.

Apart from the peculiar tenets of individual thinkers, there is also in the world at large an increasing inclination to stretch unduly the powers of society over the individual, both by the force of opinion and even by that of legislation; and as the tendency of all the changes taking place in the world is to strengthen society, and diminish the power of the individual, this encroachment is not one of the evils which tend spontaneously to disappear, but, on the contrary, to grow more and more formidable. The disposition of mankind, whether as rulers or as fellow-citizens, to impose their own opinions and inclinations as a rule of conduct on others, is so energetically supported by some of the best and by some of the worst feelings incident to human nature, that it is hardly ever kept under restraint by anything but want of power; and as the power is not declining, but growing, unless a strong barrier of moral conviction can be raised against the mischief, we must expect, in the present circumstances of the world, to see it increase. . . .

We have now recognized the necessity to the mental well-being of mankind (on which all their other well-being depends) of freedom of opinion, and freedom of the expression of opinion, on four distinct grounds; which we will now briefly recapitulate.

First, if any opinion is compelled to silence, that opinion may, for aught we can certainly know, be true. To deny this is to assume our own infallibility.

Secondly, though the silenced opinion be an error, it may, and very commonly does, contain a portion of truth; and since the general or prevailing opinion on any subject is rarely or never the whole truth, it is only by the collision of adverse opinions that the remainder of the truth has any chance of being supplied.

Thirdly, even if the received opinion

be not only true, but the whole truth; unless it is suffered to be, and actually is, vigorously and earnestly contested, it will, by most of those who receive it, be held in the manner of a prejudice, with little comprehension or feeling of its rational grounds. And not only this, but, fourthly, the meaning of the doctrine itself will be in danger of being lost, or enfeebled, and deprived of its vital effect on the character and conduct: the dogma becoming a mere formal profession, inefficacious for good, but cumbering the ground, and preventing the growth of any real and heartfelt conviction, from reason or personal experience.

23. *Why I Am Not a Communist**

MORRIS R. COHEN (1880–1947)

Like many others who are not Communists, I hold no brief for the injustices and stupidities of the present capitalist regime. Indeed, I have never ceased to be grateful for the illumination on historic and contemporary social issues which I found in studying Marx's *Das Kapital*. It prepared me to see that the present general breakdown of capitalist economy is not an unforeseeable accident but a consequence of the private ownership of the machinery of production, whereby the processes of industry are directed for the profit of individual capitalists rather than for the satisfaction of our common needs. The old optimistic but essentially anarchistic notion that the good of all will best be promoted by "rugged individualism," by each pursuing his own selfish economic gain, is a cruel superstition which no man possessed of both reason and a decent amount of human sympathy can maintain in the face of the hideous miseries of our present disorder. When

good crops turn out to be calamitous to the farmers who toil to raise them, because the city workers cannot with their needed labor buy the cereals and cotton which they need for food and clothing, the bankruptcy of capitalism is as clear as anything in human affairs can be.

But while the foregoing or essentially similar criticism of the evils of capitalism is largely used by Communists, it is not peculiar to them. They share it not only with other Marxian socialists—whom, with self-defeating unfairness, they characterize as Fascists or social-fascists—but also with many liberal social reformers. For Marx himself freely borrowed his ideas from bourgeois historians as well as from Saint-Simon, Fourier, and their followers, whom he, with the characteristic human failing of borrowers, belittled as Utopians. (Note, for instance, how closely the *Communist Manifesto* follows Victor Considérant's *Principes du Socialisme, Manifeste de la Démocratie,* not only in ideas but also in their linguistic expression.) What distinguishes present-day Communists is not, therefore, their professed ultimate goal or their analysis of our economic ills,

* Reprinted from the *Modern Monthly* (April 1934) in *The Faith of a Liberal: Selected Essays,* by Morris R. Cohen (Henry Holt and Co., New York, 1946), pp. 110-119.

but their political remedy or program—to wit, the seizure of power by armed rebellion [1] and the setting up of a dictatorship by the leaders of the Communist Party. To be sure, this dictatorship is to be in the name of the *proletariat,* just as the fascist dictatorship is in the name of *the whole nation.* But such verbal tricks cannot hide the brute facts of tyrannical suppression necessarily involved in all dictatorship. For the wielders of dictatorial power are few, they are seldom if ever themselves toilers, and they can maintain their power only by ruthlessly suppressing all expression of popular dissatisfaction with their rule. And where there is no freedom of discussion, there is no freedom of thought.

This program of civil war, dictatorship, and the illiberal or fanatically intolerant spirit which war psychology always engenders may bring more miseries than those that the Communists seek to remove; and the arguments to prove that such war is desirable or inevitable seem to me patently inadequate.

Communists ignore the historic truth that civil wars are much more destructive of all that men hold dearest than are wars between nations; and all the arguments that they use against the latter, including the late "war to end war," are much more cogent against civil wars. Wars between nations are necessarily restricted in scope and do not prevent—to a limited extent they even stimulate—co-operation within a community. But civil wars necessarily dislocate all existing social organs and leave us with little social capital or machinery to rebuild a better society. The hatreds which fratricidal wars develop are more persistent and destructive than those developed by wars that terminate in treaties or agreements.

---

[1] Since this article was written armed intervention seems to have largely replaced armed rebellion as a technique for the seizure of power.

Having lived under the tyranny of the Czar, I cannot and do not condemn all revolutions. But the success and benefits of any revolution depend on the extent to which—like the American Revolution of 1776, the French Revolution of 1789, and the anti-Czarist Revolution of March 1917—it approximates national unanimity in the co-operation of diverse classes. When armed uprisings have been undertaken by single oppressed classes, as in the revolt of the gladiators in Rome, the various peasant revolts in England, Germany, and Russia, the French Commune of 1871, or the Moscow uprising of 1905, they have left a deplorably monotonous record of bloody massacres and oppressive reaction. The idea that armed rebellion is the only or the always effective cure for social ills seems to me no better than the old superstition of medieval medicine that bloodletting is the only and the sovereign remedy for all bodily ills.

Communists may feel that the benefits of their Revolution of 1917 outweigh all the terrific hardships which the Russian people have suffered since then. But reasonable people in America will do well to demand better evidence than has yet been offered that they can improve their lot by blindly imitating Russia. Russian breadlines, and famine without breadlines, are certainly not *prima facie* improvements over American conditions. At best a revolution is a regrettable means to bring about greater human welfare. It always unleashes the forces that thrive in disorder, the brutal executions, imprisonments, and, what is even worse, the sordid spying that undermines all feeling of personal security. These forces, once let loose, are difficult to control and they tend to perpetuate themselves. If, therefore, human well-being, rather than mere destruction, is our aim, we must be as critically-minded in considering the consequences of armed revolution as in considering the evils of the existing regime.

One of the reasons that lead Communists to ignore the terrific destruction which armed rebellion must bring about is the conviction that "the revolution" is inevitable. In this they follow Marx, who, dominated by the Hegelian dialectic, regarded the victory of the proletariat over the bourgeoisie as inevitable,[2] so that all that human effort can hope to achieve is "to shorten and lessen the birth pangs" of the new order.[3] There is, however, very little scientific value in this dialectic argument, and many Communists are quite ready to soft-pedal it and admit that some human mistake or misstep might lead to the triumph of fascism. The truth is that the dialectic method which Marx inherited from Hegel and Schelling is an outgrowth of speculations carried on in theologic seminaries. The "system" of production takes the place of the councils or the mills of the gods. Such Oriental fatalism has little support in the spirit and method of modern science. Let us therefore leave the pretended dialectic proof and examine the contention on an historical basis.

Historically, the argument is put thus: When did any class give up its power without a bloody struggle? As in most rhetorical questions, the questioner does not stop for an answer, assuming that his ignorance is conclusive as to the facts. Now, it is not difficult to give instances of ruling classes giving up their sovereignty without armed resistance. The English landed aristocracy did it in the Reform Bill of 1832; and the Russian nobility did it in 1863 when they freed their serfs, though history showed clearly that in this way not only their political power but their very existence was doomed (for money income has never been so secure as direct revenue from the land, and life in cities reduced the absolute number of noble families).

In our own country, the old seaboard aristocracy, which put over the United States Constitution and controlled the government up to the Jacksonian era, offered no armed resistance when the backwoods farmers outvoted them and removed church and property qualifications for office and for the franchise.

But it is not necessary to multiply such instances. It is more important to observe that history does not show that any *class* ever gained its enfranchisement through a bloody rebellion carried out by its own unaided efforts. When ruling classes are overthrown it is generally by a combination of groups that have risen to power only after a long process. For the parties to a rebellion cannot succeed unless they have more resources than the established regime. Thus the ascendancy of the French bourgeoisie was aided by the royal power which Richelieu and Colbert used in the seventeenth century to transform the landed barons into dependent courtiers. Even so, the French Revolution of 1789 would have been impossible without the co-operation of the peasantry, whose opposition to their ancient seigneurs was strengthened as the latter ceased to be independent rulers of the land. This is in a measure also true of the supposedly purely Communist Revolution in Russia. For in that revolution, too, the peasantry had a much greater share than is ordinarily assumed. After all, the amount of landed communal property (that of the crown, the church, etc.) which was changed by the peasants into individual ownership may have been greater than the amount of private property made communal by the Soviet regime. Even the system of collective farms is, after all, a return to the old *mir* system, using modern machinery. The success of the Russian Revolution was largely due to the landlords' agents who, in their endeavor to restore the rule of the landlords, threw the peasantry into the arms of the Bolshevists. Indeed,

---

[2] *Capital* (Tr. by Untermann, 1932), I, p. 837.

[3] *Ibid.*, p. 14-15.

the strictly Marxian economics, with its ideology of surplus-value due to the ownership of the means of production, is inherently inapplicable to the case of the peasant who cultivates his own piece of ground.

Even more important, however, is it to note that no amount of repetition can make a truth of the dogma that the capitalist class alone rules this country and like the Almighty can do what it pleases. It would be folly to deny that, as individuals or as a class, capitalists have more than their proportionate share of influence in the government, and that they have exercised it unintelligently and with dire results. But it is equally absurd to maintain that they have governed or can govern without the co-operation of the farmers and the influential middle classes. None of our recent constitutional amendments—not the income-tax amendment, not the popular election of the United States Senators, not woman suffrage, neither prohibition nor its repeal—nor any other major bit of legislation can be said to have been imposed on our country in the interests of the capitalist class. The farmers, who despite mortgages still cling to the private ownership of their land, are actually the dominant political group even in industrial states like New York, Pennsylvania, and Illinois.

The Communist division of mankind into workingmen and capitalists suffers from the fallacy of simplism. Our social structure and effective class divisions are much more complicated. As the productivity of machinery increases, the middle classes increase rather than decrease. Hence a program based entirely on the supposed exclusive interests of the proletariat has no reasonable prospect. Any real threat of an armed uprising will only strengthen the reactionaries, who are not less intelligent than the Communist leaders, understand just as well how to reach and influence our people,

and have more ample means for organization. If our working classes find it difficult to learn what their true interests are and do not know how to control their representatives in the government and in the trade unions, there is little prospect that they will be able to control things better during a rebellion or during the ensuing dictatorship.

If the history of the past is any guide at all, it indicates that real improvements in the future will come like the improvements of the past—namely, through co-operation among different groups, each of which is wise enough to see the necessity of compromising with those with whom we have to live together and whom we cannot or do not wish to exterminate.

I know that this notion of compromise or of taking counsel as the least wasteful way of adjusting differences is regarded as hopelessly antiquated and bourgeois, but I do not believe that the ideas of so-called Utopian socialists have really been refuted by those who arrogate the epithet "scientific" to themselves. The Communists seem to me to be much more Utopian and quite unscientific in their claims that the working class alone can by its own efforts completely transform our social order.

I do not have very high expectations from the efforts of sentimental benevolence. Yet I cannot help noticing that the leaders of the Communists and of other revolutionary labor movements—Engels, Marx, Lassalle, Luxemburg, Liebknecht, Lenin, and Trotsky—have not been drawn to it by economic solidarity. They were not workingmen nor even all of workingmen's families. They were driven to their role by human sympathy. Sympathy with the sufferings of our fellow men is a human motive that cannot be read out of history. It has exerted tremendous social pressure. Without it you cannot explain the course of nineteenth-century factory legislation, the freeing of serfs and slaves, or the elimination of the grosser forms of human exploitation. Though some who regard themselves as followers of Karl Marx are constantly denouncing reformers who believe in piecemeal improvement and hope rather that things will get worse so as to drive people into a revolution, Marx himself did not always take that view. Very wisely he attached great importance to English factory legislation which restricted the number of hours per working day, for he realized that every little bit that strengthens the workers strengthens their resistance to exploitation. Those who are most oppressed and depressed, the inhabitants of the slums, do not revolt—they have not energy enough to think of it. When, therefore, Mr. Strachey and others criticize the socialists for not bringing about the millennium when they get into power, I am not at all impressed. I do not believe that the socialists or the Labor Party in England have been free from shameful error. But neither have the Communists, or any other human group, been free from it. Trite though it sounds, it is nevertheless true that no human arrangement can bring about perfection on earth. And while the illusion of omniscience may offer great consolation, it brings endless inhumanity when it leads us to shut the gates of mercy. Real as are our human conflicts, our fundamental identity of interest in the face of hostile nature seems to me worthy of more serious attention than the Communists have been willing to accord it.

If liberalism were dead, I should still maintain that it deserved to live, that it had not been condemned in the court of human reason, but lynched outside of it by the passionate and uncompromisingly ruthless war spirit, common to Communists and Fascists. But I do not believe that liberalism is dead, even though it is under eclipse. There still seems to

me enough reason left to which to appeal against reckless fanaticism.

It is pure fanaticism to belittle the gains that have come to mankind from the spirit of free inquiry, free discussion, and accommodation. No human individual or group of individuals can claim omniscience. Hence society can only suffer serious loss when one group suppresses the opinions and criticisms of all others. In purely abstract questions compromise may often be a sign of confusion. One cannot really believe inconsistent principles at the same time. But in the absence of perfect or even adequate knowledge in regard to human affairs and their future, we must adopt an experimental attitude and treat principles not as eternal dogmas, but as hypotheses, to be tried to the extent that they indicate the general direction of solution to specific issues. But as the scientist must be ever ready to modify his own hypothesis or to recognize wherein a contrary hypothesis has merits or deserves preference, so in practical affairs we must be prepared to learn from those who differ with us, and to recognize that however contradictory diverse views may appear in discourse they may not be so in their practical applications.

Thus, the principles of Communism and individualism may be held like theologic dogmas, eternally true and on no occasion ever to be contaminated one by the other. But in fact, when Communists get into power they do not differ so much from others. No one ever wished to make everything communal property. Nor does anyone in his senses believe that any individual will ever with impunity be permitted to use his "property" in an antisocial way when the rest of the community is aroused thereby. In actual life, the question how far Communism shall be pushed depends more upon specific analyses of actual situations—that is, upon factual knowledge.

There can be no doubt that individualism à la Herbert Hoover has led millions to destruction. Nevertheless, we must not forget that a Communist regime will, after all, be run by individuals who will exercise a tremendous amount of power, no less than do our captains of industry or finance today. There is no real advantage in assuming that under Communism the laboring classes will be omniscient. We know perfectly well how labor leaders like John Lewis keep their power by bureaucratic rather than democratic methods. May it not be that the Stalins also keep their power by bureaucratic rather than democratic methods?

Indeed the ruthless suppression of dissent within the Communist Party in Russia and the systematic glorification of the national heroes and military objectives of Czarist days suggest that the Bolshevik Revolution was not so complete a break with the Russian past as most of its friends and enemies assumed in earlier days. In any event we have witnessed in the history of the Communist movement since 1917 a dramatic demonstration of the way in which the glorification of power—first as a means of destroying a ruling class, then as a means of defending a beleaguered state from surrounding enemies, and finally as a means of extending Communism to neighboring lands—comes imperceptibly to displace the ends or objectives which once formed the core of Communist thought. Thus, one by one, the worst features of capitalist society and imperialism, against which Communism cut its eye teeth in protest—extreme inequality in wages, speed-up of workers, secret diplomacy, and armed intervention as a technique of international intercourse—have been taken over by the Soviet Union, with only a set of thin verbal distinctions to distinguish the "good" techniques of Communism from the corresponding "bad" techniques used by capitalism. As is always the case, the glorification of power dulls the sense of righteousness to which any movement for bettering the basic conditions of human living must appeal.

The Communist criticism of liberalism seems to me altogether baseless and worthless. One would suppose from it that liberalism is a peculiar excrescence of capitalism. This is, however, not true. The essence of liberalism—freedom of thought and inquiry, freedom of discussion and criticism—is not the invention of the capitalist system. It is rather the mother of Greek and modern science, without which our present industrial order and the labor movement would be impossible. The plea that the denial of freedom is a temporary necessity is advanced by all militarists. It ignores the fact that, when suppression becomes a habit, it is not readily abandoned. Thus, when the Christian Church after its alliance with the Roman Empire began the policy of "compelling them to enter," it kept up the habit of intolerant persecution for many centuries. Those who believe that many of the finer fruits of civilization were thereby choked should be careful about strengthening the forces of intolerance.

When the Communists tell me that I must choose between their dictatorship and Fascism, I feel that I am offered the choice between being shot and being hanged. It would be suicide for liberal civilization to accept this as exhausting the field of human possibility. I prefer to hope that the present wave of irrationalism and of fanatical intolerance will recede and that the great human energy which manifests itself in free thought will not perish. Often before, it has emerged after being swamped by passionate superstitions. There is no reason to feel that it may not do so again.

SUGGESTED FURTHER READINGS
FOR CHAPTER THREE

Aristotle, *Politics*.

Barnard, Oppenheimer, Thomas, Winne, and Lilienthal, *A Report on the International Control of Atomic Energy*.

Bosanquet, *Philosophy of the State*.

Cicero, *On the Ends of Things*.

Cohen, Dewey, Eddy, Russell: *Why I Am Not a Communist* (ed. S. Hook).

Cohen, M. R., *The Meaning of Human History*.

Croce, B., *History*.

Grotius, *On the Art of War and Peace*.

Hegel, *Philosophy of History; Philosophy of Right*.

Hobbes, *Leviathan*.

Holmes, Oliver W., Justice, *The Common Law*.

Kant, *Essay on Perpetual Peace*.

Kropotkin, *Mutual Aid*.

Locke, *On Civil Government*.

Machiavelli, *The Prince*.

Montesquieu, *Spirit of Laws*.

Niehbuhr, Reinhold, *Faith and History: A Comparison of Christian and Modern Views of History*.

Ortega y Gasset, José, *Toward a Philosophy of History*.

Plato, *Republic*.

Rousseau, *Social Contract*.

Sabine, George, *The History of Political Theory*.

Smith, Adam, *Wealth of Nations*.

Spinoza, *Tractatus Theologico-Politicus*.

The Atlantic Charter.

Tolstoy, *War and Peace*.

Toynbee, Arnold J., *A Study of History*.

Chapter Four

PHILOSOPHY OF SCIENCE

INTRODUCTION

I T was once possible—as late as the eighteenth century—for philosophers to master nearly everything that was known scientifically, and even to be also leaders in one or more other fields of learning. Such was the case with Aristotle, whose scientific texts supplied Western civilization for almost 2,000 years with the foundations of every science. Another classical example of a philosopher-scientist is Leibniz (1646-1716), whose contributions to mathematics and the logic of the sciences were as fruitful as the scientific societies he helped organize all over seventeenth-century Europe. In this classical tradition the love of wisdom and the cultivation of the sciences were inseparable. But the rapid growth of specialized sciences in the last few hundred years makes it practically impossible for one person to keep abreast of all the sciences and to synthesize their results in a philosophical system. Philosophers of science hence nowadays deal with problems underlying (1) the logical structure or common methodological features of the sciences, (2) their interrelations, and (3) the relations of the growing sciences to other phases of civilization, namely, morals, politics, art, and religion. These three sets of problems concerning the rapidly changing sciences require for their solution philosophical principles that are in consonance with the presuppositions and method of science.

I. Logic of Science

Despite the great number of specialized branches and sub-branches of every science, each with its own problems, techniques, and nomenclature, there are certain features common to all scientific inquiry which constitute scientific method. The chief elements of scientific method, as Huxley indicates, are hypothesis, deduction, and verification. An hypothesis is a tentative or proposed solution to the problem which initiated the inquiry. Suppose the problem is to ascertain the cause of cancer. Then the idea that a specific physical or chemical irritation of certain tissues regularly produces cancer would be considered an hypothesis. Deduction would be the drawing of consequences from the hypothesis. For example, if such and such physical or chemical irritants are applied in such and such manner to such tissues, then cancerous growth will ensue. Deductions are more precisely made when the condi-

226

tions are defined and the procedure specified. We may need to know how much of an irritation is required, or at what rate cancerous growth takes place. Experiment and measurement are thus involved in verification, which is the testing of the consequences deduced from an hypothesis. There are *a priori* an infinite number of hypotheses the scientist might test, but in practice he limits himself to those grounded in previous knowledge or related by analogy to similar situations.

There are many important questions which the philosophic student of scientific method will have to face; for example, What is meant by causation? Hume challenged the idea that there was a necessary connection between cause and effect such as we have between a statement and what is logically deduced from it.* If empirical relations are contingent but not necessary, then how can we establish a generalization that goes beyond our limited previous experience to an unlimited future, as we do when we say that all men are mortal because men have to date been mortal? This is the problem of induction: How can we logically justify generalizations that refer to more than what has been experienced? To ask whether all statements of empirical fact are probable is to raise another basic question: What do we mean by probability? Some philosophers challenge the theory of knowledge which appeals to the "certainties" of common sense, such as "I know for certain that I see red or feel pain, etc." We shall discuss theories of knowledge in the next chapter, but we shall here note some of the differences between common sense and science which do not preclude their continuity and similarity in other regards.

The scientific method of checking the consequences of hypotheses by experimental verification generally differs in certain respects from common sense, first of all, by specifying the problem and defining the terms of its hypotheses more carefully and exactly; secondly, by the systematic use of experimental controls of isolated factors; thirdly, by free and open discussion of ideas in collaboration with other investigators. Though a scientist may obtain his hypotheses from any source, he has to submit his reasoning and claims of verification to his co-workers. We have already seen in Chapter One ("Methodology") how scientific method differs from the more prevailing methods of tenacity, authority, and *apriorism*. Insofar as the latter three ways of fixing belief and tradition influence common sense, scientific method is more critical, more flexible, and more progressive than the fossilized features of common sense. The common observation of the rising and setting of the sun, moon, and other heavenly bodies led people to cling tenaciously to the view that the earth was stationary until the astronomers showed that patiently accumulated facts about the positions and motions of heavenly bodies required us to abandon the once common belief.

On the other hand, Huxley's view shows that common sense is not to be rejected when it practically or crudely but satisfactorily copes with everyday situations and problems, correcting itself, like science, on the basis of well-tried experience and tested habits. Scientists and philosophers both naturally rely on such tested common sense in matters requiring neither the precision nor generality of scientific laws or philosophical principles. Furthermore, the basic and often concealed assumptions

---

* See Selection 32.

of science and philosophy are subject to critical examination and revision just as those of common sense, though this is more openly recognized as a desirable thing to do by scientists and scientific philosophers than by the general public.

The following selections have been written by men eminent for their scientific attainments and reflections on the foundations of the sciences.

Poincaré is a mathematical physicist who has thought profoundly about the logical foundations of his science. The problem he discusses is one that occurs in all scientific generalization: how can we make predictions from what we have experienced? We measure the acceleration of falling bodies at different places and times, and accept the hypothesis that, under similar conditions, the same results of measurement will be obtained within the limits of error of our measuring instruments. But there is no *a priori* guarantee that exactly similar conditions will obtain. Hence, our generalization that there is a constant acceleration of freely falling bodies at a given place on the earth contains several general ideas: (1) Bodies fall freely; (2) they are accelerated uniformly towards the center of the earth; (3) their constant acceleration is not affected materially by other very distant or remote events. These ideas are not given by direct observation, for the ideas are general while our observations are particular. Are the general ideas mere fictions or figments of the scientist's imagination, or are they representations of objective laws of nature? This is the problem known throughout the history of philosophy as the problem of universals. The medieval "realist" asserted the objective reality of universals in the very fabric of nature, whereas the "nominalist" claimed that universals exist only as names of similarities or uniformities of particular experiences of essentially individual realities. Now, Poincaré's position is an intermediate one, called "conceptualism." It regards generalizations as hypotheses suggested by the uniformities or similarities of experience. But once the generalization is framed as a hypothesis, the mind reasons to certain conclusions that are valid regardless of the truth or falsity of the hypothesis. These reasonings, however, are applicable to the phenomena studied only so long as there is a certain uniformity of behavior or homogeneity of structure present throughout the observations.

Charles Peirce was thoroughly grounded in physics and chemistry as well as in logic, metaphysics, and the history of science and philosophy. Specimens of the fruits of his life-long study of the methods and foundations of the sciences appear respectively in the selection 5 (Ch. 1), and in the following "Notes on Scientific Philosophy." Although he called himself a "laboratory philosopher," he firmly believed that all the sciences rested on categories like causality, quality, relation, which are taken for granted by the scientist, but which ought to be logically analyzed by the philosopher of science. The logical analysis of relations and of such concepts as probability, infinity, and continuity of which Peirce gives us a glimpse has been one of the major achievements of modern logic. It encouraged Russell to conceive of logic as the essence of philosophy.

II. Interrelations of the Sciences

Peirce aimed at a synthesis of physical, biological, and psychological sciences by means of a systematic elaboration of the ideas of chance, continuity, and feeling. Chance designates the absolute spontaneity and variety in nature. There is always an element of irregularity in natural phenomena that eludes the most exact scientific formulas. Hence, probable errors attach to all scientific laws no matter how precise our instruments of measurement. Continuity explains how regularity or law can evolve from chance variations. Belief in the objective reality of general ideas made Peirce a "realist" in the medieval sense, as distinguished from "nominalists," who regard such ideas as mere names or labels for a sum of particular objects of experience. Peirce's illustrations of such objective universal ideas include physical constants, for example, the value of g, and qualities like the hardness of diamonds. There are also, in social studies, more elusive things like the commercial or nationalistic "spirit of an age," which are as real for Peirce as the merchants or rulers of a nation. But the universals of physical or social science do not exist apart from observable individuals. Specialists trained in the exact mathematical and physical sciences may err in extending their authority beyond their fields, for they may not have enough clear knowledge of the more complex phenomena of biology, psychology, and the social sciences to make generalizations that would hold for all the sciences. Peirce exposes himself to criticism in his cosmic speculations on some rather inexact ideas about evolution and habit formation (with which biologists and psychologists are still experimenting) as a basis for metaphysical generalizations about all the sciences, for example, when he describes the laws of nature as "habits," as if nature were an organism that grows and acquires habits. Whether such a vast analogy is sound or not, it illustrates the sort of speculative philosophy of science which has often stimulated more critical studies (cf. Broad's distinction between speculative and critical philosophy in Chapter Nine). Also, there is no restriction on where a scientist may go to obtain suggestions for his hypotheses. The important concept of probability originated in problems of gambling, and was used at first in sociology (insurance, population changes, and so forth) and biology (birth and death rates, medical statistics) more extensively than in physics, where it plays such a major role today, as Peirce predicted it would.

Russell distinguishes science as a body of results obtained for the sake or love of knowledge from science as a technique of dealing with problems for the sake of increasing man's power over nature (technology or applied science) and over other men (politics in practice). He does not subscribe to a narrowly pragmatic dictum that knowledge is merely power, for he regards the pursuit of science as an esthetic delight or intrinsic good somewhat like the Platonic love of truth. He fears that this esthetic value of science as pure knowledge will be lost by the religious philosophizing of certain contemporary scientists, for example, Eddington, Jeans, and Millikan. Eddington and Jeans have espoused subjectivistic theories of knowledge which would make the presuppositions of empirical science, even of the most rigorous mathematical sciences, purely arbitrary products of the scientist's sensations and imagination. Certain technical changes in the presuppositions of physical measurement, namely, the Heisenberg principle of indeterminacy and the statistical conception of law, have led these scientists (and those who uncritically accept their philosophies of science) to revive the metaphysical and religious doctrines of free will and of God as a mathematical creator of the universe. Russell thinks they are misled and shows how the old logical difficulties in these doctrines remain.

The issue between materialism and idealism as the philosophic foundation for science is restated by Russell in terms of the more fruitful question: Are the laws of physics basic to biology and psychology? His answer is affirmative, and he defends it against idealistic denials. The view that life and mind have properties which are not reducible to physical properties, but require purposive laws of their own occurs in the arguments of "emergent" or "creative evolutionists" (Lloyd Morgan, Bergson, Whitehead), whom Russell calls "evolutionary theologians." They, on the other hand, would indict Russell's physicalism for harboring a fallacy, the fallacy of *reductionism*,[1] that is, of reducing the qualities and values of living, thinking creatures to the purely quantitative, spatial elements of purposeless physical laws. Russell's answer is based on the experimental gains of bio-physics and bio-chemistry and of behavioristic psychology. He insists that scientific laws are entirely neutral with respect to human values. Also, he regards the process of evolution as entirely negative to the idea of divine purpose or cosmic plan. Peirce, on the other hand, attempted boldly to interpret the very laws of nature as part of a cosmic evolutionary growth of reasonableness.

The student should note that the problem is not one that can be settled by a technical knowledge of physics and biology, since the evolutionary view involves a generalization about the whole of nature as known to the biological and psychological sciences as well as to physics. The problem is the logical one of the interrelations of various sciences, and expert knowledge of any one of these sciences cannot settle the question by the sheer weight of specialized authority. In other words, the philosophy of science requires a knowledge of the basic presuppositions and logical interrelations of the sciences, but cannot dictate any final comprehensive interpretation of nature by merely referring to the results of these sciences. It is a common historical fact that the sciences borrow fruitful ideas from one another, but the test of any generalization remains within the logic of consistency and verification. It is in this sense that the philosophy of science is co-ordinate with scientific method, rather than based on a higher authority that can legitimately impose its views on the sciences.

III. *Cultural Implications of Scientific Method*

Quite often philosophers seek a superior realm of objects as more permanent or more important than the transitory world of common sense and science. Some of these philosophers follow Plato in placing objects on three different levels: common sense, which deals confusedly with particular things; science, which discovers empirical uniformities; and philosophy, which discovers eternal truth and purpose in a "higher" world order. "Higher" may mean more comprehensive or more important, but the former logical meaning is independent of the latter ethical sense. This hierarchy of common sense, science and philosophy is acceptable to a theological or metaphysical system which makes philosophy the handmaid of that system and subordinates science to both. Examples of such systems are found not only in those who advocate the medieval and modern Catholic subordination of the phi-

---

[1] Cf. Chapter 6.

losophy of science to theology,[2] but also in those who seek to find an eternal frame-work of philosophic categories within which to interpret the sciences. Russell attacks the extension of biological and psychological categories to the vaster regions of physical events, and recent positivists would agree with Russell on the pluralistic approach of the various sciences, on the externality of perceived events, and on the dubiousness of metaphysical speculations over the organic constitution of nature.

The anti-metaphysical viewpoint of modern positivistic philosophy of science [3] goes back historically to Hume, Auguste Comte, and Ernst Mach, although it advances beyond them on the basis of modern logic and physics. Comte distinguished three stages of cultural and intellectual history: the theological, the metaphysical, and the positive or scientific. It would be wrong to regard these as inevitable his-torical stages, since we find each of them in all periods of intellectual history. Comte also accepted the classical view of nature's laws as necessary relations among observed phenomena, and erected a hierarchy of sciences (mathematics, physics, chemistry, biology, psychology, and sociology) terminating in a high priesthood of sociologists. Mach was a more critical scientific thinker who tried to rid the sciences of all *a priori* or metaphysical notions like substance, causality, and teleology by offering an "anti-metaphysical" view of scientific laws. On this view, a scientific law is simply a functional relation asserted to hold for directly or indirectly observed elements or sensations. It was David Hume who analyzed the notion of causality to show there was no proof of necessary connection between cause and effect, al-though Hume does not distinguish clearly enough the logical and the psychological aspects of the problem. Like Mach, modern positivists go back to Galileo's functional descriptions of observed and measured phenomena for the understanding of scien-tific laws. These empirical descriptions are not intuitions of any necessary causal relations which the classical philosophy of science regarded as purely logical. This is an *a priori* tendency from which even Galileo is not free in his extra-scientific philosophical speculations. If Galileo could have freed his philosophizing from the rationalistic metaphysics of his times, and simply analyzed the experiments by which he established his laws of falling bodies, he would have realized that he had discov-ered a most probable relation between the distance and time of fall, not because of any *a priori* rational necessity, but because the relation of uniform acceleration re-curs in a constant way, which can be verified by further experimentation. On the frequency theory of probability which Peirce and Reichenbach have developed, a statistical view replaces mechanical necessity in their notions of scientific law which can thus be extended to social sciences, as more recent developments indicate.

The types of relations asserted in a scientific law will depend on the kinds of methods of observation and calculation that are required to establish them. Not all physical or social phenomena are directly observable, but only certain large-scale or macroscopic events like the motions of terrestrial and heavenly bodies or political trends. As Reichenbach shows, in the microscopic world of the atom and its sub-atomic components, we can observe with the proper instruments only the net effects

---

[2] Cf. Chapter 9, Maritain.
[3] Cf. the selection from Schlick in Chapter 9.

of large numbers of minute changes, and only a statistical correlation can serve as the basis of any generalization. The statistical conception of law is applicable to any physical or social phenomena involving large numbers of individuals whose behavior is collectively and not individually observable or predictable. We thus have in the functional, statistical view of scientific laws a logical basis common to the natural and social sciences, and perhaps more fruitful for the further development of both than the traditional metaphysical conceptions of either mechanistic or organismic philosophies of science. In any case, Reichenbach's "anti-metaphysical" view of science makes it obligatory upon students of philosophy to reconsider the traditional theories of knowledge and views of the world which have hitherto dominated our thinking.

The cultural values of science are not limited to the useful products of technology, important as these are for reducing the drudgery of menial labor, for improving the health and living standards of an industrial civilization. As Professor Nagel indicates, the growth of science affects men's lives and minds by "challenging established beliefs about the cosmos and its parts, and inducing emendations in habitual modes of thought." Science has and still can rid us of many superstitions and ungrounded fears that prevent the mind from exercising its creative functions. It can help break down prejudice and hatred in human relations when they rest on ignorance or on false guarantees of certainty about human happiness. The "brave new world" of a scientific society, satirized by Aldous Huxley as leading to a regimented mechanical conformity of belief and taste, is a caricature of the patience, diversity of opinion, and fallibilism that actually characterize the specific practice of science, although it is true to say that the best scientist outside his field of specialization is heir to all the prejudices of laymen. The value of the philosophy of science consists in discouraging such one-sided use of intelligence and in suggesting ways of humanizing the scientific temper of mind. Tolerance of new ideas no matter what race, nation, religion, or social class the originator comes from, freedom to question all beliefs, intellectual honesty, and willingness to submit one's ideas to public criticism—these are some of the cultural values of science without which no liberal culture can thrive.

P. P. W.

24. *We Are All Scientists**

T. H. HUXLEY (1825–1895)

Scientific investigation is not, as many people seem to suppose, some kind of modern black art. You might easily gather this impression from the manner in which many persons speak of scientific inquiry, or talk about inductive and deductive philosophy, or the principles of the "Baconian philosophy." I do protest that, of the vast number of cants in this world, there are none to my mind, so contemptible as the pseudo-scientific cant which is talked about the "Baconian philosophy."

To hear people talk about the great Chancellor—and a very great man he certainly was—you would think that it was he who had invented science, and that there was no such thing as sound reasoning before the time of Queen Elizabeth! Of course, you say that cannot possibly be true; you perceive, on a moment's reflection, that such an idea is absurdly wrong. . . .

The method of scientific investigation is nothing but the expression of the necessary mode of working of the human mind. It is simply the mode at which all phenomena are reasoned about, rendered precise and exact. There is no more difference, but there is just the same kind of difference, between the mental operations of a man of science and those of an ordinary person, as there is between the operations and methods of a baker or of a butcher weighing out his goods in common scales, and the

operations of a chemist in performing a difficult and complex analysis by means of his balance and finely-graduated weights. It is not that the action of the scales in the one case, and the balance in the other, differ in the principles of their construction or manner of working; but the beam of one is set on an infinitely finer axis than the other, and of course turns by the addition of a much smaller weight.

You will understand this better, perhaps, if I give you some familiar example. You have all heard it repeated, I dare say, that men of science work by means of induction and deduction, and that by the help of these operations, they, in a sort of sense, wring from Nature certain other things, which are called natural laws, and causes, and that out of these, by some cunning skill of their own, they build up hypotheses and theories. And it is imagined by many, that the operations of the common mind can be by no means compared with these processes, and that they have to be acquired by a sort of special apprenticeship to the craft. To hear all these large words, you would think that the mind of a man of science must be constituted differently from that of his fellow men; but if you will not be frightened by terms, you will discover that you are quite wrong, and that all these terrible apparatus are being used by yourselves every day and every hour of your lives.

There is a well-known incident in one of Molière's plays, where the author

* From Thomas Henry Huxley's *Darwiniana* (London, 1863).

makes the hero express unbounded delight on being told that he had been talking prose during the whole of his life. In the same way, I trust, that you will take comfort, and be delighted with yourselves, on the discovery that you have been acting on the principles of inductive and deductive philosophy during the same period. Probably there is not one who has not in the course of the day had occasion to set in motion a complex train of reasoning, of the very same kind, though differing of course in degree, as that which a scientific man goes through in tracing the causes of natural phenomena.

A very trivial circumstance will serve to exemplify this. Suppose you go into a fruiterer's shop, wanting an apple,—you take up one, and, on biting it, you find it is sour; you look at it, and see that it is hard and green. You take up another one, and that too is hard, green, and sour. The shopman offers you a third; but, before biting it, you examine it, and find that it is hard and green, and you immediately say that you will not have it, as it must be sour, like those that you have already tried.

Nothing can be more simple than that, you think; but if you will take the trouble to analyse and trace out into its logical elements what has been done by the mind, you will be greatly surprised. In the first place, you have performed the operation of induction. You found that, in two experiences, hardness and greenness in apples went together with sourness. It was so in the first case, and it was confirmed by the second. True, it is a very small basis, but still it is enough to make an induction from; you generalise the facts, and you expect to find sourness in apples where you get hardness and greenness. You found upon that a general law, that all hard and green apples are sour; and that, so far as it goes, is a perfect induction. Well, having got your natural law in this way,

when you are offered another apple which you find is hard and green, you say, "All hard and green apples are sour; this apple is hard and green, therefore this apple is sour." That train of reasoning is what logicians call a syllogism, and has all its various parts and terms—its major premiss, its minor premiss, and its conclusion. And, by the help of further reasoning, which, if drawn out, would have to be exhibited in two or three other syllogisms, you arrive at your final determination, "I will not have that apple." So that, you see, you have, in the first place, established a law by induction, and upon that you have founded a deduction, and reasoned out the special conclusion of the particular case. Well now, suppose, having got your law, that at some time afterwards, you are discussing the qualities of apples with a friend: you will say to him, "It is a very curious thing,—but I find that all hard and green apples are sour!" Your friend says to you, "But how do you know that?" You at once reply, "Oh, because I have tried them over and over again, and have always found them to be so." Well, if we were talking science instead of common sense, we should call that an experimental verification. And, if still opposed, you go further, and say, "I have heard from the people in Somersetshire and Devonshire, where a large number of apples are grown, that they have observed the same thing. It is also found to be the case in Normandy, and in North America. In short, I find it to be the universal experience of mankind wherever attention has been directed to the subject." Whereupon, your friend, unless he is a very unreasonable man, agrees with you, and is convinced that you are quite right in the conclusion you have drawn. He believes, although perhaps he does not know he believes it, that the more extensive verifications are,—that the more frequently experiments have been made, and results of the same kind arrived at, —that the more varied the conditions under which the same results are attained, the more certain is the ultimate conclusion, and he disputes the question no further. He sees that the experiment has been tried under all sorts of conditions, as to time, place, and people, with the same result; and he says with you, therefore, that the law you have laid down must be a good one, and he must believe it.

In science we do the same thing;—the philosopher exercises precisely the same faculties, though in a much more delicate manner. In scientific inquiry it becomes a matter of duty to expose a supposed law to every possible kind of verification, and to take care, moreover, that this is done intentionally, and not left to a mere accident, as in the case of the apples. And in science, as in common life, our confidence in a law is in exact proportion to the absence of variation in the result of our experimental verifications. For instance, if you let go your grasp of an article you may have in your hand, it will immediately fall to the ground. That is a very common verification of one of the best established laws of nature—that of gravitation. The method by which men of science establish the existence of that law is exactly the same as that by which we have established the trivial proposition about the sourness of hard and green apples. But we believe it in such an extensive, thorough, and unhesitating manner because the universal experience of mankind verifies it, and we can verify it ourselves at any time; and that is the strongest possible foundation on which any natural law can rest.

So much, then, by way of proof that the method of establishing laws in science is exactly the same as that pursued in common life. Let us now turn to another matter (though really it is but another phase of the same question),

and that is, the method by which, from the relations of certain phenomena, we prove that some stand in the position of causes towards the others.

I want to put the case clearly before you, and I will therefore show you what I mean by another familiar example. I will suppose that one of you, on coming down in the morning to the parlour of your house, finds that a tea-pot and some spoons which had been left in the room on the previous evening are gone, —the window is open, and you observe the mark of a dirty hand on the window-frame, and perhaps, in addition to that, you notice the impress of a hob-nailed shoe on the gravel outside. All these phenomena have struck your attention instantly, and before two seconds have passed you say, "Oh, somebody has broken open the window, entered the room, and run off with the spoons and the tea-pot!" That speech is out of your mouth in a moment. And you will probably add, "I know there has; I am quite sure of it!" You mean to say exactly what you know; but in reality you are giving expression to what is, in all essential particulars, an hypothesis. You do not *know* it at all; it is nothing but an hypothesis rapidly framed in your own mind. And it is an hypothesis founded on a long train of inductions and deductions.

What are those inductions and deductions, and how have you got at this hypothesis? You have observed, in the first place, that the window is open; but by a train of reasoning involving many inductions and deductions, you have probably arrived long before at the general law—and a very good one it is— that windows do not open of themselves; and you therefore conclude that something has opened the window. A second general law that you have arrived at in the same way is, that tea-pots and spoons do not go out of a window spontaneously, and you are satisfied that, as they are not now where you left them, they have been removed. In the third place, you look at the marks on the window-sill, and the shoe-marks outside, and you say that in all previous experience the former kind of mark has never been produced by anything else but the hand of a human being; and the same experience shows that no other animal but man at present wears shoes with hob-nails in them such as would produce the marks in the gravel. I do not know, even if we could discover any of those "missing links" that are talked about, that they would help us to any other conclusion! At any rate the law which states our present experience is strong enough for my present purpose. You next reach the conclusion, that as these kinds of marks have not been left by any other animals than men, or are liable to be formed in any other way than by a man's hand and shoe, the marks in question have been formed by a man in that way. You have, further, a general law, founded on observation and experience, and that, too, is, I am sorry to say, a very universal and unimpeachable one,—that some men are thieves; and you assume at once from all these premises—and that is what constitutes your hypothesis—that the man who made the marks outside and on the window-sill, opened the window, got into the room, and stole your tea-pot and spoons. You have now arrived at a *vera causa;* —you have assumed a cause which, it is plain, is competent to produce all the phenomena you have observed. You can explain all these phenomena only by the hypothesis of a thief. But that is a hypothetical conclusion, of the justice of which you have no absolute proof at all; it is only rendered highly probable by a series of inductive and deductive reasonings.

I suppose your first action, assuming that you are a man of ordinary common sense, and that you have established this hypothesis to your own satisfaction, will very likely be to go for the police, and set them on the track of the burglar, with the view to the recovery of your property. But just as you are starting with this object, some person comes in, and on learning what you are about, says, "My good friend, you are going on a great deal too fast. How do you know that the man who really made the marks took the spoons? It might have been a monkey that took them, and the man may have merely looked in afterwards." You would probably reply, "Well, that is all very well, but you see it is contrary to all experience of the way tea-pots and spoons are abstracted; so that, at any rate, your hypothesis is less probable than mine." While you are talking the thing over in this way, another friend arrives. And he might say, "Oh, my dear sir, you are certainly going on a great deal too fast. You are most presumptuous. You admit that all these occurrences took place when you were fast asleep, at a time when you could not possibly have known anything about what was taking place. How do you know that the laws of Nature are not suspended during the night? It may be that there has been some kind of supernatural interference in this case." In point of fact, he declares that your hypothesis is one of which you cannot at all demonstrate the truth and that you are by no means sure that the laws of Nature are the same when you are asleep as when you are awake.

Well, now, you cannot at the moment answer that kind of reasoning. You feel that your worthy friend has you somewhat at a disadvantage. You will feel perfectly convinced in your own mind, however, that you are quite right, and you say to him, "My good friend, I can only be guided by the natural probabilities of the case, and if you will be kind enough to stand aside and permit me to pass, I will go and fetch the police."

Well, we will suppose that your journey is successful, and that by good luck you meet with a policeman; that eventually the burglar is found with your property on his person, and the marks correspond to his hand and to his boots. Probably any jury would consider those facts a very good experimental verification of your hypothesis, touching the cause of the abnormal phenomena observed in your parlour, and would act accordingly.

Now, in this suppositious case, I have taken phenomena of a very common kind, in order that you might see what are the different steps in an ordinary process of reasoning, if you will only take the trouble to analyse it carefully. All the operations I have described, you will see, are involved in the mind of any man of sense in leading him to a conclusion as to the course he should take in order to make good a robbery and punish the offender. I say that you are led, in that case, to your conclusion by exactly the same train of reasoning as that which a man of science pursues when he is endeavouring to discover the origin and laws of the most occult phenomena. The process is, and always must be, the same; and precisely the same mode of reasoning was employed by Newton and Laplace in their endeavours to discover and define the causes of the movements of the heavenly bodies, as you, with your own common sense, would employ to detect a burglar. The only difference is, that the nature of the inquiry being more abstruse, every step has to be most carefully watched, so that there may not be a single crack or flaw in your hypothesis. A flaw or crack in many of the hypotheses of daily life may be of little or no moment as affecting the general correctness of the conclusions at which we may arrive; but, in a scientific inquiry, a fallacy, great or small, is always of importance, and is sure to be in the long run constantly productive of mischievous, if not fatal results.

Do not allow yourselves to be misled by the common notion that an hypothesis is untrustworthy simply because it is an hypothesis. It is often urged, in respect to some scientific conclusion, that, after all, it is only an hypothesis. But what more have we to guide us in nine-tenths of the most important affairs of daily life than hypotheses, and often very ill-based ones? So that in science, where the evidence of an hypothesis is subjected to the most rigid examination, we may rightly pursue the same course. You may have hypotheses and hypotheses. A man may say, if he likes, that the moon is made of green cheese: that is an hypothesis. But another man, who has devoted a great deal of time and attention to the subject, and availed himself of the most powerful telescopes and the results of the observations of others, declares that in his opinion it is probably composed of materials very similar to those of which our own earth is made up: and that is also only an hypothesis. But I need not tell you that there is an enormous difference in the value of the two hypotheses. That one which is based on sound scientific knowledge is sure to have a corresponding value; and that which is a mere hasty random guess is likely to have but little value. Every great step in our progress in discovering causes has been made in exactly the same way as that which I have detailed to you. A person observing the occurrence of certain facts and phenomena asks, naturally enough, what process, what kind of operation known to occur in Nature applied to the particular case, will unravel and explain the mystery? Hence you have the scientific hypothesis; and its value will be proportionate to the care and completeness with which its basis has been tested and verified. It is in these matters as in the commonest affairs of practical life: the guess of the fool will be folly, while the guess of the wise man will contain wisdom. In all cases, you see that the value of the result depends on the patience and faithfulness with which the investigator applies to his hypothesis every possible kind of verification. . . .

25. *Science and Hypothesis**

HENRI POINCARÉ (1854–1912)

Hypotheses in Physics

The Rôle of Experiment and Generalization. Experiment is the sole source of truth. It alone can teach us anything new; it alone can give us certainty. These are two points that cannot be questioned.

But then, if experiment is everything, what place will remain for mathematical physics? What has experimental physics to do with such an aid, one which seems useless and perhaps even dangerous?

And yet mathematical physics exists, and has done unquestionable service. We have here a fact that must be explained.

The explanation is that merely to observe is not enough. We must use our observations, and to do that we must generalize. This is what men always have done; only as the memory of past errors has made them more and more careful, they have observed more and more, and generalized less and less.

Every age has ridiculed the one before it, and accused it of having generalized too quickly and too naïvely. Descartes pitied the Ionians; Descartes, in his turn, makes us smile. No doubt

* H. Poincaré, *Science and Hypothesis,* translated by G. B. Halsted. New York: The Science Press. 1905. Ch. IX, with the kind permission of the publisher.

our children will some day laugh at us.

But can we not then pass over immediately to the goal? Is not this the means of escaping the ridicule that we foresee? Can we not be content with just the bare experiment?

No, that is impossible; it would be to mistake utterly the true nature of science. The scientist must set in order. Science is built up with facts, as a house is with stones. But a collection of facts is no more a science than a heap of stones is a house.

And above all the scientist must foresee. Carlyle has somewhere said something like this: "Nothing but facts are of importance. John Lackland passed by here. Here is something that is admirable. Here is a reality for which I would give all the theories in the world." Carlyle was a fellow countryman of Bacon; but Bacon would not have said that. That is the language of the historian. The physicist would say rather: "John Lackland passed by here; that makes no difference to me, for he never will pass this way again."

We all know that there are good experiments and poor ones. The latter will accumulate in vain; though one may have made a hundred or a thousand, a single piece of work by a true master, by a Pasteur, for example, will suffice to tumble them into oblivion. Bacon would have well understood this; it is he who invented the phrase *Experimentum crucis*. But Carlyle would not have understood it. A fact is a fact. A pupil has read a certain number on his thermometer; he has taken no precaution; no matter, he has read it, and if it is only the fact that counts, here is a reality of the same rank as the peregrinations of King John Lackland. Why is the fact that this pupil has made this reading of no interest, while the fact that a skilled physicist had made another reading might be on the contrary very important? It is because from the first reading we could not infer anything. What then is a good experiment? It is that which informs us of something besides an isolated fact; it is that which enables us to foresee, that is, that which enables us to generalize.

For without generalization foreknowledge is impossible. The circumstances under which one has worked will never reproduce themselves all at once. The observed action then will never recur; the only thing that can be affirmed is that under analogous circumstances an analogous action will be produced. In order to foresee, then, it is necessary to invoke at least analogy, that is to say, already then to generalize.

No matter how timid one may be, still it is necessary to interpolate. Experiment gives us only a certain number of isolated points. We must unite these by a continuous line. This is a veritable generalization. But we do more; the curve that we shall trace will pass between the observed points and near these points; it will not pass through these points themselves. Thus one does not restrict himself to generalizing the experiments, but corrects them; and the physicist who should try to abstain from these corrections and really be content with the bare experiment, would be forced to enunciate some very strange laws.

The bare facts, then, would not be enough for us; and that is why we must have science ordered, or rather organized.

It is often said experiments must be made without a preconceived idea. That is impossible. Not only would it make all experiment barren, but that would be attempted which could not be done. Every one carries in his mind his own conception of the world, of which he can not so easily rid himself. We must, for instance, use language; and our language is made up only of preconceived ideas and can not be otherwise. Only these are unconscious preconceived ideas, a thousand times more dangerous than the others.

Shall we say that if we introduce others, of which we are fully conscious, we shall only aggravate the evil? I think not. I believe rather that they will serve as counterbalances to each other—I was going to say as antidotes; they will in general accord ill with one another; they will come into conflict with one another, and thereby force us to regard things under different aspects. This is enough to emancipate us. He is no longer a slave who can choose his master.

Thus, thanks to generalization, each fact observed enables us to foresee a great many others; only we must not forget that the first alone is certain, that all others are merely probable. No matter how solidly founded a prediction may appear to us, we are never *absolutely* sure that experiment will not contradict it, if we undertake to verify it. The probability, however, is often so great that practically we may be content with it. It is far better to foresee even without certainty than not to foresee at all.

One must, then, never disdain to make a verification when opportunity offers. But all experiment is long and difficult; the workers are few; and the number of facts that we need to foresee is immense.

Compared with this mass the number of direct verifications that we can make will never be anything but a negligible quantity.

Of this few that we can directly attain, we must make the best use; it is very necessary to get from every experiment the greatest possible number of predictions, and with the highest possible degree of probability. The problem is, so to speak, to increase the yield of the scientific machine.

Let us compare science to a library that ought to grow continually. The librarian has at his disposal for his purchases only insufficient funds. He ought to make an effort not to waste them.

It is experimental physics that is entrusted with the purchases. It alone, then, can enrich the library.

As for mathematical physics, its task will be to make out the catalogue. If the catalogue is well made, the library will not be any richer, but the reader will be helped to use its riches.

And even by showing the librarian the gaps in his collections, it will enable him to make a judicious use of his funds; which is all the more important because these funds are entirely inadequate.

Such, then, is the rôle of mathematical physics. It must direct generalization in such a manner as to increase what I just now called the yield of science. By what means it can arrive at this, and how it can do it without danger, is what remains for us to investigate.

The Unity of Nature. Let us notice first of all, that every generalization implies in some measure the belief in the unity and simplicity of nature. As to the unity there can be no difficulty. If the different parts of the universe were not like the members of one body, they would not act on one another, they would know nothing of each other; and we in particular would know only one of these parts. We do not ask, then, if nature is one, but how it is one.

As for the second point, that is not such an easy matter. It is not certain that nature is simple. Can we without danger act as if it were?

There was a time when the simplicity of Mariotte's [Boyle's] law was an argument invoked in favor of its accuracy; when Fresnel himself, after having said in a conversation with Laplace that nature was not concerned about analytical difficulties, felt himself obliged to make explanations, in order not to strike too hard at prevailing opinion.

To-day ideas have greatly changed; and yet, those who do not believe that natural laws have to be simple, are still often obliged to act as if they did. They could not entirely avoid this necessity without making impossible all generalization, and consequently all science.

It is clear that any fact can be generalized in an infinity of ways, and it is a question of choice. The choice can be guided only by considerations of simplicity. Let us take the most commonplace case, that of interpolation. We pass a continuous line, as regular as possible, between the points given by observation. Why do we avoid points making angles, and too abrupt turns? Why do we not make our curve describe the most capricious zigzags? It is because we know beforehand, or believe we know, that the law to be expressed can not be so complicated as all that.

We may calculate the mass of Jupiter from either the movement of its satellites, or the perturbations of the major planets, or those of the minor planets. If we take the averages of the determinations obtained by these three methods, we find three numbers very close together, but different. We might interpret this result by supposing that the coefficient of gravitation is not the same in the three cases. The observations would certainly be much better represented. Why do we reject this interpretation? Not because it is absurd, but because it is needlessly complicated. We shall only accept it when we are forced to, and that is not yet.

To sum up, ordinarily every law is held to be simple till the contrary is proved.

This custom is imposed upon physicists by the causes that I have just explained. But how shall we justify it in the presence of discoveries that show us every day new details that are richer and more complex? How shall we even reconcile it with the belief in the unity of nature? For if everything depends on everything, relationships where so many diverse factors enter can no longer be simple.

If we study the history of science, we see happen two inverse phenomena, so to speak. Sometimes simplicity hides under complex appearances; sometimes it is the simplicity which is apparent, and which disguises extremely complicated realities.

What is more complicated than the confused movements of the planets? What simpler than Newton's law? Here nature, making sport, as Fresnel said, of analytical difficulties, employs only simple means, and by combining them produces I know not what inextricable tangle. Here it is the hidden simplicity which must be discovered.

Examples of the opposite abound. In the kinetic theory of gases, one deals with molecules moving with great velocities, whose paths, altered by incessant collisions, have the most capricious forms and traverse space in every direction. The observable result is Mariotte's simple law. Every individual fact was complicated. The law of great numbers has reestablished simplicity in the average. Here the simplicity is merely apparent, and only the coarseness of our senses prevents our perceiving the complexity.

Many phenomena obey a law of proportionality. But why? Because in these phenomena there is something very small. The simple law observed, then, is only a result of the general analytical rule that the infinitely small increment of a function is proportional to the increment of the variable. As in reality our increments are not infinitely small, but very small, the law of proportionality is only approximate, and the simplicity is only apparent. What I have just said applies to the rule of the superposition of small motions, the use of which is so fruitful, and which is the basis of optics.

And Newton's law itself? Its simplicity, so long undetected, is perhaps only apparent. Who knows whether it is not due to some complicated mechanism, to the impact of some subtle matter animated by irregular movements, and whether it has not become simple only through the action of averages and of great numbers? In any case, it is difficult not to suppose that the true law contains complementary terms, which would become sensible at small distances. If in astronomy they are negligible as modifying Newton's law, and if the law thus regains its simplicity, it would be only because of the immensity of celestial distances.

No doubt, if our means of investigation should become more and more penetrating, we should discover the simple under the complex, then the complex under the simple, then again the simple under the complex, and so on, without our being able to foresee what will be the last term.

We must stop somewhere, and that science may be possible, we must stop when we have found simplicity. This is the only ground on which we can rear the edifice of our generalizations. But this simplicity being only apparent, will the ground be firm enough? This is what must be investigated.

For that purpose, let us see what part is played in our generalizations by the belief in simplicity. We have verified a simple law in a good many particular cases; we refuse to admit that this agreement, so often repeated, is simply the result of chance, and conclude that the law must be true in the general case.

Kepler notices that a planet's positions, as observed by Tycho, are all on one ellipse. Never for a moment does he have the thought that by a strange play of chance, Tycho never observed the heavens except at a moment when the real orbit of the planet happened to cut this ellipse.

What does it matter then whether the simplicity be real, or whether it covers a complex reality? Whether it is due to the influence of great numbers, which levels down individual differences, or to the greatness or smallness of certain quantities, which allows us to neglect certain terms, in no case is it due to chance. This simplicity, real or apparent, always has a cause. We can always follow, then, the same course of reasoning, and if a simple law has been observed in several particular cases, we can legitimately suppose that it will still be true in analogous cases. To refuse to do this would be to attribute to chance an inadmissible rôle.

There is, however, a difference. If the simplicity were real and essential, it would resist the increasing precision of our means of measure. If then we believe nature to be essentially simple, we must, from a simplicity that is approximate, infer a simplicity that is rigorous. This is what was done formerly; and this is what we no longer have a right to do.

The simplicity of Kepler's laws, for example, is only apparent. That does not prevent their being applicable, very nearly, to all systems analogous to the solar system; but it does prevent their being rigorously exact.

The Rôle of Hypothesis. All generalization is a hypothesis. Hypothesis, then, has a necessary rôle that no one has ever contested. Only, it ought always, as soon as possible and as often as possible, to be subjected to verification. And, of course, if it does not stand this test, it ought to be abandoned without reserve. This is what we generally do, but sometimes with rather an ill humor.

Well, even this ill humor is not justified. The physicist who has just renounced one of his hypotheses ought, on the contrary, to be full of joy; for he has found an unexpected opportunity for discovery. His hypothesis, I imagine, had not been adopted without consideration; it took account of all the known factors that it seemed could enter into the phenomenon. If the test does not support it, it is because there is something unexpected and extraordinary; and because there is going to be something found that is unknown and new.

Has the discarded hypothesis, then, been barren? Far from that, it may be said it has rendered more service than a true hypothesis. Not only has it been the occasion of the decisive experiment, but, without having made the hypothesis, the experiment would have been made by chance, so that nothing would have been derived from it. One would have seen nothing extraordinary; only one fact the more would have been catalogued without deducing from it the least consequence.

Now on what condition is the use of hypothesis without danger?

The firm determination to submit to experiment is not enough; there are still dangerous hypotheses; first, and above all, those which are tacit and unconscious. Since we make them without knowing it, we are powerless to abandon them. Here again, then, is a service that mathematical physics can render us. By the precision that is characteristic of it, it compels us to formulate all the hypotheses that we should make without it, but unconsciously.

Let us notice besides that it is important not to multiply hypotheses beyond measure, and to make them only one after the other. If we construct a theory based on a number of hypotheses, and if experiment condemns it, which of our premises is it necessary to change? It will be impossible to know. And inversely, if the experiment succeeds, shall we believe that we have demonstrated all the hypotheses at once? Shall we believe that with one single equation we have determined several unknowns?

We must equally take care to distinguish between the different kinds of hypotheses. There are first those which are perfectly natural and from which one can scarcely escape. It is difficult not to suppose that the influence of bodies very remote is quite negligible, that small movements follow a linear law, that the effect is a continuous function of its cause. I will say as much of the conditions imposed by symmetry. All these hypotheses form, as it were, the common basis of all the theories of mathematical physics. They are the last that ought to be abandoned.

There is a second class of hypotheses, that I shall term neutral. In most questions the analyst assumes at the beginning of his calculations either that matter is continuous or, on the contrary, that it is formed of atoms. He might have made the opposite assumption without changing his results. He would only have had more trouble to obtain them; that is all. If, then, experiment confirms his conclusions, will he think that he has demonstrated, for instance, the real existence of atoms? ...

These neutral hypotheses are never dangerous, if only their character is not misunderstood. They may be useful, either as devices for computation, or to aid our understanding by concrete images, to fix our ideas as the saying is. There is, then, no occasion to exclude them.

The hypotheses of the third class are the real generalizations. They are the ones that experiment must confirm or invalidate. Whether verified or condemned, they will always be fruitful. But for the reasons that I have set forth, they will only be fruitful if they are not too numerous.

Origin of Mathematical Physics. Let us penetrate further, and study more closely the conditions that have permitted the development of mathematical physics. We observe at once that the efforts of scientists have always aimed to resolve the complex phenomenon directly given by experiment into a very large number of elementary phenomena.

This is done in three different ways: first, in time. Instead of embracing in its entirety the progressive development of a phenomenon, the aim is simply to connect each instant with the instant immediately preceding it. It is admitted that the actual state of the world depends only on the immediate past, without being directly influenced, so to speak, by the memory of a distant past. Thanks to this postulate, instead of studying directly the whole succession of phenomena, it is possible to confine ourselves to writing its 'differential equation.' For Kepler's laws we substitute Newton's law.

Next we try to analyze the phenomenon in space. What experiment gives us is a confused mass of facts presented on a stage of considerable extent. We must try to discover the elementary phenomenon, which will be, on the contrary, localized in a very small region of space.

Some examples will perhaps make my thought better understood. If we wished to study in all its complexity the distribution of temperature in a cooling solid, we could never succeed. Everything becomes simple if we reflect that one point of the solid can not give up its heat directly to a distant point; it will give up its heat only to the points in the immediate neighborhood, and it is by degrees that the flow of heat can reach other parts of the solid. The elementary phenomenon is the exchange of heat between two contiguous points. It is strictly localized, and is relatively simple, if we admit, as is natural, that it is not influenced by the temperature of molecules whose distance is sensible.

I bend a rod. It is going to take a very complicated form, the direct study of which would be impossible. But I shall be able, however, to attack it, if I observe that its flexure is a result only of the deformation of the very small elements of the rod, and that the deformation of each of these elements depends only on the forces that are directly applied to it, and not at all on those which may act on the other elements.

In all these examples, which I might easily multiply, we admit that there is no action at a distance, or at least at a great distance. This is a hypothesis. It is not always true, as the law of gravitation shows us. It must, then, be submitted to verification. If it is confirmed, even approximately, it is precious, for it will enable us to make mathematical physics, at least by successive approximations.

If it does not stand the test, we must look for something else analogous; for there are still other means of arriving at the elementary phenomenon. If several bodies act simultaneously, it may happen that their actions are independent and are simply added to one another, either as vectors or as scalars. The elementary phenomenon is then the action of an isolated body. Or again, we have to deal with small movements, or more generally, with small variations, which obey the well-known law of superposition. The observed movement will then be decomposed into simple movements, for example, sound into its harmonics, white light into its monochromatic components.

When we have discovered in what direction it is advisable to look for the elementary phenomenon, by what means can we reach it?

First of all, it will often happen that in order to detect it, or rather to detect the part of it useful to us, it will not be necessary to penetrate the mechanism; the law of great numbers will suffice.

Let us take again the instance of the propagation of heat. Every molecule emits rays towards every neighboring molecule. According to what law, we do not need to know. If we should make any supposition in regard to this, it would be a neutral hypothesis and consequently useless and incapable of verification. And, in fact, by the action of averages and thanks to the symmetry of the medium, all the differences are leveled down, and whatever hypothesis may be made, the result is always the same.

The same circumstance is presented in the theory of electricity and in that of capillarity. The neighboring molecules attract and repel one another. We do not need to know according to what law; it is enough for us that this attraction is sensible only at small distances, that the molecules are very numerous, that the medium is symmetrical, and we shall only have to let the law of great numbers act.

Here again the simplicity of the elementary phenomenon was hidden under the complexity of the resultant observable phenomenon; but, in its turn, this simplicity was only apparent, and concealed a very complex mechanism.

The best means of arriving at the elementary phenomenon would evidently be experiment. We ought by experimental contrivance to dissociate the complex sheaf that nature offers to our researches, and to study with care the elements as much isolated as possible. For example, natural white light would be decomposed into monochromatic lights by the aid of the prism, and into polarized lights by the aid of the polarizer.

Unfortunately that is neither always possible nor always sufficient, and sometimes the mind must outstrip experiment. I shall cite only one example, which has always struck me forcibly.

If I decompose white light, I shall be able to isolate a small part of the spectrum, but however small it may be, it will retain a certain breadth. Likewise the natural lights called *monochromatic*, give us a very narrow line, but not, however, infinitely narrow. It might be supposed that by studying experimentally the properties of these natural lights, by working with finer and finer lines of the spectrum, and by passing at last to the limit, so to speak, we should succeed in learning the properties of a light strictly monochromatic.

That would not be accurate. Suppose that two rays emanate from the same source, that we polarize them first in two perpendicular planes, then bring them back to the same plane of polarization, and try to make them interfere. If the light were *strictly* monochromatic, they would interfere. With our lights, which are nearly monochromatic, there will be no interference, and that no matter how narrow the line. In order to be otherwise it would have to be several million times as narrow as the finest known lines.

Here, then, the passage to the limit would have deceived us. The mind must outstrip the experiment, and if it has done so with success, it is because it has allowed itself to be guided by the instinct of simplicity.

The knowledge of the elementary fact enables us to put the problem in an equation. Nothing remains but to deduce from this by combination the complex fact that can be observed and verified. This is what is called *integration,* and is the business of the mathematician.

It may be asked why, in physical sciences, generalization so readily takes the mathematical form. The reason is now easy to see. It is not only because we have numerical laws to express; it is because the observable phenomenon is due to the superposition of a great number of elementary phenomena *all alike.* Thus quite naturally are introduced differential equations. . . .

It is then thanks to the approximate homogeneity of the matter studied by physicists, that mathematical physics could be born.

In the natural sciences, we no longer find these conditions: homogeneity, relative independence of remote parts, simplicity of the elementary fact; and this is why naturalists are obliged to resort to other methods of generalization.

26. *Notes on Scientific Philosophy**

CHARLES S. PEIRCE (1839–1914)

§ 1. Laboratory and Seminary Philosophies †

The kind of philosophy which interests me and must, I think, interest everybody is that philosophy, which uses the most rational methods it can devise, for finding out the little that can as yet be found out about the universe of mind and matter from those observations which every person can make in every hour of his waking life. It will not include matters which are more conveniently studied by students of special sciences, such as psychology. Thus, everybody has remarked that there are four prominent qualities of the sense of taste, sweet, sour, salt, and bitter. But there may be other tastes, not so readily made out without special study; and in any case tastes are conveniently studied in connexion with flavors and odors, which make a difficult experimental inquiry. Besides, the four tastes are altogether special and throw no light on the problems which, on account of their extreme generality, will naturally be examined by a class of researchers of entirely different aptitudes from those which adapt men to the discovery of recondite facts.

If anybody asks what there is in the study of obvious phenomena to make it particularly interesting, I will give two answers. The first is the one which seems to me the strongest; the other is that which nobody can fail to feel the force of. The first answer is that the spirit in which, as it seems to me, philosophy ought to be studied is the spirit in which every branch of science ought to be studied; namely, the spirit of joy in learning ourselves and in making others acquainted with the glories of God. Each person will feel this joy most in the particular branch of science to which his faculties are best adapted. It is not a sin to have no taste for philosophy as I define philosophy. As a matter of fact, however, almost everybody does feel an interest in philosophical problems, especially at that time of life at which he is spoiling for an intellectual tussle.

It is true that philosophy is in a lamentably crude condition at present; that very little is really established about it; while most philosophers set up a pretension of knowing all there is to know—a pretension calculated to disgust anybody who is at home in any real science. But all we have to do is to turn our backs upon all such truly vicious conduct, and we shall find ourselves enjoying the advantages of having an

* Reprinted by the permission of the publishers from *Collected Papers of Charles Sanders Peirce,* edited by Charles Hartshorne & Paul Weiss. Vol. I, p. 50 ff. Cambridge, Mass.: Harvard University Press, 1931.

† From "Introduction showing the point of view from which Philosophy appears to the author to be an interesting subject to a man of common-sense," in the Notebook, "Sketch of Some Proposed Chapters on the Sect of Philosophy Called Pragmatism," c. 1905.

almost virgin soil to till, where a given amount of really scientific work will bring in an extraordinary harvest, and that a harvest of very fundamental truth of exceptional value from every point of view.

This consideration touches upon the second reason for studying laboratory-philosophy (as contradistinguished from seminary-philosophy). It is that the special sciences are obliged to take for granted a number of most important propositions, because their ways of working afford no means of bringing these propositions to the test. In short, they always rest upon metaphysics. At one time, for example, we find physicists, Kelvin, Maxwell and others, assuming that a body cannot act where it is not, meaning by "where it is not" where its lines of force do not centre. At another time, we find them assuming that the laws of mechanics (including the principles of metric geometry) hold good for the smallest corpuscles. Now it is one thing to infer from the laws of little things how great things, that consist of little things, will act; but it is quite a different thing to infer from the phenomena presented by great things how single things billions of times smaller will act. It is like inferring that because in any country one man in so many will commit suicide, therefore every individual, once in such a period of time, will make an attempt at suicide. The psychical sciences, especially psychology, are, if possible, even more necessitated to assume general principles that cannot be proved or disproved by their ordinary methods of work. The philosopher alone is equipped with the facilities for examining such "axioms" and for determining the degree to which confidence may safely be reposed in them. Find a scientific man who proposes to get along without any metaphysics—not by any means every man who holds the ordinary reasonings of metaphysicians in scorn—

and you have found one whose doctrines are thoroughly vitiated by the crude and uncriticized metaphysics with which they are packed. We must philosophize, said the great naturalist Aristotle [1]—if only to avoid philosophizing. Every man of us has a metaphysics, and has to have one; and it will influence his life greatly. Far better, then, that metaphysics should be criticized and not be allowed to run loose. A man may say "I will content myself with common sense." I, for one, am with him there, in the main. I shall show why I do not think there can be any *direct* profit in going behind common sense—meaning by common sense those ideas and beliefs that man's situation absolutely forces upon him. We shall later see more definitely what is meant. I agree, for example, that it is better to recognize that some things are red and some others blue, in the teeth of what optical philosophers say, that it is merely that some things are resonant to shorter ether waves and some to longer ones. But the difficulty is to determine what really is and what is not the authoritative decision of common sense and what is merely *obiter dictum*. In short, there is no escape from the need of a critical examination of "first principles."

§ 2. *Axioms* ‡

The science which, next after logic, may be expected to throw the most light upon philosophy, is mathematics. It is historical fact, I believe, that it was the mathematicians Thales, Pythagoras, and Plato who created metaphysics, and that metaphysics has always been the ape of mathematics. Seeing how the propositions of geometry flowed demonstratively from a few postulates, men got the notion that the same must be true in philosophy. But of late mathematicians

---

[1] *Metaphysics,* bk. I, 982b-3a.
‡ Unpaginated fragment, c. 1893.

have fully agreed that the axioms of geometry (as they are wrongly called) are not by any means evidently true. Euclid, be it observed, never pretended they were evident; he does not reckon them among his κοιναὶ ἔννοιαι, or things every body knows,[2] but among the αἰτήματα, postulates, or things the author must beg you to admit, because he is unable to prove them. At any rate, it is now agreed that there is no reason whatever to think the sum of the three angles of a triangle precisely equal to 180 degrees. It is generally admitted that the evidence is that the departure from 180 degrees (if there is any) will be greater the larger the triangle, and in the case of a triangle having for its base the diameter of the earth's orbit and for its apex the furthest star, the sum hardly can differ, according to observation, so much as 0.1″. It is probable the discrepancy is far less. Nevertheless, there is an infinite number of different possible values, of which precisely 180 degrees is only one; so that the probability is as 1 to ∞ or 0 to 1, that the value is just 180 degrees. In other words, it seems for the present impossible to suppose the postulates of geometry precisely true. The matter is reduced to one of evidence; and as absolute precision [is] beyond the reach of direct observation, so it can never be rendered probable by evidence, which is indirect observation.

Thus, the postulates of geometry must go into the number of things approximately true. It may be thousands of years before men find out whether the sum of the three angles of a triangle is greater or less than 180 degrees; but the presumption is, it is one or the other.

Now what is metaphysics, which has always formed itself after the model of mathematics, to say to this state of things? The mathematical axioms being discredited, are the metaphysical ones to remain unquestioned? I trow not. There is one proposition, now held to be very certain, though denied throughout antiquity, namely that every event is precisely determined by general laws, which evidently never can be rendered probable by observation, and which, if admitted, must, therefore, stand as self-evident. This is a metaphysical postulate closely analogous to the postulates of geometry. Its fate is sealed. The geometrical axioms being exploded, this is for the future untenable. Whenever we attempt to verify a physical law, we find discrepancies between observation and theory, which we rightly set down as errors of observation. But now it appears we have no reason to deny that there are similar, though no doubt far smaller, discrepancies between the law and the real facts. As Lucretius says,[3] the atoms swerve from the paths to which the laws of mechanics would confine them. I do not now inquire whether there is or not any positive evidence that this is so. What I am at present urging is that this arbitrariness is a conception occurring in logic, encouraged by mathematics, and ought to be regarded as a possible material to be used in the construction of a philosophical theory, should we find that it would suit the facts. We observe that phenomena approach very closely to satisfying general laws; but we have not the smallest reason for supposing that they satisfy them precisely.

§ 3. The Observational Part of Philosophy

Every science has a mathematical part, a branch of work that the mathe-

---

[2] Except the proposition that two lines cannot enclose a space, though only one of the three best manuscripts places even this in the list. But what Euclid meant was that two straight lines can have but one intersection, which *is* evident.

[3] *De Rerum Natura*, bk. II, 1, 216 ff.

matician is called in to do. We say, "Here, mathematician, suppose such and such to be the case. Never you mind whether it is really so or not; but tell us, supposing it to be so, what will be the consequence." Thus arise mathematical psychology, mathematical stylometry, mathematical economics, mathematical physics, mathematical chemistry, mathematical meteorology, mathematical biology, mathematical geology, mathematical astronomy, etc., etc., etc. But there is none of these mathematical offices which constitutes quite so large a proportion of the whole science to which it is annexed as mathematical philosophy, for the obvious reason that the observational part of philosophy is a simple business, compared, for example, with that of anatomy or biography, or any other special science.

To assume, however, that the observational part of philosophy, because it is not particularly laborious, is therefore easy, is a dreadful mistake, into which the student is very apt to fall, and which gives the death-blow to any possibility of his success in this study. It is, on the contrary, extremely difficult to bring our attention to elements of experience which are continually present. For we have nothing in experience with which to contrast them; and without contrast, they cannot excite our attention. We can only contrast them with imaginary states of things; but even what we imagine is but a crazy-quilt of bits snipped off from actual experiences. The result is that roundabout devices have to be resorted to, in order to enable us to perceive what stares us in the face with a glare that, once noticed, becomes almost oppressive with its insistency. This circumstance alone would be sufficient to render philosophical observation difficult—much more difficult, for example, than the kind of observation which the painter has to exercise. Yet this is the least of the difficulties of philosophy. Of the various

hindrances more serious still, I may mention once more the notion that it is an extremely easy thing to perceive what is before us every day and hour. But quite the worst is, that every man becomes more or less imbued with philosophical opinions, without being clearly aware of it. Some of these, it is true, may be right opinions; if he is a quite uneducated man, they doubtless will be so. But even if they are right, or nearly right, they prevent true observation as much as a pair of blue spectacles will prevent a man from observing the blue of the sky. The man will hold the right opinion, but not knowing that it might be founded upon direct observation, he will class it among articles of faith of a pretty dubious character. The more a man is educated in other branches, but not trained in philosophy, the more certain it is that two-thirds of his stock of half-conscious philosophical opinions will be utterly wrong, and will completely blind him to the truth, which he will gradually become unable so much as to conceive. I remember a really eminent French *savant,* who had sojourned for very many months in America, but who must have imbibed in his childhood the notion, then common in France, that Englishmen and Americans interject into every second sentence a certain word which the French imagine to be English. He belonged to one of the most observant of races; he was naturally a keen observer; and he was trained in an observational science; and yet, in order to assimilate himself as much as possible to American ways, he used to think it necessary to greet one every morning with a "How do you do, goddam?" and to keep it up all day. He actually believed that he had observed that such was the American style. The educated man who is a beginner in philosophy is just like that man, who (be it remembered) had been moving about in America for years;—and by a beginner in philosophy I wish to be understood as meaning, in the case of an educated man, one who has not been seriously, earnestly, and single-mindedly devoted to the study of it for more than six or eight years. For there is no other science for which the preparatory training requires to be nearly so severe and so long, no matter how great the natural genius of the student may be. For a plain man or a boy who should be early taken in hand by an instructor capable of making him comprehend both sides of every question, the time, without doubt, can be greatly reduced, with untiring industry and energy on the pupil's part.

§ 4. The First Rule of Reason *

Upon this first, and in one sense this sole, rule of reason, that in order to learn you must desire to learn, and in so desiring not be satisfied with what you already incline to think, there follows one corollary which itself deserves to be inscribed upon every wall of the city of philosophy:

Do not block the way of inquiry.

Although it is better to be methodical in our investigations, and to consider the economics of research, yet there is no positive sin against logic in *trying* any theory which may come into our heads, so long as it is adopted in such a sense as to permit the investigation to go on unimpeded and undiscouraged. On the other hand, to set up a philosophy which barricades the road of further advance toward the truth is the one unpardonable offence in reasoning, as it is also the one to which metaphysicians have in all ages shown themselves the most addicted.

Let me call your attention to four familiar shapes in which this venomous error assails our knowledge:

The first is the shape of absolute assertion. That we can be sure of nothing

in science is an ancient truth. The Academy taught it. Yet science has been infested with overconfident assertion, especially on the part of the third-rate and fourth-rate men, who have been more concerned with teaching than with learning, at all times. No doubt some of the geometries still teach as a self-evident truth the proposition that if two straight lines in one plane meet a third straight line so as to make the sum of the internal angles on one side less than two right angles, those two lines will meet on that side if sufficiently prolonged. Euclid, whose logic was more careful, only reckoned this proposition as a *Postulate,* or arbitrary Hypothesis. Yet even he places among his axioms the proposition that a part is less than its whole, and falls into several conflicts with our most modern geometry in consequence. But why need we stop to consider cases where some subtilty of thought is required to see that the assertion is not warranted when every book which applies philosophy to the conduct of life lays down as positive certainty propositions which it is quite as easy to doubt as to believe?

The second bar which philosophers often set up across the roadway of inquiry lies in maintaining that this, that, and the other never can be known. When Auguste Comte was pressed to specify any matter of positive fact to the knowledge of which no man could by any possibility attain, he instanced the knowledge of the chemical composition of the fixed stars; and you may see his answer set down in the *philosophie positive.*[4] But the ink was scarcely dry upon the printed page before the spectroscope was discovered and that which he had deemed absolutely unknowable was well on the way of getting ascertained. It is easy enough to mention a question the answer to which is not known to me

---

* From unpaginated ms. "F. R. L.," c. 1899.

[4] 19me leçon.

today. But to aver that that answer will not be known tomorrow is somewhat risky; for oftentimes it is precisely the least expected truth which is turned up under the ploughshare of research. And when it comes to positive assertion that the truth never will be found out, that, in the light of the history of our time, seems to me more hazardous than the venture of Andrée.[5]

The third philosophical stratagem for cutting off inquiry consists in maintaining that this, that, or the other element of science is basic, ultimate, independent of aught else, and utterly inexplicable— not so much from any defect in our knowing as because there is nothing beneath it to know. The only type of reasoning by which such a conclusion could possibly be reached is *retroduction*.[6] Now nothing justifies a retroductive inference except its affording an explanation of the facts. It is, however, no explanation at all of a fact to pronounce it *inexplicable*. That, therefore, is a conclusion which no reasoning can ever justify or excuse.

The last philosophical obstacle to the advance of knowledge which I intend to mention is the holding that this or that law or truth has found its last and perfect formulation—and especially that the ordinary and usual course of nature never can be broken through. "Stones do not fall from heaven," said Laplace, although they had been falling upon inhabited ground every day from the earliest times. But there is no kind of inference which can lend the slightest probability to any such absolute denial of an unusual phenomenon.

---

[5] In 1897 Salomon August Andrée attempted to fly over the polar regions in a balloon. He died in the attempt.

[6] "Retroduction" is Peirce's name for the method of reasoning which leads to an explanatory *hypothesis*. Peirce also used the term "abduction" (as the complement of "induction" and "deduction") for reasoning to a hypothesis.

P. P. W.

§ 5. *Fallibilism*

All positive reasoning is of the nature of judging the proportion of something in a whole collection by the proportion found in a sample. Accordingly, there are three things to which we can never hope to attain by reasoning, namely, absolute certainty, absolute exactitude, absolute universality. We cannot be absolutely certain that our conclusions are even approximately true; for the sample may be utterly unlike the unsampled part of the collection. We cannot pretend to be even probably exact; because the sample consists of but a finite number of instances and only admits special values of the proportion sought. Finally, even if we could ascertain with absolute certainty and exactness that the ratio of sinful men to all men was as 1 to 1; still among the infinite generations of men there would be room for any finite number of sinless men without violating the proportion. The case is the same with a seven legged calf.

Now if exactitude, certitude, and universality are not to be attained by reasoning, there is certainly no other means by which they can be reached.

Somebody will suggest *revelation*. There are scientists and people influenced by science who laugh at revelation; and certainly science has taught us to look at testimony in such a light that the whole theological doctrine of the "Evidences" seems pretty weak. However, I do not think it is philosophical to reject the possibility of a revelation. Still, granting that, I declare as a logician that revealed truths—that is, truths which have nothing in their favor but revelations made to a few individuals— constitute by far the most uncertain class of truths there are. There is here no question of universality; for revelation is itself sporadic and miraculous. There is no question of mathematical exactitude; for no revelation makes any pretension to that character. But it does pretend to be *certain;* and against that there are three conclusive objections. First, we never can be absolutely certain that any given deliverance really is inspired; for that can only be established by reasoning. We cannot even prove it with any very high degree of probability. Second, even if it is inspired, we cannot be sure, or nearly sure, that the statement is true. We know that one of the commandments was in one of the Bibles printed with[out] a *not* in it.[7] All inspired matter has been subject to human distortion or coloring. Besides we cannot penetrate the counsels of the most High, or lay down anything as a principle that would govern his conduct. We do not know his inscrutable purposes, nor can we comprehend his plans. We cannot tell but he might see fit to inspire his servants with errors. In the third place, a truth which rests on the authority of inspiration only is of a somewhat incomprehensible nature; and we never can be sure that we rightly comprehend it. As there is no way of evading these difficulties, I say that revelation, far from affording us any certainty, gives results less certain than other sources of information. This would be so even if revelation were much plainer than it is.

But, it will be said, you forget the laws which are known to us *a priori,* the axioms of geometry, the principles of logic, the maxims of *causality,* and the like. Those are absolutely certain, without exception and exact. To this I reply that it seems to me there is the most positive historic proof that innate truths are particularly uncertain and mixed up with error, and therefore *a fortiori* not without exception. This historical proof is, of course, not infallible; but it is very strong. Therefore, I ask *how do you know* that *a priori* truth is certain, ex-

[7] The "Wicked Bible" of 1631 omitted "not" from the Seventh Commandment.

ceptionless, and exact? You cannot know it by *reasoning.* For that would be subject to uncertainty and inexactitude. Then, it must amount to this that you know it *a priori;* that is, you take *a priori* judgments at their own valuation, without criticism or credentials. That is barring the gate of inquiry.

Ah! but it will be said, you forget direct experience. Direct experience is neither certain nor uncertain, because it affirms nothing—it just *is.* There are delusions, hallucinations, dreams. But there is no mistake that such things really do appear, and direct experience means simply the appearance. It involves no error, because it testifies to nothing but its own appearance. For the same reason, it affords no certainty. It is not *exact,* because it leaves much vague; though it is not *inexact* either; that is, it has no false exactitude.

All this is true of direct experience at its first presentation. But when it comes up to be criticized it is past, itself, and is represented by *memory.* Now the deceptions and inexactitude of memory are proverbial.

. . . On the whole, then, we cannot in any way reach perfect certitude nor exactitude. We never can be absolutely sure of anything, nor can we with any probability ascertain the exact value of any measure or general ratio.

This is my conclusion, after many years study of the logic of science; and it is the conclusion which others, of very different cast of mind, have come to, likewise. I believe I may say there is no tenable opinion regarding human knowledge which does not legitimately lead to this corollary. Certainly there is nothing new in it; and many of the greatest minds of all time have held it for true.

Indeed, most everybody will admit it until he begins to see what is involved in the admission—and then most people will draw back. It will not be admitted by persons utterly incapable of philosophical reflection. It will not be fully admitted by masterful minds developed exclusively in the direction of action and accustomed to claim practical infallibility in matters of business. These men will admit the incurable fallibility of all opinions readily enough; only, they will always make exception of their own. The doctrine of fallibilism will also be denied by those who fear its consequences for science, for religion, and for morality. But I will take leave to say to these highly conservative gentlemen that however competent they may be to direct the affairs of a church or other corporation, they had better not try to manage science in that way. Conservatism—in the sense of a dread of consequences—is altogether out of place in science—which has on the contrary always been forwarded by radicals and radicalism, in the sense of the eagerness to carry consequences to their extremes. Not the radicalism that is cocksure, however, but the *radicalism that tries experiments*. Indeed, it is precisely among men animated by the spirit of science that the doctrine of fallibilism will find supporters.

Still, even such a man as that may well ask whether I propose to say that it is not quite certain that twice two are four—and that it is even not probably quite exact! But it would be quite misunderstanding the doctrine of fallibilism to suppose that it means that twice two is probably not exactly four. As I have already remarked, it is not my purpose to doubt that people can usually *count* with accuracy. Nor does fallibilism say that men cannot attain a sure knowledge of the creations of their own minds. It neither affirms nor denies that. It only says that people cannot attain absolute certainty concerning questions of fact. Numbers are merely a system of names devised by men for the purpose of counting. It is a matter of real fact to say that in a certain room there are two persons. It is a matter of fact to say that each person has two eyes. It is a matter of fact to say that there are four eyes in the room. But to say that *if* there are two persons and each person has two eyes there *will be* four eyes is not a statement of fact, but a statement about the system of numbers which is our own creation.

27. *Morality and Science**

HENRI POINCARÉ (1854–1912)

The dream of creating a scientific morality appeared often in the last half of the nineteenth century. It was not enough to praise the educational value of science, the benefits obtained by the human mind for its own improvement

* Translated from Poincaré's *Dernières Pensées*, pp. 223 ff.—P. P. W.

thanks to direct commerce with truth. It was expected that science would put moral truths on an indisputable plane, along with mathematical theorems and the laws formulated by physicists.

Religions can wield a great deal of power on believers, but not everybody is a believer for faith falls only to some, whereas reason should appeal to all. So we must address ourselves to reason, and I do not mean the reason of the metaphysician whose constructions are brilliant but ephemeral, like soap-bubbles amusing us for an instant and then bursting. Science alone builds solidly; it built astronomy and physics; it is building biology today; by the same procedures it will build morality. Its prescriptions will reign indivisibly, nobody will be able to murmur against them, or dream of rebelling against the moral law any more than of revolting today against the Pythagorean theorem or law of gravitation.

But on the other side there were people who imputed every evil possible to science and saw in it a school for immorality. The reason was not merely that science is too materialistic, or that it deprives us of the sense of respect, for we respect highly only the things we dare not look at. But its conclusions seemed to be the negation of morality. As some well known author, whose name I forget, put it, science goes about to extinguish the lights of heaven or at least rob them of their mystery in order to reduce them to the lowly state of gas jets. Science tends to expose the tricks of the Creator who will thereby lose something of his prestige. It is not good to let children into the wings for that might inspire doubts in them about the existence of the puppet Croquemitaine. If you let the scientists have their way, it will be the end of morality.

What are we to think of the hopes on one side of the argument and of the fears on the other side? I reply without hesitation: they are both equally vain. There can be no scientific morals; but neither can there be any immoral science. And the reason for this is simple; the reason, how else shall I put it, is simply a grammatical one.

If the premises of a syllogism are both in the indicative mood, the conclusion will also be in the indicative mood. In order for the conclusion to be put into the imperative mood, it would be necessary for at least one of the premises to be in the imperative. Now the principles of science and the postulates of geometry are and can only be in the indicative; this is also the mood in which experimental truths are stated, and at the base of the sciences, there is not and cannot be any other mood. Whence it follows, that no matter how the subtlest dialectician wishes to juggle and combine these principles, one on top of the other, everything he concludes will be in the indicative. He will never obtain a proposition which will say: Do this or do not do that; that is to say, he will not produce a proposition which confirms or contradicts morals.

This difficulty is one that moralists often encounter. They try hard to demonstrate moral law; they must be pardoned because that is their vocation. They wish to rest morals on something, as if it could be made to rest on anything but itself. Science shows us that man can only degrade himself by living in such and such a manner; but what if I don't care about degrading myself, or if what you call degrading I baptize as a mark of progress? Metaphysics invites us to conform to the universal law of the moral order it claims to have discovered; but one can reply, I prefer to obey my own personal law. I don't know what metaphysics will reply, but I can assure you that it will not have the last word.

Will religious ethics be more fortunate than science or metaphysics? Obey because God orders it, and because he is a master who breaks down all resistance. Is that a demonstration and can we not maintain that it is in vain to stand up against Omnipotence, or that in the duel between Jupiter and Prometheus the true conqueror is the tortured Prometheus? But then to yield to force is not to obey, and the obedience of the heart cannot be coerced. . . .

28. *The Scientific Outlook**

BERTRAND RUSSELL (1872–   )

Introduction

To say that we live in an age of science is a commonplace, but like most commonplaces it is only partially true. From the point of view of our predecessors, if they could view our society, we should, no doubt, appear to be very scientific, but from the point of view of our successors it is probable that the exact opposite would seem to be the case.

Science as a factor in human life is exceedingly recent. Art was already well developed before the last glacial epoch, as we know from the admirable pictures in caves; of the antiquity of religion we cannot speak with equal confidence, but it is highly probable that it is coeval with art. At a guess one might suppose that both have existed for some eighty thousand years. Science as an important force begins with Galileo, and has therefore existed for some three hundred years. During the first half of that short period it remained a pursuit of the learned, which did not affect the thoughts or habits of ordinary men. It is only during the last hundred and fifty years that science has become an important factor in determining the everyday life of everyday people. In that short time it has caused greater changes than

had occurred since the days of the ancient Egyptians. One hundred and fifty years of science have proved more explosive than five thousand years of pre-scientific culture. It would be absurd to suppose that the explosive power of science is exhausted, or has even reached its maximum. It is far more likely that science will continue for centuries to come to produce more and more rapid changes. One may suppose that a new equilibrium will ultimately be reached, either when so much is known that a lifetime is not sufficient to reach the frontiers of knowledge, and therefore further discovery must await some considerable increase of longevity, or when men become bored with the new toy, become weary of the strenuousness required in the making of scientific advances, and become content to enjoy the fruits of former labours, as the late Romans enjoyed the aqueducts built by their predecessors. Or again it may prove that no scientific society is capable of stability and that a reversion to barbarism is a necessary condition of the continuance of human life.

Such speculations, however, though they may amuse an idle moment, are too nebulous to have any practical importance. What is important at the present time is that the influence of science upon our thoughts, our hopes, and our habits is continually increasing and likely to increase for several centuries at least.

* From *The Scientific Outlook,* by Bertrand Russell, published by W. W. Norton & Company, Inc., with the permission of the author and publishers.

Science, as its name implies, is primarily knowledge; by convention it is knowledge of a certain kind, the kind, namely, which seeks general laws connecting a number of particular facts. Gradually, however, the aspect of science as knowledge is being thrust into the background by the aspect of science as the power of manipulating nature. It is because science gives us the power of manipulating nature that it has more social importance than art. Science as the pursuit of truth is the equal, but not the superior, of art. Science as a technique, though it may have little intrinsic value, has a practical importance to which art cannot aspire.

Science as a technique has a further consequence of which the implications are not yet fully evident, namely, that it makes possible, and even necessary, new forms of human society. It has already profoundly modified the forms of economic organizations and the functions of States, it is beginning to modify family life, and is almost certain to do so to a much greater extent in the not very distant future.

In considering the effect of science upon human life we have therefore three more or less separate matters to examine. The first is the nature and scope of scientific knowledge, the second the increased power of manipulation derived from scientific technique, and the third the changes in social life and in traditional institutions which must result from the new forms of organization that scientific technique demands. Science as knowledge of course underlies the other two, since all the effects which science produces are the outcome of the knowledge which it provides. Man hitherto has been prevented from realizing his hopes by ignorance as to means. As this ignorance disappears he becomes increasingly able to mould his physical environment, his social milieu and himself into the forms which he deems best. In so far as

he is wise this new power is beneficent; in so far as he is foolish it is quite the reverse. If, therefore, a scientific civilization is to be a good civilization it is necessary that increase in knowledge should be accompanied by increase in wisdom. I mean by wisdom a right conception of the ends of life. This is something which science in itself does not provide. Increase of science by itself, therefore, is not enough to guarantee any genuine progress, though it provides one of the ingredients which progress requires.

In the following pages we shall be concerned with science rather than with wisdom. It is well to remember, however, that this preoccupation is one-sided and needs to be corrected if a balanced view of human life is to be achieved.

CHAPTER V

Science and Religion

In recent times, the bulk of eminent physicists and a number of eminent biologists have made pronouncements stating that recent advances in science have disproved the older materialism, and have tended to reestablish the truths of religion. The statements of the scientists have as a rule been somewhat tentative and indefinite, but the theologians have seized upon them and extended them, while the newspapers in turn have reported the more sensational accounts of the theologians, so that the general public has derived the impression that physics confirms practically the whole of the Book of Genesis. I do not myself think that the moral to be drawn from modern science is at all what the general public has thus been led to suppose. In the first place, the men of science have not said nearly as much as they are thought to have said, and in the second place what they have said in the way of support for traditional religious beliefs has been said by them not in their cautious, scientific capacity, but rather in their capacity of good citizens, anxious to defend virtue and property. The War, and the Russian Revolution, have made all timid men conservative, and professors are usually temperamentally timid. Such considerations, however, are beside the point. Let us examine what science really has to say.

(1) *Free Will.* Until very recent times theology, while in its Catholic form it admitted free will in human beings, showed an affection for natural law in the universe, tempered only by belief in occasional miracles. In the eighteenth century, under the influence of Newton, the alliance between theology and natural law became very close. It was held that God had created the world in accordance with a Plan, and that natural laws were the embodiment of this Plan. Until the nineteenth century theology remained hard and intellectual and definite. In order to meet the assaults of atheistic reason, however, it has, during the last hundred years, aimed more and more at appealing to sentiment. It has tried to catch men in their intellectually relaxed moods; and from having been a strait-jacket it has become a dressing-gown. In our day, only the fundamentalists and a few of the more learned Catholic theologians maintain the old respectable intellectual tradition. All the other religious apologists are engaged in blunting the edge of logic, appealing to the heart instead of the head, maintaining that our feelings can demonstrate the falsity of a conclusion to which our reason has been driven. As Lord Tennyson nobly says:

And like a man in wrath the heart
Stood up and answered "I have felt."

In our day the heart has feelings about atoms, about the respiratory system, about the growth of sea-urchins and other such topics, concerning which, but

for science, it would remain indifferent.

One of the most remarkable developments in religious apologetics in recent times is the attempt to rescue free will in man by means of ignorance as to the behaviour of atoms. The older laws of mechanics which governed the movements of bodies large enough to be seen remain true to a very close approximation as regards such bodies, but are found to be not applicable to single atoms, still less to single electrons and protons. It is not yet known with any certainty whether there are laws governing the behaviour of single atoms in all respects, or whether the behaviour of such atoms is in part random. It is thought possible that the laws governing the behaviour of large bodies may be merely statistical laws, expressing the average result of a large number of random motions. Some, such as the second law of thermodynamics, are known to be statistical laws, and it is possible that others may be. In the atom there are various possible states which do not merge continuously into each other, but are separated by small finite gaps. An atom may hop from one of these states to another, and there are various different hops that it may make. At present no laws are known to decide which of the possible hops will take place on any given occasion, and it is suggested that the atom is not subject to laws at all in this respect, but has what might be called, by analogy, "free will." Eddington, in his book on the *Nature of the Physical World,* has made great play with this possibility (p. 311 ff.). He thinks, apparently, that the mind can decide the atoms in the brain to make one or another of the possible transitions at a given moment, and thus, by means of some kind of trigger action, produce large-scale results in accordance with its volition. The volition itself, he thinks, is uncaused. If he is right, the course of the physical world, even where fairly large masses are concerned, is not completely predetermined by physical laws, but is liable to be altered by the uncaused volitions of human beings.

Before examining this position I should like to say a few words about what is called "the Principle of Indeterminacy." This principle was introduced into physics in 1927 by Heisenberg, and has been seized on by clergymen—chiefly, I think, on account of its name—as something capable of giving them an escape from thraldom to mathematical laws. It is, to my mind, somewhat surprising that Eddington should countenance this use of the principle (see page 306). The Principle of Indeterminacy states that it is impossible to determine with precision both the position and the momentum of a particle; there will be a margin of error in each, and the product of the two errors is constant. That is to say, the more accurately we determine the one, the less accurately we shall be determining the other, and *vice versa*. The margin of error involved is, of course, very small. I am surprised, I repeat, that Eddington should have appealed to this principle in connexion with the question of free will, for the principle does nothing whatever to show that the course of nature is not determined. It shows merely that the old space-time apparatus is not quite adequate to the needs of modern physics, which, in any case, is known on other grounds. Space and time were invented by the Greeks, and served their purpose admirably until the present century. Einstein replaced them by a kind of centaur which he called "space-time," and this did well enough for a couple of decades, but modern quantum mechanics has made it evident that a more fundamental reconstruction is necessary. The Principle of Indeterminacy is merely an illustration of this necessity, not of the failure of physical laws to determine the course of nature.

As J. E. Turner has pointed out (*Nature*, December 27, 1930), "The use to which the Principle of Indeterminacy has been put is largely due to an ambiguity in the word 'determined.'" In one sense a quantity is determined when it is measured, in the other sense an event is determined when it is caused. The Principle of Indeterminacy has to do with measurement, not with causation. The velocity and position of a particle are declared by the Principle to be undetermined in the sense that they cannot be accurately measured. This is a physical fact causally connected with the fact that the measuring is a physical process which has a physical effect upon what is measured. There is nothing whatever in the Principle of Indeterminacy to show that any physical event is uncaused. As Turner says: "Every argument that, since some change cannot be 'determined' in the sense of 'ascertained,' it is therefore not 'determined' in the absolutely different sense of 'caused,' is a fallacy of equivocation."

Returning now to the atom and its supposed free will, it should be observed that it is not known that the behaviour of the atom is capricious. It is false to say the behaviour of the atom is known to be capricious, and it is also false to say the behaviour is known to be not capricious. Science has quite recently discovered that the atom is not subject to the laws of the older physics, and some physicists have somewhat rashly jumped to the conclusion that the atom is not subject to laws at all. Eddington's argument about the effect of the mind on the brain inevitably reminds one of Descartes's argument on the same subject. Descartes knew of the conservation of *vis viva*, but not of the conservation of momentum. He therefore thought that the mind could alter the direction of the motion of the animal spirits, though not its amount. When, shortly after the publication of his theory, the conservation of momentum was discovered, Descartes's view had to be abandoned. Eddington's view, similarly, is at the mercy of the experimental physicists, who may at any moment discover laws regulating the behaviour of individual atoms. It is very rash to erect a theological superstructure upon a piece of ignorance which may be only momentary. And the effects of this procedure, so far as it has any, are necessarily bad, since they make men hope that new discoveries will not be made.

There is, moreover, a purely empirical objection to the belief in free will. Wherever it has been possible to subject the behaviour of animals or of human beings to careful scientific observation, it has been found, as in Pavlov's experiments, that scientific laws are just as discoverable as in any other sphere. It is true that we cannot predict human actions with any completeness, but this is quite sufficiently accounted for by the complication of the mechanism, and by no means demands the hypothesis of complete lawlessness, which is found to be false wherever it can be carefully tested.

Those who desire caprice in the physical world seem to me to have failed to realize what this would involve. All inference in regard to the course of nature is causal, and if nature is not subject to causal laws all such inference must fail. We cannot, in that case, know anything outside of our personal experience; indeed, strictly speaking, we can only know our experience in the present moment, since all memory depends upon causal laws. If we cannot infer the existence of other people, or even of our own past, how much less can we infer God, or anything else that the theologians desire. The principle of causality may be true or may be false, but the person who finds the hypothesis of its falsity cheering is failing to realize the implications of his own theory. He usually retains

unchallenged all those causal laws which he finds convenient, as, for example, that his food will nourish him and that his bank will honour his cheques so long as his account is in funds, while rejecting all those that he finds inconvenient. This, however, is altogether too *naïve* a procedure.

There is, in fact, no good reason whatever for supposing that the behaviour of atoms is not subject to law. It is only quite recently that experimental methods have been able to throw any light on the behaviour of individual atoms, and it is no wonder if the laws of this behaviour have not yet been discovered. To prove that a given set of phenomena is not subject to laws is essentially and theoretically impossible. All that can be affirmed is that the laws, if any, have not yet been discovered. We may say, if we choose, that the men who have been investigating the atom are so clever that they must have discovered the laws if there were any. I do not think, however, that this is a sufficiently solid premise upon which to base a theory of the universe.

(2) *God as Mathematician.* Eddington deduces religion from the fact that atoms do not obey the laws of mathematics. Jeans deduces it from the fact that they do. Both these arguments have been accepted with equal enthusiasm by the theologians, who hold, apparently, that the demand for consistency belongs to the cold reason and must not interfere with our deeper religious feelings.

We have examined Eddington's argument from the way that atoms jump. Let us now examine Jeans's argument from the way that stars cool. Jeans's God is Platonic. He is not, we are told, a biologist or an engineer, but a pure mathematician (*The Mysterious Universe*, p. 134). I confess to a preference for this type of God rather than the one that is conceived after the analogy of big business; but that, no doubt, is because I prefer thinking to doing. This suggests a treatise dealing with the influence of muscular tone upon theology. The man whose muscles are taut believes in a God of action, while the man whose muscles are relaxed believes in a God of thought and contemplation. Jeans, confident no doubt in his own theistic arguments, is not very complimentary to those of the evolutionists. His book on the Mysterious Universe begins with a biography of the sun, one might almost say an epitaph. It seems that not more than one star in about one hundred thousand has planets, but that some two thousand million years ago the sun had the good fortune to have a fruitful meeting with another star, which led to the existing planetary offspring. The stars that do not have planets cannot give rise to life, so that life must be a very rare phenomenon in the universe. "It seems incredible," says Jeans, "that the universe can have been designed primarily to produce life like our own: had it been so, surely we might have expected to find a better proportion between the magnitude of the mechanism and the amount of the product." And even in this rare corner of the universe the possibility of life exists only during an interlude between weather that is too hot and weather that is too cold. "It is a tragedy of our race that it is probably destined to die of cold, while the greater part of the substance of the universe still remains too hot for life to obtain a footing." Theologians who argue as if human life were the purpose of creation seem to be as faulty in their astronomy as they are excessive in their estimation of themselves and their fellow-creatures. I shall not attempt to summarize Jeans's admirable chapters on modern physics, matter and radiation, and relativity and the ether; they are already as brief as possible, and no summary can do them justice. I will, however, quote Jeans's own summary in order to whet the reader's appetite.

"To sum up, a soap-bubble with irregularities and corrugations on its surface is perhaps the best representation, in terms of simple and familiar materials, of the new universe revealed to us by the theory of relativity. The universe is not the interior of the soap-bubble but its surface, and we must always remember that, while the surface of the soap-bubble has only two dimensions, the universe-bubble has four—three dimensions of space and one of time. And the substance out of which this bubble is blown, the soap-film, is empty space welded on to empty time."

The last chapter of the book is concerned to argue that this soap-bubble has been blown by a mathematical Deity because of His interest in its mathematical properties. This part has pleased the theologians. Theologians have grown grateful for small mercies, and they do not much care what sort of God the man of science gives them so long as he gives them one at all. Jeans's God, like Plato's, is one who has a passion for doing sums, but being a pure mathematician, is quite indifferent as to what the sums are about. By prefacing his argument by a lot of difficult and recent physics, the eminent author manages to give it an air of profundity which it would not otherwise possess. In essence the argument is as follows: since two apples and two apples together make four apples, it follows that the Creator must have known that two and two are four. It might be objected that, since one man and one woman together sometimes make three, the Creator was not yet quite as well versed in sums as one could wish. To speak seriously: Jeans reverts explicitly to the theory of Bishop Berkeley, according to which the only things that exist are thoughts, and the quasi-permanence which we observe in the external world is due to the fact that

God keeps on thinking about things for quite a long time. Material objects, for example, do not cease to exist when no human being is looking at them, because God is looking at them all the time, or rather because they are thoughts in His mind at all times. The universe, he says, "can best be pictured, although still very imperfectly and inadequately, as consisting of pure thought, the thought of what, for want of a wider word, we must describe as a mathematical thinker." A little later we are told that the laws governing God's thoughts are those which govern the phenomena of our waking hours, but not apparently of our dreams.

The argument is, of course, not set out with the formal precision which Jeans would demand in a subject not involving his emotions. Apart from all detail, he has been guilty of a fundamental fallacy in confusing the realms of pure and applied mathematics. Pure mathematics at no point depends upon observation; it is concerned with symbols, and with proving that different collections of symbols have the same meaning. It is because of this symbolic character that it can be studied without the help of experiment. Physics, on the contrary, however mathematical it may become, depends throughout on observation and experiment, that is to say, ultimately upon sense perception. The mathematician provides all kinds of mathematics, but only some of what he provides is useful to the physicist. And what the physicist asserts when he uses mathematics is something totally different from what the pure mathematician asserts. The physicist asserts that the mathematical symbols which he is employing can be used for the interpretation, colligation, and prediction of sense impressions. However abstract his work may become, it never loses its relation to experience. It is found that mathematical formulae can express certain laws governing the world that we observe.

Jeans argues that the world must have been created by a mathematician for the pleasure of seeing these laws in operation. If he had ever attempted to set out this argument formally, I cannot doubt that he would have seen how fallacious it is. To begin with, it seems probable that any world, no matter what, could be brought by a mathematician of sufficient skill within the scope of general laws. If this be so, the mathematical character of modern physics is not a fact about the world, but merely a tribute to the skill of the physicist. In the second place, if God were as pure a pure mathematician as His knightly champion supposes, He would have no wish to give a gross external existence to His thoughts. The desire to trace curves and make geometrical models belongs to the schoolboy stage, and would be considered *infra dig* by a professor. Nevertheless it is this desire that Jeans imputes to his Maker. The world, he tells us, consists of thoughts; of these there are, it would seem, three grades: the thoughts of God, the thoughts of men when they are awake, and the thoughts of men when they are asleep and have bad dreams. One does not quite see what the two latter kinds of thought add to the perfection of the universe, since clearly God's thoughts are the best, and one does not quite see what can have been gained by creating so much muddle-headedness. I once knew an extremely learned and orthodox theologian who told me that as the result of long study he had come to understand everything except why God created the world. I commend this puzzle to the attention of Jeans, and I hope that he will comfort the theologians by dealing with it at no distant date.

(3) *God as Creator*. One of the most serious difficulties confronting science at the present time is the difficulty derived from the fact that the universe appears to be running down. There are, for ex-

ample, radio-active elements in the world. These are perpetually disintegrating into less complex elements, and no process by which they can be built up is known. This, however, is not the most important or difficult respect in which the world is running down. Although we do not know of any natural process by which complex elements are built up out of simpler ones, we can imagine such processes, and it is possible that they are taking place somewhere. But when we come to the second law of thermodynamics we encounter a more fundamental difficulty.

The second law of thermodynamics states, roughly speaking, that things left to themselves tend to get into a muddle and do not tidy themselves up again. It seems that once upon a time the universe was all tidy, with everything in its proper place, and that ever since then it has been growing more and more disorderly, until nothing but a drastic spring-cleaning can restore it to its pristine order. In its original form the second law of thermodynamics asserted something much less general: namely, that when there was a difference of temperature between two neighbouring bodies, the hotter one would cool and the colder one would get warmer until they reached an equal temperature. In this form the law states a fact familiar to everyone: if you hold up a red-hot poker, it will get cool while the surrounding air gets warm. But the law was soon seen to have a much more general meaning. The particles of very hot bodies are in very rapid motion, while those of cold bodies move more slowly. In the long run, when a number of swiftly moving particles and a number of slowly moving particles find themselves in the same region, the swift ones will bump into the slow ones until both sets acquire on the average equal velocities. A similar truth applies to all forms of energy. Whenever there is a great deal

of energy in one region and very little in a neighbouring region, energy tends to travel from the one region to the other, until equality is established. This whole process may be described as a tendency towards democracy. It will be seen that this is an irreversible process, and that in the past energy must have been more unevenly distributed than it is now. In view of the fact that the material universe is now considered to be finite, and to consist of some definite though unknown number of electrons and protons, there is a theoretical limit to the possible heaping-up of energy in some places as opposed to others. As we trace the course of the world backwards in time, we arrive after some finite number of years (rather more than four thousand and four, however), at a state of the world which could not have been preceded by any other, if the second law of thermodynamics was then valid. This initial state of the world would be that in which energy was distributed as unevenly as possible. As Eddington says: [1]

The difficulty of an infinite past is appalling. It is inconceivable that we are the heirs of an infinite time of preparation; it is not less inconceivable that there was once a moment with no moment preceding it.

This dilemma of the beginning of time would worry us more were it not shut out by another overwhelming difficulty lying between us and the infinite past. We have been studying the running-down of the universe; if our views are right, somewhere between the beginning of time and the present day we must place the winding up of the universe.

Travelling backwards into the past we find a world with more and more organization. If there is no barrier to stop us earlier we must reach a moment when the energy of the world was wholly organized with none of the random element in it. It is impossible to go back any further under the present

[1] Eddington, *The Nature of the Physical World*, 1928, p. 83 ff., with the kind permission of The Macmillan Co.

system of natural law. I do not think the phrase "wholly organized' begs the question. The organization we are concerned with is exactly definable, and there is a limit at which it becomes perfect. There is not an infinite series of states of higher and still higher organization; nor, I think, is the limit one which is ultimately approached more and more slowly. Complete organization does not tend to be more immune from loss than incomplete organization.

There is no doubt that the scheme of physics as it has stood for the last three-quarters of a century postulates a date at which either the entities of the universe were created in a state of high organization, or pre-existing entities were endowed with that organization which they have been squandering ever since. Moreover, this organization is admittedly the antithesis of chance. It is something which could not occur fortuitously.

This has long been used as an argument against a too aggressive materialism. It has been quoted as scientific proof of the intervention of the Creator at a time not infinitely remote from to-day. But I am not advocating that we draw any hasty conclusions from it. Scientists and theologians alike must regard as somewhat crude the naïve theological doctrine which (suitably disguised) is at present to be found in every textbook of thermodynamics, namely, that some billions of years ago God wound up the material universe and has left it to chance ever since. This should be regarded as the working-hypothesis of thermodynamics rather than its declaration of faith. It is one of those conclusions from which we can see no logical escape—only it suffers from the drawback that it is incredible. As a scientist I simply do not believe that the present order of things started off with a bang; unscientifically I feel equally unwilling to accept the implied discontinuity in the Divine nature. But I can make no suggestion to evade the deadlock.

It will be seen that Eddington, in this passage, does not infer a definite act of creation by a Creator. His only reason for not doing so is that he does not like the idea. The scientific argument leading to the conclusion which he rejects is much stronger than the argument in favour of free will, since that is based upon ignorance, whereas the one we are now considering is based upon knowledge. This illustrates the fact that the theological conclusions drawn by scientists from their science are only such as please them, and not such as their appetite for orthodoxy is insufficient to swallow, although the argument would warrant them. We must, I think, admit that there is far more to be said for the view that the universe had a beginning in time at some not infinitely remote period, than there is for any of the other theological conclusions which scientists have recently been urging us to admit. The argument does not have demonstrative certainty. The second law of thermodynamics may not hold in all times and places, or we may be mistaken in thinking the universe spatially finite; but as arguments of this nature go, it is a good one, and I think we ought provisionally to accept the hypothesis that the world had a beginning at some definite, though unknown, date.

Are we to infer from this that the world was made by a Creator? Certainly not, if we are to adhere to the canons of valid scientific inference. There is no reason whatever why the universe should not have begun spontaneously, except that it seems odd that it should do so; but there is no law of nature to the effect that things which seem odd to us must not happen. To infer a Creator is to infer a cause, and causal inferences are only admissible in science when they proceed from observed causal laws. Creation out of nothing is an occurrence which has not been observed. There is, therefore, no better reason to suppose that the world was caused by a Creator than to suppose that it was uncaused; either equally contradicts the causal laws that we can observe.

Nor is there, so far as I can see, any particular comfort to be derived from the hypothesis that the world was made by a Creator. Whether it was, or whether it was not, it is what it is. If somebody tried to sell you a bottle of very nasty wine, you would not like it any better for being told that it had been made in a laboratory and not from the juice of the grape. In like manner, I see no comfort to be derived from the supposition that this very unpleasing universe was manufactured of set purpose.   ·

Some people—among whom, however, Eddington is not included—derive comfort from the thought that if God made the world, He may wind it up again when it has completely run down. For my part, I do not see how an unpleasant process can be made less so by the reflection that it is to be indefinitely repeated. No doubt, however, that is because I am lacking in religious feeling.

The purely intellectual argument on this point may be put in a nutshell: is the Creator amenable to the laws of physics or is He not? If He is not, He cannot be inferred from physical phenomena, since no physical causal law can lead to Him; if He is, we shall have to apply the second law of thermodynamics to Him and suppose that He also had to be created at some remote period. But in that case He has lost His *raison d'être*. It is curious that not only the physicists, but even the theologians, seem to find something new in the arguments from modern physics. Physicists, perhaps, can scarcely be expected to know the history of theology, but the theologians ought to be aware that the modern arguments have all had their counterparts at earlier times. Eddington's argument about free will and the brain is, as we saw, closely parallel to Descartes's. Jeans's argument is a compound of Plato and Berkeley, and has no more warrant in physics than it had at the time of either of these philosophers. The argument that the world

must have had a beginning in time is set forth with great clearness by Kant, who, however, supplements it by an equally powerful argument to prove that the world had no beginning in time. Our age has been rendered conceited by the multitude of new discoveries and inventions, but in the realm of philosophy it is much less in advance of the past than it imagines itself to be.

We hear a great deal nowadays about the old-fashioned materialism, and its refutation by modern physics. As a matter of fact, there has been a change in the technique of physics. In old days, whatever philosophers might say, physics proceeded technically on the assumption that matter consisted of hard little lumps. Now it no longer does so. But few philosophers ever believed in the hard little lumps at any date later than that of Democritus. Berkeley and Hume certainly did not; no more did Leibniz, Kant and Hegel. Mach, himself a physicist, taught a completely different doctrine, and every scientist with even a tincture of philosophy was ready to admit that the hard little lumps were no more than a technical device. In that sense materialism is dead, but in another and more important sense it is more alive than it ever was. The important question is not whether matter consists of hard little lumps or of something else, but whether the course of nature is determined by the laws of physics. The progress of biology, physiology, and psychology has made it more probable than it ever was before that all natural phenomena are governed by the laws of physics; and this is the really important point. To prove this point, however, we must consider some of the dicta of those who deal with the sciences of life.

(4) *Evolutionary Theology.* Evolution, when it was new, was regarded as hostile to religion, and is still so considered by fundamentalists. But a whole

school of apologists has grown up who see in evolution evidence of a Divine Plan slowly unfolding through the ages. Some place this Plan in the mind of a Creator, while others regard it as immanent in the obscure strivings of living organisms. In the one view we fulfil God's purposes; in the other we fulfil our own, though these are better than we know. Like most controversial questions, the question of the purposiveness of evolution has become entangled in a mass of detail. When, long ago, Huxley and Mr. Gladstone debated the truth of the Christian religion in the pages of the *Nineteenth Century,* this great issue was found to turn upon the question whether Gadarene swine had belonged to a Jew or a Gentile, since in the latter case, but not in the former, their destruction involved an unwarrantable interference with private property. Similarly the question of purpose in evolution becomes entangled in the habits of the amophila, the behaviour of sea-urchins when turned upside-down, and the aquatic or terrestrial habits of the axolotl. But such questions, grave as they are, we may leave to specialists.

In passing from physics to biology one is conscious of a transition from the cosmic to the parochial. In physics and astronomy we are dealing with the universe at large, and not only with that corner of it in which we happen to live, nor with those aspects of it which we happen to exemplify. From a cosmic point of view, life is a very unimportant phenomenon: very few stars have planets; very few planets can support life. Life, even on the earth, belongs to only a very small proportion of the matter close to the earth's surface. During the greater part of the past existence of the earth, it was too hot to support life; during the greater part of its future existence, it will be too cold. It is by no means impossible that there is, at this moment, no life anywhere in the universe except on the earth; but even if, taking a very liberal estimate, we suppose that there are scattered through space some hundred thousand other planets on which life exists, it must still be admitted that living matter makes rather a poor show if considered as the purpose of the whole creation. There are some old gentlemen who are fond of prosy anecdotes leading at last to a "point"; imagine an anecdote longer than any you have ever heard, and the "point" shorter, and you will have a fair picture of the activities of the Creator according to the biologists. Moreover, the "point" of the anecdote, even when it is reached, appears hardly worthy of so long a preface. I am willing to admit that there is merit in the tail of the fox, the song of the thrush, or the horns of the ibex. But it is not to these things that the evolutionary theologian points with pride: it is to the soul of man. Unfortunately, there is no impartial arbiter to decide on the merits of the human race; but for my part, when I consider their poison gases, their researches into bacteriological warfare, their meannesses, cruelties and oppressions, I find them, considered as the crowning gem of the creation, somewhat lacking in lustre. But let that pass.

Is there anything in the process of evolution that demands the hypothesis of a purpose, whether immanent or transcendent? This is the crucial question. For one who is not a biologist it is difficult to speak otherwise than with hesitation on this question. I am, however, entirely unconvinced by the arguments in favour of purpose that I have seen.

The behaviour of animals and plants is on the whole such as to lead to certain results, which the observing biologist interprets as the purpose of the behaviour. In the case of plants, at any rate, he is generally willing to concede that this purpose is not consciously entertained by the organism; but that is all the better if he wishes to prove that it is the purpose of a Creator. I am, however, quite unable to see why an intelligent Creator should have the purposes which we must attribute to Him if He has really designed all that happens in the world of organic life. Nor does the progress of scientific investigation afford any evidence that the behaviour of living matter is governed by anything other than laws of physics and chemistry. Take, for example, the process of digestion. The first step in this process is the seizing of food. This has been carefully studied in many animals, more particularly in chickens. New-born chickens have a reflex which causes them to peck at any object having more or less the shape and size of edible grains. After some experience this unconditioned reflex becomes transformed into a conditioned reflex, exactly after the manner studied by Pavlov. The same thing may be observed in babies: they suck not only their mothers' breasts, but everything physically capable of being sucked; they endeavour to extract food out of shoulders and hands and arms. It is only after months of experience that they learn to confine their efforts after nourishment to the breast. Sucking in infants is at first an unconditioned reflex, and by no means an intelligent one. It depends for its success upon the intelligence of the mother. Chewing and swallowing are at first unconditioned reflexes, though through experience they become conditioned. The chemical processes which the food undergoes at various stages of digestion have been minutely studied, and none of them require the invocation of any peculiar vital principle.

Or take again reproduction, which, though not universal throughout the animal kingdom, is nevertheless one of its most interesting peculiarities. There is now nothing in this process that can rightly be called mysterious. I do not

mean to say that it is all fully understood, but that mechanistic principles have explained enough of it to make it probable that, given time, they will explain the whole. Jacques Loeb, over twenty years ago, discovered means of fertilizing an ovum without the intervention of a spermatozoon. He sums up the results of his experiments and those of other investigators in the sentence: "We may, therefore, state that the complete imitation of the developmental effect of the spermatozoon by certain physico-chemical agencies has been accomplished." [2]

Take again the question of heredity, which is closely associated with that of reproduction. The present [3] state of scientific knowledge in regard to this matter is set forth very ably by Professor Hogben in his book on *The Nature of Living Matter*, more particularly in the chapter on the atomistic view of parenthood. In this chapter the reader can learn all that a layman needs to know about the Mendelian theory, chromosomes, mutants, etc. I do not see how anybody can, in view of what is now known on these subjects, maintain that there is anything in the theory of heredity requiring us to bow down before a mystery. The experimental stage of embryology is still recent, yet it has achieved remarkable results: it has shown that the conception of an organism which had dominated biology is not nearly so rigid as had been supposed.

To graft the eye of one salamander tadpole on to the head of another individual is now a commonplace of experimental embryology. Five-legged and two-headed newts are now manufactured in the laboratory.[4]

But all this, the reader may say, is concerned only with the body; what are we

---

[2] *The Mechanistic Conception of Life,* 1912, p. 11.

[3] 1931.

[4] Hogben, op. cit., p. 111.

to say concerning the mind? As to this, the question is not quite so simple. We may observe, to begin with, that the mental processes of animals are purely hypothetical, and that the scientific treatment of animals must confine itself to their behaviour and to their physical processes, since these alone are observable. I do not mean that we should deny that animals have minds; I mean merely that in so far as we are scientific we should say nothing about their minds one way or the other. As a matter of fact, the behaviour of their bodies appears to be causally self-contained, in the sense that its explanation does not, at any point, demand the intervention of some unobservable entity which we could call a mind. The theory of the conditioned reflex deals satisfactorily with all those cases in which it was formerly thought that a mental causation is essential for explaining the behaviour of the animal. When we come to human beings, we seem still able to explain the behaviour of human bodies on the assumption that there is no extraneous agent called mind acting upon them. But in the case of human beings this statement is much more questionable than in the case of other animals, both because the behaviour of human beings is more complex, and because we know, or think we know, through introspection, that we have minds. There is no doubt that we do know something about ourselves which is commonly expressed by saying that we have minds; but, as often happens, although we know something it is very difficut to say what we know. More particularly it is difficult to show that the causes of our bodily behaviour are not purely physical. It seems to introspection as though there were something called the will which causes those movements that we call voluntary. It is, however, quite possible that such movements have a complete chain of physical causes to which the will (whatever it may be)

is a mere concomitant. Or perhaps, since the subject matter of physics is no longer matter in the old sense, it may be that what we call our thoughts are ingredients of the complexes with which physics has replaced the old conception of matter. The dualism of mind and matter is out-of-date: matter has become more like mind, and mind has become more like matter, than seemed possible at an earlier stage of science. One is led to suppose that what really exists is something intermediate between the billiard-balls of old-fashioned materialism and the soul of old-fashioned psychology.

There is here, however, an important distinction to be made. There is, on the one hand, the question as to the sort of stuff the world is made of, and on the other hand, the question as to its causal skeleton. Science has been from its inception, though at first not exclusively, a form of what may be called power-thought: that is to say, it has been concerned to understand what causes the processes we observe rather than to analyse the ingredients of which they are composed. The highly abstract scheme of physics gives, it would seem, the causal skeleton of the world, while leaving out all the colour and variety and individuality of the things that compose the world. In suggesting that the causal skeleton supplied by physics is, in theory, adequate to give the causal laws governing the behaviour of human bodies, we are not suggesting that this bare abstraction tells us anything about the contents of human minds, or for that matter about the actual constitution of what we regard as matter. The billiard-balls of old-fashioned materialism were far too concrete and sensible to be admitted into the framework of modern physics, but the same is true of our thoughts. The concrete variety of the actual world seems to be largely irrelevant when we are investigating these causal processes. Let us take an illustration. The principle of the lever is simple and easily understood. It depends only upon the relative positions of the fulcrum, force, and resistance. It may happen that the actual lever employed is covered with exquisite pictures by a painter of genius; although these may be of more importance from the emotional point of view than the mechanistic properties of the lever, they do not in any way affect those properties, and may be wholly omitted in an account of what the lever can do. So it is with the world. The world as we perceive it is full of a rich variety: some of it is beautiful, some of it is ugly; parts seem to us good, parts bad. But all this has nothing to do with the purely causal properties of things, and it is these properties with which science is concerned. I am not suggesting that if we knew these properties completely we should have a complete knowledge of the world, for its concrete variety is an equally legitimate object of knowledge. What I am saying is that science is that sort of knowledge which gives causal understanding, and that this sort of knowledge can in all likelihood be completed, even where living bodies are concerned, without taking account of anything but their physical and chemical properties. In saying this we are, of course, going beyond what can at present be said with any certainty, but the work that has been done in recent times in physiology, biochemistry, embryology, the mechanism of sensation,[5] and so on, irresistibly suggests the truth of our conclusion.

One of the best statements of the point of view of a religiously-minded biologist is to be found in Lloyd Morgan's *Emergent Evolution* (1923) and *Life, Mind and Spirit* (1926). Lloyd Morgan believes that there is a Divine

---

[5] See e. g. *The Basis of Sensation*, by E. D. Adrian, 1928.

Purpose underlying the course of evolution, more particularly of what he calls "emergent evolution." The definition of emergent evolution, if I understand it rightly, is as follows: it sometimes happens that a collection of objects arranged in a suitable pattern will have a new property which does not belong to the objects singly, and which cannot, so far as we can see, be deduced from their several properties together with the way in which they are arranged. He considers that there are examples of the same kind of thing even in the inorganic realm. The atom, the molecule, and the crystal will all have properties which, if I understand Lloyd Morgan aright, he regards as not deducible from the properties of their constituents. The same holds in a higher degree of living organisms, and most of all with those higher organisms which possess what are called minds. Our minds, he would say, are, it is true, associated with the physical organism, but are not deducible from properties of that organism considered as an arrangement of atoms in space. "Emergent evolution," he says, "is from first to last a revelation and manifestation of that which I speak of as Divine Purpose." Again he says: "Some of us, and I for one, end with a concept of activity, under acknowledgment, as part and parcel of Divine Purpose." Sin, however, is not contributory to the manifestation of the Divine Purpose (p. 288).

It would be easier to deal with this view if any reasons were advanced in its favour, but so far as I have been able to discover from Professor Lloyd Morgan's pages, he considers that the doctrine is its own recommendation and does not need to be demonstrated by appeals to the mere understanding. I do not pretend to know whether Professor Lloyd Morgan's opinion is false. For aught I know to the contrary, there may be a Being of infinite power who chooses that children should die of meningitis, and older people of cancer; these things occur, and occur as the result of evolution. If, therefore, evolution embodies a Divine Plan, these occurrences must also have been planned. I have been informed that suffering is sent as a purification for sin, but I find it difficult to think that a child of four or five years old can be sunk in such black depths of iniquity as to deserve the punishment that befalls not a few of the children whom our optimistic divines might see any day, if they chose, suffering torments in children's hospitals. Again, I am told that though the child himself may not have sinned very deeply, he deserves to suffer on account of his parents' wickedness. I can only repeat that if this is the Divine sense of justice it differs from mine, and that I think mine superior. If indeed the world in which we live has been produced in accordance with a Plan, we shall have to reckon Nero a saint in comparison with the Author of that Plan. Fortunately, however, the evidence of Divine Purpose is non-existent; so at least one must infer from the fact that no evidence is adduced by those who believe in it. We are, therefore, spared the necessity for that attitude of impotent hatred which every brave and humane man would otherwise be called upon to adopt towards the Almighty Tyrant.

We have reviewed in this chapter a number of different apologies for religion on the part of eminent men of science. We have seen that Eddington and Jeans contradict each other, and that both contradict the biological theologians, but all agree that in the last resort science should abdicate before what is called the religious consciousness. This attitude is regarded by themselves and by their admirers as more optimistic than that of the uncompromising rationalist. It is, in fact, quite the opposite: it is the outcome of discouragement and loss of faith. Time was when religion was believed with whole-hearted fervour, when men went on crusades and burned each other at the stake because of the intensity of their convictions. After the wars of religion theology gradually lost this intense hold on men's minds. So far as anything has taken its place, its place has been taken by science. In the name of science we revolutionize industry, undermine family morals, enslave coloured races, and skilfully exterminate each other with poison gases. Some men of science do not altogether like these uses to which science is being put. In terror and dismay they shrink from the uncompromising pursuit of knowledge and try to find refuge in the superstitions of an earlier day. As Professor Hogben says:

The apologetic attitude so prevalent in science to-day is not a logical outcome of the introduction of new concepts. It is based upon the hope of reinstating traditional beliefs with which science was at one time in open conflict. This hope is not a by-product of scientific discovery. It has its roots in the social temper of the period. For half a decade the nations of Europe abandoned the exercise of reason in their relations with one another. Intellectual detachment was disloyalty. Criticism of traditional belief was treason. Philosophers and men of science bowed to the inexorable decree of herd suggestion. Compromise to traditional belief became the hall-mark of good citizenship. Contemporary philosophy has yet to find a way out of the intellectual discouragement which is the heritage of a World War.[6]

It is not by going backward that we shall find an issue from our troubles. No slothful relapses into infantile fantasies will direct the new power which men have derived from science into the right channels; nor will philosophic scepticism as to the foundations arrest the course of scientific technique in the world of affairs. Men need a faith which is robust and real, not timid and half-

[6] Hogben, op. cit., p. 28.

hearted. Science is in its essence nothing but the systematic pursuit of knowledge, and knowledge, whatever ill-uses bad men may make of it, is in its essence good. To lose faith in knowledge is to lose faith in the best of man's capacities;

and therefore I repeat unhesitatingly that the unyielding rationalist has a better faith and a more unbending optimism than any of the timid seekers after the childish comforts of a less adult age.

29. *Atom and Cosmos* *

HANS REICHENBACH (1891–1953)

Causality and Probability

The interpretation of quantum mechanics, as we have seen, arrives at a renunciation of the strict concept of law with which physics had previously operated in all its theories. The fundamental principle that law rules universally is also called the principle of causality; and now that quantum mechanics uses, in its place, the concept of a connection between events that is ruled merely by probability, it is the problem of causality and probability which must concern us. Since we have here a problem of fundamental importance, we will subject these questions to a more careful investigation; and with that investigation we will begin the last section of our presentation, in which those consequences of modern physics are to be treated, which are most important for the philosophy of nature.

The idea of the strict causal connection of all that happens has been regarded as a mark of modern natural science, and, in truth, it was the decisive conceptual trend by which alone modern

thought in this field became possible. To be sure, the Ancient World also knew the idea of a predetermination of future happening, and, in the concept of destiny, *fatum*, which dictates the decisive turn of every life without regard for mortals' wishes, the men of that day had created a formula for their conception of the course of events. And yet the classical concept of destiny is essentially different from the causal concept of modern physics; for, although the Greeks also recognised a law at work in all that occurs in nature, that law was of an entirely different type. The predetermination of an event was, for the Greek, a *connection of meanings;* it is the destiny of Oedipus that he shall some day kill his father—but as to the ways and means by which this event is to be realised, nothing is determined, and the struggle of man with fate consists precisely in his consciously escaping from one means of fulfilling his destiny only the more surely to fall victim to it in another, unforeseen manner. The predetermination characterising Western thought, however, is a connection without a superimposed meaning. The cause fixes one, and only one, effect; the present event B occurs because another defi-

---

* Chapter 18, with the permission of The Macmillan Co.

nite event A preceded it; it is, then, determined solely by the past, by a *cause*, and not by a future *purpose*. The rule of the causal law is blind, in contrast to the seeing government of destiny; according to the causal conception, it is strictly determined in advance at what place Oedipus is to slay his father, and, indeed, at what points on his sword the separate drops of blood will be spattered by this murder—whereas a slight difference in the initial conditions, such as the delay of Oedipus' birth by a half-hour, might conceivably lead to an entirely different career, quite free from patricide. Causality is a blind concatenation through causes; its symbol is the machine, which moves its piston only because a certain pressure of gas acts on it, not for the sake of any meaningful function.

How does natural science come to such a strange and yet far-reaching assertion? The observation of man and his spiritual fate, such as stood in the foreground of the ancients' field of vision, could not lead to it. It was the rigorous study of nature, the attempt to understand all natural happenings, uninfluenced by the colouring of human thought, and with the greatest possible faithfulness, which led to such a causal concept. Galileo is called the creator of modern natural science, not because he gathered a great wealth of new material for knowledge, but because he was the first to connect inductive questioning with the mathematical formula. When he counted the seconds required by falling balls, he recognised the concept of the mathematical function in nature, the strict "if . . . then," that decisive connection which sees a natural quantity B as fixed in its value *if* another natural quantity takes on its determinate value A. The whole development of natural science in the following centuries is a single triumph of this great idea. Newton's mechanics, tested in the exact

measurements of astronomy, the discovery of new forces of nature in electricity, or in unsuspected chemical energy, all furnished evidence for the fundamental idea of cause. The construction of machines of unexampled technical perfection, which was the practical result of such a science, was at the same time an ever-repeated confirmation of the underlying causal hypothesis, and no engineer would ever attempt to build or repair a machine, using any but a causal point of view. The French mathematician Laplace gave this determinism its classical formulation: if there were a perfect intelligence, its supreme spirit could comprise all happenings of the world in one formula, from which, by the insertion of definite numerical values for the variable time, the state of the world at any desired future, or, for that matter, past time could be calculated.

This conception is least obvious in biology, and attempts have ever again been made on the part of that science to justify laws of their own for living beings, and thus a deviation from strict causal connection. And yet biology was unable to keep away from the triumphal progress of the causal idea, above all since physiology taught the occurrence of chemical and electrical processes in the animal organism, and had explained such phenomena as digestion, respiration, the heart's activity—yes, even the activity of the brain—as physico-chemical processes. The mechanistic idea celebrated triumphs in biology; only in the most recent time were vitalistic hypotheses again able to become prominent, after the mechanistic method of explanation seemed to have reached its bounds in biology. Nevertheless, such objections availed nothing against the causal concept, so long as the idea of causation triumphed in physics, the most exact of all natural sciences, for the consideration could not be neglected that physiological processes must ultimately be reducible to mechanical motions of atoms and molecules, and that, accordingly, all the imperfection of causal explanations which we observe can be only provisional, and non-existent for the spirit imagined by Laplace, which can compute the motions of the milliards of atoms in advance, just as well as we do those of the planets.

It is only now, therefore, that we have to speak of a real crisis for the causal concept, when doubts as to the perfect determination of all natural happenings gain ground even in physics, and when, as we have shown, these doubts, precisely in the mechanics of the interior of the atom, have led to conscious renunciation of causal conceptions. And yet this step of quantum mechanics is not so new as it might seem; for anyone who has followed the development of physics in the last century could see that all conceptual work leading up to the new step had been done, and that this is only the last step in a consistent line of development.

We have met these approaches to a more general concept of law in the theory of heat, when we showed how the second law of thermodynamics, the law regarding the direction in which all events move, can be referred back to statistical considerations (Chapter 10). According to it, the mingling of hurrying molecules is directed by a smoothing-out tendency, which cannot be regarded as a causal law, but as a statistical one—that is, a law of probability. And this statistical law transformed one which had previously been regarded as strictly universal, the law of increase of entropy, into a mere law of averages. Here, already, the substitution of a probability law for a strict one had taken place.

Since the statistical justification of the second law of heat, therefore, the idea has repeatedly been expressed that it might possibly be the destiny of all exact laws of nature to be restricted to purely statistical validity, that the regularity which we see in large-scale nature cannot be brought into small dimensions, and turns out, on closer inspection, to be the average regularity of a molecular chaos. Opinions on this point have gone this way and that. Some, in close connection with Kant's philosophy, upheld the idea that such a conception is inadmissible, that there must under no circumstances be any doubt as to the validity of the strictly causal principle for small dimensions; while others pointed out that we do not have sufficiently exact knowledge of single molecular events, and that a reasoning by analogy from the large to the small is not necessarily conclusive. A third view, finally, held that the question could, on principle, not be answered; according to this view, nothing but direct observation of molecular processes could warrant a decision, whereas only an *inference* as to molecular events from macroscopic observations is really possible for us human beings.

For a time, however, the problem was not further followed from the physical side, as it was not immediately in the circle of the problems then interesting physics. It was investigations of a philosophical direction which next looked into this question; and, specifically, they proceeded from an analysis of the probability concept. The central significance of this concept had never been recognised in earlier epistemological discussion. It had been regarded as more or less parallel to human imperfection; that is, the merely probable correctness of prophecies as to nature was regarded as a result of human ignorance, which one endowed with perfect powers of learning could avoid. This point of view seemed to be especially well supported by the position of the probability concept in its original home, in games of chance. There has hardly ever been serious doubt that, for instance, the result of every throw of a die is absolutely fixed by its initial conditions, such as the original position of the die and the force used by the player. If, nevertheless, we forgo an exact advance computation and simply make the assumption that all sides of the die are *equally* likely to be uppermost, although only one side, in principle predetermined, will appear, that is, in substance, a subterfuge of human ignorance, necessitated by the inability of our degree of experimental accuracy to investigate the initial conditions exactly. The symbolical idea of Laplace, which we have already mentioned, grew precisely out of such conceptions. It is found in a work of his on the philosophy of the theory of probability; and Laplace wished thereby to express the opinion that a superhuman intelligence would not need the laws of probability, but would foretell the result of a game of chance, just as astronomers foretell the courses of the planets. This conception is named the subjective theory of probability; it leads to determinism, the doctrine that all which happens in nature follows flawless principles, and that all uncertainty of prophecy is occasioned by human weakness only.

The philosophical critics of the probability concept, on the other hand, held that a subjective theory can never prove the objective validity for reality of assumptions concerning probability, as that reality is expressed in the frequency laws of statistics. It is, in fact, not at all clear why, for instance, each face of a die should be uppermost about a hundred times out of six hundred throws, if the equal probability of the faces corresponds only to human ignorance; we cannot imagine that nature should pay such close attention to man's incapacity. This argument against the subjective theory of probability is conclusive, and an objective theory was therefore set up, which attempts to present the validity of laws of probability as an objective fact in the occurrences of nature, just as the validity of causal laws signified such a fact. According to the objective theory, the regularity of statistical processes, such as those of aggregates of molecules, means a fundamental trend in natural events, the understanding of whose laws is quite as much the task of natural science as is the understanding of causal laws. From this point of view it seems senseless to see anything merely provisional in the use of statistical laws; even the Laplacian superman—as the French mathematician Cournot remarked in the 'forties of the last century—would not renounce the use of statistical laws, but, on summing up the computations concerning the separate casts of the die, would still discover that, on the average, all sides appear with equal frequency.

Starting from such a view of the probability concept, it was possible to take the next step, uniting the concept of probability to that of cause; for both concepts, as we have pointed out, present objective realities. In fact, the two are firmly chained together, and it can even be shown that the causal principle would be an empty, useless assumption, if the principle of probability were not also there. It is not at all true that we ever find strict laws in nature. For all that we observe, each time, is that a law has been approximately fulfilled; a hurled stone, a flowing electrical current, a deflected ray of light, when exactly measured, will never show the course prescribed by the mathematical formula, but there will always be little deviations, so-called errors of observation, which may be decreased by better experimental devices, but can never be fully eliminated. How far, however, such errors influence the result of advance calculation can never be told *with certainty*. It can only be said that the errors will *very probably* occasion but a slight disturbance—but that is already a statement containing the concept of probability. Thus the idea of probability unavoidably enters the formulation of all laws of nature, if these laws are to be stated with complete conceptual rigour.

In daily life, too, the concept of probability finds much more far-reaching application than is generally believed. We fail to notice that it is implied in many statements, because the probability involved is very high and so can be treated practically as if it were absolute certainty. We may, for instance, rely on the figures in a railway guide, and so reckon that the train stands in the station at a certain moment; yet this is by no means sure, since any disturbances might work against the railway's punctuality. In such a case, indeed, we are slightly aware of the intrusion of probability, because, after all, every one is likely to have suffered some disappointment through the tardiness of a train. But, in principle, even those assertions which we hold to be much more certain involve probability—as when we believe that an iron bridge will hold us as we walk over it, or rely on the sun's rising the next day; even this cannot be prophesied with certainty, as there might, for example, be a cosmic catastrophe in the night, which would throw the earth off its course. It is especially in such cases that we are not troubled by the disturbing possibilities, as they are too improbable. But we have also learned to get along with much smaller probabilities. Thus a merchant knows that he can reckon on success in his business, at best, with some probability. He protects himself by undertaking as many different operations as possible in different directions; he then assumes that, at any rate, the projects will not all fail *at once,* and that he can therefore rely on some average gain. This procedure is very characteristic of our attitude toward problems involving probability. By passing to a large number of cases, we change the low probability of the single case into the high probability of average success. In this way we succeed in mastering probability; it is the same procedure as the scientist uses, when, for instance, he makes statements about the average motions of molecules in kinetic gas theory.

Now there is, to be sure, another way of bettering the probability of a prophecy than that of passing to greater numbers. When the meteorologist foretells the weather for the next day, he knows that his forecast can hope for correctness with but a certain probability. But he knows, too, that he can substantially improve the reliability of his forecast, if he investigates the state of the weather to-day more carefully, taking into account, it may be, not only the direction of the wind, but the distribution of atmospheric pressure over a considerable area, cloudiness, temperature, etc. That is, he betters his prophecy when he investigates the case in question with the greatest possible thoroughness—in other words, when he looks for as many factors of influence as he can, and takes them into account in his forecast. In much the same way the physicist improves his prediction of the course of a projectile when he considers, in addition to the initial speed, the resistance of the air, the influence of the earth's rotation, and so on; and the astronomer obeys the same fundamental principle, when, in order to foretell the position of a planet, he considers, not only the elements of the orbit of the satellite in question—the planet's velocity, the orbit's diameter, etc.—but also the perturbations from the force of attraction exerted by neighbouring planets. This is, in very essence, the procedure of exact research; one broadens his assumptions by the inclusion of ever more factors of influence, and thus gives greater and greater probability to the prediction.

Shall we be able to progress in this way for ever? Shall we, in the end, paying closest attention to all causes, succeed in changing probability into certainty? Presumably no one has ever said in earnest that we should ever *succeed* in this. We can, indeed, be quite well satisfied, if we can raise the probability to such a point, at least, that it means *practical* certainty. But are we, then, sure that the road is open even that far?

It was formerly the general belief that it was; and yet it must be considered an unanswered question whether such an unbounded improvement of precision will always be possible. For reflection shows that such a demand cannot necessarily be said to be justified. At bottom, we have here a question of a property of nature; it might well be that there is an absolute limit, short of certainty, to the increase of accuracy. In that case it would be impossible, by taking a greater number of factors into consideration, eventually to arrive at the making of certain predictions (or even predictions of approximate certainty).

This possibility, already foreseen in philosophical investigations at an earlier date,[1] must to-day be regarded as that case which is actually realised in nature. For the development which quantum mechanics has taken in Heisenberg's uncertainty principle corresponds exactly to this state of affairs. It is, according to Heisenberg, impossible to determine both place and speed of an electron at the same time with the maximum precision, and it is therefore impossible to compute the electron's future path with arbitrary exactness. Objective barriers are drawn to advance calculation. Objective barriers—that means that even the

---

[1] In this connection, see H. Reichenbach, "Das Kausalproblem in der Physik," *Die Naturwissenschaften*, Vol. 19, 1931, pp. 713, 716. [Cf. H. Reichenbach's more recent work, *The Philosophic Foundations of Quantum Mechanics*, 1945.]

Laplacian superman could not pass them, but would also have to be satisfied with a "probability." Nature is simply not completely determined. It is not to be compared to the precise functioning of a machine, for chance rules in small dimensions; and it is only in the large that the numberless separate atomic events combine in processes of such great probability that we can treat them in practice as certain.

Although, then, there is no perceptible change in our practical activity, the revolution in our theoretical knowledge is all the more profound. What happens is not predetermined in all details, as determinism, distorting world history into the mechanical performance of a clock movement, maintains; the course of all events is much more like a continual game of dice, so that each separate step corresponds to a new throw. The decision, as between a causal and a statistical view of the world, has fallen in favour of statistics. It cannot be said that it is a lack of knowledge which leads to this renunciation of strict causality; it is, on the contrary, a very positive knowledge, the mathematical and empirical relations concentrated in quantum mechanics, which has led to this decision.

Even though this conception means a radical break with the causal picture of the world which classical physics had constructed—that is, with that fundamental tendency in which we had found the contrast of modern natural science with the ancient concept of destiny—it cannot be said that, at one stroke, it solves all those riddles which the anti-causal conception of psychical and physiological happening has proposed; for men's ways of acting, which seem to have purpose and meaning, the government of action by the will, and the associated feeling of freedom—these are all questions which have by no means yet been answered by the reduction of world history to a game of chance. We believe, nevertheless, that the desired solution finds new possibilities in the framework of these ideas, and that, in the end, this solution will be discovered. It is of crucial importance that the solid barrier which determinism erects against every non-deterministic solution of the problem of life and freedom has fallen, that we can no longer speak of objective predetermination of the future, and that the concept of possibility and of becoming takes on an entirely new aspect when we no longer need regard it as an illusion due to human ignorance, as a mere substitute for the description of real and objectively existing facts, which are only subjectively withheld from us human beings.

And here, therefore, the development of modern physics is confronted by problems which have always been the subject of philosophical speculation, but of which it has hitherto been impossible to offer a notionally rigorous solution. Nevertheless, it is only by the philosophic consideration of these problems that a solution can be found. We do not believe, to be sure, that further results are to be won by holding fast to traditional methods of philosophic thought; the problems which have received more precise formulation at the hands of exact science demand essentially new methods of philosophical research. Such progress, however, can be made only by a philosophy which has ceased to depend on the traditional methods of philosophical exposition, but seeks its own paths, determined by the problems in question. It will be a new philosophy of nature, which, in closest contact with the investigations and concepts of modern natural science, and the formation of scientific concepts, once more develops the problem of knowledge from its very foundations.

30. *The Perspectives of Science and the Prospects of Men** *

ERNEST NAGEL (1901–   )

There are two modes in which human life is influenced by new developments in theoretical science. Since the beginnings of systematic inquiry in classical antiquity, advances in fundamental knowledge have prepared the way for a more effective practical mastery of the environment; and the technological in-

novations to which they frequently give rise—in agriculture, industry, medicine, or warfare—have produced radical transformations in traditional patterns of social living. This aspect of science is now a commonplace in the writings of modern historians and students of human affairs. It is certainly not neglected in recent popular literature on the wonders wrought by present-day inventions. Indeed, many distinguished scien-

* Reprinted from *Perspectives U.S.A.* (Spring, 1954) with the kind permission of the author and publishers.

tists with an attentive eye on the ultimate source of financial support for pure research are now stressing the practical fruits often gathered from investigations which initially do not promise such a harvest; and the utilitarian values of science undoubtedly loom large in the minds of those who today eventually foot the staggering costs of modern research. However, there is a second and less publicized way in which scientific developments affect men's lives: by challenging established beliefs about the cosmos and its parts, and inducing emendations in habitual modes of thought. Revisions of ancient creeds and alterations in intellectual habits are not exclusively the products of major theoretical revolutions like those of Newton and Darwin; they may also be called forth by relatively minor additions to knowledge like those associated with voyages of exploration and the study of ancient or primitive cultures. The flood of books and articles in our own day on the bearing of current scientific discoveries upon inherited conceptions of nature and man is visible testimony to this aspect of the impact of science on human life.

Although there are different channels through which scientific developments exert their influence, changes in knowledge eventually lead to a re-examination of the ideals which express man's basic aspirations, of the principles by which men evaluate their actions, and of the methods which men employ in deciding between alternative moral claims. Technological innovations of any magnitude often make it difficult, if not impossible, to continue customary modes of conduct; and they may produce fashions of living that are not congruous with, or are not envisaged by, traditional moral ideals. Moreover, though new theoretical and factual discoveries do not always introduce any overt changes in social practice, they may nevertheless become highly pertinent in the evaluation of

social policy and in the justification of moral attitudes. An ideal of human life which seems eminently reasonable on one set of factual assumptions may be utterly without cogency when viewed in the perspective of altered scientific conclusions. Accordingly, an integrated system of moral commitments can be disrupted by developments in science; and, individually as well as collectively, men are sometimes made distraught by felt incompatibilities between traditional moral standards and new advances in knowledge. Reflective men are thus perennially confronted with a threefold task of criticism: of clarifying the bearing of trends in scientific inquiry upon pervasive conceptions of man's place in nature; of making explicit the intellectual methods by which responsibly held beliefs are achieved; and of interpreting inherited beliefs and institutions in the light of current additions to knowledge—all this, in order to exhibit the enduring wisdom which may be embodied in them.

It has been the traditional office of philosophy, whether lay or professional, to contribute to this difficult task. Professional philosophers frequently engage in heated debate concerning the subject matter and the problems that are proper to their discipline. Although their conclusions are often in sharp disagreement with each other, the record of history leaves little room for doubt as to what in the main their ultimate concern has been. Indeed, even the recurrent disputes over the legitimate scope and method of philosophy illustrate the conception of philosophy as a critical commentary on science, and as a continuing interpretation of human experience in the perspective of fresh scientific achievements. It is certainly a striking fact that some of the most brilliant periods in the history of Western philosophy coincide with eras during which frontiers of knowledge were being pushed back vigorously. It is hardly an accident that the flowering of philosophic thought in Greek antiquity came on the heels of fundamental discoveries in mathematics and biology; that the influential speculative and critical philosophies of the seventeenth and eighteenth centuries were produced during the decades which saw the rise and consolidation of modern physical science; or that the ambitious philosophies of evolution in the nineteenth century were developed at a time when knowledge of the human past as well as of the history of other forms of organic life was being rapidly expanded. The adequacy of these various philosophies as systems of warranted truth is a matter of controversy, upon which general agreement is hardly likely in the foreseeable future. These systems, nevertheless, exhibit the historical role of philosophy as the examination of the significance of science for human weal and woe; and this role is easily discerned in the literature of contemporary philosophy as well. In a readily identifiable sense, all of philosophy has been, and continues to be, a critique of science. And while what is today commonly designated as the philosophy of science is the investigation of a loosely defined set of special problems, the boundaries of the philosophy of science are in fact the boundaries of philosophy itself.

For several decades, however, in Western Europe and America, philosophical reflection on science has been largely directed to logical and methodological issues generated both by the remarkable theoretical innovations of physical science and by new approaches in the study of human society. These developments have not only upset deeply rooted certainties concerning the structure of the physical universe and the behavior of the human individual; they have also compelled a re-examination of supposedly firm criteria of intelligibility and

the grounds of cognitive certitude. Euclidean geometry has been displaced from its age-old status as the only conceivable foundation for a comprehensive theory of nature. A system of chronometry has been introduced which is sharply at variance with customary notions of temporal order. Apparently cogent reasons have been found for curtailing the scope of regulative and constitutive principles, like those of causality and continuity, which have long been regarded as paradigms of absolute universality and necessity. Evidence has accumulated for conceptions concerning the springs of human action which are deeply disturbing to widely held assumptions about the basis of human rationality and responsible action. And comprehensive theoretical explanations of newly discovered phenomena have become current which, despite their enormous success in accounting for detailed facts, postulate an executive order of nature that seems alien to human experience and appears paradoxical even to expertly skilled scientists.

It is not altogether surprising that intellectual changes of the magnitude here only briefly indicated have found interpreters who see in the latest findings of science renewed grounds for comforting superstitions, or who defend in the very name of science itself creeds to which the use of a disciplined but free intelligence is basically hateful. If such interpretations seem plausible to many, this is partly because scientists have in the main failed to clarify for themselves as well as for others the actual content of their new theories and the rationale of their intellectual methods. Indeed, distinguished workers in the sciences have themselves sometimes supplied commentaries on current reorientations in scientific theory that are at best examples of uncontrolled fancy, and are frequently exercises in obscurantism.

This situation is not quite as anomalous as it may appear at first glance. To be sure, skill and understanding are at their best, as Santayana noted, when they adorn the same mind. Nor is there much doubt that perhaps the most illuminating analyses of scientific achievements and procedure have been made by philosophical-minded practicing scientists. What is loosely called "scientific method," however, is generally a habit of workmanship that skilled investigators possess, and not a codified set of principles which they explictly acknowledge. Those who are successfully engaged in specialized research usually show no serious interest in methodological analysis which does not contribute directly to the solution of specific research tasks. Their philosophy of science is often hardly more than the echo of philosophic ideas uncritically acquired during their early schooling. There is little agreement among scientific workers on the broad significance of their theories or on the logic of their procedure, despite their remarkable virtuosity in handling complex intellectual tools, and in striking contrast to the eventual unanimity which they achieve on solutions for specific technical problems. There are, indeed, no uniform standards of competent workmanship, whether among scientists or professional philosophers, which control the analysis of such matters. There is still lacking a generally adequate technique for unravelling the enormously complex maze of symbolism involved in the construction and the use of scientific theory.

The symbolic nature of scientific theory is certainly not a recent discovery. Nevertheless, the subtle and indirect ways in which theories function as schemata of representation have not been widely noted or appreciated until fairly recently. A century ago, it was common to think of a theory—even a theory in physics—as an inductive gen-eralization derived by abstraction from directly observed occurrences. A theory was assumed to be simply a compact description of regularities that obtain between phenomena. The successful development of theories which ostensibly postulate inherently unobservable entities and processes made evident the superficiality of this account. For a time the view then became prevalent that postulations of "unobservables" are nothing but convenient though fictional modes of speech. This amended version of the "simple description" notion of theory became incredible, however, when impressive experimental evidence was found for the "reality" of molecules, atoms, electrons, and the like. Many thinkers have therefore concluded that the fundamental theories of modern physics and chemistry are about an order of things and events that are existentially and causally prior to the things and events encountered in daily life.

The unobservable but basic entities of nature, however, ostensibly possess few if any of the traits that characterize the objects of familiar experience. Moreover, they seem in many respects to be incommensurably unlike the latter. The relation of the "world" of gross experience to the "world" disclosed by physics thus became an acute problem. Some writers resolved it by relegating one or the other of these "worlds" to a realm of metaphysical appearance. Others sought to overcome it by construing the postulated scientific objects in terms of the categories of human experience, and thereby clothing the unobservable entities of physics with properties analogous to those distinctive of the human organism. Still others solved it by postulating a progressive evolution or emergence of levels of being. But the proposed solutions raise more issues than they settle; and they are all based on the dubious assumption that each constituent part of a theory is the intellectual image of an identifiable item in the subject matter of inquiry. On this assumption a theory is therefore a description of some fixed realm of ultimate fact. But the assumption simply ignores the complex structure of theoretical symbolism. Those who make this assumption fail to appreciate the flexible uses of theoretical expressions, the variety of special meanings which are associated with them in different contexts of inquiry, the multiple regulative roles which theories play, or the different logical functions which grammatically similar statements may possess. These matters are more fully understood at present. Contemporary philosophy of science has succeeded in dispelling much of the mystery that is produced when the elliptic formulations of mathematical physics are construed in a myopically literal manner.

Indeed, much of the recent literature of the philosophy of science is a self-conscious attempt at articulating modes of symbolic signification, and a search for effective criteria of meaningful discourse. This search is often controlled by the therapeutic objective of eliminating pseudo-problems both within science proper and in the philosophic interpretations of science. In the pursuit of this objective, variants of Charles Peirce's "pragmatic maxim" for making our ideas clear have played a prominent role. According to that maxim, our conception of an object of thought consists entirely of the "practical" bearings which we suppose that object to have. The adoption of the maxim leads, on the one hand, to the rejection as spurious of many allegedly profound puzzles raised by commentators on science, and, on the other hand, to the detailed study of scientific formulations in terms of the concrete procedures and habits of usage that alone invest them with significance. Peirce himself noted, for example, that the term "force" in physics does not represent a "mysterious entity," as was commonly believed by many of his contemporaries. On the contrary, the term is completely understood when its role in the equations of physics is made explicit, and when the use in inquiry of those equations is indicated. It is therefore absurd to claim, as many eminent scientists have done, that while we may understand the effects of force we do not understand what force itself is. Many thinkers in Europe and America, in many instances without having been exposed to the influence of Peirce's writings, have adopted his maxim in a variety of forms. They have extended the type of analysis he proposed for the notion of force to a large number of other ideas in physics, biology, psychology, and social science. In consequence, fundamental contributions have been made not only to the clarification of specific theoretical concepts, but also to the understanding of the structure and operation of scientific symbolism in general.

It must be acknowledged, however, that oversimplified versions of the Peircean maxim have gained wide currency, and that injudicious use of them has frequently darkened counsel. Many contemporary writers have supposed that a criterion of meaning contains in capsule form the solutions for all mortal ills, and in consequence they have made grotesque claims for their approach to the analysis of scientific discourse. Other writers have espoused simple-minded tests of significance, and have shown themselves insensitive to the influence of context upon the meaning and function of statements. They have thereby been compelled to classify as species of "nonsense" nearly all statements of science. But in spite of the quantity of material, incompetent, trivial, and irrelevant, that has been published in consequence, there has been substantial achievement as well. In the hands of analysts competently familiar with the actual operations of scientific inquiry and with the role played in it by theoretical constructions, the Peircean maxim in some of its variant forms has undoubtedly been an instrument of genuine illumination.

It is difficult to exaggerate in this connection the far-reaching and salutary influence of the theory of relativity upon current philosophy of science. For the Einsteinian critique of classical mechanics called attention to the importance of construing scientific notions by way of the actual operations which control their range of application; and it made impressively clear that apparently significant statements often possess no physical content, precisely because crucial terms occurring in them are associated with no specified procedures of application. Einstein's analysis also made evident that the construction of a theory involves, among other things, a series of decisions between alternate modes of representing and organizing relevant features of a subject matter— for example, in the case of mechanics, decisions between alternate geometries and alternate chronometries. Such decisions are logically arbitrary, since they are not implied by experimental data; they can nevertheless be evaluated in the light of their effectiveness in systematizing fields of inquiry. Furthermore, the theory of relativity reveals unmistakably that when the range of application of a scientific symbol is enlarged, the symbol may undergo fundamental changes in meaning. This has been the history of such terms as "mass" and "energy" in physics, "species" and "image" in biology and psychology, and "class" and "property" in social science. Subtle analogies may control the process of enlarging the scope of application of a symbol. Nevertheless, it is in general a blunder to interpret the more inclusive use of an expression in terms of its initially more restricted meaning. It is this blunder which underlies much of the

alleged "unintelligibility" commonly attributed to modern physics. These methodological observations are, however, pertinent for the understanding not merely of a special physical theory but of all theoretical constructions. They have rendered valuable service to thinkers seeking to develop a generalized account of knowledge that is founded on the realities of scientific procedure and on the actual character of scientific explanation.

The classical conception of scientific knowledge was formed under the influence of demonstrative geometry as traditionally taught, and rests on three fundamental assumptions: Genuine scientific knowledge is demonstrative knowledge, and science seeks to "save the phenomena" by exhibiting the events and regularities of nature as consequences of universal truths. Secondly, since every demonstration must start from premises which are not themselves demonstrable, there must be transparently luminous universal truths which the intellect can grasp as self-evident. Thirdly, if the particulars of sense are to be truly explained, the basic premises of a science must be necessary truths, which are better known and more certain than anything explained by them. These assumptions have dominated scientific, philosophic, and popular thought since antiquity. For example, it was a widespread supposition a half-century ago that the axioms of Newtonian mechanics conform to the classical requirements for the first principles of a science. The discovery soon thereafter that the Newtonian system is not fully adequate to the facts therefore appeared to a number of commentators as a symptom of "the bankruptcy of science."

Many thinkers continue to demand of genuine knowledge the characteristics postulated by the classical ideal of science. The first requirement in that ideal undoubtedly does represent a permanent though partial objective of scientific research. But the remaining components in that ideal are not, and cannot be, achieved by the actual methods of any positive inquiry. Contemporary analyses of the kind previously mentioned have shown, for example, that a theory is never uniquely determined by any set of empirical data, however numerous and varied these may be. Alternate explanations are always possible in principle; and the supposition that a unique explanatory principle is embedded in the phenomena, and shines forth to the attentive intellect, is therefore radically mistaken. It follows that scientific research is not a passive beholding and codifying of self-evident structures in things. On the contrary, the construction of theories, like the construction of works of art, makes serious demands upon powers of imagination and invention. Scientists have repeatedly noted the "free creation of concepts" embodied in their theoretical foundations. As one of them has remarked, the work of Newton, Leverrier, Maxwell, and Hertz "was an expression of their personality just as surely as the work of Giotto, of Shakespeare, or of Bach." This does not mean that the scientist is a demiurge who creates the things he studies. It does mean that an explanatory theory is but one among several possible techniques for representing and analyzing systematically an indefinitely large set of specific processes. When a scientific theory is constructed in terms of its functions in inquiry, the supposition that the fundamental principles of a science can be established by appeals to self-evidence is thus not even plausible. Indeed, the traditional conception of the relation between a theory and the facts it explains must be partially reversed. A theory does make "intelligible" the occurrences of nature by indicating their interrelations. Nevertheless, the theory is itself "intelligible" not because of its self-luminous necessity and certainty, but because of the manner in which it analyzes and organizes the concrete facts of experience. In short, abstract theory and matters of observation mutually clarify each other. If it is a task of science to "save the phenomena" by making them intelligible in the light of a theory, it is equally its task to "save the abstracta" by making them intelligible in the light of the phenomena they coordinate. Maxwell's electro-magnetic theory, for example, explains a host of electrical, magnetic, and optical phenomena. But the content of the theory becomes clear only when it is understood how its equations are employed for directing specific inquiries and for interpreting matters of observation.

One important outcome of this altered view of scientific knowledge is a correspondingly altered conception of the grounds of scientific certitude. Neither the first principles of a science nor the formulations of concrete happenings are incorrigible. And if the findings of science are reliable, they are reliable neither because they follow from necessarily true basic premises nor because they are derivable from indubitable data of observation. What does support claims to warranted knowledge is the use of a general method (or logic) for establishing a particular claim. Inquiries into different subject matters employ different special techniques of investigation; but underlying them all is a common pattern of procedure for gathering, interpreting and evaluating evidence. A distinctive feature of this method is its doubly self-corrective character. No conclusion of an inquiry is exempt from the challenge of further inquiry, provoked perhaps by doubts raised because of new theoretical constructions or fresh experimental data. And every schema for evaluating the weight of evidence is subject to revision, if further analysis should reveal that the use of a given schema leads to conclusions which are too frequently undependable. The quest for certainty is perhaps an inherent aspect of the scientific enterprise. But current clarifications of the self-corrective method of science have made evident that scientific certitude cannot be equated with infallibility. The reliability of a scientific conclusion, it is now clear, is a function of the thoroughness with which it has been tested by methods that on repeated application yield conclusions in good agreement with observed fact. While any given claim to knowledge may be mistaken, some claims are better warranted than others; but the warrant itself ultimately derives from the character of the general policy which science adopts for evaluating all claims.

Considerations such as these have contributed to the formation of a naturalistic conception of human reason and scientific intelligence. Scientific knowledge does not depend on the possession of an esoteric capacity for grasping the necessary structure of some superior reality, nor does it require modes of warranting beliefs which are discontinuous with operations of thought, identifiable and effective in the ordinary affairs of human life. The achievements of science are the products of a cooperative social enterprise, which has refined and extended skills encountered in the meanest employments of the human intellect. The principles of human reason, far from representing the immutable traits of all possible being, are socially cultivated standards of competent intellectual workmanship. The life of reason as embodied in the community of scientific effort is thus a pattern of life that generates an autonomous yet controlling ideal. That ideal requires disciplined dedication without servitude to any ultimate authority, imposes responsibility for performance upon individual judg-

ment but demands responsiveness to the criticism of others, and calls for adherence to a tradition of workmanship without commitment to any system of dogma. To many commentators, the ideals realized in the enterprise of science are also the ideals which are indispensable to the successful operation of any society of free men. Many thinkers, indeed, like John Dewey in America, have based their hopes for the future of mankind upon the extension of the habits of scientific intelligence to every stratum of communal life and to every form of social organization.

Philosophers often suppose themselves to possess avenues to truth—truth which is not accessible to the empirically controlled analytic methods of the sciences. Certainly no shortage exists today of oracular metaphysical pronouncements on the spiritual foundations of the universe or on the ultimate nature and destiny of human effort. It is not difficult to perceive the reasons why, in a period of acute social tension such as ours, there should be large audiences for philosophies that thrive on obscurantism and which see the shape of things through a glass clouded by anguish and fear. To those who seek from philosophy assurance that life is worth living or that the universe is mindful of human aspirations, contemporary philosophy of science has on the whole nothing significant to say. On the other hand, it has had an unmistakable influence on the development of new approaches in Anglo-American psychology and social science; and it has made an impress on a substantial majority of Anglo-American philosophers, even when their chief concerns are only peripherally related to the analysis of science. A comparison of current philosophical writing in English-speaking countries with similar publications a half-century ago, reveals a greater responsiveness today to the requirements of clarity and cogency than was customary then. There is now a diminished tendency to fall back on *a priori* methods for settling issues that can be resolved, if they can be resolved at all, only by experimental trial and factual study. There is less reliance today on outmoded conceptions of scientific procedure in discussions on the theory of knowledge. There is a greater awareness at present of the dangers implicit in using debatable or half-digested conclusions of factual inquiry as foundation stones for comprehensive systems of political and ethical theory. And greater caution is now practiced when current findings about physical or biological processes are invoked to decide issues in moral and aesthetic analysis.

These are in the main negative achievements for which contemporary philosophy of science is in part responsible. But it can also be credited with an invaluable positive achievement, quite apart from its detailed contributions to the clarification of scientific procedures. For it has given vigorous support and expression to an attitude, at once critical and experimental, toward the perennial as well as the current issues of human life; and it has thereby been a champion of the central values of liberal civilization. The basis for a general outlook on the place of man in nature is supplied by detailed knowledge of the structure of things supplied by the special sciences— an outlook that contemporary philosophy of science has helped to articulate and defend. In the perspective of that outlook, the human creature is not an autonomous empire in the vast entanglement of events and forces constituting the human environment. Nevertheless, no antecedent limits can be set to the power of scientific reason to acquire theoretical mastery over natural and social processes. Every doctrine which pretends to set such limits contains within itself the seeds of intolerance and repression. Moreover, in the perspective of that scientifically grounded outlook, human aspirations are expressions of impulses and needs which, whether these be native or acquired, constitute the ultimate point of reference for every justifiable moral judgment. The adequacy of such aspirations must therefore be evaluated in terms of the structures of human capacities and the order of human preferences. Accordingly, though the forces of nature may one day extinguish the human scene, those forces do not define valid human ideals, and they do not provide the measure of human achievement. But an indispensable condition for the just definition and the realization of those ideals is the employment and extension of the method of intelligence embodied in the scientific enterprise. A judicious confidence in the power of reason to ennoble the human estate may seem shallow to an age in which, despite the dominant position in it of scientific technology, there is a growing and pervasive distrust of the operations of free intelligence. It may indeed be the case that the temper of mind essential to the exercise of such intelligence has no immediate social future. But the cultivation of that intellectual temper is a fundamental condition for every liberal civilization. By making manifest the nature of scientific reason and the grounds for a continued confidence in it, contemporary philosophy of science has been a servant of men's noblest and most relevant ideals.

SUGGESTED FURTHER READINGS
FOR CHAPTER FOUR

Archimedes, *On Method* (ed. Heiberg).
Aristotle, *Posterior Analytics; Parts of Animals; Metaphysics.*
Bacon, Francis, *The Advancement of Learning; The New Atlantis.*
Burtt, E. A., *Metaphysical Foundations of Modern Science.*
Butterfield, H., *The Origins of Modern Science.*
Cassirer, Ernst, *Substance and Function.*
Cohen, M. R., *Reason and Nature; Studies in the Philosophy of Science.*
Darwin, Charles, *The Origin of Species; Descent of Man.*
Duhem, P., *The Aim and Structure of Physical Theory.*
Feigl and Brodbeck, *Readings in the Philosophy of Science.*
Frank, Ph., *Modern Science and Its Philosophy.*
Galileo, *Sidereal Messenger; Dialogue on the Great World Systems.*
Lewis, C. I., *Mind and the World Order; Analysis of Knowledge and Valuation.*
Mach, Ernst, *Historical Development of the Science of Mechanics.*
Peirce, Charles S., *Collected Papers,* 7 volumes.
Pledge, H. T., *Science Since 1500.*
Poincaré, H., *Foundations of Science.*
Russell, B., *Human Knowledge: Its Scope and Limits.*
Von Mises, R., *Positivism.*
Whewell, W., *Philosophy of the Inductive Sciences.*
Whitehead, A. N., *Science and the Modern World.*
Wiener, Philip P. (ed.), *Readings in Philosophy of Science.*

Chapter Five

THEORY OF KNOWLEDGE

INTRODUCTION

THE reader who has come this far has probably begun to wonder, considering the many different points of view on each subject, whether anything in philosophy can pass muster as genuine knowledge, not to be contradicted by some philosopher. To take this matter up would require a discussion of the nature of philosophy, a subject we have reserved for the final chapter. It is pertinent at this point, however, to remark that this puzzlement or wonder is a good sign, since, if followed by reflection and analysis, it can become the generating force of a philosophical inquiry. In fact, it is this very bewilderment over the many tongues and diverse opinions of man that has prompted him to study the nature of human knowledge—how it arises and how it can be grounded.

We all have a natural desire for knowledge, which is attested by our interest in what is perceived by our senses. Not content, however, with enjoying the sights and sounds that come to us without any effort on our part, we instinctively strive, by co-ordinating them, to locate their origin in material things—as when we hear the faint drone of a motor, we turn to look for a speck in the sky which we identify as a plane. Then we may be interested in tracing a causal chain and in anticipating the future; where did the plane come from, and what is its mission? In a similar way men have studied eclipses, growth, disease, and so on. Thus there gradually developed the sciences of astronomy, biology, medicine, and the others. Success in the scientific enterprise is rewarded by understanding, which may serve practical purposes, but is also, by the satisfaction it brings, its own reward. And failure, when recognized as such, can be a stimulus to search for hidden causes and to construct subtler explanations. The difficulties encountered in achieving knowledge of natural phenomena were not only a stimulus to the discovery of new scientific techniques. They were also the starting point of an inquiry into the nature of knowledge and how it differs from error. In fact, if nature had not proved baffling and man's grasp limited, the theory of knowledge might never have arisen. For it is the discovery of something apparently inexplicable and the desire to override error in human understanding that gave birth to this branch of philosophy. With error the inquirer into nature is brought up short; and because he wishes to avoid it, he is enticed to wander off on a side road, inquiring first into the sources of human error and then whether sense-perception or memory can give us genuine knowledge—free from the danger of error. Before long he is likely to find himself in the heart of the philosophic forest considering the question: Is any reliable knowledge of nature possible?

Whoever entertains this question, provided it is prompted by real doubt, or answers it in the negative, has joined the camp of the skeptic. There he will be in the company of many famous philosophers, though most of them remain for only a short visit. Descartes, as we have seen (see the selection 3, Chap. One), adopts universal doubt as a methodological device to help him rid his mind of illusions, prejudices, and the false notions taught him at school. His doubt, however, is only provisional. What he wants to show is that there are items of knowledge so indubitable that they can resist the most radical skepticism. In his theory of knowledge Descartes is anything but skeptical. Once he proves to his own satisfaction that God exists, he casts away doubt, affirming his readiness to believe anything which seems true to him, since he is convinced that God would not deceive him.

While Descartes, who begins his philosophy by sweeping the slate clean and resolving to admit nothing about which the least doubt can be raised, ends by demonstrating an unbounded faith in the power of the human mind to discover the nature of the world, George Berkeley, who proclaims his opposition to the skeptics, aims to convince us that no matter how hard we try to "conceive the existence of external bodies, we are all the while only contemplating our own ideas."

Berkeley begins by attacking certain basic assumptions which had been taken for granted by scientists and philosophers for centuries. Among these was the view that we can perceive the existence of material bodies outside and independent of the mind by means of images or mental representations which are more or less faithful copies of the qualities of these bodies. This theory of representative perception (sometimes called "the copy theory of knowledge") was coupled with a distinction between qualities like extension and mobility which inhere in things (the primary or physical qualities), and the qualities like color, sound, taste, and so on, which are not in the objects themselves, but are effects produced by them on the mind (the secondary or sense-qualities).[1]

John Locke accepted this view though it presents insuperable problems for his theory of knowledge. This theory contains the two following assumptions:

(1) that the mind can directly perceive only its own contents, which are variously called images, impressions, ideas; and

(2) that these ideas are distinct from one another.

The question that arises is: How can we know that our ideas truly represent the properties of existing things, since we can never perceive the things themselves, but only our own ideas of them? Locke struggled with this difficulty, but confessed he had no solution. He believed that our innate feeling of certainty was a sufficient guarantee of the validity of natural knowledge. As he himself puts it:

The notice we have by our senses, of the existence of things without us, though it be not altogether so certain as our intuitive knowledge, or the deductions of our reason employed

---

[1] It is interesting to note that the primary qualities were those which were amenable to the processes of measurement; the secondary qualities were thought to be incapable of measurement, and were regarded as subjective.

about the clear abstract ideas of our own minds; yet it is an assurance that deserves the name of knowledge. If we persuade ourselves that our faculties act and inform us right, concerning the existence of those objects that affect them, it cannot pass for an ill-grounded confidence; for I think nobody can, in earnest, be so skeptical, as to be uncertain of the existence of those things which he sees and feels.

To the two epistemological premises which Locke assumed, Berkeley and Hume added a third, namely:

(3) that the existence of things "out there" which react on one another as well as on our mind can be accepted only if it can be validly inferred from the first two premises. In this respect they were more influenced than was Locke by the Cartesian method of doubt and quest for certainty. For both Berkeley and Hume the mind is encased in a framework of its own sensations and ideas from which it vainly endeavors to escape. Berkeley embraces this skeptical doctrine enthusiastically and with remarkable consistency. Hume, on the contrary, does so regretfully and haltingly. At times his own arguments fail to convince him, but he sees no way of answering them.

Berkeley and Hume undermine the confidence which Locke felt in the validity of our knowledge of nature—Berkeley concluding that there is nothing in the universe but minds, or spirits, and Hume that our knowledge of nature is restricted to a succession of disconnected events. Hume holds that the notion of an order of nature in which events are necessarily connected with other events is an illusion engendered by a mental habit. The British philosophers have a reputation for being hard-headed men of common sense, but those three epistemological premises (p. 287) had so thoroughly infected their theory of knowledge with the germ of skepticism that the dictates of common sense were all but submerged.

To common sense it seems obvious that the "objects of knowledge" are chairs, tables, rivers and oceans, animals and other men, and not more or less reasonable facsimiles of the same. As Bertrand Russell has remarked, only philosophers with a long training in absurdity could have succeeded in believing otherwise. However, it is one thing to point out where the epistemology of Locke, Berkeley, and Hume does violence to common sense. It is quite another to construct an alternative theory of knowledge, based on common sense, which gives an adequate account of the nature of knowledge in such diverse fields as mathematics, natural science, and history. Many philosophers who have made such an attempt found in the end that they had to depart more or less from common-sense notions. Perhaps the "principles of common sense" are not as clear, when analyzed, as they appear to be. Perhaps they cannot be integrated into a consistent philosophy. In that case, instead of demanding that a theory of knowledge satisfy certain vague "principles of common sense," we should make it serve the purpose of clarifying and helping to reformulate those principles.

So far we have been discussing one facet of the theory of knowledge—its relation to skepticism. Closely connected with questions concerning the significance and reliability of our knowledge of nature is an issue prominent in the history of philosophy, which has been the subject of a long debate between empiricists, who adhere to the views of Locke, Berkeley, and Hume, and rationalists who follow Descartes and Kant. Is all knowledge derived from experience as the former maintain, or are there truths known *a priori,* such as the law of causality [2] and the principle of induction,[3] which are presupposed for the significant interpretation of experience, as the latter insist?

Immanuel Kant, who writes that Hume's skeptical criticism of knowledge awakened him from his dogmatic slumbers, is credited by some with having successfully answered Hume's arguments. Kant's "answer" is in his *Critique of Pure Reason,* a work which has profoundly influenced modern philosophy. The gist of Kant's epistemology (theory of knowledge) is that all knowledge is compounded out of two factors: (1) what is given in experience, and (2) what is contributed by the interpretation of the mind. The "given in experience" is formless and chaotic and can enter into knowledge only by being transformed and ordered by the faculties of the mind. Far from being a blank tablet on which experience writes (Locke's view), the mind, for Kant, is the agency whose activity makes cognitive experience possible. Knowledge is not received by a passive intellect, but must be constructed by the mind, which impresses on the given, its own notions of *space* and *time* (called by Kant forms of intuition) and its own conceptions of *substance, quantity, quality, relation, causality* (categories of the understanding). These forms of intuition and categories of the understanding Kant believed were common possessions of all human minds. Reality can be known only as it is screened through the forms and categories of the mind. It then becomes what Kant calls a *phenomenon.* The "thing-in-itself," something which has an independent existence, is not and cannot be an object of knowledge; it is unknowable. For to know it, the mind would first have to impart to it its own forms of organization, thus transforming it. For this reason, in the opinion of some philosophers, the shadow of doubt which Hume cast over our knowledge of the natural world is not only not removed by Kant, but is converted by him into a curtain effectively placed between the external reality and the mind, thereby making knowledge a delusion. Philosophers have also questioned Kant's right to assume the existence of fixed and permanent faculties in all human minds; for this is an empirical question which Kant is deciding by an *ad hoc* hypothesis, a hypothesis which has not received the needed confirmation by psychologists and philosophers outside the Kantian schools. But interpreters of Kant are legion and they are far from unanimous in their reading and evaluation of the master's position. There is no doubt that the active, dominant role in knowledge which Kant assigned to the mind proved to be a needed and welcome change from the Humean conception of the mind as a discontinuous series of inert, momentary perceptions, no one of which contains within itself any inkling of a past or a future. The many post-

---

[2] The law of causality, which is a favorite example of an *a priori* law, is difficult to state briefly and precisely; it has usually been taken to mean that every event has a cause and the same cause always has the same effect. See footnote, p. 3.

[3] The principle of induction states that the repeated association of a group of things, events, or properties in the past affords a ground for believing that they will be so ordered in the future; and that the more often such an association of things has been observed, the stronger is the ground for inferring that they are universally connected in that way. Hume's skepticism is based on his attempt to undermine the law of causality and the principle of induction. See, for example, p. 302 ff.

Kantian and neo-Kantian movements which took their inspiration from Kant's philosophy, even while departing from it in many respects, are, in themselves, evidence enough of the suggestive and stimulating character of his thought.

In contemporary philosophy the emphasis in the theory of knowledge has been shifted and many new refinements have been introduced, but the problems discussed are, in the main, variations on the old themes rather than new problems. More attention is being paid today than formerly to the rôle of language in knowledge, and there has been a revival of interest in semantics and the science of semiotic—the study of the nature of signs and of their relations to what is signified by them.[4] A fundamental change which markedly affects the tenor of recent philosophy has occurred in the conception of the goal of knowledge. Certainty in the Cartesian sense, thought to be the aim of knowledge when science was in its infancy, is now for the most part [5] regarded as a will o' the wisp. This, as we shall see, is particularly evident in the philosophy of George Santayana.

In introducing his system of philosophy to his readers, Santayana writes that his philosophy is "no phase of any current movement"; yet it bears the stamp of contemporary trends and shows the influence of previous philosophers. He conceives of his system of philosophy as the natural outcome of a detached survey of the realm of eternal essences and the obvious facts of existence. This is his meaning, perhaps, when he writes:

In the past or in the future, my language or my borrowed knowledge would have been different, but under whatever sky I had been born, since it is the same sky, I should have had the same philosophy.

But if the personal and historical factors have no part in the creation of a philosophy one wonders why Santayana's philosophy did not come to flower among the ancient Greeks or in Oriental civilization. Be that as it may, the student of philosophy will soon discover that every philosopher, ancient or modern, Platonist or Kantian, idealist or naturalist, whatever his persuasion and wherever he has lived, has believed, as Santayana believes, that his philosophy "rests on public experience" and is "justified by the facts before every man's eyes." What none of them satisfactorily explains is how these inescapable facts could have escaped the other philosophers.

Santayana has attempted to recapture and reformulate the common-sense view of the world. Those who hold such a view suffered many a rude shock, as we have seen, from the psychologizing philosophy of the British empiricists. Santayana proceeds by an explicit denial of the first and third premises (p. 287) which led to Hume's skeptical conclusions. The immediate data of experience which Berkeley called "the objects of knowledge" are, for Santayana, not objects of knowledge at all, but what he calls "essences." Essences, however, are not restricted to what is present to the mind in sensation, but embrace all objects of possible contemplation,

---

[4] The interest in semiotic and the abandonment of the Cartesian quest for certainty are traceable, at least in America, to the influence of Charles Peirce (see Selection 5 and 26). Semantics and the general theory of signs were studied with great care by the medieval philosophers.

[5] Exceptions are Bergson and Maritain. Their views are presented in Chapters One and Nine, respectively.

whether fanciful or analytic, aesthetic or religious, scientific or speculative. The cloudy images of a dreamer and the perspicuous conceptions of the mathematician are alike essences. They are not abstractions from things, nor do they reside in the mind. They can, however, be revealed to the mind in the process of "intuition." This intuition, it should be noted, is not a substitute for knowledge or a higher form of knowledge.[6] It is not knowledge at all. It cannot err or be challenged, since it posits no existence and asserts no fact. Essences, for Santayana, do not exist.

They may, however, become signs to an intelligent observer of some thing or event which is inferred to exist at some place or time. This inference, which may be perception, memory, or anticipation, is an act of knowledge. And since it involves a passage from what is given to something beyond which is presumed to exist, it is fallible. Santayana calls it "animal faith." The kinship of Santayana's conception of knowledge as animal faith, with Hume's view that our knowledge of causal relations is the projection into nature of a habit of the human mind, is apparent.

Santayana finds much less difficulty than Descartes in proving the existence of material things. Their existence, he holds, is proclaimed to us at every turn by the shocks they produce on our animal body. But here the skeptic rears his head. This knowledge of existence is only an act of faith and may be a mere illusion.

It is instructive to compare Santayana's skepticism with Descartes'. Both begin their system of philosophy with doubts concerning the validity of ordinary knowledge. But whereas Descartes finds a way, or thinks he does, of overcoming those doubts, Santayana never rescues our knowledge of existence from the limbo of uncertainty. For Descartes, universal doubt is instrumental, a prelude to an ultimate objective, embraced temporarily in the search for certain knowledge and then discarded as a scaffolding after the house is built. In Santayana also, doubt is instrumental, rather than integral and fundamental as it is in Hume; though it withers whatever it touches, including all of existence, at the same time it opens the way to the realm of essence, a beautiful castle in the air where the weary traveler can find surcease from the pain, boredom, and disappointment of animal life. Santayana carries skepticism to its utmost limits. Fortunately it has limits. It is only a part of himself, his intelligence, that entertains doubts, and since these doubts can affect only existence, he finds them impotent to disturb the placid enjoyment of essences which is native to another part of himself, intuition. Though the skeptic may prove conclusively that certain knowledge is an illusion, certainty is still attainable as intuition of essences, and knowledge is still possible as an act of animal faith. Does Santayana succeed in recovering the common-sense philosophy? Is there such a philosophy? These questions are left to the reader.

Although Descartes resolved to doubt everything and to scrutinize all beliefs, no matter how widely accepted, before admitting them as true,[7] there are some beliefs which it never occurred to him to doubt. For example, he did not doubt that there is some agency responsible for reasoning, remembering, imagining, doubting. And he did not doubt that if there is thinking, which is undeniable, then there must be a

---

[6] As it is in Bergson. Cf. Chapter One.

[7] See Selection 3, p. 23.

thinking thing; else, what could be doing the thinking? Descartes calls this thinking thing a *substance,* which means that he believed it existed as a distinct thing and not as a dependent part of a larger whole.

But then the question arises as to how this thinking thing could act on the body or be affected by it. Since Descartes tries to describe the body's changes as if they were part of a mechanical system, while the mind belongs to a totally different, spiritual realm, the contemporary British philosopher, Gilbert Ryle (Selection 34) has labeled Descartes' view "the theory of the ghost in the machine." We have long realized that the body is very far from being a machine. And Ryle thinks it is about time we got rid of the ghost.

D. J. B.

31. *Of the Principles of Human Knowledge*

GEORGE BERKELEY (1685–1753)

1. It is evident to any one who takes a survey of the *objects of human knowledge,* that they are either *ideas* actually imprinted on the senses; or else such as are perceived by attending to the passions and operations of the mind; or lastly, *ideas* formed by help of memory and imagination—either compounding, dividing, or barely representing those originally perceived in the aforesaid ways. By sight I have the ideas of light and colours, with their several degrees and variations. By touch I perceive hard and soft, heat and cold, motion and resistance; and of all these more and less either as to quantity or degree. Smelling furnishes me with odours; the palate with tastes; and hearing conveys sounds to the mind in all their variety of tone and composition.

And as several of these are observed to accompany each other, they come to be marked by one name, and so to be reputed as one *thing.* Thus, for example, a certain colour, taste, smell, figure and consistence having been observed to go together, are accounted one distinct thing, signified by the name apple; other collections of ideas constitute a stone, a tree, a book, and the like sensible things; which as they are pleasing or disagreeable excite the passions of love, hatred, joy, grief, and so forth.

2. But, besides all that endless variety of ideas or objects of knowledge, there is likewise Something which knows or perceives them; and exercises divers operations, as willing, imagining, remembering, about them. This perceiving, active being is what I call *mind, spirit, soul,* or *myself.* By which words I do not denote any one of my ideas, but a thing entirely distinct from them, wherein they exist, or, which is the same thing,

whereby they are perceived; for the existence of an idea consists in being perceived.

3. That neither our thoughts, nor passions, nor ideas formed by the imagination, exist without the mind is what everybody will allow. And to me it seems no less evident that the various sensations or ideas imprinted on the Sense, however blended or combined together (that is, whatever objects they compose), cannot exist otherwise than in a mind perceiving them. I think an intuitive knowledge may be obtained of this, by any one that shall attend to what is meant by the term *exist* when applied to sensible things. The table I write on I say exists; that is, I see and feel it: and if I were out of my study I should say it existed; meaning thereby that if I was in my study I might perceive it, or that some other spirit actually does perceive it. There was an odour, that is, it was smelt; there was a sound, that is, it was heard; a colour or figure, and it was perceived by sight or touch. This is all that I can understand by these and the like expressions. For as to what is said of the *absolute* existence of unthinking things, without any relation to their being perceived, that is to me perfectly unintelligible. Their *esse* is *percipi;* nor is it possible they should have any existence out of the minds or thinking things which perceive them.

4. It is indeed an opinion strangely prevailing amongst men, that houses, mountains, rivers, and in a word all sensible objects, have an existence, natural or real, distinct from their being perceived by the understanding. But, with how great an assurance and acquiescence soever this Principle may be entertained in the world, yet whoever shall find in his heart to call it in question may, if I mistake not, perceive it to involve a manifest contradiction. For, what are the forementioned objects but the things we perceive by sense? and what do we perceive besides our own ideas or sensations? and is it not plainly repugnant that any one of these, or any combination of them, should exist unperceived?

5. If we thoroughly examine this tenet it will, perhaps, be found at bottom to depend on the doctrine of *abstract ideas.* For can there be a nicer strain of abstraction than to distinguish the existence of sensible objects from their being perceived, so as to conceive them existing unperceived? Light and colours, heat and cold, extension and figures—in a word the things we see and feel—what are they but so many sensations, notions, ideas, or impressions on the sense? and is it possible to separate, even in thought, any of these from perception? For my part, I might as easily divide a thing from itself. I may, indeed, divide in my thoughts, or conceive apart from each other, those things which perhaps I never perceived by sense so divided. Thus, I imagine the trunk of a human body without the limbs, or conceive the smell of a rose without thinking on the rose itself. So far, I will not deny, I can abstract; if that may properly be called *abstraction* which extends only to the conceiving separately such objects as it is possible may really exist or be actually perceived asunder. But my conceiving or imagining power does not extend beyond the possibility of real existence or perception. Hence, as it is impossible for me to see or feel anything without an actual sensation of that thing, so is it impossible for me to conceive in my thoughts any sensible thing or object distinct from the sensation or perception of it. (In truth, the object and the sensation are the same thing, and cannot therefore be abstracted from each other.)

6. Some truths there are so near and obvious to the mind that a man need only open his eyes to see them. Such I take this important one to be, viz. that

all the choir of heaven and furniture of the earth, in a word all those bodies which compose the mighty frame of the world, have not any subsistence without a mind; that their *being* is to be perceived or known; that consequently so long as they are not actually perceived by me, or do not exist in my mind, or that of any other created spirit, they must either have no existence at all, or else subsist in the mind of some Eternal Spirit: it being perfectly unintelligible, and involving all the absurdity of abstraction, to attribute to any single part of them an existence independent of a spirit. (To be convinced of which, the reader need only reflect, and try to separate in his own thoughts the *being* of a sensible thing from its *being perceived*.)

7. From what has been said it is evident there is not any other Substance than *Spirit,* or that which perceives. But, for the fuller proof of this point, let it be considered the sensible qualities are colour, figure, motion, smell, taste, and such like, that is, the ideas perceived by sense. Now, for an idea to exist in an unperceiving thing is a manifest contradiction; for to have an idea is all one as to perceive: that therefore wherein colour, figure, and the like qualities exist must perceive them. Hence it is clear there can be no unthinking substance or *substratum* of those ideas.

8. But, say you, though the ideas themselves do not exist without the mind, yet there may be things like them, whereof they are copies or resemblances; which things exist without the mind, in an unthinking substance. I answer, an idea can be like nothing but an idea; a colour or figure can be like nothing but another colour or figure. If we look but never so little into our thoughts, we shall find it impossible for us to conceive a likeness except only between our ideas. Again, I ask whether those supposed *originals,* or external things, of which our ideas are the pictures or representations, be themselves perceivable or no? If they are, then *they* are ideas, and we have gained our point: but if you say they are not, I appeal to any one whether it be sense to assert a colour is like something which is invisible; hard or soft, like something which is intangible; and so of the rest.

9. Some there are who make a distinction betwixt *primary* and *secondary* qualities. By the former they mean extension, figure, motion, rest, solidity or impenetrability, and number; by the latter they denote all other sensible qualities, as colours, sounds, tastes, and so forth. The ideas we have of these last they acknowledge not to be the resemblances of anything existing without the mind, or unperceived; but they will have our ideas of the *primary qualities* to be patterns or images of things which exist without the mind, in an unthinking substance which they call Matter. By Matter, therefore, we are to understand an inert, senseless substance, in which extension, figure, and motion do actually subsist. But it is evident, from what we have already shown, that extension, figure, and motion are only ideas existing in the mind, and that an idea can be like nothing but another idea; and that consequently neither they nor their archetypes can exist in an unperceiving substance. Hence, it is plain that the very notion of what is called *Matter,* of *corporeal substance,* involves a contradiction in it. . . .

18. But, though it were possible that solid, figured, moveable substances may exist without the mind, corresponding to the ideas we have of bodies, yet how is it possible for us to know this? Either we must know it by Sense or by Reason. As for our senses, by them we have the knowledge only of our sensations, ideas, or those things that are immediately perceived by sense, call them what you will: but they do not inform us that things exist without the mind, or unper-

ceived, like to those which are perceived. This the materialists themselves acknowledge. It remains therefore that if we have any knowledge at all of external things, it must be by reason inferring their existence from what is immediately perceived by sense. But [I do not see] what reason can induce us to believe the existence of bodies without the mind, from what we perceive, since the very patrons of Matter themselves do not pretend there is any necessary connexion betwixt them and our ideas? I say it is granted on all hands (and what happens in dreams, frensies, and the like, puts it beyond dispute) that it is possible we might be affected with all the ideas we have now, though no bodies existed without resembling them. Hence it is evident the supposition of external bodies is not necessary for the producing our ideas; since it is granted they are produced sometimes, and might possibly be produced always, in the same order we see them in at present, without their concurrence.

19. But, though we might possibly have all our sensations without them, yet perhaps it may be thought easier to conceive and explain the manner of their production, by supposing external bodies in their likeness rather than otherwise; and so it might be at least probable there are such things as bodies that excite their ideas in our minds. But neither can this be said. For, though we give the materialists their external bodies, they by their own confession are never the nearer knowing how our ideas are produced; since they own themselves unable to comprehend in what manner body can act upon spirit, or how it is possible it should imprint any idea in the mind. Hence it is evident the production of ideas or sensations in our minds, can be no reason why we should suppose Matter or corporeal substances; since that is acknowledged to remain equally inexplicable with or without this supposition. If therefore it were possible for bodies to exist without the mind, yet to hold they do so must needs be a very precarious opinion; since it is to suppose, without any reason at all, that God has created innumerable beings that are entirely useless, and serve to no manner of purpose.

20. In short, if there were external bodies, it is impossible we should ever come to know it; and if there were not, we might have the very same reasons to think there were that we have now. Suppose—what no one can deny possible —an intelligence, without the help of external bodies, to be affected with the same train of sensations or ideas that you are, imprinted in the same order and with like vividness in his mind. I ask whether that intelligence hath not all the reason to believe the existence of Corporeal Substances, represented by his ideas, and exciting them in his mind, that you can possibly have for believing the same thing? Of this there can be no question. Which one consideration were enough to make any reasonable person suspect the strength of whatever arguments he may think himself to have, for the existence of bodies without the mind. . . .

23. But, say you, surely there is nothing easier than for me to imagine trees, for instance, in a park, or books existing in a closet, and nobody by to perceive them. I answer, you may so, there is no difficulty in it. But what is all this, I beseech you, more than framing in your mind certain ideas which you call *books* and *trees,* and at the same time omitting to frame the idea of any one that may perceive them? But do not you yourself perceive or think of them all the while? This therefore is nothing to the purpose: it only shews you have the power of imagining, or forming ideas in your mind; but it does not shew that you can conceive it possible the objects of your thought may exist without the mind. To

make out this, it is necessary that you conceive them existing unconceived or unthought of; which is a manifest repugnancy. When we do our utmost to conceive the existence of external bodies, we are all the while only contemplating our own ideas. But the mind, taking no notice of itself, is deluded to think it can and does conceive bodies existing unthought of, or without the mind, though at the same time they are apprehended by, or exist in, itself. A little attention will discover to any one the truth and evidence of what is here said, and make it unnecessary to insist on any other proofs against the existence of *material substance*. . . .

33. The ideas imprinted on the Senses by the Author of nature are called *real things:* and those excited in the imagination, being less regular, vivid, and constant, are more properly termed *ideas* or *images of* things, which they copy and represent. But then our *sensations,* be they never so vivid and distinct, are nevertheless ideas: that is, they exist in the mind, or are perceived by it, as truly as the ideas of its own framing. The ideas of Sense are allowed to have more reality in them, that is, to be more strong, orderly, and coherent than the creatures of the mind; but this is no argument that they exist without the mind. They are also less dependent on the spirit or thinking substance which perceives them, in that they are excited by the will of another and more powerful Spirit: yet still they are *ideas:* and certainly no idea, whether faint or strong, can exist otherwise than in a mind perceiving it.

34. Before we proceed any farther it is necessary we spend some time in answering Objections which may probably be made against the Principles we have hitherto laid down. In doing of which, if I seem too prolix to those of quick apprehensions, I desire I may be excused, since all men do not equally apprehend things of this nature; and I am willing to be understood by every one.

First, then, it will be objected that by the foregoing principles all that is real and substantial in nature is banished out of the world, and instead thereof a chimerical scheme of *ideas* takes place. All things that exist exist only in the mind; that is, they are purely notional. What therefore becomes of the sun, moon, and stars? What must we think of houses, rivers, mountains, trees, stones; nay, even of our own bodies? Are all these but so many chimeras and illusions on the fancy? To all which, and whatever else of the same sort may be objected, I answer, that by the Principles premised we are not deprived of any one thing in nature. Whatever we see, feel, hear, or any wise conceive or understand, remains as secure as ever, and is as real as ever. There is a *rerum natura,* and the distinction between realities and chimeras retains its full force. . .

35. I do not argue against the existence of any one thing that we can apprehend, either by sense, or reflection. That the things I see with my eyes and touch with my hands do exist, really exist, I make not the least question. The only thing whose existence we deny is that which *philosophers* call Matter or corporeal substance. And in doing of this there is no damage done to the rest of mankind, who, I dare say, will never miss it. The Atheist indeed will want the colour of an empty name to support his impiety; and the Philosophers may possibly find they have lost a great handle for trifling and disputation. (But that is all the harm that I can see done.)

36. If any man thinks this detracts from the existence or reality of things, he is very far from understanding what hath been premised in the plainest terms I could think of. Take here an abstract of what has been said:—There are spiritual substances, minds, or human souls, which will or excite ideas in themselves

at pleasure; but these are faint, weak, and unsteady in respect of others they perceive by sense: which, being impressed upon them according to certain rules or laws of nature, speak themselves the effects of a Mind more powerful and wise than human spirits. These latter are said to have *more reality* in them than the former;—by which is meant that they are more affecting, orderly, and distinct, and that they are not fictions of the mind perceiving them. And in this sense the sun that I see by day is the real sun, and that which I imagine by night is the idea of the former. In the sense here given of *reality,* it is evident that every vegetable, star, mineral, and in general each part of the mundane system, is as much a *real being* by our principles as by any other. Whether others mean anything by the term *reality* different from what I do, I entreat them to look into their own thoughts and see.

37. It will be urged that thus much at least is true, to wit, that we take away all *corporeal substances.* To this my answer is, that if the word *substance* be taken in the vulgar sense, for a *combination* of sensible qualities, such as extension, solidity, weight, and the like—this we cannot be accused of taking away: but if it be taken in a philosophic sense, for the support of accidents or qualities without the mind—then indeed I acknowledge that we take it away, if one may be said to take away that which never had any existence, not even in the imagination.

38. But after all, say you, it sounds very harsh to say we eat and drink ideas, and are clothed with ideas. I acknowledge it does so—the word *idea* not being used in common discourse to signify the several combinations of sensible qualities which are called *things;* and it is certain that any expression which varies from the familiar use of language will seem harsh and ridiculous. But this doth not concern the truth of the proposition, which in other words is no more than to say, we are fed and clothed with those things which we perceive immediately by our senses. The hardness or softness, the colour, taste, warmth, figure, and such-like qualities, which combined together constitute the several sorts of victuals and apparel, have been shewn to exist only in the mind that perceives them: and this is all that is meant by calling them *ideas;* which word, if it was as ordinarily used as *thing,* would sound no harsher nor more ridiculous than it. I am not for disputing about the propriety, but the truth of the expression. If therefore you agree with me that we eat and drink and are clad with the immediate objects of sense, which cannot exist unperceived or without the mind, I shall readily grant it is more proper or conformable to custom that they should be called *things* rather than *ideas.*

39. If it be demanded why I make use of the word *idea,* and do not rather in compliance with custom call them *things;* I answer, I do it for two reasons: —First, because the term *thing,* in contradistinction to *idea,* is generally supposed to denote somewhat existing without the mind: Secondly, because *thing* hath a more comprehensive signification than *idea,* including spirits, or thinking things, as well as ideas. Since therefore the objects of sense exist only in the mind, and are withal thoughtless and inactive, I chose to mark them by the word *idea;* which implies those properties.

40. But, say what we can, some one perhaps may be apt to reply, he will still believe his senses, and never suffer any arguments, how plausible soever, to prevail over the certainty of them. Be it so; assert the evidence of sense as high as you please, we are willing to do the same. That what I see, hear, and feel doth exist, that is to say, is perceived by

me, I no more doubt than I do of my own being. But I do not see how the testimony of sense can be alleged as a proof for the existence of anything which is *not* perceived by sense. We are not for having any man turn sceptic and disbelieve his senses; on the contrary, we give them all the stress and assurance imaginable; nor are there any principles more opposite to Scepticism than those we have laid down, as shall be hereafter clearly shewn.

41. *Secondly*, it will be objected that there is a great difference betwixt real fire for instance, and the idea of fire, betwixt dreaming or imagining oneself burnt, and actually being so. (If you suspect it to be only the idea of fire which you see, do but put your hand into it and you will be convinced with a witness.) This and the like may be urged in opposition to our tenets. To all which the answer is evident from what hath been already said; and I shall only add in this place, that if real fire be very different from the idea of fire, so also is the real pain that it occasions very different from the idea of the same pain, and yet nobody will pretend that real pain either is, or can possibly be, in an unperceiving thing, or without the mind, any more than its idea.

32. An Enquiry Concerning Human Understanding*

DAVID HUME (1711–1776)

SECTION IV

Sceptical Doubts Concerning the Operations of the Understanding

PART I

All the objects of human reason or enquiry may naturally be divided into two kinds, to wit, *Relations of Ideas,* and *Matters of Fact.* Of the first kind are the sciences of Geometry, Algebra, and Arithmetic; and in short, every affirmation which is either intuitively or demonstratively certain. *That the square of the hypothenuse is equal to the square of the two sides,* is a proposition which expresses a relation between these fig-ures. *That three times five is equal to the half of thirty,* expresses a relation between these numbers. Propositions of this kind are discoverable by the mere operation of thought, without dependence on what is anywhere existent in the universe. Though there never were a circle or triangle in nature, the truths demonstrated by Euclid would for ever retain their certainty and evidence.

Matters of fact, which are the second objects of human reason, are not ascertained in the same manner; nor is our evidence of their truth, however great, of a like nature with the foregoing. The contrary of every matter of fact is still possible; because it can never imply a contradiction, and is conceived by the mind with the same facility and distinct·

---

* Section IV and part of Section V.

ness, as if ever so conformable to reality. *That the sun will not rise tomorrow* is no less intelligible a proposition, and implies no more contradiction than the affirmation, *that it will rise*. We should in vain, therefore, attempt to demonstrate its falsehood. Were it demonstratively false, it would imply a contradiction and could never be distinctly conceived by the mind.

It may, therefore, be a subject worthy of curiosity, to enquire what is the nature of that evidence which assures us of any real existence and matter of fact, beyond the present testimony of our senses, or the records of our memory. This part of philosophy, it is observable, has been little cultivated, either by the ancients or moderns; and therefore our doubts and errors, in the prosecution of so important an enquiry, may be the more excusable; while we march through such difficult paths without any guide or direction. They may even prove useful, by exciting curiosity, and destroying that implicit faith and security, which is the bane of all reasoning and free enquiry. The discovery of defects in the common philosophy, if any such there be, will not, I presume, be a discouragement, but rather an incitement, as is usual, to attempt something more full and satisfactory than has yet been proposed to the public.

All reasonings concerning matter of fact seem to be founded on the relation of *Cause and Effect*. By means of that relation alone we can go beyond the evidence of our memory and senses. If you were to ask a man, why he believes any matter of fact, which is absent; for instance, that his friend is in the country, or in France; he would give you a reason; and this reason would be some other fact; as a letter received from him, or the knowledge of his former resolutions and promises. A man finding a watch or any other machine in a desert island, would conclude that there had once been men on that island. All our reasonings concerning fact are of the same nature. And here it is constantly supposed that there is a connexion between the present fact and that which is inferred from it. Were there nothing to bind them together, the inference would be entirely precarious. The hearing of an articulate voice and rational discourse in the dark assures us of the presence of some person: Why? because these are the effects of the human make and fabric, and closely connected with it. If we anatomize all the other reasonings of this nature, we shall find that they are founded on the relation of cause and effect, and that this relation is either near or remote, direct or collateral. Heat and light are collateral effects of fire, and the one effect may justly be inferred from the other.

If we would satisfy ourselves, therefore, concerning the nature of that evidence, which assures us of matters of fact, we must enquire how we arrive at the knowledge of cause and effect.

I shall venture to affirm, as a general proposition, which admits of no exception, that the knowledge of this relation is not, in any instance, attained by reasonings *a priori;* but arises entirely from experience, when we find that any particular objects are constantly conjoined with each other. Let an object be presented to a man of ever so strong natural reason and abilities; if that object be entirely new to him, he will not be able, by the most accurate examination of its sensible qualities, to discover any of its causes or effects. Adam, though his rational faculties be supposed, at the very first, entirely perfect, could not have inferred from the fluidity and transparency of water that it would suffocate him, or from the light and warmth of fire that it would consume him. No object ever discovers, by the qualities which appear to the senses, either the causes which produced it, or the effects which will arise from it; nor can our reason, unassisted by experience, ever draw any inference concerning real existence and matter of fact.

This proposition, *that causes and effects are discoverable, not by reason but by experience,* will readily be admitted with regard to such objects, as we remember to have once been altogether unknown to us; since we must be conscious of the utter inability, which we then lay under, of foretelling what would arise from them. Present two smooth pieces of marble to a man who has no tincture of natural philosophy; he will never discover that they will adhere together in such a manner as to require great force to separate them in a direct line, while they make so small a resistance to a lateral pressure. Such events, as bear little analogy to the common course of nature, are also readily confessed to be known only by experience; nor does any man imagine that the explosion of gunpowder, or the attraction of a loadstone, could ever be discovered by arguments *a priori.* In like manner, when an effect is supposed to depend upon an intricate machinery or secret structure of parts, we make no difficulty in attributing all our knowledge of it to experience. Who will assert that he can give the ultimate reason, why milk or bread is proper nourishment for a man, not for a lion or a tiger?

But the same truth may not appear, at first sight, to have the same evidence with regard to events, which have become familiar to us from our first appearance in the world, which bear a close analogy to the whole course of nature, and which are supposed to depend on the simple qualities of objects, without any secret structure of parts. We are apt to imagine that we could discover these effects by the mere operation of our reason, without experience. We fancy, that were we brought on a sudden

into this world, we could at first have inferred that one Billiard-ball would communicate motion to another upon impulse; and that we needed not to have waited for the event, in order to pronounce with certainty concerning it. Such is the influence of custom, that, where it is strongest, it not only covers our natural ignorance, but even conceals itself, and seems not to take place, merely because it is found in the highest degree.

But to convince us that all the laws of nature, and all the operations of bodies without exception, are known only by experience, the following reflections may, perhaps, suffice. Were any object presented to us, and were we required to pronounce concerning the effect, which will result from it, without consulting past observation; after what manner, I beseech you, must the mind proceed in this operation? It must invent or imagine some event, which it ascribes to the object as its effect; and it is plain that this invention must be entirely arbitrary. The mind can never possibly find the effect in the supposed cause, by the most accurate scrutiny and examination. For the effect is totally different from the cause, and consequently can never be discovered in it. Motion in the second Billiard-ball is a quite distinct event from motion in the first; nor is there anything in the one to suggest the smallest hint of the other. A stone or piece of metal raised into the air, and left without any support, immediately falls: but to consider the matter *a priori,* is there anything we discover in this situation which can beget the idea of a downward, rather than an upward, or any other motion, in the stone or metal?

And as the first imagination or invention of a particular effect, in all natural operations, is arbitrary, where we consult not experience; so must we also esteem the supposed tie or connexion between the cause and effect, which binds them together, and renders it impossible that any other effect could result from the operation of that cause. When I see, for instance, a Billiard-ball moving in a straight line towards another; even suppose motion in the second ball should by accident be suggested to me, as the result of their contact or impulse; may I not conceive, that a hundred different events might as well follow from that cause? May not both these balls remain at absolute rest? May not the first ball return in a straight line, or leap off from the second in any line or direction? All these suppositions are consistent and conceivable. Why then should we give preference to one, which is no more consistent or conceivable than the rest? All our reasonings *a priori* will never be able to show us any foundation for this preference.

In a word, then, every effect is a distinct event from its cause. It could not, therefore, be discovered in the cause, and the first invention or conception of it, *a priori,* must be entirely arbitrary. And even after it is suggested, the conjunction of it with the cause must appear equally arbitrary; since there are always many other effects, which, to reason, must seem fully as consistent and natural. In vain, therefore, should we pretend to determine any single event, or infer any cause or effect, without the assistance of observation and experience.

Hence we may discover the reason why no philosopher, who is rational and modest, has ever pretended to assign the ultimate cause of any natural operation, or to show distinctly the action of that power, which produces any single effect in the universe. It is confessed, that the utmost effort of human reason is to reduce the principles, productive of natural phenomena, to a greater simplicity, and to resolve the many particular effects into a few general causes, by

means of reasonings from analogy, experience, and observation. But as to the causes of these general causes, we should in vain attempt their discovery; nor shall we ever be able to satisfy ourselves, by any particular explication of them. These ultimate springs and principles are totally shut up from human curiosity and enquiry. Elasticity, gravity, cohesion of parts, communication of motion by impulse; these are probably the ultimate causes and principles which we shall ever discover in nature; and we may esteem ourselves sufficiently happy, if, by accurate enquiry and reasoning, we can trace up the particular phenomena to, or near to, these general principles. The most perfect philosophy of the natural kind only staves off our ignorance a little longer: as perhaps the most perfect philosophy of the moral or metaphysical kind serves only to discover larger portions of it. Thus the observation of human blindness and weakness is the result of all philosophy, and meets us at every turn, in spite of our endeavours to elude or avoid it.

Nor is geometry, when taken into the assistance of natural philosophy, ever able to remedy this defect, or lead us into the knowledge of ultimate causes, by all that accuracy of reasoning for which it is so 'justly celebrated. Every part of mixed mathematics proceeds upon the supposition that certain laws are established by nature in her operations; and abstract reasonings are employed, either to assist experience in the discovery of these laws, or to determine their influence in particular instances, where it depends upon any precise degree of distance and quantity. Thus, it is a law of motion, discovered by experience, that the moment or force of any body in motion is in the compound ratio or proportion of its solid contents and its velocity; and consequently, that a small force may remove the greatest obstacle or raise the greatest weight, if, by any contrivance or machinery, we can increase the velocity of that force, so as to make it an overmatch for its antagonist. Geometry assists us in the application of this law, by giving us the just dimensions of all the parts and figures which can enter into any species of machine; but still the discovery of the law itself is owing merely to experience, and all the abstract reasonings in the world could never lead us one step towards the knowledge of it. When we reason *a priori,* and consider merely any object or cause, as it appears to the mind, independent of all observation, it never could suggest to us the notion of any distinct object, such as its effect; much less, show us the inseparable and inviolable connexion between them. A man must be very sagacious who could discover by reasoning that crystal is the effect of heat, and ice of cold, without being previously acquainted with the operation of these qualities.

PART II

But we have not yet attained any tolerable satisfaction with regard to the question first proposed. Each solution still gives rise to a new question as difficult as the foregoing, and leads us on to farther enquiries. When it is asked, *What is the nature of all our reasonings concerning matter of fact?* the proper answer seems to be, that they are founded on the relation of cause and effect. When again it is asked, *What is the foundation of all our reasonings and conclusions concerning that relation?* it may be replied in one word, Experience. But if we still carry on our sifting humour, and ask, *What is the foundation of all conclusions from experience?* this implies a new question, which may be of more difficult solution and explication. Philosophers, that give themselves airs of superior wisdom and sufficiency, have a hard task when they encounter persons of inquisitive dispositions, who push them from every corner to which they retreat, and who are sure at last to bring them to some dangerous dilemma. The best expedient to prevent this confusion, is to be modest in our pretensions; and even to discover the difficulty ourselves before it is objected to us. By this means, we may make a kind of merit of our very ignorance.

I shall content myself, in this section, with an easy task, and shall pretend only to give a negative answer to the question here proposed. I say then, that, even after we have experience of the operations of cause and effect, our conclusions from that experience are *not* founded on reasoning, or any process of the understanding. This answer we must endeavour both to explain and to defend.

It must certainly be allowed, that nature has kept us at a great distance from all her secrets, and has afforded us only the knowledge of a few superficial qualities of objects; while she conceals from us those powers and principles on which the influence of those objects entirely depends. Our senses inform us of the colour, weight, and consistence of bread; but neither sense nor reason can ever inform us of those qualities which fit it for the nourishment and support of a human body. Sight or feeling conveys an idea of the actual motion of bodies; but as to that wonderful force or power, which would carry on a moving body for ever in a continued change of place, and which bodies never lose but by communicating it to others; of this we cannot form the most distant conception. But notwithstanding this ignorance of natural powers and principles, we always presume, when we see like sensible qualities, that they have like secret powers, and expect that effects, similar to those which we have experienced, will follow from them. If a body of like colour and consistence with that bread, which we have formerly eaten, be presented to us, we make no scruple of repeating the experiment, and foresee, with certainty, like nourishment and support. Now this is a process of the mind or thought, of which I would willingly know the foundation. It is allowed on all hands that there is no known connexion between the sensible qualities and the secret powers; and consequently, that the mind is not led to form such a conclusion concerning their constant and regular conjunction, by anything which it knows of their nature. As to past *Experience*, it can be allowed to give *direct* and *certain* information of those precise objects only, and that precise period of time, which fell under its cognizance: but why this experience should be extended to future times, and to other objects, which for aught we know, may be only in appearance similar; this is the main question on which I would insist. The bread, which I formerly ate, nourished me; that is, a body of such sensible qualities was, at that time, endued with such secret powers: but does it follow, that other bread must also nourish me at another time, and that like sensible qualities must always be attended with like secret powers? The consequence seems nowise necessary. At least, it must be acknowledged that there is here a consequence drawn by the mind; that there is a certain step taken; a process of thought, and an inference, which wants to be explained. These two propositions are far from being the same, *I have found that such an object has always been attended with such an effect,* and *I foresee, that other objects, which are, in appearance, similar, will be attended with similar effects.* I shall allow, if you please, that the one proposition may justly be inferred from the other: I know, in fact, that it always is inferred. But if you insist that the inference is made by a chain of reasoning, I desire you to produce that reasoning. The connexion between these propositions is not intuitive. There is required a medium, which may enable the mind to draw such an inference, if indeed it be drawn by reasoning and argument. What that medium is, I must confess, passes my comprehension; and it is incumbent on those to produce it, who assert that it really exists, and is the origin of all our conclusions concerning matter of fact.

This negative argument must certainly, in process of time, become altogether convincing, if many penetrating and able philosophers shall turn their enquiries this way and no one be ever able to discover any connecting proposition or intermediate step, which supports the understanding in this conclusion. But as the question is yet new, every reader may not trust so far to his own penetration, as to conclude, because an argument escapes his enquiry, that therefore it does not really exist. For this reason it may be requisite to venture upon a more difficult task; and enumerating all the branches of human knowledge, endeavour to show that none of them can afford such an argument.

All reasonings may be divided into two kinds, namely, demonstrative reasoning, or that concerning relations of ideas, and moral reasoning, or that concerning matter of fact and existence. That there are no demonstrative arguments in the case seems evident; since it implies no contradiction that the course of nature may change, and that an object, seemingly like those which we have experienced, may be attended with different or contrary effects. May I not clearly and distinctly conceive that a body, falling from the clouds, and which, in all other respects, resembles snow, has yet the taste of salt or feeling of fire? Is there any more intelligible proposition than to affirm, that all the trees will flourish in December and January, and decay in May and June? Now whatever is intelligible, and can be distinctly conceived, implies no contradiction, and can never be proved false by any demonstrative argument or abstract reasoning *a priori*.

If we be, therefore, engaged by arguments to put trust in past experience, and make it the standard of our future judgment, these arguments must be probable only, or such as regard matter of fact and real existence, according to the division above mentioned. But that there is no argument of this kind, must appear, if our explication of that species of reasoning be admitted as solid and satisfactory. We have said that all arguments concerning existence are founded on the relation of cause and effect; that our knowledge of that relation is derived entirely from experience; and that all our experimental conclusions proceed upon the supposition that the future will be conformable to the past. To endeavour, therefore, the proof of this last supposition by probable arguments, or arguments regarding existence, must be evidently going in a circle, and taking that for granted, which is the very point in question.

In reality, all arguments from experience are founded on the similarity which we discover among natural objects, and by which we are induced to expect effects similar to those which we have found to follow from such objects. And though none but a fool or madman will ever pretend to dispute the authority of experience, or to reject that great guide of human life, it may surely be allowed a philosopher to have so much curiosity at least as to examine the principle of human nature, which gives this mighty authority to experience, and makes us draw advantage from that similarity which nature has placed among different objects. From causes which appear *similar* we expect similar effects. This is the sum of all our experimental conclusions. Now it seems evident that, if this conclusion were formed by reason, it would be as perfect at first, and upon one instance, as after ever so long a course of experience. But the case is far otherwise. Nothing so like as eggs; yet no one, on account of this appearing similarity, expects the same taste and relish in all of them. It is only after a long course of uniform experiments in any kind, that we attain a firm reliance and security with regard to a particular event. Now where is that process of reasoning which, from one instance, draws a conclusion, so different from that which it infers from a hundred instances that are nowise different from that single one? This question I propose as much for the sake of information, as with an intention of raising difficulties. I cannot find, I cannot imagine any such reasoning. But I keep my mind still open to instruction, if any one will vouchsafe to bestow it on me.

Should it be said that, from a number of uniform experiments, we *infer* a connexion between the sensible qualities and the secret powers; this, I must confess, seems the same difficulty, couched in different terms. The question still recurs, on what process of argument this *inference* is founded? Where is the medium, the interposing ideas, which join propositions so very wide of each other? It is confessed that the colour, consistence, and other sensible qualities of bread appear not, of themselves, to have any connexion with the secret powers of nourishment and support. For otherwise we could infer these secret powers from the first appearance of these sensible qualities, without the aid of experience; contrary to the sentiment of all philosophers, and contrary to plain matter of fact. Here, then, is our natural state of ignorance with regard to the powers and influence of all objects. How is this remedied by experience? It only shows us a number of uniform effects, resulting from certain objects, and teaches us that those particular objects, at that particular time, were endowed with such powers and forces. When a new object, endowed with similar sensible qualities, is produced, we expect similar powers and forces, and look for a like effect. From a body of like colour and consistence with bread we expect like nourishment and support. But this surely is a step or progress of the mind, which wants to be explained. When a man says, *I have found, in all past instances, such sensible qualities conjoined with such secret powers:* And when he says, *Similar sensible qualities will always be conjoined with similar secret powers,* he is not guilty of a tautology, nor are these propositions in any respect the same. You say that the one proposition is an inference from the other. But you must confess that the inference is not intuitive; neither is it demonstrative: Of what nature is it, then? To say it is experimental, is begging the question. For all inferences from experience suppose, as their foundation, that the future will resemble the past, and that similar powers will be conjoined with similar sensible qualities. If there be any suspicion that the course of nature may change, and that the past may be no rule for the future, all experience becomes useless, and can give rise to no inference or conclusion. It is impossible, therefore, that any arguments from experience can prove this resemblance of the past to the future; since all these arguments are founded on the supposition of that resemblance. Let the course of things be allowed hitherto ever so regular; that alone, without some new argument or inference, proves not that, for the future, it will continue so. In vain do you pretend to have learned the nature of bodies from your past experience. Their secret nature, and consequently all their effects and influence, may change, without any change in their sensible qualities. This happens sometimes, and with regard to some objects: Why may it not happen always, and with regard to all objects? What logic, what process of argument

secures you against this supposition? My practice, you say, refutes my doubts. But you mistake the purport of my question. As an agent, I am quite satisfied in the point; but as a philosopher, who has some share of curiosity, I will not say scepticism, I want to learn the foundation of this inference. No reading, no enquiry has yet been able to remove my difficulty, or give me satisfaction in a matter of such importance. Can I do better than propose the difficulty to the public, even though, perhaps, I have small hopes of obtaining a solution? We shall at least, by this means, be sensible of our ignorance, if we do not augment our knowledge.

I must confess that a man is guilty of unpardonable arrogance who concludes, because an argument has escaped his own investigation, that therefore it does not really exist. I must also confess that, though all the learned, for several ages, should have employed themselves in fruitless search upon any subject, it may still, perhaps, be rash to conclude positively that the subject must, therefore, pass all human comprehension. Even though we examine all the sources of our knowledge, and conclude them unfit for such a subject, there may still remain a suspicion, that the enumeration is not complete, or the examination not accurate. But with regard to the present subject, there are some considerations which seem to remove all this accusation of arrogance or suspicion of mistake.

It is certain that the most ignorant and stupid peasants—nay infants, nay even brute beasts—improve by experience, and learn the qualities of natural objects, by observing the effects which result from them. When a child has felt the sensation of pain from touching the flame of a candle, he will be careful not to put his hand near any candle; but will expect a similar effect from a cause which is similar in its sensible qualities and appearance. If you assert, therefore, that the understanding of the child is led into this conclusion by any process of argument or ratiocination, I may justly require you to produce that argument; nor have you any pretence to refuse so equitable a demand. You cannot say that the argument is abstruse, and may possibly escape your enquiry; since you confess that it is obvious to the capacity of a mere infant. If you hesitate, therefore, a moment, or if, after reflection, you produce any intricate or profound argument, you, in a manner, give up the question, and confess that it is not reasoning which engages us to suppose the past resembling the future, and to expect similar effects from causes which are, to appearance, similar. This is the proposition which I intended to enforce in the present section. If I be right, I pretend not to have made any mighty discovery. And if I be wrong, I must acknowledge myself to be indeed a very backward scholar; since I cannot now discover an argument which, it seems, was perfectly familiar to me long before I was out of my cradle.

SECTION V

Sceptical Solution of These Doubts

PART I

The passion for philosophy, like that for religion, seems liable to this inconvenience, that, though it aims at the correction of our manners, and extirpation of our vices, it may only serve, by imprudent management, to foster a predominant inclination, and push the mind, with more determined resolution, towards that side which already *draws* too much, by the bias and propensity of the natural temper. It is certain that, while we aspire to the magnanimous firmness of the philosophic sage,

and endeavour to confine our pleasures altogether within our own minds, we may, at last, render our philosophy like that of Epictetus, and other *Stoics*, only a more refined system of selfishness, and reason ourselves out of all virtue as well as social enjoyment. While we study with attention the vanity of human life, and turn all our thoughts towards the empty and transitory nature of riches and honours, we are, perhaps, all the while flattering our natural indolence, which, hating the bustle of the world, and drudgery of business, seeks a pretence of reason to give itself a full and uncontrolled indulgence. There is, however, one species of philosophy which seems little liable to this inconvenience, and that because it strikes in with no disorderly passion of the human mind, nor can mingle itself with any natural affection or propensity; and that is the Academic or Sceptical philosophy. The academics always talk of doubt and suspense of judgment, of danger in hasty determinations, of confining to very narrow bounds the enquiries of the understanding, and of renouncing all speculations which lie not within the limits of common life and practice. Nothing, therefore, can be more contrary than such a philosophy to the supine indolence of the mind, its rash arrogance, its lofty pretensions, and its superstitious credulity. Every passion is mortified by it, except the love of truth; and that passion never is, nor can be, carried to too high a degree. It is surprising, therefore, that this philosophy, which, in almost every instance, must be harmless and innocent, should be the subject of so much groundless reproach and obloquy. But, perhaps, the very circumstance which renders it so innocent is what chiefly exposes it to the public hatred and resentment. By flattering no irregular passion, it gains few partizans: By opposing so many vices and follies, it raises to itself abundance of enemies, who stigmatize it as libertine, profane, and irreligious.

Nor need we fear that this philosophy, while it endeavours to limit our enquiries to common life, should ever undermine the reasonings of common life, and carry its doubts so far as to destroy all action, as well as speculation. Nature will always maintain her rights, and prevail in the end over any abstract reasoning whatsoever. Though we should conclude, for instance, as in the foregoing section, that, in all reasonings from experience, there is a step taken by the mind which is not supported by any argument or process of the understanding; there is no danger that these reasonings, on which almost all knowledge depends, will ever be affected by such a discovery. If the mind be not engaged by argument to make this step, it must be induced by some other principle of equal weight and authority; and that principle will preserve its influence as long as human nature remains the same. What that principle is may well be worth the pains of enquiry.

Suppose a person, though endowed with the strongest faculties of reason and reflection, to be brought on a sudden into this world; he would, indeed, immediately observe a continual succession of objects, and one event following another; but he would not be able to discover anything farther. He would not, at first, by any reasoning, be able to reach the idea of cause and effect; since the particular powers, by which all natural operations are performed, never appear to the senses; nor is it reasonable to conclude, merely because one event, in one instance, precedes another, that therefore the one is the cause, the other the effect. Their conjunction may be arbitrary and casual. There may be no reason to infer the existence of one from the appearance of the other. And in a word, such a person, without more experience, could never employ his conjec-

ture or reasoning concerning any matter of fact, or be assured of anything beyond what was immediately present to his memory and senses.

Suppose, again, that he has acquired more experience, and has lived so long in the world as to have observed familiar objects or events to be constantly conjoined together; what is the consequence of this experience? He immediately infers the existence of one object from the appearance of the other. Yet he has not, by all his experience, acquired any idea or knowledge of the secret power by which the one object produces the other; nor is it, by any process of reasoning, he is engaged to draw this inference. But still he finds himself determined to draw it: And though he should be convinced that his understanding has no part in the operation, he would nevertheless continue in the same course of thinking. There is some other principle which determines him to form such a conclusion.

This principle is Custom or Habit. For wherever the repetition of any particular act or operation produces a propensity to renew the same act or operation, without being impelled by any reasoning or process of the understanding, we always say, that this propensity is the effect of *Custom*. By employing that word, we pretend not to have given the ultimate reason of such a propensity. We only point out a principle of human nature, which is universally acknowledged, and which is well known by its effects. Perhaps we can push our enquiries no farther, or pretend to give the cause of this cause; but must rest contented with it as the ultimate principle, which we can assign, of all our conclusions from experience. It is sufficient satisfaction, that we can go so far, without repining at the narrowness of our faculties because they will carry us no farther. And it is certain we here advance a very intelligible proposition at least, if not a true one, when we assert that, after the constant conjunction of two objects—heat and flame, for instance, weight and solidity—we are determined by custom alone to expect the one from the appearance of the other. This hypothesis seems even the only one which explains the difficulty, why we draw, from a thousand instances, an inference which we are not able to draw from one instance, that is, in no respect, different from them. Reason is incapable of any such variation. The conclusions which it draws from considering one circle are the same which it would form upon surveying all the circles in the universe. But no man, having seen only one body move after being impelled by another, could infer that every other body will move after a like impulse. All inferences from experience, therefore, are effects of custom, not of reasoning.

Custom, then, is the great guide of human life. It is that principle alone which renders our experience useful to us, and makes us expect, for the future, a similar train of events with those which have appeared in the past. Without the influence of custom, we should be entirely ignorant of every matter of fact beyond what is immediately present to the memory and senses. We should never know how to adjust means to ends, or to employ our natural powers in the production of any effect. There would be an end at once of all action, as well as of the chief part of speculation.

But here it may be proper to remark, that though our conclusions from experience carry us beyond our memory and senses, and assure us of matters of fact which happened in the most distant places and most remote ages, yet some fact must always be present to the senses or memory, from which we may first proceed in drawing these conclusions. A man, who should find in a desert country the remains of pompous buildings, would conclude that the country had, in ancient times, been cultivated by civilized inhabitants; but did nothing of this nature occur to him, he could never form such an inference. We learn the events of former ages from history; but then we must peruse the volumes in which this instruction is contained, and thence carry up our inferences from one testimony to another, till we arrive at the eyewitnesses and spectators of these distant events. In a word, if we proceed not upon some fact, present to the memory or senses, our reasonings would be merely hypothetical; and however the particular links might be connected with each other, the whole chain of inferences would have nothing to support it, nor could we ever, by its means, arrive at the knowledge of any real existence. If I ask why you believe any particular matter of fact, which you relate, you must tell me some reason; and this reason will be some other fact, connected with it. But as you cannot proceed after this manner, *in infinitum,* you must at last terminate in some fact, which is present to your memory or senses; or must allow that your belief is entirely without foundation.

What, then, is the conclusion of the whole matter? A simple one; though, it must be confessed, pretty remote from the common theories of philosophy. All belief of matter of fact or real existence is derived merely from some object, present to the memory or senses, and a customary conjunction between that and some other object. Or in other words; having found, in many instances, that any two kinds of objects—flame and heat, snow and cold—have always been conjoined together; if flame or snow be presented anew to the senses, the mind is carried by custom to expect heat or cold, and to *believe* that such a quality does exist, and will discover itself upon a nearer approach. This belief is the necessary result of placing the mind in such circumstances. It is an operation of the soul, when we are so situated, as unavoidable as to feel the passion of love, when we receive benefits; or hatred, when we meet with injuries. All these operations are a species of natural instincts, which no reasoning or process of the thought and understanding is able either to produce or to prevent.

33. *Scepticism and Animal Faith**

George Santayana (1863–1952)

In the claims of memory I have a typical instance of what is called knowledge. In remembering I believe that I am taking cognisance not of a given essence but of a remote existence, so that, being myself here and now, I can consider and describe something going on at another place and time. This leap, which renders knowledge essentially faith, may come to seem paradoxical or impossible like the leap of physical being from place to place or from form to form which is called motion or change, and which some philosophers deny, as they deny knowledge. Is there such a leap in knowing? Am I really here and now when I apprehend some remote thing? Certainly, if by myself I understand the psyche within my body, which directs my outer organs, reacts on external things, and shapes the history and character of the individual animal that bears my name. In this sense I am a physical being in the midst of nature, and my knowledge is a name for the effects which surrounding things have upon me, in so far as I am quickened by them, and readjusted to them. I am certainly confined at each moment to a limited space and time, but may be quickened by the

influence of things at any distance, and may be readjusting myself to them. For the naturalist there is accordingly no paradox in the leap of knowledge other than the general marvel of material interaction and animal life.

If by myself, however, I meant pure spirit, or the light of attention by which essences appear and intuitions are rendered actual, it would not be true that I am confined or even situated in a particular place and time, nor that in considering things remote from my body, my thoughts are taking any unnatural leap. The marvel, from the point of view of spirit, is rather that it should need to be planted at all in the sensorium of some living animal, and that, being rooted there, it should take that accidental station for its point of view in surveying all nature, and should dignify one momentary phase of that animal life with the titles of the Here and the Now. It is only spirit, be it observed, that can do this. In themselves all the points of space-time are equally central and palpitating, and every phase of every psyche is a focus for actual readjustments to the whole universe. How then can the spirit, which would seem to be the principle of universality and justice, take up its station in each of these atoms and fight its battles for it, and prostitute

* All of Chapter XVIII, entitled: "Knowledge is faith mediated by symbols," reprinted by permission of Chas. Scribner's Sons.

its own light in the service of that desperate blindness? Can reason do nothing better than supply the eloquence of prejudice? Such are the puzzles which spirit might find, I will not say in the leap of knowledge, but in the fatality which links the spirit to a material organ so that, in order to reach other things, it is obliged to leap; or rather can never reach other things, because it is tethered to its starting-point, except by its intent in leaping, and cannot even discover the stepping-stone on which it stands because its whole life is the act of leaping away from it. There is no reason, therefore, in so far as knowledge is an apanage of spirit, why knowledge should not bathe all time and all existence in an equal light, and see everything as it is, with an equal sympathy and immediacy. The problem for the spirit is how it could ever come to pick out one body or another for its cynosure and for its instrument, as if it could not see save through such a little eye-glass, and in such a violent perspective. This problem, I think, has a ready answer, but it is not one that spirit could ever find of itself, without a long and docile apprenticeship in the school of animal faith. This answer is that spirit, with knowledge and all its other prerogatives, is intrinsically and altogether a function of animal life; so that if it were not lodged in some body and expressive of its rhythms and relations, spirit would not exist at all. But this solution, even when spirit is humble enough to accept it, always seems to it a little disappointing and satirical.

Spirit, therefore, has no need to leap in order to know, because in its range as spirit it is omnipresent and omnimodal. Events which are past or future in relation to the phase of the psyche which spirit expresses in a particular instance, or events which are remote from that psyche in space, are not for that reason remote from spirit, or out of its cognitive

range: they are merely hidden, or placed in a particular perspective for the moment, like the features of a landscape by the hedges and turns of a road. Just as all essences are equally near to spirit, and equally fit and easy to contemplate, if only a psyche with an affinity to those essences happens to arise; so all existing things, past, future, or infinitely distant, are equally within the range of knowledge, if only a psyche happens to be directed upon them, and to choose terms, however poor or fantastic, in which to describe them. In choosing these terms the psyche creates spirit, for they are essences given in intuition; and in directing her action or endeavour, backward or forward, upon those remote events, she creates intent in the spirit, so that the given essences become descriptions of the things with which the psyche is then busied.

But how, I may ask, can intent distinguish its hidden object, so that an image, distorted or faithful, may be truly or falsely projected *there,* or used to describe *it?* How does the spirit divine that there is such an object, or where it lies? And how can it appeal to a thing which is hidden, the object of mere intent, as to a touchstone or standard for its various descriptions of that object, and say to them, as they suggest themselves in turn: You are too vague, You are absurd, You are better, You are absolutely right?

I answer that it does so by animal presumption, positing whatsoever object instinct is materially predisposed to cope with, as in hunger, love, fighting, or the expectation of a future. But before developing this reply, let me make one observation. Since intuition of essence is not knowledge, knowledge can never lie in an overt comparison of one datum with another datum given at the same time; even in pure dialectic, the comparison is with a datum *believed* to have been given formerly. If both terms were simply given they would compose a complex essence, without the least signification. Only when one of the terms is indicated by intent, without being given exhaustively, can the other term serve to define the first more fully, or be linked with it in an assertion which is not mere tautology. An object of faith—and knowledge is one species of faith—can never, even in the most direct perception, come within the circle of intuition. Intuition of things is a contradiction in terms. If philosophers wish to abstain from faith, and reduce themselves to intuition of the obvious, they are free to do so, but they will thereby renounce all knowledge, and live on passive illusions. No fact, not even the fact that these illusions exist, would ever be, or would ever have been, anything but the false idea that they had existed. There would be nothing but the realm of essence, without any intuition of any part of it, nor of the whole: so that we should be driven back to a nihilism which only silence and death could express consistently; since the least actual assertion of it, by existing, would contradict it.

Even such acquaintance with the realm of essence as constitutes some science or recognisable art—like mathematics or music—lies in intending and positing great stretches of essence not now given, so that the essences now given acquire significance and become pregnant, to my vital feeling, with a thousand things which they do not present actually, but which I know where to look for eventually, and how to await. Suppose a moment ago I heard a clap of thunder, loud and prolonged, but that the physical shock has subsided and I am conscious of repose and silence. I may find some difficulty, although the thing was so recent, in *rehearsing* even now the exact volume, tone, and rumblings of that sound; yet I *know* the theme perfectly, in the sense that when

it thunders again, I can say with assurance whether the second crash was longer, louder, or differently modulated. In such a case I have no longer an intuition of the first thunder-clap, but a memory of it which is knowledge; and I can define on occasion, up to a certain point and not without some error, the essence given in that particular past intuition. Thus even pure essences can become objects of intent and of tentative knowledge when they are not present in intuition but are approached and posited indirectly, as the essences given on another particular occasion or signified by some particular word. The word or the occasion are natural facts, and my knowledge is focussed upon them in the first instance by ordinary perception or conception of nature: and the essence I hope to recover is elicited gradually, imaginatively, perhaps incorrectly, at the suggestion of those assumed facts, according to my quickness of wit, or my familiarity with the conventions of that art or science. In this way it becomes possible and necessary to learn about essences as if they were things, not initially by a spontaneous and complete intuition, but by coaxing the mind until possibly, at the end, it beholds them clearly. This is the sort of intuition which is mediated by language and by works of fine art; also by logic and mathematics, as they are learned from teachers and out of books. It is not happy intuition of some casual datum: it is laborious recovery, up to a certain point, of the *sort* of essence somebody else may have intuited. Whereas intuition, which reveals an essence directly, is not knowledge, because it has no ulterior object, the designation of some essence by some sign does convey knowledge, to an intelligent pupil, of what that essence was. Obviously such divination of essences present elsewhere, so that they become present here also, in so far as it is knowledge, is trebly faith. Faith first in the document, as a genuine natural fact and not a vapid fancy of my own; for instance, belief that there is a book called the Bible, really handed down from the ancient Jews and the early Christians, and that I have not merely dreamt of such a book. Faith then in the significance of that document, that it means some essence which it is not; in this instance, belief that the sacred writers were not merely speaking with tongues but were signifying some intelligible points in history and philosophy. Faith finally in my success in interpreting that document correctly, so that the essences it suggests to me now are the very essences it expressed originally: in other words, the belief that when I read the Bible I understand it as it was meant, and not fantastically.

I revert now to the question how it is possible to posit an object which is not a datum, and how without knowing positively what this object is I can make it the criterion of truth in my ideas. How can I test the accuracy of descriptions by referring them to a subject-matter which is not only out of view now but which probably has never been more than an object of intent, an event which even while it was occurring was described by me only in terms native to my fancy? If I know a man only by reputation, how should I judge if the reputation is deserved? If I know things only by representations, are not the representations the only things I know?

This challenge is fundamental, and so long as the assumptions which it makes are not challenged in turn, it drives critics of knowledge inexorably to scepticism of a dogmatic sort, I mean to the assertion that the very notion of knowledge is absurd. One assumption is that knowledge should be intuition: but I have already come to the conclusion that intuition is not knowledge. So long as a knowledge is demanded that shall be intuition, the issue can only be laughter or

despair; for if I attain intuition, I have only a phantom object, and if I spurn that and turn to the facts, I have renounced intuition. This assumption alone suffices, therefore, to disprove the possibility of knowledge. But in case the force of this disproof escaped us, another assumption is at hand to despatch the business, namely, the assumption that in a true description—if we grant knowledge by description—the terms should be identical with the constituents of the object, so that the idea should *look like* the thing that it knows. This assumption is derived from the other, or is a timid form of it: for it is supposed that I know by intuiting my idea, and that unless that idea resembled the object I wish to know, I could not even by courtesy be said to have discovered the latter. But the intuition of an idea, let me repeat, is not knowledge; and if a thing resembling that idea happened to exist, my intuition would still not be knowledge of it, but contemplation of the idea only.

Plato and many other philosophers, being in love with intuition (for which alone they were perhaps designed by nature), have identified science with certitude, and consequently entirely condemned what I call knowledge (which is a form of animal faith) or relegated it to an inferior position, as something merely necessary for life. I myself have no passionate attachment to existence, and value this world for the intuitions it can suggest, rather than for the wilderness of facts that compose it. To turn away from it may be the deepest wisdom in the end. What better than to blow out the candle, and to bed! But at noon this pleasure is premature. I can always hold it in reserve, and perhaps nihilism is a system—the simplest of all—on which we shall all agree in the end. But I seem to see very clearly now that in doing so we should all be missing the truth: not indeed by any false assertion, such as may separate us from the truth now, but by dumb ignorance—a dumb ignorance which, when proposed as a solution to actual doubts, is the most radical of errors, since it ignores and virtually denies the pressure of those doubts, and their living presence. Accordingly, so long as I remain awake and the light burning, that total dogmatic scepticism is evidently an impossible attitude. It requires me to deny what I assert, not to mean what I mean, and (in the sense in which seeing is believing) not to believe what I see. If I wish, therefore, to formulate in any way my actual claim to knowledge—a claim which life, and in particular memory, imposes upon me —I must revise the premises of this nihilism. For I have been led to it not by any accidental error, but by the logic of the assumption that knowledge should be intuition of fact. It is this presumption that must be revoked.

Knowledge is no such thing. It is not intramental nor internal to experience. Not only does it not require me to compare two given terms and to find them similar or identical, but it positively excludes any intuitive possession of its object. Intuition subsists beneath knowledge, as vegetative life subsists beneath animal life, and within it. Intuition may also supervene upon knowledge, when all I have learned of the universe, and all my concern for it, turn to a playful or a hypnotising phantom; and any poet or philosopher, like any flower, is free to prefer intuition to knowledge. But in preferring intuition he prefers ignorance. Knowledge is knowledge because it has compulsory objects that pre-exist. It is incidental to the predicaments and labour of life: also to its masterful explorations and satirical moods. It is reflected from events as light is reflected from bodies. It expresses in discourse the modified habits of an active being, plastic to experience, and capable of readjusting its organic attitude to other

things on the same material plane of being with itself. The place and the pertinent functions of these several things are indicated by the very attitude of the animal who notices them; this attitude, physical and practical, determines the object of intent, which discourse is about.

When the proverbial child cries for the moon, is the object of his desire doubtful? He points at it unmistakably; yet the psychologist (not to speak of the child himself) would have some difficulty in recovering exactly the sensations and images, the gathering demands and fumbling efforts, that traverse the child's mind while he points. Fortunately all this fluid sentience, even if it could be described, is irrelevant to the question; for the child's sensuous experience is not his object. If it were, he would have attained it. What his object is, his fixed gaze and outstretched arm declare unequivocally. His elders may say that he doesn't know what he wants, which is probably true of them also: that is, he has only a ridiculously false and inconstant idea of what the moon may be in itself. But his attention is arrested in a particular direction, his appetition flows the same way; and if he may be said to know anything, he knows there is something there which he would like to reach, which he would like to know better. He is a little philosopher; and his knowledge, if less diversified and congealed, is exactly like science.

The attitude of his body in pointing to the moon, and his tears, fill full his little mind, which not only reverberates to this physical passion, but probably observes it: and this felt attitude *identifies the object* of his desire and knowledge *in the physical world*. It determines what particular thing, in the same space and time with the child's body, was the object of that particular passion. If the object which the body is after is identified, that which the soul is after is identified too: no one, I suppose, would carry dualism so far as to assert that when the mouth waters at the sight of one particular plum, the soul may be yearning for quite another.

The same bodily attitude of the child *identifies the object in the discourse of an observer*. In perceiving what his senses are excited by, and which way his endeavour is turned, I can see that the object of his desire is the moon, which I too am looking at. That I am looking at the same moon as he can be proved by a little triangulation: our glances converge upon it. If the child has reached the inquisitive age and asks: "What is that?" I understand what he means by "that" and am able to reply sapiently "That is the moon," only because our respective bodies, in one common space, are discoverably turned towards one material object, which is stimulating them simultaneously. Knowledge of discourse in other people, or of myself at other times, is what I call literary psychology. It is, or may be, in its texture, the most literal and adequate sort of knowledge of which a mind is capable. If I am a lover of children, and a good psycho-analyst, I may feel for a moment exactly as the child feels in looking at the moon: and I may know that I know his feeling, and very likely he too will know that I know it, and we shall become fast friends. But this rare adequacy of knowledge, attained by dramatic sympathy, goes out to an object which in its existence is known very indirectly: because poets and religious visionaries feel this sort of sympathy with all sorts of imaginary persons, of whose existence and thoughts they have only intuition, not knowledge. If I ask for evidence that such an object exists, and is not an *alter ego* of my private invention, I must appeal to my faith in nature, and to my conventional assumption that this child and I are animals of the same species, in the same habitat, looking at the same moon, and likely to have the same feelings: and finally the psychology of the tribe and the crowd may enable me half to understand how we know that we have the same feelings at once, when we actually share them.

The attitude of the child's body also *identifies the object for him, in his own subsequent discourse*. He is not likely to forget a moon that he cried for. When in stretching his hand towards it he found he could not touch it, he learned that this bright good was not within his grasp, and he made a beginning in the experience of life. He also made a beginning in science, since he then added the absolutely true predicate "out of reach" to the rather questionable predicates "bright" and "good" (and perhaps "edible") with which his first glimpse had supplied him. That active and mysterious thing, co-ordinate with himself, since it lay in the same world with his body, and affected it—the thing that attracted his hand, was evidently the very thing that eluded it. His failure would have had no meaning and would have taught him nothing—that is, would not have corrected his instinctive reactions—if the object he saw and the object he failed to reach had not been identical; and certainly that object was not brightness nor goodness nor excitements in his brain or psyche, for these are not things he could ever have attempted or expected to touch. It is only things on the scale of the human senses and in the field of those instinctive reactions which sensation calls forth, that can be the primary objects of human knowledge: no other things can be discriminated at first by an animal mind, or can interest it, or can be meant and believed in by it. It is these instinctive reactions that select the objects of attention, designate their locus, and impose faith in their existence. But these reactions may be modified by experience, and the description the mind gives of the objects reacted upon can be revised, or the objects themselves discarded, and others discerned instead. Thus the child's instinct to touch the moon was as spontaneous and as confident at first as his instinct to look at it; and the object of both efforts was the same, because the same external agency aroused them, and with them the very heterogeneous sensations of light and of disappointment. These various terms of sense or of discourse, by which the child described the object under whose attractions and rebuffs he was living, were merely symbols to him, like words. An animal naturally has as many signs for an object as he has sensations or emotions in its presence. These signs are miscellaneous essences—sights, sounds, smells, contacts, tears, provocations— and they are alternative or supplementary to one another, like words in different languages. The most diverse senses, such as smell and sight, if summoned to the same point in the environment, and guiding a single action, will report upon a single object. Even when one sense brings all the news I have, its reports will change from moment to moment with the distance, variation, or suspension of the connection between the object and my body: and this without any relevant change in the object itself. Nay, often the very transformation of the sensation bears witness that the object is unchanged; as music and laughter, overheard as I pass a tavern, are felt and known to continue unabated, and to be no merriment of mine, just because they fade from my ears as I move away.

The object of knowledge being that designated in this way by my bodily attitude, the aesthetic qualities I attribute to it will depend on the particular sense it happens to affect at the moment, or on the sweep and nature of the reaction which it then calls forth on my part. This diversity in signs and descriptions

for a single thing is a normal diversity. Diversity, when it is not contradiction, irritates only unreasonably dogmatic people; they are offended with nature for having a rich vocabulary, and sometimes speaking a language, or employing a syntax, which they never heard at home. It is an innocent prejudice, and it yields easily in a generous mind to pleasure at the wealth of alternatives which animal life affords. Even such contradictions as may arise in the description of things, and may truly demand a solution, reside in the implication of the terms, not in their sensuous or rhetorical diversity: they become contradictory only when they assign to the object contrary movements or contrary effects, not when they merely exhibit its various appearances. Looking at the moon, one man may call it simply a light in the sky; another, prone to dreaming awake, may call it a virgin goddess; a more observant person, remembering that this luminary is given to waxing and waning, may call it the crescent; and a fourth, a full-fledged astronomer, may say (taking the aesthetic essence before him merely for a sign) that it is an extinct and opaque spheroidal satellite of the earth, reflecting the light of the sun from a part of its surface. All these descriptions envisage the same object—otherwise no relevance, conflict, or progress could obtain among them. What that object is in its complete constitution and history will never be known by man; but that this object exists in a known space and time and has traceable physical relations with all other physical objects is a fact posited from the beginning; it was posited by the child when he pointed, and by me when I saw him point. If it did not so exist and (as sometimes happens) he and I were suffering from a hallucination, in thinking we were pointing at the moon we should be discoverably pointing at vacancy: exploration would eventually satisfy us of that fact, and any bystander would vouch for it. But if in pointing at it we were pointing to it, its identity would be fixed without more ado; disputes and discoveries concerning it would be pertinent and soluble, no matter what diversity there might be in the ideal essences—light, crescent, goddess, or satellite—which we used as rival descriptions of it while we pointed.

I find that the discrimination of essence brings a wonderful clearness into this subject. All data and descriptions—light, crescent, goddess, or satellite—are equally essences, terms of human discourse, inexistent in themselves. What exists in any instance, besides the moon and our various reactions upon it, is some intuition, expressing those reactions, evoking that essence, and lending it a specious actuality. The terms of astronomy are essences no less human and visionary than those of mythology; but they are the fruit of a better focussed, more chastened, and more prolonged attention turned upon what actually occurs; that is, they are kept closer to animal faith, and freer from pictorial elements and the infusion of reverie. In myth, on the contrary, intuition wanders idly and uncontrolled; it makes epicycles, as it were, upon the reflex arc of perception; the moonbeams bewitch some sleeping Endymion, and he dreams of a swift huntress in heaven. Myth is nevertheless a relevant fancy, and genuinely expressive; only instead of being guided by a perpetual fresh study of the object posited by animal faith and encountered in action, it runs into marginal comments, personal associations, and rhetorical asides; so that even if based originally on perception, it is built upon principles internal to human discourse, as are grammar, rhyme, music, and morals. It may be admirable as an expression of these principles, and yet be egregiously false if asserted of the object, without discounting the human

medium in which it has taken form. Diana is an exquisite symbol for the moon, and for one sort of human loveliness; but she must not be credited with any existence over and above that of the moon, and of sundry short-skirted Dorian maidens. She is not other than they: she is an image of them, the best part of their essence distilled in a poet's mind. So with the description of the moon given by astronomers, which is not less fascinating; this, too, is no added object, but only a new image for the moon known even to the child and me. The space, matter, gravitation, time, and laws of motion conceived by astronomers are essences only, and mere symbols for the use of animal faith, when very enlightened: I mean in so far as they are alleged to constitute knowledge of a world which I must bow to and encounter in action; for if astronomy is content to be a mathematical exercise without any truth, an object of pure intuition, its terms and its laws will, of course, be ultimate realities, apart from what happens to exist: realities in the realm of essence. In the description of the natural world, however, they are mere symbols, mediating animal faith. Science at any moment may recast or correct its conceptions (as it is doing now) giving them a different colour; and the nerve of truth in them will be laid bare and made taut in proportion as the sensuous and rhetorical vesture of these notions is stripped off, and the dynamic relations of events, as found and posited by material exploration, are nakedly recorded.

Knowledge accordingly is belief: belief in a world of events, and especially of those parts of it which are near the self, tempting or threatening it. This belief is native to animals, and precedes all deliberate use of intuitions as signs or descriptions of things; as I turn my head to see who is there, before I see who it is. Furthermore, knowledge is true belief. It is such an enlightening of the self by intuitions arising there, that what the self imagines and asserts of the collateral thing, with which it wrestles in action, is actually true of that thing. Truth in such presumptions or conceptions does not imply adequacy, nor a pictorial identity between the essence in intuition and the constitution of the object. Discourse is a language, not a mirror. The images in sense are parts of discourse, not parts of nature: they are the babble of our innocent organs under the stimulus of things; but these spontaneous images, like the sounds of the voice, may acquire the function of names; they may become signs, if discourse is intelligent and can recapitulate its phases, for the things sought or encountered in the world. The truth which discourse can achieve is truth in its own terms, appropriate description: it is no incorporation or reproduction of the object in the mind. The mind notices and intends; it cannot incorporate or reproduce anything not an intention or an intuition. Its objects are no part of itself even when they are essences, much less when they are things. It thinks the essences, with that sort of immediate and self-forgetful attention which I have been calling intuition; and if it is animated, as it usually is, by some ulterior interest or pursuit, it takes the essences before it for messages, signs, or emanations sent forth to it from those objects of animal faith; and they become its evidences and its description for those objects. Therefore any degree of inadequacy and originality is tolerable in discourse, or even requisite, when the constitution of the objects which the animal encounters is out of scale with his organs, or quite heterogeneous from his possible images. A sensation or a theory, no matter how arbitrary its terms (and all language is perfectly arbitrary), will be true of the object, if it expresses some true relation in which that object stands to the self, so that these terms are not misleading as signs, however poetical they may be as sounds or as pictures.

Finally, knowledge is true belief grounded in experience, I mean, controlled by outer facts. It is not true by accident; it is not shot into the air on the chance that there may be something it may hit. It arises by a movement of the self sympathetic or responsive to surrounding beings, so that these beings become its intended objects, and at the same time an appropriate correspondence tends to be established between these objects and the beliefs generated under their influence.

In regard to the original articles of the animal creed—that there is a world, that there is a future, that things sought can be found, and things seen can be eaten—no guarantee can possibly be offered. I am sure these dogmas are often false; and perhaps the event will some day falsify them all, and they will lapse altogether. But while life lasts, in one form or another this faith must endure. It is the initial expression of animal vitality in the sphere of mind, the first announcement that anything is going on. It is involved in any pang of hunger, of fear, or of love. It launches the adventure of knowledge. The object of this tentative knowledge is things in general, whatsoever may be at work (as I am) to disturb me or awake my attention. The effort of knowledge is to discover what sort of world this disturbing world happens to be. Progress in knowledge lies open in various directions, now in the scope of its survey, now in its accuracy, now in its depth of local penetration. The ideal of knowledge is to become natural science: if it trespasses beyond that, it relapses into intuition, and ceases to be knowledge.

34. Descartes' Myth[*]

GILBERT RYLE (1900–   )

(1) *The Official Doctrine.*

There is a doctrine about the nature and place of minds which is so prevalent among theorists and even among laymen that it deserves to be described as the official theory. Most philosophers, psychologists and religious teachers subscribe, with minor reservations, to its main articles and, although they admit certain theoretical difficulties in it, they tend to assume that these can be overcome without serious modifications being made to the architecture of the theory. It will be argued here that the central principles of the doctrine are unsound and conflict with the whole body of what we know about minds when we are not speculating about them.

The official doctrine, which hails chiefly from Descartes, is something like this. With the doubtful exceptions of idiots and infants in arms every human being has both a body and a mind. Some would prefer to say that every human being is both a body and a mind. His body and his mind are ordinarily harnessed together, but after death of the body his mind may continue to exist and function.

Human bodies are in space and are subject to the mechanical laws which govern all other bodies in space. Bodily processes and states can be inspected by external observers. So a man's bodily life is as much a public affair as are the lives of animals and reptiles and even as the careers of trees, crystals and planets.

But minds are not in space, nor are their operations subject to mechanical laws. The workings of one mind are not witnessable by other observers; its career is private. Only I can take direct cognisance of the states and processes of my own mind. A person therefore lives through two collateral histories, one consisting of what happens in and to his body, the other consisting of what happens in and to his mind. The first is public, the second private. The events in the first history are events in the physical world, those in the second are events in the mental world.

It has been disputed whether a person does or can directly monitor all or only some of the episodes of his own private history; but, according to the official doctrine, of at least some of these episodes he has direct and unchallengeable cognisance. In consciousness, self-consciousness and introspection he is directly and authentically apprised of the present states and operations of his mind. He may have great or small uncertainties about concurrent and adjacent episodes in the physical world, but he can have none about at least part of what is momentarily occupying his mind.

It is customary to express this bifurcation of his two lives and of his two

---

    [*] An excerpt from Chapters 1 and 2 of *The Concept of Mind,* by Gilbert Ryle, published by Hutchinson's University Library, 1949, and reprinted with their permission.

worlds by saying that the things and events which belong to the physical world, including his own body, are external, while the workings of his own mind are internal. This antithesis of outer and inner is of course meant to be construed as a metaphor, since minds, not being in space, could not be described as being spatially inside anything else, or as having things going on spatially inside themselves. But relapses from this good intention are common and theorists are found speculating how stimuli, the physical sources of which are yards or miles outside a person's skin, can generate mental responses inside his skull, or how decisions framed inside his cranium can set going movements of his extremities.

Even when 'inner' and 'outer' are construed as metaphors, the problem how a person's mind and body influence one another is notoriously charged with theoretical difficulties. What the mind wills, the legs, arms and the tongue execute; what affects the ear and the eye has something to do with what the mind perceives; grimaces and smiles betray the mind's moods and bodily castigations lead, it is hoped, to moral improvement. But the actual transactions between the episodes of the private history and those of the public history remain mysterious, since by definition they can belong to neither series. They could not be reported among the happenings described in a person's autobiography of his inner life, but nor could they be reported among those described in some one else's biography of that person's overt career. They can be inspected neither by introspection nor by laboratory experiment. They are theoretical shuttlecocks which are forever being bandied from the physiologist back to the psychologist and from the psychologist back to the physiologist.

Underlying this partly metaphorical representation of the bifurcation of a person's two lives there is a seemingly more profound and philosophical assumption that there are two different kinds of existence or status. What exists or happens may have the status of physical existence, or it may have the status of mental existence. Somewhat as the faces of coins are either heads or tails, or somewhat as living creatures are either male or female, so, it is supposed, some existing is physical existing, other existing is mental existing. It is a necessary feature of what has physical existence that it is in space and time; it is a necessary feature of what has mental existence that it is in time but not in space. What has physical existence is composed of matter, or else is a function of matter; what has mental existence consists of consciousness, or else is a function of consciousness.

There is thus a polar opposition between mind and matter, an opposition which is often brought out as follows. Material objects are situated in a common field, known as 'space', and what happens to one body in one part of space is mechanically connected with what happens to other bodies in other parts of space. But mental happenings occur in insulated fields, known as 'minds', and there is, apart maybe from telepathy, no direct causal connection between what happens in one mind and what happens in another. Only through the medium of the public physical world can the mind of one person make a difference to the mind of another. The mind is its own place and in his inner life each of us lives the life of a ghostly Robinson Crusoe. People can see, hear and jolt one another's bodies, but they are irremediably blind and deaf to the workings of one another's minds and inoperative upon them.

What sort of knowledge can be secured of the workings of a mind? On the one side, according to the official theory, a person has direct knowledge of the best imaginable kind of the workings of his own mind. Mental states and processes are (or are normally) conscious states and processes, and the consciousness which irradiates them can engender no illusions and leaves the door open for no doubts. A person's present thinkings, feelings and willings, his perceivings, rememberings and imaginings are intrinsically 'phosphorescent'; their existence and their nature are inevitably betrayed to their owner. The inner life is a stream of consciousness of such a sort that it would be absurd to suggest that the mind whose life is that stream might be unaware of what is passing down it.

True, the evidence adduced recently by Freud seems to show that there exist channels tributary to this stream, which run hidden from their owner. People are actuated by impulses the existence of which they vigorously disavow; some of their thoughts differ from the thoughts which they acknowledge; and some of the actions which they think they will to perform they do not really will. They are thoroughly gulled by some of their own hypocrisies and they successfully ignore facts about their mental lives which on the official theory ought to be patent to them. Holders of the official theory tend, however, to maintain that anyhow in normal circumstances a person must be directly and authentically seized of the present state and workings of his own mind.

Besides being currently supplied with these alleged immediate data of consciousness, a person is also generally supposed to be able to exercise from time to time a special kind of perception, namely inner perception, or introspection. He can take a (non-optical) 'look' at what is passing in his mind. Not only can he view and scrutinize a flower through his sense of sight and listen to and discriminate the notes of a bell through his sense of hearing; he can also reflectively or introspectively

watch, without any bodily organ of sense, the current episodes of his inner life. This self-observation is also commonly supposed to be immune from illusion, confusion or doubt. A mind's reports of its own affairs have a certainty superior to the best that is possessed by its reports of matters in the physical world. Sense-perceptions can, but consciousness and introspection cannot, be mistaken or confused.

On the other side, one person has no direct access of any sort to the events of the inner life of another. He cannot do better than make problematic inferences from the observed behaviour of the other person's body to the states of mind which, by analogy from his own conduct, he supposes to be signalised by that behaviour. Direct access to the workings of a mind is the privilege of that mind itself; in default of such privileged access, the workings of one mind are inevitably occult to everyone else. For the supposed arguments from bodily movements similar to their own to mental workings similar to their own would lack any possibility of observational corroboration. Not unnaturally, therefore, an adherent of the official theory finds it difficult to resist this consequence of his premisses, that he has no good reason to believe that there do exist minds other than his own. Even if he prefers to believe that to other human bodies there are harnessed minds not unlike his own, he cannot claim to be able to discover their individual characteristics, or the particular things that they undergo and do. Absolute solitude is on this showing the ineluctable destiny of the soul. Only our bodies can meet.

As a necessary corollary of this general scheme there is implicitly prescribed a special way of construing our ordinary concepts of mental powers and operations. The verbs, nouns and adjectives, with which in ordinary life we describe the wits, characters and higher-grade performances of the people with whom we have to do, are required to be construed as signifying special episodes in their secret histories, or else as signifying tendencies for such episodes to occur. When someone is described as knowing, believing or guessing something, as hoping, dreading, intending or shirking something, as designing this or being amused at that, these verbs are supposed to denote the occurrence or specific modifications in his (to us) occult stream of consciousness. Only his own privileged access to this stream in direct awareness and introspection could provide authentic testimony that these mental-conduct verbs were correctly or incorrectly applied. The onlooker, be he teacher, critic, biographer or friend, can never assure himself that his comments have any vestige of truth. Yet it was just because we do in fact all know how to make such comments, make them with general correctness and correct them when they turn out to be confused or mistaken, that philosophers found it necessary to construct their theories of the nature and place of minds. Finding mental-conduct concepts being regularly and effectively used, they properly sought to fix their logical geography. But the logical geography officially recommended would entail that there could be no regular or effective use of these mental-conduct concepts in our descriptions of, and prescriptions for, other people's minds.

(2) *The Absurdity of the Official Doctrine.*

Such in outline is the official theory. I shall often speak of it, with deliberate abusiveness, as 'the dogma of the Ghost in the Machine'. I hope to prove that it is entirely false, and false not in detail but in principle. It is not merely an assemblage of particular mistakes. It is one big mistake and a mistake of a spe-

cial kind. It is, namely, a category-mistake. It represents the facts of mental life as if they belonged to one logical type or category (or range of types or categories), when they actually belong to another. The dogma is therefore a philosopher's myth. In attempting to explode the myth I shall probably be taken to be denying well-known facts about the mental life of human beings, and my plea that I aim at doing nothing more than rectify the logic of mental-conduct concepts will probably be disallowed as mere subterfuge.

I must first indicate what is meant by the phrase 'Category-mistake'. This I do in a series of illustrations.

A foreigner visiting Oxford or Cambridge for the first time is shown a number of colleges, libraries, playing fields, museums, scientific departments and administrative offices. He then asks 'But where is the University? I have seen where the members of the Colleges live, where the Registrar works, where the scientists experiment and the rest. But I have not yet seen the University in which reside and work the members of your University.' It has then to be explained to him that the University is not another collateral institution, some ulterior counterpart to the colleges, laboratories and offices which he has seen. The University is just the way in which all that he has already seen is organized. When they are seen and when their coordination is understood, the University has been seen. His mistake lay in his innocent assumption that it was correct to speak of Christ Church, the Bodleian Library, the Ashmolean Museum *and* the University, to speak, that is, as if 'the University' stood for an extra member of the class of which these other units are members. He was mistakenly allocating the University to the same category as that to which the other institutions belong.

The same mistake would be made by

a child witnessing the march-past of a division, who, having had pointed out to him such and such battalions, batteries, squadrons, etc., asked when the division was going to appear. He would be supposing that a division was a counterpart to the units already seen, partly similar to them and partly unlike them. He would be shown his mistake by being told that in watching the battalions, batteries and squadrons marching past he had been watching the division marching past. The march-past was not a parade of battalions, batteries, squadrons *and* a division; it was a parade of the battalions, batteries and squadrons *of* a division.

One more illustration. A foreigner watching his first game of cricket learns what are the functions of the bowlers, the batsmen, the fielders, the umpires and the scorers. He then says 'But there is no one left on the field to contribute the famous element of team-spirit. I see who does the bowling, the batting and the wicket-keeping; but I do not see whose role it is to exercise *esprit de corps.*' Once more, it would have to be explained that he was looking for the wrong type of thing. Team-spirit is not another cricketing-operation supplementary to all of the other special tasks. It is, roughly, the keenness with which each of the special tasks is performed, and performing a task keenly is not performing two tasks. Certainly exhibiting team-spirit is not the same thing as bowling or catching, but nor is it a third thing such that we can say that the bowler first bowls *and* then exhibits team-spirit or that a fielder is at a given moment *either* catching *or* displaying *esprit de corps.*

These illustrations of category-mistakes have a common feature which must be noticed. The mistakes were made by people who did not know how to wield the concepts *University, division* and *team-spirit.* Their puzzles arose from inability to use certain items in the English vocabulary.

The theoretically interesting category-mistakes are those made by people who are perfectly competent to apply concepts, at least in the situations with which they are familiar, but are still liable in their abstract thinking to allocate those concepts to logical types to which they do not belong. An instance of a mistake of this sort would be the following story. A student of politics has learned the main differences between the British, the French and the American Constitutions, and has learned also the differences and connections between the Cabinet, Parliament, the various Ministries, the Judicature and the Church of England. But he still becomes embarrassed when asked questions about the connections between the Church of England, the Home Office and the British Constitution. For while the Church and the Home Office are institutions, the British Constitution is not another institution in the same sense of that noun. So inter-institutional relations which can be asserted or denied to hold between the Church and the Home Office cannot be asserted or denied to hold between either of them and the British Constitution. 'The British Constitution' is not a term of the same logical type as 'the Home Office' and 'the Church of England'. In a partially similar way, John Doe may be a relative, a friend, an enemy or a stranger to Richard Roe; but he cannot be any of these things to the Average Taxpayer. He knows how to talk sense in certain sorts of discussions about the Average Taxpayer, but he is baffled to say why he could not come across him in the street as he can come across Richard Roe.

It is pertinent to our main subject to notice that, so long as the student of politics continues to think of the British Constitution as a counterpart to the other institutions, he will tend to describe it as a mysteriously occult institution; and so long as John Doe continues to think of the Average Taxpayer as a fellow-citizen, he will tend to think of him as an elusive insubstantial man, a ghost who is everywhere yet nowhere.

My destructive purpose is to show that a family of radical category-mistakes is the source of the double-life theory. The representation of a person as a ghost mysteriously ensconced in a machine derives from this argument. Because, as is true, a person's thinking, feeling and purposive doing cannot be described solely in the idioms of physics, chemistry and physiology, therefore they must be described in counterpart idioms. As the human body is a complex organised unit, so the human mind must be another complex organised unit, though one made of a different sort of stuff and with a different sort of structure. Or, again, as the human body, like any other parcel of matter, is a field of causes and effects, so the mind must be another field of causes and effects, though not (Heaven be praised) mechanical causes and effects.

(3) The Origin of the Category-mistake.

One of the chief intellectual origins of what I have yet to prove to be the Cartesian category-mistake seems to be this. When Galileo showed that his methods of scientific discovery were competent to provide a mechanical theory which should cover every occupant of space, Descartes found in himself two conflicting motives. As a man of scientific genius he could not but endorse the claims of mechanics, yet as a religious and moral man he could not accept, as Hobbes accepted, the discouraging rider to those claims, namely that human nature differs only in degree of complexity from clockwork. The mental could not be just a variety of the mechanical.

He and subsequent philosophers nat-

urally but erroneously availed themselves of the following escape-route. Since mental-conduct words are not to be construed as signifying the occurrence of mechanical processes, they must be construed as signifying the occurrence of non-mechanical processes; since mechanical laws explain movements in space as the effects of other movements in space, other laws must explain some of the non-spatial workings of minds as the effects of other non-spatial workings of minds. The difference between the human behaviours which we describe as intelligent and those which we describe as unintelligent must be a difference in their causation; so, while some movements of human tongues and limbs are the effects of mechanical causes, others must be the effects of non-mechanical causes, i.e. some issue from movements of particles of matter, others from workings of the mind.

The differences between the physical and the mental were thus represented as differences inside the common framework of the categories of 'thing', 'stuff', 'attribute', 'state', 'process', 'change', 'cause' and 'effect'. Minds are things, but different sorts of things from bodies; mental processes are causes and effects, but different sorts of causes and effects from bodily movements. And so on. Somewhat as the foreigner expected the University to be an extra edifice, rather like a college but also considerably different, so the repudiators of mechanism represented minds as extra centres of causal processes, rather like machines but also considerably different from them. Their theory was a para-mechanical hypothesis.

That this assumption was at the heart of the doctrine is shown by the fact that there was from the beginning felt to be a major theoretical difficulty in explaining how minds can influence and be influenced by bodies. How can a mental process, such as willing, cause spatial movements like the movements of the tongue? How can a physical change in the optic nerve have among its effects a mind's perception of a flash of light? This notorious crux by itself shows the logical mould into which Descartes pressed his theory of the mind. It was the self-same mould into which he and Galileo set their mechanics. Still unwittingly adhering to the grammar of mechanics, he tried to avert disaster by describing minds in what was merely an obverse vocabulary. The workings of minds had to be described by the mere negatives of the specific descriptions given to bodies; they are not in space, they are not motions, they are not modifications of matter, they are not accessible to public observation. Minds are not bits of clockwork, they are just bits of not-clockwork.

As thus represented, minds are not merely ghosts harnessed to machines, they are themselves just spectral machines. Though the human body is an engine, it is not quite an ordinary engine, since some of its workings are governed by another engine inside it—this interior governor-engine being one of a very special sort. It is invisible, inaudible and it has no size or weight. It cannot be taken to bits and the laws it obeys are not those known to ordinary engineers. Nothing is known of how it governs the bodily engine.

A second major crux points the same moral. Since, according to the doctrine, minds belong to the same category as bodies and since bodies are rigidly governed by mechanical laws, it seemed to many theorists to follow that minds must be similarly governed by rigid non-mechanical laws. The physical world is a deterministic system, so the mental world must be a deterministic system. Bodies cannot help the modifications that they undergo, so minds cannot help pursuing the careers fixed for them.

Responsibility, choice, merit and *demerit* are therefore inapplicable concepts —unless the compromise solution is adopted of saying that the laws governing mental processes, unlike those governing physical processes, have the congenial attribute of being only rather rigid. The problem of the Freedom of the Will was the problem how to reconcile the hypothesis that minds are to be described in terms drawn from the categories of mechanics with the knowledge that higher-grade human conduct is not of a piece with the behaviour of machines.

It is an historical curiosity that it was not noticed that the entire argument was broken-backed. Theorists correctly assumed that any sane man could already recognise the differences between, say, rational and non-rational utterances or between purposive and automatic behaviour. Else there would have been nothing requiring to be salved from mechanism. Yet the explanation given presupposed that one person could in principle never recognise the difference between the rational and the irrational utterances issuing from other human bodies, since he could never get access to the postulated immaterial causes of some of their utterances. Save for the doubtful exception of himself, he could never tell the difference between a man and a Robot. It would have to be conceded, for example, that, for all that we can tell, the inner lives of persons who are classed as idiots or lunatics are as rational as those of anyone else. Perhaps only their overt behaviour is disappointing; that is to say, perhaps 'idiots' are not really idiotic, or 'lunatics' lunatic. Perhaps, too, some of those who are classed as sane are really idiots. According to the theory, external observers could never know how the overt behaviour of others is correlated with their mental powers and processes and so they could never know or even plausibly conjecture whether their applications of mental-conduct concepts to these other people were correct or incorrect. It would then be hazardous or impossible for a man to claim sanity or logical consistency even for himself, since he would be debarred from comparing his own performances with those of others. In short, our characterisations of persons and their performances as intelligent, prudent and virtuous or as stupid, hypocritical and cowardly could never have been made, so the problem of providing a special causal hypothesis to serve as the basis of such diagnoses would never have arisen. The question, 'How do persons differ from machines?' arose just because everyone already knew how to apply mental-conduct concepts before the new causal hypothesis was introduced. This causal hypothesis could not therefore be the source of the criteria used in those applications. Nor, of course, has the causal hypothesis in any degree improved our handling of those criteria. We still distinguish good from bad arithmetic, politic from impolitic conduct and fertile from infertile imaginations in the ways in which Descartes himself distinguished them before and after he speculated how the applicability of these criteria was compatible with the principle of mechanical causation.

He had mistaken the logic of his problem. Instead of asking by what criteria intelligent behaviour is actually distinguished from non-intelligent behaviour, he asked 'Given that the principle of mechanical causation does not tell us the difference, what other causal principle will tell it us?' He realised that the problem was not one of mechanics and assumed that it must therefore be one of some counterpart to mechanics. Not unnaturally psychology is often cast for just this role.

When two terms belong to the same category, it is proper to construct conjunctive propositions embodying them.

Thus a purchaser may say that he bought a left-hand glove and a right-hand glove, but not that he bought a left-hand glove, a right-hand glove and a pair of gloves. 'She came home in a flood of tears and a sedan-chair' is a well-known joke based on the absurdity of conjoining terms of different types. It would have been equally ridiculous to construct the disjunction 'She came home either in a flood of tears or else in a sedan-chair'. Now the dogma of the Ghost in the Machine does just this. It maintains that there exist both bodies and minds; that there occur physical processes and mental processes; that there are mechanical causes of corporeal movements and mental causes of corporeal movements. I shall argue that these and other analogous conjunctions are absurd; but, it must be noticed, the argument will not show that either of the illegitimately conjoined propositions is absurd in itself. I am not, for example, denying that there occur mental processes. Doing long division is a mental process and so is making a joke. But I am saying that the phrase 'there occur mental processes' does not mean the same sort of thing as 'there occur physical processes', and, therefore, that it makes no sense to conjoin or disjoin the two.

If my argument is successful, there will follow some interesting consequences. First, the hallowed contrast between Mind and Matter will be dissipated, but dissipated not by either of the equally hallowed absorptions of Mind by Matter or of Matter by Mind, but in quite a different way. For the seeming contrast of the two will be shown to be as illegitimate as would be the contrast of 'she came home in a flood of tears' and 'she came home in a sedan-chair'. The belief that there is a polar opposition between Mind and Matter is the belief that they are terms of the same logical type.

It will also follow that both Idealism and Materialism are answers to an improper question. The 'reduction' of the material world to mental states and processes, as well as the 'reduction' of mental states and processes to physical states and processes, presuppose the legitimacy of the disjunction 'Either there exist minds or there exist bodies (but not both)'. It would be like saying, 'Either she bought a left-hand and a right-hand glove or she bought a pair of gloves (but not both)'.

It is perfectly proper to say, in one logical tone of voice, that there exist minds and to say, in another logical tone of voice, that there exist bodies. But these expressions do not indicate two different species of existence, for 'existence' is not a generic word like 'coloured' or 'sexed'. They indicate two different senses of 'exist', somewhat as 'rising' has different senses in 'the tide is rising', 'hopes are rising', and 'the average age of death is rising'. A man would be thought to be making a poor joke who said that three things are now rising, namely the tide, hopes and the average age of death. It would be just as good or bad a joke to say that there exist prime numbers and Wednesdays and public opinions and navies; or that there exist both minds and bodies. In the succeeding chapters I try to prove that the official theory does rest on a batch of category-mistakes by showing that logically absurd corollaries follow from it. The exhibition of these absurdities will have the constructive effect of bringing out part of the correct logic of mental-conduct concepts.

(4) *Historical Note.*

It would not be true to say that the official theory derives solely from Descartes' theories, or even from a more widespread anxiety about the implications of seventeenth century mechanism. Scholastic and Reformation theology had schooled the intellects of the scientists as well as of the laymen, philosophers and clerics of that age. Stoic-Augustinian theories of the will were embedded in the Calvinist doctrines of sin and grace; Platonic and Aristotelian theories of the intellect shaped the orthodox doctrines of the immortality of the soul. Descartes was reformulating already prevalent theological doctrines of the soul in the new syntax of Galileo. The theologian's privacy of conscience became the philosopher's privacy of consciousness, and what had been the bogy of Predestination reappeared as the bogy of Determinism.

It would also not be true to say that the two-worlds myth did no theoretical good. Myths often do a lot of theoretical good, while they are still new. One benefit bestowed by the para-mechanical myth was that it partly superannuated the then prevalent para-political myth. Minds and their Faculties had previously been described by analogies with political superiors and political subordinates. The idioms used were those of ruling, obeying, collaborating and rebelling. They survived and still survive in many ethical and some epistemological discussions. As, in physics, the new myth of occult Forces was a scientific improvement on the old myth of Final Causes, so, in anthropological and psychological theory, the new myth of hidden operations, impulses and agencies was an improvement on the old myth of dictations, deferences and disobediences. . . .

(4) *The Motives of the Intellectualist Legend.*

Why are people so strongly drawn to believe, in the face of their own daily experience, that the intelligent execution of an operation must embody two processes, one of doing and another of theorising? Part of the answer is that they are wedded to the dogma of the ghost in the machine. Since doing is often an overt muscular affair, it is written off as a merely physical process. On the assumption of the antithesis between 'physical' and 'mental', it follows that muscular doing cannot itself be a mental operation. To earn the title 'skilful', 'cunning', or 'humorous', it must therefore get it by transfer from another counterpart act occurring not 'in the machine' but 'in the ghost'; for 'skilful', 'cunning' and 'humorous' are certainly mental predicates.

It is, of course, perfectly true that when we characterise as witty or tactful some piece of overt behaviour, we are not considering only the muscular movements which we witness. A parrot might have made the same remark in the same situation without our crediting it with a sense of humour, or a lout might have done precisely what the tactful man did, without our thinking him tactful. But if one and the same vocal utterance is a stroke of humour from the humorist, but a mere noise-response, when issuing from the parrot, it is tempting to say that we are ascribing wit not to something that we hear but to something else that we do not hear. We are accordingly tempted to say that what makes one audible or visible action witty, while another audibly or visibly similar action was not, is that the former was attended by another inaudible and invisible action which was the real exercise of wit. But to admit, as we must, that there may be no visible or audible difference between a tactful or witty act and a tactless or humourless one is not to admit that the difference is constituted by the performance or non-performance of some extra secret acts.

The cleverness of the clown may be exhibited in his tripping and tumbling. He trips and tumbles just as clumsy people do, except that he trips and tumbles on purpose and after much rehearsal and at the golden moment and where

the children can see him and so as not to hurt himself. The spectators applaud his skill at seeming clumsy, but what they applaud is not some extra hidden performance executed 'in his head'. It is his visible performance that they admire, but they admire it not for being an effect of any hidden internal causes but for being an exercise of a skill. Now a skill is not an act. It is therefore neither a witnessable nor an unwitnessable act. To recognise that a performance is an exercise of a skill is indeed to appreciate it in the light of a factor which could not be separately recorded by a camera. But the reason why the skill exercised in a performance cannot be separately recorded by a camera is not that it is an occult or ghostly happening, but that it is not a happening at all. It is a disposition, or complex of dispositions, and a disposition is a factor of the wrong logical type to be seen or unseen, recorded or unrecorded. Just as the habit of talking loudly is not itself loud or quiet, since it is not the sort of term of which 'loud' and 'quiet' can be predicated, or just as a susceptibility to headaches is for the same reason not itself unendurable or endurable, so the skills, tastes and bents which are exercised in overt or internal operations are not themselves overt or internal, witnessable or unwitnessable. The traditional theory of the mind has misconstrued the type-distinction between disposition and exercise into its mythical bifurcation of unwitnessable mental causes and their witnessable physical effects.

The clown's trippings and tumblings are the workings of his mind, for they are his jokes; but the visibly similar trippings and tumblings of a clumsy man are not the workings of that man's mind. For he does not trip on purpose. Tripping on purpose is both a bodily and a mental process, but it is not two processes, such as one process of purposing to trip and, as an effect, another process of tripping. Yet the old myth dies hard. We are still tempted to argue that if the clown's antics exhibit carefulness, judgment, wit, and appreciation of the moods of his spectators, there must be occurring in the clown's head a counterpart performance to that which is taking place on the sawdust. If he is thinking what he is doing, there must be occurring behind his painted face a cogitative shadow-operation which we do not witness, tallying with, and controlling, the bodily contortions which we do witness. Surely the thinking of thoughts is the basic activity of minds and surely, too, the process of thinking is an invisible and inaudible process. So how can the clown's visible and audible performance be his mind at work?

To do justice to this objection it is necessary to make a verbal concession. There has fairly recently come into general use a certain special sense of the words 'mental' and 'mind'. We speak of 'mental arithmetic', of 'mind-reading' and of debates going on 'in the mind', and it certainly is the case that what is in this sense mental is unwitnessable. A boy is said to be doing 'mental arithmetic' when instead of writing down, or reciting aloud, the numerical symbols with which he is operating, he says them to himself, performing his calculations in silent soliloquy. Similarly a person is said to be reading the mind of another when he describes truly what the other is saying or picturing to himself in auditory or visual images. That these are special uses of 'mental' and 'mind' is easily shown. For a boy who does his calculating aloud, or on paper, may be reasoning correctly and organising his steps methodically; his reckoning is not the less a careful intellectual operation for being conducted in public instead of in private. His performance is therefore an exercise of a mental faculty in the normal sense of 'mental.'

Now calculating does not first acquire the rank of proper thinking when its author begins to do it with his lips closed and his hands in his pockets. The sealing of the lips is no part of the definition of thinking. A man may think aloud or half under his breath; he may think silently, yet with lip-movements conspicuous enough to be read by a lip-reader; or he may, as most of us have done since nursery-days, think in silence and with motionless lips. The differences are differences of social and personal convenience, of celerity and of facility. They need import no more differences into the coherence, cogency or appropriateness of the intellectual operations performed than is imported into them by a writer's preference for pencils over pens, or for invisible ink over ordinary ink. A deaf and dumb person talks in manual signs. Perhaps, when he wants to keep his thoughts to himself, he makes these signs with his hands kept behind his back or under the table. The fact that these signs might happen to be observed by a Paul Pry would not lead us or their maker to say that he was not thinking.

This special use of 'mental' and 'mind' in which they signify what is done 'in one's head' cannot be used as evidence for the dogma of the ghost in the machine. It is nothing but a contagion from that dogma. The technical trick of conducting our thinking in auditory word-images, instead of in spoken words, does indeed secure secrecy for our thinking, since the auditory imaginings of one person are not seen or heard by another (or, as we shall see, by their owner either). But this secrecy is not the secrecy ascribed to the postulated episodes of the ghostly shadow-world. It is merely the convenient privacy which characterises the tunes that run in my head and the things that I see in my mind's eye.

Moreover the fact that a person says things to himself in his head does not entail that he is thinking. He can babble deliriously, or repeat jingles in inner speech, just as he can in talking aloud. The distinction between talking sense and babbling, or between thinking what one is saying and merely saying, cuts across the distinction between talking aloud and talking to oneself. What makes a verbal operation an exercise of intellect is independent of what makes it public or private. Arithmetic done with pencil and paper may be more intelligent than mental arithmetic, and the public tumblings of the clown may be more intelligent than the tumblings which he merely 'sees' in his mind's eye or 'feels' in his mind's legs, if, as may or may not be the case, any such imaginings of antics occur.

SUGGESTED FURTHER READINGS FOR CHAPTER FIVE

Berkeley, George, *Three Dialogues between Hylas and Philonous.*
Blanshard, Brand, *The Nature of Thought,* two volumes.
Descartes, René, *Meditations on First Philosophy.*
Dewey, John, *The Quest for Certainty* (or *Intelligence in the Modern World,* Modern Library edition of Dewey's Works (ed. Ratner), p. 305-343).
Eaton, R. M., *Symbolism and Truth.*
Feigel, H. and Sellars, Wilfrid, *Readings in Philosophical Analysis.*
Hume, David, *Treatise on Human Nature.*
———, *An Enquiry concerning Human Understanding.*
Kant, Immanuel, *Prolegomena to any Future Metaphysics.*
———, *Critique of Pure Reason.*
Leibniz, Gottfried Wilhelm, *New Essays.*
Lewis, C. I., *Mind and the World Order.*
Locke, John, *An Essay Concerning Human Understanding.*
McKeon, Richard (ed.), *Selections from Medieval Philosophers* (The Modern Student's Library, published by Charles Scribner's Sons).
Plato, *Theaetetus.*
Royce, Josiah, *Lectures on Modern Idealism.*
Russell, Bertrand, *Problems of Philosophy.*
———, *Our Knowledge of the External World.*
Ryle, Gilbert, *The Concept of Mind.*
Santayana, George, *Scepticism and Animal Faith.*
Spinoza, Benedict, *On the Improvement of the Understanding.*

Chapter Six

THEORIES OF ART AND AESTHETIC EXPERIENCE

INTRODUCTION

TO the realm of art and aesthetic experience one hesitates to bring critical reflection. Before art's products one stands in rapture; the word that expresses one's feeling in such a state is the word "ineffable," and the ineffable is not prone to analysis. Yet if not at the moment of aesthetic experience, at a later moment questions begin to rise. What was it that moved us so deeply in hearing a certain musical piece? Why did we say that the painting we saw was beautiful? Has the ugly or the neutral any place in art? Why do we call certain objects works of art? Do they all have some common trait? Why is it that we consider certain works of art as great and others as inferior? Are there absolute standards of taste or are they merely relative? Has art any function in civilization, and if so, what is it? These and similar questions when fully analyzed become the basis of one's philosophy of art and aesthetic experience.

Before examining some of these questions one ought briefly to define art and aesthetic experience. *Art,* in its inclusive sense, refers to any manipulation of objects or events for any human purpose whatsoever. We speak of the art of masonry, the art of weaving, the art of speech, the art of writing, the art of politics, the art of war. Usually art is divided into two types: useful or technical art and fine art. Technical art refers to any human product that is useful for an end other than aesthetic effect. The central notion here is utility. A car, a machine, a tool are examples of technical art. Fine art, on the other hand, refers to products whose end is aesthetic effect, commonly referred to as "beauty." A painting, a statue, a poem, a piece of music are examples of fine art. In the present discussion art will be used in the sense of fine art unless otherwise specified. Similarly, the expression *aesthetic experience* is much wider in its general meaning than the sense in which it will here be used. The word *aesthetic,* derived originally from the Greek, referred to anything that is perceptive. Gradually, however, it came to be applied to the realms of art and beauty. By aesthetic experience we shall mean, therefore, whatever experience has relevance to art, whether the experience be that of the creative artist or of the appreciator. Some of the major theories of art and aesthetic experience will now be examined;

and in the course of the examination there will be occasion to analyze philosophical questions concerning the nature and function of art.

I. Art as Imitation

One of the oldest theories of art is that art is essentially imitation. Plato gives expression to this theory, though this is not the only theory of art that Plato presents. Plato describes the art of painting, for example, as an imitation of appearances, say of a tree or a bed with such similitude that one may mistake the copy for the real thing. In his own words: "A painter will paint a cobbler, carpenter, or any other artist, though he knows nothing of their arts; and, if he is a good artist, he may deceive children or simple persons when he shows them his picture of a carpenter from a distance, and they will fancy that they are looking at a real carpenter." But it is just because the poets and the painters are imitators that they are incapable of discerning what is good and what is bad. There is no place for the artist in Plato's State. "When we have anointed him with myrrh, and set a garland upon his head, we shall send him away to another city."

In his *Poetics,* Aristotle presents a modified form of the imitation theory of art. For Aristotle, poetry springs from the instinct for harmony and rhythm. The instinct of imitation "is implanted in man from childhood, one difference between him and the other animals being that he is the most imitative of living creatures and through imitation he learns his earliest lessons." Aristotle not only finds the source of poetry in the mimetic instinct but he indicates that it is "also natural for all to delight in works of imitation."

The theory of art as imitation is too simple a theory to be satisfactory. If art is merely an exact imitation of the original, why, as Socrates points out, should we go to art? Is not the original much superior? An imitative painting of a tree or of a river can never completely capture the colors or the nuances of their beauty. And if fine art is merely an imitation, it is at best something second rate. And, again, the imitation theory of art fails to account for significant forms of art. Such major forms of art as architecture, poetry, and music may occasionally make use of imitation, such as in a floral motif or in the sound of joy or sorrow or of a thunderstorm, but these are merely minor aspects of these arts. Art is not so much an imitation as an enrichment of human experience through objective forms; imitation is passive, but art is essentially a creative construction.

II. Art as Insight into Reality

Another theory of art and aesthetic experience that will be considered is a more metaphysical one. According to this theory the aesthetic experience is a species of knowledge. Sometimes the claim is that the aesthetic experience is insight into some transcendental reality, independent of observed particular objects. Beauty, for example, in this view is not a mundane quality of certain objects in their natural environment but is a universal, something over and above all particular beautiful objects. And sometimes, though less frequently, the claim is that art and aesthetic experience are not so much insight into or an intuition of universals as of particular objects and situations. In both cases the fundamental belief is that art is a form of cognition.

Plato, who is the source of so many major theories of art, argues in some of his dialogues—especially in the *Symposium* and the *Phaedrus*—that beauty, with truth and goodness, is an eternal, changeless reality. Beauty belongs to the realm of Ideas or Forms, and these for him are perfect, absolute, immutable. A given beautiful object only partially expresses and vaguely reminds one of the absolute beauty. Absolute beauty cannot be perceived in our ordinary experience. One must go through a spiritual struggle to attain the vision of the transcendent beauty. In the *Symposium* Plato describes the steps of this ascent. To attain the final vision of absolute beauty one should begin early in life to be sensitive to physical beauty. One should then gradually learn to go beyond the attraction of physical beauty and learn to love the beauty of soul even when it is not expressed in outward comeliness. Next, he should learn to love beauty as revealed in laws and institutions, and then advance to "science." But even here one has not reached the end of the ascent. The final step is the one that will reward one with the vision of the supreme beauty which was all along the object of one's search. Beauty at this highest level is eternal and perfect, above mutability. Particular beautiful objects are mere echoes, imitations, reminders of the absolute beauty.

In modern philosophy it is Schopenhauer who most effectively maintains the notion that art is a form of insight into reality. For Schopenhauer, reality at its core is *Will;* the so-called objective world as idea is merely the outward side of the will, only the appearance of the real world. The universal will, of which everything is an expression, has grades of objectification. The will objectifies itself first of all as Ideas, as universal types. These Ideas are eternal and changeless. Next come particular things which exemplify the Ideas. In such a philosophy our everyday knowledge is knowledge for action. As such, it is only an instrument through which the will seeks to fulfill itself. Yet there is a kind of knowledge that can rise above this purely practical status. This happens when the mind fixes its attention on the Platonic Ideas and contemplates them for their own sake, that is, as independent of the desires of the will. Such knowledge is no longer the instrument of the will; on the contrary, it frees one from the will in the latter's eternal character of desire. It is through this kind of contemplation that art comes into being. The artistic genius is one capable of this kind of contemplation; going beyond the practical bearing of the objects around him, he penetrates to the inner meaning of these objects, that is, apprehends the Platonic Ideas of which they are a particular expression. Though most of us do not have this sheer power of genius, we may yet in a limited sense partake of the same kind of experience.

Schopenhauer applies his theory of art to various forms of art. These constitute a hierarchy. Architecture as a fine art seizes on the most inarticulate manifestation of the will; that is, it sets forth the Platonic Ideas of such purely material manifestations as gravity, cohesion, rigidity. Great architecture holds all of these properties in balance. As we pass to the paintings of animals or to their sculptural representation we come to a higher form of art than architecture, since life uncontrolled by intellect is a higher stage of will's objectification than the purely inanimate or material. Next in the order of ascent come statues and paintings of human beings. Sculpture sets forth the outward beauty of the human being; painting comes nearer to portraying his inner life. The highest of the arts that reveal Ideas is poetry which represents significant characters in significant actions. And tragedy is the highest form of poetry, for in tragedy we feel most directly the blindness of the striving will. Music for Schopenhauer stands by itself; it is different from all other arts. The latter reveal the Ideas, but music penetrates behind the Ideas to the will itself. The other arts are copies of copies, while music is a copy of the original.

According to the classic view, as we have seen, art is a species of cognition: for Plato an apprehension of the Forms, for Schopenhauer a like apprehension in the matrix of his own type of philosophy. Croce retains the fundamental thesis that art is cognitive, though for him the object of knowledge is the individual thing and not the universal or the Idea in the Platonic sense. For Croce reality is spirit developing in several independent ways. The various aspects of reality do not have to be reduced to one another. In the activity of the spirit one may distinguish between contemplation and action. We perceive, know, and also act. The perceptive aspect of experience may be assigned to intuition; the intellectual aspect to concept-formation. Art belongs to the realm of intuition. For Croce art is intuition, and intuition includes all that is concrete and immediate in experience. Intuition involves sense-data; it also involves memory, imagination, feeling. Croce also defines art as expression, but intuition and expression are identical for him. "To intuit is to express, and nothing else." Expression takes the form of images: color-images, line-images, word-images. These images are not mere passive impressions but are meaningful and charged with feeling. Aesthetic experience is thus expression in images; and the physical creative work of art, such as a painting, a statue, or a poem, is nothing but a copy of what the artist has experienced.

Alexander's elegant discussion on beauty should be studied carefully as a corrective of Croce's neglect of the physical in his definition of art. Croce's interpretation of art in terms of intuition tends to drift towards extreme subjectivism. Alexander rightly points out that art both in its origin as well as in its creation depends on external material. As he expresses it: "Art grows out of craft and goes beyond it, when the worker handles his materials not, or not only, as a means of reaching a certain practical end but for their own sakes, and becomes contemplative instead of merely practical." And, again, as on the nature of artistic creation, he writes: "The mind is mixed in artistic creation with its materials because the impulses initiated in it the course of construction are reflected in the materials or worked up into their artistic form."

We need not examine here the basic ideas of Plato's, Schopenhauer's, and Croce's philosophical systems. The issues are complex and would lead us too far from the present subject. Yet it is important to note that valuable ideas of these philosophers about art and aesthetic experience can be retained without necessarily consenting to their theories of reality. Plato's insistence that the vision of beauty can be attained only through a spiritual ascent; Schopenhauer's analysis of art as contemplation, and specially his suggestive characterization of specific forms of art; Croce's account of aesthetic experience as intuition and expression: all these views may have a permanent value. One may accept the empirical insights of these philosophers into different phases of aesthetic experience without submitting to their more doubtful and speculative metaphysics.

III. Art as Play

The view of art as insight into reality usually places the alleged absolute beauty above the mundane realm and emphasizes the contemplation and vision of this beauty. Yet to make art and its experience more intelligible and vital, greater continuity has to be established between art and other activities of life. Art occupies too wide an area of human life to be exclusively identified with the rare insights of geniuses. The play theory of art, with its emphasis on activity, origins, and functions, is an attempt to meet this need. A variety of thinkers have found this theory of art fruitful. The theory has its beginnings in some of the Greek philosophers, but one must go primarily to the writings of Schiller, Spencer, and Groos to find its full development and implications.

The first point of interest in the play theory of art is its description of the genesis of art. For Schiller, the genesis of art is to be sought in the play impulse, and play for him is the expression of superfluous energy. "The beast *labors,* when a want is the incitement to its activity, and it *plays,* when profusion of vigor is the incitement, when superfluous life is its own stimulus to activity." But the spirit of play is also expressed in the imagination of man, which, not unlike his corporeal organs, has "its free emotion and its material play, in which it merely enjoys its native power and liberty, without any reference to shape." Thus far imagination is not yet aesthetic, since the images flow in a free and unconstrained manner; but the activity of the imagination becomes aesthetic play when taste asserts itself and imposes form upon the products of this activity. Similarly, Spencer finds the origin of play and aesthetic activity in surplus energy. Though Spencer got the suggestion from Schiller, he gave the idea a fuller evolutionary description. As superior animals evolve, "having faculties more efficient and more numerous," they "begin to spend their time and strength not merely for immediate needs." Better nutrition, gained by superiority, "occasionally yields surplus of vigour," and the basic appetites being satisfied, the surplus vigour and energy are diverted to all kinds of play. Groos, who also advocates the play theory of art, is critical of some of Schiller's and Spencer's ideas on the origin of art. For Groos surplus energy is a favourable condition for play, "but it is not its motive cause, nor . . . a necessary condition of its existence." A playful act, he argues, is no more dependent on surplus energy than a serious act. When a kitten claws, for example, at a rolling ball of twine nothing more is needed, he claims, than when a cat moves toward a mouse. For Groos, play is instinctive in origin, though not all play is purely instinctive in character. As we ascend "in the scale of existence the richer and finer become the psychological phenomena that supplement the natural impulse, ennobling it, elevating it, and tending to conceal it under added details."

The second point of interest in the play theory of art is its analysis of the relation between play and aesthetic activity. Are play and art the same thing? Or, if they differ, in what respect do they differ? For Schiller, in the beginning at least, play and art are identical, but gradually, as earlier pointed out, he somewhat modifies this identity. Art goes beyond the wild excesses and unconstrained motions of the play impulse. Even the play of imagination does not become aesthetic until it is regulated and controlled. In art, according to Schiller, form takes possession of the material, and imposes the standards of taste. This activity is independent of physical needs, and eventually the beautiful becomes an end in itself. Spencer also emphasizes the similarities and relative differences between play and aesthetic activity. According to Spencer, in normal circumstances primary actions result in immediate gratification, in the increased ability that comes from exercise, and in the achievement of some objective. On the other hand, secondary actions, and Spencer places play and aesthetic activity in this class, issue only in the first two results. To this extent play and aesthetic activities are the same. And yet they also differ. Though both emerge in the process of organic evolution, play is the activity of "lower powers," and art is the activity of "higher powers."

Finally, the play theory of art attempts to explain the function of art in human life. In this connection Schiller's views are of special significance. Schiller develops his conception of the role of art within the framework of the Kantian philosophy. Kant had introduced a rigid separation between two realms, the realm of necessary phenomena and the realm of transcendent freedom. Freedom, for Kant, was limited to moral action controlled by the supra-empirical conception of duty. Schiller attempts to escape this rigid dualism by suggesting that play and art may occupy an intermediate, transitional place between these two realms by serving to educate man in the responsibilities of freedom. Play may do this because it is an ideal union of the "sensuous" and the "formal" instincts. Play's mediating capacity enables man to experience his world both in its sensuous and rational aspects. In play, man need submit neither to the extreme abstracting power of the instinct for form nor to the compulsions of passion subsequent upon the operations of the "sensuous" instinct. "Man only plays when in the full meaning of the word he is a man, and he is only completely a man when he plays." Groos also gives considerable thought to the function of play and art. Play develops the crude powers and matures them for life's uses. The child, helpless at birth and cared for by its parents, develops gradually its capacities to meet the problems and difficulties of life. This gradual development is achieved by the child's playful activities. There is also the impulse for "imitation," which strengthens the hereditary foundations of the activity imitated. The potentialities of the child are thus actualized by means of a "preparatory practice" and "imitation." The boy plays at fighting and engages in mimic warfare in preparation for the career of soldier. The girl plays at nursery games in anticipation of and preparation for motherhood.

The play theory of art has been fruitful in several ways: by providing a genetic theory of art, by emphasizing the place of action in art (an aspect of art ignored by many theories), and by recognizing the function of art in the larger context of life. Yet it has certain limitations. Of these the major one is that play, at least in most of its forms, is recreative, whereas art is essentially creative. The player of a game has to function within the limits set by specific regulations; and though the artist is likewise bound by the limitations inherent in form and matter, both the art-object and the mood it induces are truly creative in proportion to the richness with which the artist's imagination functions.

IV. *Art as Expression of Feeling and Desire*

We referred to art as insight into reality and as play. One conception emphasizes the cognitive aspect, while the other stresses the active. It remained to more recent theories of art to make crucial the conative and affective aspects. Common to the theories of art that will now be examined is the fact that art and aesthetic experience are primarily concerned with the expression and intensification of human feelings, desires, and wishes. There are, of course, wide differences within this general frame.

One of the earlier theories of art in terms of human feeling and desires is that of Tolstoi. For Tolstoi, art is primarily the language of feeling; it is a means by which men transmit feeling, in the same way that as by speech they transmit thought. "Art is a human activity, consisting in this that one man consciously, by means of certain external signs, hands on to others feelings he has lived through, and that other people are infected by these feelings, and also experience them." The criterion of art is thus its degree of infectiousness, its ability to evoke in the observer or reader the feeling of the artist. These feelings are transmitted by means of movements, lines, colors, sounds, and words. The subject matter of art is as wide as the life of humanity itself. The relation of man to his world is constantly taking on new aspects, and this fact provides unlimited material for artists. Yet the feelings connected with pleasure are quite limited, since they consist almost exclusively of pride, sex-expression, and weariness with life. In any case, they have long ago been interpreted by artists, so that their field is exhausted. In order to produce a real work of art, the artist must move on the level of the highest conception of humanity and must experience the emotion that flowers on this level.

Another theory of art that is expressed in terms of feeling is that of Santayana who has written extensively on art and on its various phases. He first makes a distinction between the pleasures of the senses and the pleasure that is traceable to the sense of beauty. The former involves no assertion beyond the individual's experience, while the latter claims universality. When something gives me pleasure I do not assert that it must give pleasure to others too, but when I judge something to be beautiful my judgment means that "the thing is beautiful in itself, or ... that it should seem so to everybody." Yet theoretically Santayana thinks it is difficult to defend the universality of aesthetic judgment. There is, for example, no universal agreement among men on aesthetic matters, and whatever agreement one does observe seems to stem from similarity of origin and circumstances. And, again, it is unreasonable to insist that what appears beautiful to one person *ought* to appear beautiful to another. How shall we, then, explain beauty's claim of universality? Santayana resorts to the psychological tendency to objectification. At an early stage of mental development the tendency of men was to objectify every sensation and emotion, and thus consider them as qualities of external objects. In our own scientific era we tend to regard as qualities of objects only such qualities as extension and other physically measurable properties. Santayana believes that in our experience of beauty we have a survival of the primitive and pre-scientific tendency to objectification. The fact that we try to get other men to share our aesthetic experience shows that we tend to regard beauty as in the object rather than in our minds. Santayana thus reaches his definition: "Beauty is pleasure regarded as the quality of a thing."

Santayana's definition of beauty sums up a variety of ideas. First of all, beauty for Santayana is a value, that is, it is not the perception of a fact but rather of "an emotion, an affection of our volitional and appreciative nature." Secondly, beauty as value is something positive. In our appreciation of beauty we feel ourselves in the presence of something good. Thirdly, the pleasure that we get from beauty is not derived from utility but from the immediate perception. For Santayana, beauty is ultimate good, "a positive value that is intrinsic; it is pleasure." Finally, the pleasure that comes from beauty, in contrast to the pleasures of the senses, tends to be objectified, thus appearing as the quality of things rather than the mere experience of our private consciousness. The transition from the one to the other is gradual, yet the distinction is significant for Santayana. There is no sharp line between our ordinary sensations and our experiences of beauty: "it depends upon the degree of objectivity my feeling has attained at the moment whether I say it pleases me or it is beautiful." The more remote, interwoven, and inextricable the pleasure is, the more we tend to objectify it.

And finally, there is Parker's view that art is the imaginative expression of a wish. According to him wishes may be satisfied in two ways: in the real way and in the dream way. The first is the practical way: one satisfies one's hunger by getting food. The second is the imaginary way—here "there is no acquisitive interaction with environment; the wish is satisfied by something that occurs entirely within myself, within my own mind and body in the realm of fantasy." Parker goes further to show some of the characteristics of dream experience. One of these is the "as if" attitude. Things seen in a day-dream or in a dream at night are regarded by us "as if" they were real, yet for the time being we do not take them to be merely imaginary but actual.

Parker applies his view of the imagination and the dream to various forms of art and tries to show that they are all modes of make-believe which satisfy wishes both of the creator and beholder. That such arts as painting, sculpture, literature, and drama can be made to conform to his theory seems clear enough, but he claims the same conformity for music, the dance, and architecture. When I watch a dance, I enact in the imagination the movements of the dancer and vicariously enjoy her ease and joy. In the case of music the experience is the same; the moods of the musician are awakened and fulfilled in me. Music is beautiful as a voice that I hear "storming, sobbing, making merry, lamenting, rejoicing, as the case may be, and it is as if that voice were my own." And for architecture the argument is the same. When I am in the presence of a beautiful building, especially if I am inside of it, "I feel all about me life variously and magnificently eloquent, uttering a meaning which, to be sure, I cannot put into words ... meaning that comes to me, not by the avenues of sound, but by that of sight, and through subtle arousals of imaginative touch and movement."

Yet there are differences, for Parker, between ordinary dreams and art. A dream in the ordinary sense is an inner fact existing wholly in the realm of imagination, but art belongs also to the outer world, to the world of the senses. In art the dream is given sensuous shape; it is expressed in colors, lines, sounds, and so on. The artist creates something external that can charm the senses. Yet despite the sensuous side of art, art does not leave the world of the imagination; rather the artist takes the senses into the imagination. A work of art possesses objectivity, the tang of reality, while still remaining a dream. Because of this objectivity, a work of art not only satisfies a wish as does any sort of dream, but it also becomes a means for "the clarification and communication of imagination." Art, for Parker, is expression; yet this expression, unlike that of the practical or scientific kind, "is expression for the sake of expression because in the process of expression a dream is embodied, a wish satisfied."

Interpretations of art in terms of desire, wish, and imagination make art and the aesthetic experience more intelligible than the other views that have been considered. They place the creative activity of the artist and the experience of the beholder in a natural setting; they establish a continuity between the biological drives or impulses and the idealized experiences we call aesthetic. In these views art retains all its ideal and creative qualities without becoming something transcendental or esoteric. Yet these interpretations leave many problems to be explored. What is an adequate conception of feeling, desire, imagination? What is the nature of the aesthetic mood? What is the relation between aesthetic symbol and symbol in general? What specific variations do these ideas assume in the different modes of art? These and similar questions need full analysis in the light of modern psychology and in terms of the techniques of the arts before the empirical theories of art can be wholly satisfactory.

V. Art, Criticism, and Morality

We have been discussing, primarily, different theories of art; yet there are many other problems in the philosophy of art: the analysis of form and expression in art, the examination of the standards of criticism, the determination of the place of art in society, and the relation of art to science, religion, morality, and civilization. Of these problems two have been selected: examination of the standards of criticism, and the relation of morality to art.

Ducasse gives a clear and persuasive analysis of the issues involved in art criticism. He defends a relativistic view. As he writes: "Beauty is relative to the individual observer. Beauty being . . . dependent upon the constitution of the individual observer, it will be as variable as the constitution. An object which one person properly calls beautiful will, with equal propriety be not so judged by another." An extreme alternative to Ducasse's view would be the claim that there are absolute standards and truths of art which everyone must accept. Yet it may be that one may develop a theory of standards that would do justice to both relativism and absolutism. It may be that through long aesthetic experience we may develop certain functional absolutes in art that may help to regulate our taste and critical judgments.

Perry, in his sensitive, fair, and suggestive analysis of the relation of art to morality points out that "the aesthetic life of man is embedded in his moral life." The aesthetic interest, though independent of morality, has a vital relation to it. "Because the aesthetic interest operates in the realm of the imagination, it enjoys a peculiar freedom to multiply and entertain ideal possibilities. It tends to emancipate men's minds from habit, authority, and *status quo,* and thus readily allies itself with the forces of progress and life—realization." On the other hand, the aesthetic interest may tend to be "a passive complacency, a narrow absorption, and an irresponsibility toward that very social organization on which aesthetic life itself depends." Aesthetic rapture may become "so obsessive as to make men indifferent to its evil effect—of commission or omission—on the lives of other men." How should one resolve this possible conflict arising between morality and art? This is not an easy question to be determined. For Plato and Tolstoi, for instance, the demands of morality and religion must be the ruling factors. Yet Perry rightly refers to the dangers to which art may be exposed from moral and social controls. As he puts it: "Art will flourish best when it is allowed to germinate, grow, and prolificate in obedience to its own nature." There may be occasions when the conflict between morality and art need not be settled by suppression of one interest in favor of the other, but rather by acceptance of the conflict as an inevitable part of experience—as something to be lived through and endured.

Y.H.K.

35. *Art as Imitation**

PLATO (B.C. 427–347)

Of the many excellences which I perceive in the order of our State, there is none which upon reflection pleases me better than the rule about poetry.

To what do you refer?

To the rejection of imitative poetry, which certainly ought not to be received; as I see far more clearly now that the parts of the soul have been distinguished.

What do you mean?

Speaking in confidence, for I should not like to have my words repeated to the tragedians and the rest of the imitative tribe—but I do not mind saying to you, that all poetical imitations are ruinous to the understanding of the hearers, and that the knowledge of their true nature is the only antidote to them.

Explain the purpose of your remark.

Well, I will tell you, although I have always from my earliest youth had an awe and love of Homer, which even now makes the words falter on my lips, for he

* From *The Republic,* Book X, translated by Benjamin Jowett (by permission from Oxford University Press).

is the great captain and teacher of the whole of that charming tragic company; but a man is not to be reverenced more than the truth, and therefore I will speak out.

Very good, he said.

Listen to me then, or rather, answer me.

Put your question.

Can you tell me what imitation is? for I really do not know.

A likely thing, then, that I should know.

Why not? for the duller eye may often see a thing sooner than the keener.

Very true, he said; but in your presence, even if I had any faint notion, I could not muster courage to utter it. Will you inquire yourself?

Well then, shall we begin the inquiry in our usual manner: Whenever a number of individuals have a common name, we assume them to have also a corresponding idea or form:—do you understand me?

I do.

Let us take any common instance; there are beds and tables in the world—plenty of them, are there not?

Yes.

But there are only two ideas or forms of them—one the idea of a bed, the other of a table.

True.

And the maker of either of them makes a bed or he makes a table for our use, in accordance with the idea—that is our way of speaking in this and similar instances—but no artificer makes the ideas themselves: how could he?

Impossible.

And there is another artist,—I should like to know what you would say of him.

Who is he?

One who is the maker of all the works of all other workmen.

What an extraordinary man!

Wait a little, and there will be more reason for your saying so. For this is he who is able to make not only vessels of every kind, but plants and animals, himself and all other things—the earth and heaven, and the things which are in heaven or under the earth; he makes the gods also.

He must be a wizard and no mistake.

Oh! you are incredulous, are you? Do you mean that there is no such maker or creator, or that in one sense there might be a maker of all these things but in another not? Do you see that there is a way in which you could make them all yourself?

What way?

An easy way enough; or rather, there are many ways in which the feat might be quickly and easily accomplished, none quicker than that of turning a mirror round and round—you would soon enough make the sun and the heavens, and the earth and yourself, and other animals and plants, and all the other things of which we were just now speaking, in the mirror.

Yes, he said; but they would be appearances only.

Very good, I said, you are coming to the point now. And the painter too is, as I conceive, just such another—a creator of appearances, is he not?

Of course.

But then I suppose you will say that what he creates is untrue. And yet there is a sense in which the painter also creates a bed?

Yes, he said, but not a real bed.

And what of the maker of the bed? were you not saying that he too makes, not the idea which, according to our view, is the essence of the bed, but only a particular bed?

Yes, I did.

Then if he does not make that which exists he cannot make true existence, but only some semblance of existence; and if any one were to say that the work of the maker of the bed, or of any other workman, has real existence, he could hardly be supposed to be speaking the truth.

At any rate, he replied, philosophers would say that he was not speaking the truth.

No wonder, then, that his work too is an indistinct expression of truth.

No wonder.

Suppose now that by the light of the examples just offered we inquire who this imitator is?

If you please.

Well then, here are three beds: one existing in nature, which is made by God, as I think that we may say—for no one else can be the maker?

No.

There is another which is the work of the carpenter?

Yes.

And the work of the painter is a third?

Yes.

Beds, then, are of three kinds, and there are three artists who superintend them: God, the maker of the bed, and the painter?

Yes, there are three of them.

God, whether from choice or from necessity, made one bed in nature and one only; two or more such ideal beds neither ever have been nor ever will be made by God.

Why is that?

Because even if He had made but two, a third would still appear behind them which both of them would have for their idea, and that would be the ideal bed and not the two others.

Very true, he said.

God knew this, and He desired to be the real maker of a real bed, not a particular maker of a particular bed, and therefore He created a bed which is essentially and by nature one only.

So we believe.

Shall we, then, speak of Him as the natural author or maker of the bed?

Yes, he replied; inasmuch as by the natural process of creation He is the author of this and of all other things.

And what shall we say of the carpenter—is not he also the maker of the bed?

Yes.

But would you call the painter a creator and maker?

Certainly not.

Yet if he is not the maker, what is he in relation to the bed?

I think, he said, that we may fairly designate him as the imitator of that which the others make.

Good, I said; then you call him who is third in the descent from nature an imitator?

Certainly, he said.

And the tragic poet is an imitator, and therefore, like all other imitators, he is thrice removed from the king and from the truth?

That appears to be so.

Then about the imitator we are agreed. And what about the painter?—I would like to know whether he may be thought to imitate that which originally exists in nature, or only the creation of artists?

The latter.

As they are or as they appear? you have still to determine this.

What do you mean?

I mean, that you may look at a bed from different points of view, obliquely or directly from any other point of view, and the bed will appear different, but there is no difference in reality. And the same of all things.

Yes, he said, the difference is only apparent.

Now let me ask you another question: Which is the art of painting designed to be—an imitation of things as they are, or as they appear—of appearance or of reality?

Of appearance.

Then the imitator, I said, is a long way off the truth, and can do all things because he lightly touches on a small part of them, and that part an image. For example: A painter will paint a cobbler, carpenter, or any other artist, though he knows nothing of their arts; and, if he is a good artist, he may deceive children or simple persons, when he shows them his picture of a carpenter from a distance, and they will fancy that they are looking at a real carpenter.

Certainly.

And whenever any one informs us that he has found a man who knows all the arts, and all things else that anybody knows, and every single thing with a higher degree of accuracy than any other man—whoever tells us this, I think that we can only imagine him to be a simple creature who is likely to have been deceived by some wizard or actor whom he met, and whom he thought all-knowing, because he himself was unable to analyse the nature of knowledge and ignorance and imitation.

Most true.

And so, when we hear persons saying that the tragedians, and Homer, who is at their head, know all the arts and all things human, virtue as well as vice, and divine things too, for that the good poet cannot compose well unless he knows his subject, and that he who has not this knowledge can never be a poet, we ought to consider whether here also there may not be a similar illusion. Perhaps they may have come across imitators and been deceived by them; they may not have remembered when they saw their works that these were but imitations thrice removed from the truth, and could easily be made without any knowledge of the truth, because they are appearances only and not realities? Or, after all, they may be in the right, and poets do really know the things about which they seem to the many to speak so well?

The question, he said, should by all means be considered.

Now do you suppose that if a person were able to make the original as well as the image, he would seriously devote himself to the image-making branch? Would he allow imitation to be the ruling principle of his life, as if he had nothing higher in him?

I should say not.

The real artist, who knew what he was imitating, would be interested in realities and not in imitations; and would desire to leave as memorials of himself works many and fair; and, instead of being the author of encomiums, he would prefer to be the theme of them.

Yes, he said, that would be to him a source of much greater honour and profit.

Then, I said, we must put a question to Homer; not about medicine, or any of the arts to which his poems only incidentally refer: we are not going to ask him, or any other poet, whether he has cured patients like Asclepius, or left behind him a school of medicine such as the Asclepiads were, or whether he only talks about medicine and other arts at second-hand; but we have a right to know respecting military tactics, politics, education, which are the chiefest and noblest subjects of his poems, and we may fairly ask him about them. 'Friend Homer,' then we say to him, 'if you are only in the second remove from truth in what you say of virtue, and not in the third—not an image maker or imitator—and if you are able to discern what pursuits make men better or worse in private or public life, tell us what State was ever better governed by your help? The good order of Lacedaemon is due to Lycurgus, and many other cities great and small have been similarly benefited by others; but who says that you have been a good legislator to them and have done them any good? Italy and Sicily boast of Charondas, and there is Solon who is renowned among us; but what city has anything to say about you?' Is there any city which he might name?

I think not, said Glaucon; not even the Homerids themselves pretend that he was a legislator.

Well, but is there any war on record

which was carried on successfully by him, or aided by his counsels, when he was alive?

There is not.

Or is there any invention [1] of his, applicable to the arts or to human life, such as Thales the Milesian or Anacharsis the Scythian, and other ingenious men have conceived, which is attributed to him?

There is absolutely nothing of the kind.

But, if Homer never did any public service, was he privately a guide or teacher of any? Had he in his lifetime friends who loved to associate with him, and who handed down to posterity an Homeric way of life, such as was established by Pythagoras who was so greatly beloved for his wisdom, and whose followers are to this day quite celebrated for the order which was named after him?

Nothing of the kind is recorded of him. For surely, Socrates, Creophylus, the companion of Homer, that child of flesh, whose name always makes us laugh, might be more justly ridiculed for his stupidity, if, as is said, Homer was greatly neglected by him and others in his own day when he was alive?

Yes, I replied, that is the tradition. But can you imagine, Glaucon, that if Homer had really been able to educate and improve mankind—if he had possessed knowledge and not been a mere imitator—can you imagine, I say, that he would not have had many followers, and been honoured and loved by them? Protagoras of Abdera, and Prodicus of Ceos, and a host of others, have only to whisper to their contemporaries: 'You will never be able to manage either your own house or your own State until you appoint us to be your ministers of education'—and this ingenious device of theirs has such an effect in making men love

them that their companions all but carry them about on their shoulders. And is it conceivable that the contemporaries of Homer, or again of Hesiod, would have allowed either of them to go about as rhapsodists, if they had really been able to make mankind virtuous? Would they not have been as unwilling to part with them as with gold, and have compelled them to stay at home with them? Or, if the master would not stay, then the disciples would have followed him about everywhere, until they had got education enough?

Yes, Socrates, that, I think, is quite true.

Then must we not infer that all these poetical individuals, beginning with Homer, are only imitators; they copy images of virtue and the like, but the truth they never reach? The poet is like a painter who, as we have already observed, will make a likeness of a cobbler though he understands nothing of cobbling; and his picture is good enough for those who know no more than he does, and judge only by colours and figures.

Quite so.

In like manner the poet with his words and phrases [2] may be said to lay on the colours of the several arts, himself understanding their nature only enough to imitate them; and other people, who are as ignorant as he is, and judge only from his words, imagine that if he speaks of cobbling, or of military tactics, or of anything else, in metre and harmony and rhythm, he speaks very well—such is the sweet influence which melody and rhythm by nature have. And I think that you must have observed again and again what a poor appearance the tales of poets make when stripped of the colours which music puts upon them, and recited in simple prose.

Yes, he said.

----

[1] Omitting εἰς.

[2] Or, "with his nouns and verbs."

They are like faces which were never really beautiful, but only blooming; and now the bloom of youth has passed away from them?

Exactly.

Here is another point: The imitator or maker of the image knows nothing of true existence; he knows appearances only. Am I not right?

Yes.

Then let us have a clear understanding, and not be satisfied with half an explanation.

Proceed.

Of the painter we say that he will paint reins, and he will paint a bit?

Yes.

And the worker in leather and brass will make them?

Certainly.

But does the painter know the right form of the bit and reins? Nay, hardly even the workers in brass and leather who make them; only the horseman who knows how to use them—he knows their right form.

Most true.

And may we not say the same of all things?

What?

That there are three arts which are concerned with all things, one which uses, another which makes, a third which imitates them?

Yes.

And the excellence or beauty or truth of every structure, animate or inanimate, and of every action of man, is relative to the use for which nature or the artist has intended them.

True.

Then the user of them must have the greatest experience of them, and he must indicate to the maker the good or bad qualities which develop themselves in use; for example, the flute-player will tell the flute-maker which of his flutes is satisfactory to the performer; he will tell him how he ought to make them, and

the other will attend to his instructions?

Of course.

The one knows and therefore speaks with authority about the goodness and badness of flutes, while the other, confiding in him, will do that what he is told by him?

True.

The instrument is the same, but about the excellence or badness of it the maker will only attain to a correct belief; and this he will gain from him who knows, by talking to him and being compelled to hear what he has to say, whereas the user will have knowledge?

True.

But will the imitator have either? Will he know from use whether or no his drawing is correct or beautiful? or will he have right opinion from being compelled to associate with another who knows and gives him instructions about what he should draw?

Neither.

Then he will no more have true opinion than he will have knowledge about the goodness or badness of his imitations?

I suppose not.

The imitative artist will be in a brilliant state of intelligence about his own creations?

Nay, very much the reverse.

And still he will go on imitating without knowing what makes a thing good or bad, and may be expected therefore to imitate only that which appears to be good to the ignorant multitude?

Just so.

Thus far then we are pretty well agreed that the imitator has no knowledge worth mentioning of what he imitates. Imitation is only a kind of play or sport, and the tragic poets, whether they write in Iambic or in Heroic verse, are imitators in the highest degree?

Very true.

And now tell me, I conjure you, has not imitation been shown by us to be concerned with that which is thrice removed from the truth?

Certainly.

And what is the faculty in man to which imitation is addressed?

What do you mean?

I will explain: The body which is large when seen near, appears small when seen at a distance?

True.

And the same objects appear straight when looked at out of the water, and crooked when in the water; and the concave becomes convex, owing to the illusion about colours to which the sight is liable. Thus every sort of confusion is revealed within us; and this is that weakness of the human mind on which the art of conjuring and of deceiving by light and shadow and other ingenious devices imposes, having an effect upon us like magic.

True.

And the arts of measuring and numbering and weighing come to the rescue of the human understanding—there is the beauty of them—and the apparent greater or less, or more or heavier, no longer have the mastery over us, but give way before calculation and measure and weight?

Most true.

And this, surely, must be the work of the calculating and rational principle in the soul?

To be sure.

And when this principle measures and certifies that some things are equal, or that some are greater or less than others, there occurs an apparent contradiction?

True.

But were we not saying that such a contradiction is impossible—the same faculty cannot have contrary opinions at the same time about the same thing?

Very true.

Then that part of the soul which has an opinion contrary to measure is not the same with that which has an opinion in accordance with measure?

True.

And the better part of the soul is likely to be that which trusts to measure and calculation?

Certainly.

And that which is opposed to them is one of the inferior principles of the soul?

No doubt.

This was the conclusion at which I was seeking to arrive when I said that painting or drawing, and imitation in general, when doing their own proper work, are far removed from truth, and the companions and friends and associates of a principle within us which is equally removed from reason, and that they have no true or healthy aim.

Exactly.

The imitative art is an inferior who marries an inferior, and has inferior offspring.

Very true. . . .

36. Tragedy*

ARISTOTLE (B.C. 384–322)

Let us proceed now to the discussion of Tragedy; before doing so, however, we must gather up the definition resulting from what has been said. A tragedy, then, is the imitation of an action that is serious and also, as having magnitude, complete in itself; in language with pleasurable accessories, each kind brought in separately in the parts of the work; in a dramatic, not in a narrative form; with incidents arousing pity and fear, wherewith to accomplish its catharsis of such emotions. Here by 'language with pleasurable accessories' I mean that with rhythm and harmony or song superadded; and by 'the kinds separately' I mean that some portions are worked out with verse only, and others in turn with song.

I. As they act the stories, it follows that in the first place the Spectacle (or stage-appearance of the actors) must be some part of the whole; and in the second Melody and Diction, these two being the means of their imitation. Here by 'Diction' I mean merely this, the composition of the verses; and by 'Melody', what is too completely understood to require explanation. But further: the subject represented also is an action; and the action involves agents, who must necessarily have their distinctive qualities both of character and thought, since it is from these that

we ascribe certain qualities to their actions. There are in the natural order of things, therefore, two causes, Thought and Character, of their actions, and consequently of their success or failure in their lives. Now the action (that which was done) is represented in the play by the Fable or Plot. The Fable, in our present sense of the term, is simply this, the combination of the incidents, or things done in the story; whereas Character is what makes us ascribe certain moral qualities to the agents; and Thought is shown in all they say when proving a particular point or, it may be, enunciating a general truth. There are six parts consequently of every tragedy, as a whole (that is) of such or such quality, viz. a Fable or Plot, Characters, Diction, Thought, Spectacle, and Melody; two of them arising from the means, one from the manner, and three from the objects of the dramatic imitation; and there is nothing else besides these six. Of these, its formative elements, then, not a few of the dramatists have made due use, as every play, one may say, admits of Spectacle, Character, Fable, Diction, Melody, and Thought.

II. The most important of the six is the combination of the incidents of the story. Tragedy is essentially an imitation not of persons but of action and life, of happiness and misery. All human happiness or misery takes the form of action; the end for which we live is a certain kind of activity, not a quality. Character gives us qualities, but it is in our

* From the *Poetics*. Oxford translation. Reprinted by kind permission of the Oxford University Press.

actions—what we do—that we are happy or the reverse. In a play accordingly they do not act in order to portray the Characters; they include the Characters for the sake of the action. So that it is the action in it, i.e. its Fable or Plot, that is the end and purpose of the tragedy; and the end is everywhere the chief thing. Besides this, a tragedy is impossible without action, but there may be one without Character. The tragedies of most of the moderns are characterless—a defect common among poets of all kinds, and with its counterpart in painting in Zeuxis as compared with Polygnotus; for whereas the latter is strong in character, the work of Zeuxis is devoid of it. And again: one may string together a series of characteristic speeches of the utmost finish as regards Diction and Thought, and yet fail to produce the true tragic effect; but one will have much better success with a tragedy which, however inferior in these respects, has a Plot, a combination of incidents, in it. And again: the most powerful elements of attraction in Tragedy, the Peripeties and Discoveries, are parts of the Plot. A further proof is in the fact that beginners succeed earlier with the Diction and Characters than with the construction of a story; and the same may be said of nearly all the early dramatists. We maintain, therefore, that the first essential, the life and soul, so to speak, of Tragedy is the Plot; and that the Characters come second—compare the parallel in painting, where the most beautiful colours laid on without order will not give one the same pleasure as a simple black-and-white sketch of a portrait. We maintain that Tragedy is primarily an imitation of action, and that it is mainly for the sake of the action that it imitates the personal agents. Third comes the element of Thought, i.e. the power of saying whatever can be said, or what is appropriate to the occasion. This is what, in the speeches in

Tragedy, falls under the arts of Politics and Rhetoric; for the older poets make their personages discourse like statesmen, and the moderns like rhetoricians. One must not confuse it with Character. Character in a play is that which reveals the moral purpose of the agents, i.e. the sort of thing they seek or avoid, where that is not obvious—hence there is no room for Character in a speech on a purely indifferent subject. Thought, on the other hand, is shown in all they say when proving or disproving some particular point, or enunciating some universal proposition. Fourth among the literary elements is the Diction of the personages, i.e., is as before explained, the expression of their thoughts in words, which is practically the same thing with verse as with prose. As for the two remaining parts, the Melody is the greatest of the pleasurable accessories of Tragedy. The Spectacle, though an attraction, is the least artistic of all the parts, and has least to do with the art of poetry. The tragic effect is quite possible without a public performance and actors; and besides, the getting-up of the Spectacle is more a matter for the costumier than the poet.

Having thus distinguished the parts, let us now consider the proper construction of the Fable or Plot, as that is at once the first and the most important thing in Tragedy. We have laid it down that a tragedy is an imitation of an action that is complete itself, as a whole of some magnitude; for a whole may be of no magnitude to speak of. Now a whole is that which has beginning, middle, and end. A beginning is that which is not itself necessarily after anything else, and which has naturally something else after it; an end is that which is naturally after something itself, either as its necessary or usual consequent, and with nothing else after it; and a middle, that which is by nature after one thing and has also another after it. A well-constructed Plot, therefore, cannot either begin or end at any point one likes; beginning and end in it must be of the forms just described. Again: to be beautiful, a living creature, and every whole made up of parts, must not only present a certain order in its arrangement of parts, but also be of certain definite magnitude. Beauty is a matter of size and order, and therefore impossible either (1) in a very minute creature, since our perception becomes indistinct as it approaches instantaneity; or (2) in a creature of vast size—one, say, 1,000 miles long—as in that case, instead of the object being seen all at once, the unity and wholeness of it is lost to the beholder. Just in the same way, then, as a beautiful whole made up of parts, or a beautiful living creature, must be of some size, but a size to be taken in by the eye, so a story or Plot must be of some length, but of a length to be taken in by the memory. As for the limit of its length, so far as that is relative to public performances and spectators, it does not fall within the theory of poetry. If they had to perform a hundred tragedies, they would be timed by water-clocks, as they are said to have been at one period. The limit, however, set by the actual nature of the thing is this: the longer the story, consistently with its being comprehensible as a whole, the finer it is by reason of its magnitude. As a rough general formula, 'a length which allows of the hero passing by a series of probable or necessary stages from misfortune to happiness, or from happiness to misfortune,' may suffice as a limit for the magnitude of the story.

The Unity of a Plot does not consist, as some suppose, in its having one man as its subject. An infinity of things befall that one man, some of which it is impossible to reduce to unity; and in like manner there are many actions of one man which cannot be made to form one action. One sees, therefore, the mistake of all the poets who have written a *Heracleid*, a *Theseid*, or similar poems; they suppose that, because Heracles was one man, the story also of Heracles must be one story. Homer, however, evidently understood this point quite well, whether by art or instinct, just in the same way as he excels the rest in every other respect. In writing an *Odyssey*, he did not make the poem cover all that ever befell his hero—it befell him, for instance, to get wounded on Parnassus and also to feign madness at the time of the call to arms, but the two incidents had no necessary or probable connexion with one another—instead of doing that, he took as the subject of the *Odyssey*, as also of the *Iliad*, an action with a Unity of the kind we are describing. The truth is that, just as in the other imitative arts one imitation is always of one thing, so in poetry the story, as an imitation of action, must represent one action, a complete whole, with its several incidents so closely connected that the transposal or withdrawal of any one of them will disjoin and dislocate the whole. For that which makes no perceptible difference by its presence or absence is no real part of the whole.

From what we have said it will be seen that the poet's function is to describe, not the thing that has happened, but a kind of thing that might happen, i.e. what is possible as being probable or necessary. The distinction between historian and poet is not in the one writing prose and the other verse—you might put the work of Herodotus into verse, and it would still be a species of history; it consists really in this, that the one describes the thing that has been, and the other a kind of thing that might be. Hence poetry is something more philosophic and of graver import than history, since its statements are of the nature rather of universals, whereas those of history are singulars. By a universal statement I mean one as to what such or such a kind of man will probably or necessarily say or do—which is the aim of poetry, though it affixes proper names to the characters; by a singular statement, one as to what, say, Alcibiades did or had done to him. In Comedy this has become clear by this time; it is only when their Plot is already made up of probable incidents that they give it a basis of proper names, choosing for the purpose any names that may occur to them, instead of writing like the old iambic poets about particular persons. In Tragedy, however, they still adhere to the historic names; and for this reason: what convinces is the possible; now whereas we are not yet sure as to the possibility of that which has not happened, that which has happened is manifestly possible, else it would not have come to pass. Nevertheless even in Tragedy there are some plays with but one or two known names in them, the rest being inventions; and there are some without a single known name, e.g. Agathon's *Antheus*, in which both incidents and names are of the poet's invention; and it is no less delightful on that account. So that one must not aim at a rigid adherence to the traditional stories on which tragedies are based. It would be absurd, in fact, to do so, as even the known stories are only known to a few, though they are a delight none the less to all.

It is evident from the above that the poet must be more the poet of his stories or Plots than of his verses, inasmuch as he is a poet by virtue of the imitative element in his work, and it is actions that he imitates. And if he should come to take a subject from actual history, he is none the less a poet for that; since some historic occurrences may very well be in the probable and possible order of things; and it is in that aspect of them that he is their poet.

Of simple Plots and actions the episodic are the worst. I call a Plot episodic when there is neither probability nor necessity in the sequence of its episodes. Actions of this sort bad poets construct through their own fault, and good ones on account of the players. His work being for public performance, a good poet often stretches out a Plot beyond its capabilities, and is thus obliged to twist the sequence of incident.

Tragedy, however, is an imitation not only of a complete action, but also of incidents arousing pity and fear. Such incidents have the very greatest effect on the mind when they occur unexpectedly and at the same time in consequence of one another; there is more of the marvellous in them then than if they happened of themselves or by mere chance. Even matters of chance seem most marvellous if there is an appearance of design as it were in them; as for instance the statue of Mitys at Argos killed the author of Mitys' death by falling down on him when a looker-on at a public spectacle; for incidents like that we think to be not without a meaning. A Plot, therefore, of this sort is necessarily finer than others.

Plots are either simple or complex, since the actions they represent are naturally of this twofold description. The action, proceeding in the way defined, as one continuous whole, I call simple, when the change in the hero's fortunes takes place without Peripety or Discovery; and complex, when it involves one or the other, or both. These should each of them arise out of the structure of the Plot itself, so as to be the consequence, necessary or probable, of the antecedents. There is a great difference between a thing happening *propter hoc* and *post hoc*.

A Peripety is the change of the kind described from one state of things within the play to its opposite, and that too in the way we are saying, in the probable or necessary sequence of events; as it is for instance in *Oedipus:* here the opposite state of things is produced by the Messenger, who, coming to gladden Oedipus and to remove his fears as to his mother, reveals the secret of his birth. And in *Lynceus:* just as he is being led off for execution, with Danaus at his side to put him to death, the incidents preceding this bring it about that he is saved and Danaus put to death. A Discovery is, as the very word implies, a change from ignorance to knowledge, and thus to either love or hate, in the personages marked for good or evil fortune. The finest form of Discovery is one attended by Peripeties, like that which goes with the Discovery in *Oedipus*. There are no doubt other forms of it; what we have said may happen in a way in reference to inanimate things, even things of a very casual kind; and it is also possible to discover whether some one has done or not done something. But the form most directly connected with the Plot and the action of the piece is the first-mentioned. This, with a Peripety, will arouse either pity or fear—actions of that nature being what Tragedy is assumed to represent; and it will also serve to bring about the happy or unhappy ending. The Discovery, then, being of persons, it may be that of one party only to the other, the latter being already known; or both the parties may have to discover themselves. Iphigenia, for instance, was discovered to Orestes by sending the letter; and another Discovery was required to reveal him to Iphigenia.

Two parts of the Plot, then, Peripety and Discovery, are on matters of this sort. A third part is Suffering; which we may define as an action of a destructive or painful nature, such as murders on the stage, tortures, woundings, and the like. The other two have been already explained. . . .

The next points after what we have said above will be these: (1) What is the poet to aim at, and what is he to avoid, in constructing his Plots? and (2) What are the conditions on which the tragic effect depends?

We assume that, for the finest form of Tragedy, the Plot must be not simple but complex; and further, that it must imitate actions arousing fear and pity, since that is the distinctive function of this kind of imitation. It follows, therefore, that there are three forms of Plot to be avoided. (1) A good man must not be seen passing from happiness to misery, or (2) a bad man from misery to happiness. The first situation is not fear-inspiring or piteous, but simply odious to us. The second is the most untragic that can be; it has no one of the requisites of Tragedy; it does not appeal either to the human feeling in us, or to our pity, or to our fears. Nor, on the other hand, should (3) an extremely bad man be seen falling from happiness into misery. Such a story may arouse the human feeling in us, but it will not move us to either pity or fear; pity is occasioned by undeserved misfortune, and fear by that of one like ourselves; so that there will be nothing either piteous or fear-inspiring in the situation. There remains, then, the intermediate kind of personage, a man not pre-eminently virtuous and just, whose misfortune, however, is brought upon him not by vice and depravity but by some error of judgment, of the number of those in the enjoyment of great reputation and prosperity; e.g. Oedipus, Thyestes, and the men of note of similar families. The perfect Plot, accordingly, must have a single, and not (as some tell us) a double issue; the change in the hero's fortunes must be not from misery to happiness, but on the contrary from happiness to misery; and the cause of it must lie not in any depravity, but in some great error on his part; the man himself being either such as we have described, or better, not worse, than that.

Fact also confirms our theory. Though

the poets began by accepting any tragic story that came to hand, in these days the finest tragedies are always on the story of some few houses, on that of Alcmeon, Oedipus, Orestes, Meleager, Thyestes, Telephus, or any others that may have been involved, as either agents or sufferers, in some deed of horror. The theoretically best tragedy, then, has a Plot of this description. The critics, therefore, are wrong who blame Euripides for taking this line in his tragedies, and giving many of them an unhappy ending. It is, as we have said, the right line to take. The best proof is this: on the stage, and in the public performances, such plays, properly worked out, are seen to be the most truly tragic; and Euripides, even if his execution be faulty in every other point, is seen to be nevertheless the most tragic certainly of the dramatists. After this comes the construction of Plot which some rank first, one with a double story (like the *Odyssey*) and an opposite issue for the good and the bad personages. It is ranked as first only through the weakness of the audiences; the poets merely follow their public, writing as its wishes dictates. But the pleasure here is not that of Tragedy. It belongs rather to Comedy, where the bitterest enemies in the piece (e.g. Orestes and Aegisthus) walk off good friends at the end, with no slaying of any one by any one.

The tragic fear and pity may be aroused by the Spectacle; but they may also be aroused by the very structure and incidents of the play—which is the better way and shows the better poet. The Plot in fact should be so framed that, even without seeing the things take place, he who simply hears the account of them shall be filled with horror and pity at the incidents; which is just the effect that the mere recital of the story in *Oedipus* would have on one. . . .

The Dénouement should arise out of the Plot itself, and not depend on a stage-artifice, as in *Medea,* or in the story of the (arrested) departure of the Greeks in the *Iliad.* The artifice must be reserved for matters outside the play— for past events beyond human knowledge, or events yet to come, which require to be foretold or announced; since it is the privilege of the Gods to know everything. There should be nothing improbable among the actual incidents. If it be unavoidable, however, it should be outside the Tragedy, like the improbability in the *Oedipus* of Sophocles. But to return to the Characters. As Tragedy is an imitation of personages better than the ordinary man, we in our way should follow the example of good portrait-painters, who reproduce the distinctive features of a man, and at the same time, without losing the likeness, make him handsomer than he is. The poet in like manner, in portraying men quick or slow to anger, or with similar infirmities of character, must know how to represent them as such, and at the same time as good men, as Agathon and Homer have represented Achilles.

37. *Platonic Idea and the Object of Art**

ARTHUR SCHOPENHAUER (1788–1860)

The knowledge of the beautiful always supposes at once and inseparably the pure knowing subject and the known Idea as object. Yet the source of aesthetic satisfaction will sometimes lie more in the comprehension of the known Idea, sometimes more in the blessedness and spiritual peace of the pure knowing subject freed from all willing, and therefore from all individuality, and the pain that proceeds from it. And, indeed, this predominance of one or the other constituent part of aesthetic feeling will depend upon whether the intuitively grasped Idea is a higher or a lower grade of the objectivity of will. Thus in aesthetic contemplation (in the real, or through the medium of art) of the beauty of nature in the inorganic and vegetable worlds, or in works of architecture, the pleasure of pure willless knowing will predominate, because the Ideas which are here apprehended are only low grades of the objectivity of will, and are therefore not manifestations of deep significance and rich content. On the other hand, if animals and man are objects of aesthetic contemplation or representation, the pleasure will consist rather in the comprehension of these Ideas, which are the most distinct revelation of will; for they exhibit the greatest multiplicity of forms, the greatest richness and deep significance of

phenomena, and reveal to us most completely the nature of will, whether in its violence, its terribleness, its satisfaction or its aberration (the latter in tragic situations), or finally in its change and self-surrender, which is the peculiar theme of Christian painting; as the Idea of the will enlightened by full knowledge is the object of historical painting in general, and of the drama. We shall now go through the fine arts one by one, and this will give completeness and distinctness to the theory of the beautiful which we have advanced. . . .

If now we consider *architecture* simply as a fine art and apart from its application to useful ends, in which it serves the will and not pure knowledge, and therefore ceases to be art in our sense; we can assign to it no other aim than that of bringing to greater distinctness some of those ideas, which are the lowest grades of the objectivity of will; such as gravity, cohesion, rigidity, hardness, those universal qualities of stone, those first, simplest, most inarticulate manifestations of will; the bass notes of nature; and after these light, which in many respects is their opposite. Even at these low grades of the objectivity of will we see its nature revealing itself in discord; for properly speaking the conflict between gravity and rigidity is the sole aesthetic material of architecture; its problem is to make this conflict appear with perfect distinctness in a multitude of different ways. It solves it by

---

* Part of Book III in *The World as Will and Idea*.

depriving these indestructible forces of the shortest way to their satisfaction, and conducting them to it by a circuitous route, so that the conflict is lengthened and the inexhaustible efforts of both forces become visible in many different ways. The whole mass of the building, if left to its original tendency, would exhibit a mere heap or clump, bound as closely as possible to the earth, to which gravity, the form in which the will appears here, continually presses, while rigidity, also objectivity of will, resists. But this very tendency, this effort, is hindered by architecture from obtaining direct satisfaction, and only allowed to reach it indirectly and by roundabout ways. The roof, for example, can only press the earth through columns, the arch must support itself, and can only satisfy its tendency towards the earth through the medium of the pillars, and so forth. But just by these enforced digressions, just by these restrictions, the forces which reside in the crude mass of stone unfold themselves in the most distinct and multifarious ways; and the purely aesthetic aim of architecture can go no further than this. Therefore the beauty, at any rate, of a building lies in the obvious adaptation of every part, not to the outward arbitrary end of man (so far the work belongs to practical architecture), but directly to the stability of the whole, to which the position, dimensions, and form of every part must have so necessary a relation that, where it is possible, if any one part were taken away, the whole would fall to pieces. For just because each part bears just as much as it conveniently can, and each is supported just where it requires to be and just to the necessary extent, this opposition unfolds itself, this conflict between rigidity and gravity, which constitutes the life, the manifestation of will, in the stone, becomes completely visible, and these lowest grades of the objectivity of will

reveal themselves distinctly. In the same way the form of each part must not be determined arbitrarily, but by its end, and its relation to the whole. The column is the simplest form of support, determined simply by its end: the twisted column is tasteless; the four-cornered pillar is in fact not so simple as the round column, though it happens that it is easier to make it. The forms also of frieze, rafter, roof, and dome are entirely determined by their immediate end, and explain themselves from it. The decoration of capitals, &c., belongs to sculpture, not to architecture, which admits it merely as extraneous ornament, and could dispense with it. According to what has been said, it is absolutely necessary, in order to understand the aesthetic satisfaction afforded by a work of architecture, to have immediate knowledge through perception of its matter as regards its weight, rigidity, and cohesion, and our pleasure in such a work would suddenly be very much diminished by the discovery that the material used was pumice-stone; for then it would appear to us as a kind of sham building. We would be affected in almost the same way if we were told that it was made of wood, when we had supposed it to be of stone, just because this alters and destroys the relation between rigidity and gravity, and consequently the significance and necessity of all the parts, for these natural forces reveal themselves in a far weaker degree in a wooden building. Therefore no real work of architecture as a fine art can be made of wood, although it assumes all forms so easily; this can only be explained by our theory. If we were distinctly told that a building, the sight of which gave us pleasure, was made of different kinds of material of very unequal weight and consistency, but not distinguishable to the eye, the whole building would become as utterly incapable of affording us pleasure as a poem in an unknown language. All this proves that architecture does not affect us mathematically, but also dynamically, and that what speaks to us through it, is not mere form and symmetry, but rather those fundamental forces of nature, those first Ideas, those lowest grades of the objectivity of will. The regularity of the building and its parts is partly produced by the direct adaptation of each member to the stability of the whole, partly it serves to facilitate the survey and comprehension of the whole, and finally, regular figures to some extent enhance the beauty because they reveal the constitution of space as such. But all this is of subordinate value and necessity, and by no means the chief concern; indeed, symmetry is not invariably demanded, as ruins are still beautiful. . . .

Ideas are essentially perceptible; if, therefore, in poetry only abstract conceptions are directly communicated through words, it is yet clearly the intention to make the hearer perceive the Ideas of life in the representatives of these conceptions, and this can only take place through the assistance of his own imagination. But in order to set the imagination to work for the accomplishment of this end, the abstract conceptions, which are the immediate material of poetry as of dry prose, must be so arranged that their spheres intersect each in such a way that none of them can remain in its abstract universality; but, instead of it, a perceptible representative appears to the imagination; and this is always further modified by the words of the poet according to what his intention may be. As the chemist obtains solid precipitates by combining perfectly clear and transparent fluids; the poet understands how to precipitate, as it were, the concrete, the individual, the perceptible idea, out of the abstract and transparent universality of the concepts by the manner in which he combines them. For the Idea can only be

known by perception; and knowledge of the Idea is the end of art. The skill of a master, in poetry as in chemistry, enables us always to obtain the precise precipitate we intended. This end is assisted by the numerous epithets in poetry, by means of which the universality of every concept is narrowed more and more till we reach the perceptible.

"Where gentle winds from the blue heavens sigh,
There stand the myrtles still, the laurel high,"—

calls up before the imagination by means of a few concepts the whole delight of a southern clime.

Rhythm and rhyme are quite peculiar aids to poetry. I can give no other explanation of their incredibly powerful effect than that our faculties of perception have received from time, to which they are essentially bound, some quality on account of which we inwardly follow, and, as it were, consent to each regularly recurring sound. In this way rhythm and rhyme are partly a means of holding our attention, because we willingly follow the poem read, and partly they produce in us a blind consent to what is read prior to any judgment, and this gives the poem a certain emphatic power of convincing independent of all reasons. . . .

Tragedy is to be regarded, and is recognised as the summit of poetical art, both on account of the greatness of its effect and the difficulty of its achievement. It is very significant for our whole system, and well worthy of observation, that the end of this highest poetical achievement is the representation of the terrible side of life. The unspeakable pain, the wail of humanity, the triumph of evil, the scornful mastery of chance, and the irretrievable fall of the just and innocent, is here presented to us; and in this lies a significant hint of the nature of the world and of existence. It is the strife of will with itself, which here, completely unfolded at the highest grade of its objectivity, comes into fearful prominence. It becomes visible in the suffering of men, which is now introduced, partly through chance and error, which appear as the rulers of the world, personified as fate, on account of their insidiousness, which even reaches the appearance of design; partly it proceeds from man himself, through the self-mortifying efforts of a few, through the wickedness and perversity of most. It is one and the same will that lives and appears in them all, but whose phenomena fight against each other and destroy each other. In one individual it appears powerfully, in another more weakly; in one more subject to reason, and softened by the light of knowledge, in another less so, till at last, in some single case, this knowledge, purified and heightened by suffering itself, reaches the point at which the phenomenon, the veil of Maya, no longer deceives it. It sees through the form of the phenomenon, the principle of individuation. The egoism which rests on this perishes with it, so that now the *motives* that were so powerful before have lost their might, and instead of them the complete knowledge of the nature of the world, which has a *quieting* effect on the will, produces resignation, the surrender not merely of life, but of the very will to live. Thus we see in tragedies the noblest men, after long conflict and suffering, at last renounce the ends they have so keenly followed, and all the pleasures of life for ever, or else freely and joyfully surrender life itself. So is it with the steadfast prince of Calderon; with Gretchen in "Faust"; with Hamlet, whom his friend Horatio would willingly follow, but is bade remain a while, and in this harsh world draw his breath in pain, to tell the story of Hamlet, and clear his memory; so also is it with the Maid of Orleans, the Bride of Messina;

they all die purified by suffering, *i. e.*, after the will to live which was formerly in them is dead. In the "Mohammed" of Voltaire this is actually expressed in the concluding words which the dying Palmira addresses to Mohammed: "The world is for tyrants: live!" On the other hand, the demand for so-called poetical justice rests on entire misconception of the nature of tragedy, and, indeed, of the nature of the world itself. It boldly appears in all its dulness in the criticisms which Dr. Samuel Johnson made on particular plays of Shakespeare, for he very naïvely laments its entire absence. And its absence is certainly obvious, for in what has Ophelia, Desdemona, or Cordelia offended? But only the dull, optimistic, Protestant-rationalistic, or peculiarly Jewish view of life will make the demand for poetical justice, and find satisfaction in it. The true sense of tragedy is the deeper insight, that it is not his own individual sins that the hero atones for, but original sin, *i. e.*, the crime of existence itself:

"Pues el delito mayor
    Del hombre es haber nacido;"

("For the greatest crime of man
    Is that he was born;")

as Calderon exactly expresses it.

I shall allow myself only one remark, more closely concerning the treatment of tragedy. The representation of a great misfortune is alone essential to tragedy. But the many different ways in which this is introduced by the poet may be brought under three specific conceptions. It may happen by means of a character of extraordinary wickedness, touching the utmost limits of possibility, who becomes the author of the misfortune; examples of this kind are Richard III., Iago in "Othello," Shylock in "The Merchant of Venice," Franz Moor, Phædra of Euripides, Creon in the "Antigone," &c., &c. Secondly, it may happen through blind fate, *i. e.*, chance and error; a true pattern of this kind is the Œdipus Rex of Sophocles, the "Trachiniæ" also; and in general most of the tragedies of the ancients belong to this class. Among modern tragedies, "Romeo and Juliet," "Tancred" by Voltaire, and "The Bride of Messina," are examples. Lastly, the misfortune may be brought about by the mere position of the *dramatis personœ* with regard to each other, through their relations; so that there is no need either for a tremendous error or an unheard-of accident, nor yet for a character whose wickedness reaches the limits of human possibility; but characters of ordinary morality, under circumstances such as often occur, are so situated with regard to each other that their position compels them, knowingly and with their eyes open, to do each other the greatest injury, without any one of them being entirely in the wrong. This last kind of tragedy seems to me far to surpass the other two, for it shows us the greatest misfortune, not as an exception, not as something occasioned by rare circumstances or monstrous characters, but as arising easily and of itself out of the actions and characters of men, indeed almost as essential to them, and thus brings it terribly near to us. In the other two kinds we may look on the prodigious fate and the horrible wickedness as terrible powers which certainly threaten us, but only from afar, which we may very well escape without taking refuge in renunciation. But in the last kind of tragedy we see that those powers which destroy happiness and life are such that their path to us also is open at every moment; we see the greatest sufferings brought about by entanglements that our fate might also partake of, and through actions that perhaps we also are capable of performing, and so could not complain of injustice; then shuddering we feel ourselves already in

the midst of hell. This last kind of tragedy is also the most difficult of achievement; for the greatest effect has to be produced in it with the least use of means and causes of movement, merely through the position and distribution of the characters; therefore even in many of the best tragedies this difficulty is evaded. Yet one tragedy may be referred to as a perfect model of this kind, a tragedy which in other respects is far surpassed by more than one work of the same great master; it is "Clavigo." "Hamlet" belongs to a certain extent to this class, as far as the relation of Hamlet to Laertes and Ophelia is concerned. "Wallenstein" has also this excellence. "Faust" belongs entirely to this class, if we regard the events connected with Gretchen and her brother as the principal action; also the "Cid" of Corneille, only that it lacks the tragic conclusion, while on the contrary the analogous relation of Max to Thecla has it. . . .

The (Platonic) Ideas are the adequate objectification of will. To excite or suggest the knowledge of these by means of the representation of particular things (for works of art themselves are always representations of particular things) is the end of all the other arts, which can only be attained by a corresponding change in the knowing subject. Thus all these arts objectify the will indirectly only by means of the Ideas; and since our world is nothing but the manifestation of the Ideas in multiplicity, though their entrance into the principle of individuality (the form of the knowledge possible for the individual as such), music also, since it passes over the Ideas, is entirely independent of the phenomenal world, ignores it altogether, could to a certain extent exist if there was no world at all, which cannot be said of the other arts. Music is as *direct* an objectification and copy of the whole *will* as the world itself, nay, even as the Ideas, whose multiplied manifestation constitutes the world of individual things. Music is thus by no means like the other arts, the copy of the Ideas, but the *copy of the will itself,* whose objectivity the Ideas are. This is why the effect of music is so much more powerful and penetrating than that of the other arts, for they speak only of shadows, but it speaks of the thing itself. . . .

Now the nature of man consists in this, that his will strives, is satisfied and strives anew, and so on for ever. Indeed, his happiness and well-being consist simply in the quick transition from wish to satisfaction, and from satisfaction to a new wish. For the absence of satisfaction is suffering, the empty longing for a new wish, languor, *ennui.* And corresponding to this the nature of melody is a constant digression and deviation from the keynote in a thousand ways, not only to the harmonious intervals to the third and dominant, but to every tone, to the dissonant sevenths and to the superfluous degrees; yet there always follows a constant return to the keynote. In all these deviations melody expresses the multifarious efforts of will, but always its satisfaction also by the final return to an harmonious interval, and still more, to the key-note. The composition of melody, the disclosure in it of all the deepest secrets of human willing and feeling, is the work of genius, whose action, which is more apparent here than anywhere else, lies far from all reflection and conscious intention, and may be called an inspiration. The conception is here, as everywhere in art, unfruitful. The composer reveals the inner nature of the world, and expresses the deepest wisdom in a language which his reason does not understand; as a person under the influence of mesmerism tells things of which he has no conception when he awakes. Therefore in the composer, more than in any other artist, the man is entirely separated and distinct from the artist. Even in the expla-

nation of this wonderful art, the concept shows its poverty and limitation. I shall try, however, to complete our analogy. As quick transition from wish to satisfaction, and from satisfaction to a new wish, is happiness and well-being, so quick melodies without great deviations are cheerful; slow melodies, striking painful discords, and only winding back through many bars to the key-note are, as analogous to the delayed and hardly won satisfaction, sad. The delay of the new excitement of will, languor, could have no other expression than the sustained key-note, the effect of which would soon be unbearable; very monotonous and unmeaning melodies approach this effect. The short intelligible subjects of quick dance-music seem to speak only of easily attained common pleasure. On the other hand, the *Allegro maestoso,* in elaborate movements, long passages, and wide deviations, signifies a greater, nobler effort towards a more distant end, and its final attainment. The *Adagio* speaks of the pain of a great and noble effort which despises a trifling happiness. But how wonderful is the effect of the *minor* and *major!* How astounding that the change of half a tone, the entrance of a minor third instead of a major, at once and inevitably forces upon us an anxious painful feeling, from which again we are just as instantaneously delivered by the major. The *Adagio* lengthens in the minor the expression of the keenest pain, and becomes even a convulsive wail. Dance-music in the minor seems to indicate the failure of that trifling happiness which we ought rather to despise, seems to speak of the attainment of a lower end with toil and trouble. The inexhaustibleness of possible melodies corresponds to the inexhaustibleness of Nature in difference of individuals, physiognomies, and courses of life. The transition from one key to an entirely different one, since it altogether breaks the connection with what went before, is like death, for the individual ends in it; but the will which appeared in this individual lives after him as before him, appearing in other individuals, whose consciousness, however, has no connection with his.

But it must never be forgotten, in the investigation of all these analogies I have pointed out, that music has no direct, but merely an indirect relation to them, for it never expresses the phenomenon, but only the inner nature, the in-itself of all phenomena, the will itself. It does not therefore express this or that particular and definite joy, this or that sorrow, or pain, or horror, or delight, or merriment, or peace of mind; but joy, sorrow, pain, horror, delight, merriment, peace of mind *themselves,* to a certain extent in the abstract, their essential nature, without accessories, and therefore without their motives. Yet we completely understand them in this extracted quintessence. Hence it arises that our imagination is so easily excited by music, and now seeks to give form to that invisible yet actively moved spirit-world which speaks to us directly, and clothe it with flesh and blood, *i. e.,* to embody it in an analogous example. This is the origin of the song with words, and finally of the opera, the text of which should therefore never forsake that subordinate position in order to make itself the chief thing and the music a mere means of expressing it, which is a great misconception and a piece of utter perversity; for music always expresses only the quintessence of life and its events, never these themselves, and therefore their differences do not always affect it. It is precisely this universality, which belongs exclusively to it, together with the greatest determinateness, that gives music the high worth which it has as the panacea for all our woes. Thus, if music is too closely united to the words, and tries to form itself according to the events, it is striving to speak a language

which is not its own. No one has kept so free from this mistake as Rossini; therefore his music speaks *its own language* so distinctly and purely that it requires no words, and produces its full effect when rendered by instruments alone.

I might still have something to say about the way in which music is perceived, namely, in and through time alone, with absolute exclusion of space, and also apart from the influence of the knowledge of causality, thus without understanding; for the tones make the aesthetic impression as effect, and without obliging us to go back to their causes, as in the case of perception. I do not wish, however, to lengthen this discussion, as I have perhaps already gone too much into detail with regard to some things in this Third Book, or have dwelt too much on particulars. But my aim made it necessary, and it will be the less disapproved if the importance and high worth of art, which is seldom sufficiently recognised, be kept in mind. For if, according to our view, the whole visible world is just the objectification, the mirror, of the will, conducting it to knowledge of itself, and, indeed, as we shall soon see, to the possibility of its deliverance; and if, at the same time, the world as idea, if we regard it in isolation, and, freeing ourselves from all volition, allow it alone to take possession of our consciousness, is the most joy-giving and the only innocent side of life; we must regard art as the higher ascent, the more complete development of all this, for it achieves essentially just what is achieved by the visible world itself, only with greater concentration, more perfectly, with intention and intelligence, and therefore may be called, in the full significance of the word, the flower of life. If the whole world as idea is only the visibility of will, the work of art is to render this visibility more distinct. It is the *camera obscura* which shows the objects more purely, and enables us to survey them and comprehend them better. It is the play within the play, the stage upon the stage in "Hamlet."

The pleasure we receive from all beauty, the consolation which art affords, the enthusiasm of the artist, which enables him to forget the cares of life,—the latter an advantage of the man of genius over other men, which alone repays him for the suffering that increases in proportion to the clearness of consciousness, and for the desert loncliness among men of a different race,—all this rests on the fact that the in-itself of life, the will, existence itself, is, as we shall see farther on, a constant sorrow, partly miserable, partly terrible; while, on the contrary, as idea alone, purely contemplated, or copied by art, free from pain, it presents to us a drama full of significance. This purely knowable side of the world, and the copy of it in any art, is the element of the artist. He

is chained to the contemplation of the play, the objectification of will; he remains beside it, does not get tired of contemplating it and representing it in copies; and meanwhile he bears himself the cost of the production of that play, i. e., he himself is the will which objectifies itself, and remains in constant suffering. That pure, true and deep knowledge of the inner nature of the world becomes now for him an end in itself: he stops there. Therefore it does not become to him a quieter of the will, as, we shall see in the next book, it does in the case of the saint who has attained to resignation; it does not deliver him for ever from life, but only at moments, and is therefore not for him a path out of life, but only an occasional consolation in it, till his power, increased by this contemplation and at last tired of the play, lays hold on the real. The St. Cecilia of Raphael may be regarded as a representation of this transition.

38. Letters Upon the Aesthetical Education of Man*

FRIEDRICH SCHILLER (1759–1805)

No doubt nature has given more than is necessary to unreasoning beings; she has caused a gleam of freedom to shine even in the darkness of animal life. When the lion is not tormented by hunger, and when no wild beast challenges

* Part of Letter XXVII, from *Letters upon the Aesthetical Education of Man*. By kind permission of the publishers, G. Bell & Sons, Ltd., London.

him to fight, his unemployed energy creates an object for himself; full of ardour, he fills the re-echoing desert with his terrible roars, and his exuberant force rejoices in itself, showing itself without an object. The insect flits about rejoicing in life in the sunlight, and it is certainly not the cry of want that makes itself heard in the melodious song of the bird; there is undeniably freedom in these movements, though it is not emancipation from want in general, but from a determinate external necessity.

The animal *works,* when a privation is the motor of its activity, and it *plays* when the plenitude of force is this motor, when an exuberant life is excited to action. Even in inanimate nature a luxury of strength and a latitude of determination are shown, which in this material sense might be styled play. The tree produces numberless germs that are abortive without developing, and it sends forth more roots, branches and leaves, organs of nutrition, than are used for the preservation of the species. Whatever this tree restores to the elements of its exuberant life, without using it, or enjoying it, may be expended by life in free and joyful movements. It is thus that nature offers, in her material sphere, a sort of prelude to the limitless, and that even there she suppresses partially the chains from which she will be completely emancipated in the realm of form. The constraint of superabundance or *physical play,* answers as a transition from the constraint of necessity, or of *physical seriousness,* to aesthetical play; and before shaking off, in the supreme freedom of the beautiful, the yoke of any special aim, nature already approaches, at least remotely, this independence, by the *free movement* which is itself its own end and means.

The imagination, like the bodily organs, has in man its free movement and its material play, a play in which, without any reference to form, it simply takes pleasure in its arbitrary power and in the absence of all hindrance. These plays of fancy, inasmuch as form is not mixed up with them, and because a free succession of images makes all their charm, though confined to man, belong exclusively to animal life, and only prove one thing—that he is delivered from all external sensuous constraint—

without our being entitled to infer that there is in it an independent plastic force.

From this play of *free association* of ideas, which is still quite material in nature and is explained by simple natural laws, the imagination, by making the attempt of creating a free form, passes at length at a jump to the aesthetic play: I say at one leap, for quite a new force enters into action here; for here, for the first time, the legislative mind is mixed with the acts of a blind instinct, subjects the arbitrary march of the imagination to its eternal and immutable unity, causes its independent permanence to enter in that which is transitory, and its infinity in the sensuous. Nevertheless, as long as rude nature, which knows of no other law than running incessantly from change to change, will yet retain too much strength, it will oppose itself by its different caprices to this necessity; by its agitation to this permanence; by its manifold needs to this independence, and by its insatiability to this sublime simplicity. It will be also troublesome to recognise the instinct of play in its first trials, seeing that the sensuous impulsion, with its capricious humour and its violent appetites, constantly crosses. It is on that account that we see the taste, still coarse, seize that which is new and startling, the disordered, the adventurous and the strange, the violent and the savage, and fly from nothing so much as from calm and simplicity. It invents grotesque figures, it likes rapid transitions, luxurious forms, sharply marked changes, acute tones, a pathetic song. That which man calls beautiful at this time, is that which excites him, that which gives him matter; but that which excites him to give his personality to the object, that which gives matter to a *possible plastic operation,* for otherwise it would not be the beautiful for him. A remarkable change has therefore taken place in the form of his judgments; he searches for these objects, not because they affect him, but because they furnish him with the occasion of acting; they please him, not because they answer to a want, but because they satisfy a law, which speaks in his breast, although quite low as yet.

Soon it will not be sufficient for things to please him; he will wish to please: in the first place, it is true, only by that which belongs to him; afterwards by that which he is. That which he possesses, that which he produces, ought not merely to bear any more the traces of servitude, nor to mark out the end, simply and scrupulously, by the form. Independently of the use to which it is destined, the object ought also to reflect the enlightened intelligence which imagines it, the hand which shaped it with affection, the mind free and serene which chose it and exposed it to view. Now, the ancient German searches for more *magnificent* furs, for more *splendid* antlers of the stag, for more elegant drinking horns; and the Caledonian chooses the prettiest shells for his festivals. The arms themselves ought to be no longer only objects of terror, but also of pleasure; and the skilfully worked scabbard will not attract less attention than the homicidal edge of the sword. The instinct of play, not satisfied with bringing into the sphere of the necessary an aesthetic superabundance for the future more free, is at last completely emancipated from the bonds of duty, and the beautiful becomes of itself an object of man's exertions. He adorns himself. The free pleasure comes to take a place among his wants, and the useless soon becomes the best part of his joys. Form, which from the outside gradually approaches him, in his dwelling, his furniture, his clothing, begins at last to take possession of the man himself, to transform him, at first exteriorly, and afterwards in the interior. The disor-

dered leaps of joy become the dance, the formless gesture is changed into an amiable and harmonious pantomime, the confused accents of feeling are developed, and begin to obey measure and adapt themselves to song. When, like the flight of cranes, the Trojan army rushes on to the field of battle with thrilling cries, the Greek army approaches in silence and with a noble and measured step. On the one side we see but the exuberance of a blind force, on the other the triumph of form and the simple majesty of law.

Now, a nobler necessity binds the two sexes mutually, and the interests of the heart contribute in rendering durable an alliance which was at first capricious and changing like the desire that knits it. Delivered from the heavy fetters of desire, the eye, now calmer, attends to the form, the soul contemplates the soul, and the interested exchange of pleasure becomes a generous exchange of mutual inclination. Desire enlarges and rises to love, in proportion as it sees humanity dawn in its object; and, despising the vile triumphs gained by the senses, man tries to win a nobler victory over the will. The necessity of pleasing subjects the powerful nature to the gentle laws of taste; pleasure may be stolen, but love must be a gift. To obtain this higher recompense it is only through the form and not through matter that it can carry on the contest. It must cease to act on feeling as a force, to appear in the intelligence as a simple phenomenon; it must respect liberty, as it is liberty it wishes to please. The beautiful reconciles the contrast of different natures in its simplest and purest expression. It also reconciles the eternal contrast of the two sexes, in the whole complex framework of society, or at all events it seeks to do so; and, taking as its model the free alliance it has knit between manly strength and womanly gentleness, it strikes to place in harmony, in the moral world, all the elements of gentleness and of violence. Now, at length, weakness becomes sacred, and an unbridled strength disgraces; the injustice of nature is corrected by the generosity of chivalrous manners. The being whom no power can make tremble, is disarmed by the amiable blush of modesty, and tears extinguish a vengeance that blood could not have quenched. Hatred itself hears the delicate voice of honour, the conqueror's sword spares the disarmed enemy, and a hospitable hearth smokes for the stranger on the dreaded hill-side where murder alone awaited him before.

In the midst of the formidable realm of forces, and of the sacred empire of laws, the aesthetic impulse of form creates by degrees a third and a joyous realm, that of play and of the appearance, where she emancipates man from fetters, in all his relations, and from all that is named constraint, whether physical or moral.

If in the dynamic state of rights men mutually move and come into collision as forces, in the moral (ethical) state of duties, man opposes to man the majesty of the laws, and chains down his will. In this realm of the beautiful or the aesthetic state, man ought to appear to man only as a form, and an object of free play. To give freedom through freedom is the fundamental law of this realm.

The dynamic state can only make society simply possible by subduing nature through nature; the moral (ethical) state can only make it morally necessary by submitting the will of the individual to the general will. The aesthetic state alone can make it real, because it carries out the will of all through the nature of the individual. If necessity alone forces man to enter into society, and if his reason engraves on his soul principles, it is beauty only that can give him a social *character;* taste alone brings harmony into society, because it creates harmony

in the individual. All other forms of perception divide the man, because they are based exclusively either in the sensuous or in the spiritual part of his being. It is only the perception of beauty that makes of him an entirety, because it demands the co-operation of his two natures. All other forms of communication divide society, because they apply exclusively either to the receptivity or to the private activity of its members, and therefore to what distinguishes men one from the other. The aesthetic communication alone unites society, because it applies to what is common to all its members. We only enjoy the pleasures of sense as individuals, without the nature of the race in us sharing in it; accordingly, we cannot generalise our individual pleasures, because we cannot generalise our individuality. We enjoy the pleasures of knowledge as a race, dropping the individual in our judgment; but we cannot generalise the pleasures of the understanding, because we cannot eliminate individuality from the judgments of others as we do from our own. Beauty alone can we enjoy both as individuals and as a race, that is, as representing a race. Good appertaining to sense can only make one person happy, because it is founded on inclination, which is always exclusive; and it can only make a man partially happy, because his real personality does not share in it. Absolute good can only render a man happy conditionally, for truth is only the reward of abnegation, and a pure heart alone has faith in a pure will. Beauty alone confers happiness on all, and under its influence every being forgets that he is limited.

Taste does not suffer any superior or absolute authority, and the sway of beauty is extended over appearance. It extends up to the seat of reason's supremacy, suppressing all that is material. It extends down to where sensuous impulse rules with blind compulsion, and form is undeveloped. Taste ever maintains its power on these remote borders, where legislation is taken from it. Particular desires must renounce their egotism, and the agreeable, otherwise tempting the senses, must in matters of taste adorn the mind with the attractions of grace.

Duty and stern necessity must change their forbidding tone, only excused by resistance, and do homage to nature by a nobler trust in her. Taste leads our knowledge from the mysteries of science into the open expanse of common sense, and changes a narrow scholasticism into the common property of the human race. Here the highest genius must leave its particular elevation, and make itself familiar to the comprehension even of a child. Strength must let the Graces bind it, and the arbitrary lion must yield to the reins of love. For this purpose taste throws a veil over physical necessity, offending a free mind by its coarse nudity, and dissimulating our degrading parentage with matter by a delightful illusion of freedom. Mercenary art itself rises from the dust; and the bondage of the bodily, at its magic touch, falls off

from the inanimate and animate. In the aesthetic state the most slavish tool is a free citizen, having the same rights as the noblest; and the intellect which shapes the mass to its intent must consult it concerning its destination. Consequently in the realm of aesthetic appearance, the idea of equality is realised, which the political zealot would gladly see carried out socially. It has often been said that perfect politeness is only found near a throne. If thus restricted in the material, man has, as elsewhere appears, to find compensation in the ideal world.

Does such a state of beauty in appearance exist, and where? It must be in every finely harmonised soul; but as a fact, only in select circles, like the pure ideal of the church and state—in circles where manners are not formed by the empty imitations of the foreign, but by the very beauty of nature; where man passes through all sorts of complications in all simplicity and innocence, neither forced to trench on another's freedom to preserve his own, nor to show grace at the cost of dignity.

39. *What Is Art?* *

BENEDETTO CROCE (1866–1952)

The question as to what is art,—I will say at once, in the simplest manner, that art is *vision* or *intuition*. The artist produces an image or a phantasm; and he who enjoys art turns his gaze upon the

point to which the artist has pointed, looks through the chink which he has opened, and reproduces that image in himself. "Intuition," "vision," "contemplation," "imagination," "fancy," "figurations," "representations," and so on, are words continually recurring, like synonyms, when discoursing upon art, and they all lead the mind to the same

* Part of Chapter I in *Breviary of Aesthetic*. Published in *The Book of the Opening of the Rice Institute*, Vol. II. By kind permission of the Rice Institute.

conceptual sphere which indicates general agreement.

But this reply, that art is intuition, obtains its force and meaning from all that it implicitly denies and from which it distinguishes art. What negations are implicit in it? I shall indicate the principal, or at least those that are the most important for us at this present moment of our culture.

It denies, above all, that art is a *physical fact:* for example, certain determined colours, or relations of colours; certain definite forms of bodies; certain definite sounds, or relations of sounds; certain phenomena of heat or of electricity—in short, whatsoever be designated as "physical." The inclination toward this error of physicising art is already present in ordinary thought, and as children who touch the soap-bubble and would wish to touch the rainbow, so the human spirit, admiring beautiful things, hastens spontaneously to trace out the reasons for them in external nature, and proves that it must think, or believes that it should think, certain colours beautiful and certain other colours ugly, certain forms beautiful and certain other forms ugly. But this attempt has been carried out intentionally and with method on several occasions in the history of thought: from the "canons" which the Greek and Renaissance theoreticians and artists fixed for the beauty of bodies, through the speculations as to the geometrical and numerical relations of figures and sounds, down to the researches of the aestheticians of the nineteenth century (Fechner, for example), and to the "communications" presented in our day by the inexpert, at philosophical, psychological, and natural science congresses, concerning the relations of physical phenomena with art. And if it be asked why art cannot be a physical fact, we must reply, in the first place, that physical facts *do not possess reality,* and that art, to which so many devote their whole lives and which fills all with a divine joy, is *supremely real;* thus it cannot be a physical fact, which is something unreal. This sounds at first paradoxical, for nothing seems more solid and secure to the ordinary man than the physical world; but we, in the seat of truth, must not abstain from the good reason and substitute for it one less good, solely because the first should have the appearance of a lie; and besides, in order to surpass what of strange and difficult may be contained in that truth, to become at home with it, we may take into consideration the fact that the demonstration of the unreality of the physical world has not only been proved in an indisputable manner and is admitted by all philosophers (who are not crass materialists and are not involved in the strident contradictions of materialism), but is professed by these same physicists in the spontaneous philosophy which they mingle with their physics, when they conceive physical phenomena as products of principles that are beyond experience, of atoms or of ether, or as the manifestation of an Unknowable: besides, the matter itself of the materialists is a supermaterial principle. Thus physical facts reveal themselves, by their internal logic and by common consent, not as reality, but as a *construction of our intellect for the purposes of science.* Consequently, the question whether art be a physical fact must rationally assume this different signification: that is to say, *whether it be possible to construct art physically.* And this is certainly possible, for we indeed carry it out always, when, turning from the sense of a poem and ceasing to enjoy it, we set ourselves, for example, to count the words of which the poem is composed and to divide them into syllables and letters; or, disregarding the aesthetic effect of a statue, we weigh and measure it: a most useful performance for the packers of statues, as is the other for the typographers who have to "compose" pages of poetry; but most useless for the contemplator and student of art, to whom it is neither useful nor licit to allow himself to be "distracted" from his proper object. Thus art is not a physical fact in this second sense, either; which amounts to saying that when we propose to ourselves to penetrate its nature and mode of action, to construct it physically is of no avail.

Another negation is implied in the definition of art as intuition: if it be intuition, and intuition is equivalent to *theory* in the original sense of contemplation, art cannot be a utilitarian act; and since a utilitarian act aims always at obtaining a pleasure and therefore at keeping off a pain, art, considered in its own nature, has nothing to do with the *useful* and with *pleasure* and *pain,* as such. It will be admitted, indeed, without much difficulty, that a pleasure as a pleasure, any sort of pleasure, is not of itself artistic; the pleasure of a drink of water that slakes thirst, or a walk in the open air that stretches our limbs and makes our blood circulate more lightly, or the obtaining of a longed-for post that settles us in practical life, and so on, is not artistic. Finally, the difference between pleasure and art leaps to the eyes in the relations that are developed between ourselves and works of art, because the figure represented may be dear to us and represent the most delightful memories, and at the same time the picture may be ugly; or, on the other hand, the picture may be beautiful and the figure represented hateful to our hearts, or the picture itself, which we approve as beautiful, may also cause us rage and envy, because it is the work of our enemy or rival, for whom it will procure advantage and on whom it will confer new strength: our practical interests, with their relative pleasures and pains, mingle and sometimes become confused with art and disturb, but are never *iden-*

tified with, our aesthetic interest. At the most it will be affirmed, with a view to maintaining more effectively the definition of art as the pleasurable, that it is not the pleasurable in general, but a *particular* form of the pleasurable. But such a restriction is no longer a defence, it is indeed an abandonment of that thesis; for given that art is a particular form of pleasure, its distinctive character would be supplied, not by the pleasurable, but by what distinguishes that pleasurable from other pleasurables, and it would be desirable to turn the attention to that distinctive element—more than pleasurable or different from pleasurable. Nevertheless, the doctrine that defines art as the pleasurable has a special denomination (hedonistic aesthetic), and a long and complicated development in the history of aesthetic doctrines: it showed itself in the Graeco-Roman world, prevailed in the eighteenth century, reflowered in the second half of the nineteenth, and still enjoys much favour, being especially well received by beginners in aesthetic, who are above all struck by the fact that art causes pleasure. The life of this doctrine has consisted of proposing in turn one or another class of pleasures, or several classes together (the pleasure of the superior senses, the pleasure of play, of consciousness of our own strength, of love, etc., etc.), or of adding to it elements differing from the pleasurable, the useful for example (when understood as distinct from the pleasurable), the satisfaction of cognoscitive and moral wants, and the like. And its progress has been caused just by this restlessness, and by its allowing foreign elements to ferment in its bosom, which it introduces through the necessity of somehow bringing itself into agreement with the reality of art, thus attaining to its dissolution as hedonistic doctrine and to the unconscious promotion of a new doctrine, or at least to drawing attention to its necessity. And since every error has its ele- ment of truth (and that of the physical doctrine has been seen to be the possibil- ity of the physical "construction" of art as of any other fact), the hedonistic doctrine has its eternal element of truth in the placing in relief the hedonistic accompaniment, or pleasure, common to the aesthetic activity as to every form of spiritual activity, which it has not at all been intended to deny in absolutely denying the identification of art with the pleasurable, and in distinguishing it from the pleasurable by defining it as intuition.

A third negation, effected by means of the theory of art as intuition, is that art is a *moral act;* that is to say, that form of practical act which, although neces- sarily uniting with the useful and with pleasure and pain, is not immediately utilitarian and hedonistic, and moves in a superior spiritual sphere. But the in- tuition, in so far as it is a theoretic act, is opposed to the practical of any sort. And in truth, art, as has been remarked from the earliest times, does not arise as an act of the will; good will, which con- stitutes the honest man, does not consti- tute the artist. And since it is not the result of an act of will, so it escapes all moral discrimination, not because a priv- ilege of exemption is accorded to it, but simply because moral discrimination cannot be applied to art. An artistic image portrays an act morally praise- worthy or blameworthy; but this image, as image, is neither morally praiseworthy nor blameworthy. Not only is there no penal code that can condemn an image to prison or to death, but no moral judg- ment, uttered by a rational person, can make of it its object: we might just as well judge the square moral or the tri- angle immoral as the Francesca of Dante immoral or the Cordelia of Shakespeare moral, for these have a purely artistic function, they are like musical notes in the souls of Dante and of Shakespeare.

Further, the moralistic theory of art is also represented in the history of aes- thetic doctrines nor is it entirely dead today, though much discredited in the common opinion of our times, not only on account of its intrinsic demerit, but also, in some measure, owing to the moral demerit of certain tendencies of our times, which render possible, owing to psychological dislike, that refutation of it which should be made—and which we here make—solely for logical reasons. The end attributed to art, of directing the good and inspiring horror of evil, of correcting and ameliorating customs, is a derivation of the moralistic doctrine; and so is the demand addressed to artists to collaborate in the education of the lower classes, in the strengthening of the national or bellicose spirit of a people, in the diffusion of the ideals of a modest and laborious life; and so on. These are all things that art cannot do, any more than geometry, which, however, does not lose anything of its importance on ac- count of its inability to do this; and one does not see why art should do so, either. That it cannot do these things was partially perceived by the moralistic aestheticians also; who very readily effected a transaction with it, permitting it to provide pleasures that were not moral, provided they were not openly dishonest, or recommending it to employ to a good end the dominion that, owing to its hedonistic power, it possessed over souls, to gild the pill, to sprinkle sweet- ness upon the rim of the glass contain- ing the bitter draught—in short, to play the courtezan (since it could not get rid of its old and inborn habits), in the serv- ice of holy church or of morality: *mere- trix ecclesiae*. On other occasions they have sought to avail themselves of it for purposes of instruction, since not only virtue but also science is a difficult thing, and art could remove this difficulty and render pleasant and attractive the en- trance into the ocean of science—indeed, lead them through it as through a garden of Armida, gaily and voluptuously, without their being conscious of the lofty protection they had obtained, or of the crisis of renovation which they were preparing for themselves. We cannot now refrain from a smile when we talk of these theories, but should not forget that they were once a serious matter corresponding to a serious effort to understand the nature of art and to elevate the conception of it; and that among those who believed in it (to limit ourselves to Italian literature) were Dante and Tasso, Parini and Alfieri, Manzoni and Mazzini. And the moralistic doctrine of art was and is and will be perpetually beneficial by its very contradictions; it was and will be an effort, however unhappy, to separate art from the merely pleasing, with which it is sometimes confused, and to assign to it a more worthy post: and it, too, has its true side, because, if art be beyond morality, the artist is neither this side of it nor that, but under its empire, in so far as he is a man who cannot withdraw himself from the duties of man, and must look upon art itself—art, which is not and never will be moral—as a mission to be exercised as a priestly office.

Again (and this is the last and perhaps the most important of all the general negations that it suits me to recall in relation to this matter), with the definition of art as intuition, we deny that it has the character of *conceptual knowledge*. Conceptual knowledge, in its true form, which is the philosophical, is always realistic, aiming at establishing reality against unreality, or at lowering unreality by including it in reality as a subordinate moment of reality itself. But intuition means, precisely, indistinction of reality and unreality, the image with its value as mere image, the pure ideality of the image, and opposing the intuitive or sensible knowledge to the conceptual or intelligible, the aesthetic to the noetic, it aims at claiming the autonomy of this more simple and elementary form of knowledge, which has been compared to the dream (the dream, and not the sleep) of the theoretic life, in respect to which philosophy would be the waking. And indeed, whoever should ask, when examining a work of art, whether what the artist has expressed be metaphysically and historically true or false, asks a question that is without meaning, and commits an error analogous to his who should bring the airy images of the fancy before the tribunal of morality: without meaning, because the discrimination of true and false always concerns an affirmation of reality, or a judgment, but it cannot fall under the head of an image or of a pure subject, which is not the subject of a judgment, since it is without qualification or predicate. It is useless to object that the individuality of the image cannot subsist without reference to the universal, of which that image is the individuation, because we do not here deny that the universal, as the spirit of God, is everywhere and animates all things with itself, but we deny that the universal is rendered logically explicit and is thought in the intuition. Useless also is the appeal to the principle of the unity of the spirit, which is not broken, but, on the contrary, strengthened by the clear distinction of fancy from thought, because from the distinction comes opposition, and from opposition concrete unity. . . . Certainly art is symbol, all symbol—that is, all significant; but symbol of what? What does it mean? The intuition is truly artistic, it is truly intuition, and not a chaotic mass of images, only when it has a vital principle that animates it, making it all one with itself; but what is this principle?

The answer to such a question may be said to result from the examination of the greatest ideal strife that has ever taken place in the field of art (and is not

368 BENEDETTO CROCE

confined to the epoch that took its name from it and in which it was predominant): the strife between *romanticism* and *classicism*. Giving the general definition, here convenient, and setting aside minor and accidental determinations, romanticism asks of art, above all, the spontaneous and violent effusion of the affections, of love and hate, of anguish and jubilation, of desperation and elevation; and is willingly satisfied and pleased with vaporous and indeterminate images, broken and allusive in style, with vague suggestions, with approximate phrases, with powerful and troubled sketches: while classicism loves the peaceful soul, the wise design, figures studied in their characteristics and precise in outline, ponderation, equilibrium, clarity; and resolutely tends toward *representation,* as the other tends toward *feeling.* And whoever puts himself at one or the other point of view finds crowds of reasons for maintaining it and for confuting the opposite point of view; because (say the romantics), What is the use of an art, rich in beautiful images, which, nevertheless, does not speak to the heart? And if it do speak to the heart, what is the use if the images be not beautiful? And the others will say, What is the use of the shock of the passions, if the spirit do not rest upon a beautiful image? And if the image be beautiful, if our taste be satisfied, what matters the absence of those emotions which can all of them be obtained outside art, and which life does not fail to provide, sometimes in greater quantity than we desire?—But when we begin to feel weary of the fruitless defence of both partial views; above all, when we turn away from the ordinary works of art produced by the romantic and classical schools, from works convulsed with passion or coldly decorous, and fix them on the works, not of the disciples, but of the masters, not of the mediocre, but of the supreme, we see the contest disap-

pear in the distance and find ourselves unable to call the great portions of these works, romantic or classic representative, because they are both classic and romantic, feelings and representations, a vigorous feeling which has become all most brilliant representation. Such, for example, are the works of Hellenic art, and such those of Italian poetry and art: the transcendentalism of the Middle Ages became fixed in the bronze of the Dantesque *terzina;* melancholy and suave fancy, in the transparency of the songs and sonnets of Petrarch; sage experience of life and badinage with the fables of the past, in the limpid *ottava rima* of Ariosto; heroism and the thought of death, in the perfect blank verse hendecasyllabics of Foscolo; the infinite variety of everything, in the sober and austere songs of Giacomo Leopardi. Finally (be it said in parenthesis and without intending comparison with the other examples adduced), the voluptuous refinements and animal sensuality of international decadentism have received their most perfect expression in the prose and verse of an Italian, D'Annunzio. All these souls were profoundly passionate (all, even the serene Lodovico Ariosto, who was so amorous, so tender, and so often represses his emotion with a smile); their works of art are the eternal flower that springs from their passions.

These expressions and these critical judgments can be theoretically resumed in the formula, that what gives coherence and unity to the intuition is feeling: the intuition is really such because it represents a feeling, and can only appear from and upon that. Not the idea, but the feeling, is what confers upon art the airy lightness of the symbol: an aspiration enclosed in the circle of a representation—that is art; and in it the aspiration alone stands for the representation, and the representation alone for the aspiration. Epic and lyric, or drama and lyric, are scholastic divisions of the indivisible: art is always lyrical—that is, epic and dramatic in feeling. What we admire in genuine works of art is the perfect fanciful form which a state of the soul assumes; and we call this life, unity, solidity of the work of art. What displeases us in the false and imperfect forms is the struggle of several different states of the soul not yet unified, their stratification, or mixture, their vacillating method, which obtains apparent unity from the will of the author, who for this purpose avails himself of an abstract plan or idea, or of extra-aesthetic, passionate emotion. A series of images which seem to be, each in turn, rich in power of conviction, leaves us nevertheless deluded and diffident, because we do not see them generated from a state of the soul, from a "sketch" (as the painters call it), from a motive; and they follow one another and crowd together without that precise intonation, without that accent, which comes from the heart. And what is the figure cut out from the background of the picture or transported and placed against another background, what is the personage of drama or of romance outside his relation with all the other personages and with the general action? And what is the value of this general action if it be not an action of the spirit of the author? The secular disputes concerning dramatic unity are interesting in this connection; they are first applied to the unity of "action" when they have been obtained from an extrinsic determination of time and place, and this finally applied to the unity of "interest," and the interest would have to be in its turn dissolved in the interest of the spirit of the poet—that is, in his intimate aspiration, in his feeling. The negative issue of the great dispute between classicists and romanticists is interesting, for it resulted in the negation both of the art which strives to distract and

illude the soul as to the deficiency of the image with mere feeling, with the practical violence of feeling, with feeling that has not become contemplation, and of the art which, by means of the superficial clearness of the image, of drawing correctly false, of the word falsely correct, seeks to deceive as to its lack of inspiration and its lack of an aesthetic reason to justify what it has produced. A celebrated sentence uttered by an English critic, and become one of the commonplaces of journalism, states that "all the arts tend to the condition of music;" but it would have been more accurate to say that all the arts are music, if it be thus intended to emphasise the genesis of aesthetic images in feeling, excluding from their number those mechanically constructed or realistically ponderous. And another not less celebrated utterance of a Swiss semi-philosopher, which has had the like good or bad fortune of becoming trivial, discovers that "every landscape is a state of the soul:" which is indisputable, not because the landscape is landscape, but because the landscape is art.

Artistic intuition, then, is always *lyrical* intuition: this latter being a word that is not present as an adjective or definition of the first, but as a synonym, another of the synonyms that can be united to the several that I have mentioned already, and which, all of them, designate the intuition. And if it be some times convenient that instead of appearing as a synonym, it should assume the grammatical form of the adjective, that is only to make clear the difference between the intuition-image, or nexus of images (for what is called image is always a nexus of images, since image-atoms do not exist any more than thought-atoms), which constitutes the organism, and, as organism, has its vital principle, which is the organism itself,— between this, which is true and proper intuition, and that false intuition which is a heap of images put together in play or intentionally or for some other practical purpose, the connection of which, being practical, shows itself to be not organic, but mechanic, when considered from the aesthetic point of view. But the word *lyric* would be redundant save in this explicative or polemical sense; and art is perfectly defined when it is simply defined as *intuition*.

40. Beauty *

S. ALEXANDER (1859–1938)

Beauty, like pleasure in Wordsworth's line, is "spread through the world"; and those who begin their inquiry into beauty with the beauty of nature are apt to conclude that beauty is a quality of things, independent of us, which we discover as we discover the other qualities of things. But the conclusion may be premature. Nature is beautiful only to the mind which is prepared to apprehend her beauty, to contemplate her for her own sake apart from the practical delight she brings. We distinguish the mere pleasure which she gives to the eye or ear from the pleasure of her beauty. A green field is doubtless pleasant to the eye of the cow, as well as grateful to her hunger. But does she find it beautiful? "Pleased when the sylvan world displays its raptures to the feeding gaze"—those raptures are not mere delight of the eye. There has been selection of what suits the feeder. Nature is not beautiful because she pleases but, to borrow a famous phrase of Hume which we shall elsewhere find enlightening, because she pleases after a particular manner. To discover in what manner, let us turn to the beauty of fine art.

Art of all kinds, including fine art,

constructs the work of art out of physical materials, wood or stone or pigments or words or, as in music, tones or, it may be, bodily movements as in the dance. A poem, whatever else may be said of it, is made of words, a picture of paints, a sonata of tones. There may be beauty of imagery or of thoughts. But images are images of things, and so in some more difficult sense are thoughts, when they are thoughts of physical things, physical too. The objects of the mind's internal visions are drawn in the lines and colours of external things. . . . In any case it is always well in dealing with intricate matters to take the simplest cases first. Art, then, is the construction of material works of art, and fine art of beautiful material or physical things.

Man is not the first artificer. He is preceded by the swallow which builds its nest, by the beaver which builds its dam, by the bee which constructs the hive, by the nightingale who sings to his mate. This impulse (or instinct) of construction may be identified as the impulse which in a qualified form produces in man fine art, and is the foundation of the impulse towards beauty. But such animal constructiveness falls far short of fine art. It is exhausted in practice and serves practical ends which the animal itself may be unaware of. Nest-

* From *Beauty and Other Forms of Value*, pp. 15-26. By permission of the publishers, The Macmillan Company.

building of birds and burrowing of wasps are spontaneous outflows of impulses whose end is the preservation of the young. The beaver and the bee construct for storage of food. The nightingale's song, however lovely to our aesthetic ears, is an incident in the practical arrangements of mating. It is not fine art, it is not even craft.

Craft is the next state upwards from animal construction and differs from it in that the end is purposed and not merely attained. Accordingly all manner of thinking and devices may enter into it. The craftsman is full of ideas of what he means to do, on the whole and in detail. The main feature, however, of his work is that he constructs his materials for practical ends, to give his clay the shape of a pot, or to weave his yarn into the pattern of cloth. Craft is more than spontaneous construction, because the result is willed, and less than fine art. At the same time craft is at every moment passing over into fine art. The craftsman as such is not an artist. The good craftsman constructs his product as perfectly as he can, he takes faithfully the steps necessary to that end. He becomes an artist in so far as he treats his materials also for themselves, and the craftsman may be and is perpetually besieged by dreams of beauty in his work. From skill he proceeds to good taste and from taste to charm and beauty. So constantly may the faithful craftsman be mixed with the creative artist. On the other hand the artist, if he is to be a good artist, must possess craft, and though a defect in his craft may be atoned for by excellence of creative handling, his work loses in artistic rank, just as contrariwise he may fail of greatness because his creativeness may be unequal to the craft of the 'perfect painter.'

Moreover, the greater part of what is commonly known as fine art is not art at all—and in future when I say art I shall mean fine art—but is craft. The paintings which cover the walls of our exhibitions are largely skilful or competent representations, good rather than beautiful, half-way between photographs, which are the artistry of the sun, and those truly beautiful representative paintings which I shall later describe as the prose of painting. The larger part of the houses and other buildings of our towns are not so much architecture, many of them are not even made by architects, but workman-like constructions, and sometimes they are even positively ugly because they defy architectural form. The greater part of our writing, in books and still more in newspapers, is competent narrative or exposition, skilled but not beautiful or artistic writing such as deserves the name of literature. And this is in no way intended in depreciation of such works of craft. For craftsmanship is not only the prerequisite of artistry but is itself precious and good and attained only by much labour and experience, and exercised only with pains and devotion.

Art grows out of craft and goes beyond it, when the worker handles his materials not, or not only, as a means of reaching a certain practical end but for their own sakes, and becomes contemplative instead of merely practical. How does this difference arise? We have seen how practical observation of things becomes theoretical when the practical issue of grasping the object is diverted into another practical issue, that of naming. But the fine art of speech goes beyond naming and introduces into speech magic and beauty. How does construction become thus contemplative? The question has to be asked, for the act of the artist, like that of the craftsman, primarily conforms to the type of behaviour already exhibited in ordinary cognition of a thing or colour. The artist is excited by some subject or other, a scene in nature, a woman, a commission to build a house, the thought of a chivalrous deed; and his excitement issues in external action, in the use of the hands with chisel or paint-brush or burin, or of the voice or other instrument for producing tones, or of the limbs in dance, or in speech. Some of these instruments of his utterance are native to him, others are acquired. In all cases he uses materials which as in building he finds ready to be used, or as in speech and singing he himself provides and constructs into certain arrangements. But the artist, unlike the craftsman, uses the materials not practically but contemplatively, for this is the meaning of the phrase which I use, 'the use of materials for their own sake,' which means simply that the materials are used without practical purpose as in craft, though of course without excluding the practical purpose in the craft which underlies the art. It does not mean that the materials are considered in themselves as if words should be regarded in their history or derivation as the philologist uses, or pigments in their chemical composition, or stones as geological formations. That is precisely what the artist does not do.

How is this transition effected? The answer is to be found in an old phrase which describes the work of art—*homo additus naturae,* the addition of man to nature. It is because the artist mixes himself with his materials. Not only does he arrange the materials in a form which they themselves, as he finds them, have not; the craftsman also does that, which is implied in mere construction. He introduces into his materials, through the form he gives them, characters, or rather the appearance of characters, which in their practical use they do not possess. He gives the bronze breath and living features to the marble, according to the Virgilian phrases, *spirantia aera, vivos ducent de marmore voltus.* He does not merely interpret as we do in ordinary perception the data of sense by his past experience of things, perceiving

the orange which he merely sees as fragrant and juicy fruit, and so add to things as he experiences them characters which they do actually possess in practical experience. He imputes to his materials characters which in practical experience they do not possess. The exact import and the range of this procedure will be discussed presently. The fact is certain, most easily verified in the statue which looks living or the flat picture which looks solid. In virtue of this addition of the artist to his work, which in special cases may be replaced by subtraction, the work to be what it is, to convey its meaning, demands the presence of the artist's mind in its creation, or of his substitute the spectator in appreciation. Without them the marble has no appearance of life, and its form, however remarkable, has no significance. If we found such strange shapes scattered among shapeless blocks or masses of clay, they would be mere curiosities of nature.

Now it is the admixture to the given material of meaning imported from the artist himself, and not belonging to the material itself, which detaches the materials from their mere natural use in practice and makes them objects treated for their own sakes. The meanings which we add to the objects of sense in perceiving a sensible object, where the supplements imputed by the perceiver are verified by the thing itself in fact, have no such effect. But the imputation of meanings which do not belong to the material itself raises both those meanings and the sensible materials to which they are imputed into objects of intrinsic contemplation. Possessed by the excitement which is produced in him by the subject which occupies him, let us say the face of a 'beautiful' woman, and by the feel of the material in which he works in consequence of his excitement (for the mere touch of clay or the mere sound of a word may excite him into production, as the feel of the fresh grass sets a horse upon a wild scamper); under these excitements, the artist constructs spontaneously out of the fulness of his constructive impulse, but, moulding his material as he does to a shape which, to use inaccurate language which will be corrected hereafter, 'expresses' his own mind, his materials acquire an attachment to himself which detaches them from the mere world of nature. The constructive impulse, once provoked, indulges itself in its own enjoyment, the artist surrenders himself to what we may loosely call ideas beyond the direct information conveyed by the subject matter, and these promptings of his mind issue into the shaping of his material. It is thus that the materials, those he finds and the adventitious form he gives them, become for him materials to be used contemplatively. For I observe again that not merely the significance added through the form is contemplated, but the material to which it is added becomes transfigured in the process. The meadows Shakespeare speaks of in the lovely song I shall quote presently— 'painted' as they are 'with delight', are no longer the mere meadows that please the animal's eyes, and the words themselves are no longer mere names of actual meadows. The marble ceases through its significant form to be mere marble. The same thing holds of natural objects when they are seen to be beautiful. The thunderstorm when it is felt to be sublime has lost in part at least the terrors it possesses as a natural event, becomes a source of delight, and approaches to the condition of a painted storm.

Ruskin rightly defines beauty in this way: "Any material object which can give us pleasure in the simple contemplation of its outward qualities without any direct and definite exertion of the intellect, I call in some way or in some degree beautiful." But the saving notion of contemplation which distinguishes such contemplation from practical observation is left unexplained. We, however, after this history of its origin, are free to say that the beautiful is the object (and perhaps we may even add, the satisfaction) of the constructive impulse when that impulse has become contemplative instead of practical.

Instead of sculpture, which has been chosen because it is the easiest example, we may illustrate what has been said from artistic speech; remembering at the same time that speech may be used for its own sake, apparently, at an early period but still not strictly for its own sake but practically. For example, barbaric chants which are no more literature than the wild dances of the orgy are art. Much singing has a liturgical purpose or even a hypnotic one. Let us take the case then of speech and ask how speech becomes artistic, whether poetry or prose. Speech is creative, and that fact offers such foundation as there is for a doctrine that has acquired authority in our own time, that linguistics and aesthetics are the same subject. That doctrine misses the difference of aesthetic from ordinary speech. For speech of itself is a construction for practical purpose. Either it is the means of creating theory or speculative consideration of things, and then it has the practical purpose of description, as in science. Or else it is manifestly practical, because it is the indication of our needs. To say 'I am cold' means in general 'help me to get warm'. It is a winter's night and friends are gathered together, and one says it would be comfortable to have more fire. That is constructive practical speech, and it may require not only for scientific description, but even for practical needs, much skill and niceness in the construction. Compare now those words with familiar ones:

Dissolve frigus, ligna super foco
Large reponens.

"Thaw away the cold, piling generous logs upon the fire." The subject is indeed practical, but the words are not practical speech; they are used lovingly as words, though they express the same practical thought as before. They are not indeed striking differences; take any accurate description of spring and the appearance of the fields at that time, which would be practical speech, and compare it with

> When daisies pied and violets blue,
>   And lady-smocks all silver white,
> And cuckoo-buds of yellow hue,
>   Do paint the meadows with delight.

There, at least in the last line, is enchantment, not from the thought alone but from the words.

But I have only illustrated and not explained. How do words get diverted from their practical use, and become enchanted? How does the magic get in? When physical objects, instead of being apprehended through practice, as originally they are, are apprehended theoretically, it was, we saw, because the normal response was diverted into another response and primarily into speech. But when speech itself, instead of being used as a practical means, becomes the end, there is no other response into which the speech-response can be diverted. If there were, we should be contemplating the words theoretically, as indeed we do in the science of them. Now the very thing which the poet does not do is to contemplate his words theoretically. He makes an artistic and not a scientific use of them. Since then there is no other action to detach words from practice, except the action of poetic construction itself, what is it which effects the detachment?

It is, I suggest, the constructive excitement itself which attaches the words to the artist and detaches them from their practical issues. The constructed object (the word), instead of leading the mind on to its practical effect, stimulates

or serves as a signal for the continuance of the constructive activity itself, and leads on to the next constructed object (word) in the connected work. Just as to pass from one thing to another in a train of ideas loosens the first thing from its practical urgency and makes it an object of theory, so the first element in a constructional whole may lead on, through the constructive process, to the next element, without regard for the practical outcome. Then we have art. In the constructive process the objects then are held or possessed by the constructor. The poet makes himself one with his words and so holds them to himself, and detaches them from the subject matter which excited his constructive impulse. In practical speech or the use of speech for the practical means of description, there may indeed be constructive passion, as anyone may attest who recalls the effort of bare accurate description. But it is the subject described which interests him: his use of speech, his constructiveness, is a means to describing the subject, which remains outside him and he a looker-on. It is the subject which excites his constructive passion and he has to use his constructions in order to satisfy the subject matter. The poetic excitement of constructiveness, on the other hand, seeks to satisfy the poet himself, at least to satisfy himself as well as be adequate to the subject matter. And in this passionate constructive effort he blends himself with his materials, which are words, holds them to himself, and thus constructiveness in speech becomes contemplative.

The statement that in art the artist mixes his mind with the materials demands explanation but it conceals no mystery, and implies no miracle. There is no literal blending of the mind with physical materials, as if such an idea could even be intelligible. It used to be said of a famous cricketer that he bowled or batted, I forget which, with his head. The use of his head was exhibited in the cunning direction which he gave to the ball. In the same way, the mixing of the artist's mind with his materials means that elements in the work of art, whether actual new material, or the form given to the material before him, are supplied at the initiative of the mind instead of that of something outside him. Let us take for convenience the simple case of a portrait bust, and for the moment disregard the difference of the matter which the artist uses and the form he gives to his clay. He is no photographer and does not reproduce the subject's head mechanically as it may be reproduced in marble by a cutting instrument which follows directly or indirectly the form of the head. He may be aware in himself of no ideas of the character of the person he is representing, and may to his own mind be copying the head faithfully. In fact he stresses here, and omits there, so that the result embodies his vision but yet is a study of the original. The major part of the work is suggested from the model; but some elements are suggested in the working of the artist's mind. He makes his bust live by importing into the dead clay the life which he sees in the model or subject. With his hand he imputes life to the clay.

The process is familiar from ordinary perception in which, according to James's well-known phrase, half comes from the object and half from the observer's mind. The observer interprets what he sees. But what he adds to what he sees is of the same order as what he sees, is physical and not mental. What goes on in his mind is the mental act, the conation, of which the object is the physical addition he makes to the thing he perceives. That conation is started in his mind, in virtue of his past experience, by the mental act provoked in him by the external object. He complicates that simple mental process by enlargement. The elements he adds may have been first entertained by him consciously in the form of an imaginative act. But most commonly his supplementary act does not reach the level of imagination. Rather it is 'ideal supplementation', 'tied ideas', as when we see the ice cold. Or it may not reach the conscious level at all. In every case what happens is that, for one reason or another, an impulse or conation is started internally and to that interior conation an external object corresponds, which is a modification of the actual external thing which would have provoked such internal conation. The object so brought before the mind forms part of the whole perceived external object because the conation to which it corresponds is linked into a unity with the conations evoked by the presented external thing. This is the simple process of imputation, and the imputation characteristic of the work of art is precisely of this nature. The mind is mixed in artistic creation with its materials because the impulses initiated in it in the course of construction are reflected in the materials as worked up into their artistic form.

41. The Analysis of Art *

DeWitt H. Parker (1885–1949)

For those who delight in thinking, the most fascinating problems are the most elusive. There is an initial discouragement in approaching them and a continuing humility, yet stronger than either is the attraction of their mystery and the hardihood of trying again where so many have failed. That shall be my excuse, as it has been others', for attempting the *pons asinorum* of defining art. No definition of so living a thing as art can be wholly adequate; yet a good definition should at least seize the distinctive characteristics of art, and thus make the mind more vividly aware of art against the background of things that are not art. The hope of framing such a definition has been greatly increased in recent years through the new insight into the nature of art which has come to us from several sources. Yet from none of these sources can one get precisely what a satisfactory theory of art should provide, namely, insight into the differentia, the distinguishing characteristics of art. The chief reason for their failure is the mistaken faith that some single, simple formula can contain the essence of art, whereas art is a very complex, and also a very special sort of thing, that requires a correspondingly complex formula to do it justice. Most of the statements that men have made

about art are true enough, but unfortunately they are also true of many other things, or else leave out of account aspects of art equally essential. The well-known formulae that come to mind, the 'objectified pleasure' of Santayana; 'intuition' of Croce and Fiedler; the 'expression of feeling' of Véron and Tolstoy; 'significant form' of Clive Bell— these are, one and all, illuminating, but inadequate, either because they fit other things besides works of art or because they omit characteristics of art as important as those they emphasize. And yet one cannot reach the truth about art by merely piecing these and other descriptions together; for that would leave unrevealed the strikingly organic, unified nature of art. Only the sort of definition that would follow and unfold the living structure of art could be successful at all. For this reason, while gratefully making use of the ideas of others, I shall seek to describe art as good painters have always sought to paint nature, from the model rather than from mere information or academic canons and formulae. We shall find that art has no inescapably threefold complexity, as imagination, as language, and as design, but that nevertheless it has its own unity and uniqueness.

That art belongs to the sphere of the imagination has long been recognized. It is true that this recognition has not been so complete and general as it

* Part of Chapter I in *The Analysis of Art*. By kind permission of the publishers, Yale University Press.

should be, owing to the classical theory of art as 'imitation'; yet whereas the classical theory has always found difficulty in squaring itself with such obviously fantastic forms of art as *Alice in Wonderland* or the Barberini Faun, there is no trouble in finding a place for imitation within imagination. For, despite its creativeness, the imagination derives its elements from nature, and by reproducing nature can include it. Only recently, however, has the full significance of the imaginative character of art come to light. The now demonstrated kinship between art, day-dreaming, dreaming at night, and mythology has opened new avenues of insight, and also, as we shall see, given rise to new problems and some false suggestions.

The most valuable result that has emerged is the proof that the imagination itself, including all its forms, not excepting art, is no independent, autonomous thing, functioning according to mechanical laws of similarity or contiguity, but is, in a sense, secondary, being always under the control of what, without too much misunderstanding, we may still venture to call a 'wish.' The imagination exists for a purpose, to provide satisfaction for moods and desires. That this is true of day-dreams is clear to every one; that it is also true of night-dreams has been rendered almost certain by Freud. There are two ways in which wishes may find satisfaction; one of which may be called the real way, and the other, the dream way. The first is the practical method, to appropriate from the environment what is needed. Thus I satisfy hunger by procuring food, or ambition by inducing other people to provide me with the place and advantages that I desire. In the second mode of satisfaction of wishes, there is no acquisitive interaction with the environment; the wish is satisfied by something that occurs entirely within myself, within my own mind and body, in the realm of my fantasy. And, strangely, this mode of satisfaction of a wish is as genuine as the other; for the time being, at least, my wish is fulfilled, and I am content. Theoretically, to every real satisfaction, there corresponds a possible imaginary, or ideal, satisfaction. So, we are told, hungry and thirsty men, crossing the desert, find satisfaction in dreaming that they are feasting, and in an idle hour every ambitious man dreams that he has won his prize, and every lover that his mistress has favored him. Any wish, frustrated or postponed or only partially satisfied, may generate a dream, a fantasy, in which it finds a substitute satisfaction. Thus it is that we 'get even' with fate, and, however bound by the world, achieve freedom in our dreams. The importance of such satisfactions in the life of man is immense; for whenever he is not busy doing things or planning to do them, he is secretly dreaming that he has done them successfully.

The typical characteristics of dream experiences are now pretty well known. One of the most fundamental of these we may call, after Vaihinger, the 'as if' attitude, the analogue of the 'conscious self-deception' (*bewusste Selbst-Täuschung*) of Gross and Lange. Things seen in a dream, be it a day-dream or a dream at night, are to us 'as if' they were real; for the time being, at least, we do not treat them as imaginary, but as actual. And the interest that we take in them depends upon the fact that we do accept them as real. They must seem to us to be real or our wish would not be able to fulfil itself in them. Nevertheless, the acceptance of objects and occurrences in a dream as real is seldom entire; there is always, in the fringe of consciousness, an awareness that, after all, they are unreal. One part of ourselves believes in them, but another part refuses its assent; and it is this unique combination of belief and unbelief which creates the 'as if' attitude, the attitude of make-believe. There is a dissociation of certain elements of the mind, which form a little island of belief, from the wider sea of consciousness which maintains the point of view of ordinary life and condemns the dream as unreal. These two diverse points of view toward the same thing coexist in the same mind; so that it is almost true to say that we at once believe and do not believe. Sometimes one and sometimes another of the two attitudes will dominate; in dreams at night there is partial, if not complete, submergence of the doubter; complete submergence occurs only in the delusions of the insane, when dream passes into reality; in the day-dream the doubter is still active, but overruled for the time being by the dreamful believer; in art and in play there is equipoise, and we dream on, knowing full well and luminously that we are dreaming.

In accordance with the foregoing, it should be possible to show that works of art, as products of the imagination, are at once characterized by the 'as if' attitude and are satisfactions of wishes. That the 'as if' attitude dominates the aesthetic appreciation of the normal types of painting and sculpture is evident. But even when we look at the Cézanne landscape ... it is for us as if there were hills and trees and skies before us; great as the schematization is, they are to us as if they were real, and they evoke in us some, at least, of the interests and feelings called forth by real things. There is, as we shall see, absolutely no test of good drawing or painting except the capacity of the artist to make us believe; his work may be realistic or highly stylized, either method is good as art, so long as it creates an image in which we believe. Or when, for example, we look at MacMonnies' Bac-

chante, it is as if the divinely frenzied girl and her child were alive in our presence and we were witnesses of their ecstasy in the festival of the god. To induce us to make believe this is the triumph of the artist. But equally, when we look at Brancusi's Miss Pogany, for all the geometrization of the head, we get a feeling of reality. So, likewise, we demand of every novel and play, every dramatic and narrative poem, that it create the semblance of reality.

That such arts as painting, sculpture, literature, and the drama belong to the realm of the imagination seems clear enough, but music, the dance, and architecture do not so obviously belong there. The character of make-believe, of the 'as if' attitude, may seem to be absent. For is not music real sound, and the dance real motion, and a building real marble? And yet, so far as these things are beautiful, that is not the whole truth about them. Let us consider the dance first. We must distinguish from the outset the aesthetic experience of the dancer from that of one who is watching the dance. Now the latter is clearly an imaginative experience; for when I watch a dance, I enjoy it fully only when it is as if I, too, were dancing; when, in the imagination, I move with the motions of the dancer, experiencing vicariously her ease and her joy. The dancer's experience is, of course, different. She really moves, no make-believe that. Yet, even so, her experience possesses the essential character of imagination. For it is a satisfaction of impulses through occurrences within her own mind and body. For the moment it is as if she were having her way, only not through some purposive adjustment to her environment, but through action within her own self. To be sure, that action is not confined to her mind, as it is with me who watch her, but overflows into the body; but who has ever set the limits of the mind or the body? And even in my case when I watch her, something more than the mind is really involved, for imagination tends to translate itself into action, and there are impulses to movement, inhibited for obvious reasons, all through my muscles. In this enlarged sense of imagination, therefore, which nevertheless retains its fundamental meaning as a satisfaction of desire from within the system of the mind and body, dancing belongs with the other arts to imagination.

The case is similar with music. And, in parallel fashion, let us distinguish between music which we ourselves make and music which we merely listen to. And let us, furthermore, confine our attention entirely to absolute music, where no definite ideas or images are summoned to mind. I exclude programme music, because it is obviously imaginative; one cannot listen to the Golliwogs' Cake Walk, for example, without having the experience as if the Golliwogs were dancing. Suppose, then, I just hum a tune, say the motif from the first movement of Beethoven's Second Symphony. Well, why do I hum it? Perhaps my neighbor does not understand, but I do: I hum the tune because it pleases me; because some wish, some emotion of mine, is satisfied thus—an emotion which I feel none the less strongly because I am unable to tell what it is about or just what it means. At all events, in this little world of sound that I am making, it is as if I were having my way perfectly, and that is enough reason for humming: I so seldom have my way in real life! Thus, as in dancing, I am securing the satisfaction of my wish, not through some practical relation to the environment, but by way of an occurrence that is entirely within my own mind and body, and, for the time being at least, it is for me as if the satisfaction were real; and that, let me say once more, is the essence of imagination. The fact that my wishes may be objectless, that I do not attach them to some fancied situation or happening, is irrelevant. But suppose now, instead of humming the tune, I listen to some one play it. Then, first of all, I apprehend what Hanslick called an arabesque, a pattern of sound. But my experience is richer than that. For on hearing the sound, various wishes, moods, emotions, are awakened in me, the same, in fact, that I felt when I, myself, hummed the tune, and these emotions and wishes find expression and fulfilment, as before, in the sounds. Thus there is no important difference in what happens within me whether I make or only listen to the music. Music is beautiful as a voice that I hear storming, sobbing, making merry, lamenting, rejoicing, as the case may be, and it is as if that voice were my own. Hence music, too, belongs to the world of the imagination, in the larger and truer sense.

The demonstration of the imaginative quality of beautiful architecture is not so simple, and in place of the scientific analysis that should be given I beg leave to report a personal experience, which is, I believe, universal. Whenever I am in the presence of a beautiful building, and especially when I am inside it, I seem not to be in the neighborhood of a mere thing. I am not alone, as I am alone when surrounded by buildings unbeautiful or indifferent, as when at night I walk down the undistinguished streets of a large city; on the contrary, I am richly companioned; I feel all about me a life variously and magnificently eloquent; uttering a meaning which, to be sure, I cannot put into words—any more than I can translate music into words—but which I seem to understand; a meaning that comes to me, not by the avenues of sound, but by that of sight, and through subtle arousals of imaginative touch and movement. Every beautiful building is not only fit to house, but itself possesses or is a personality; a personality as distinct, as unique, as the faces of friends. Amiens, Rheims, Ulm, St. Mark's; piles of stone, yes, of course; but how much more; and that more is, so tells my sober reason, mere make-believe, pure fancy; yet essential to beauty. A beautiful building makes us dream, becomes itself a dream. And what I have said of beautiful architecture applies, if in lower key, to beautiful specimens of the potter's art, to color paintings, to oriental carpets; if they have for us the quality of beauty, they are not dead things, but things possessed of an imagined life. When you look at an oriental carpet it may seem to you at first no more than a mere pattern of colors and lines, but as you linger over it, you observe a change. The lines begin to run or shoot like arrows, the colors tingle; everything seems to move, or if not moving, rests—not really, of course, but in the mind, in the imagination. . . .

Thus far I have accepted the familiar comparison between art and dream, but certain differences between them are of the utmost importance. For a dream is an inner fact only, an affair wholly of the imagination, while a work of art belongs also to the outer world, to the senses. It is something to be seen, heard, perhaps even touched. A work of art is born only when imaginative vision is wedded to sensuous shape. The inner vision must be expressed, in the etymological meaning of the term, put out into color and line, word-sound or tone. To be an artist always involves being more than a dreamer or seer; it involves mastery of a material as well; the mere dreamers are only half artists. The painter is one who can translate his visions of nature into visible line and color; the poet is one fertile in words as well as in ideas; the sculptor does not

exist until he is able to model. Art is a 'gift of tongues,' of language. The artist must be able to create, in the external world, something to charm the senses as well as to speak to the mind. It is as if the artist were not content to realize his wishes in the closed room of the imagination, but desired to step out into reality and find satisfaction there. Yet the artist never does, of course, achieve reality. In the words of Bacon, he submits the mere *shows* of things to the desires of the mind. He takes the senses into the imagination, he does not leave the world of the imagination. His work remains a show, a make-believe, to the end; or rather it makes of reality itself such a show. It is a play, not of images merely, as in a dream, but of sensations. These are chosen partly for their ability to embody the dream, but also for their own intrinsic beauty. Thus in a song, like Der Erlkönig, the musical tones are not merely an embodiment in sound of Goethe's ideas as Schubert made them his own; but independently, as mere sound, they are an expression of vague moods and desires; and the colors in a painting are not only the right colors from the point of view of representation, but beautiful on their own account, apart from any representation. A picture is, first of all, a pattern of expressive colors and lines, just as music is first of all an arabesque of beautiful sound. Thus the sense medium is itself a part of the dream and an expression of the artist's desire.

That, despite its sensuous side, a work of art remains within the sphere of imagination, can easily be seen from another point of view. Consider, for example, Vermeer's Young Woman with a Water Jug. The pigments and the canvas are, of course, physical objects, as real as sun and moon; no dream work, no mere imagination they. Yet the paint and the canvas are relevant to the aesthetic experience only through what can be seen of them in the picture; as parts of the aesthetic object, they are only visual sensations in the mind of the beholder; they might as well be a hallucination. Moreover, the colors there are the colors of the woman's face, of her garments, of the casement and the map. Now admittedly all those things are not real; despite the convincing art of the painter, they are a make-believe, that is all. And notwithstanding their intrinsic beauty, the colors are, for aesthetic appreciation, constituents of these make-believe objects, nothing more.

Yet certain transformations accrue to the dream through sensuous embodiment; or, in order to avoid the possibility of misunderstanding (as if in artistic work the vision must precede expression when, as a matter of fact, the two usually go hand in hand), let me say rather that a dream expressed differs in important ways from a mere dream. It possesses a poignancy, an objectivity, an additional tang of reality, while remaining nevertheless a dream. Through its connection with the sense world, it is partly dissociated from the rest of the self, and so seems to be external, like the color or sound in which it is embodied. It belongs to the outer as well as to the inner world; it confronts us; it draws attention to itself; we are awake to it, not asleep in it, as we are in a dream. It is "the dream of a man awake." It possesses a steadiness, clarity, and independence that permit us to observe it, as we cannot observe a dream. In the experience of beauty there are two, the work of art and myself. This fact renders inadequate every comparison of the aesthetic experience to hypnosis or the mystical experience, where the distinction between subject and object disappears in utter oneness. So far may the process of dissociation go that the poet's passion is no longer felt as his

own, after expression; and the novelist's characters, for all that they are bits of himself, may seem to be doing their own wills, not his. . . .

But even now our analysis of art is incomplete; for we have barely mentioned one of the most striking characteristics of art, aesthetic form or design. . . . By design I mean, of course, harmony, balance, rhythm, and the like. A poem is not only an expression of feeling, it is patterned words; a musical composition is not only an embodiment of mood, it has a very elaborate harmonic and rhythmic structure; a picture or statue is never merely the representation of some object in nature, it is besides a harmony of lines and colors and space elements. A beautiful building is never one that is merely well adapted to its purpose, it possesses besides proportion and expressive lines and space forms. No matter how interesting and noble be the imagination of the artist, without design there is no picture or statue or poem or beautiful building. Moreover, the fundamental principles underlying aesthetic design are universal; they are exemplified in primitive art as well as in civilized art; in oriental as well as in occidental art; in the art of the black, the white, and the yellow man. Arguing from the universality of design some students of art, called formalists, have claimed that design was the essence of art, the very thing we call beauty.

Yet despite the importance of design in art, the claim of the formalist is unjustified. For the underlying impulse to art is the demand for satisfaction of wishes in the imagination; design is a necessary, not a sufficient, condition of beauty, as many a faultless but cold and meaningless work attests. Moreover, design is no independent thing, imposed as from the outside upon imaginative expression, but a perfectly natural and inevitable development of expression, when it is an end in itself. For . . . design is the form of all experience when it is satisfactory. Whenever experience is most delightful, it possesses rhythm, balance, unity in variety, and a cumulative movement—these are not peculiar to art, except in their perfect realization, and they are perfect there because the artist, unlike other men, has complete control of his material. Building up in the imagination a little world that shall satisfy his wishes, and embodying it in a medium over which, as expert technician, he is master, it would be strange if the artist did not give that world design. Design is the inevitable consummation of the artistic impulse. And it is right that artists and critics should place stress upon that which gives to art its perfection.

42. *Standards of Criticism**

C. J. DUCASSE (1881–   )

#1

Criticism is (a) *judgment,* (b) *of worth,* (c) *mediate or immediate, and* (d), *respectively fallible or infallible.* Criticism is judgment concerning questions of worth, value. All criticism involves reference to some character, the possession of which by the object criticized is regarded by the critic as being in some way good, or the lack of it, bad. The object is then examined with respect to that character, and pronounced good or bad in the degree in which it possesses it or lacks it. Such a character so used constitutes a standard of criticism. The character used may be one the possession of which makes an object *mediately good;* or on the other hand it may be one that makes the object *immediately good.* The object is said to be mediately or instrumentally good, when the character used as standard of goodness, and possessed by the object, is that of being an adequate instrument to or a necessary condition of the production or preservation in certain other objects, or characters which confer upon those objects immediate goodness of some sort. An object, on the other hand, is said to be immediately good when the character used as standard of goodness, and possessed by the object, is that of being directly and immediately a source of active or passive pleasure to some conscious being. That is to say, the object is called immediately good when it is, to the sentient being in terms of whose point of view it is asserted to be good, a source of pleasure *directly through its* relation to him, and apart from any pleasure which it may also procure him indirectly through its actual or potential effects upon other objects. The conscious being in terms of whose point of view the assertion of immediate goodness is made may be one person or a class of persons; it may be oneself or someone else; it may be a self considered in someone only of its aspects, which may be an active or a passive one; or it

* From *The Philosophy of Art.* By permission of publishers. The Dial Press.

may be a self, such only as it is at a given time or in given circumstances. But any doubt as to which such sort of self is referred to when goodness is predicated of anything, will leave the import of the predication hopelessly ambiguous.

The instrumental goodness of an object can be proved or disproved, if there is agreement as to the end, being a means to or condition of which constitutes the object's goodness; for it is then only a matter of showing whether or not the object does under the sort of conditions in view, cause or make possible in other objects effects of the sort desired. Thus it is possible to prove to someone who doubts or disbelieves it, that a given chisel is a good, or as the case may be, a bad chisel. As to instrumental goodness, mistakes can be made.

But the immediate goodness of an object cannot be proved or disproved to the self in terms of whose point of view immediate goodness is asserted to be possessed by the object. Such immediate goodness being a matter of the pleasure which *that* self experiences through his direct relation to the object, he himself is the final and infallible judge of it; for, as to pleasure, appearance and reality are identical. His actual pleasure or displeasure when in direct relation to the object, constitutes the proof or disproof *to others,* of any assertions or predictions that *they* may have made as to what, in terms of his point of view, is, or will turn out to be, immediately good. Such an other, to whom the prediction may have been made, may of course be, or have been, living under the same skin as the self who verifies the prediction; but it cannot be strictly the same self.

#10

Beauty is relative to the individual observer. Beauty ... was defined as the capacity of an object esthetically contemplated to yield feelings that are pleasant. This definition cannot be characterized simply either as objective, or as subjective. According to it, "beautiful" is an adjective properly predicable only of objects, but what that adjective does predicate of an object is that the feelings of which it constitutes the esthetic symbol for a contemplating observer, are pleasurable. Beauty being in this definite sense dependent upon the constitution of the individual observer, it will be as variable as that constitution. That is to say, an object which one person properly calls beautiful will, with equal propriety be not so judged by another, or indeed by the same person at a different time.

There is, then, no such thing as authoritative opinion concerning the beauty of a given object. There is only the opinion of this person or that; or the opinion of persons of some specified sort. When one has stated the opinion and mentioned the person or class of persons who hold it, one has gone as far as it is possible to go in the direction of a scientifically objective statement relating to the beauty of the object. When some matter (as that of beauty) is not of the sort which "is so," or "not so," in an *absolute* sense, the nearest approach that one can make to the wished-for absoluteness lies in furnishing, as fully as possible, the data to which the matter in question is *relative;* and this is what one does in the case of beauty when one indicates just who it happens to be, that judges the given object beautiful or the reverse.

All that was said above concerning esthetic connoisseurship, i.e., concerning superior capacity for experiencing difference in esthetic feeling in the presence of slight differences in the esthetic object, applies equally here, where differences in the pleasantness of the feelings are particularly in question. There are connoisseurs of beauty, or, more often, of particular sorts of beauty; but their judgments of beauty are "binding" on no one. Indeed it is hard to see what could possibly be meant by "binding" in such a connection, unless it were an obligation on others to lie or dissemble concerning the esthetic feelings which in fact they have or do not have on a given occasion. There is, of course, such a thing as good taste, and bad taste. But good taste, I submit, means either my taste, or the taste of people who are to my taste, or the taste of people to whose taste I want to be. There is no objective test of the goodness or badness of taste, in the sense in which there is an objective test of the goodness or badness of a person's judgment concerning, let us say, the fitness of a given tool to a given task.

#11

Why we have a natural inclination to think otherwise. What makes it so difficult for us to acknowledge that judgments of esthetic value, i.e., of beauty and ugliness, which are truly judgments about objects, are not universally and necessarily valid, but on the contrary valid, except by chance, only for the individuals who make them, is that we are so constantly occupied otherwise with judgments concerning instrumental values. These have to do with relations of the object judged, *to other objects,* and such relations are socially observable, and the judgments concerning them socially valid. That a given railroad bridge is a good bridge can be proved or disproved by running over it such trains as we wished it to carry, and observing whether or not it does carry them. But there is no similar test by which the beauty of a landscape could be proved or disproved. Judgments of beauty (which is an immediate value) have to do with the relation of the object judged to the individual's own pleasure experience, of which he himself is the sole possible observer and judge. Judgments of

beauty are therefore in this respect exactly on a par with judgments of the pleasantness of foods, wines, climates, amusements, companions, etc. Like these they are ultimately matters of the individual's own taste. It is of course quite possible that two persons, or two million, should have similar tastes, i.e., should happen alike to find pleasure in a given food or wine, or to obtain pleasurable feelings in contemplating esthetically a given picture, melody, etc. But such community in the experience of pleasure, even then remains a bare matter of fact concerning just the persons who have it in common, and leaves wholly untouched the equally bare fact that other persons—whether many, few, or only one—find not pleasure but displeasure in the very same objects.

. . . . . .

#12

Beauty cannot be proved by appeal to consensus, or to the "test of time," or to the type of person who experiences it in a given case. In the light of what precedes, it is obvious that the familiar attempts to prove the beauty of certain works of art by appeal to the consensus of opinion, or to the test of continued approval through long periods of time in the life either of society or of the individual, are, like the appeal to the connoisseur's verdict, entirely futile. Such tests cannot possibly prove the object's beauty to those who do not perceive any in it; and to those who do, they are needless. They prove nothing whatever, except that beauty is found in the object . . . by such as do find it there.

We might attempt to rank beauties on the basis of the particular aspect of human nature, or type of human being, that experiences esthetic pleasure in given cases. This would lead to a classifying of beauties as, for instance, sentimental, intellectual, sexual, spiritual, utilitarian, sensuous, social, etc. We might well believe in some certain order of worth or dignity in the human faculties respectively concerned, but this would not lead to any esthetically objective ranking of beauties. To suggest it would be as ludicrous as a proposal to rank the worth of various religions according to the average cost of the vestments of their priests. For a ranking of beauties, there are available only such principles as the relative intensity of the pleasure felt, its relative duration, relative volume, and relative freedom from admixture of pain. These principles, however, do not in the least release us from the need of relying upon the individual's judgment; on the contrary their application rests wholly upon it.

#13

Beauty cannot be proved by appeal to technical principles or canons. It may yet be thought, however, that there are certain narrower and more technical requirements in the various fields of art, without the fulfilling of which no work can be beautiful. Among such alleged canons of beauty may be mentioned the rules of so-called "harmony" in music; various precepts concerning literary composition; unity; truth to nature; such requirements as consistency, relevance, and unambiguity; and so on. There are indeed "rules" or "principles" of that sort, some of which are, I will freely declare, valid for me; so that when I find myself confronted by flagrant violations of them, I am apt to feel rather strongly, and to be impatient or sarcastic about "that sort of stuff." And indeed, on occasions when I have found myself inadvertently guilty of having drawn some line or written some sentence in violation of my own esthetic canons, I have at times felt as ashamed of the line or the sentence as I should of having picked somebody's pocket. I ad-

mit having pronounced opinions about the beauty or ugliness of various things, and what is more, in many cases I am able to *give reasons* for my opinions.

But of what nature are those reasons? They are, ultimately, of the same nature as would be that offered by a man arguing that my pen had to fall when I let go of it a moment ago, *because of gravitation.* Gravitation is but the name we give to the general fact that unsupported objects *do* fall, and at a certain rate; but it is not a reason, or cause, or proof of that fact. To say that something always happens, is not to give any reason why it ever does. Therefore when I say that a certain design is ugly because it is against the "law of symmetry," I am not giving a reason why it *had* to give me esthetic displeasure, but only mentioning the fact that it resembles in a stated respect certain others which as a bare matter of fact also do displease me. This character which displeases me and many persons, may, however, please others. And, what is more directly to the point, it not only may but it does,—jazzy or uncouth though I may call the taste of such persons. But what most obstinately drives me to the acquisition of a certain, at least abstract, sense of humor concerning the ravening intolerance and would-be-authoritativeness of my own pet canons of beauty, is the fact that they have changed in the past, and that I see no reason why they should not change again in the future. For all I can see to prevent it, I may well to-morrow, next year, or in some future incarnation, burn what I esthetically adore to-day, and adore what I now would burn. If this happens, I have no doubt at all that I shall then smugly label the change a progress and a development of my taste; whereas to-day I should no less smugly describe the possibility of a change of that sort in me, as a possibility that my taste may go to the devil. And, let it be noted, the sole foundation upon which either of the two descriptions would rest, would be the fact that the describer *actually* possesses at the time the sort of taste which he does. Tastes can be neither proved nor refuted, but only "called names," i.e., praised or reviled.

Certain limited and empirical generalizations have been found possible concerning factors upon which the esthetic pleasure of most people, or of some kinds of people, appears to depend. Precarious generalizations of this sort may be found for instance in manuals of design and of pictorial composition, where they are often dignified by the name of "principles." People familiar with them may then be heard to say that a given picture, perhaps, is well composed and why; or that the tones, the masses, or the values are, as the case may be, well or ill balanced, and so on. Other statements that we may hear and which also imply "principles," would be that the color is clean, or else muddy; that the drawing is, perhaps, distorted; that the surfaces are well modelled; that the lines are rhythmical; that the color combinations are impossible; that the masses lack volume or solidity, etc. The words beauty and ugliness may not occur once, but it is nevertheless obvious that all such statements are not merely descriptive, but *critical*. They are not direct assertions of esthetic value or disvalue, viz., of beauty or ugliness, but, taking it as an obvious fact, they attempt to trace it to certain definite sorts of features in the work. The more intelligent and better informed kind of art-criticism is of this analytical and diagnostic sort, and there is nothing beyond this that the art-critic could do.

All such comments, worded in the technical jargon of the particular craft, have the imposing sound of expert judgments based upon authoritative principles, and are likely to make the lay consumer of art feel very small and uninitiated. Therefore it cannot be too much emphasized here that a given picture is not ugly because the composition of it, or the color combinations in it, are against the rules; but that the rule against a given type of composition or of color combination is authoritative only because, or if, or for whom, or when, compositions or combinations of that type are *actually* found displeasing. All rules and canons and theories concerning what a painting or other work of art should or should not be, derive such authority as they have over you or me or anyone else, solely from the capacity of such canons *to predict to us* that we shall feel esthetic pleasure here, and esthetic pain there. If a given rule predicts this accurately for a given person, that person's *actual* feeling of esthetic pleasure or displeasure then, proves that that rule *was* a valid one so far as *he* is concerned. That is, the feeling judges the rule, not the rule the feeling. The rule may not be valid for someone else, and it may at any time cease to be valid for the given person, since few things are so variable as pleasure. The *actual* experience of beauty or ugliness by somebody is the final test of the validity of all rules and theories of painting, music, etc., and that test absolutely determines how far, and when, and for whom any given rule or theory holds or does not hold.

The difference between the criticisms of the professionals, and those of the people who, having humbly premised that they "know nothing about art," find little more to say than that a given work is in their judgment beautiful, or as the case may be, ugly or indifferent; —the difference, I say, between the criticisms of professionals and of laymen is essentially that the former are able to trace the esthetic pleasure or displeasure which they feel, to certain features of the object, while the latter are not able to do it. From this, however, it does not in the least follow that the evaluations of the professionals ultimately rest on any basis less subjective and less a matter of individual taste than do those of the layman. Indeed, so far as the non-professionals really judge at all, i.e., do not merely echo an opinion which they have somehow been bluffed into accepting as authoritative, their judgment is based on the fact that they actually feel something. The artists and professional critics, on the other hand, are exposed to a danger which does not threaten people who know nothing of the factors on which esthetic pleasure or displeasure has in the past been found to depend for most people, or for some particular class of people,—the danger, namely, of erecting such empirical findings into fixed and rigid rules, and of judging the work of art no longer by the esthetic pleasure it actually gives them, but by that which they think it "ought" to give them according to such rules. This danger is really very great, especially for the artist, who, in the nature of the case, is constantly forced to give attention to the technical means by which the objective expression of his feeling is alone to be achieved. Having thus all the time to solve technical problems, it is fatally easy for him to become interested in them for their own sake, and, without knowing it, to be henceforth no longer an artist expressing what he feels, but a restless virtuoso searching for new stunts to perform. This may be the reason why so many of the pictures displayed in our exhibits, although well-enough painted, make one feel as though one were receiving a special-delivery, registered, extra-postage letter, . . . just to say, perhaps, that after Thursday comes Friday!

Listening to the comments of artists and of some critics on a picture will quickly convince one that, strange as it sounds, they are as often as not almost incapable of seeing the picture about which they speak. What they see instead is brush work, values, edges, dark against light, colored shadows, etc. They are thus often not more but less capable than the untrained public of giving the picture *esthetic* attention, and of getting from it genuinely esthetic enjoyment. The theory that *esthetic* appreciation of the products of a given art is increased by cultivating an amateur's measure of proficiency in that art, is therefore true only so far as such cultivation results in more intimate and thoroughgoing *esthetic* acquaintance with the products of that art. This is likely to be the case in an interpretative art like music (not music-composing). But in an art which, like painting, is not so largely interpretative, and is at the same time dependent on rather elaborate technical processes, the amateur practitioner's attention is from the very first emphatically directed to these processes; and, when it is directed to extant works of art it is directed to them as examples of a technique to be studied, not as esthetic objects to be contemplated. The danger is then that such technical matters will come to monopolize his attention habitually, and that even in the face of nature he will forget to look at her, wondering instead whether the water or the sky be the brighter, or what color would have to be used to reproduce the appearance of a given shadow. Attention to technique is of course indispensable to the acquisition of it; and mastery of technique is in turn necessary to the production of art on any but the most humble scale. The risk is that the outcome of technical training will be not mastery of technique, but slavery to it. This risk disappears only when the technical apparatus has become as intimately a part of the artist as the hand is of the body for ordinary purposes, and is used without requiring attention. The attention can then turn from the means to the ends of art, viz., to the objective expression of feeling. But the stage at which technique has so become second-nature as to be forgotten, is not often fully reached. With most artists, what we may call their technical *savoir-faire* creaks more or less, as does the social *savoir-faire* of people who have become emily-posted but lately. Like the nouveaux gentlemen, such artists are too conscious of their technical manners, and forget what they are for.

#14

Beauty and accuracy of representation. Among the special criteria by which the merit of works of art—especially paintings—is judged by many, there is one about which something should be said here, namely, accuracy of representation. Accuracy of representation is important from the standpoint of esthetic criticism only so far as beauty happens to be conditioned by it. Representation, in painting, is a relation between the perceptual varicolored canvas and the esthetic object, when that esthetic object is not simply a flat design as such, but contains imaginal and conceptual elements. Accuracy of representation of the intended esthetic object, by the perceptual canvas is thus not in itself an esthetic but a noematic merit. Nevertheless it is a merit which is indispensable since without it the intended esthetic object (in the sort of cases considered), would be set up before the attention either not at all, or only in altered form.

Accuracy of representation of the esthetic object is of course not at all the same thing as accuracy of representation of the model. An accurate representation of a model is, merely as such, not a work of art at all, but only a document, —a piece of reliable information about the appearance of an existing object. If it is accurate, the copy will indeed have more or less the same esthetic import and value as the model itself, but that

copy as such will none the less be only a work of imitative skill. It will not be a work of art unless it also constitutes the conscious objective expression of a feeling experienced by the painter. Accuracy of representation of the esthetic object, on the other hand, means only that the perceptual canvas sets up clearly before the ideational attention just the esthetic object that embodies the feeling which it is intended should be obtained in contemplation.

Photographic accuracy of drawing, and faithfulness of representation of persons or things, provokes the pleasure of recognition, and admiration of the painter's capacity to act as a color camera. But this does not mean that his work is a work of art; nor even that he has created something beautiful, if the object which he has "photographed" happens not to be so. On the other hand, the fact that various elements are out of drawing in some pictures in which the artist is expressing himself in terms of represented objects, does not mean that they are necessarily ugly. What is important for beauty is *not truth but plausibility*. A dramatic entity represented may in fact be distorted, but it is not on this account ugly if it does not *look* distorted. Contrariwise, if something which in fact is photographically accurate looks distorted or unplausible, it will be disagreeable in esthetic effect. The works of El Greco, who is famous for his distortions of drawing, illustrate this. Some people have thought that something was wrong with his eyes; but the true explanation of his distortions is much more probably his preoccupation with the design-aspect of his paintings. When his design needed a line or thing of a particular shape and size at a certain place, and the object represented at that place happened to be, say, a human leg incapable of the needed shape and size, then it was so much the worse for the leg. Either design or accuracy of representation had to be sacrificed, and in such cases El Greco did not hesitate to sacrifice the latter. Whether ugliness is produced thereby, however, depends on whether the sacrifice is obvious,—the inaccuracy flagrant. In many places it is not; and it does not there constitute an esthetic fault. Where the distortion is not plausible, on the other hand, but thrusts itself upon our notice as distortion, it gives rise to ugliness and is therefore to that extent esthetically bad, whatever esthetic gains it may otherwise involve.

Only the addicts of design, who are satisfied with but a half of what an esthetically complete beholder demands, fail to see this. On the other hand, to the painter who justifies this or that bad part of his picture by insisting that "nature looked just like that," the answer is that even if she did, she ought not to have, so far as beauty was concerned. As often has been said, when truth is stranger than fiction, it does not make good fiction, but only news for the papers.

43. *Art and Morality* *

Ralph Barton Perry (1876–   )

The aesthetic life of man is embedded in his total life, and its internal standard is only one among many standards by which it may be judged. The critique of art by external standards of education has played an important role in controversy over the place of art in civilization. The critique of art by religious standards played a considerable part in the rise of protestantism, and in disputes among protestant sects. The omission of these topics here is practically compensated by the fact that these critiques are largely concerned with the relation of art to morality. The examination of the moral and cognitive critiques of art is more fundamental and calls for special consideration.

In the appraisal of man's major institutions of conscience, polity, law, and economy, the moral standard is internal.

These forms of human life are essentially moral institutions, that is, their very being lies in their more or less successful solution of the problem created by the conflict of interests. The aesthetic activities and enjoyments, on the other hand, are only accidentally moral; they become so because the aesthetic interest is one among many interests with which it will conflict or harmonize, and because morality itself may be an object of the aesthetic interest.

It may be argued that these relations of the moral and the aesthetic are necessary and not accidental. Thus it may be argued that there is a positive correlation between the value of art and the moral character of the artist. But this is notoriously contrary to fact. Indeed the aesthetic interest seems peculiarly capable of flourishing in the absence of morality; indulgence of moral laxity is considered a price to pay for the contributions of artistic genius. It is by no

* From *Realms of Value*, pp. 342-346. By permission of the publishers. Harvard University Press.

means clear that an excess of passion beyond the bounds of virtue, and even extended to vices highly offensive to the conscience of the community, may not positively enhance artistic creativity. A distinguished musical critic has described Wagner's looseness of living, his sponging on his friends, his cruelty to his opponents, his infidelities, childish tantrums, ingratitude, egotism, insolence, and dishonesty. He was, in short, a moral monstrosity—a social parasite. It is clear that a society of Wagners could not exist. The writer goes on to say:

And the curious thing about this record is that it doesn't matter in the least. . . . When you consider what he wrote—thirteen operas and music dramas, eleven of them still holding the stage, eight of them unquestionably worth ranking among the world's great musico-dramatic masterpieces—when you listen to what he wrote, the debts and heartaches that people had to endure from him don't seem much of a price. . . . The miracle is that what he did in the little space of seventy years could have been done at all, even by a great genius. Is it any wonder that he had no time to be a man? *

It is often argued that art must choose a moral object; or that if it deals with human life at all, it must point a moral. William Dean Howells was a comparatively moderate exponent of this view:

If a novel flatters the passions, and exalts them above the principles, it is poisonous; it may not kill, but it will certainly injure; and this test will alone exclude an entire class of fiction, of which eminent examples will occur to all. Then the whole spawn of so-called unmoral romances, which imagine a world where the sins of sense are unvisited by the penalties following, swift or slow, but inexorably sure, in the real world, are deadly poison: these do kill.

This argument would seem to contradict the same writer's contention that fiction should be true to life. But are "sins of sense" invariably visited by

penalties? Is the critic not representing what would happen in a just world? And if so, on what artistic ground can he demand that a writer omit the tragic fact that vice *is* sometimes rewarded and virtue penalized?

There is a persistent strain of European thought which identifies the aesthetic and the moral through the principle of harmony:

Harmony, which might be called an aesthetic principle, is also the principle of health, of justice, and of happiness. Every impulse, not the aesthetic mood alone, is innocent and irresponsible in its origin and precious in its own eyes; but every impulse or indulgence, including the aesthetic, is evil in its effect, when it renders harmony impossible in the general tenor of life, or produces in the soul division and ruin.

But the aesthetic value of harmony and the moral value of harmony are not the same value. The aesthetic value of harmony is the enjoyment of the whole in contemplation; the moral value of harmony is benefit to the parts from nonconflict and coöperation.

The distinction between the aesthetic and moral standards paves the way to the understanding of their relations. Insofar as harmony is one of the constituents of beauty a moral society is beautiful, that is, good to contemplate. But many, indeed, most, harmonies fail to meet the requirements of morality; and are under no *aesthetic* obligation to do so. The moral standard is one of many external standards which are applicable to art.[1]

Assuming the aesthetic interest to have a peculiar and independent bias of its own, it may be asked how far this bias happily coincides with morality, and how far it diverges and resists. The aesthetic interest, like the cognitive in-

---

* D. Taylor, *Of Men and Music*, pp. 7-8.

[1] There are indefinitely many external standards which are applicable to art—including, for example, the dealer's standard, and the collector's standard.

terest, is amenable to morality because it is non-preëmptive, that is, does not appropriate its object exclusively. In the act of enjoying its object it does not deprive other subjects of its enjoyment. On the contrary, its enjoyment is enhanced by participation. Not only does it possess this original innocence, but it disposes men to friendly association. Because it does not need to take away from other interests it is unlikely to be associated with combativeness—with an impulse to weaken or destroy competitors.

Because the aesthetic interest operates in the realm of the imagination, it enjoys a peculiar freedom to multiply and entertain ideal possibilities. It tends to emancipate men's minds from habit, authority, and the *status quo,* and thus readily allies itself with the forces of progress and liberalization. It can dream utopias without hindrance, and through giving them vividness and permanence can provide direction to the moral life and to all aspiration. It can add to the attractiveness of any goal, including the goal of harmonious happiness; and can thus provide an additional motivation for ends which would otherwise suffer from their remotenes or abstractness. Art provides symbols for the moral cause. In its symbolic role the aesthetic object helps to preserve the identity of the goal amidst the vicissitudes of fortune, and to make it clearly manifest. Like the flag it can be hauled up where it can be seen; like the flag it can rally armies, regiments, and companies, and their successive replacements, to the same standard. And finally, the aesthetic interest can fortify moral courage by compensating life's practical and theoretical failures, and enable men to face the grimmer aspects of reality by presenting them in their tragic beauty. It thus contributes to that general auspiciousness of outlook which constitutes happiness.

The same traits of the aesthetic interest which render it morally propitious account for its moral dangers. Its detachment from the competitive struggle does, it is true, render art comparatively innocent, but there is a selfishness of innocence which consists in a withdrawal from affairs. The aesthetic interest does, it is true, tend to non-aggression, but it may tend to a passive complacency, a narrow absorption, and an irresponsibility toward that very social organization on which the aesthetic life itself depends. In his Olympian detachment the artist or man of contemplation is likely to forget that Olympus rises from the plain of organized society and that he owes his privileges to those who guard its approaches.

Aesthetic rapture does not escape the danger which attends all raptures. It tends to be so obsessive as to make men indifferent to its evil effects—of commission or omission—on the lives of other men. Nero would not have been less morally blameworthy if he had been Jascha Heifetz.

The aesthetic interest evades the problems of knowledge and action, instead of solving them; for their real solution it substitutes that pseudo-solution which is called "aestheticism" or "escapism." The aesthetic interest may render the ideal so vivid and reassuring that it is mistaken for the real: and men may perish from aesthetic illusion, as they die of thirst in the desert through the allurement of the mirage. Because the aesthetic interest renders the evil of life palatable it weakens the will to remove it.

Aesthetic enjoyment can add to the appeal of the good and strengthen the moral passion; but it can also strengthen evil passion. It has a promiscuity similar to that of science. "Music hath charms to soothe the savage breast"; but it has other charms, and may debase the civilized man to savagery. There are "Dorian and Phrygian harmonies" which incite men to courage and temperance, but there are also Lydian, Ionian, and other harmonies which incite men to voluptuousness, to idleness, or to sexual excesses.[2] The fine arts can be used to give force to any propaganda, whether totalitarian or democratic; the actor can play any part and give it dramatic value; the poet can make Satan more appealing than God.

The fact that art can be put to bad as well as to good uses, and that the aesthetic motive cannot be trusted, when left to itself, to take the side of the angels, raises the question of its social control. It cannot be controlled as effectively as science, nor is its control so deadly. Under the present regime of Soviet Russia art is explicitly subjected to the state and to Communist ideology, but we are told that "there are thinkers and artists, living perfectly respectable lives, but forever struggling to introduce into their official epics of stereotyped verbosity disguised glimpses of an inner vision personal to themselves." [3] And in art, at least, this struggle is more or less successful. Science is more readily controlled, because it depends on access to

evidence, and on the facilities of organized experimentation. The "inner vision" escapes external control, and its disguise is not easily penetrated by the grosser eye of the censor. Whatever restrictions are placed on men's overt conduct, there is always food for aesthetic contemplation, and some room for the play of the imagination.

But in principle the objection to social control is the same in art as in science. The artist renders his particular form of service through being free to follow his particular vocation. Art appraised by rulers and police is no longer judged by its own standard. Art harnessed to ideology becomes a dependent interest, deriving its motive from an ulterior end. In proportion as it is thus enslaved, art is destroyed at its source; it can no longer give other interests that very enhancement for the sake of which it was controlled. The effect of control is likely to be wholly negative. It can destroy and prevent better than it can create. Art will flourish best when it is allowed to germinate, grow, and proliferate in obedience to its own nature.[4]

---

[2] Plato's *Republic,* tr. by Jowett, Bk. III, 398-9.

[3] E. Crankshaw, *Russia and the Russians,* 1948, p. 187.

[4] Political and ideological controls are not the only alien controls by which the aesthetic part of life may be frustrated. There is also a commercial control, less palpable, but all the more insidious.

SUGGESTED FURTHER READINGS
FOR CHAPTER SIX

Alexander, S., *Beauty and Other Forms of Value.*
Aristotle, *Poetics.*
Bell, C., *Art.*
Bosanquet, B., *Three Lectures on Aesthetics.*
Dewey, J., *Art as Experience.*
Hegel, G. W. F., *The Philosophy of Art.*
Housman, A. E., *The Name and Nature of Poetry.*
Lee, Vernon, *The Beautiful.*
Marshall, H. R., *Pain, Pleasure and Aesthetic.*
Prall, D. W., *The Aesthetic Analysis.*

Chapter Seven

THE PHILOSOPHY OF RELIGION

INTRODUCTION

RELIGION is an important aspect of human life. In some form or other it functions in every society; its symbols and activities exist through the whole length and breadth of the world. Something as complex and diverse as it is difficult to describe, yet its essential traits may be indicated. First, it should be noted that the motives and the driving forces in religion are the basic human wants and desires —survival, growth, well-being, self-realization. There is nothing distinctive in this phase of religion. And if all human desires could be naturally fulfilled, probably there would be no need of religion. Secondly, and more distinctively, religion involves belief in a supreme power or powers on whom human beings depend for their well-being. As man's wants grow, the need for greater gods grows. In the early forms of religion the religious object of worship and devotion is a number of powers or gods; in the later forms it is a supreme God. Yet this belief is not merely an intellectual attitude but a practical and active one. Thirdly, religion involves rituals which are believed to be ways of winning the favor of gods or God. Finally, it should be noted that religion, like all other major human activities, assumes a social, institutional form. The temple, the church, the synagogue, or the "beloved community" not only preserve the great religious traditions but make it possible for religion to function in the group.

Such a rich and varied aspect of human life may be approached in different ways. There is the historical approach, dealing with the origin and growth of religion. Where and when did religion begin? How did religion evolve from tribal to more universal forms? These and other historical questions may be of interest to some. There is also the psychological approach, dealing with the mental or emotional basis of religion. Does religion satisfy some deep-seated psychological craving? What, in mental or emotional terms, is conversion, or the mystic experience, or worship? A third approach to religion is the sociological, which deals with religion as a social institution. What is the organization of this institution? How does it affect other institutions, and how, in turn, is it affected by them? All three of these approaches are necessary for a full understanding of religion.

Yet there remains another approach to religion—what is sometimes called "the philosophy of religion." This expression, however, is rather ambiguous, having at least two different meanings which must be carefully distinguished. It may refer, on the one hand, to the beliefs which a religious person or group entertains; or it may refer, on the other hand, to the critical examination of these beliefs. It is in the latter sense that the phrase "philosophy of religion" will be used here. By philosophy of religion will be meant a reflective, critical examination and analysis of the meanings and the beliefs involved in religion. This examination may lead to a firmer attachment to religious beliefs or it may awaken doubts about them. In other words, we shall take the philosopher to be the *seeker* who inquires into the meaning of religious experience and into the truth of religious beliefs, rather than the dogmatic *knower* who tells us what to believe and what not to believe.

I. Religion and Theism

Various aspects of religion are material for philosophical reflection; but the one aspect of religion that is of crucial importance is the idea of God. It is on this issue that most severe and fundamental conflicts have occurred in the field of theology and in the philosophy of religion. Some of the major views on this issue will be indicated.

Some conceive of God as a transcendent, supernatural being. And this supernatural being is also believed to be a personal God. In the great monotheistic religions—Judaism, Christianity, Mohammedanism—the idea of the supernatural God is central. This view is usually called *theism.* In theism God is the creator and the sustainer of the world. There are, however, differences among the theists. Some are absolute theists, who maintain that God is all-knowing, all-good, and all-powerful. Absolute theists feel that the object of religious worship must be infinite and ideal perfection. Other theists, primarily to meet the intellectual difficulties in the existence of evil, advocate belief in a finite God. According to them, as with James, God is all-good but not all-powerful. What, one may ask, is the basis for a belief in the theistic God, be he infinite or finite?

To validate belief in a supernatural, personal God, the method of authority has sometimes been relied upon. The authority may be a sacred book, a religious institution, or a person. The authoritarian method has been influential in theistic religions and still has a firm hold on many people. There is, however, more than one authority, and different authorities conflict. Christians have their Bible, Jews their Talmud, Mohammedans their Koran. Which should be taken as *the* authority? But an even graver difficulty confronts the authoritarians: the need of justifying, rationally, the claim of authority. Why should one accept authority? Especially those who are philosophically inclined tend to distrust authority, since they are committed to thinking for themselves and are reluctant to forego independence of judgment.

A second means of determining the truth of theism has been through the "proofs" of the existence of God. This argumentative method does not resort to authority, but claims that certain arguments can substantiate the existence of God. There are three arguments of this kind: (1) The cosmological argument, which affirms that the existence of nature demands a "first" cause, while this in turn is identified with God. In this argument one must determine whether the same demand does not attach to the "first" cause. (2) The teleological argument, which affirms that the designful structure and activities of nature prove the existence of a supreme designer. One must examine here whether nature is as designful as it is claimed to be, and even if designful, whether it is possible to explain design by causality or chance. (3) The ontological argument, which affirms that the idea of perfection that is attributed to God implies His existence, since a being that lacked existence would not be perfect. In analyzing this argument one must consider carefully whether the idea of perfection necessarily implies existence, or, for that matter, whether existential truth can be established by mere logical argument. In the past these arguments were discussed by philosophers in great detail, and at present they are receiving new formulations which deserve careful study.

A third way of determining the truth of theism has been through moral and practical considerations. Kant and James are important representatives of this approach. According to Kant, man must act in accordance with moral law; therefore he must be free to do so. Faith in freedom, therefore, is a necessary correlate of the existence of a moral law. And, again, since the ideal of moral perfection can be made real only through an unending series of acts, immortality is an imperative belief. Finally, since ultimately the determining factor in reality must be favorable to the absolute good of man, and thus provide immortality for him, belief in God is a moral necessity. According to James, the practical argument for God arises from the possibility of choice between two alternative conceptions that are equally logical. James argues that where knowledge in the strict sense of the word is impossible but where a choice between hypotheses is forced upon one in the interests of effective living, one has the right to make the choice. The religious question—namely, belief in God—presents to James such a genuine option. We have, therefore, the right to believe in God. This is James' famous doctrine of the "will to believe." Kant's and James' approach to religion have appealed to many, especially to liberal theists. Yet the arguments upon which this approach is based should be closely examined. Is it true that morality demands that we postulate God, as Kant argues? Or is the theistic belief necessary for effective and dynamic living, as James insists? Or, again, have we the right to believe as we hope if our hope is not sufficiently borne out by the facts? These and similar questions must be fully explored before this approach can establish its validity.

Recently a fourth way of determining the truth of theism has been suggested. Trueblood gives a clear account of this approach. According to this view the ultimate appeal of theism is not to arguments but to actual religious experience. The claim is that in religious experience we are confronted with a Reality of which only theistic interpretation is an adequate account. This empirical approach appeals to the modern mind, but to make it really acceptable one would have to examine the nature of religious experience as well as the nature of empirical method.

II. Religion, Pantheism, and Mysticism

Thus far we have been considering the theistic view of God. But there are others for whom God is not a separate, supernatural being but is reality in its complete unity. This view is sometimes called pantheism. In pantheism God is conceived as the whole of reality in its meaningful unity. Everything is believed to have its logical and purposeful place in the scheme of things.

Some mystics drift to what is essentially pantheism. Mystics usually emphasize the oneness of all things and the union of the finite self with the infinite God. In the mystic vision there are not two things—God and the individual—but one. The seer and the seen are one; the finite individual is mingled with the Divine. "My Me is God, nor do I recognize any other Me, except God himself. My being is God, not by simple participation but by a true transformation." (St. Catherine of Genoa.) This ultimate unity of things, the mystic claims, may be intuited but cannot be described. "The One is an Absolute transcending all thought." (Plotinus.) He may be adored in silence, but He cannot be described by the intellect. The nearest descriptions are by negatives. "To God as Godhead appertains neither will nor knowledge nor manifestations, nor anything that we can measure, or say, or conceive." (*Theologia Germanica*.) Yet mystical pantheism on the whole tends to claim that God is all, rather than that all is God. For the mystic, material objects in space, as well as events in time, are deceptive. The mystical vision leaves behind perceptual objects. "The soul to find God must go out from all things, and all things must be to it as if they existed not." (St. John of the Cross.) Similarly, time vanishes. Past and present are like dreams for the mystic. Time and place are hindrances, for God is above them. "The soul has two eyes; the right beholds eternity, and the left eye, time. Both cannot perform their work at once. If the soul would see into eternity, the left eye must be closed." (*Theologia Germanica*.) Finally, evil and ugliness do not come within the range of mystical contemplation; they are as if they were not. Since God is all, and God is absolutely good, there can be no evil. What seems evil is only an illusory appearance in the deluded mortal mind. "Evil is merely a negation and lies entirely outside the knowledge of God, who only knows and wills the good.... For God evil is not. It has existence only in the sphere of time." (Scotus Erigena.) [1]

Mystics are convinced that in their mystical experience they have direct contact and union with Divine Reality and that this Divine Reality or God is all. This claim, however, cannot be so easily settled. That there is a type of experience which corresponds to the so-called mystical experience may not be doubted, but the problem of interpreting this experience is difficult and controversial. Some regard the mystical experience as giving direct knowledge of a supernatural, divine being; others consider it as a union with an all-inclusive Reality; still others interpret it as an expression of an abnormal pathological state. It is also worth observing that different cultures have given different accounts of the mystics' claim. The account of Hindu mystics differs from that of Neo-Platonic mystics, and the account of the latter, in turn, differs from that of later mystics.

Sometimes rationalistic philosophers are led to the pantheistic belief. Most rationalists take the function of philosophy to be "the quest for the world's unity." The formula that God is all and all is God seems to be the supreme goal of such a quest. In this respect Spinoza is uniquely significant. Spinoza has a mystical aspect,

---

[1] For a fuller analysis of mysticism, see D. C. Macintosh, *The Problem of Religious Knowledge*, Chapter 2.

but for the present we are primarily concerned with his more rigorous, rationalistic philosophy and its bearing on religion. Spinoza uses the terms Substance, Nature, and God to denote the ultimate reality. God—nature, universe, substance—is the all-inclusive unity. He is self-caused, self-dependent, infinite, and eternal. God is infinite, else He would be dependent upon something else; but two such realities cannot exist, for if they did, each would be limited by the other and so not really be infinite. And again, God is eternal, since if He were not, He would have been preceded and produced by something else and therefore not be self-sufficient. Similar logical arguments are offered for other traits of God. Yet God or the all-inclusive reality is not a mere undifferentiated unity. God has certain attributes, such as thought and extension. Yet Spinoza's superlative God has none of the ordinary characteristics of the theists' God. Spinoza's God, for example, is not the creator of the world. God did not design or make the world; He *is* the world; He is the immanent cause of all that is. God, again, does not act for the benefit of men. Being perfect, all-inclusive, He has no aims or desires to attain. Good, evil, beauty are merely human values and not the characteristics of God. Man is part of the whole—of God. Man arises in God and lives in God. Thus, the religious person does not think of the universe in terms of his limited finite hopes and desires but sees things "under the aspect of eternity." Redemption lies in the knowledge that the mind exists in indissoluble union with the whole of reality. This is what he means by the knowledge of God, Who is the true and eternal good for which our whole being yearns and in which we find our peace. He who becomes one with God's infinite and eternal nature attains freedom from all the vicissitudes of finite human life.

III. Religion and Naturalism

There is still a third view of religion and of its basic belief, God. This view insists that religion should be concerned neither with belief in a supernatural God nor with belief related to alleged perfection of reality as a whole. The claim is that religion should limit itself to human hopes in the context of natural existence; should the word "God" be retained, it should be applied to some ideal phase of human experience, such as the hope for a better world, the aspiration for a happier society, the ideal of a nobler individual life. This philosophy of religion, which is sometimes called the naturalistic-humanistic view of religion, starts with the basic belief that it is only through science that questions of fact can be determined. "That which science refuses to grant to religion is not its right to exist," writes Durkheim, "but its right to dogmatize upon the nature of things and the special competence which it claims for itself for knowing man and the world." It is true that there are supernaturalistic ideas of God, but these ideas, the naturalists argue, must be so reinterpreted that they will not rival scientific truth but become intelligible within the natural and social human setting. Though there are many types of naturalistic-humanistic philosophies of religion, they all agree in the denial of a supernaturalistic God; they differ only in their specific formulation of religion and their idea of God.

About a hundred years ago Ludwig Feuerbach gave a naturalistic interpretation of religion by emphasizing the strictly human or psychological aspect of religion.

For Feuerbach religion is man's earliest and indirect form of self-knowledge. Religion is "the child-like condition of humanity: in childhood a man is an object to himself under the form of another man." Consciousness of God for Feuerbach is "self-consciousness, knowledge of God is self-knowledge." Freud, in turn, gives a psychiatric description of religion. For the child, Freud argues, the mother is the first "love-object"; she was the first to satisfy its hunger. But the mother is soon superseded by the stronger father. And God, for Freud, is exalted-father. Gods have a three-fold task: to exorcise the terrors of nature, to reconcile one to the cruelty of fate, and to make amends for the sufferings that the communal life imposes on the individual. A more sociological interpretation is given by Emil Durkheim. For Durkheim the idea of God is rooted in totemism. "The notion of the great god is due entirely to the sentiment . . . observed in the genesis of the most specifically totemic beliefs; this is the tribal sentiment. . . . Totemism was . . . always elaborated in the body of a tribe which was to some degree conscious of its unity. . . . It is this same sentiment of a tribal unity which is expressed in the conception of a supreme God, common to the tribe as a whole."

In this country Santayana and Dewey have given interpretations of religion more strictly in terms of ideal human aspiration. For Santayana science and religion have different functions, and the way to avoid conflict between these two enterprises is not to confuse their functions. It is to science that one must turn for truth about matters of fact. The belief that religion may also convey literal truth is an impossible view for Santayana. Whenever religion attempts to give truth about the nature of the world, the result is pseudo-science or superstition. Santayana thus rejects all forms of supernaturalistic religion. What, then, is religion for Santayana? It is poetry or mythology. But for him the poetic conception has no disparaging implications. Religion as poetry has a moral function, and it is this function that defines religion. The poetic conception of religion also makes it possible for one to respect the fantastic beliefs of religions. The belief in animal gods, or in certain eschatological expectations when regarded as myth, can be appreciated as expressions of human pathos and desires. There should, therefore, be no conflict between religions on the ground that one is truer than another. At most one religion may be better than another in the efficacy of its symbols. From Santayana's point of view it naturally follows that "God" is not the name for a transcendent, supernaturalistic being but rather the poetic symbol for human ideals of truth, beauty, and goodness. The different gods of religion symbolize different human ideals—Ahura Mazda that of goodness, Zeus that of power, and Yahweh that of justice, while the God of the great monotheistic religions symbolizes the unified ideal of perfection.

Dewey, like Santayana, feels the necessity of giving a naturalistic account of religion which will preserve both the validity of science and the ideal values of religion. Dewey approaches his task by making a distinction between "religion" and "the religious." By the former he means organized religion, primarily supernatural religion, and by the latter an attitude. Dewey is anxious to preserve the latter. What, then, is the religious attitude for Dewey? The religious attitude signifies the general attitude that guides our action, a fundamental perspective that gives direction to life. We may, therefore, reverse the usual statement and say "that whatever introduces genuine perspective is religious, not that religion is something that introduces it." The religious attitude as pursuit of ideals refers to natural possibilities, that is, to possibilities which belong to natural things and to natural creatures. Dewey's naturalistic account of religion leads him to restate the traditional religious ideas. The term "God," if it is to be used, stands for "the ideal ends that at a given time and place one acknowledges as having authority over his volition and emotion, the values to which one is supremely devoted." And, again, religious faith is used by Dewey not in relation to some alleged religious truths as being other than or superior to scientific truths, but as loyalty and steadfast adherence to one's ideals. Such a faith is obviously not opposed to science but is the result of free inquiry. The scientific attitude, when perfectly adhered to, is itself one of the ideals of this religious attitude.

Naturalistic-humanistic forms of religion lack the rich tradition and symbolism of the older forms of religion. They also fail to give the same degree of guarantee as theism does for the final triumph of man's deep desires. Their strength seems to lie in not being in conflict with science and in offering more effective methods to ameliorate human conditions. Whether naturalistic forms of religion will ever become a significant factor in our civilization has yet to be determined.

IV. God, Evil, and Immortality

The central problem of religion is the nature and existence of God. Most of the readings on religion are concerned with this issue. Yet a belief in God, especially a belief in a personal God, is not an isolated abstract problem; it has its vital relation to human destiny. This relationship becomes obvious in considering the problem of evil and the hope of immortality.

Let us first consider the problem of evil. That there is evil in our world—pain, suffering, defeat, injustice, and inevitable death—hardly demands argument. Even should evil be illusion, as some argue, there would still be the evil of illusion. The theological issue that has been a source of endless controversy through the ages is: How can one reconcile the existence of evil with a God that is perfect in power as well as in goodness?

The usual answer to this question has been that evil is in some sense less real than good is, and that evil is ultimately a means for the fruition of good. Some, for example, consider evil as necessary to "the good of the whole." There are many variations of this view: evil as good "in disguise," evil as "something torn of its context," evil as "illusory." Others think of evil as a means for the growth and strengthening of character. Hardship, sorrow, defeat have, it is claimed their salutary effects. They are the means for "soul-making." Still others justify evil as something that heightens the danger and excitement of life. Without evil life would be insipid; there would be no drama, no high tragedy of existence. All these theories in some way consider evil as a means for good.

Sheldon, in his attempt to defend the thesis that the existence of evil and perfection of God (in power and goodness) are not contradictory, does not resort to the view that evil is in some sense not fully real. Evil for Sheldon is real and he is not concerned with the question why evil is permitted. Sheldon's interest is primarily a negative one. As he puts it, "We have only a negative task; to show that the contradiction alleged is not necessary." Evil "being actual—*need not* imply any lack of perfection in the Divine nature." Sheldon tries to establish his claim through the highly dubious notion of reincarnation, through the more defensible notions that we do not know the given order of God's plan and purpose; that later experience includes and transmutes the earlier; that responsibility means acceptance of the consequences of one's acts. Sheldon presents his views fairly and persuasively.

Yet there are philosophers who reject Sheldon's formulation of the problem. William James and contemporary personal idealists like Brightman and Hartshorne try to ease the problem by claiming that God is all-good but not all-powerful. Brightman finds God's limitation in his own internal constitution, while Hartshorne finds it in the powers of His creatures, who try to thwart His purposes. Others, like Dewey, take a more radical step. Dewey limits the problem of evil to practical action. As he puts it: "The position of natural intelligence is that there exists a *mixture* of good and evil, and that reconstruction in the direction of the good which is indicated by ideal ends, must take place, if at all, through continued cooperative effort."

Hope in immortality is also vitally related to a belief in God and is a central dogma of the Christian religion. Of all evils death is the supreme evil for it brings individual life to final, inevitable shipwreck. Religion with its ultimate optimism holds the faith that no final disaster can destroy man.

Macintosh, a great theologian, formerly of the Yale Divinity School, presents some of the weightiest arguments for immortality. Starting with the premise that conservation of spiritual values involves the conservation of persons, he first argues that mind is independent of physical body. And if mind is independent of body it is plausible that it may exist and act when set free from the body at death. In the fact of human freedom Macintosh finds a more assured argument for the possibility of immortality. Human freedom being granted, it follows "that mind or the self acts in an originative manner." Mind for Macintosh is an agent and not a mere phenomenon. Finally, and more significantly from the theistic viewpoint, Macintosh finds assurance for immortality in the belief in God, that is, in a Power great enough and good enough to conserve the human individual in spite of bodily death. All these arguments for immortality deserve careful examination.

Yet here again the student of philosophy must examine other serious possible answers to the questions before he comes to a final decision. Moreover, he must ask which of the alternative theories does greater justice to human aspirations, to experience, to known facts. One such alternative view is found in Professor W. E. Hocking's philosophy. Hocking, a leading contemporary idealist, argues that immortality is not something assured, but conditional on the type of life we live. "There is such a thing as losing one's soul: . . . the destiny of our own deeds, great and small, is an integral part of whatever future there may be for us. To deserve to endure is the only guarantee of enduring. I have no faith in an intrinsic indestructibility of the substance of consciousness. One life is given us; another may be acquired." Still another alternative to Macintosh's view is that of the materialists and naturalists. Since these schools deny the independence of mind from body and the existence of a supernatural

Deity, they consider this world as the only abode of human existence. Centuries ago the great Hindu materialist Carvaka succinctly expressed this view: "There is no other world, death is the end of all." It is quite clear that one's belief in immortality is primarily determined by one's metaphysics and theory of evidence. In the end one must answer these questions: What constitutes evidence? What evidence is there for immortality?

V. The Function of Religion

We have been analyzing and contrasting theistic, pantheistic, and naturalistic views of religion. But religion is not merely a matter of intellectual belief, it is a practical thing. Kant and James justify belief in God not on theoretical grounds, which they could not find, but on moral and practical grounds. Similarly, Spinoza, Santayana, and Dewey in different ways emphasize the practical aspect of religion. What, then, are the practical functions of religions which are common to all different interpretations of religion? Only some of the major ones can be indicated here.

One such function is the integration of the individual life. An individual, as James defined him, "is a fighter for ends." Devotion to God or to a supreme ideal unifies and therefore integrates conflicting desires. The religious experience called "salvation" is primarily this process of unification of the self in the light of some inclusive and worthy object. Theists, pantheists, and naturalists, in different ways, emphasize this function of religion. Yet one should approach this function of religion with a critical attitude. Some gods and some ends are not sufficiently moral or inclusive to be an adequate object of devotion. Therefore, in such inadequate religions, the unifications of the self would tend to make a person fanatic, narrow, and arrogant. It is dangerous to assume that whatever is related to religion is thereby morally worthy. Actions motivated by religion must be critically examined in the light of moral standards.

Another major function of religion is to idealize and sanctify social morals or customs. Religion sanctifies birth and death, marriage and celibacy, peace and war. Terms like "Father," "King of Kings," and "Lord," and expressions like "Kingdom of God" and "Blessed Community" are social in their implications. Sometimes religion has been socially beneficial by promoting philanthropy, education, and the arts, by pressing for greater economic equality, by opposing despotic political power, or by emphasizing internationalism. But at other times religion has been socially harmful, by opposing scientific thought and philosophic freedom, by defending vested economic interests, by sanctifying political tyranny, or by idealizing fanatic nationalism. Religious institutions are human institutions. Their social policies must always be examined in relation to secular, human interests. Religious institutions as social agencies must never be allowed special privileges, but must always remain subject to social criticism, while at the same time they should be encouraged to use their power towards humane ends.

Finally, religion has the function of lending cosmic support to human aspirations. Life is full of inscrutable evils and crushing tragedies that many find it almost impossible to face without belief in a power that will ultimately bring triumph. Theism provides this sanction in the form of a personal God who is benevolent and powerful; pantheism, in the perfection of the whole; and naturalistic religion, in the genuine possibilities for good in nature. As with the other functions of religion, this one too should not be accepted without critical scrutiny. It is true that certain religious beliefs, especially the one in a personal God, have given hope and courage to many; yet these very beliefs have made many unduly passive and patient before evil and suffering. Passively hoping that good must triumph over evil, human beings have failed to apply their intelligence to strengthen the good. Religion, to be satisfactory, must be intellectually acceptable and morally conducive to a worthy life.

Y. H. K.

*44. Mysticism**

Douglas Clyde Macintosh (1877–1948)

That religious mysticism in its characteristic form is religious realism ... does not admit of doubt. The religious Object, God or the Absolute, is regarded as a reality, existing independently of all subjective human experience and realization of His power and presence. Furthermore, the mystical form of religious realism is religious empiricism. It is through a special variety of religious experience that revelatory contact is made with God, it is claimed, and truth learned about him. ... Finally, as claiming *knowledge* of God rather than mere belief or faith in him, the mystic may be said to be a gnostic, in a broad interpretation of the term, and not an agnostic. A few samples selected out of the superabundant evidence in support of this interpretation of religious mysticism as monistic realism, or realistic monism, with regard to God, or in the realm of religion, may now be offered.

There is no more characteristic doctrine of mysticism than that God is to be looked for and eventually found in the mystic's own inner experience. Among the technical terms employed by the mystics "introversion" is used to designate "the beholding of God as immanent in the soul." There is marked unanimity among the mystics in laying claim to an experience which they thus interpret:

"To mount to God is to enter into one's self" (Albertus Magnus).

"God is nearer to me than I am to myself." "Where the soul is, there is God." "I have a capacity in my soul for taking in God entirely." "When I saw into myself, I saw God in me." "Ye men, why do ye look without for that which is within you?" (Meister Eckhart).

"The soul finds God in its own depths" (Ruysbroeck).

"We should seek God in our own interior" (St. Teresa).

"God is hidden within the soul, and the true contemplative will seek him there in love" (St. John of the Cross).

"The main point of mystic theology is to speak with and hearken to God in the recesses of the heart" (St. Francis de Sales).

* From *The Problem of Religious Knowledge*, Chapter II. By kind permission of Harper and Brothers Publishers.

"Every man has an open gate to God in his soul." "Begin to search and dig in thy own field for this pearl of eternity that lieth hidden in it. . . . Heaven is . . . a treasure hidden in the center of our own souls" (William Law).

Madame Guyon quotes her confessor to whom she went with her difficulties about prayer, as replying, "You seek without what you have within. Accustom yourself to see God in your heart, and you will find him there." "These words," she tells us, "were like a dart which penetrated my heart. They brought into my heart what I had been seeking so many years; or rather they discovered to me what was there, and which I had not enjoyed for want of knowing it! O my God, Thou wast in my heart, and demanded only a simple turning of my mind inward, to make me perceive Thy presence."

The mystics claim that this experience of Divine Reality in the inner depths of the soul is not mediated by representative ideas, but is direct and immediate. They are thus in the religious realm what the so-called "new realists" of a generation ago were in the realm of sense-experience, epistemological monists as well as realists. According to Ruysbroeck, "the divine union is effected without medium"; the mystics "enjoy God without intermediary." He continues, "The reason of the soul is like the eye of the bat," but in the mystic state "the soul is like the eagle, gazing with unmoved pupil on the rays of the sun; for so does the simple eye of the loving spirit receive, without medium and above reason, the irradiation of the divine glory." St. Francis de Sales agrees that in the experience of God intellectual representation is transcended, "for who wants to represent that which the soul actually enjoys?"

On the basis of this immediate experience, claim is made to religious knowledge, knowledge of God. Any other supposed source of such knowledge is correspondingly disparaged. The mystics are very emphatic about this:

In "the school of the Holy Spirit" "a person can learn more in the twinkling of an eye than all the doctors can teach him" (Meister Eckhart).

"If ye keep watch over your hearts and listen for the voice of God, and learn of Him, in one short hour ye can learn more from Him than ye could learn from man in a thousand years" (John Tauler).

"The soul is made to know in an instant, by means of a new light above itself, all that God desires it to know" (St. Catherine of Genoa).

"God gives the soul an ever-increasing perceptive light, by which the understanding continues to penetrate deeper and deeper in the knowledge of its divine attraction" (Francis de Sales).

"The soul doth swim in knowledge" (Angela of Foligno).

"The book of God's image was given to me to read, and therein have I studied. I have no need of any other book." "The Gate was opened unto me, so that in one quarter of an hour I saw and knew more than if I had been many years together at a University." "I saw and knew the Being of all beings" (Jacob Boehme).

On the basis, then, of the mystical experience taken as revelation of reality, the claim is made that the central object of religious interest, commonly called God, is known to exist. This knowledge is proclaimed as immediate and, for one who has had the experience, indubitable. God, for the mystic, is actual, religiously accessible, and, presumably, religiously adequate. Indeed "adequate" would seem altogether too mild and colorless a term to express what is so deeply, if at the same time but vaguely, felt. Such emotional terms as "infinite" and "ineffable" are more suitable for voicing the mystical conviction and feeling.

It is an interesting fact that whereas

some critical philosophers claim to be able to say *what* God would be, but confess themselves unable to say *that* he is, the mystic is very sure *that* God is, but is very insistent that he cannot express in intelligible terms just *what* he is. One is tempted to ask just what it can mean to say that a being exists if no conception can be formed as to what the being is. On the other hand it may seem that the mystic is only struggling with an especially acute instance of the common difficulty of putting first-hand experience of reality into definite, communicable concepts. Convinced after many trials that he cannot express at all adequately what he has experienced of Divine Reality, he concludes, whether justifiably or not, that this is because the Divine Reality itself is by nature ineffable. At this point again there is practical unanimity among the outstanding mystics. The following excerpts from the literature of mysticism are typical.

"He who knows the Tao does not care to speak about it; he who is ever ready to speak about it does not know it." "The great everlasting infinite First Cause can neither be defined nor named." "Something exists which is incomprehensible, which is perfect, and which existed before heaven and earth were.... Its name I know not, but I call it Tao. Were I to give it yet another name, I should call it the Great" (Lao-Tze).

"I knew a man ... that was caught up into paradise and heard unspeakable words, which it is not possible for a man to utter" (St. Paul).

"The One is an Absolute transcending all thought and is even beyond Being." "If anyone, seeing God, knows what he sees, it is by no means God that he so sees, but something created and knowable" (Plotinus).

"I awoke in Thee and saw Thee infinite." "God is best adored in silence; best known by nescience, best described by negatives" (St. Augustine).

"God is known through not knowing during union above mind." "By understanding nothing, understand after a manner above all intelligence." "We pray to enter into the superbright gloom, and through not seeing and not knowing to see and to know that not to see nor to know is itself the above-sight and above-knowledge. For this is veritably to see and to know and to celebrate superessentially the superessential." "Never is it true to say that we know God." "The superessential Trinity and Over-God ... is neither an object of intellectual nor of sensible perception, nor is he absolutely anything of things existing.... He is all in all and nothing in none." "He is neither soul, nor intellect, ... nor is he spirit, as we know spirit." "He can neither be affirmed nor denied." "God is far above all predicates." "No monad nor triad can express the all-transcending hiddenness of the all-transcending superessential superexisting super-Deity" (Dionysius).

"To know God is to know Him as unknowable" (Eckhart).

"The simple eye beholds, in the divine light with simple gaze and look, whatever God is. The intellectual eye follows the gaze, desiring to explore and have experience in the same light; but at the sight of God, reason, with all that is distinct, succumbs and fails. It sees something, but what? It cannot tell; for the faculty of understanding is lifted up in a kind of knowledge without mode or form of any kind. What it beholds it cannot come up to or apprehend." But "where the intellect stops short, love advances and goes in" (Ruysbroeck).

"Thou askest me, 'How shall I think on Himself, and what is He?' and to this I cannot answer thee but this, 'I wot not.' For thou hast brought me with thy question into that same darkness and into that same cloud of unknowing that I would thou wert in thyself.... Of God Himself can no man think. He may well be loved, but not thought. By love He may be gotten and holden; but by thought never" (*The Cloud of Unknowing*).

"What [the mystical state] is and how it comes to pass is easier to experience than to describe. All that I have said of it is as poor and unlike it as a point of a needle is to the heavens above us." "The being of God is unfathomable." "The Divine Darkness is dark from its surpassing brightness, ... as the shining of the sun is as darkness to weak eyes." "Man experiences something in himself, but he cannot describe it; it is above all words; he cannot give it in images and forms" (John Tauler).

"All that we can say is as nothing in comparison with that which it really is." "After learning the secrets of God I can speak some few words with certainty; yet are my words outside of those divine and ineffable workings, and in no way do they approach nigh unto them, but rather do they spoil and blaspheme" (Angela of Foligno).

"To explain in our defective language what I saw would seem to me like blaspheming the Lord or dishonoring him by my speech; so great is the distance between what the intellect, when rapt and illumined and strengthened by God apprehends and what can be expressed with words, that they seem almost contradictory" (St. Catherine of Siena).

"All that can be said of God is not God." "So long as a person can still talk of things divine, he has not yet come to port" (St. Catherine of Genoa).

"To God as Godhead appertains neither will nor knowledge nor manifestation, nor anything that we can measure, or say, or conceive" (*Theologia Germanica*).

"God wills the understanding to understand that it understands nothing of that which His Majesty places before it." "The understanding makes no reflection, but is occupied with the fruition of God. ... It is understood that the fruition is a certain good containing in itself all good together at once; but this good is not comprehended." "O wonderful secrets of God! I should never be satisfied with endeavoring to make them understand, if I thought I should succeed, and thus I will say a thousand foolish things, provided I may happen but once to speak to the point" (St. Teresa).

"All that the understanding may comprehend, all that the will may be satisfied with, all that the imagination may conceive, is most unlike God and most disproportionate to him" (St. John of the Cross).

"That which you have seen in my writings is but a glimpse of the mysteries, for a person cannot write them" (Boehme).

"Remember that it is always good to speak like one that knows not, and not like one who knows" (Molinos).

"O God, what shall I say thou art, when thou canst not be named? What shall I speak of thee, when speaking of thee I speak nothing but contradiction?" (Jacob Bottomley, 1650, quoted by R. M. Jones, in Hastings' *Encyclopaedia of Religion and Ethics,* Vol. X, p. 579a).

"Oh, if I could express what I conceive of this state! But I can only stammer about it." "The soul knows God only, of whom it can say nothing" (Madame Guyon).

"It is not possible for me to describe all the things which I have seen in visions of the spiritual world, because the language and illustrations of this world are inadequate to express these spiritual realities; and the very attempt to reduce to ordinary language the glory of the things seen is likely to result in misunderstanding" (Sadhu Sundar Singh).

"My eyes were opened, and for the first time in all my life I caught a glimpse of the ecstatic beauty of reality. ... It was not an experience for words. It was an emotion, a rapture of the heart. ... I knew that every man, woman, bird and tree, and every living thing before me was extravagantly beautiful and extravagantly important. ... Yet what the importance was, I did not grasp. If my heart could have seen just a little further, I should have understood" (M. P. Montague, "Twenty

Minutes of Reality," *Atlantic Monthly,*
May, 1916).

"To describe God as this or that is
blasphemy." "I am dealing here with a
reality which is experienced, not with
metaphysical speculations or blasphe-
mous definitions of God." "Every human conception of God is a crime *lèse
majesté*. ... God is *not* or God is *all*—
the one, as the other, is proof of the
helplessness of human powers of expression" (J. Anker Larsen, *With the
Door Open,* 1931, pp. 102-103).

For the present it may suffice to point
out that the naturalness of the suggestion is no proof of the doctrine that the
ineffableness of the mystical experience
reflects a similar ineffableness in the
religious object, and to remark that
negative experience is commonly not so
good evidence of what a reality is not,
as positive experience is evidence of
what it is.

The mystic state, claiming as it does
to be a vision or perception of God, is
inevitably one of intense concentration
of attention, at first more or less voluntary, either upon God himself or it may
be at first upon something else from
which it is later transferred to the religious Object. This passes over into an
involuntary rapt contemplation, and
finally, in extreme instances, into an
ecstatic seizure often culminating in an
apparently unconscious trance. Now
concentration of attention upon one
object involves a corresponding withdrawal of attention from other objects,
and rapt contemplation of God will naturally lead to inattention to and temporary unconsciousness of the environing
world of events and things. The intensified mystical concentration of consciousness upon God and the consequent
unconsciousness, during the mystical
state, of all that is not God, naturally
tend to be taken as revelation not only
of the reality of God but of the unreality
of all that is not God. For instance, the
world of material objects in space and

of events in time or time-space comes to
be regarded as but deceptive appearance,
as compared with the one eternal and
unchangeable reality, God. First with
regard to the material and spatial:

"By persistent commerce with mystic visions, leave behind sensible perception" (Dionysius).

"Matter has no real being" (Scotus
Erigena).

"All creatures are absolutely nothing. I do not say that they are small or
anything else, but that they are absolutely nothing" (J. Tauler).

"The soul is fast asleep as to worldly
things and is like one dead to the
world" (St. Teresa).

"There is one loftiest point of the
soul which knows nothing of body."
"No form was ever seen at the summit
of the soul" (Eckhart).

"The soul to find God must go out
from all things, and all things must be
to it as if they existed not." "This
draught of God's most deep wisdom
makes the soul forget all the things of
this world" (St. John of the Cross).

"The outward senses are locked up
by holy abstraction; all things are as
nothing" (Boehme).

"Thou sleepest and what thou seest
are dream pictures" (A Persian mystic, quoted by Lehmann, *Mysticism in
Heathendom and Christendom,* p. 66).

"The great soul ... throws off *Maya*
and takes up God only." "In divine
love one entirely forgets the external
world, even one's own body. ... In ecstasy the whole mind remains absolutely fixed upon the supreme. ... He
whose heart earnestly longs after the
Deity has no time for anything else"
(Ramakrishna).

"Everything is here. ... I sat in my
garden, but there was no place in the
world where I was not. ... When one
has met the eternal Now, it is East
everywhere and Mecca is the very spot
on which one stands" (J. Anker Larsen, *op. cit.,* pp. 52, 73, 102).

Similarly, on the basis of the psychological fact that in the state of absorbed contemplation of the religious Object the tendency is to take no note of the passing of time, so that the time thus spent comes to seem very short, or even as if it were not of any duration at all, the mystic commonly claims either to have transcended the temporal process or to have seen into the unreality of time.

"All the past and present vanish like a dream" (Amelios).

"All things in the noumenal world co-exist in an eternal now" (Plotinus).

"Time and place hinder attaining to knowledge of God. God can only be known outside time and place, since He is above them. If the soul is to see God it must look at nothing in time. While occupied with time and place, it cannot recognize God.... The Divine Light lifts the soul above the turmoil of temporal things." "There is one loftiest part of the soul which stands above time and knows nothing of time or of body." "When we rise past our own mind to the summit of mind [we have] an inkling of the perfection and stability of eternity, for there is neither time nor space, neither before nor after, but everything present in one new fresh-springing now, where millenniums last no longer than the twinkling of an eye." "God is truth, but things in time are not truth" (Eckhart).

"All is present. God contemplates himself in an eternal now, without before or after" (Ruysbroeck).

"The soul neither sees, nor heeds, nor understands, nor perceives, all the time she is in this state, and this time is short; and indeed it seems shorter than it is. It is extremely difficult to know how long, because the senses are all in suspense" (St. Teresa).

"When I am in this state I do remember naught else" (Angela of Foligno).

"The soul has two eyes; the right eye beholds eternity, and the left eye, time. Both cannot perform their work at once. If the soul would see into eternity the left eye must be closed" (*Theologia Germanica*).

"There is no past nor future; everything is now.... There is no beginning and no end.... Eternity is now and accessible now" (J. Anker Larsen, *op. cit.*, pp. 53, 73, 94).

It may be pointed out in passing that if time be wholly unreal, there is no now at all, much less an everlasting now. The timeless validity of abstract truth and ideal value may be admitted, without committing oneself to the confused and self-contradictory concept of timeless existence. We can think of existence at all times, but we cannot think without contradiction of a real being which never has existed in the past, does not exist in the present, and will never exist in the future. If, *per impossibile*, there chanced to be something corresponding to such a figment of confused thinking, it would be not only ineffable and unknowable, but inconceivable.

Another phase of the mystical experience resulting from the extreme concentration of attention upon the religious Object is a temporary lapse of self-consciousness. Not the self, but only God is consciously contemplated, and when in retrospect the intense awareness of God is taken as revelation of the reality of God, recollection that there was no consciousness of the self tends similarly to be taken as revelation of the *unreality* of the separate finite self as such, either during the interval of the rapt mystical contemplation or more permanently. If one may speak of degrees within the extreme, the former interpretation may be said to be the less extreme, the latter the more extreme, holding as it does to the sole reality of God, man being real only as identified with or included in God. In the following excerpts from mystical writings one can detect on the one hand the description of the psychological state in which the mystic's distinct self-consciousness lapses, and on the other hand both the less extreme doctrine of temporary loss of individuality through the absorption of the self in the Absolute, or God, and the more extreme doctrine of the unreality of the finite self as distinct from the Absolute Self, or God. But attention may also be called to the fact that there is a tendency, particularly among mystics who belong in the Christian tradition, to correct or modify the doctrine of the unreality or temporary loss of individual selfhood. This, presumably, is in recognition of moral obligation and individual responsibility. Passages making such corrections will be italicized.

The mystic "belongs to God and is one with him, like two concentric circles." "He will be that which he sees, if indeed it is possible any longer to distinguish seer and seen." "Since in the vision there were not two things, but seer and seen were one, if a man could preserve the memory of what he was when he was mingled with the Divine, he would have in himself an image of God. For he was then one with God.... Caught up in an ecstasy, tranquil and alone with God, ... he turned not even to himself" (Plotinus).

"By persistent commerce with mystic visions [one is] raised aloft unknowingly to union with Him" (Dionysius).

"God's center is everywhere, and his circumference nowhere." "Through ecstasy of contemplation blessed Francis [of Assisi] passed over into God" (St. Bonaventura).

"The eye with which I see is the same eye with which he sees me." "If thy soul is to know God, it must forget itself and lose itself, for as long as it contemplates itself it cannot contemplate God." "Man is turned into God." "The soul may arrive at such an intimate union that God at last draws it to Himself altogether, so that there is no distinction left, in the soul's consciousness, between itself and God—*though God still regards it as a creature* (Eckhart).

"We can only behold that which we are." "The contemplative who has renounced himself is no longer conscious of himself except as an immense conflagration sensible of its own heat. But there comes a moment in the conflagration when simplicity throws a veil over the abyss [between man and God], and the spirit sees nothing more; nothing but pure unity." "Lost in the bliss of our eternal blending, we perceive no distinction between ourselves and God." "Even if the divine union be effected without medium, we must understand that *God and the creatures can never be confounded; union can never become confusion; the distinction remains forever inviolable.*" "By virtue of love we are plunged and absorbed in His bliss; we lose ourselves in it, *not as to our substance,* but as to the feeling of joy. In speaking of union between God and man, I have said and wish to repeat that *there is no question of unity of nature or of essence,* but unity of love. *God does not become the creature*" (Ruysbroeck).

"When man cometh into true poverty, he must transfer himself with One into One, without any distinction." "When the Divine Sun ariseth in the soul, all other lights change into the Divine Light." "Whoever attaineth to a true contemplative life, him God draweth to Himself." "The spirit is placed in an equality and entereth into God and is embraced by God; the spirit loseth its name, so that it is called rather God than spirit—*not that it is God, but only divine*" (Tauler).

The mystic may "divest himself of himself, pass into God, and become wholly one with Him, as a drop of water mingles with a cask of wine" (Suso).

"I saw no difference between God and our substance, but as it were all God; and yet mine understanding took it that our substance is in God; that is to say, *God is God, and our substance is a creature in God*" (Julian of Norwich).

"The soul is so entirely made one with God and God with it, that it knoweth and enjoyeth with God the most high things" (Angela of Foligno).

"My Me is God, nor do I recognize any other Me, except God Himself. My Being is God, not by simple participation but by a true transformation of my Being." "I will have nothing to do with a love that would be *for* God or *in* God; this is a love which pure love cannot bear, since pure love is God Himself. I cannot abide to see that word *for* and that word *in,* since they denote to my mind a something that stands between God and myself" (St. Catherine of Genoa).

"God can be known only by God." "He who shall or will love God, loveth ... One in All as All in One" (*Theologia Germanica*).

"I am as great as God, He is as small as I am; He is not above me, nor I below Him" (Angelus Silesius).

The understanding "makes no reflections, but is occupied with the fruition of God." In "the prayer of union," "the soul is thoroughly awake to God, though fast asleep as to ourselves." In "real union," "the soul neither understands nor knows anything, for all the faculties are lost and absorbed" (St. Teresa).

In "the perfect union of love," "the soul becomes divine, and, by participation, God, *so far as it is possible in this life.*" In this "deification" "the soul is detached not only from all outward things, but even from itself. It passes out of itself into the Beloved." "The soul loves God with the will and strength of God Himself" (St. John of the Cross).

"The very climax of loving ecstasy is to merge the will, not in one's own content, but in that of God." "The soul flows forth and loses itself, not merely by union with the Beloved, but by being utterly mingled with and merged in Him. ... It is carried wholly beyond its natural limits; it is swallowed up and absorbed in God." "There is an ever increasing union of soul with God" (St. Francis de Sales).

"God heareth and seeth through thee, being now the organ of His Spirit" (Boehme).

"When the soul is in God, her progress is infinite, seeing it is that of God Himself. Having become one with God, it can see nothing but God; having lost all separateness, self-possession and distinction, the soul no longer exists; it no longer acts, but God acts, and it is the instrument" (Madame Guyon).

"I am God. I am He whom I love, and He whom I love is I. ... If thou seest me, thou seest Him; and if thou seest Him, thou seest us both" (Husayn ibn Mansur).

"Myself with mine own eye I saw most clearly, but when I looked with God's eye, only God I saw" (Baba Kuhi).

"There is no such thing as I. As by continually peeling off the skin of the onion, so by analyzing the ego it will be found that there is not any real entity corresponding to the ego. The ultimate result of all such analysis is God." "All men are divided into three classes: those who, like stone in water, are so worldly that they will not absorb the least drop of true knowledge; those who, like cloth in water, are true lovers of Bhakta and become full of Divine bliss and knowledge; and finally, those who, like salt in water, merge themselves in the Absolute and all-pervading Self, and become one with it" (Ramakrishna).

"I have met God, seen God. To say *meet* or *see* is still too superficial and external to exhaust the consciousness of the moment. It was a confluence, a union of me with God; at that moment I myself became almost melted away with the reality of God. I became God" (R. Tsunashima, as quoted by M. Anesaki, *The Religious and Social Problems of the Orient,* Macmillan, 1923, p. 19).

Rapt mystical contemplation of the Divine Being is naturally accompanied by a "serene and blessed mood," amounting at times, in the case of some mystics, to ecstatic joy. Evil and ugliness do not come within the range of mystical contemplation; to the mystic, for the time being at least, they are as if they were not. And so it comes as a natural suggestion, especially when what is consciously experienced in the mystic state is taken as revelation, that God, the sole object of consciousness in the mystical revelation, is the sole reality, and that since God is all and God is absolutely good, all is good, there is no evil. What seems such is but an illusory appearance which reality takes on in deluded mortal mind. And so, psychology is made to teach ontology; the doctrine of the unreality of evil is based upon the bliss of ecstatic mysticism. Here again the evidence from the writings of the mystics is forthcoming and abundant.

"Evil is nohow, nowhere, no thing. God sees evil as good" (Dionysius).

"Evil is merely a negation and lies entirely outside the knowledge of God, who only knows and wills the good. . . . For God evil is not. It has meaning only in the sphere of time" (Scotus Erigena).

"If a man really abides in God's will, even the pains of hell would be a joy to him." "If I say God is good, it is not true; for what is good can grow better; what can grow better can grow best. Now these three things (good, better, best) are far from God, for he is above all" (Eckhart).

"The soul doth feel the presence of God with such love and divine fire that it loseth all love for itself and for the body. . . . God doth implant most sweet love in the soul. . . . It experienceth within itself the fulness of the goodness of God." "The soul doth swim in joyfulness and in knowledge." "I felt a sweetness so peaceful, quiet and great that I know not how to describe it." "I beheld a thing as fixed and stable as it was indescribable, and more than this I cannot say, save that it was all good." "Since God hath left me I am remained as contented as an angel; for I love toads and serpents, and even fools and demons, and nothing that I see them do, even sins committed against others, can displease me, inasmuch as I believe that God doth justly

permit and desire that it should be done" (Angela of Foligno).

"All shall be well, and all manner of things shall be well." "I saw no sin" (Julian of Norwich).

"If a man truly loves God and has no will but to do God's will, the whole force of the River Rhine may run at him and will not disturb him nor break his peace" (J. Tauler).

"I stood so occupied in seeing the work of Love, that if it had thrown me soul and body into hell, hell itself would have appeared to me to be nothing but love and consolation." "If of that which this heart of mine is feeling one drop were to fall into hell, hell itself would become all life eternal." "O my God, all mine, everything is mine, because all that belongs to God seems all to belong to me" (St. Catherine of Genoa).

There is an "inward peace which can break through all the assaults and crosses of oppression, suffering, misery and humiliation," possessing which "the apostles and martyrs suffered willingly all that was done to them." "All that is is good, in so far as it hath Being. The devil is good in so far as he hath Being. In this sense nothing is evil, or not good" (*Theologia Germanica*).

"Fruition is a certain good, containing in itself all good together at once" (St. Teresa).

"The soul feels itself filled with all good, emptied and delivered from all evil" (St. John of the Cross).

"I lay still in secret fruition of a joy unspeakable, . . . I had an inexpressible satisfaction and joy in suffering." "The soul drawn out of itself experiences an inward ecstasy. O unutterable happiness! Here all is God to the soul. . . . I believe that if such a soul were taken to hell, it would suffer all the cruel tortures of its fall in a complete contentment." "The soul sees only God everywhere, and all is God" (Madame Guyon).

"To the man of God right and wrong are alike." (Jalaluddin Rumi).

"Happiness is one of the marks of the Cosmic Sense." "There is no sense of sin in cosmic consciousness" (R. M. Burke).

"I saw no new thing but I saw all the usual things in a new miraculous light—in what I believe is their true light. I saw for the first time how wildly beautiful and joyous, beyond any words of mine to describe, is the whole of life.... For those fleeting lovely moments I did indeed and in truth love my neighbor as myself." "Heaven, in all its springtide and beauty, is here and now, before our very eyes, surging up to our very feet, lapping against our hearts; but we, alas, know not how to let it in" (M. P. Montague).

"I have now come to a stage of realization in which I see that God is walking in every human form and manifesting Himself alike through the sage and the sinner, the virtuous and the vicious.... Therefore when I meet different people I say to myself, 'God in the form of the saint, God in the form of the sinner, God in the form of the righteous, God in the form of the unrighteous.' He who has attained to such realization goes beyond good and evil, above virtue and vice, and realizes that the divine will is working everywhere." "Says God, 'I am the snake that biteth and the charmer that healeth; I am the judge that condemneth and the executioner that whippeth.' God tells the thief to go and steal, and at the same time warns the householder against the thief." "Everything that exists is God" (Ramakrishna).

"I say there is in fact no evil.... Clear and sweet is my soul, and clear and sweet is all that is not my soul" (Walt Whitman).

45. Knowledge of the Divine Truth*

Thomas Aquinas (1225?–1274?)

In what way it is possible to make known the divine truth.... Now in those things which we hold about God there is truth in two ways. For certain things that are true about God wholly surpass the capability of human reason, for instance that God is three and one: while there are certain things to which even natural reason can attain, for instance that God is, that God is one, and others like these, which even the philosophers proved demonstratively of God, being guided by the light of natural reason.

That certain divine truths wholly surpass the capability of human reason, is most clearly evident. For since the principle of all the knowledge which the reason acquires about a thing, is the understanding of that thing's essence, because according to the Philosopher's teaching the principle of a demonstration is *what a thing is,* it follows that our knowledge about a thing will be in proportion to our understanding of its essence. Wherefore, if the human intellect comprehends the essence of a particular thing, for instance a stone or a

* From *The Summa Contra Gentiles,* Volume I, pages 4-16, translated by the English Dominican Fathers. Reprinted by kind permission of Benziger Brothers, New York, and Burns Oates Washbourne Ltd., London.

triangle, no truth about that thing will surpass the capability of human reason. But this does not happen to us in relation to God, because the human intellect is incapable by its natural power of attaining to the comprehension of His essence: since our intellect's knowledge, according to the mode of the present life, originates from the senses: so that things which are not objects of sense cannot be comprehended by the human intellect, except in so far as knowledge of them is gathered from sensibles. Now sensibles cannot lead our intellect to see in them what God is, because they are effects unequal to the power of their cause. And yet our intellect is led by sensibles to the divine knowledge so as to know about God that He is, and other such truths, which need to be ascribed to the first principle. Accordingly some divine truths are attainable by human reason, while others altogether surpass the power of human reason.

Again. The same is easy to see from the degrees of intellects. For if one of two men perceives a thing with his intellect with greater subtlety, the one whose intellect is of a higher degree understands many things which the other is altogether unable to grasp; as instanced in a yokel who is utterly incapable of grasping the subtleties of philosophy. Now the angelic intellect surpasses the human intellect more than the intellect of the cleverest philosopher surpasses that of the most uncultured. For an angel knows God through a more excellent effect than does man, for as much as the angel's essence, through which he is led to know God by natural knowledge, is more excellent than sensible things, even than the soul itself, by which the human intellect mounts to the knowledge of God. And the divine intellect surpasses the angelic intellect much more than the angelic surpasses the human. For the divine intellect by its capacity equals the divine essence,

wherefore God perfectly understands of Himself what He is, and He knows all things that can be understood about Him: whereas the angel knows not what God is by his natural knowledge, because the angel's essence, by which he is led to the knowledge of God, is an effect unequal to the power of its cause. Consequently an angel is unable by his natural knowledge to grasp all that God understands about Himself: nor again is human reason capable of grasping all that an angel understands by his natural power. Accordingly just as a man would show himself to be a most insane fool if he declared the assertions of a philosopher to be false because he was unable to understand them, so, and much more, a man would be exceedingly foolish, were he to suspect of falsehood the things revealed by God through the ministry of His angels, because they cannot be the object of reason's investigations.

Furthermore. The same is made abundantly clear by the deficiency which every day we experience in our knowledge of things. For we are ignorant of many of the properties of sensible things, and in many cases we are unable to discover the nature of those properties which we perceive by our senses. Much less therefore is human reason capable of investigating all the truths about that most sublime essence . . .

That the truth about divine things which is attainable by reason is fittingly proposed to man as an object of belief. While then the truth of the intelligible things of God is twofold, one to which the inquiry of reason can attain, the other which surpasses the whole range of human reason, both are fittingly proposed by God to man as an object of belief. We must first show this with regard to that truth which is attainable by the inquiry of reason, lest it appears to some, that since it can be attained by reason, it was useless to make it an object of faith by supernatural inspiration. Now three disadvantages would result if this truth were left solely to the inquiry of reason. One is that few men would have knowledge of God: because very many are hindered from gathering the fruit of diligent inquiry, which is the discovery of truth, for three reasons. Some indeed on account of an indisposition of temperament, by reason of which many are naturally indisposed to knowledge: so that no efforts of theirs would enable them to reach to the attainment of the highest degree of human knowledge, which consists in knowing God. Some are hindered by the needs of household affairs. For there must needs be among men some that devote themselves to the conduct of temporal affairs, who would be unable to devote so much time to the leisure of contemplative research as to reach the summit of human inquiry, namely the knowledge of God. And some are hindered by laziness. For in order to acquire the knowledge of God in those things which reason is able to investigate, it is necessary to have a previous knowledge of many things: since almost the entire consideration of philosophy is directed to the knowledge of God: for which reason metaphysics, which is about divine things, is the last of the parts of philosophy to be studied. Wherefore it is not possible to arrive at the inquiry about the aforesaid truth except after a most laborious study: and few are willing to take upon themselves this labour for the love of a knowledge, the natural desire for which has nevertheless been instilled into the mind of man by God.

The second disadvantage is that those who would arrive at the discovery of the aforesaid truth would scarcely succeed in doing so after a long time. First, because this truth is so profound, that it is only after long practice that the human intellect is enabled to grasp it by means of reason. Secondly, because many

things are required beforehand, as stated above. Thirdly, because at the time of youth, the mind, when tossed about by the various movements of the passions, is not fit for the knowledge of so sublime a truth, whereas *calm gives prudence and knowledge.* Hence mankind would remain in the deepest darkness of ignorance, if the path of reason were the only available way to the knowledge of God: because the knowledge of God which especially makes men perfect and good, would be acquired only by the few, and by these only after a long time.

The third disadvantage is that much falsehood is mingled with the investigations of human reason, on account of the weakness of our intellect in forming its judgments, and by reason of the admixture of phantasms. Consequently many would remain in doubt about those things even which are most truly demonstrated, through ignoring the force of the demonstration: especially when they perceive that different things are taught by the various men who are called wise. Moreover among the many demonstrated truths, there is sometimes a mixture of falsehood that is not demonstrated, but assumed for some probable or sophistical reason which at times is mistaken for a demonstration. Therefore it was necessary that definite certainty and pure truth about divine things should be offered to man by the way of faith.

Accordingly the divine clemency has made this salutary commandment, that even some things which reason is able to investigate must be held by faith: so that all may share in the knowledge of God easily, and without doubt or error . . .

That those things which cannot be investigated by reason are fittingly proposed to man as an object of faith. It may appear to some that those things which cannot be investigated by reason ought not to be proposed to man as an object of faith: because divine wisdom provides for each thing according to the mode of its nature. We must therefore prove that it is necessary also for those things which surpass reason to be proposed by God to man as an object of faith.

For no man tends to do a thing by his desire and endeavor unless it be previously known to him. Wherefore since man is directed by divine providence to a higher good than human frailty can attain in the present life, as we shall show in the sequel, it was necessary for his mind to be bidden to something higher than those things to which our reason can reach in the present life, so that he might learn to aspire, and by his endeavors to tend to something surpassing the whole state of the present life. And this is especially competent to the Christian religion, which alone promises goods spiritual and eternal: for which reason it proposes many things surpassing the thought of man: whereas the old law which contained promises of temporal things, proposed few things that are above human inquiry. It was with this motive that the philosophers, in order to wean men from sensible pleasures to virtue, took care to show that there are other goods of greater account than those which appeal to the senses, the taste of which things affords much greater delight to those who devote themselves to active or contemplative virtues.

Again it is necessary for this truth to be proposed to man as an object of faith in order that he may have truer knowledge of God. For then alone do we know God truly, when we believe that He is far above all that man can possibly think of God, because the divine essence surpasses man's natural knowledge, as stated above. Hence by the fact that certain things about God are proposed to man, which surpass his reason, he is strengthened in his opinion that God is far above what he is able to think.

There results also another advantage from this, namely the checking of presumption which is the mother of error. For some there are who presume so far on their wits that they think themselves capable of measuring the whole nature of things by their intellect, in that they esteem all things true which they see, and false which they see not. Accordingly, in order that man's mind might be freed from this presumption, and seek the truth humbly, it was necessary that certain things far surpassing his intellect should be proposed to man by God.

Yet another advantage is made apparent by the words of the Philosopher. For when a certain Simonides maintained that man should neglect the knowledge of God, and apply his mind to human affairs, and declared that *a man ought to relish human things, and a mortal, mortal things:* the Philosopher contradicted him, saying that *a man ought to devote himself to immortal and divine things as much as he can.* Hence he says that though it is but little that we perceive of higher substances, yet that little is more loved and desired than all the knowledge we have of lower substances. He says also that when questions about the heavenly bodies can be answered by a short and probable solution, it happens that the hearer is very much rejoiced. All this shows that however imperfect the knowledge of the highest things may be, it bestows very great perfection on the soul: and consequently, although human reason is unable to grasp fully things that are above reason, it nevertheless acquires much perfection, if at least it hold things, in any way whatever, by faith . . .

That it is not a mark of levity to assent to the things that are of faith, al-

though they are above reason. Now those who believe this truth, of *which reason affords a proof,* believe not lightly, as though *following foolish fables.* For divine Wisdom Himself, Who knows all things most fully, deigned to reveal to man *the secrets of God's wisdom:* and by suitable arguments proves His presence, and the truth of His doctrine and inspiration, by performing works surpassing the capability of the whole of nature, namely, the wondrous healing of the sick, the raising of the dead to life, a marvellous control over the heavenly bodies, and what excites yet more wonder the inspiration of human minds, so that unlettered and simple persons are filled with the Holy Ghost, and in one instant are endowed with the most sublime wisdom and eloquence. And after considering these arguments, convinced by the strength of the proof, and not by the force of arms, nor by the promise of delights, but—and this is the greatest marvel of all—amidst the tyranny of persecutions, a countless crowd of not only simple but also of the wisest men, embraced the Christian faith, which inculcates things surpassing all human understanding, curbs the pleasure of the flesh, and teaches contempt of all worldly things. That the minds of mortal beings should assent to such things, is both the greatest of miracles, and the evident work of divine inspiration, seeing that they despise visible things and desire only those that are invisible. And that this happened not suddenly nor by chance, but by the disposition of God, is shown by the fact that God foretold that He would do so by the manifold oracles of the prophets, whose books we hold in veneration as bearing witness to our faith. This particular kind of proof is alluded to in the words of Heb ii 3, 4; *Which* namely the salvation of mankind, *having begun to be declared by the Lord, was confirmed with us by them that heard Him, God also bearing witness by signs and wonders, and divers . . . distributions of the Holy Ghost.*

Now such a wondrous conversion of the world to the Christian faith is a most indubitable proof that such signs did take place, so that there is no need to repeat them, seeing that there is evidence of them in their result. For it would be the most wondrous sign of all if without any wondrous signs the world were persuaded by simple and lowly men to believe things so arduous, to accomplish things so difficult, and to hope for things so sublime. Although God ceases not even in our time to work miracles through His saints in confirmation of the faith. . . .

That the truth of reason is not in opposition to the truth of the Christian faith. Now though the aforesaid truth of the Christian faith surpasses the ability of human reason, nevertheless those things which are naturally instilled in human reason cannot be opposed to this truth. For it is clear that those things which are implanted in reason by nature, are most true, so much so that it is impossible to think them to be false. Nor is it lawful to deem false that which is held by faith, since it is so evidently confirmed by God. Seeing then that the false alone is opposed to the true, as evidently appears if we examine their definitions, it is impossible for the aforesaid truth of faith to be contrary to those principles which reason knows naturally.

Again. The same thing which the disciple's mind receives from its teacher is contained in the knowledge of the teacher, unless he teach insincerely, which it were wicked to say of God. Now the knowledge of naturally known principles is instilled into us by God, since God Himself is the author of our nature. Therefore the divine Wisdom also contains these principles. Consequently whatever is contrary to these principles, is contrary to the divine Wisdom; wherefore it cannot be from God. Therefore those things which are received by faith from divine revelation cannot be contrary to our natural knowledge.

Moreover. Our intellect is stayed by contrary arguments, so that it cannot advance to the knowledge of truth. Wherefore if conflicting knowledges were instilled into us by God, our intellect would thereby be hindered from knowing the truth. And this cannot be ascribed to God.

Furthermore. Things that are natural are unchangeable so long as nature remains. Now contrary opinions cannot be together in the same subject. Therefore God does not instill into man any opinion or belief contrary to natural knowledge. . . .

In what relation human reason stands to the truth of faith. It would also seem well to observe that sensible things from which human reason derives the source of its knowledge, retain a certain trace of likeness to God, but so imperfect that it proves altogether inadequate to manifest the substance itself of God. For effects resemble their causes according to their own mode, since like action proceeds from like agent; and yet the effect does not always reach to a perfect likeness to the agent. Accordingly human reason is adapted to the knowledge of the truth of faith, which can be known in the highest degree only by those who see the divine substance, in so far as it is able to put together certain probable arguments in support thereof, which nevertheless are insufficient to enable us to understand the aforesaid truth as though it were demonstrated to us or understood by us in itself. And yet however weak these arguments may be, it is useful for the human mind to be practised therein, so long as it does not pride itself on having comprehended or demonstrated: since although our view of the sublimest things is limited and weak, it is most pleasant to be able to catch but a glimpse of them. . . .

46. *Proofs of the Existence of God**

GEORGE GALLOWAY (1862–1933)

The importance of the traditional proofs of the existence of God has greatly diminished in modern times. No one, remarks the late Prof. Pfleiderer, now holds it possible to prove the divine existence from an abstract conception of

* From *The Philosophy of Religion*, pp. 381–394. By kind permission of publishers, Charles Scribner's Sons

God, or, from an abstract conception of the world, to reach by inference a God who is separate from the world. Nor can it be said that these proofs have ever played a part in producing religious conviction where it did not already exist; their ostensible function has rather been to confirm religious belief than to create it. The proofs themselves do not set out from religious presuppositions, either explicit or implicit. The presuppositions from which they start are quite general and abstract; and the standing difficulty in the argument has always been, that the concrete reality at which they aim contains more than is to be found in the premises. Those who developed the Theistic Arguments had a clear idea of what they wanted to reach, and they hoped to reach it by logical thinking. The misfortune was that they were not fully conscious of the disparity between the means and the end. The 'proofs' have been a favourite theme of comment and criticism; in truth, the subject has been treated so often by theologians and philosophers that it has been worn threadbare, and it has become well-nigh impossible to say anything new on the topic. There is a consensus of opinion that the arguments are not valid in their present form; but some who admit this believe that they can be reconstructed so as to have weight, though the weight does not amount to demonstration. It will be necessary to refer to these reconstructions, and the whole subject, however familiar, can hardly be passed over here: for it is of historic interest, and shows the way in which thought has come to the aid of faith by offering rational proof that the object of faith is real. The proofs represent modes in which the human mind, through the exercise of reasoning meant to be universal and cogent, sought to justify to itself the truth of its religious conviction. A short discussion and criticism of these proofs will help to define more clearly in our minds the nature of the problem before us. And when we understand where certain solutions have failed, and why they failed, we shall see better the lines on which a solution may be profitably attempted.

The proof which is usually taken first is the Ontological. It is the one which raises the deepest philosophical issues, and, as we shall see, the other proofs implicitly assume its validity. The On-tological Argument has been stated in slightly different ways, but its essential contention is, that the *reality* of God is involved in the *idea* of God. There is something, it is urged, unique in the idea of God, so that it cannot be a mere idea. Anselm (1033–1109) presented this proof in its scholastic form. It runs thus: God is a Being than which a greater cannot be conceived (*id quo majus cogitari nequit*); but an idea which existed only *in intellectu* would not be so great as one which existed *in re* as well as *in intellectu;* therefore God must be thought as necessarily existing. This argument has been set forth in a simpler and less artificial form by Descartes. He omits the step which declares that what exists in fact as well as in idea is greater than what exists merely in idea, and affirms that the very notion of God, the most perfect Being, carries existence as necessarily with it as the idea of a triangle carries with it the equality of the sum of its angles to two right angles. In short, reality belongs, and is clearly perceived to belong, to the very notion of God. Descartes is well aware that this line of reasoning will not hold in regard to other objects of thought, but he maintains the idea of God to be unique in the respect that it involves existence. This specific claim is the crux of the argument. A second form of proof was offered by Descartes. In this case the argument asserts that the idea of God, who is infinite and perfect, cannot be formed in man by any finite object, and must be caused by God himself. It is implied here that the idea of the Infinite is positive and cannot be reached *via negationis*. But, even if this were not open to objection, the term Infinite connotes much less than is signified by God. Still, taken simply as a probable argument, the thought is suggestive and not without weight, that man's knowledge of God is due to God himself. He is the sufficient reason of the idea of himself in man....

At the hands of Kant the Ontological Proof was subjected to a penetrating criticism, and since Kant's day it has ceased to be put forward seriously in the old form. His criticism proceeds on the principle that existence is no part of the content of an idea. "Being is evidently not a real predicate, that is, a conception of something that is capable of being added to the conception of a thing. . . . I add nothing to my conception, which expresses merely the possibility of the object, by simply placing its object before me in thought, and saying that it *is*. The real contains no more than the possible. A hundred real dollars do not contain a cent more than a hundred possible dollars." [1] Kant has shown conclusively, that it is not possible from the analysis of a conception to deduce from it existence as a predicate. Even when we feel that existence does belong to an idea or combination of ideas, we are not entitled to say that the union of existence and idea is more than a union in idea. It has, however, been objected that, while Kant's reasoning may hold of the idea of a particular thing,—say a sum of money —the idea of God as the absolute Being is in a different position. . . .

The source of the vitality of the Ontological Argument—of the lingering belief that, after all, there is something in it—must be sought elsewhere than in the cogency of its logic. It lies, as Lotze has pointed out, in the rooted disinclination of the human spirit to believe that the Supreme Being, who is the Supreme Value, is only a fiction of the mind.[2] The refusal to entertain the thought is not due to convincing argument, but to the demands of inner experience. The Ontological Proof, in its traditional form, represents an artificial way in which men sought to justify to themselves a faith,

of the truth of which they felt sure on other grounds.

In its method the second of the Theistic Proofs, the Cosmological, is sounder than the Ontological. It sets out from the world as given, and from the character of the world infers the existence of a God to explain it. This line of thought was at least suggested by Plato in the *Timæus*, where he says that every created thing must be created by some cause.[3] It is also hinted at by Augustine: "And I beheld the other things below Thee, and I perceived that they neither are absolutely existent nor absolutely non-existent. For they are, since they are from Thee, but are not, because they are not what Thou art. For that truly is which remains unchangeably." [4] The Cosmological Proof has two forms. In the first instance we set out from the contingency of facts within the world: they may either be or not be—so it is said, and there is no element of necessity in them. This contingency, however, must lead up to something which is necessary, and we have to posit a necessary Being as the ground of the contingent. The other form of proof makes use of the principle of causality. In our experienced world effects are always preceded by causes, and these in turn are the effects of other causes. So the chain of causality runs back step by step. But an infinite line of causes is impossible, and there must come a point in the series at which we arrive at a First or Uncaused Cause. This First Cause of all the different series of causes is God.

Kant was no doubt right when he said that this proof could not yield a necessary Being over and above the given series of facts. Moreover, we are not justified in assuming, without evidence, that data within our world are contingent; and even if this were so, it would

---

[1] *Transcendental Dialectic,* Prof. Watson's translation, pp. 208-209.

[2] *Microcosmus,* Eng. tr., vol. ii, p. 671. Cp. also *Religionsphilosophie,* pp. 9-10.

[3] *Tim.,* p. 27 ff.

[4] *Confessions,* Bk. vii, cap. xi.

not follow that the world itself in its totality is contingent. Again, it may be asked, Why is the Unconditioned Being said to be necessary? The necessary, in the current use of the word, is that which is conditioned, in other words determined to be what it is and not something else; and this idea of necessity should not be predicated uncritically of the Unconditioned. Nor is it apparent how a world of *contingent* facts could be derived from a necessary Being. On the other hand, if we think the line of regress under the notion of effects and causes, there are just as good reasons for saying the series can be prolonged indefinitely as that it must end in a First Cause. Then the causal series in the world are manifold, and it is not legitimate to assume that all the lines converge upon and end in a single Cause. Why not a plurality of First Causes? Finally, there is the objection that the notion of cause is a category by which we connect and organise elements within experience, and ought not to be applied without some reason and explanation to a Being supposed to exist beyond the experienced world. The truth is that, while the principle is sound that we should argue from the facts of experience to a ground of experience, the Cosmological Proof gives effect to this principle in a faulty and one-sided way. It tries to reach a certain goal by setting out from data and using a method which preclude it from reaching the goal. This line of proof, even were it purified of flaws, could not take us beyond the world-system; it could not lead us to God in the theistic sense of the word.

The third of the traditional proofs, the Teleological, is rather an extension, or a special application, of the Cosmological than a separate argument. Like the latter, it infers that a particular aspect or character of the world requires the existence of God to explain it. The Teleological Proof bases itself on the presence of order in the world; this order it takes to be the token of design, and concludes that God must be the source of that design. Of all the Proofs this, to the ordinary mind, is the most simple and striking. The existence of design in nature at first blush seems so transparent, and the need for applying the human analogy of the designer and his material so obvious. The Teleological Argument is consequently an old one; and Plato has in substance made use of it when he suggested that the principle that mind orders all things was the only one worthy of the world around us and the heavens above us. The natural tendency of thought in this matter is fairly reflected by the words of Bacon: "For while the mind of man looketh upon second causes scattered, it may sometimes rest upon them and go no farther; but when it beholdeth the chain of them confederate and linked together, it must needs fly to Providence and Deity." And Kant, it is well known, treated the Teleological Proof more tenderly than the others, and said that "it must be always mentioned with respect." But he very pertinently remarked: "All that the argument from design can possibly prove is an *architect* of the world, who is very much limited by the adaptability of the material in which he works." On the evidence it is inadmissible to say that such a Being is supreme, omnipotent, and the creator of the world. The human designer is hampered by an intractable element in the matter which he manipulates, and the way in which he overcomes this intractability is a token of his intelligence and foresight. It is obvious that this conception cannot be consistently applied to a Being supposed to be omnipotent, who cannot therefore be limited by his material in the way that man is. Moreover, while it may well be that so-called matter is incapable of producing order and adaptation, those who argue from design ought not to take this for granted. The physico-theological proof, as it is sometimes called, fails owing to the mechanical and external way in which it deals with order and adaptation in nature, and it has lost much of its former force owing to the growth and influence of the idea of evolution in modern times. I have already referred to the transformation of teleological ideas by the modern principle of development in the previous chapter, and I need not repeat here what was said there. The result has been that the notion of external design has been replaced by that of immanent adaptation, and the complex harmony of parts in organisms is regarded as a continuous development from simpler forms. It may be well to repeat that the presence of immanent ends in the world does not prove the existence of an intelligence which is above or part from the world-system. We have already tried to show that this inward finalism is consistent with theism, but it certainly does not point to a theistic conception of the universe as its only possible explanation.

As Kant explained,-the three Theistic Proofs are intimately related to one another. The teleological proof leans back on the cosmological, and the cosmological in turn leans back on the ontological. If we follow the natural progress of the human mind in its endeavour to rise by reflexion to the idea of God, we have to reverse the order in which we have taken the proofs. The evidences of design, which he seemed to find in the world around him, led man in the first instance to think of a designer, and this designer he identified with God. Further reflexion served to show that the argument must be extended to embrace the world as a whole, and the world, it was inferred, must have a First Cause who was God. But it is plain that both these arguments imply the principle which is stated explicitly in the Ontological Argument. They presuppose the principle that what we find ourselves obliged to think holds of reality; and this is the nerve of the Ontological Proof. In short, all the arguments involve the validity and trustworthiness of thought. We have already indicated in what sense, and with what qualifications this far-reaching principle is to be understood; and in any case, whatever stress is laid on this principle, the premisses of the traditional proofs are not such that they could yield the existence of God for their logical conclusion.

Two further arguments fall to be mentioned—the Moral Proof and the Historical Proof. Though it is usual to speak of them as proofs, they are not proofs in the true sense of the word, and they do not claim to be so. The first of these, the Moral Argument, seeks to show that in the existence of God we find the best solution to the problems of the moral life. The form which this argument received at the hands of Kant is peculiar, and it is not satisfactory. Kant says it is a demand of the moral self that the highest Good be realised. But in the highest Good there are two elements, virtue and happiness: the consciousness of duty fulfilled and of desire satisfied. Now, for Kant, virtue and happiness belong to two different worlds, the former to the intelligible and the latter to the phenomenal world. How can the union of these diverse elements demanded by the Supreme Good be assured? Kant replies by the postulate of God as the teleological ground of both worlds: God then guarantees the union of virtue and happiness, and therefore the realisation of the Chief Good. All this is very artificial. It is not a psychological description of the motives which lead men to postulate a God; nor is it consistent with Kant's own premisses that an empirical and sensuous product, which he deems happiness to be, should be raised to a constituent of the Supreme Good. Yet if we disentangle Kant's argument from the adventitious elements which hamper it, we can present it in a form which is not without force. While not committing ourselves to the Kantian doctrine of a noumenal and a phenomenal world, we are justified in accepting the existence of an ethical and a natural order, a material and a spiritual world. The moral consciousness demands the realisation of its ideal of Good, but this demand presupposes that the natural world is adapted to the ends of the spirit. The possibility of this adaptation is contained in the conception of an ethical God who is ground of both worlds and pledge of their harmony. Though we do not demonstrate God's existence in this way, we at least show how the postulate of his existence solves an urgent ethical problem. Nor can the argument from the moral consciousness be made to yield more than this. The feeling of obligation —the sense of duty—cannot be explained from beneath: no naturalistic theory of evolution can account for the birth of the word *ought* in the mind of man. The thought therefore lies to hand that it must be explained from above, through man's relation to a Moral Power that governs the world. It is a fact of deepest significance that man, a moral being with a sense of right and wrong, has developed within the universe, and we rightly ask: What must the character of that universe be which gives birth to such a being? When we postulate a God in answer to this question we are basing our postulate on the demands of the moral consciousness. And this is the legitimate use of the Moral Argument.

The Historical Proof is the name often given to the argument *e consensu gentium*. What we have here is not, of course, a proof, but a suggestion that the only sufficient reason of the widespread consciousness of God in human minds is God himself. The thought conveyed is closely related to the Moral Proof, which finds an explanation of the facts of the moral consciousness in the existence of an ethical Deity.[5] Unfortunately, if we take the argument for what it originally professed to be, an inference from human agreement, the historical evidences do not show us the agreement which is necessary. For to agree that God is, means little unless there is some concord in regard to *what* he is. Now there is a consensus of belief on the part of mankind in some Power above them, but in regard to the nature of this Power beliefs are very confused and conflicting, and they range from gross materialism to refined spiritualism. If we take these ideas as they stand, in their variety and mutual inconsistency, we cannot build any solid argument upon them. On the other hand, if we revise the proof and state it in the light of the idea of development, it assumes a sounder and more hopeful form. The reality of God then becomes a postulate of the developing spiritual experience of humanity. The long upward journey of the race, during which the idea of a spiritual God has gradually taken form and substance in human minds, becomes a meaningless movement if there be no Reality corresponding to the idea. We may add, the argument from history does not depend on a metaphysical theory of the process of development, nor on a speculative conception of the relation of God to man. It rests on an unbiassed view of the development of religion, and it puts the case with studious moderation when it declares, that it is hard to believe that this growing consciousness of God as a spiritual and ethical Being has not its source and ground in God himself.[6]

When we look back on these well-

---

[5] The Historical Proof was put forward in substance by Descartes, as the reader will remember, though in a metaphysical rather than in a historical form.

[6] It was the same motive which lent vitality to the Ontological Proof—the demand of the spiritual consciousness that the Supreme Value be real.

meant endeavours to demonstrate the existence of God, we can only reiterate the judgment we formed by the way: as proofs they break down. They suggest probabilities, probabilities of greater or less degree; but they carry no conviction to the minds of those who demand cogent logic. Proof means logical connexion or implication, and to infer God from the world and its character is to put more into the conclusion than is contained in the premises. God in the sense that spiritual religion demands can never be reached by any deductive argument; and there is truth in the trenchant words of the late Professor James: "The attempt to demonstrate by purely intellectual processes the truth of the deliverances of direct religious experience is absolutely hopeless." [7] Unfortunately, it took men a long time to discover this. But though these Proofs are in principle unsound, they are not on that account entirely valueless. For one thing, they testify to the confidence of the human spirit that reason can support the claims of faith, that the God who is necessary to the inner life can also be justified by reflective thinking. The Theistic Proofs are, in their own fashion, a witness to a per-

sisting conviction on man's part that his religion is not a non-rational attitude of mind. The attempt to reach God by rational deduction may be taken as the symptom and expression of a constant tendency of the human spirit, which is central in the religious consciousness. This movement carries the spiritual self beyond its environment, beyond the world, to gain a deeper ground of thought and life in the Being whom it calls God. The religious man, it is true, does not reach this goal by inference from the world or what is in it: he is prompted to take this course by his practical and experimental knowledge that "the world and the desire thereof" cannot satisfy him. The inspiring motive, alike of the arguments for the existence of God and of the Godward movement of the religious spirit, is the sincere conviction that the world is imperfect and needs a deeper Reality to complete it. Both for thought and for spiritual experience the world proves unsatisfying, and so impels men to go beyond it to find its true explanation and value. The Theistic Proofs, despite their shortcomings, recognise this, and they have worth as the symptom and the symbol of the general movement of the religious mind.

[7] *Varieties of Religious Experience,* p. 435.

47. *The Evidential Value of Religious Experience** *

D. E. TRUEBLOOD (1900–   )

Most of the arguments which have become classic in the support of the hy-

* From *The Logic of Belief,* Ch. XII. By kind permission of publishers, Harper and Brothers, Publishers.

pothesis of God as objectively real have been based on inference. We find, that is, that there are aspects of the world which are not understandable if theism is not true, but are understandable if theism is true. These arguments, as we have seen in an earlier chapter, are parallel to many used to arrive at scientific conclusions, the example given being that of the conclusion about the existence of atoms.

This kind of evidence is good evidence and can never be despised, inasmuch as we necessarily rely on it in so many areas of experience. Nevertheless, it is generally recognized that such inferential experience would be greatly strengthened if, in addition to it, there could be direct experience. If, in any situation, inferential arguments could show what logically ought to be the case, and if, furthermore, there could be a direct observation showing that the inference had the support of immediate experience, the impetus to believe would be very strong indeed. This is the procedure which has actually been followed in regard to certain astronomical discoveries, the most striking example being that of the discovery of the planet Neptune. The existence of the planet was first inferred as a necessary hypothesis in order to explain certain observed phenomena, and then by use of the telescope the inferred body was actually seen. It is conceivable that something like this may occur in regard to atoms, with the perfection of the new electron microscopes, which use electrical fields rather than light as their means of amplification.

The fortunate situation in the field of religious belief is that here the opportunity for the corroboration of inferential evidence by direct evidence is very great. One of the most amazing failures of historic theology has been the failure to employ, in the substantiation of religious belief, the same kind of empirical evidence which has long been used in support of scientific belief. The failure to make use of empirical evidence in religion is the more amazing when we begin to realize how abundant the evidence is, and how truly it has been the

real basis of belief in actual practice. "I had heard of thee by the hearing of the ear, but now mine eye seeth thee," is echoed in every generation.

A. The Primary Datum of Religion

That fact that religious experience occurs is a fact with which every philosophy must eventually deal. The claim which such experience makes, the claim to actual contact, not merely with persons and things, but with the Creator and Sustainer of the universe, is so stupendous and so insistent that it cannot be neglected. Our philosophy must either explain it away or construct a world view consistent with it.

The reasonable procedure is to look at religious experience as we look at any other datum. It is the primary datum of religion, and it awaits analysis. If we are scientifically minded we approach experience without prejudice and with humility. The scientific temper demands that we neither *accept* the data of experience uncritically nor *reject* it uncritically. We do not know what any experience is worth in the verification of belief until we analyze it, subjecting it to all the appropriate tests available. The mere fact that millions have reported that they have known God directly is not absolute proof that they have really done so, but, on the other hand, to assume, prior to critical testing, that they have not really done so would be unscientific in the extreme.

It must be made clear that we are not referring to *belief* in this connection, but to *reported experience*. The two are different. Belief may arise from many sources, some of them intellectually respectable and some of them not respectable. There can be belief *because* of direct experience and there can be belief *apart from* direct experience. The point we are making is not that millions of men have believed in God, something almost too obvious to bother to mention, but rather that millions of men have reported and continue to report that they have known God with the directness and intimacy with which they know other persons or physical objects.

Not all religious experience is the same, but there are characteristic features which appear with astonishing regularity and which are not especially difficult to describe. Normally it is not some experience wholly separated from other experiences, but a particular way in which all reality is apprehended. It comes about most naturally in the mood of prayer or workship, but is by no means limited to stated times for these, either individually or collectively. Ordinarily religious experience has nothing to do with visions, ecstasies, raptures or other phenomena which are usually considered abnormal. It is true that some mystics have experienced these exalted states of consciousness or unconsciousness, but they are no part of *normative* religious experience.[1] It, on the contrary, is as unspectacular as breathing or sleeping. For most men and women religious experience has been a calm assurance of the reality of a relationship which gives meaning to existence. . . .

B. Normative Religious Experience

Interesting as may be the study of peculiar mental phenomena, that is no part of our present purpose. We are concerned with the logical structure of belief, and, for this purpose, we are interested in the unspectacular. This normative experience may be described by making certain definite propositions about it which are related to one another as steps in the progressive narrowing of the field.

(1) *Religious experience is percep-*

---

[1] Unusual mental states, such as "speaking with tongues," have frequently been minimized, even by those reporting them personally.

tual. By this we mean that experience, as reported, is not a matter of either speculation or imagination, but of something independent of the observer with which the observer has established contact. God might be either imagined or perceived, just as a tree might be imagined or perceived. We say the tree is perceived when the tree is experienced as external to the mind of the perceiver. Imagination is free to indulge in wishful thinking; perception is limited by the nature of the real as known. The point is that religious experience reports itself as so limited.

Perhaps it is necessary to remind the reader that perceptual and sensory are not identical concepts. Perception refers to a relation to an *object* and is thus distinct from *conception,* as well as from imagination. Sensation, on the other hand, refers to the kind of experience which comes through the instrumentality of end organs, of which ears and eyes are conspicuous examples. There can be nonperceptual sensation, as a blow on the head may easily demonstrate, and, unless normative religion is a delusion, there is a vast amount of non-sensory perception, i.e., real contact with a perceived object, *without* the instrumentality of the sensory end organs. If God is really known, as so many have claimed to know Him, it is clear that He is not known by means of our auditory, optic or tactual nerves. Sometimes the language of sense has been used in the reports of vivid religious experience, but nearly always such language is consciously figurative. This is well illustrated by the Psalmist's appeal, "O taste and see that the Lord is good." The very fact that men speak so often of an *inward* sense is evidence that they are not talking about the actual sensory apparatus. What they mean is that their awareness of God is *as vivid, as incontestable,* as any sensory experience ever is. One of the great seventeenth century interpreters of such experience attempted, in the following words, to tell his Dutch friend Heer Paets, what he meant by an "inward sense."

An example of an inward, supernatural sense is when the heart or soul of a pious man feels in itself divine motions, influences and operations, which sometimes are as the voice or speech of God, sometimes as a most pleasant and glorious illustration or visible object to the inward eye, sometimes as a most sweet savour or taste, sometimes as a heavenly and divine warmness or (so to speak) melting of the soul in the love of God.[2]

It would be stupid to minimize the value of expressions like those of Barclay on the ground that they are figures of speech. The more important any disclosure is, the more necessary figures of speech become. The necessity for figures of speech arises from the fact that intelligible language is used for the purpose of making known what was formerly unknown, and this can only be done by establishing some similarity with what is already known. Thus we seek to make the experience of color understandable to the congenitally blind by comparing color with musical tone, though we are well aware that the two are not the same. Similarly, those who have tried to make religious experience understandable to others not conscious of it, have used the language of sense, while recognizing that it is not really sensory. They mean that it has the vividness, the certitude, the striking quality of that which impinges on ears, eyes, and other organs. An impressive testimony to this effect is that of Newman, when, speaking of his *inward conversion*, he affirmed years later that he was still more certain of it "than that I have hands and feet." [3]

It was, apparently, in an effort to em-phasize the perceptual character of his own religious experience that the celebrated French mathematician, Blaise Pascal, used the word "Fire" in capital letters, as the central feature of the record of his life-shaking experience. This record, which Pascal's servant found sewed into the scholar's coat, at the time of his death, was made up largely of interjections, the normal language of assured contact. The word "Fire" was most emphasized, probably in the effort to show that what he perceived had about it the same indubitable quality that we find in the flame, which warms, lights, and even burns.

Perhaps there is need to remark in passing that when we speak of perception as *contact with an object,* we are not necessarily referring to a *physical* object. The object is that which is perceived, whatever it is. It would be both unphilosophical and unscientific to assert dogmatically that the only objects of perception are physical bodies. The kinds of object in which we must believe depend wholly on the kind of evidence which is available. The correct method is not to decide in advance whether or not there are nonphysical objects of perception, but rather to begin with the data of experience and wait to see to what conclusions we are led by the analysis of this experience.

(2) *Religious experience is cognitive,* in that it claims to be the kind of perception which gives the perceiver actual knowledge of God. In short it is possible, in religious experience, to go beyond Pascal's memorable hour, when there was certainty of contact, but little more. The prophets, in all generations, claim that their experience of God is such that they learn something about His nature, and His will for men. We are not discussing now the correctness of this knowledge, since such discussion should come later in this chapter; we are saying merely that the primary datum of re-

---

[2] Robert Barclay, *Truth Triumphant,* p. 897.
[3] John Henry Newman, *Apologia pro Vita Sua,* Everyman edition, p. 31.

ligion includes a "knowledge claim."

Naturally it is not easy for men to tell others *what* they know, since language here becomes more inadequate than it ordinarily is, and poetry becomes inevitable, but this is not the important point. The point is that knowledge is claimed, though never perfect knowledge. The devout man in all generations says with St. Paul, "I know in part." It has long been recognized that men, in their knowledge of God, can touch no more than the hem of His garment. But to know in part, is to know something.

(3) *Religious experience is personal,* not in the sense that every devout man has consciously believed that God is a "Person," but that the experience characteristically recorded is of the kind which we normally associate with persons. The experience has about it, as aesthetic experience has, the augustness which we cannot expect contact with a mere "thing" to inspire. In many cases, and most strikingly in the experience of Jesus, the relationship is consciously personal. God is addressed in prayer as "O Father," and the second person is used when a pronoun is employed.

This personal aspect of religious experience becomes more clear when we note that what men try to describe is not so much a quest as a response to a revelation. If religion were a quest, we might seek our object as we seek a precious stone. All the personal qualities would be in *us,* not in the object sought and known. But it is not a mere quest. This seems to be the meaning of the ancient rhetorical question, "Canst thou by searching find out God?"[4]

Religion is not so much the thrill of discovery, as the awareness of being assaulted. The witness to this comes from testimonies as far apart as Francis Thompson's *Hound of Heaven* and Karl Barth's theology of crisis. Religion is not

----

[4] Job, 11:7.

so much finding God, as reaction to the Reality which has found us. It is not so much man's bargain with God, as it is man's response to God's grace. But the point of all this, to which there is abundant testimony covering the greater part of three thousand years, is that this is the way we react to the tremendous, soul-stirring experience of *being loved. It is persons who do the loving.* Thus it is true to say that normative experience is personal, either explicitly or implicitly.

C. Subject and Object

Assuming that the foregoing brief description of religious experience is sufficient for our present purposes, we can proceed to show the main structure of the argument based upon it. All that we know arises in experience. Our reason for believing that there is a physical order is the fact that millions of men report an experience of such an order. In a similar manner millions of men in all times and places have experienced God as the Sustainer of their lives. Therefore, God is.

The only reason for not accepting this forthright empirical evidence is the fact that experience can be delusory. Not everything that men experience exists. Two experiences given at a court trial and referring to the same event are sometimes contradictory. Though we cannot dispense with the ultimate appeal to experience we cannot take experience at its face value. But this applies to sensory experience just as truly as it applies to religious experience. Why, then, are there so many who deny the evidential value of religious experience while they accept the evidential value of sensory experience? The fact that men may make mistakes about the interpretation of their sense perceptions does not lead the ordinary intelligent person to the conclusion that sense perception is a purely subjective affair, but the fact that some men have had religious experiences which we must regard as illusory has led a number of otherwise critical persons to the conclusion that religious experience is a purely subjective affair and no revelation of the real. It is indeed a curious leap to conclude, from the fact that men make mistakes, that there is no reality which they are making mistakes *about....*

D. *The Tests of Veracity*

To know precisely what belongs to the objective order is a problem of the greatest difficulty, and one never fully solved in any extended area. We solve the problem, insofar as we solve it at all, not by the application of some special *means,* but rather by the humble process of noting converging lines of agreement with experience as known. If Karl Pearson's lonely telephone operator finds that fire alarms are coming in simultaneously on many of his wires and if the alarms refer to the same place, he is justified in believing that there really is a fire. When people, who differ in many ways, have substantial agreement about one item, we consider it more reasonable to posit objective status than to accept a miracle of coincidence. In this we may be wrong, but we have no suitable alternative.

The agreement, of course, must be of a particular kind to have any value. In testing the veracity of religious experience four tests are of especial importance.

(1) *Number of reporters.* Other things being equal an experience has more veracity if it is widely shared. One reason for doubting the objective status of the animals seen in *delirium tremens* is that those who see them are so badly outnumbered.

By the most conservative estimate the number of persons who have reported religious experience, not in the sense of ecstatic trance, and not in the sense of mere inference from the order of nature,

but with a deep assurance of the divine undergirding, is many millions and, indeed, it is difficult to think of any similar data that are so numerous. The abundance of such reports in the Old and New Testament is enough to give us pause, but this is by no means the end of the story. When we think of the humble souls who have made their testimony in Christian lands in the intervening years, as well as many more quite outside the Christian tradition, we begin to see that we are dealing with one of the best attested experiences in the world. "The simple fact is," as Canon Raven has said, "that those who would explain away religion are hardly aware of the greatness of the task or of the qualifications necessary for it." [5]

The evidence upon which we can depend comes to us chiefly in three ways. (a) In the first place there is the vocal testimony, especially that which has appeared in gatherings similar to the Methodist "class meeting." Some of this can be discounted, especially when it follows the fashionable religious pattern of the day, but, taken as a whole, the vocal testimonies are so numerous and so sincere that it is impossible for a reasonable person to dismiss them as unworthy of attention.

(b) A second source of evidence is found in literary records, especially those of spiritual autobiography. This material, as is well known, is an important part of our literature from Augustine's *Confessions* to Newman's *Apologia* and beyond.[6] Even the Quaker journals alone make an impressive showing *and all of them were written in order to provide the very data with which we are here concerned.*

[5] Charles E. Raven, *Jesus and the Gospel of Love,* London, 1931, p. 73.
[6] Reliable modern studies of this rich deposit are available in Gaius Glenn Atkins' *Pilgrims of the Lonely Road,* and Willard L. Sperry's Lowell Lectures, *Strangers and Pilgrims.*

(c) If these two sources were the only ones the evidence would be impressive, but they do not exhaust the data. The experiences of most people cannot be known by their own direct report, since they are too modest or are lacking in facility of expression. Accordingly we must learn what their experience is from the worship in which they share, the reading which they prize, and the prayers to which they turn for the expression of their own devotional life. Thus the Hebrew Psalms tell us something, not merely about the experience of the few persons who originally composed them, but chiefly about the experience of the millions, of all creeds, who have found in the Psalms the best expression of what they would like to say and cannot. The satisfaction found in the use of hymns, many of which are forthright testimonies to divine acquaintance, gives us similar evidence. The testimony implicit in prayer is similarly great. We cannot know how many pray, but all will agree that the number is enormous. Anyone who believes in prayer is bearing witness thereby to direct contact between the human and the divine, inasmuch as God is supposed to hear our prayers. Of course this relationship need not be mutual, but the chief reasons for denying the objective reality of what devout men experience is already overcome, if there is the real contact which prayer entails.

Any thorough study of the number of the reports must include some reference to the fact that the report is not universal in the human race. There is not space here for an exhaustive treatment of this matter, but two relevant points can be made briefly. One is that *no* human experience, not even sight, is strictly universal, for experience depends in part on receptive powers. The higher we go, as in music for example, the less universal experience is. The other point is that failure to report experience has no evidential value, *unless* the individual

concerned has met the appropriate conditions. The testimony of those who have not met the requirements has no logical weight and need not be seriously considered, whatever their qualifications in other ways. *The religious opinions of the unreligious are no more valuable than are the scientific opinions of the unscientific.*

(2) *The quality of the reporters* is more important than the numbers. Great numbers are not sufficient unless they include those who have qualitative fitness. The majority has frequently been wrong. Is there a substantial body of evidence coming from sensitive men, who are in command of their faculties, and properly qualified, on both moral and intellectual grounds, so that they inspire trust in that to which they bear testimony? We want to be sure of a substantial body of men and women of sufficiently good character not to engage in deliberate deceit and of sufficiently critical intelligence not to be self-deceived.

That answer is that there is a substantial body of evidence which meets these qualifications. That the great majority of reporters have been honest needs little support. It is not credible that the increase in personal effectiveness and power would come if men were consciously deceiving others in what they say on the deepest questions. This personal effectiveness is recognized even by those who reject the evidential value of the testimony. Furthermore, no serious reader can look at the written testimony of men like Pascal, Newman, and Fox and suppose that these men were engaged in a grand hoax. . . .

(3) *The agreement of the reports* is our third test of veracity. Even if the reports are numerous, and the reporters persons of proven integrity as well as critical judgment, the evidence is not good unless there is fundamental agreement in what is said. Part of the reason

for doubting the objective reference to the animals "seen" by patients suffering from *delirium tremens* is that two or more patients do not "see" the same snakes.

Upon a superficial view, it is easy to conclude that the reports of the religious consciousness are more remarkable for their diversity than for their convergence. This conclusion is strengthened by the development of many sects. As we consider the matter carefully, however, we discover that the obvious differences, so easily recognized by the populace, refer chiefly to matters of organization and liturgical details, on the one hand, and to differences of creed on the other. It is when we concentrate on the actual record of experience that we are struck with the great degree of convergence in the testimony. There is, indeed, the most distressing divergency on all questions *about* religion, but not in the experience *of* religion. To use William James' familiar distinction, that on which men have argued is "knowledge about," and that on which they have agreed is "acquaintance with." The conclusion to which James came as a result of his long empirical inquiry was that there is "a certain composite photograph of universal saintliness, the same in all religions, of which the features can easily be traced." [7]

Such conclusions are enforced by a simple experiment. Take a number of records of direct religious experience, read them to listeners, putting all into the same tongue, and see what success the listeners have in separating and locating them. In many cases there is no way to identify the reports at all, and an ancient Hindu testimony is sometimes mistaken for a modern Christian testimony. "We need not trouble ourselves to ask," writes Dr. Inge, "and we could seldom guess without asking, whether a paragraph describing the highest spiritual experiences was written in the Middle Ages or in modern times, in the north or south of Europe, by a Catholic or by a Protestant." [8] As a specific test we may submit the following testimony:

And he hath many times refreshed my soul in his presence, and given me assurance that I knew that estate in which He will never leave me, nor suffer me to be drawn from all which he has graciously fulfilled; for though various infirmities and temptations beset me, yet my heart cleaveth unto the Lord, in the everlasting bonds that cannot be broken.

The saints all tell the same story and this is the story they tell. It is hard to see how this impressive agreement can be accounted for apart from the hypothesis that the object to which so many severally point is a genuine one.

(4) *The fourth and final test of the veracity of religious experience is the difference it makes.* It is not necessary to be a pragmatist in order to recognize that the pragmatic test is one among others. That there has been a new quality of life in countless persons as a result of religious experience is beyond serious doubt.

In religion we cannot reasonably look for a mark on photographic plates, but we can reasonably look for a mark on human lives. If the experience of God is what men claim it is, we should expect to see a general change in their character; we should expect them to walk with a new step. It is this that we can check abundantly in a way that should be convincing to the open-minded. The evidence of altered lives, including both new strength and new tenderness, is so great that only a small portion of it has ever been committed to print. Not all of those who have reported religious experience have demonstrated "the fruits of

---

[7] William James, *The Varieties of Religious Experience*, p. 271.

[8] W. R. Inge, *Studies of English Mystics*, p. 35.

the spirit," but, in considering evidence of this kind, we are concerned not so much with what is universal as with what is typical. We can show the typical verification through moral strength, by pointing to characteristic experiences in different settings.

The sense of God's presence has been sufficient to make men courageous in the face of persecution, to sensitize their consciences to social wrong, such as that of slavery and poverty, and, above all, has suffused entire lives with joy. It was this last point, as noted earlier, which the scientific mind of Romanes was unable to explain away.

The pragmatic test of the veracity of religious experience has seldom been more vividly illustrated than in the letters of German pastors, which have been written in concentration camps during the last few dreadful years. The following expressions are characteristic:

"I cannot tell you how thankful I am for the inner experience I have been permitted to have in these days. Though I walk through the valley of the shadow, I fear no evil, for Thou art with me. This presence of God in such a situation becomes even now a precious reality. And how good it is that our faith may now manifest itself really as faith, not merely in words, but in deeds and in the attitude in which we stand ready to take upon ourselves unpleasantness for the sake of the faith, if God thus permits it that men oppress us for our faith's sake. No one will be able to say any more what formerly in foolishness was sometimes said: He merely talks that way because he is paid for it . . .

"God's ways are wonderful. And where He leads through dark ways, there one experiences his glory most. And again and again the experience is repeated: 'You thought to bring evil upon me, but God thought to turn it to good.' I am sure that all this, too, which we are now going through will serve 'only more

for the furtherance of the gospel' in our congregation, without the congregation's needing to get into unwise (imprudent or reckless) agitation if our church services are forbidden.

"God has thrown us Christian people in our church to-day out of all safe nests, out of all the nests of earthly security and human calculations and plans, cast us out as it were into emptiness, into nothingness. In sudden shock and terror we may have felt sometimes in these years as if we were plunging into a bottomless abyss, sinking away into nothingness. What are we now to do? Now we must fly if we do not want to be borne away by the storms of oppression into the yawning chasms of despair. But if we only really learn to believe, yes, learn really to believe in God, and in firm belief and trusting prayer spread our wings, then we shall experience—and how many times in these years we have already experienced it with amazement and awe—that we do not sink away; there is a power there which holds us, we are borne by God's eternal father-arms, we are sustained in the storms." [9]

What can we say in the face of testimonies so tremendous, testimonies repeated in so many generations? Drugs and delusions may sustain men for a time, but here is something which wears out all opposition. It makes weak men bold and proud men humble. Words seem impertinent and silence the only adequate response. If that which sustains men and makes them praise God in both bright and dark hours be not reality, where is reality to be found?

Thus we see that the empirical evidence for the hypothesis of God as real is the strongest evidence of all. It is the most difficult to escape, especially in a scientific age when experience is re-

---

[9] From *Und Lobten Gott,* private translation of my colleague, Helena Nye. The Student Christian Movement has brought out a translation, *I Was in Prison.*

spected. We need, however, to integrate this evidence with the other evidence which comes from our knowledge of nature and of our own being. The full strength of each line of evidence appears, not in isolation, but in conjunction.

The conclusion to which we are driven is that in religion we have a situation in which the evidence of objectivity is even better than it is in natural science be-cause the corroboration comes from such a long time and from such widely separated areas. The miracle of coincidence is so great that it is bound to be unacceptable to thoughtful persons. Yet what other alternative is there unless belief in God as objectively real is accepted? Herein lies part of the deep significance of the ancient saying that it is hard to believe, but harder still to disbelieve.

48. *The Will to Believe*[*]

WILLIAM JAMES (1842–1910)

In the recently published Life by Leslie Stephen of his brother, Fitz-James, there is an account of a school to which the latter went when he was a boy. The teacher, a certain Mr. Guest, used to converse with his pupils in this wise: "Gurney, what is the difference between justification and sanctification?—Stephen, prove the omnipotence of God!" etc. In the midst of our Harvard freethinking and indifference we are prone to imagine that here at your good old orthodox College conversation continues to be somewhat upon this order; and to show you that we at Harvard have not lost all interest in these vital subjects, I have brought with me to-night something like a sermon on justification by faith to read to you,—I mean an essay in justification *of* faith, a defence of our right to adopt a believing attitude in religious matters, in spite of the fact that our merely logical intellect may not have been coerced. 'The Will to Believe,' accordingly, is the title of my paper.

I have long defended to my own students the lawfulness of voluntary adopted faith; but as soon as they have got well imbued with the logical spirit, they have as a rule refused to admit my contention to be lawful philosophically, even though in point of fact they were personally all the time chock-full of some faith or other themselves. I am all the while, however, so profoundly convinced that my own position is correct, that your invitation has seemed to me a good occasion to make my statements more clear. Perhaps your minds will be more open than those with which I have hitherto had to deal. I will be as little technical as I can, though I must begin by setting up some technical distinctions that will help us in the end.

* Part of *The Will to Believe*. Published in *The New World*, June, 1896.

I

Let us give the name of *hypothesis* to anything that may be proposed to our belief; and just as the electricians speak of live and dead wires, let us speak of any hypothesis as either *live* or *dead*. A live hypothesis is one which appeals as a real possibility to him to whom it is proposed. If I ask you to believe in the Mahdi, the notion makes no electric connection with your nature,—it refuses to scintillate with any credibility at all. As an hypothesis it is completely dead. To an Arab, however (even if he be not one of the Mahdi's followers), the hypothesis is among the mind's possibilities: it is alive. This shows that deadness and liveness in an hypothesis are not intrinsic properties, but relations to the individual thinker. They are measured by his willingness to act. The maximum of liveness in an hypothesis means willingness to act irrevocably. Practically, that means belief; but there is some believing tendency wherever there is willingness to act at all.

Next, let us call the decision between two hypotheses an *option*. Options may be of several kinds. They may be—1, *living* or *dead;* 2, *forced* or *avoidable;* 3, *momentous* or *trivial;* and for our purposes we may call an option a *genuine* option when it is of the forced, living, and momentous kind.

1. A living option is one in which both hypotheses are live ones. If I say to you: "Be a theosophist or be a Mohammedan," it is probably a dead option, because for you neither hypothesis is likely to be alive. But if I say: "Be an agnostic or be a Christian," it is otherwise: trained as you are, each hypothesis makes some appeal, however small, to your belief.

2. Next, if I say to you: "Choose between going out with your umbrella or without it," I do not offer you a genuine option, for it is not forced. You can

easily avoid it by not going out at all. Similarly, if I say, "Either love me or hate me," "Either call my theory true or call it false," your option is avoidable. You may remain indifferent to me, neither loving nor hating, and you may decline to offer any judgment as to my theory. But if I say, "Either accept this truth or go without it," I put on you a forced option, for there is no standing place outside of the alternative. Every dilemma based on a complete logical disjunction, with no possibility of not choosing, is an option of this forced kind.

3. Finally, if I were Dr. Nansen and proposed to you to join my North Pole expedition, your option would be momentous; for this would probably be your only similar opportunity, and your choice now would either exclude you from the North Pole sort of immortality altogether or put at least the chance of it into your hands. He who refuses to embrace a unique opportunity loses the prize as surely as if he tried and failed. *Per contra*, the option is trivial when the opportunity is not unique, when the stake is insignificant, or when the decision is reversible if it later prove unwise. Such trivial options abound in the scientific life. A chemist finds an hypothesis live enough to spend a year in its verification: he believes in it to that extent. But if his experiments prove inconclusive either way, he is quit for his loss of time, no vital harm being done.

It will facilitate our discussion if we keep all these distinctions well in mind....

IV

The thesis I defend is, briefly stated, this: *Our passional nature not only lawfully may, but must, decide an option between propositions, whenever it is a genuine option that cannot by its nature be decided on intellectual grounds; for to say, under such circumstances, "Do not decide, but leave the question open," is itself a passional decision,—just like deciding yes or no,—and is attended with the same risk of losing the truth.* The thesis thus abstractly expressed will, I trust, soon become quite clear. . . .

VIII

And now, after all this introduction, let us go straight at our question. I have said, and now repeat it, that not only as a matter of fact do we find our passional nature influencing us in our opinions, but that there are some options between opinions in which this influence must be regarded both as an inevitable and as a lawful determinant of our choice.

I fear here that some of you my hearers will begin to scent danger, and lend an inhospitable ear. Two first steps of passion you have indeed had to admit as necessary,—we must think so as to avoid dupery, and we must think so as to gain truth; but the surest path to those ideal consummations, you will probably consider, is from now onwards to take no further passional step.

Well, of course, I agree as far as the facts will allow. Wherever the option between losing truth and gaining it is not momentous, we can throw the chance of *gaining truth* away, and at any rate save ourselves from any chance of *believing falsehood,* by not making up our minds at all till objective evidence has come. In scientific questions, this is almost always the case; and even in human affairs in general, the need of acting is seldom so urgent that a false belief to act on is better than no belief at all. Law courts, indeed, have to decide on the best evidence attainable for the moment, because a judge's duty is to make law as well as to ascertain it, and (as a learned judge once said to me) few cases are worth spending much time over: the great thing is to have them decided on *any* acceptable principle, and got out of the way. But in our dealings with objective nature we obviously are recorders, not makers, of the truth; and

decisions for the mere sake of deciding promptly and getting on to the next business would be wholly out of place. Throughout the breadth of physical nature facts are what they are quite independently of us, and seldom is there any such hurry about them that the risks of being duped by believing a premature theory need be faced. The questions here are always trivial options, the hypotheses are hardly living (at any rate not living for us spectators), the choice between believing truth or falsehood is seldom forced. The attitude of sceptical balance is therefore the absolutely wise one if we would escape mistakes. What difference, indeed, does it make to most of us whether we have or have not a theory of the Röntgen rays, whether we believe or not in mind-stuff, or have a conviction about the causality of conscious states? It makes no difference. Such options are not forced on us. On every account it is better not to make them, but still keep weighing reasons *pro et contra* with an indifferent hand.

I speak, of course, here of the purely judging mind. For purposes of discovery such indifference is to be less highly recommended, and science would be far less advanced than she is if the passionate desires of individuals to get their own faiths confirmed had been kept out of the game. See for example the sagacity which Spencer and Weismann now display. On the other hand, if you want an absolute duffer in an investigation, you must, after all, take the man who has no interest whatever in its results: he is the warranted incapable, the positive fool. The most useful investigator, because the most sensitive observer, is always he whose eager interest in one side of the question is balanced by an equally keen nervousness lest he become deceived.[1] Science has organized this

---

[1] Compare Wilfrid Ward's Essay, "The Wish to Believe," in his *Witnesses to the Unseen,* Macmillan & Co., 1893.

nervousness into a regular *technique,* her so-called method of verification; and she has fallen so deeply in love with the method that one may even say she has ceased to care for truth by itself at all. It is only truth as technically verified that interests her. The truth of truths might come in merely affirmative form, and she would decline to touch it. Such truth as that, she might repeat with Clifford, would be stolen in defiance of her duty to mankind. Human passions, however, are stronger than technical rules. "Le coeur a ses raisons," as Pascal says, "que la raison ne connait pas"; and however indifferent to all but the bare rules of the game the umpire, the abstract intellect, may be, the concrete players who furnish him the materials to judge of are usually, each one of them, in love with some pet 'live hypothesis' of his own. Let us agree, however, that wherever there is no forced option, the dispassionately judicial intellect with no pet hypothesis, saving us, as it does, from dupery at any rate, ought to be our ideal.

The question next arises: Are there not somewhere forced options in our speculative questions, and can we (as men who may be interested at least as much in positively gaining truth as in merely escaping dupery) always wait with impunity till the coercive evidence shall have arrived? It seems *a priori* improbable that the truth should be so nicely adjusted to our needs and powers as that. In the great boarding-house of nature, the cakes and the butter and the syrup seldom come out so even and leave the plates so clean. Indeed, we should view them with scientific suspicion if they did.

IX

Moral questions immediately present themselves as questions whose solution cannot wait for sensible proof. A moral question is a question not of what sensibly exists, but of what is good, or would be good if it did exist. Science can tell us what exists; but to compare the *worths,* both of what exists and of what does not exist, we must consult not science, but what Pascal calls our heart. Science herself consults her heart when she lays it down that the infinite ascertainment of fact and correction of false belief are the supreme goods for man. Challenge the statement, and science can only repeat it oracularly, or else prove it by showing that such ascertainment and correction bring man all sorts of other goods which man's heart in turn declares. The question of having moral beliefs at all or not having them is decided by our will. Are our moral preferences true or false, or are they only odd biological phenomena, making things good or bad for *us,* but in themselves indifferent? How can your pure intellect decide? If your heart does not *want* a world of moral reality, your head will assuredly never make you believe in one. Mephistophelian scepticism, indeed, will satisfy the head's play-instincts much better than any rigorous idealism can. Some men (even at the student age) are so naturally cool-hearted that the moralistic hypothesis never has for them any pungent life, and in their supercilious presence the hot young moralist always feels strangely ill at ease. The appearance of knowingness is on their side, of *naïveté* and gullibility on his. Yet, in the inarticulate heart of him, he clings to it that he is not a dupe, and that there is a realm in which (as Emerson says) all their wit and intellectual superiority is no better than the cunning of a fox. Moral scepticism can no more be refuted or proved by logic than intellectual scepticism can. When we stick to it that there *is* truth (be it of either kind), we do so with our whole nature, and resolve to stand or fall by the results. The sceptic with his whole nature adopts the doubting attitude; but which of us is the wiser, Omniscience only knows.

Turn now from these wide questions of good to a certain class of questions of fact, questions concerning personal relations, states of mind between one man and another. *Do you like me or not?*— for example. Whether you do or not depends, in countless instances, on whether I meet you half-way, am willing to assume that you must like me, and show you trust and expectation. The previous faith on my part in your liking's existence is in such cases what makes your liking come. But if I stand aloof, and refuse to budge an inch until I have objective evidence, until you shall have done something apt, as the absolutists say, *ad extorquendum assensum meum,* ten to one your liking never comes. How many women's hearts are vanquished by the mere sanguine insistence of some man that they *must* love him! he will not consent to the hypothesis that they cannot. The desire for a certain kind of truth here brings about that special truth's existence; and so it is in innumerable cases of other sorts. Who gains promotions, boons, appointments, but the man in whose life they are seen to play the part of live hypotheses, who discounts them, sacrifices other things for their sake before they have come, and takes risks for them in advance? His faith acts on the powers above him as a claim, and creates its own verification.

A social organism of any sort whatever, large or small, is what it is because each member proceeds to his own duty with a trust that the other members will simultaneously do theirs. Wherever a desired result is achieved by the co-operation of many independent persons, its existence as a fact is a pure consequence of the precursive faith in one another of those immediately concerned. A government, an army, a commercial system, a ship, a college, an athletic team, all exist on this condition, without which not

only is nothing achieved, but nothing is even attempted. A whole train of passengers (individually brave enough) will be looted by a few highwaymen, simply because the latter can count on one another, while each passenger fears that if he makes a movement of resistance, he will be shot before any one else backs him up. If we believed that the whole car-full would rise at once with us, we should each severally rise, and train-robbing would never even be attempted. There are, then, cases where a fact cannot come at all unless a preliminary faith exists in its coming. *And where faith in a fact can help create the fact,* that would be an insane logic which should say that faith running ahead of scientific evidence is the 'lowest kind of immorality' into which a thinking being can fall. Yet such is the logic by which our scientific absolutists pretend to regulate our lives!

X

In truths dependent on our personal action, then, faith based on desire is certainly a lawful and possibly an indispensable thing.

But now, it will be said, these are all childish human cases, and have nothing to do with great cosmical matters, like the question of religious faith. Let us then pass on to that. Religions differ so much in their accidents that in discussing the religious question we must make it very generic and broad. What then do we now mean by the religious hypothesis? Science says things are; morality says some things are better than other things; and religion says essentially two things.

First, she says that the best things are the more eternal things, the overlapping things, the things in the universe that throw the last stone, so to speak, and say the final word. "Perfection is eternal,"— this phrase of Charles Secrétan seems a good way of putting this first affirmation of religion, an affirmation which obviously cannot yet be verified scientifically at all.

The second affirmation of religion is that we are better off even now if we believe her first affirmation to be true.

Now, let us consider what the logical elements of this situation are *in case the religious hypothesis in both its branches be really true.* (Of course, we must admit that possibility at the outset. If we are to discuss the question at all, it must involve a living option. If for any of you religion be a hypothesis that cannot, by any living possibility be true, then you need go no farther. I speak to the 'saving remnant' alone.) So proceeding, we see, first, that religion offers itself as a *momentous* option. We are supposed to gain, even now, by our belief, and to lose by our non-belief, a certain vital good. Secondly, religion is a *forced* option, so far as that good goes. We cannot escape the issue by remaining sceptical and waiting for more light, because, although we do avoid error in that way *if religion be untrue,* we lose the good, *if it be true,* just as certainly as if we positively chose to disbelieve. It is as if a man should hesitate indefinitely to ask a certain woman to marry him because he was not perfectly sure that she would prove an angel after he brought her home. Would he not cut himself off from that particular angel-possibility as decisively as if he went and married some one else? Scepticism, then, is not avoidance of option; it is option of a certain particular kind of risk. *Better risk loss of truth than chance of error,*—that is your faith-vetoer's exact position. He is actively playing his take as much as the believer is; he is backing the field against the religious hypothesis, just as the believer is backing the religious hypothesis against the field. To preach scepticism to us as a duty until 'sufficient evidence' for religion be found, is tantamount therefore to telling us, when in presence of the religious hypothesis, that to yield to our fear of its being error is wiser and better than to yield to our hope that it may be true. It is not intellect against all passions, then; it is only intellect with one passion laying down its law. And by what, forsooth, is the supreme wisdom of this passion warranted? Dupery for dupery, what proof is there that dupery through hope is so much worse than dupery through fear? I, for one, can see no proof; and I simply refuse obedience to the scientist's command to imitate his kind of option, in a case where my own stake is important enough to give me the right to choose my own form of risk. If religion be true and the evidence for it be still insufficient, I do not wish, by putting your extinguisher upon my nature (which feels to me as if it had after all some business in this matter), to forfeit my sole chance in life of getting upon the winning side,—that chance depending, of course, on my willingness to run the risk of acting as if my passional need of taking the world religiously might be prophetic and right.

All this is on the supposition that it really may be prophetic and right, and that even, to us who are discussing the matter, religion is a live hypothesis which may be true. Now, to most of us religion comes in a still further way that makes a veto on our active faith even more illogical. The more perfect and more eternal aspect of the universe is represented in our religions as having personal form. The universe is no longer a mere *It* to us, but a *Thou,* if we are religious; and any relation that may be possible from person to person might be possible here. For instance, although in one sense we are passive portions of the universe, in another we show a curious autonomy, as if we were small active centres on our own account. We feel, too, as if the appeal of religion to us were made to our own active good-will, as if evidence might be forever withheld from us unless we met the hypothesis half-way. To take a trivial illustration: just as a man who in a company of gentlemen made no advances, asked a warrant for every concession, and believed no one's word without proof, would cut himself off by such churlishness from all the social rewards that a more trusting spirit would earn,—so here, one who should shut himself up in snarling logicality and try to make the gods extort his recognition willy-nilly, or not get it at all, might cut himself off forever from his only opportunity of making the gods' acquaintance. This feeling, forced on us we know not whence, that by obstinately believing that there are gods (although not to do so would be so easy both for our logic and our life) we are doing the universe the deepest service we can, seems part of the living essence of the religious hypothesis. If the hypothesis *were* true in all its parts, including this one, then pure intellectualism, with its veto on our making willing advances, would be an absurdity; and some participation of our sympathetic nature would be logically required. I, therefore, for one, cannot see my way to accepting the agnostic rules for truth-seeking, or wilfully agree to keep my willing nature out of the game. I cannot do so for this plain reason, that *a rule of thinking which would absolutely prevent me from acknowledging certain kinds of truth if those kinds of truth were really there, would be an irrational rule.* That for me is the long and short of the formal logic of the situation, no matter what the kinds of truth might materially be.

I confess I do not see how this logic can be escaped. But sad experience makes me fear that some of you may still shrink from radically saying with me, *in abstracto,* that we have the right to believe at our own risk any hypothesis that is live enough to tempt our will. I suspect, however, that if this is so, it is because you have got away from the abstract logical point of view altogether, and are thinking (perhaps without realizing it) of some particular religious hypothesis which for you is dead. The freedom to 'believe what we will' you apply to the case of some patent superstition; and the faith you think of is the faith defined by the schoolboy when he said, "Faith is when you believe something that you know ain't true." I can only repeat that this is misapprehension. *In concreto,* the freedom to believe can only cover living options which the intellect of the individual cannot by itself resolve; and living options never seem absurdities to him who has them to consider. When I look at the religious question as it really puts itself to concrete men, and when I think of all the possibilities which both practically and theoretically it involves, then this command that we shall put a stopper on our heart, instincts, and courage, and *wait—* acting of course meanwhile more or less as if religion were *not* true [1]—till doomsday, or till such time as our intellect and senses working together may have raked in evidence enough,—this command, I say, seems to me the queerest idol ever manufactured in the philosophic cave. Were we scholastic absolutists, there might be more excuse. If we had an infallible intellect with its objective certitudes, we might feel ourselves disloyal

---

[1] Since belief is measured by action, he who forbids us to believe religion to be true, necessarily also forbids us to act as we should if we did believe it to be true. The whole defence of religious faith hinges upon action. If the action required or inspired by the religious hypothesis is in no way different from that dictated by the naturalistic hypothesis, then religious faith is a pure superfluity, better pruned away, and controversy about its legitimacy is a piece of idle trifling, unworthy of serious minds. I myself believe, of course, that the religious hypothesis gives to the world an expression which specifically determines our reactions, and makes them in a large part unlike what they might be on a purely naturalistic scheme of belief.

to such a perfect organ of knowledge in not trusting to it exclusively, in not waiting for its releasing word. But if we are empiricists, if we believe that no bell in us tolls to let us know for certain when truth is in our grasp, then it seems a piece of idle fantasticality to preach so solemnly our duty of waiting for the bell. Indeed we *may* wait if we will,—I hope you do not think that I am denying that, —but if we do so, we do so at our peril as much as if we believed. In either case we *act*, taking our life in our hands. No one of us ought to issue vetoes to the other, nor should we bandy words of abuse. We ought, on the contrary, delicately and profoundly to respect one another's mental freedom: then only shall we bring about the intellectual republic; then only shall we have that spirit of inner tolerance without which all our outer tolerance is soulless, and which is empiricism's glory; then only shall we live and let live, in speculative as well as in practical things.

I began by a reference to Fitz-James Stephen; let me end by a quotation from him. "What do you think of yourself? What do you think of the world? ... These are questions with which all must deal as it seems good to them. They are riddles of the Sphinx, and in some way or other we must deal with them. ... In all important transactions of life we have to take a leap in the dark. ... If we decide to leave the riddles unanswered, that is a choice; if we waver in our answer, that, too, is a choice: but whatever choice we make, we make it at our peril. If a man chooses to turn his back altogether on God and the future, no one can prevent him; no one can show beyond reasonable doubt that he is mistaken. If a man thinks otherwise and acts as he thinks, I do not see that any one can prove that *he* is mistaken. Each must act as he thinks best; and if he is wrong, so much the worse for him. We stand on a mountain pass in the midst of whirling snow and blinding mist, through which we get glimpses now and then of paths which may be deceptive. If we stand still we shall be frozen to death. If we take the wrong road we shall be dashed to pieces. We do not certainly know whether there is any right one. What must we do? 'Be strong and of a good courage.' Act for the best, hope for the best, and take what comes. ... If death ends all, we cannot meet death better." [2]

[2] Liberty, Equality, Fraternity, p. 353, 2d edition. London, 1874.

49. How Religion May Be an Embodiment of Reason [*]

GEORGE SANTAYANA (1863–1952)

Experience has repeatedly confirmed that well-known maxim of Bacon's, that "a little philosophy inclineth man's mind to atheism, but depth in philosophy bringeth men's minds about to religion." In every age the most comprehensive thinkers have found in the religion of

[*] Chapter I, *Reason in Religion*. By kind permission of the publishers, Charles Scribner's Sons.

their time and country something they could accept, interpreting and illustrating that religion so as to give it depth and universal application. Even the heretics and atheists, if they have had profundity, turn out after a while to be forerunners of some new orthodoxy. What they rebel against is a religion alien to their nature; they are atheists only by accident, and relatively to a convention which inwardly offends them, but they yearn mightily in their own souls after the religious acceptance of a world interpreted in their own fashion. So it appears in the end that their atheism and loud protestation were in fact the hastier part of their thought, since what emboldened them to deny the poor world's faith was that they were too impatient to understand it. Indeed, the enlightenment common to young wits and worm-eaten old satirists, who plume themselves on detecting the scientific ineptitude of religion—something which the blindest half see—is not nearly enlightened enough; it points to notorious facts incompatible with religious tenets literally taken, but it leaves unexplored the habits of thought from which those tenets sprang, their original meaning, and their true function. Such studies would bring the sceptic face to face with the mystery and pathos of mortal existence. They would make him understand why religion is so profoundly moving and in a sense so profoundly just. There must needs be something humane and necessary in an influence that has become the most general sanction of virtue, the chief occasion for art and philosophy, and the source, perhaps, of the best human happiness. If nothing, as Hooker said, is "so malapert as a splenetic religion," a sour irreligion is almost as perverse.

At the same time, when Bacon penned the sage epigram we have quoted he forgot to add that the God to whom depth in philosophy brings back men's minds is far from being the same from whom a little philosophy estranges them. It would be pitiful indeed if mature reflection bred no better conceptions than those which have drifted down the muddy stream of time, where tradition and passion have jumbled everything together. Traditional conceptions, when they are felicitous, may be adopted by the poet, but they must be purified by the moralist and disintegrated by the philosopher. Each religion, so dear to those whose life it sanctifies, and fulfilling so necessary a function in the society that has adopted it, necessarily contradicts every other religion, and probably contradicts itself. What religion a man shall have is a historical accident, quite as much as what language he shall speak. In the rare circumstances where a choice is possible, he may, with some difficulty, make an exchange; but even then he is only adopting a new convention which may be more agreeable to his personal temper but which is essentially as arbitrary as the old.

The attempt to speak without speaking any particular language is not more hopeless than the attempt to have a religion that shall be no religion in particular. A courier's or a dragoman's speech may indeed be often unusual and drawn from disparate sources, not without some mixture of personal originality; but that private jargon will have a meaning only because of its analogy to one or more conventional languages and its obvious derivation from them. So travellers from one religion to another, people who have lost their spiritual nationality, may often retain a neutral and confused residuum of belief, which they may egregiously regard as the essence of all religion, so little may they remember the graciousness and naturalness of that ancestral accent which a perfect religion should have. Yet a moment's probing of the conceptions surviving in such minds will show them to be nothing but vestiges of old beliefs, creases which thought, even if emptied of all dogmatic tenets, has not been able to smooth away at its first unfolding. Later generations, if they have any religion at all, will be found either to revert to ancient authority, or to attach themselves spontaneously to something wholly novel and immensely positive, to some faith promulgated by a fresh genius and passionately embraced by a converted people. Thus every living and healthy religion has a marked idiosyncrasy. Its power consists in its special and surprising message and in the bias which that revelation gives to life. The vistas it opens and the mysteries it propounds are another world to live in; and another world to live in—whether we expect ever to pass wholly into it or no—is what we mean by having a religion.

What relation, then, does this great business of the soul, which we call religion, bear to the Life of Reason? That the relation between the two is close seems clear from several circumstances. The Life of Reason is the seat of all ultimate values. Now the history of mankind will show us that whenever spirits at once lofty and intense have seemed to attain the highest joys, they have envisaged and attained them in religion. Religion would therefore seem to be a vehicle or a factor in rational life, since the ends of rational life are attained by it. Moreover, the Life of Reason is an ideal to which everything in the world should be subordinated; it establishes lines of moral cleavage everywhere and makes right eternally different from wrong. Religion does the same thing. It makes absolute moral decisions. It sanctions, unifies, and transforms ethics. Religion thus exercises a function of the Life of Reason. And a further function which is common to both is that of emancipating man from his personal limitations. In different ways religions promise to transfer the soul to better

conditions. A supernaturally favoured kingdom is to be established for posterity upon earth, or for all the faithful in heaven, or the soul is to be freed by repeated purgations from all taint and sorrow, or it is to be lost in the absolute, or it is to become an influence and an object of adoration in the places it once haunted or wherever the activities it once loved may be carried on by future generations of its kindred. Now reason in its way lays before us all these possibilities: it points to common objects, political and intellectual, in which an individual may lose what is mortal and accidental in himself and immortalise what is rational and human; it teaches us how sweet and fortunate death may be to those whose spirit can still live in their country and in their ideas; it reveals the radiating effects of action and the eternal objects of thought.

Yet the difference in tone and language must strike us, so soon as it is philosophy that speaks. That change should remind us that even if the function of religion and that of reason coincide, this function is performed in the two cases by very different organs. Religions are many, reason one. Religion consists of conscious ideas, hopes, enthusiasms, and objects of worship; it operates by grace and flourishes by prayer. Reason, on the other hand, is a mere principle or potential order, on which, indeed, we may come to reflect, but which exists in us ideally only, without variation or stress of any kind. We conform or do not conform to it; it does not urge or chide us, nor call for any emotions on our part other than those naturally aroused by the various objects which it unfolds in their true nature and proportion. Religion brings some order into life by weighting it with new materials. Reason adds to the natural materials only the perfect order which it introduces into them. Rationality is nothing but a form, an ideal constitution which experience may more or less embody. Religion is a part of experience itself, a mass of sentiments and ideas. The one is an inviolate principle, the other a changing and struggling force. And yet this struggling and changing force of religion seems to direct man toward something eternal. It seems to make for an ultimate harmony within the soul and for an ultimate harmony between the soul and all the soul depends upon. So that religion, in its intent, is a more conscious and direct pursuit of the Life of Reason than is society, science, or art. For these approach and fill out the ideal life tentatively and piecemeal, hardly regarding the goal or caring for the ultimate justification of their instinctive aims. Religion also has an instinctive and blind side, and bubbles up in all manner of chance practices and intuitions; soon, however, it feels its way toward the heart of things, and, from whatever quarter it may come, veers in the direction of the ultimate.

Nevertheless, we must confess that this religious pursuit of the Life of Reason has been singularly abortive. Those within the pale of each religion may prevail upon themselves to express satisfaction with its results, thanks to a fond partiality in reading the past and generous draughts of hope for the future; but any one regarding the various religions at once and comparing their achievements with what reason requires, must feel how terrible is the disappointment which they have one and all prepared for mankind. Their chief anxiety has been to offer imaginary remedies for mortal ills, some of which are incurable essentially, while others might have been really cured by well-directed effort. The Greek oracles, for instance, pretended to heal our natural ignorance, which has its appropriate though difficult cure, while the Christian vision of heaven pretended to be an antidote to our natural death,

the inevitable correlate of birth and of a changing and conditioned existence. By methods of this sort little can be done for the real betterment of life. To confuse intelligence and dislocate sentiment by gratuitous fictions is a short-sighted way of pursuing happiness. Nature is soon avenged. An unhealthy exaltation and a one-sided morality have to be followed by regrettable reactions. When these come, the real rewards of life may seem vain to a relaxed vitality, and the very name of virtue may irritate young spirits untrained in any natural excellence. Thus religion too often debauches the morality it comes to sanction, and impedes the science it ought to fulfil.

What is the secret of this ineptitude? Why does religion, so near to rationality in its purpose, fall so far short of it in its texture and in its results? The answer is easy: Religion pursues rationality through the imagination. When it explains events or assigns causes, it is an imaginative substitute for science. When it gives precepts, insinuates ideals, or remoulds aspiration, it is an imaginative substitute for wisdom—I mean for the deliberate and impartial pursuit of all good. The conditions and the aims of life are both represented in religion poetically, but this poetry tends to arrogate to itself literal truth and moral authority, neither of which it possesses. Hence the depth and importance of religion become intelligible no less than its contradictions and practical disasters. Its object is the same as that of reason, but its method is to proceed by intuition and by unchecked poetical conceits. These are repeated and vulgarised in proportion to their original fineness and significance, till they pass for reports of objective truth and come to constitute a world of faith, superposed upon the world of experience and regarded as materially enveloping it, if not in space at least in time and in existence. The only truth of religion comes from its interpretation of life, from its symbolic rendering of that moral experience which it springs out of and which it seeks to elucidate. Its falsehood comes from the insidious misunderstanding which clings to it, to the effect that these poetic conceptions are not merely representations of experience as it is or should be, but are rather information about experience or reality elsewhere—an experience and reality which, strangely enough, supply just the defects betrayed by reality and experience here.

Thus religion has the same original relation to life that poetry has; only poetry, which never pretends to literal validity, adds a pure value to existence, the value of a liberal imaginative exercise. The poetic value of religion would initially be greater than that of poetry itself, because religion deals with higher and more practical themes, with sides of life which are in greater need of some imaginative touch and ideal interpretation than are those pleasant or pompous things which ordinary poetry dwells upon. But this initial advantage is neutralised in part by the abuse to which religion is subject, whenever it symbolic rightness is taken for scientific truth. Like poetry, it improves the world only by imagining it improved, but not content with making this addition to the mind's furniture—an addition which might be useful and ennobling—it thinks to confer a more radical benefit by persuading mankind that, in spite of appearances, the world is really such as that rather arbitrary idealisation has painted it. This spurious satisfaction is naturally the prelude to many a disappointment, and the soul has infinite trouble to emerge again from the artificial problems and sentiments into which it is thus plunged. The value of religion becomes equivocal. Religion remains an imaginative achievement, a symbolic representation of moral reality which may have a most important function in

vitalising the mind and in transmitting, by way of parables, the lessons of experience. But it becomes at the same time a continuous incidental deception; and this deception, in proportion as it is strenuously denied to be such, can work indefinite harm in the world and in the conscience.

On the whole, however, religion should not be conceived as having taken the place of anything better, but rather as having come to relieve situations which, but for its presence, would have been infinitely worse. In the thick of active life, or in the monotony of practical slavery, there is more need to stimulate fancy than to control it. Natural instinct is not much disturbed in the human brain by what may happen in that thin superstratum of ideas which commonly overlays it. We must not blame religion for preventing the development of a moral and natural science which at any rate would seldom have appeared; we must rather thank it for the sensibility, the reverence, the speculative insight which it has introduced into the world.

We may therefore proceed to analyse the significance and the function which religion has had at its different stages, and, without disguising or in the least condoning its confusion with literal truth, we may allow ourselves to enter as sympathetically as possible into its various conceptions and emotions. They have made up the inner life of many sages, and of all those who without great genius or learning have lived steadfastly in the spirit. The feeling of reverence should itself be treated with reverence, although not at a sacrifice of truth, with which alone, in the end, reverence is compatible. Nor have we any reason to be intolerant of the partialities and contradictions which religions display. Were we dealing with a science, such contradictions would have to be instantly solved and removed; but when we are concerned with the poetic interpretation of experience, contradiction means only variety, and variety means spontaneity, wealth of resource, and a nearer approach to total adequacy.

If we hope to gain any understanding of these matters we must begin by taking them out of that heated and fanatical atmosphere in which the Hebrew tradition has enveloped them. The Jews had no philosophy, and when their national traditions came to be theoretically explicated and justified, they were made to issue in a puerile scholasticism and a rabid intolerance. The question of monotheism, for instance, was a terrible question to the Jews. Idolatry did not consist in worshipping a god who, not being ideal, might be unworthy of worship, but rather in recognising other gods than the one worshipped in Jerusalem. To the Greeks, on the contrary, whose philosophy was enlightened and ingenuous, monotheism and polytheism seemed perfectly innocent and compatible. To say God or the gods was only to use different expressions for the same influence, now viewed in its abstract unity and correlation with all existence, now viewed in its various manifestations in moral life, in nature, or in history. So that what in Plato, Aristotle, and the Stoics meets us at every step—the combination of monotheism with polytheism—is no contradiction, but merely an intelligent variation of phrase to indicate various aspects or functions in physical and moral things. When religion appears to us in this light its contradictions and controversies lose all their bitterness. Each doctrine will simply represent the moral plane on which they live who have devised or adopted it. Religions will thus be better or worse, never true or false. We shall be able to lend ourselves to each in turn, and seek to draw from it the secret of its inspiration.

50. *Faith and Its Object**

JOHN DEWEY (1859–1952)

All religions, as I pointed out in the preceding chapter, involve specific intellectual beliefs, and they attach—some greater, some less—importance to assent to these doctrines as true, true in the intellectual sense. They have literatures held especially sacred, containing historical material with which the validity of the religions is connected. They have developed a doctrinal apparatus it is incumbent upon "believers" (with varying degrees of strictness in different religions) to accept. They also insist that there is some special and isolated channel of access to the truths they hold.

No one will deny, I suppose, that the present crisis in religion is intimately bound up with these claims. The skepticism and agnosticism that are rife and that from the standpoint of the religionist are fatal to the religious spirit are directly bound up with the intellectual contents, historical, cosmological, ethical, and theological, asserted to be indispensable in everything religious. There

* Part II in *A Common Faith*. By kind permission of the publishers, Yale University Press.

is no need for me here to go with any minuteness into the causes that have generated doubt and disbelief, uncertainty and rejection, as to these contents. It is enough to point out that all the beliefs and ideas in question, whether having to do with historical and literary matters, or with astronomy, geology and biology, or with the creation and structure of the world and man, are connected with the supernatural, and that this connection is the factor that has brought doubt upon them; the factor that from the standpoint of historic and institutional religions is sapping the religious life itself.

The obvious and simple facts of the case are that some views about the origin and constitution of the world and man, some views about the course of human history and personages and incidents in that history, have become so interwoven with religion as to be identified with it. On the other hand, the growth of knowledge and of its methods and tests has been such as to make acceptance of these beliefs increasingly onerous and even impossible for large numbers of cultivated men and women. With such persons, the result is that the more these ideas are used as the basis and justification of a religion, the more dubious that religion becomes.

Protestant denominations have largely abandoned the idea that particular ecclesiastic sources can authoritatively determine cosmic, historic and theological beliefs. The more liberal among them have at least mitigated the older belief that individual hardness and corruption of heart are the causes of intellectual rejection of the intellectual apparatus of the Christian religion. But these denominations have also, with exceptions numerically insignificant, retained a certain indispensable minimum of intellectual content. They ascribe peculiar religious force to certain literary documents and certain historic person-

ages. Even when they have greatly reduced the bulk of intellectual content to be accepted, they have insisted at least upon theism and the immortality of the individual.

It is no part of my intention to rehearse in any detail the weighty facts that collectively go by the name of the conflict of science and religion—a conflict that is not done away with by calling it a conflict of science with theology, as long as even a minimum of intellectual assent is prescribed as essential. The impact of astronomy not merely upon the older cosmogony of religion but upon elements of creeds dealing with historic events—witness the idea of ascent into heaven—is familiar. Geological discoveries have displaced creation myths which once bulked large. Biology has revolutionized conceptions of soul and mind which once occupied a central place in religious beliefs and ideas, and this science has made a profound impression upon ideas of sin, redemption, and immortality. Anthropology, history and literary criticism have furnished a radically different version of the historic events and personages upon which Christian religions have built. Psychology is already opening to us natural explanations of phenomena so extraordinary that once their supernatural origin was, so to say, the natural explanation.

The significant bearing for my purpose of all this is that new methods of inquiry and reflection have become for the educated man today the final arbiter of all questions of fact, existence, and intellectual assent. Nothing less than a revolution in the "seat of intellectual authority" has taken place. This revolution, rather than any particular aspect of its impact upon this and that religious belief, is the central thing. In this revolution, every defeat is a stimulus to renewed inquiry; every victory won is the open door to more discoveries, and every discovery is a new seed planted in the soil of intelligence, from which grow fresh plants with new fruits. The mind of man is being habituated to a new method and ideal: There is but one sure road of access to truth—the road of patient, coöperative inquiry operating by means of observation, experiment, record and controlled reflection.

The scope of the change is well illustrated by the fact that whenever a particular outpost is surrendered it is usually met by the remark from a liberal theologian that the particular doctrine or supposed historic or literary tenet surrendered was never, after all, an intrinsic part of religious belief, and that without it the true nature of religion stands out more clearly than before. Equally significant is the growing gulf between fundamentalists and liberals in the churches. What is not realized— although perhaps it is more definitely seen by fundamentalists than by liberals —is that the issue does not concern this and that piecemeal *item* of belief, but centers in the question of the method by which any and every item of intellectual belief is to be arrived at and justified.

The positive lesson is that religious qualities and values if they are real at all are not bound up with any single item of intellectual assent, not even that of the existence of the God of theism; and that, under existing conditions, the religious function in experience can be emancipated only through the surrender of the whole notion of special truths that are religious by their own nature, together with the idea of peculiar avenues of access to such truths. For were we to admit that there is but one method for ascertaining fact and truth—that conveyed by the word "scientific" in its most general and generous sense—no discovery in any branch of knowledge and inquiry could then disturb the faith that is religious. I should describe this faith as the unification of the self through allegiance to inclusive ideal ends, which imagination presents to us and to which the human will responds as worthy of controlling our desires and choices.

It is probably impossible to imagine the amount of intellectual energy that has been diverted from normal processes of arriving at intellectual conclusions because it has gone into rationalization of the doctrines entertained by historic religions. The set that has thus been given the general mind is much more harmful, to my mind, than are the consequences of any one particular item of belief, serious as have been those flowing from acceptance of some of them. The modern liberal version of the intellectual content of Christianity seems to the modern mind to be more rational than some of the earlier doctrines that have been reacted against. Such is not the case in fact. The theological philosophers of the Middle Ages had no greater difficulty in giving rational form to all the doctrines of the Roman church than has the liberal theologian of today in formulating and justifying intellectually the doctrines he entertains. This statement is as applicable to the doctrine of continuing miracles, penance, indulgences, saints and angels, etc., as to the trinity, incarnation, atonement, and the sacraments. The fundamental question, I repeat, is not of this and that article of intellectual belief but of intellectual habit, method and criterion.

One method of swerving aside the impact of changed knowledge and method upon the intellectual content of religion is the method of division of territory and jurisdiction into two parts. Formerly these were called the realm of nature and the realm of grace. They are now often known as those of revelation and natural knowledge. Modern religious liberalism has no definite names for them, save, perhaps, the division, referred to in the last chapter, between scientific and religious experience. The implication is that in one territory the supremacy of scientific knowledge must be acknowledged, while there is another region, not very precisely defined, of intimate personal experience wherein other methods and criteria hold sway.

This method of justifying the peculiar and legitimate claim of certain elements of belief is always open to the objection that a positive conclusion is drawn from a negative fact. Existing ignorance or backwardness is employed to assert the existence of a division in the nature of the subject-matter dealt with. Yet the gap may only reflect, at most, a limitation now existing but in the future to be done away with. The argument that because some province or aspect of experience has not yet been "invaded" by scientific methods, it is not subject to them, is as old as it is dangerous. Time and time again, in some particular reserved field, it has been invalidated. Psychology is still in its infancy. He is bold to the point of rashness who asserts that intimate personal experience will never come within the ken of natural knowledge.

It is more to the present point, however, to consider the region that is claimed by religionists as a special preserve. It is mystical experience. The difference, however, between mystic experience and the theory about it that is offered to us must be noted. The experience is a fact to be inquired into. The theory, like any theory, is an interpretation of the fact. The idea that by its very nature the experience is a veridical realization of the direct presence of God does not rest so much upon examination of the facts as it does upon importing into their interpretation a conception that is formed outside them. In its dependence upon a prior conception of the supernatural, which is the thing to be proved, it begs the question.

History exhibits many types of mystic experience, and each of these types is contemporaneously explained by the concepts that prevail in the culture and the circle in which the phenomena occur. There are mystic crises that arise, as among some North American Indian tribes, induced by fasting. They are accompanied by trances and semi-hysteria. Their purpose is to gain some special power, such perhaps as locating a person who is lost or finding objects that have been secreted. There is the mysticism of Hindoo practice now enjoying some vogue in Western countries. There is the mystic ecstasy of Neoplatonism with its complete abrogation of the self and absorption into an impersonal whole of Being. There is the mysticism of intense aesthetic experience independent of any theological or metaphysical interpretation. There is the heretical mysticism of William Blake. There is the mysticism of sudden unreasoning fear in which the very foundations seem shaken beneath one—to mention but a few of the types that may be found.

What common element is there between, say, the Neoplatonic conception of a super-divine Being wholly apart from human needs and conditions and the medieval theory of an immediate union that is fostered through attention to the sacraments or through concentration upon the heart of Jesus? The contemporary emphasis of some Protestant theologians upon the sense of inner personal communion with God, found in religious experience, is almost as far away from medieval Christianity as it is from Neoplatonism or Yoga. Interpretations of the experience have not grown from the experience itself with the aid of such scientific resources as may be available. They have been imported by borrowing without criticism from ideas that are current in the surrounding culture.

The mystic states of the shaman and of some North American Indians are frankly techniques for gaining a special power—*the* power as it is conceived by some revivalist sects. There is no especial intellectual objectification accompanying the experience. The knowledge that is said to be gained is not that of Being but of particular secrets and occult modes of operation. The aim is not to gain knowledge of superior divine power, but to get advice, cures for the sick, prestige, etc. The conception that mystic experience is a normal mode of religious experience by which we may acquire knowledge of God and divine things is a nineteenth-century interpretation that has gained vogue in direct ratio to the decline of older methods of religious apologetics.

There is no reason for denying the existence of experiences that are called mystical. On the contrary, there is every reason to suppose that, in some degree of intensity, they occur so frequently that they may be regarded as normal manifestations that take place at certain rhythmic points in the movement of experience. The assumption that denial of a particular interpretation of their objective content proves that those who make the denial do not have the experience in question, so that if they had it they would be equally persuaded of its objective source in the presence of God, has no foundation in fact. As with every empirical phenomenon, the occurrence of the state called mystical is simply an occasion for inquiry into its mode of causation. There is no more reason for converting the experience itself into an immediate knowledge of its cause than in the case of an experience of lightning or any other natural occurrence.

My purpose, then, in this brief reference to mysticism is not to throw doubt upon the existence of particular experiences called mystical. Nor is it to propound any theory to account for them. I have referred to the matter merely as an illustration of the general tendency to mark off two distinct realms in one of which science has jurisdiction, while in

the other, special modes of immediate knowledge of religious objects have authority. This dualism as it operates in contemporary interpretation of mystic experience in order to validate certain beliefs is but a reinstatement of the old dualism between the natural and the supernatural, in terms better adapted to the cultural conditions of the present time. Since it is the conception of the supernatural that science calls in question, the circular nature of this type of reasoning is obvious.

Apologists for a religion often point to the shift that goes on in scientific ideas and materials as evidence of the unreliability of science as a mode of knowledge. They often seem peculiarly elated by the great, almost revolutionary, change in fundamental physical conceptions that has taken place in science during the present generation. Even if the alleged unreliability were as great as they assume (or even greater), the question would remain: Have we any other recourse for knowledge? But in fact they miss the point. Science is not constituted by any particular body of subject-matter. It is constituted by a method, a method of changing beliefs by means of tested inquiry as well as of arriving at them. It is its glory, not its condemnation, that its subject-matter develops as the method is improved. There is no special subject-matter of belief that is sacrosanct. The identification of science with a particular set of beliefs and ideas is itself a hold-over of ancient and still current dogmatic habits of thought which are opposed to science in its actuality and which science is undermining.

For scientific method is adverse not only to dogma but to doctrine as well, provided we take "doctrine" in its usual meaning—a body of definite beliefs that need only to be taught and learned as true. This negative attitude of science to doctrine does not indicate indifference to truth. It signifies supreme loyalty to the method by which truth is attained. The scientific-religious conflict ultimately is a conflict between allegiance to this method and allegiance to even an irreducible minimum of belief so fixed in advance that it can never be modified.

The method of intelligence is open and public. The doctrinal method is limited and private. This limitation persists even when knowledge of the truth that is religious is said to be arrived at by a special mode of experience, that termed "religious." For the latter is assumed to be a very special kind of experience. To be sure it is asserted to be open to all who obey certain conditions. Yet the mystic experience yields, as we have seen, various results in the way of belief to different persons, depending upon the surrounding culture of those who undergo it. As a method, it lacks the public character belonging to the method of intelligence. Moreover, when the experience in question does not yield conciousness of the presence of God, in the sense that is alleged to exist, the retort is always at hand that it is not a genuine religious experience. For by definition, only that experience *is* religious which arrives at this particular result. The argument is circular. The traditional position is that some hardness or corruption of heart prevents one from having the experience. Liberal religionists are now more humane. But their logic does not differ.

It is sometimes held that beliefs about religious matters are symbolic, like rites and ceremonies. This view may be an advance upon that which holds to their literal objective validity. But as usually put forward it suffers from an ambiguity. Of what are the beliefs symbols? Are they symbols of things experienced in other modes than those set apart as religious, so that the things symbolized have an independent standing? Or are they symbols in the sense of standing for some transcendental reality—transcendental because not being the subject-matter of experience generally? Even the fundamentalist admits a certain quality and degree of symbolism in the latter sense in objects of religious belief. For he holds that the objects of these beliefs are so far beyond finite human capacity that our beliefs must be couched in more or less metaphorical terms. The conception that faith is the best available substitute for knowledge in our present estate still attaches to the notion of the symbolic character of the materials of faith; unless by ascribing to them a symbolic nature we mean that these materials stand for something that is verifiable in general and public experience.

Were we to adopt the latter point of view, it would be evident not only that the intellectual articles of a creed must be understood to be symbolic of moral and other ideal values; but that the facts taken to be historic and used as concrete evidence of the intellectual articles are themselves symbolic. These articles of a creed present events and persons that have been made over by the idealizing imagination in the interest, at their best, of moral ideals. Historic personages in their divine attributes are materializations of the ends that enlist devotion and inspire endeavor. They are symbolic of the reality of ends moving us in many forms of experience. The ideal values that are thus symbolized also mark human experience in science and art and the various modes of human association: they mark almost everything in life that rises from the level of manipulation of conditions as they exist. It is admitted that the objects of religion are ideal in contrast with our present state. What would be lost if it were also admitted that they have authoritative claim upon conduct just because they are ideal? The assumption that these objects of religion exist already in some realm of Being seems to add nothing to their force, while it weakens their claim over us as ideals, in so far as it bases that claim upon matters that are intellectually dubious. The question narrows itself to this: Are the ideals that move us genuinely ideal or are they ideal only in contrast with our present estate?

The import of the question extends far. It determines the meaning given to the word "God." On one score, the word can mean only a particular Being. On the other score, it denotes the unity of all ideal ends arousing us to desire and actions. Does the unification have a claim upon our attitude and conduct because it is already, apart from us, in realized existence, or because of its own inherent meaning and value? Suppose for the moment that the word "God" means the ideal ends that at a given time and place one acknowledges as having authority over his volition and emotion, the values to which one is supremely devoted, as far as these ends, through imagination, take on unity. If we make this supposition, the issue will stand out clearly in contrast with the doctrine of religions that "God" designates some kind of Being having prior and therefore non-ideal existence.

The word "non-ideal" is to be taken literally in regard to some religions that have historically existed, to all of them as far as they are neglectful of moral qualities in their divine beings. It does not apply in the same *literal* way to Judaism and Christianity. For they have asserted that the Supreme Being has moral and spiritual attributes. But it applies to them none the less in that these moral and spiritual characters are thought of as properties of a particular existence and are thought to be of religious value for us because of this embodiment in such an existence. Here, as far as I can see, is the ultimate issue as to the difference between *a* religion and

the religious as a function of experience.

The idea that "God" represents a unification of ideal values that is essentially imaginative in origin when the imagination supervenes in conduct is attended with verbal difficulties owing to our frequent use of the word "imagination" to denote fantasy and doubtful reality. But the reality of ideal ends as ideals is vouched for by their undeniable power in action. An ideal is not an illusion because imagination is the origin through which it is apprehended. For *all* possibilities reach us through the imagination. In a definite sense the only meaning that can be assigned the term "imagination" is that things unrealized in fact come home to us and have power to stir us. The unification effected through imagination is not fanciful, for it is the reflex of the unification of practical and emotional attitudes. The unity signifies not a single Being, but the unity of loyalty and effort evoked by the fact that many ends are one in the power of their ideal, or imaginative, quality to stir and hold us.

We may well ask whether the power and significance in life of the traditional conceptions of God are not due to the ideal qualities referred to by them, the hypostatization of them into an existence being due to a conflux of tendencies in human nature that converts the object of desire into an antecedent reality (as was mentioned in the previous chapter) with beliefs that have prevailed in the cultures of the past. For in the older cultures the idea of the supernatural was "natural," in the sense in which "natural" signifies something customary and familiar. It seems more credible that religious persons have been supported and consoled by the reality with which ideal values appeal to them than that they have been upborne by sheer matter of fact existence. That, when once men are inured to the idea of the union of the ideal and the physical, the two should be so bound together in emotion that it is difficult to institute a separation, agrees with all we know of human psychology.

The benefits that will accrue, however, from making the separation are evident. The dislocation frees the religious values of experience once for all from matters that are continually becoming more dubious. With that release there comes emancipation from the necessity of resort to apologetics. The reality of ideal ends and values in their authority over us is an undoubted fact. The validity of justice, affection, and that intellectual correspondence of our ideas with realities that we call truth, is so assured in its hold upon humanity that it is unnecessary for the religious attitude to encumber itself with the apparatus of dogma and doctrine. Any other conception of the religious attitude, when it is adequately analyzed, means that those who hold it care more for force than for ideal values—since all that an Existence can add is force to establish, to punish, and to reward. There are, indeed, some persons who frankly say that their own faith does not require any guarantee that moral values are backed up by physical force, but who hold that the masses are so backward that ideal values will not affect their conduct unless in the popular belief these values have the sanction of a power that can enforce them and can execute justice upon those who fail to comply.

There are some persons, deserving of more respect, who say: "We agree that the beginning must be made with the primacy of the ideal. But why stop at this point? Why not search with the utmost eagerness and vigor for all the evidence we can find, such as is supplied by history, by presence of design in nature, which may lead on to the belief that the ideal is already extant in a Personality having objective existence?"

One answer to the question is that we are involved by this search in all the problems of the existence of evil that have haunted theology in the past and that the most ingenious apologetics have not faced, much less met. If these apologists had not identified the existence of ideal goods with that of a Person supposed to originate and support them —a Being, moreover, to whom omnipotent power is attributed—the problem of the occurrence of evil would be gratuitous. The significance of ideal ends and meanings is, indeed, closely connected with the fact that there are in life all sorts of things that are evil to us because we would have them otherwise. Were existing conditions wholly good, the notion of possibilities to be realized would never emerge.

But the more basic answer is that while if the search is conducted upon a strictly empirical basis there is no reason why it should not take place, as a matter of fact it is always undertaken in the interest of the supernatural. Thus it diverts attention and energy from ideal values and from the exploration of actual conditions by means of which they may be promoted. History is testimony to this fact. Men have never fully used the powers they possess to advance the good in life, because they have waited upon some power external to themselves and to nature to do the work they are responsible for doing. Dependence upon an external power is the counterpart of surrender of human endeavor. Nor is emphasis on exercising our own powers for good an egoistical or a sentimentally optimistic recourse. It is not the first, for it does not isolate man, either individually or collectively, from nature. It is not the second, because it makes no assumption beyond that of the need and responsibility for human endeavor, and beyond the conviction that, if human desire and endeavor were enlisted in behalf of natural ends, conditions would be bettered. It involves no expectation of a millennium of good.

Belief in the supernatural as a necessary power for apprehension of the ideal and for practical attachment to it has for its counterpart a pessimistic belief in the corruption and impotency of natural means. That is axiomatic in Christian dogma. But this apparent pessimism has a way of suddenly changing into an exaggerated optimism. For according to the terms of the doctrine, if the faith in the supernatural is of the required order, regeneration at once takes place. Goodness, in all essentials, is thereby established; if not, there is proof that the established relation to the supernatural has been vitiated. This romantic optimism is one cause for the excessive attention to individual salvation characteristic of traditional Christianity. Belief in a sudden and complete transmutation through conversion and in the objective efficacy of prayer, is too easy a way out of difficulties. It leaves matters in general just about as they were before; that is, sufficiently bad so that there is additional support for the idea that only supernatural aid can better them. The position of natural intelligence is that there exists a *mixture* of good and evil, and that reconstruction in the direction of the good which is indicated by ideal ends, must take place, if at all, through continued cooperative effort. There is at least enough impulse toward justice, kindliness, and order so that if it were mobilized for action, not expecting abrupt and complete transformation to occur, the disorder, cruelty, and oppression that exist would be reduced.

The discussion has arrived at a point where a more fundamental objection to the position I am taking needs consideration. The misunderstanding upon which this objection rests should be pointed out. The view I have advanced is sometimes treated as if the identification of the divine with ideal ends left the ideal wholly without roots in existence and without support from existence. The objection implies that my view commits one to such a separation of the ideal and the existent that the ideal has no chance to find lodgment even as a seed that might grow and bear fruit. On the contrary, what I have been criticizing is the *identification* of the ideal with a particular Being, especially when that identification makes necessary the conclusion that this Being is outside of nature, and what I have tried to show is that the ideal itself has its roots in natural conditions; it emerges when the imagination idealizes existence by laying hold of the possibilities offered to thought and action. There are values, goods, actually realized upon a natural basis—the goods of human association, of art and knowledge. The idealizing imagination seizes upon the most precious things found in the climacteric moments of experience and projects them. We need no external criterion and guarantee for their goodness. They are had, they exist as good, and out of them we frame our ideal ends.

Moreover, the ends that result from our projection of experienced goods into objects of thought, desire and effort exist, only they exist *as* ends. Ends, purposes, exercise determining power in human conduct. The aims of philanthropists, of Florence Nightingale, of Howard, of Wilberforce, of Peabody, have not been idle dreams. They have modified institutions. Aims, ideals, do not exist simply in "mind"; they exist in character, in personality and action. One might call the roll of artists, intellectual inquirers, parents, friends, citizens who are neighbors, to show that purposes exist in an *operative* way. What I have been objecting to, I repeat, is not the idea that ideals are linked with existence and that they themselves exist, through human embodiment, as forces, but the idea that their authority and value depend upon some prior complete embodiment—as if the efforts of human beings in behalf of justice, or knowledge or beauty, depended for their effectiveness and validity upon assurance that there already existed in some supernal region a place where criminals are humanely treated, where there is no serfdom or slavery, where all facts and truths are already discovered and possessed, and all beauty is eternally displayed in actualized form.

The aims and ideals that move us are generated through imagination. But they are not made out of imaginary stuff. They are made out of the hard stuff of the world of physical and social experience. The locomotive did not exist before Stevenson, nor the telegraph before the time of Morse. But the conditions for their existence were there in physical material and energies and in human capacity. Imagination seized hold upon the idea of a rearrangement of existing things that would evolve new objects. The same thing is true of a painter, a musician, a poet, a philanthropist, a moral prophet. The new vision does not arise out of nothing, but emerges through seeing, in terms of possibilities, that is, of imagination, old things in new relations serving a new end which the new end aids in creating.

Moreover the process of creation is experimental and continuous. The artist, scientific man, or good citizen, depends upon what others have done before him and are doing around him. The sense of new values that become ends to be realized arises first in dim and uncertain form. As the values are dwelt upon and carried forward in action they grow in definiteness and coherence. Interaction between aim and existent conditions improves and tests the ideal; and conditions are at the same time modified. Ideals change as they are applied in existent conditions. The process endures and advances with the life of humanity. What one person and one group accomplish becomes the standing ground and starting point of those who succeed them.

When the vital factors in this natural process are generally acknowledged in emotion, thought and action, the process will be both accelerated and purified through elimination of that irrelevant element that culminates in the idea of the supernatural. When the vital factors attain the religious force that has been drafted into supernatural religions, the resulting reinforcement will be incalculable.

These considerations may be applied to the idea of God, or, to avoid misleading conceptions, to the idea of the divine. This idea is, as I have said, one of ideal possibilities unified through imaginative realization and projection. But this idea of God, or of the divine, is also connected with all the natural forces and conditions—including man and human association—that promote the growth of the ideal and that further its realization. We are in the presence neither of ideals completely embodied in existence nor yet of ideals that are mere rootless ideals, fantasies, utopias. For there are forces in nature and society that generate and support the ideals. They are further unified by the action that gives them coherence and solidity. It is this *active* relation between ideal and actual to which I would give the name "God." I would not insist that the name *must* be given. There are those who hold that the associations of the term with the supernatural are so numerous and close that any use of the word "God" is sure to give rise to misconception and be taken as a concession to traditional ideas.

They may be correct in this view. But the facts to which I have referred are there, and they need to be brought out with all possible clearness and force. There exist concretely and experimentally goods—the values of art in all its forms, of knowledge, of effort and of rest after striving, of education and fellowship, of friendship and love, of growth in mind and body. These goods are there and yet they are relatively embryonic. Many persons are shut out from generous participation in them; there are forces at work that threaten and sap existent goods as well as prevent their expansion. A clear and intense conception of a union of ideal ends with actual conditions is capable of arousing steady emotion. It may be fed by every experience, no matter what its material.

In a distracted age, the need for such an idea is urgent. It can unify interests and energies now dispersed; it can direct action and generate the heat of emotion and the light of intelligence. Whether one gives the name "God" to this union, operative in thought and action, is a matter for individual decision. But the *function* of such a working union of the ideal and actual seems to me to be identical with the force that has in fact been attached to the conception of God in all the religions that have a spiritual content; and a clear idea of that function seems to me urgently needed at the present time.

The sense of this union may, with some persons, be furthered by mystical experiences, using the term "mystical" in its broadest sense. That result depends largely upon temperament. But there is a marked difference between the union associated with mysticism and the union which I had in mind. There is nothing mystical about the latter; it is natural and moral. Nor is there anything mystical about the perception or consciousness of such union. Imagination of ideal ends pertinent to actual conditions represents the fruition of a disciplined mind. There is, indeed, even danger that resort to mystical experiences will be an escape, and that its result will be the passive feeling that the union of actual and ideal is already accomplished. But in fact this union is active and practical; it is a *uniting*, not something given.

One reason why personally I think it fitting to use the word "God" to denote that uniting of the ideal and actual which has been spoken of, lies in the fact that aggressive atheism seems to me to have something in common with traditional supernaturalism. I do not mean merely that the former is mainly so negative that it fails to give positive direction to thought, though that fact is pertinent. What I have in mind especially is the exclusive preoccupation of both militant atheism and supernaturalism with man in isolation. For in spite of supernaturalism's reference to something beyond nature, it conceives of this earth as the moral center of the universe and of man as the apex of the whole scheme of things. It regards the drama of sin and redemption enacted within the isolated and lonely soul of man as the one thing of ultimate importance. Apart from man, nature is held either accursed or negligible. Militant atheism is also affected by lack of natural piety. The ties binding man to nature that poets have always celebrated are passed over lightly. The attitude taken is often that of man living in an indifferent and hostile world and issuing blasts of defiance. A religious attitude, however, needs the sense of a connection of man, in the way of both dependence and support, with the enveloping world that the imagination feels is a universe. Use of the words "God" or "divine" to convey the union of actual with ideal may protect man from a sense of isolation and from consequent despair or defiance.

In any case, whatever the name, the meaning is selective. For it involves no miscellaneous worship of everything in general. It selects those factors in existence that generate and support our idea of good as an end to be striven for. It excludes a multitude of forces that at any given time are irrelevant to this function. Nature produces whatever gives reinforcement and direction but also what occasions discord and confusion. The "divine" is thus a term of human choice and aspiration. A humanistic religion, if it excludes our relation to nature, is pale and thin, as it is presumptuous, when it takes humanity as an object of worship. Matthew Arnold's conception of a "power not ourselves" is too narrow in its reference to operative and sustaining conditions. While it is selective, it is too narrow in its basis of selection—righteousness. The conception thus needs to be widened in two ways. The powers that generate and support the good as experienced and as ideal, work *within* as well as without. There seems to be a reminiscence of an external Jehovah in Arnold's statement. And the powers work to enforce other values and ideals than righteousness. Arnold's sense of an opposition between Hellenism and Hebraism resulted in exclusion of beauty, truth, and friendship from the list of the consequences toward which powers work within and without.

In the relation between nature and human ends and endeavors, recent science has broken down the older dualism. It has been engaged in this task for three centuries. But as long as the conceptions of science were strictly mechanical (mechanical in the sense of assuming separate things acting upon one another purely externally by push and pull), religious apologists had a standing ground in pointing out the differences between man and physical nature. The differences could be used for arguing that something supernatural had intervened in the case of man. The recent acclaim, however, by apologists for religion of the surrender by science of the classic type of mechanicalism [1] seems ill-advised from their own point of view. For the change in the modern scientific view of nature simply brings man and nature nearer together.

---

[1] I use this term because science has not abandoned its beliefs in working mechanisms in giving up the idea that they are of the nature of a strictly mechanical contact of discrete things.

We are no longer compelled to choose between explaining away what is distinctive in man through reducing him to another form of a mechanical model and the doctrine that something literally supernatural marks him off from nature. The less mechanical—in its older sense —physical nature is found to be, the closer is man to nature.

In his fascinating book, *The Dawn of Conscience,* James Henry Breasted refers to Haeckel as saying that the question he would most wish to have answered is this: Is the universe friendly to man? The question is an ambiguous one. Friendly to man in what respect? With respect to ease and comfort, to material success, to egoistic ambitions? Or to his aspiration to inquire and discover, to invent and create, to build a more secure order for human existence? In whatever form the question be put, the answer cannot in all honesty be an unqualified and absolute one. Mr. Breasted's answer, as a historian, is that nature has been friendly to the emergence and development of conscience and character. Those who will have all or nothing cannot be satisfied with this answer. Emergence and growth are not enough for them. They want something more than growth accompanied by toil and pain. They want final achievement. Others who are less absolutist may be content to think that, morally speaking, growth is a higher value and ideal than is sheer attainment. They will remember also that growth has not been confined to conscience and character; that it extends also to discovery, learning and knowledge, to creation in the arts, to furtherance of ties that hold men together in mutual aid and affection. These persons at least will be satisfied with an intellectual view of the religious function that is based on continuing choice directed toward ideal ends.

For, I would remind readers in conclusion, it is the intellectual side of the religious attitude that I have been considering. I have suggested that the religious element in life has been hampered by conceptions of the supernatural that were imbedded in those cultures wherein man had little control over outer nature and little in the way of sure method of inquiry and test. The crisis today as to the intellectual content of religious belief has been caused by the change in the intellectual climate due to the increase of our knowledge and our means of understanding. I have tried to show that this change is not fatal to the religious values in our comon experience, however adverse its impact may be upon historic religions. Rather, provided that the methods and results of intelligence at work are frankly adopted, the change is liberating.

It clarifies our ideals, rendering them less subject to illusion and fantasy. It relieves us of the incubus of thinking of them as fixed, as without power of growth. It discloses that they develop in coherence and pertinency with increase of natural intelligence. The change gives aspiration for natural knowledge a definitely religious character, since growth in understanding of nature is seen to be organically related to the formation of ideal ends. The same change enables man to select those elements in natural conditions that may be organized to support and extend the sway of ideals. All purpose is selective, and all intelligent action includes deliberate choice. In the degree in which we cease to depend upon belief in the supernatural, selection is enlightened and choice can be made in behalf of ideals whose inherent relations to conditions and consequences are understood. Were the naturalistic foundations and bearings of religion grasped, the religious element in life would emerge from the throes of the crisis in religion. Religion would then be found to have its natural place in every aspect of human experience that is concerned with estimate of possibilities, with emotional stir by possibilities as yet unrealized, and with all action in behalf of their realization. All that is significant in human experience falls within this frame.

51. *The Problem of Evil**

Wilmon Henry Sheldon (1876–   )

Man is limited in power, unhappy, and wicked. Even if the degree of these evils is nothing like what the pessimists claim, even if this is, at the other extreme, the best possible world, still there is something incredible in a Perfect God creating a world that contains any evil at all. To many people who are not professional thinkers, as well as to the professional, this argument weighs heavy. It does not on its face seem to be a theoretical matter at all. The notion of a Creator perfect in power as well as goodness seems to be directly contradicted by the *facts*. Not that a perfect Deity would

* From *God and Polarity*, pp. 266-277. By kind permission of publishers, Yale University Press.

be self-contradictory in Himself; only if He created a world containing evil things: which He has done. Surely no logical analysis, no dialectical subtlety drawing out the ultimate postulates of reason, is needed to bring home to plain common sense this grievous paradox. In fact, the less of a theorist, the more sensitive to the sufferings of his fellow men one is, the more will he feel it. Many devout people have had their faith in God shaken by the terrible injustices that are so obvious in man's life; not to dwell on the uncountable cruelties and pains of animals in the long ages of evolution. As men (including the philosophers) have grown more compassionate in modern times, the problem of evil thrusts itself on their minds with greater and greater force.

A little reflection makes the thesis of a God limited in power though not in goodness look more like a dialectical thesis. It has no experimental verification. We do not directly experience God's limitation. We do experience many evils: ugly sights, cruel deeds of men, our own ignorance. These may seem to *imply* an imperfect Creator, but so far as we know, no one claims to have experienced *directly* the Divine nature as even a little bit ugly, mean, weak, or ignorant. On the contrary—to repeat what was above said—our human experiences of Divinity point in the opposite direction. Consider the Hindu Atman, the Buddhist Nirvana, the flight of the alone to the Alone of Plotinus, the Christian's mystical ecstasy. Here is alleged no experience of imperfection or weakness of any sort. So, by such evidence as we have wherever the experiment of observing Deity has been tried, we should accept His perfection. But the modern personalist, being no mystic, in lieu of concrete witness of God's limitation, brings in his argument by implication. Imperfect creatures *imply* an imperfect Creator (at least in power) as a red-haired child implies a

red-haired progenitor; like effect, like cause. Well, is the implication certain? We know from the history of mathematics, the very home of purest implications, that many notions once deemed inconsistent have been found not so; difficult indeed it is to know what implies what.

By all precedents a long book should here be written on this problem of evil. Has any other problem of theology or philosophy filled so many volumes? How dare we presume to settle it in a few pages? But the fact is, we have only a negative task: to show that the contradiction alleged is not necessary. We don't have to explain why evil is permitted. Far from it! Enough that, being actual, it *need not* imply any lack of perfection in the Divine nature. For we make no claim to show that it is illusory, as some older views have held, nor do we spend time trying to prove it actual. Probably those who have called it illusory—and perhaps our friends the "Christian Scientists" could agree— really mean that it is *due to* an illusion, to some belief that can and ought to be removed. None of these illusionists deny the sorry *fact* of our being under an illusion. There we have no quarrel with them. The source of evil, whether illusion or obstinate denial of known truth, or what not, is not our present problem. To our negative task then.

According to classical treatment, evil for conscious beings is of three kinds: limitation of power physical or mental, pain (poena), and moral evil or guilt (culpa)—the last for man only, in our world. Begin with the first.

(1) Limitation of Power

For the Thomist, a failure of power to realize their native capacities, even in unconscious things, is evil. A stunted tree is a bad thing because something has prevented it from growing to full stature. Evil is any potency frustrated, deprived of its fulfillment; evil is privation. Good is fulfillment of a thing's intrinsic capacities. This we may accept. But the personalist, being idealist, centers his attention on the obviously conscious beings, the men and animals. If stones were unconscious he wouldn't think the category of evil (or good) applicable to them merely in themselves. So we now confine ourselves to the troubles of men and animals.

Now there is nothing bad about limitation of power, just by itself. A rock's powers are very limited. It can't leap to the sky or grow or think. But that doesn't hurt it. So of animals: a bird or beast, lacking the power of abstract thought, wouldn't be in the least injured by the lack, provided its natural wants (food, etc.,) were satisfied. Limitation of power in conscious beings is an evil only when it prevents getting what they want. The rabbit killed by the snake experiences evil because it wants to live and hasn't the power to overcome the snake. And so on. Frustration of desire, privation, or rather deprivation: that is the evil. And that is *pain:* pain in the larger, more general sense and not merely an organic sensation. The painfulness or misery of pain lies in the fact that the struggle to avoid it or get rid of it is defeated: frustrated desire, *poena* as the scholastics called it. Pass then to this well-nigh all-inclusive class of evils.

(2) *Pain*

No argument is needed to show the evil of this. To be sure, not all pains are wholly bad: the smart of the medicine that heals a wound is better than its absence, the sting of conscience in the sinner is better than its absence. Yet if in such cases we could have the result without the pain, we should all prefer it. Pain is, by very definition, any quality or datum which we inevitably want to remove, even though some further motive may lead us to endure it. There is

no theory about this, just a matter of plain everyday experience. Technically put: pain as such, pain *qua* pain, is evil. And for us men there are all sorts of pain, of qualitative data to be thrust away; from the restless fret of an unsolved theoretical problem or the shame for a wrong we have done or the disapproval of our fellows to the pangs of hunger, flesh torn or burned, fatigue, or even a little itch that we cannot scratch. There are about as many sorts of pain for men as there are sorts of being. And for animals taken collectively probably not less, since animals are of so many more kinds than man. Vastly more indeed: think of the long long epochs of past animal life with pain and death the lot of each and all. And pains of all possible degrees of intensity too, for both man and animal. The sheer magnitude of it all is beyond imagination. Now how could a perfect Creator, infinitely loving and infinitely powerful and intelligent, have made such a world? Surely there could be nothing more utterly contradictory. Yet He has made it. Very well then, He must be limited in power or goodness.

On the other hand, as just now said, some pains are at least not wholly evil. Is the sting of conscience an evil? Most people would call it a good: it shows a moral sense at least. And further, it is *deserved*. There is a justice about it. If I have knowingly done wrong, don't I deserve to suffer, at least in my own mind? Surely we can't rule out desert; a genuine human category. The self-sacrificing lover of men deserves praise, the selfish coward blame (though some loving sentimentalists would do away with blame for any one; the modern "pacifists" for instance would have no punishments for murderers, etc.). And God, so we say, is just. True, He forgives sin; but only when the sinner repents, and to repent, to feel remorse, is to suffer acute pain. Not all the argument in the world

will convince mankind that one who
gloats over the pain of another just to
show his own superiority, deserves happiness as much as one who lovingly
labors to ease the misery of his fellows.
Much of the pain of human life is doubtless deserved. How much? Certainly a
great deal of it seems to be quite undeserved: go to the work of Schopenhauer to see the evidence. Born a cripple,
mentally deficient, torn by sickness, a
helpless child beaten and abused—which
of these is to blame for this his lot? Perhaps animals do not have the exquisite
refinements of pain we men are subject
to, but they are filled with cruelty to one
another, and quantity makes up for
quality. And who can blame them; where
is the evidence that they have free choice
and responsibility? We may pass over
the human pains of discipline; they have
a good result, let us grant, though of
course the evil lies in the lot of man,
that he *needs* pains to discipline his will.
True, the tender Christian may pray for
strength to endure the suffering he cannot prevent, even the suffering of those
he loves, which is for him the maximum
of agony; and he may be given the
strength he needs. But what of those who
never heard of Christianity? What of
primitive man, man through the millions
of years of his early evolution, even
semi-civilized man before the consola-
tions of religion, *any* religion, dawned
upon his soul? The undeserved pains, the
misery that does no good that we can
see, that drives to madness or crime—
the torments of the insane, the hopeless
invalids, and last but not least, death the
supreme evil native to all living things:
who shall dare say that these are deserved? Hideously unjust they seem. So
rises intense emotion, and the sensitive
man of our modern West can listen to no
considerations on the other side. Not
wishful but resentful thinking now:
away with the stupid old-time orthodox
Christian, so coldly indifferent to human

agony; he is a wicked man himself. It is
wrong to believe in a perfect Creator.
The Western lover of mankind, loving
God too much to blame Him, finds Him
guiltless of evil intent, but limited in
power: evil only in the sense of imperfectly able to accomplish His Will. . . .

Is it logically inescapable that the
First Cause of an evil effect—partly evil
to be sure, not wholly—must be partly
evil (limited in power)? Is there any
other possibility that is consistent with
the facts? If there is, the argument is
not sound. Not, of course, that the failure of the argument proves its opposite.
We are not now asking whether God is
perfect. We ask only: are we compelled
by infallible logic to deny it?

We are not. Another hypothesis is
possible. It may not be verifiable, it may
not be probable, but if it is possible, we
have no proof that God is in any way
limited.

Start from the facts. Many people,
many animals, suffer untold miseries
without any apparent fault of their own.
It is the injustice of it that rankles. Now
why do we think these sufferers are
punished far beyond their deserts? Because we have no evidence of their having done wrong in anything like the
degree of their pains. And in the case of
very young children, they couldn't have
done so. Still less, if possible, with the
sweet-singing little bird who is devoured
by a poisonous snake. All the evidence
we have goes to show the innocence of
these helpless victims. Well now, how
much evidence have we? Are we *sure*
that these victims didn't live other and
wicked lives before the present one? The
hypothesis of transmigration is a very
old one, even Plato seemed to accept it;
many sincere people believe it today.
But, you say, there is no evidence of
transmigration. Perhaps not, perhaps
there is. The hypothesis is certainly not
a favorite with modern Western devotees
of "scientific method." It may be quite

false anyway. But it is not *disproved*. It is, so far as compelling proof goes, an open possibility. If it is a true hypothesis, it at once removes the apparent injustice of so much suffering—or rather, it makes the removal possible. *A, B,* or *C,* persons or animals, may well be paying the penalty for frightful cruelties practiced in a former incarnation. Who knows? To be sure, this leaves the problem of *moral* evil, or *culpa,* untouched. You may still say: a good God could not have permitted evil deeds that involve such punishment. You may even have yourself a theory of punishment that altogether denies the notion of desert, credit, or blame. The problem of moral evil we shall take up anon. We consider now the problem of *poena* only. And it is plain fact that the appeal of the argument from human and animal suffering to a limitation of God's power draws its strength from the burning indignation we feel at the apparently *undeserved* pain of it. No mere *theory* of punishment can quench that flame in the compassionate minds of those who follow the gospel of love, as do the personalists. Emotion blots out what cool reason might discover.

But, to be sure, these loving hearts will answer: if the only way you can save God's perfection is by such a wild, unprovable, unscientific notion as reincarnation—why then, we prefer to believe in a limited God. Precisely: they *will* prefer it. But they claim to have proved it, and they have not. The whole point is this: implications are valid only *within a given order.* As the logicians say, they follow from *given postulates.* Now, we just do not know the given order of God's plans and purposes. We do not know how He feels toward sinners, except that we believe He loves them; we do not know how far His love may take the form of chastening, how far of forgiving, how far of rewarding and punishing. Nor do the modern per-

sonalists *know* whether or not men and animals live beyond the grave or before the birth. We do know a great deal about the order of the physical world. We can draw implications within that order with a high degree of success; we predict eclipses, we infer the earth's past history, and so on. We do *not* know the make-up and the laws of the spirit realm; many even deny such a realm. That is why we cannot prove that there is unmerited suffering in the world. That is why we cannot argue from *poena* to a limitation of God's power, or love, or inner "Given" nature.

But even if reincarnation be rejected as absurd, there is another possibility. The proverb says "All's well that ends well"; and proverbs are usually based on human experience. In the experience of time, the later counts more than the earlier. Often we feel, in looking back at some past suffering, as if the knowledge we gained through it made it worth while. We say, "I am glad I went through that, I wouldn't have missed it." We feel that the later experience includes and transmutes the earlier. Our memory is not just a memory of bitterness, but of bitterness-to-be-transformed into joy. In the novels, hero and heroine pass through long tribulation, the villain all the while rejoicing; yet when at the end he is cast down and they unite in bliss we feel that the end at once justifies and overcomes the pain that went before. Happiness not only outweighs; it *transubstantiates* the griefs undergone to reach it. Happiness becomes *retroactive.* Of course you may object, "but the pain *was* real *then* and was *not* compensated: we can't get away from that! That was just straight evil." The objection disregards the empirical evidence. Time doesn't stop; the past misery was *not* just itself, for it was passing on to something else. You forget the passing on. It is the same mistake as Zeno made in his dialectic about the flying arrow. You take what the monists call an abstract view; you are false to the experience. Now to be sure this by no means uncommon experience isn't universal. Many are our pains and griefs which we don't see transformed. And if the present life for men and for animals is all, then evil remains evil to the bitter end. All we are now pointing out is that that is not *proved*. You may or may not believe it; the alternative remains a possibility. And the possibility means that *poena* may be a vanishing quantity, that God's power puts it there to be overcome, in fact to reveal God's power in the very overcoming. Again, we are not urging that this *is* the case; only that there is nothing like proof that it is *not* the case. So far: no need to limit God's power.

True, some thinkers have said that in any created world there must be some unmerited suffering. So Leibniz. To this we answer as above: there is no way of proving it. We cannot compass God's power. We cannot estimate beforehand what He can or cannot do. Grant that any created world must be less than its Creator; if it were His equal it would be Himself and such tautological behavior would leave Him where He eternally is. But to be imperfect in this sense is not necessarily to be evil. It may be perfect after its kind; all the species it contained might so cooperate as to fulfill to the limit the substantial forms of each: as for example the good angels in Christian theology. So much for *poena;* now for *culpa* or

(3) Moral Evil

Grant everything we have urged above; the problem remains, how could a perfect being permit a voluntary choice of evil on the part of creatures: Satan and his hosts if you like, human beings certainly. Here we assume for argument's sake that man exercises free choice, deliberately deciding sometimes to do what he believes (correctly or not) to be

morally wrong, or morally right. We are starting from the platform of the personalists to see if we must go with them to their conclusion.

What is the real reason why they would have the Creator permit no moral evil? Is it not that the sinful deed causes suffering to others than the sinner, and to himself in punishment? Some rigorists in morals, antihedonists, would assert that a wrong deed is wrong in itself, irrespective of consequences; just ugly, a stain on the white radiance of being. For these thinkers it need frustrate no human (or animal) wants, nor give pain to others or to one's self; it is loathsome as a hideous scene or raucous noise is loathsome. This is really an aesthetic view, due to the purely contemplative perspective. If it were the whole truth, none would knowingly do wrong.

Vice is a monster of such hideous mien
As to be hated needs but to be seen.

And no doubt it is hideous, to a later reflection; but even then *hideous* is but a word for aesthetic pain; to the moral aesthete such blots and stains are painful in the extreme. But this is not the whole truth. Temptation means two opposing lures: the drug I crave against the health I need and want, where the right act satisfies the more basic lure, the wrong frustrates the deeper want. And if the wrong act gave no pain to man, still it would (so argues the personalist too) pain God to see it. But whether or no painful consequences mark the essence of the immoral, they are there and inseparable from it. And what we human beings resent, what to us in daily life *counts* as its wrongness, is the pain it inflicts or the joy it prevents in conscious beings. . . .

It is the misery that follows wickedness that makes the sensitive lover of his fellow men ask: Why should God have permitted wickedness? We are back again at the argument from *poena*. But now remember how that argument was met. It appeared that for aught we men know every single iota of suffering is deserved. True, we cannot at present prove that it is deserved, is the result perhaps of grievous sins in some former incarnation. The possibility remains. It cannot be ruled out. Perhaps then God permits person *A* to cause misery in person *B* because *B* deserves punishment for sins he committed in a former life. Perhaps *all* the miseries of men and animals are to be justified in this way.

But of course this doesn't meet the real trouble. Why did God permit men to sin, when sin entailed punishment? Yet the answer is not hard to see. No sin without free will, responsible self-originating choice. Now such choice is (for the personalists) God's gift to man, one of man's noblest traits. It is analogous to the creative power of God Himself. True, it may be abused by man. He may choose the wrong; then he must suffer penalty. But that is not in the least God's fault; God gave him absolute freedom of choice between right and wrong, with no compulsion whatever; the slightest bit of compulsion from God would indeed have been cruel and unjust. But to punish an evil deed, freely committed, is of course perfectly right. *Not* to punish it would be a mark of imperfection, of injustice on the part of God. No unprovable possibilities have to be taken into account here, as in the case of *poena*. *Culpa* really offers no problem. If we say God should not have permitted man (or anyone else) to sin, should not for a moment have allowed such a thing, we are surreptitiously importing the responsibility which is *wholly* man's, into God's creative act. God has no whit of share in the *particular* free choice of man for evil action; once the gift of choice is bestowed as man's innate possession, man has a *separate existence* and is wholly responsible for exercising the powers granted to him. At least the pluralists accept this separate existence, this independence (within limits of course) that goes with the ultimate reality of each person, and for them the problem of moral evil should disappear. And that is the simple straightforward answer to the problem of moral evil.

But now consider the position of those today whose sensitiveness for the suffering of others is so extreme that they do not believe in the justice of *any* punishment for sin. For these people, God is merciful rather than just; He would not willingly let a Nero, an Ivan the Terrible, a Hitler, suffer any pain at all. Now whether their view is true or false, it removes for them the problem of *moral* evil. If men don't deserve punishment for wickedness, if they are not to be blamed, then God is not to be blamed either, when He permits them to do wrong. Rather we ought to feel sorry for God, that He has made that mistake, and we ought to try to make Him happier by loving and helping those wicked men. Such a view limits the power of God, for His lack of intelligence is a lack of power to bring about the good. He may be all-loving, but is not all-powerful. It is "up to us" to increase His power by taking sides with Him.

But of course this view is just another instance of man's perennial tendency to one-sided exclusions. Because love is a great good, perhaps the greatest good, it is taken as the only good. Justice is ruled out. Human nature is viewed in its *affective* phase alone, or perhaps to a degree as cognitive too; but the active phase, where dwells free choice, is overlooked. Free choice entails responsibility; what you have done is due to you, and you must take the consequences. In fact the very doctrine of love, as taught by these soft pacifists, itself implies responsibility. They say, "you *ought* to love all beings without limit." Suppose you refuse. Then you have done *wrong*.

Are you not to blame? But no, they say, you are to be pitied, and loved all the more as a poor misguided mortal. Then they shouldn't have said "you ought"; they should have said "Ah, please do." And indeed this method often works well; persuasion, where possible, is better than force, and many times *it is* possible. Better than force, yes; but free choice is not a matter of force, quite the opposite. The view here in question would leave nothing to man's free choice, and there it excludes what is the foundation stone of individual personal being. Remember how the personalists have insisted on the will as fundamental to personality. A man is this individual man, a source of events by himself, because he originates the choices that lead to his accomplishments. He *is* what he *does*. As species, as of this or that kind, he is what he inherits, what his genes and his social environment make him; as individual, he is what he *chooses* to love, to seek, to obtain. In actual daily living, we just have to treat men—and ourselves—as responsible beings. And responsibility means: you must take the consequences of your acts. The chickens come home to roost. That is what blame and credit mean. In brief, man has free choice, and as he chooses the right or wrong, love or its opposite if you will, so he should suffer or enjoy the consequences. True enough, in the order of things in this world, he who troubles others is not always troubled himself thereby. But the consequence of his evil deed is misery, deprivation, want; and he should experience that consequence himself since he is responsible for it. That is the way, the natural way, we all feel about it if we reflect coolly on the matter. That is our innate sense of justice. All the same, the emotion of the sensitive lover is so consuming that he is hardly able to see the beauty of justice, which is, as St. Thomas has taught, the beauty of balance and order. The beauty of love, the counterpart of justice, is that of aspiration.

No, we cannot exclude the motive of justice, praise or blame, punishment of wrongdoing. All theories of punishment as a human social instrument are here irrelevant. Whether it is a survival of the revenge-motive (the "vindictive" theory, as the pacifists call it), or is a way of prevention, or a means of reformation—these theories may stand or fall, but the individual-moral category of punishment stands on its own feet, a native and inevitable attitude of man's pursuit of the good life. Thereby we may see that moral evil points to no defect in God. To claim that it does is to "pass the buck."

Or is it finally argued that good is meaningless without evil; as one enjoys rest after the unrest of work, food after hunger, and so on? Doesn't everything imply its opposite? And if so, God is compelled to see that evil is not only permitted but committed, though (rather unfairly) He is unwilling to commit it Himself. Wherefore His power is limited. Again the answer is simple. There is no a priori proof that everything implies its opposite. The statement in any case is too vague to be workable. A general principle of contrast does indeed hold in many realms of being, but always it needs empirical verification. The most we can say in respect of man's moral good is that right action implies the *possibility* of wrong action. Certainly we don't have to *choose* the wrong in order to choose the right. Do you say: God is better pleased by the one sinner who repents than by the ninety and nine just men who need no repentance? And because we who love God wish to please Him, therefore we ought to sin and repent? Now here is a genuine self-contradiction. Nobody can sin that good may come when he repents. If he really means to repent he is repenting now in his heart and will not commit the sin;

repentance means abhorrence that prevents. To be sure, a man may do something which is against the moral code in which he has been brought up. He may lie to save a life which he believes to be of great value to humanity. He may kill a hopeless sufferer to put the tormented one out of his agony, provided he sees no other way of helping. These are not sins committed that good may come, whether or not they are mistakes; they are prompted by love of fellow men. We do indeed need moral codes, yet there are cases, happily rare, where the rigidity of the code must take on a little elasticity. The letter killeth, but the spirit maketh alive. As long as he sincerely believes he is contributing to the greater good of men (animals too) he is not sinning. After all there is only one absolute moral command in respect of creatures: love one another. So taught Jesus.

In sum on the whole problem of evil as related to God's power: there is no logical implication that His power be limited by the presence of evil: evil as imperfection, as pain, or as guilt. On the contrary, we poor human beings have experiences which suggest how evils may be overcome, thereby *manifesting to us* more of God's power than would be *manifested*—though it would still be there—if no evil were permitted.

52. *Immortality**

DOUGLAS CLYDE MACINTOSH (1877–1948)

Moral optimism assumes man's right to an optimistic outlook on moral conditions. As a life-attitude it is moral and critical enough to recognize the unconditional imperative of the moral law, and at the same time normal and healthy-minded enough to rest assured that he whose life is consecrated to the moral ideal, to the discovery and performance of his duty, has a right to be nobly unconcerned as to what may happen to himself. What it logically involves is the faith that no absolute and final disaster can happen to man through purely external or physical events; that, even when outside forces have done their worst, no ultimate and irremediable evil,

* From *The Reasonableness of Christianity*, pp. 64-73. By permission of publishers, Charles Scribner's Sons.

no final loss of spiritual values, can have befallen the will that was steadfastly devoted to the realization of the true ideal.

If we turn to human experience for confirmation of this conviction, we are confronted at once with the universal fact of physical death. Sooner or later each individual dies and disappears; only the race remains. Is this consistent with moral optimism? The ultimate conservation of all absolute, that is, spiritual, values, in spite of physical death, is obviously involved in the morally optimistic faith upon which we have taken our stand; for only under such conditions could the moral will be justified in facing any possible physical event with equanimity.

But the adequate conservation of spiritual values necessarily involves the conservation of persons. If all genuine spiritual values are to be conserved without final loss, the death of the body cannot mean the end of personal existence. There are spiritual values, moral and social values particularly, but other values also, which are inseparably bound up with the existence of the individuals in and for whom they exist. Since the human individual is a free agent, as we have seen, he is able creatively to produce spiritual values. This means that, given ever new opportunity for activity, he would be of infinite value as a possible means of creating such values. In other words, by virtue of his moral personality, man is of potentially infinite value as a means. Thus we find reflective support for love's intuitive certainty of the infinite value of the individual as an end. There is a cynical proverb to the effect that love is blind, and this may be true of some kinds of love. But all noble and true loves are glimpses into the infinite worth of the personal individual as such, and he who does not know from experience what true love is, is blind. Feeling has cognitive value, and, generally speaking, the true worth of personality is not discovered apart from love.

There is nothing more fundamental or essential in Christianity than this appreciation of the infinite value of the human individual, and it is in this essentially Christian insight that we find the true answer to latter-day speculations about a merely conditional immortality. Wherever a divine all-seeing love would find absolute values, actual or potential, there is something the conservation of which divine love imperatively demands. If personalities in whom such absolute values exist are allowed to sink into nothingness, then faith in the conservation of absolute values is mistaken, and moral optimism is an illusory dream.

We are aware that some high-minded persons would turn attention away from the individual to the race, urging that while the individual unit may cease to exist, the race will persist; that values produced by the individual will be conserved in the race. Now this is true enough of some of the spiritual values produced by the individual, but it is not true of all. In character and friendship are moral and social values which are inseparably bound up with the existence of the individual. Spiritual personality is of value as an end, and not merely as a means. We can view with composure the final disappearance of merely relative and instrumental values; but spiritual personality is of absolute value as an end. And spiritual personality is always individual, even when it is also social. Wherefore the moral optimism which affirms the conservation of all spiritual values cannot be satisfied with the persistence of the race alone. Besides, in spite of the speculations of some thinkers, it remains doubtful whether without the immortality of the individual there can be any immortality for the race. If, then, at last upon the physically embodied race inhabiting this gradually cooling planet the "slow, sure doom" shall fall, without personal immortality all values of and for human personality, social as well as individual, will be as if they never had been, and moral optimism will have been all along a delusion and a lie.

Just what will be involved in the undiminished conservation of spiritual personality, with its absolute values, we may not be able to surmise, except in a general way. But there must of necessity be included not only continued existence of intelligence, with experience, selective memory, and thought, but moral activity with the development of character, and social relations, with the conservation of all true friendship and love. All this, with the vision beatific, moral optimism must postulate and the conservation of absolute values include. And with this, essential Christianity is in full accord. Apart from figurative and merely negative descriptions of the ideal future life, our Christian scriptures contain statements in terms of relationship to Christ which may be regarded as expressions of a more general truth. "To be with Christ"—this stands for ideal social relations. "We shall be like Him"—this means progressive realization of ideal character. "His servants shall serve Him"—this, taken with the words of the parable of judgment, "Inasmuch as ye have done it unto one of the least of these my brethren, ye have done it unto Me," can only mean ideal human activity along lines of social service. All of this is essentially Christian and all is logically involved in moral optimism, so that if the attitude we have so designated is reasonable and true, the same may be said of this vital and essentially Christian hope.

It will be seen that from the point of view of moral optimism the question as to whether the individual desires a future life is comparatively unimportant. Whether we desire immortality or not, the conservation of every person whose will is actually or even potentially moral is as imperative as the value of every such person is absolute. We may not want to live again; but as it is our duty to act morally whether we want to or not, so it is our duty to want to live again and to do in a future existence whatever good it may then be possible for us to accomplish. The desire to live forever is not a selfish or unworthy desire, if the extension of existence is not desired for unworthily selfish purposes. If to live is in itself better than not to live, to continue to live is similarly better than not to continue to live. It could never be right to refuse or not to desire further opportunity to develop and express the good will, and any adequate appreciation of the moral ideal with its categorical imperative must be accompanied by desire amounting to an absolute demand for opportunity progressively to realize that ideal.

We have seen that belief in human immortality is logically involved in moral optimism. We have also seen that moral optimism is normal and necessary for spiritual ends, so that, finding it theoretically permissible as far as we went into the matter, we have continued to regard it as a reasonable fundamental faith. With equal cogency we conclude that belief in immortality is reasonable also. But it is always true that the more general hypothesis is tested in the tests applied to the propositions logically deduced from it, and we may raise the further question whether belief in a future life, together with the moral optimism of which it is one expression, is still theoretically permissible when we come to look further into the facts of nature and human life. It is admitted that with the morally discerning and those who have known friendship dearer than life itself, the demand for immortality is too imperious for the hope to be given up for anything short of its refutation by indubitable facts of experience. But the question remains whether, in the light of modern science, such refutation may not be forthcoming.

It must be admitted that it is the opinion of some scientists that human consciousness depends upon the brain in such a way that without that organ the conscious existence of the individual would be impossible; but this is not the teaching of science itself. As William James, William McDougall, and other eminent psychologists have said, and as every psychologist who has not needlessly sold out to materialism knows, there are no known facts concerning the relation of consciousness to the brain which require us to believe that the physical organ is indispensably necessary for conscious survival. Consciousness is instrumental to the body, without doubt; but increasingly the inverse relationship tends to establish itself. More and more as development proceeds in the individual and in the race, brain and body come to be instrumental to mind, whose interests reach out far beyond the bodily organism and its physical environment. It is not necessarily an unreasonable interpretation of the facts, therefore, when mind is regarded as destined for a position of ultimate independence with reference to the present physical body. That normal faith of the healthy mind and moral will which we have called moral optimism, leading necessarily, as it does, to belief in human immortality, cannot be dismissed as forbidden by the facts. We who are still in the body have not yet verified the future life directly. The time for that will come when this earthly physical life is over. Whether we shall ever in this life verify the other life indirectly, through completely demonstrated communication from the departed, may well be doubted. When fraud, hallucination, and mere chance coincidence have been eliminated from the phenomena to which spiritists appeal, it seems always possible to regard the facts as due to subconscious activities of the medium and others present, and to telepathy between living persons. However, it may be remarked in passing that if mind in its relation to body is independent enough to make telepathy under certain conditions a fact, it seems not unreasonable to think that mind may be independent enough to continue to exist and act when set free from the body at death.

A more assured argument for the possibility of immortality is found in the fact of human freedom, already sufficiently established as morally certain. Human freedom being granted in the sense in which we have defined the term,

it follows that mind or the self acts in an originative manner in and through the brain; and if the mind is independent enough to act thus creatively in and through the brain, it may conceivably be independent enough to act independently of this particular organism altogether. If mind is an agent and not a mere phenomenon, it may conceivably find or be furnished with another instrument when the one it is now using becomes no longer serviceable. In spite, then, of anything the pessimistic or doubting critic can show by appeal to reason or experience, belief in the undiminished survival of human personality is theoretically permissible and, in view of its foundation in moral optimism, presumably true. Considering, then, the central place the belief occupies in the Christian religious faith, we are in a position to claim, at this point also, further confirmation of essential Christianity as reasonable and so presumably true.

Before leaving the subject, however, one very important thing remains to be said. If we ask the secret of the persistence of belief in immortality in the absence of any absolute empirical demonstration of the truth of the doctrine, the answer is that, after an appreciation of the worth of human personality, the chief factor in the belief has been the idea of God, that is, of a Power great enough and good enough to conserve the human individual in spite of bodily death. If we can be adequately assured, through experience or argument, of the existence of such a Being, we can at the same time be reassured of the truth of immortality. If we can be assured that the Supreme Being in the universe loves man with an everlasting love, we can be assured that man is intended for everlasting life.

SUGGESTED FURTHER READINGS
FOR CHAPTER SEVEN

Alexander, Samuel, *Space, Time and Deity,* Vol. II.

Bergson, Henri, *The Two Sources of Morality and Religion.*

Berkeley, George, *Three Dialogues Between Hylas and Philonous.*

Bronstein, Daniel J. and Schulweis, Harold, *Approaches to the Philosophy of Religion.*

Durkheim, Emile, *The Elementary Forms of Religious Life.*

Foster, G. B., *The Function of Religion.*

Frazer, J. G., *The Golden Bough.*

Freud, Sigmund, *The Future of an Illusion.*

Fromm, Erich, *Psychoanalysis and Religion.*

Hegel, Georg W., *Lectures on the Philosophy of Religion.*

Hocking, W. E., *The Meaning of God in Human Experience.*

James, W., *Varieties of Religious Experience.*

Kant, Immanuel, *Religion Within the Limits of Reason Alone.*

Kierkegaard, S., *The Journals.*

Leuba, James H., *A Psychological Study of Religion.*

Macintosh, D. C., *The Problem of Religious Knowledge.*

McTaggart, J. M. E., *Some Dogmas of Religion.*

Malinowski, Bronislaw, *Magic, Science, and Religion.*

Mill, J. S., *Three Essays on Religion.*

Montague, W. P., *Belief Unbound.*

Pfeffer, Leo, *Church, State, and Freedom.*

Plato, *Euthyphro.*

Taylor, A. E., *Faith of a Moralist,* Vol. I, II.

Tillich, D., *The Religious Situation.*

Chapter Eight

THEORIES OF REALITY

INTRODUCTION

WE all observe many facts and go through many experiences; yet somehow we are not fully satisfied with isolated, piecemeal facts and experiences; we wish to tie them together and thus arrive at some sense of them as a whole. We make big charts of life and existence not unlike an artist who makes a sketch of what he wants to fill in with detail. We call the world good or bad, designful or chaotic, mental or material. Most of these charts or world-views, sometimes referred to as theories of reality or metaphysical systems, are mythical, fantastic, and intellectually irresponsible. Too often they are intense expressions of what we wish the world to be rather than interpretations of what the world really is. And yet, more or less, we all genuinely desire to get a critical, inclusive, and coherent perspective of the nature of things.

There are many theories of reality. In a sense every individual has his own theory of reality, for there will always be individual differences in experience and in the selection of facts. But in the history of the human race certain major theories of reality have persisted. Although these major theories have all sorts of variations within themselves, they are sufficiently definite to be regarded as types. Of these major types five will be considered here—metaphysical dualism, idealism, naturalism, process-philosophy, and existentialism.

I. Metaphysical Dualism

The first theory of reality to be considered will be dualism. Dualism is a theory of knowledge as well as a theory of reality, but it is with the latter that we are now concerned. Metaphysical dualism is based on the belief that there are two kinds of primary reality of which neither can be reduced to the other or regarded as a mere shadow of the other. These two kinds of reality may run parallel to each other or they may interact.

Earlier forms of dualism were primarily moral and religious in their emphasis. Reality was described as a struggle between good and evil forces, between Ahura Mazda and Ahriman, between God and the Devil. In Greek philosophy, however, a more metaphysical type of dualism began to emerge, in which the material tended to be contrasted with the immaterial. Mediaeval philosophy further emphasized the dichotomy between the material and the immaterial. According to it, man is a union of body and soul, of which the former is material and mortal, and the latter immaterial and immortal.

But for an incisive formulation of metaphysical dualism one must go to Descartes. Descartes inherited the dualism of St. Augustine and Scholasticism, but he was clearer in his analysis and introduced a sharper contrast between matter and mind. For Descartes there are two kinds of substances—matter and mind.[1] And he defines substance as "an existent thing which requires nothing but itself in order to exist." The distinctive characteristic of matter is extension; the distinctive characteristic of mind is thinking. These two substances or realities comprise two separate systems; what happens in one system does not depend on the laws or principles of the other system. The material world—and he includes non-human living beings in this world —is mechanical throughout. Mind, on the other hand, is outside the net of mechanism. Yet these two substances interact; there is a causal relation between them. The mind acts upon the body by initiating and regulating its motions, and matter acts upon the mind by causing its sensations and moods. But how does this happen? Descartes thought that the seat of mind was the pineal gland and that the mind regulated the body at this point. But he faced a major difficulty in this theory of interaction. How could a non-spatial thing have a spatial location and causally control a mechanical system? And again, how could a spatial thing causally affect the action of a non-spatial thing? Although this objection was raised to his theory in his own time, he never fully met it, nor have the later dualists been able to resolve it satisfactorily.

In contemporary thought it is the vitalists—represented by Bergson, Driesch, and McDougall—who most effectively carry on the tradition of metaphysical dualism.[2] They all agree that living and mental beings are more than physico-chemical systems and that this "more" is a non-spatial, non-physical agency, such as *élan vital, entelechy,* or *anima.* The arguments offered by the vitalists are complex and subtle. But on the whole, their views converge to the central claim that the teleological or near-teleological processes of life and mind are inexplicable apart from the postulate of a vitalistic agency. To explain life and mind, they believe, it is necessary to introduce the notion of guidance, and this is lacking in mechanistic explanations. Driesch, for example, claims that physico-chemical concepts are incapable of explaining the fact that when the embryo of a star-fish is cut in half, the two pieces develop into miniature star-fishes; to make this fact intelligible he feels compelled to postulate the vitalistic agency *entelechy* in addition to the physico-chemical elements. Similarly, Bergson believes that the current mechanistic and near-mechanistic evolutionary theories are incapable of explaining the development of the eye on two divergent evolutionary lines, as in the molluscs and vertebrates. According to him, such a development requires the assumption that the *élan vital* creatively guides the evolu-

---

[1] There is, however, a third reality for Descartes—God, who creates and sustains matter and mind.

[2] In Bergson, however, there is a strain that suggests a novel form of monism, since he occasionally regards matter as a deposit of universal life.

tionary process. And again, McDougall denies that psychological phenomena—such as memory, consciousness, meaning, will—can be explained in the absence of a non-physical agency like *anima*. Montague, in the selection that has been included, also defends a dualistic metaphysics by distinguishing between adjectival and substantive notions of mind and by arguing for the latter view.

It is true that many biological and psychological processes are very complex and that many of them have not yet been adequately explained; but one should hesitate before assuming that the difficulties in question are sufficient warrant for resorting to unverifiable concepts. It is important to bear in mind that the vitalistic agency is in principle unverifiable. And though it is also true that biological and psychological phenomena involve teleological processes, one should make sure whether to make these processes intelligible it is necessary to introduce, as the vitalists do, a chasm between matter and life, between body and mind.

So far, in speaking of metaphysical dualism, the reference has been only to life and mind; but dualism as a theory of reality has also a cosmic application. Metaphysical dualism usually drifts towards a type of supernaturalism. The mediaeval Thomists and the modern neo-Thomists, Descartes, and most of the contemporary vitalists, all maintain that it is necessary to believe in a supernatural supreme Spirit or God. Most of the arguments for this view were considered in some detail in the former chapter on religion.

II. Idealism

Another great historic theory of reality is idealism. The idealist's central belief is that reality is of the nature of mind. This view is both a simpler and a more complex one than dualism; it is simpler because for it there is only one type of reality, and it is more complex because in its attempt to prove that matter depends on mind, its reasoning gets involved. And, again, it is not enough to say that reality is of the nature of mind, since mind has a number of aspects—perceiving, reasoning, and willing. Idealists differ among themselves as to which of these aspects is the prime reality. Reality is for some a system of perceptions; for others, a coherent system of thought; and for still others, a form of will. There are also idealists who try to synthesize all of the aspects of mind into a system. The idealistic view might have been appropriately called Mentalism or Spiritualism, in the sense that the ultimate reality is said to be Mind or Spirit. Yet the name "idealism" has its own peculiar implications, for most idealists feel that ideals find a firmer footing in a universe that is basically mind rather than matter.

Idealism, like dualism, has a long history. Only a few of the landmarks may be mentioned. Long before its development in the West, idealism was the core of Vedantism and Brahmanism in India and of certain Buddhistic sects in China. In the West, Plato was the first great idealist, though there was always a strong dualistic strain in his philosophy. Plato's idealism is not primarily mentalistic but logical. For him the real things are Ideas, but he meant by Ideas not mental states or images but objective forms, eternal essences, prototypes. For the development of mentalistic idealism one must go to Berkeley, who is often regarded as the true founder of modern idealism. His theory that the existence of objects depends upon perception has been the cornerstone of most idealistic arguments. Kant, though not himself an idealist in the strict sense of the word, since he did not reduce the whole of reality to mind, made possible the development of Absolute Idealism through his doctrine that knowledge is in large part determined by the formal activity of the mind. Hegel is the outstanding figure in the development of post-Kantian idealism. For him, reality is rational throughout, and the rational is real. The world, one might say, is a great thought-process and to know the laws of thought one must know the laws of reality. Idealism spread to other countries, especially in the Hegelian form. In England, Green, Bradley, and Bosanquet were idealists; in Italy, Croce and Gentile; and in America, Royce and Howison.

As has just been indicated, idealism takes many forms. For metaphysical analysis, pluralistic idealism and monistic idealism are of special importance. Pluralistic idealism pictures the universe as a society of spirits. Although there may be a hierarchy of spirits culminating in a supreme Mind, individuality is never lost. God himself as a member of this society is limited in power. Pluralistic idealists, on the whole, emphasize the values of the personal life, such as freedom, individuality, change, reality of time. On the other hand, monistic idealists would unify reality in one supreme Mind or Self; they emphasize the dynamic relations and interactions that exist among different phases of reality. Monistic idealism tends to be eternalistic, deterministic, and optimistic. There have been many attempts to synthesize these polar extremes of idealism.

The first impression of idealism may be puzzling. It is not obvious that reality is a society of minds or a universal Mind. Surely common sense does not favor this philosophy. What, then, is the reasoning out of which the idealistic world-view takes its rise? The present discussion will be limited to some of Royce's arguments for idealism, since he is not only the most brilliant idealist this country has produced but also important because of his rich synthesis of the pluralistic and monistic forms of idealism. For Royce reality is a supreme Mind. This Mind he calls Self, God, Absolute, Logos. But in Royce's Absolute, individuals are not swallowed up; they are unique and indispensable parts of the whole. In such a universe nothing is dead. Nature as a whole and in its specific parts is conscious. As Royce puts it, "My hypothesis is that in case of Nature in general, as in case of the particular portions of Nature known as our fellow-men, we are dealing with phenomenal signs of a vast conscious process."

One argument which Royce offers for his idealism is based on the distinction which he makes between the World of Description and the World of Appreciation. According to him, the World of Description, which is the world of science, deals "with a realm of abstraction,—everywhere founded upon final truth although in itself not final." It is very much like describing a friend as a congeries of physical qualities, that is, by omitting what counts most—his character or his lovableness. Description emphasizes only quantitative relations and uniform laws. To understand reality fully one must go beyond and behind the World of Description. "We can't describe the unique, e.g., Shelley's sense that at the winds of spring, etc. That we have to appreciate." It is only through inner appreciation that we discover the irreplaceability of the one we love, the unity of our own selves, the social interdependence of individuals, and the organic inclusiveness of the Absolute.

Another of Royce's arguments in support of his idealism is the claim that mind is primary in the knowing process. This type of argument is fundamental for most idealists. Royce's formulation of it consists of two parts. Like Berkeley, he argues, first, that external objects depend on mind for their existence. No object can have meaning apart from the knower. This being so, the inference is drawn that objects cannot exist apart from the mind; that is, they are only ideas. What do we mean, Royce asks, by the shape of anything or by the size of anything? What is the meaning of any property that we give to the outer world? All these, he maintains, can be expressed only in terms of one's ideas. What, for instance, are trees or mountains but sensations of mind, and again, what are sound waves or ether waves but conceptions of the mind to explain the facts of nature? But the argument thus far merely attempts to establish the claim that external objects depend for their existence on mind; the reality of the Supreme Mind has not yet been proved. To prove this we must pass to the second part of Royce's argument. Our knowledge, he maintains, always looks beyond the immediate present. How do we recognize the objects in our environment if not by combining our perception of them with memories of them as perceived in the past? How do we recall a forgotten name if not by appealing to our larger self of memory which knows that name? In knowledge, Royce argues, we must always draw more on a larger self than on the immediate one. Again, how do we settle our arguments? There must be some common framework for arriving at the truth. To escape conflict of aims or the relativity of human ideas, we must assume a self-consistent system of ideas; and this system is, for Royce, our deeper Self or the Absolute.

Royce's arguments raise many fundamental issues. As his argument maintains, science does possess abstractions and ideal constructions. But do these involve neglect of facts? And, again, as his second argument points out, the known object as an object of knowledge is always related to mind [this is sometimes called "the egocentric predicament"]. But does this fact prove that the known object has no independent existence? These problems have been given a great deal of attention in modern philosophy, but no unanimous solution has as yet been reached.

III. Naturalism

Naturalism is another theory of reality that must be considered. According to this theory, nature is the whole of reality; that is, there is no other realm of reality beyond or behind nature; there is no supernatural. Nature for the naturalist is all-inclusive; everything has its origin and career in nature. But what is this all-inclusive nature and how should one approach it to find its secret? A poet may find beauty in nature, a mystic an inner spirit, a practical man useful power; but the naturalist, though he does not deny the significance or value of these approaches to nature, insists that in order to know nature one must resort to the scientific method. Wherever knowledge is possible the naturalist is committed to the application of the scientific method. He claims that every area of nature—physical, biological, psychological, or social—must be approached by this method. This does not mean that the same specialized technique and instruments must be used in every area, but that the same general canons should be used to test the truth of every claim. Thus, for the naturalist, nature is what science says it is, or, more precisely, what completed science will say it is.

Like other great metaphysical systems, naturalism has had a long history. And, again, reference will be made to only a few leading representatives. In Western thought the Greek atomists Leucippus and Democritus were the first materialists.[3] According to them the world was composed of atoms which combined and recombined by necessity. The first modern materialist of note was Thomas Hobbes, who sought to reduce all events, inclusive of the mental, to motion. In the 18th century, preceding the French Revolution, materialism was vigorously advocated by Diderot, de La Mettrie, d'Holbach, and others. But the great era of naturalism was the 19th century. The extensive developments in mathematics, physics, biology, psychology, sociology, and particularly in Darwin's theory of evolution, gave a wide vogue to naturalism. Spencer tried to generalize the idea of evolution into a formula for the whole universe. Karl Marx, at one time an admirer of Hegel, turned Hegel's philosophy of history upside down by giving the chief role not to spirit but to material and economic conditions. All these and other figures spread the naturalistic outlook. Contemporary naturalism is more complex and varied than that of the nineteenth century. Some of the leading contemporary naturalists are Dewey, Santayana, Alexander, and Russell.

There are different types of naturalists. Of these we shall examine the reductive and non-reductive types.

The reductive naturalist is one who thinks that everything in nature, living as well as non-living, mental as well as non-mental, must be explained in the most basic, elementary physical terms. Traditionally this ideal was to explain everything in terms of matter in motion or in terms of the laws of mechanics. In current thought, reductive naturalism, which is sometimes called mechanism, has a looser meaning. The reductive naturalist is now one who usually tries to explain biological, psychological, and sociological phenomena in "nothing but" physico-chemical terms—such as motion, electric charge, oxidation, and so on. From this point of view such things as adaptation, thinking, loving, or the social will are "nothing but," that is, have the same status as physico-chemical entities and processes. Sometimes materialists like Democritus, Hobbes, and certain extreme contemporary behaviorists are supposed to hold this view. In any case, those who uphold reductive naturalism are compelled to draw a distinction between appearance and reality, between illusion and true judgment. According to them, all so-called biological or psychological occurrences should be regarded as mere appearance, since only physico-chemical occurrences can be granted the status of the real. But because life, mind, and society are conditioned by the physico-chemical medium, it does not necessarily follow that they can be wholly defined in terms of the concepts of this medium. The issue is an

---

[3] For the present, no sharp distinction will be made between naturalism and materialism.

empirical one; and empirically, different modes of action are being observed—the physical, the biological, the psychological, and the social.

What might be called non-reductive naturalism differs from the reductive type by not reducing everything to physico-chemical terms. Alexander's philosophy is an example of this type, since Alexander not only states with clearness the major principles common to the non-reductive naturalists but also offers some original speculations of his own, which, though perhaps of doubtful validity, yield new perspectives. As in the case of all other major metaphysical views, no one philosopher should be regarded as the definitive representative of naturalism. Though the exponents of any one type of philosophy hold certain major principles in common, there are always differences in emphasis or terminology or speculation.

The crucial idea in Alexander's naturalistic metaphysics is emergence. The best way to understand this idea of emergence is to compare and contrast it with the central claim of reductive naturalism. Alexander, as an emergentist, agrees with the reductionists that living and mental beings are compounded of physico-chemical elements and that there is no vitalistic entity, such as *élan vital*. He also agrees with the reductionists that no biological or psychological phenomenon, such as adaptation, thinking, or willing, would be possible without physical conditions. But he disagrees with the reductionists' claim that these phenomena are "nothing but" or that their meaning can be wholly expressed in physico-chemical terms. He believes, on the contrary, that when certain elements are organized in a certain way, new distinctive qualities emerge which are not identifiable with the properties of the elements in their isolation. According to him, one should distinguish between the discrete properties of an object and its organizational properties. An object, for example, may exhibit no curvature when one examines it discretely, that is, point for point, yet it may exhibit the quality of curvature when examined organizationally. The same principle applies when defining a molecule, a cell, or a living organism. It is experience that must show what organizations should be described merely in terms of the properties of their parts and what organizations should be described in terms of new distinctive qualities that result from the organization of their parts. Alexander also insists that "higher" levels of emergence could not have been predicted from a knowledge of the "lower" levels. For instance, antecedent to the emergence of life one could not have predicted the nature of life from a knowledge of atoms and molecules. Emergencies are, for Alexander, new facts.

Moreover, according to him, there are different levels of emergence. Most emergent evolutionists agree that there are three levels of natural existence—matter, life, and mind. Alexander is more speculative on this point. For him the lowest and basic level of existence is space-time. This is the stuff of which all things consist; it is the primal substance of all things; it is the begetter of all other levels. The next level is matter with its primary qualities—size, shape, motion. At still another level secondary qualities emerge, such as color and sound. These qualities have, for Alexander, a reality apart from our minds. Though they do not inhere in objects, as the primary qualities do, they belong to objects in relation to their surroundings—in relation to light in the case of color, in relation to air in the case of sound. Life comes at a still higher level. Life possesses certain unique qualities found only in the organism. Living organisms do not possess a new entity, but they are matter organized in a distinctive way. Yet living organisms have new emergent qualities. These are primarily the organic and kinaesthetic senses: the motion of muscles and the sensations of hunger and thirst—qualities quite distinct from colors and sounds, since they inhere in organic bodies. The next higher level of emergence is mind. Yet mind is firmly embedded in nature and emerges only when certain physiological conditions concur. Mind has two main functions, contemplation and enjoyment. We contemplate objects about us as mere things external to us and to one another. We contemplate our bodies when we look at our hands and feet. But when we play a game we enjoy our playing as well as contemplate it. Alexander's term enjoyment includes not only joy but also grief, and, indeed, every experience of the inner life.

Is there any higher level of emergence than mind? Most naturalists would stop at mind; but Alexander believes that the universe is pressing forward toward still higher levels of emergence. He often uses the term Deity for the level above mind. His Deity does not belong to the past but to the future, as some thing not yet actual. And Alexander does not think of Deity in the singular. Should this higher level come into existence, there would be many individuals on this level to which the term would apply.

Alexander's naturalism is impressive and has many merits, although some of his ideas are highly speculative. Many find it hard to accept his claim that the basic stuff of existence is space-time. And many can find no evidence for his exciting idea that the universe is pressing forward to create a higher level of existence.

IV. Process-Philosophy: A. N. Whitehead

Whitehead's metaphysics is one of the most daring and magnificent philosophical creations of our time. As against the abstractions of nineteenth-century scientific materialism he emphasizes concreteness and fidelity to experience. As against the irresponsible speculation of romanticists he insists on the necessity of incorporating into one's philosophy matters of fact and the most exacting recent theories of science. As against many thin current philosophies he richly weaves together varied aspects of experience: change with permanence, causality with teleology, science with religion, modern hopes with traditional values.

The key idea in Whitehead's interpretation of reality is process, and the title of his major work, *Process and Reality,* reminds us of this fact. The notion of process was eloquently expressed in early Greek philosophy by Heraclitus: "You cannot step twice into the same river; for fresh waters are ever flowing in upon us." In modern philosophy Bergson, James, Dewey and Alexander have again made change or flux the central concept of philosophy. The transitoriness of everyday events, the principle of evolution and the recent theories of matter all favor such a view.

Whitehead's notion of process is rich and many-sided. First, process is a universal happening in the spatio-temporal world. Every point in nature is in the throes of change—some swifter, others slower. There are no permanent substances, no immutable material particles, no self-sufficient realities. In Whitehead's view, "becoming" attains greater importance metaphysically than "being." As he expresses it, "The world is always becoming, and as it becomes it passes away and perishes." Second, world-process or becoming is not sheer flux, formless continuity, but is atomized, individualized into units of process. Passing events initiate new processes. The creative activity of emerging events brings together various elements of the prior events to form new syntheses that are characterized by new qualities and activities. In time these new syntheses disintegrate and become material for future events. This pattern of world-process is endless. Whitehead calls the units of process "actual entities." These are the ultimate facts of reality; there is no going behind them to anything more real. These units are not observable objects like stones, trees or human beings; they are too microscopic and transitory. They are like a vibration or pulse; yet every object is nothing more than a complex grouping of these processes. Finally, a given process, and this is the most controversial aspect of Whitehead's suggestion, is not merely a physical event but rather a center or pulse of experience. Individualized processes are, if you like, miniatures of human experience. They have feelings and are guided by aims. Even atoms and molecules, for Whitehead, are composed of processes which possess inner experience. Thus nature is alive at every point. This does not mean that every process has "conscious" experience, but it does mean that all processes have experience in the widest sense of the term. Whitehead's metaphysics becomes essentially a type of panpsychism.

In the turmoil of the changing world there is still, for Whitehead, something permanent. All passing and perishing events exhibit certain qualities that are not exposed to the ravages of time. Fallen leaves that are carried away by the winds, joyous moods that are changed by succeeding events, have eternal characteristics. The same shade of green or the same oval contour observed in one of the drifting leaves may recur in the future; the same joyous mood may recur. Qualities like greenness, ovalness, joyfulness, usually designated "universals," Whitehead calls "eternal objects." Eternal objects, for him, do not emerge from nature to perish like other events—they invade nature, or "ingress" (to use his own term) into the events of nature.

Whitehead's thought here, with some modifications, is similar to Plato's. Plato, in his attempt to reconcile the conflict between the changing and the changeless, the temporal and the eternal, had suggested the theory of Ideas or Forms. What one perceives, he claimed, are imperfect, perishing copies of immutable, eternal models. All straight lines, for example, as perceived by the senses are only crude repetitions of an ideal straight line. Similarly, Whitehead's eternal objects are immutable. They are not confined to the spatio-temporal world, yet they may be exemplified in the transitory events of this world. But Whitehead's eternal objects, unlike Plato's Ideas, are not superior realities; they are, rather, possibilities of realization.

One further question: How does one explain the fact that eternal objects as possibilities are actualized in the world in a rational, orderly way? The world exhibits a rational order, yet it might have been a chaos. Events occur as if prescribed by certain standards, yet they might have been altogether capricious. Whitehead thinks reality must contain some principle of limitation or selection to make this orderliness possible. This principle of limitation or rationality he calls "God." One may wish to ask, "Why should there be this principle of rationality, this God?" No answer can be given to this question, since God as the principle of rationality is the ground for the presence of everything. Not even God can account for His presence.   .

Yet Whitehead's God is not merely a metaphysical principle, but an object to satisfy religious aspiration. His God is persuasive rather than coercive; not omnipotent, but a "fellow-sufferer who understands." He is "wisdom." He is the poet of the world "with tender patience leading it by his vision of truth, beauty, and goodness."

Whitehead's metaphysics has scope, depth and coherence, yet it has certain serious difficulties.

In his speculative philosophy he presents the types of claim that are denied empirical knowledge. It is true that he is scrupulously empirical whenever the matter under discussion permits; yet in his attempt to fill the gaps in our knowledge he suggests ideas which are basically not verifiable. In this respect he partly revives the classic role of philosophy as something having access to knowledge which is not open to the uninitiated. But this role seems doubtful to many. Whitehead rightly points out that a true metaphysics must do justice to all phases of experience and that one's final interpretation of reality must escape the abstractions of the specific sciences; yet to achieve such an all-embracing philosophy it should not be necessary to go beyond natural, experimental knowledge. What we need is a more empirical metaphysics than Whitehead has offered.

Consider Whitehead's basic contention that every process, even the physical one, involves inner experience, that every point in the universe has feeling and is guided by a subjective aim. This affirmation is certainly not the result of empirical knowledge. On the contrary, it is nothing more than a postulate which goes beyond inductive knowledge to satisfy the demands of concreteness and of the continuity of matter and mind. And though one must make serious attempts to meet these demands, one's procedure must not, like Whitehead's, introduce greater difficulties than one started with.

Similarly unwarranted is his claim that reality must contain a principle of limitation, by him called God, as a ground for the actualization of possibilities. Unless one adheres to Whitehead's theories of eternal objects and actual entities, which are highly controversial, there is no need of going outside of nature to make sense of natural happenings. It is true that Whitehead's metaphysical God is free from most of the obscurities of the traditional gods. But one cannot help pointing out that this postulate gets one involved in the same difficulties as characterize every non-empirical philosophy.

Whitehead's metaphysics is an impressive alternative to naturalistic philosophy. To some his philosophy may be a new source of hope for retaining beliefs which have been deeply disturbed by science; but to others his occasional flights beyond the natural world are invitations they cannot accept. Yet even the latter need not deprive themselves of Whitehead's rich and generous insights.

V. Existentialism: Jean-Paul Sartre

Existentialism is a very recent metaphysical system. At present it exerts considerable influence, primarily in religious and literary circles. Sören Kierkegaard (1813–1855) is considered its originator, though some of its basic ideas go back to Scholastic philosophy, to Fichte, and especially to Schopenhauer and Nietzsche.

Contemporary existentialists belong to one of two camps: the theistic existentialists, such as Gabriel Marcel in France and Reinhold Niebuhr, Richard Kroner and Paul Tillich in North America; and the atheistic existentialists, such as Martin Heiddegger in Germany and Jean-Paul Sartre in France. Karl Jaspers, another major representative of existentialism, seems to occupy a middle position between the two camps. Existentialists as a group adhere to a common philosophic claim, though there are important differences among them. Sartre's discussion presents some of the major tenets of the existentialists, primarily of the atheistic type.

The primary doctrine of the existentialists on which all seem to agree, is that existence is prior to essence. As Sartre expresses it: "What they [existentialists] have in common is that they think that existence precedes essence, or, if you prefer, that subjectivity must be the starting point." What does this obscure saying mean? In reading existentialist literature one has to be prepared for a pervasive fogginess. As anti-rationalists they are not primarily concerned with rational categories. Yet the attempt will be made to apply such categories.

As a preliminary step, if one is to understand the doctrine that existence precedes essence, he should bear in mind that for most of the existentialists the term existence does not refer to existence in its widest sense but rather to the existence of man. Existentialism is primarily a philosophy of man as a struggling and hopeful being. What, then, does Sartre mean when he says that in man existence precedes essence? In answering this question Sartre is quite clear. He argues, and rather eloquently, that man's fate or reality is not determined by a prior superimposed essence or universal plan, as most dogmatic religions and metaphysical systems maintain. But rather, man's fate is determined by his free decisions and actions. The chisel that carves essences into existence is man's free choice between alternative actions. And Sartre assumes absolute freedom for such actions.

Existentialism is thus a philosophy of crisis, rather than a philosophy of pure contemplation. The existentialists assert that in life one must either take the reins or be destroyed. As Kierkegaard says: "*Both-And* is the road to hell," but "*Either-Or* is the key to heaven."

A second doctrine of the existentialists is that, as man must make choices and act, he is inevitably involved in anguish, forlornness and despair. These and similar words, like terror, violence, death, and nothingness are favorites with the existentialists. Anguish, as Sartre describes it, is due to our feeling of responsibility in action, especially towards others; forlornness results from our knowledge that we live in a purposeless world and in one in which all things perish, including oneself; despair comes from the realization that ultimately all events are contingent, that there are no certainties.

Finally, despite the fact that Sartre depicts a purposeless, precarious world, he is not a quietistic, pessimistic philosopher. Anguish, forlornness, and despair are spurs, in a sense, to heroic action and creative enterprise. As he says: "Being condemned in such a purposeless world, we must create [our values]."

Sartre has important philosophic insights, such as that reality has extra-rational (though not necessarily contrarational) aspects, that human beings have freedom, that our decisions shape our destiny. Yet one has to raise many questions. Is there any pure existence without essence? Do not even our free choices exhibit evidence of certain essences, that is, do not they exhibit character, significance? And, again, in what sense, if any, might one assume absolute freedom? Is Sartre neglecting many of the determinants—physical, psychological, social—of our actions? Finally, if one is not to be hampered by reason in one's crucial decisions, religious existentialists like Marcel and Niebuhr might ask Sartre: "Why not take the ultimate leap and have faith in God?" Analysis of these and of similar questions would help one not only obtain a fuller understanding of existentialism but also clarify one's own metaphysics.

The metaphysical systems that have been considered offer different world-views; yet they have one quality in common—the aim to understand fully the nature of things. It is not strange that equally great minds should arrive at different metaphysical views, for the task is complex and difficult.

Y. H. K.

53. *Objections to Metaphysics**

F. H. BRADLEY (1846–1924)

The writer on metaphysics has a great deal against him. Engaged on a subject which more than others demands peace of spirit, even before he enters on the controversies of his own field, he finds himself involved in a sort of warfare. He is confronted by prejudices hostile to his study, and he is tempted to lean upon those prejudices, within him and around him, which seem contrary to the first. It is on the preconceptions adverse to metaphysics in general that I am going to make some remarks by way of introduction. We may agree, perhaps, to understand by metaphysics an attempt to know reality as against mere appearance, or the study of first principles or ultimate truths, or again the effort to comprehend the universe, not simply piecemeal or by fragments, but somehow as a whole. Any such pursuit will encounter a number of objections. It will have to hear that the knowledge which it desires to obtain is impossible altogether; or, if possible in some degree, is yet practically useless; or that, at all events, we can

* From *Appearance and Reality*, Introduction. By kind permission of the publishers, Ruskin House.

want nothing beyond the old philosophies. And I will say a few words on these arguments in their order.

(*a*) The man who is ready to prove that metaphysical knowledge is wholly impossible has no right here to any answer. He must be referred for conviction to the body of this treatise. And he can hardly refuse to go there, since he himself has, perhaps unknowingly, entered the arena. He is a brother metaphysician with a rival theory of first principles. And this is so plain that I must excuse myself from dwelling on the point. To say the reality is such that our knowledge cannot reach it, is a claim to know reality; to urge that our knowledge is of a kind which must fail to transcend appearance, itself implies that transcendence. For, if we had no idea of a beyond, we should assuredly not know how to talk about failure or success. And the test, by which we distinguish them, must obviously be some acquaintance with the nature of the goal. Nay, the would-be sceptic, who presses on us the contradictions of our thoughts, himself asserts dogmatically. For these contradictions might be ultimate and absolute truth, if the nature of the reality were not known to be otherwise. But this introduction is not the place to discuss a class of objections which are themselves, however unwillingly, metaphysical views, and which a little acquaintance with the subject commonly serves to dispel. So far as is necessary, they will be dealt with in their proper place; and I will therefore pass to the second main argument against metaphysics.

(*b*) It would be idle to deny that this possesses great force. "Metaphysical knowledge," it insists, "may be possible theoretically, and even actual, if you please, to a certain degree; but, for all that, it is practically no knowledge worth the name." And this objection may be rested on various grounds. I will state some of these, and will make the

answers which appear to me to be sufficient.

The first reason for refusing to enter on our field is an appeal to the confusion and barrenness which prevail there. "The same problems," we hear it often, "the same disputes, the same sheer failure. Why not abandon it and come out? Is there nothing else more worth your labour?" To this I shall reply more fully soon, but will at present deny entirely that the problems have not altered. The assertion is about as true and about as false as would be a statement that human nature has not changed. And it seems indefensible when we consider that in history metaphysics has not only been acted on by the general development, but has also reacted. But, apart from historical questions, which are here not in place, I am inclined to take my stand on the admitted possibility. If the object is not impossible, and the adventure suits us—what then? Others far better than ourselves have wholly failed—so you say. But the man who succeeds is not apparently always the man of most merit, and even in philosophy's cold world perhaps some fortunes go by favour. One never knows until one tries.

But to the question, if seriously I expect to succeed, I must, of course, answer, No. I do not suppose, that is, that satisfactory knowledge is possible. How much we can ascertain about reality will be discussed in this book; but I may say at once that I expect a very partial satisfaction. I am so bold as to believe that we have a knowledge of the Absolute, certain and real, though I am sure that our comprehension is miserably incomplete. But I dissent emphatically from the conclusion that, because imperfect, it is worthless. And I must suggest to the objector that he should open his eyes and should consider human nature. Is it possible to abstain from thought about the universe? I do not mean merely that to every one the whole body of things must come in the gross, whether consciously or unconsciously, in a certain way. I mean that, by various causes, even the average man is compelled to wonder and to reflect. To him the world, and his share in it, is a natural object of thought, and seems likely to remain one. And so, when poetry, art, and religion have ceased wholly to interest, or when they show no longer any tendency to struggle with ultimate problems and to come to an understanding with them; when the sense of mystery and enchantment no longer draws the mind to wander aimlessly and to love it knows not what; when, in short, twilight has no charm—then metaphysics will be worthless. For the question (as things are now) is not whether we are to reflect and ponder on ultimate truth—for perhaps most of us do that, and are not likely to cease. The question is merely as to the way in which this should be done. And the claim of metaphysics is surely not unreasonable. Metaphysics takes its stand on this side of human nature, this desire to think about and comprehend reality. And it merely asserts that, if the attempt is to be made, it should be done as thoroughly as our nature permits. There is no claim on its part to supersede other functions of the human mind; but it protests that, if we are to think, we should sometimes try to think properly. And the opponent of metaphysics, it appears to me, is driven to a dilemma. He must either condemn all reflection on the essence of things,—and, if so, he breaks, or, rather, tries to break, with part of the highest side of human nature,—or else he allows us to think, but not to think strictly. He permits, that is to say, the exercise of thought so long as it is entangled with other functions of our being; but as soon as it attempts a pure development of its own, guided by the principles of its own distinctive working, he prohibits it forthwith. And this appears to be a paradox, since it seems equivalent to saying, You may satisfy your instinctive longing to reflect, so long as you do it in a way which is unsatisfactory. If your character is such that in you thought is satisfied by what does not, and cannot, pretend to be thought proper, that is quite legitimate. But if you are constituted otherwise, and if in you a more strict thinking is a want of your nature, that is by all means to be crushed out. And, speaking for myself, I must regard this as at once dogmatic and absurd.

But the reader, perhaps, may press me with a different objection. Admitting, he may say, that thought about reality is lawful, I still do not understand why, the results being what they are, you should judge it to be desirable. And I will try to answer this frankly. I certainly do not suppose that it would be good for every one to study metaphysics, and I cannot express any opinion as to the number of persons who should do so. But I think it quite necessary, even on the view that this study can produce no positive results, that it should still be pursued. There is, so far as I can see, no other certain way of protecting ourselves against dogmatic superstition. Our orthodox theology on the one side, and our common-place materialism on the other side (it is natural to take these as prominent instances), vanish like ghosts before the daylight of free sceptical enquiry. I do not mean, of course, to condemn wholly either of these beliefs; but I am sure that either, when taken seriously, is the mutilation of our nature. Neither, as experience has amply shown, can now survive in the mind which has thought sincerely on first principles; and it seems desirable that there should be such a refuge for the man who burns to think consistently, and yet is too good to become a slave, either to stupid fanaticism or dishonest sophistry. That is one reason why I think that metaphysics, even if it end in total scepticism, should be studied by a certain number of persons.

And there is a further reason which, with myself perhaps, has even more weight. All of us, I presume, more or less, are led beyond the region of ordinary facts. Some in one way and some in others, we seem to touch and have communion with what is beyond the visible world. In various manners we find something higher, which both supports and humbles, both chastens and transports us. And, with certain persons, the intellectual effort to understand the universe is a principal way of thus experiencing the Deity. No one, probably, who has not felt this, however differently he might describe it, has ever cared much for metaphysics. And, wherever it has been felt strongly, it has been its own justification. The man whose nature is such that by one path alone his chief desire will reach consummation, will try to find it on that path, whatever it may be, and whatever the world thinks of it; and, if he does not, he is contemptible. Self-sacrifice is too often the "great sacrifice" of trade, the giving cheap what is worth nothing. To know what one wants, and to scruple at no means that will get it, may be a harder self-surrender. And this appears to be another reason for some persons pursuing the study of ultimate truth.

(c) And that is why, lastly, existing philosophies cannot answer the purpose. For whether there is progress or not, at all events there is change; and the changed minds of each generation will require a difference in what has to satisfy their intellect. Hence there seems as much reason for new philosophy as there is for new poetry. In each case the fresh production is usually much inferior to something already in existence; and yet it answers a purpose if it appeals more personally to the reader. What is really worse may serve better to promote, in certain respects and in a certain generation, the exercise of our best functions. And that is why, so long as we alter, we shall always want, and shall always have, new metaphysics.

I will end this introduction with a word of warning. I have been obliged to speak of philosophy as a satisfaction of what may be called the mystical side of our nature—a satisfaction which, by certain persons, cannot be as well procured otherwise. And I may have given the impression that I take the metaphysician to be initiated into something far higher than what the common herd possesses. Such a doctrine would rest on a most deplorable error, the superstition that the mere intellect is the highest side of our nature, and the false idea that in the intellectual world work done on higher subjects is for that reason higher work. Certainly the life of one man, in comparison with that of another, may be fuller of the Divine, or, again, may realize it with an intenser consciousness; but there is no calling or pursuit which is a private road to the Deity. And assuredly the way through speculation upon ultimate truths, though distinct and legitimate, is not superior to others. There is no sin, however prone to it the philosopher may be, which philosophy can justify so little as spiritual pride.

54. *Metaphysics**

ARISTOTLE (B.C. 384–322)

I. Being

There is a science which investigates being as being and the attributes which belong to this in virtue of its own nature. Now this is not the same as any of the so-called special sciences; for none of these others deals generally with being as being. They cut off a part of being and investigate the attributes of this part —this is what the mathematical sciences for instance do. Now since we are seeking the first principles and the highest causes, clearly there must be some thing to which these belong in virtue of its own nature. If then our predecessors who sought the elements of existing things were seeking these same principles, it is necessary that the elements must be elements of being not by accident but just because it *is* being. Therefore it is of being as being that we also must grasp the first causes.

There are many senses in which a thing may be said to 'be,' but they are related to one central point, one definite kind of thing, and have not merely the *epithet* 'being' in common. Everything which is healthy is related to health, one thing in the sense that it preserves health, another in the sense that it produces it, another in the sense that it is a symptom of health, another because it is capable of it. And that which is medical is relative to the medical art, one thing in the sense that it possesses it, another in the sense that it is naturally adapted to it, another in the sense that it is a function of the medical art. And we shall find other words used similarly to these. So, too, there are many senses in which a thing is said to be, but all refer to one starting-point; some things are said to be because they are substances, others because they are affections of substance, others because they are a process towards substance, or destructions or privations or qualities of substance, or productive or generative of substance, or of things which are relative to substance, or negations of some of these things or of substance itself. It is for this reason that we say even of non-being that it *is* non-being. As, then, there is one science which deals with all healthy things, the same applies in the other cases also. For not only in the case of things which have one common notion does the investigation belong to one science, but also in the case of things which are related to one common nature; for even these in a sense have one common notion. It is clear then that it is the work of one science also to study all things that are, *qua* being.—But everywhere science deals chiefly with that which is primary, and on which the other things depend, and in virtue of which they get their names. If, then, this is substance, it is of substances that the philosopher must grasp the principles and the causes.

* From *Metaphysics*. Oxford Translation. By permission of the Oxford University Press.

II. The Four Causes

'Cause' means (1) that from which (as immanent material) a thing comes into being, e.g. the bronze of the statue and the silver of the saucer, and the classes which include these. (2) The form or pattern, i.e. the formula of the essence, and the classes which include this (e.g. the ratio 2:1 and number in general are causes of the octave) and the parts of the formula. (3) That from which the change or the freedom from change first begins, e.g. the adviser is a cause of the action, and the father a cause of the child, and in general the maker a cause of the thing made and the change-producing of the changing. (4) The end, i.e. that for the sake of which a thing is, e.g. health is the cause of walking. For why does one walk? We say 'that one may be healthy,' and in speaking thus we think we have given the cause. The same is true of all the means that intervene before the end, when something else has put the process in motion (as e.g. thinning or purging or drugs or instruments intervene before health is reached); for all these are for the sake of the end, though they differ from one another in that some are instruments and others are actions.

These, then, are practically all the senses in which causes are spoken of, and as they are spoken of in several senses it follows that there are several causes of the same thing, and in no accidental sense, e.g. both the art of sculpture and the bronze are causes of the statue not in virtue of anything else but *qua* statue; not, however, in the same way, but the one as matter and the other as source of the movement. And things can be causes of one another, e.g. exercise of good condition, and the latter of exercise; not, however, in the same way, but the one as end and the other as source of movement.—Again, the same thing is sometimes a cause of contraries; for that which when present causes a particular thing, we sometimes charge, when absent, with the contrary, e.g. we impute the shipwreck to the absence of the steersman, whose presence was the cause of safety; and both—the presence and the privation—are causes as sources of movement.

All the causes now mentioned fall under four senses which are the most obvious. For the letters are the causes of syllables, and the material is the cause of manufactured things, and fire and earth and all such things are the causes of bodies, and the parts are causes of the whole, and the hypotheses are causes of the conclusion, in the sense that they are that out of which these respectively are made; but of these some are cause as *substratum* (e.g. the parts), others as *essence* (the whole, the synthesis, and the form). The semen, the physician, the adviser, and in general the agent, are all *sources of change* or of rest. The remainder are causes as the *end* and the good of the other things; for that, for the sake of which other things are, is naturally the best and the end of the other things; let us take it as making no difference whether we call it good or apparent good.

These, then, are the causes, and this is the number of their kinds, but the *varieties* of causes are many in number, though when summarized these also are comparatively few. Causes are spoken of in many senses, and even of those which are of the same kind some are causes in a prior and others in a posterior sense, e.g. both 'the physician' and 'the professional man' are causes of health, and 'the ratio 2:1' and 'number' are causes of the octave, and the classes that include any particular cause are always causes of the particular effect. Again, there are accidental causes and the classes which include these, e.g. while in one sense 'the sculptor' causes the statue, in another sense 'Polyclitus' causes it, because the sculptor happens to be Polyclitus; and the classes that include the accidental cause are also causes, e.g. 'man'—or in general 'animal'—is the cause of the statue, because Polyclitus is a man, and a man is an animal. Of accidental causes also some are more remote or nearer than others, as, for instance, if 'the white' and 'the musical' were called causes of the statue, and not only 'Polyclitus' or 'man.' But besides all these varieties of causes, whether proper or accidental, some are called causes as being able to act, others as acting, e.g. the cause of the house's being built is the builder, or the builder when building.—The same variety of language will be found with regard to the effects of causes, e.g. a thing may be called the cause of this statue or of a statue or in general of an image, and of this bronze or of bronze or of matter in general; and similarly in the case of accidental effects. Again, both accidental and proper causes may be spoken of in combination, e.g. we may say not 'Polyclitus' nor 'the sculptor,' but 'Polyclitus the sculptor.'

Yet all these are but six in number, while each is spoken of in two ways: for (1) they are causes either as the individual, or as the class that includes the individual, or as the accidental, or as the class that includes the accidental, and these either as combined, or as taken simply; and (2) all may be taken as acting or as having a capacity. But they differ inasmuch as the acting causes and the individuals exist, or do not exist, simultaneously with the things of which they are causes, e.g. this particular man who is curing, with this particular man who is recovering health, and this particular builder with this particular thing that is being built; but the potential causes are not always in this case; for the house does not perish at the same time as the builder.

III. Potentiality and Actuality

Since we have treated of the kind of potency which is related to movement, let us discuss actuality, its genus and its differentia. In the course of our analysis it will also become clear, with regard to the potential, that we not only ascribe potency to that whose nature it is to move something else, or to be moved by something else, either without qualification or in some particular way, but also use the word in another sense, in the pursuit of which we have discussed these previous senses. Actuality means the existence of the thing, not in the way which we express by 'potentially'; we say that potentially, for instance, a statue of Hermes is in the block of wood and the half-line is in the whole, because it might be separated out, and we call even the man who is not studying a man of science, if he is capable of actually studying a particular problem. Our meaning can be seen in the particular cases by induction, and we must not seek a definition of everything but be content to grasp the analogy,—that as that which is building is to that which is capable of building, so is the waking to the sleeping, and that which is seeing to that which has its eyes shut but has sight, and that which is shaped out of the matter to the matter, and that which has been wrought up to the unwrought. Let actuality be defined by one member of this antithesis, and 'the potential' by the other. But all things are not said in the *same sense* to exist actually, but only by analogy—as A is in B or to B, C is in D or to D; for some are as movement to potency, and the others as determinate substance to some sort of matter.

The infinite and the void and all similar things are said to exist potentially and actually in a different sense from that in which many other things are said so to exist, e.g. that which sees or walks or is seen. For of the latter class these predicates can at some time be truly asserted without qualification; for the seen is so called sometimes because it is being seen, sometimes because it is capable of being seen. But the infinite does not exist potentially in the sense that it

will ever actually have separate existence; its separateness is only in knowledge. For the fact that division never

ceases to be possible gives the result that
this actuality exists potentially, but not
that it exists separately.

55. *What Is Mind?* *

W. P. MONTAGUE (1873–1953)

II

*The Point at Issue: Is the Self an Adjec-
tive of the Body or Is It Substantive
in Its Own Right?*

We enter the chamber where our
friend lies dying. His voice sinks to a
whisper, his words become incoherent—
a gasp, a tremor, and it is over. Upon
our grief there supervenes a wonder and
the wonder crystallizes in a question.
Was the personality that we knew and
loved a mere aspect of the quiet thing
on the bed and of the complicated motions within its nervous system which
issued in the characteristic expressions
and responses of a living man to his environment? If we answer our question in
the affirmative, then that which we call
his *mind*, the inner kind of thing with its
thoughts, memories, and hopes that each
of us finds himself to be or have, is no
more existent. For if the self is an aspect
of the body it is an aspect not of its
mere mass but of the peculiar motions of
the mass when it was alive. That those
vital motions have ceased, never to re-

cur, is quite certain; and when a thing
ceases, its aspects, attributes, and adjectives cease also. Our memory of the man
will continue to exist, the consequences
of his deeds will continue to exist, but he
himself will exist no more.

There is, however, the other alternative. Suppose that the personality of our
friend was not an adjective of his body's
vital motions but something substantive
in its own right—in short a substance
rather than an attribute. In that case
there is no reason to assume that he has
ceased to exist. . . . The real rub is
whether the temporary assemblage of
material particles carries the self that is
within it as an inseparable attribute or
as a separable substance. Let us not be
frightened out of this simple way of
stating the issue by learned bluster concerning the term "substance." By substance we mean not substance apart
from any attribute, but only that which
is *existentially substantive*, capable of
existing concretely and in its own right
rather than as a dependent adjective of
something else. Meaning by substance
nothing but this, we shall be untouched
by charges that a "substance" would be
like the infinitely innermost core of an
onion, or that it would be a mysterious
something that would underlie its attri-

---

* Part of *The Chances of Surviving Death*.
By kind permission of the publishers, Harvard
University Press.

butes as a pin-cushion underlies the pins stuck into it. And we shall be equally cold to those who tell us that to conceive of the self as an independent substance or soul would be to conceive of it as a sort of *homunculus,* a queer little second man inside the regular man. The belief in a soul may well be false, but it cannot be laughed out of court by sophisticated phrases. Whether the soul, if it exists, would itself have, or later acquire, physical form; or whether, though not having such a form, it would impress observers as having it—whether, in short, the soul, if it existed, would be or appear to be what is called a *ghost*—is a question not only incapable of being settled, but irrelevant to the main point at issue. The point or question which is prior to all others is, we repeat, just the question as to whether the thing called the self or mind or personality is substantive in its own right or an adjective of the body and its motions. . . .

III

The Case for the Self As Adjective

The evidence for the view so widely prevalent in learned circles that the mind is an adjective of the body is enormously voluminous. It is, in fact, coextensive not only with human cerebral physiology and the associated phases of psychology, but also with a great deal of general biology, both ontogenetic and phylogenetic. Fortunately for our inquiry, this evidence, in spite of its vast number of details, is fairly homogeneous. It can all be epitomized as follows:

The mind varies as the brain varies; and to the extent that the brain ceases to function the mind ceases to produce its characteristic effects; from which it may be inferred with overwhelming probability that the mind depends upon the brain as an adjective depends on its substantive, and that when at death the brain ceases to function, the mind will cease to exist.

This is the argument in general, and its constituent particular elements comprise all the particular observations and inferences that have been made as to the correlation of mental and neural events. . . .

There is in the first place the broad biological fact that the higher the *mind* (as judged behavioristically by the adaptiveness and purposefulness of the performances of an individual) the higher or more elaborate and systematized is the *brain* (as explored by the physiologist). This holds phylogenetically when the brains of various species are correlated with their intelligence as exemplified in or inferred from their behavior. Man's *brain* is more intricately developed than that of his nearest cousins, the apes, and far more developed than the brains of still lower animals. And man's *mind* as judged by his achievements is correspondingly as much higher than that of the apes as theirs is higher than that of brutes with still simpler nervous systems. And ontogenetically there is the same sort of correlation; as the brain grows from infancy to adulthood the mental abilities grow also.

When we turn from this general correlation of cerebral development with mental development in the species and in the individual to the more specific and controllable variations in a brain which result from lesions, either natural or experimental, and from drugs or glandular secretions being added or subtracted, we find very definite and strikingly correlative changes in the mind. And in these more specific and *physiological* variations we can often supplement the indirect study of the mind through its body's behavior by the direct method of introspection; whereas in the more general and *biological* changes (except when we can compare in memory the mind of our early childhood with our mind today) we have to get at the mental changes entirely through observation of behavior.

Everybody has experienced both introspectively and behavioristically the effect on his intelligence, his emotions, and his volitions of narcotics and stimulants, of exercise, of fatigue, or of diseases and their toxins. We can observe the rise of a child's moods and mentality from cretinous idiocy to almost normal brightness, and its relapse into idiocy again, by first giving and then withholding the extract of the thyroid gland. We can observe the progressive degeneration of a personality in intellect, sentiment, and will through the ravages made in the brain by syphilis. We can observe the successive declines of intelligence in a dog or a cat as successive portions of its brain are removed. And we can observe quite analogous changes resulting in a human mind from analogous cerebral wounds.

It is difficult in the face of countless facts like these to resist the conclusion of the materialist that mind is adjectival rather than substantive, and that because it varies with the variations of the brain and its functionings it must depend entirely upon those physical structures and processes.

Is there indeed anything at all to be said against this conclusion unless new facts are found? There is, I think, one thing that may be said against the conclusiveness of the argument as thus far stated. It is not a very strong defense, but it counts for something.

Materialism has to reckon with the possibility, never to be completely removed, that the mind, which is discovered through introspection and through behavior and which varies with the body's changes, is a function not merely of that body but also of an immaterial entity or soul which, during life as we know it, must operate through the body and use it as its instrument in much the same way as a musician must use *his*

instrument to make manifest the harmonies within him. If you take the instrument on which a musician (whom you cannot see) is playing, clean it, tune it, and increase its number of strings or stops, its music will become purer and more elaborate. If, on the other hand, you take the instrument and poison it with the injection of fluids that impede its vibrations, deprive it of the air against which it beats, or "vivisect" it by cutting out one after another of its essential parts—what then will happen? Obviously the music will become imperfect, abnormal, discordant, harsh; as the process continues there will be an insane and even idiotic jumble of sounds; and, at last, will come silence and the mercy of death. Perhaps you would feel triumphant and make conscientious claim to having proved that the music is a function of the instrument, an adjective of its motion, dependent upon it, and upon it alone. And yet you would be wrong, for despite the impressive assemblage of concomitant variations between the instrument and the music, that music was not "robot" music. The instrument did not play itself; it was played upon by an invisible operator.

Please do not sneer this off as "just an argument from analogy." Of course it is an argument from analogy. What else could it be? We can conclude from the known to the unknown by taking as our premises the relations that are given and extending them by the "rule of three" method of extrapolation to what is not given. When I see you weeping I attribute to you an inner grief. I do not, to be sure, do this by any *argument* analogical or non-analogical; I do it spontaneously as an act of "animal faith." It is the "pathetic fallacy," the instinctive ascription to the outside world of what is really our inner stuff, not only our feelings but our sensory forms and conceptual relations. All men, and animals, too, live by the pathetic fallacy. Without committing it they could not carry on at all. But if, and when, I am asked to *prove* my spontaneous interpretation of your observable tears as indicative of inner grief, then I can only argue by analogy. A is to B as A' is to B'. As my own remembered weeping is to my own remembered grief, so is your observed weeping to your (by me unobservable and hence hypothetical) grief. When I put it this way I see that of course I may be mistaken in my conclusion despite the *feeling* of certainty due to my "animal faith." You may not be weeping from grief but from tear gas or onion juice or from a desire to deceive. This risk of error I must always take in inferring anything beyond the here-and-now appearance.

Whether an analogy is good or bad depends on whether the resembling relations are essential and causal, or trivial and casual. Now with regard to the analogy between a possible but unknown soul in its relation to the body and its consciousness, on the one hand, and a musician (invisible to the observer) in his relation to his instrument and its music on the other hand—I do not claim that it is convincing or even very good. I claim only that it is pedagogically clarifying and sufficiently plausible to give us pause and make us realize that the concomitant variation of one thing with another does not *prove* the adjectival dependence of the one thing on the other.

But in spite of our analogy and all that may be said for it, the materialist theory is still very strong, because of the *prior rights enjoyed by the more nearly known over the less nearly known in all sound methodology.* That there may be a soul is possible, but until it is shown on other grounds to be not merely possible but also probable, the physiological scientist and the materialistic philosopher have the right and even the duty to disregard the dualistic hypothesis. The burden of proof is on the dualist to transform an empty and sterile possibility into a possibility that shall at least be probable, even if not fruitful.

How can this transformation be effected? In only one way—by examining the nature of the mind as we know it and of the brain as we know it and demonstrating that the latter is not the *kind* of thing that could with any plausibility serve as the sole ground for the former, and that its inadequacy is such that something other than the body must be postulated as operating upon or cooperating with the body. Of such evidence there is a goodly quantity, and it constitutes the positive as distinct from the merely negative argument for the existence of a soul. Let us now proceed to examine it.

IV

The Case for the Self as Substantive

1. *The Distinctive Aspects of Mind.* There are a number of curious properties possessed by mental states and processes which are so different from the properties of bodies, or at least from those of inorganic or non-living bodies, that there is difficulty in imagining how they can be mere aspects of a mechanistic aggregate.

All of these properties are characterized by a *self-transcendence* or reference to what is other than themselves. There are four kinds of self-transcending reference—prospective, retrospective, spatial, and logical. Let us consider them in turn.

Prospective self-transcendence is the characteristic of a process in which something not yet existent appears to act as a causal determiner of the train of events that leads up to it. Processes determined in this way are called purposive or teleological. And the goal of such a process, whether it is actually attained or only approached, is called its *purpose* or *telos*.

When a purposive process is experienced from within we are conscious of the purpose or telos as a present idea of a possible future situation. Our attitude towards it is one of desire or interest; we make efforts to actualize it and characterize it as a good or a value, and whatever seems to contribute to its attainment shares this quality of value in a secondary or instrumental fashion. Correspondingly, whatever opposes or hinders our striving has the character of a bad or negative value. When such a process is accelerated we have the feeling of pleasantness, when it is retarded that of unpleasantness.

These purposive activities, so familiar in our own subjective experience, are not lacking in objective or externally observable characteristics that make them more or less easy to identify. Such objective characteristics are, however, not positive as in subjective experience, but negative. They result from the fact that an externally observable process is not adequately determined by externally observable causes. Two perfectly similar *inanimate* bodies or the same inanimate body on two successive occasions, when put in the same environmental situation will behave in the same way. And as the environment becomes specifically different the behavior of the bodies will become specifically different. There is, in short, what Professor Jennings calls Experimental Determinism. For every observable episode or element in the consequent there can be found an observable episode or element in the antecedent. Now in a purposive process such as we find subjectively to characterize mind, the situation is quite different. Two externally similar beings placed in similar environments may behave differently; and conversely, when placed in different environments they may behave in the same way. The result is that there appears to be no complete Experimental Determinism, i.e. no one-to-one correspondence between the externally observable phenomena of purposive conduct and the externally observable phenomena of the environment in which that conduct takes place. When we wish to emphasize the absence of external determination we speak of the being's *freedom;* when we wish to put the emphasis on the presence of internal causes we speak of the being's *teleology* or *purposiveness.* Whether we take the internal and subjective standpoint or the standpoint of an external observer, mind or a being endowed with mind exhibits in its behavior a curious self-transcending reference to the future situations in which that behavior will eventuate.

As mental processes are determined by, and extend forward toward, the not yet existent events of the future, so do they also extend backward to the no longer existent events of the past. When this present inclusion of the past is continuous with the sensory experience of the present moment, it is called "duration," when discontinuous, "memory." Bergson has with great clearness and originality analyzed this characteristic of conscious life. In a mind the past is not lost as in the world of physical motions, but preserved. It is not displaced by the present, but coexists with it, with the result that the mind is made up of a cumulative and growing system of memories intensively superimposed upon one another; and in addition to a three-dimensional space reference, it possesses a fourth or purely temporal dimension, not merely as a futuristic potentiality of purposive behavior but as an actually achieved and present body of past experience.

In addition to its temporal dimension the mind in most of its sensory states has a self-transcending reference to spatially distant objects. We perceive and visually imagine such objects by means of inner cerebral states. We are tempted to say, and we can say, that each being with a mind carries about inside his skull a sort of copy or map of the extra-organic world. But having said this we must immediately add that the map thus carried is no ordinary map whose puny dimensions can be perceived alongside of the large domain of which it is the copy. The mental map that is *here and now* reveals a world of objects that are *there and then,* not by being just a copy of them but by functioning as a dynamically and causally effective substitute for them. The mental map itself is never seen as such; through it and by means of it the world is seen. This is due to the fact that our mental states do not in general act in their own right and produce effects characteristic of their intrinsic sensory nature. Their behavior is governed not by what they are but by what they mean. They are comparable to marionettes whose capers are only to be understood and explained by the agents who pull them about by strings. In the hurly-burly of perceiving, remembering, and acting we cannot realize this, for we are conscious only of the objects meant and not of the sensory states that mean or reveal them.

It is only in the fourth kind of self-transcending reference, which is exemplified in abstract reflection, that we can be conscious not only of the meaning but also of the symbol that carries it. When we write "$a + b = b + a$," we are aware of the letters as well as of their meanings. The mind is, as we have said, imprisoned in the skull, but the skull is so comfortable a prison that the prisoner is hardly aware of his plight. By means of the sensory effects which he receives and preserves, he gets a free view of the world outside. It is as though the walls of his prison were transparent. He does not see them; nor does he see the effects produced upon him, just because he sees by means of them, and so through them. The effects *within* mean or "reveal" their actual or possible

external causes. To be conscious of the world without, is to have that world vicariously within you. From this standpoint the mind might be defined as a condition for the vicarious or virtual presence of events which actually are distant from it in space and in time. If you looked into the man's brain you would not see what the man saw. You could at best see only the events *by* which he saw. In this sense each field of consciousness is *private.*

And now that we have examined the mind and found it to involve as its essential character the curious function of self-transcending reference to what is not itself, let us turn to an examination of the brain with a view to discovering whether its nature is such as to enable it to have the mind as its adjective.

2. *The Distinctive Aspects of the Brain.* Even to the untutored eye, the brain is a slippery and complicated object with strange convolutions on the outside and queer caverns within. It has its exits and entrances which give it dual connections with practically every part of the body; and through the whole of it run innumerable pathways, which keep its various regions and centers even more closely and intricately connected with one another than they are with the sense organs, muscles, and glands of the body. Supplement this bird's-eye view of the layman with the carefully directed microscopic views of anatomists and histologists, and with physiological discoveries such as those of Sherrington, Pavlow, and Cannon—crucially and pitifully corroborated by the testimony of numberless dogs and cats—and the brain assumes momentous proportions. Its millions of interconnected neuronic elements are organized in hierarchies of sensori-motor arcs, and the more or less well marked levels of these hierarchies correspond most instructively to the successive levels of cerebral development displayed by the species in their evolu-

tionary ascent. Here, as elsewhere, phylogeny is recapitulated and confirmed by ontogeny.

Confronted with such knowledge one is overwhelmed. The brain, with its affiliated ramifications throughout the body, is so vast in its complexities, so marvellous in its internal and external articulations, that the proper attitude towards it would seem to be one of prayerful admiration and humble trust—a kind of religious faith that since it can do so much it can do everything, and that in the further and as yet undiscovered details of its mighty organization lie hidden the whole secret of human personality and the entire and sufficient cause of mind and spirit.

Is there any way of getting closer to the object of our worship, closer even than the physiologist can get? Yes, there is the way of the chemist. Viewed through the eyes of the chemist the cerebral landscape undergoes a rather curious change. In place of organized hierarchies involving the whole organism or large tracts of it, we get multitudes of narrowly localized chemical reactions. The atoms in the complex organic molecules are continually dissolving their associations and forming new ones. But the divorce and remarriage of atoms which the chemist studies is a piecemeal affair. Naturally it must be *observed* collectively and in the mass because of the minuteness of the parties to the transaction. But the relations inferred from the observation are in the main dyadic relations, the tête-à-tête intercourse of one molecule with another. Of course, there are the catalyzers, and there are several other indications that chemical reactions are not purely dyadic. But the factor of *Gestalt*, the influence of the structural pattern of the *whole* upon the *parts,* is almost gone. For the chemist, the nervous system and the rest of the body is a vast conglomerate of comparatively independent and separate processes, in perpetual interaction with one another, to be sure, but lacking the benefit of any presiding genius or controlling organic structure. For such a thing there is no chemical formula. This new and more intimate view if the organism brings with it a new mystery—the mystery of the regulation and self-regulation of a living system, the whole amazing conspiracy of the various chemical substances and activities to play into each other's hands and with exquisite cooperation maintain the balance of the organism and its life.

Is there any further way in which we can get even closer than the chemist to the intimate and ultimate structure of the brain? Yes, there is the way of physics. Taking this further way we now pass beyond the conglomerate of organic molecules and their chemical reactions, and see the brain dissolving before our conceptual eyes into a swarm of atom-systems, comprising as to type some dozen or so of the 92 known kinds. Each of these atoms, or atom-systems, is composed of a nucleus and outlying planets. The nucleus consists of electric particles or units of positive charge packed closely together with a lesser number of particles or units of negative charge; the planets or outlying fringe are entirely of negative charge and (apart from ionization) are just sufficient in number to balance the deficit of negative charge in the nucleus. This, or something like it, is the atom. We may leave its further details to the experts in quantum physics. For us it is sufficient to view the brain as a swarm of quintillions of tiny particles, pushing and pulling each other about and continuously moving with incredible velocities in all directions. This is the physicist's picture of the brain. It is like that of the chemist only more so. And it is vastly different from the pictures made by biologist and physiologist.

Where in this picture can we find the *Gestalt,* the ground for the self-regulating and self-perpetuating unity of pattern that does so surely pervade the nervous system as a whole? And where indeed can we find in these scudding clouds of spatially separate particles, with their motions governed by the beautifully simple laws of attraction and repulsion, any basis or ground for explaining the thing called mind—the hidden thing, stored with rich and cumulative memories of events that no longer exist, and capable of purposeful actions successfully directed to what does not yet exist? Surely in the light of this more intimate "close-up" of the brain the chance of reducing the mind to a bodily adjective seems rather remote. And the counter-hypothesis of the mind as substantive in its own right, a veritable *soul* has passed from the status of a bare and sterile possibility to one of respectable, if not overwhelming, probability.

56. The Dilemma of Determinism *

WILLIAM JAMES (1842–1910)

A common opinion prevails that the juice has ages ago been pressed out of the free-will controversy, and that no new champion can do more than warm up stale arguments which every one has heard. This is a radical mistake. I know of no subject less worn out, or in which inventive genius has a better chance of breaking open new ground,—not, perhaps, of forcing a conclusion or of coercing assent, but of deepening our sense of what the issue between the two parties really is, of what the ideas of fate and of free-will imply. . . .

The arguments I am about to urge all proceed on two suppositions: first, when we make theories about the world and discuss them with one another, we do so in order to attain a conception of things which shall give us subjective satisfaction; and, second, if there be two conceptions, and the one seems to us, on the whole, more rational than the other, we are entitled to suppose that the more rational one is the truer of the two. I hope that you are all willing to make these suppositions with me; for I am afraid that if there be any of you here who are not, they will find little edification in the rest of what I have to say. I cannot stop to argue the point; but I myself believe that all the magnificent achievements of mathematical and physical science—our doctrines of evolution, of uniformity of law, and the rest—proceed from our indomitable desire to cast the world into a more rational shape in our minds than the shape into which it is thrown there by the crude order of our experience. The world has shown itself, to a great extent, plastic to this demand of ours for rationality. How much farther it will show itself plastic no one can say. Our only means of finding out is to try; and I, for one, feel as free to try conceptions of moral as of mechanical or of logical rationality. If a certain formula for expressing the nature of the world violates my moral demand, I shall

* From an address to the Harvard Divinity Students, published in the *Unitarian Review* for September, 1884.

feel as free to throw it overboard, or at least to doubt it, as if it disappointed my demand for uniformity of sequence, for example; the one demand being, so far as I can see, quite as subjective and emotional as the other is. The principle of causality, for example,—what is it but a postulate, an empty name covering simply a demand that the sequence of events shall some day manifest a deeper kind of belonging of one thing with another than the mere arbitrary juxtaposition which now phenomenally appears? It is as much an altar to an unknown god as the one that Saint Paul found at Athens. All our scientific and philosophic ideals are altars to unknown gods. Uniformity is as much so as is free-will. If this be admitted, we can debate on even terms. But if any one pretends that while freedom and variety are, in the first instance, subjective demands, necessity and uniformity are something altogether different, I do not see how we can debate at all.

To begin, then, I must suppose you acquainted with all the usual arguments on the subject. I cannot stop to take up the old proofs from causation, from statistics, from the certainty with which we can foretell one another's conduct, from the fixity of character, and all the rest. But there are two *words* which usually encumber these classical arguments, and which we must immediately dispose of if we are to make any progress. One is the eulogistic word *freedom,* and the other is the opprobrious word *chance.* The word 'chance' I wish to keep, but I wish to get rid of the word 'freedom.' Its eulogistic associations have so far overshadowed all the rest of its meaning that both parties claim the sole right to use it, and determinists to-day insist that they alone are freedom's champions. . . .

But there *is* a problem, an issue of fact and not of words, an issue of the most momentous importance, which is often decided without discussion in one sentence,—nay, in one clause of a sentence, —by those very writers who spin out whole chapters in their efforts to show what 'true' freedom is; and that is the question of determinism, about which we are to talk to-night.

Fortunately, no ambiguities hang about this word or about its opposite, indeterminism. Both designate an outward way in which things may happen, and their cold and mathematical sound has no sentimental associations that can bribe our partiality either way in advance. Now, evidence of an external kind to decide between determinism and indeterminism is, as I intimated a while back, strictly impossible to find. Let us look at the difference between them and see for ourselves. What does determinism profess?

It professes that those parts of the universe already laid down absolutely appoint and decree what the other parts shall be. The future has no ambiguous possibilities hidden in its womb: the part we call the present is compatible with only one totality. Any other future complement than the one fixed from eternity is impossible. The whole is in each and every part, and welds it with the rest into an absolute unity, an iron block, in which there can be no equivocation or shadow of turning.

"With earth's first clay they did the last
    man knead,
And there of the last harvest sowed the
    seed.
And the first morning of creation wrote
What the last dawn of reckoning shall
    read."

Indeterminism, on the contrary, says that the parts have a certain amount of loose play on one another, so that the laying down of one of them does not necessarily determine what the others shall be. It admits that possibilities may be in excess of actualities, and that things not yet revealed to our knowledge may really in themselves be ambiguous. Of two alternative futures which we conceive, both may now be really possible; and the one become impossible only at the very moment when the other excludes it by becoming real itself. Indeterminism thus denies the world to be one unbending unit of fact. It says there is a certain ultimate pluralism in it; and, so saying, it corroborates our ordinary unsophisticated view of things. To that view, actualities seem to float in a wider sea of possibilities from out of which they are chosen; and, *somewhere,* indeterminism says, such possibilities exist, and form a part of truth.

Determinism, on the contrary, says they exist *nowhere,* and that necessity on the one hand and impossibility on the other are the sole categories of the real. Possibilities that fail to get realized are, for determinism, pure illusions: they never were possibilities at all. There is nothing inchoate, it says, about this universe of ours, all that was or is or shall be actual in it having been from eternity virtually there. The cloud of alternatives our minds escort this mass of actuality withal is a cloud of sheer deceptions, to which 'impossibilities' is the only name that rightfully belongs.

The issue, it will be seen, is a perfectly sharp one, which no eulogistic terminology can smear over or wipe out. The truth *must* lie with one side or the other, and its lying with one side makes the other false.

The question relates solely to the existence of possibilities, in the strict sense of the term, as things that may, but need not, be. Both sides admit that a volition, for instance, has occurred. The indeterminists say another volition might have occurred in its place: the determinists swear that nothing could possibly have occurred in its place. Now, can science be called in to tell us which of these two point-blank contradicters of each other is right? Science professes to draw no conclusions but such as are based on matters of fact, things that have actually happened; but how can any amount of assurance that something actually happened give us the least grain of information as to whether another thing might or might not have happened in its place? Only facts can be proved by other facts. With things that are possibilities and not facts, facts have no concern. If we have no other evidence than the evidence of existing facts, the possibility-question must remain a mystery never to be cleared up.

And the truth is that facts practically have hardly anything to do with making us either determinists or indeterminists. Sure enough, we make a flourish of quoting facts this way or that; and if we are determinists, we talk about the infallibility with which we can predict one another's conduct; while if we are indeterminists, we lay great stress on the fact that it is just because we cannot foretell one another's conduct, either in war or statecraft or in any of the great and small intrigues and businesses of men, that life is so intensely anxious and hazardous a game. But who does not see the wretched insufficiency of this so-called objective testimony on both sides? What fills up the gaps in our minds is something not objective, not external. What divides us into possibility men and anti-possibility men is different faiths or postulates,—postulates of rationality. To this man the world seems more rational with possibilities in it,—to that man more rational with possibilities excluded; and talk as we will about having to yield to evidence, what makes us monists or pluralists, determinists or indeterminists, is at bottom always some sentiment like this.

The stronghold of the deterministic sentiment is the antipathy to the idea of chance. As soon as we begin to talk indeterminism to our friends, we find a number of them shaking their heads.

This notion of alternative possibility, they say, this admission that any one of several things may come to pass, is, after all, only a roundabout name for chance; and chance is something the notion of which no sane mind can for an instant tolerate in the world. What is it, they ask, but barefaced crazy unreason, the negation of intelligibility and law? And if the slightest particle of it exist anywhere, what is to prevent the whole fabric from falling together, the stars from going out, and chaos from recommencing her topsy-turvy reign?

Remarks of this sort about chance will put an end to discussion as quickly as anything one can find. I have already told you that 'chance' was a word I wished to keep and use. Let us then examine exactly what it means, and see whether it ought to be such a terrible bugbear to us. I fancy that squeezing the thistle boldly will rob it of its sting.

The sting of the word 'chance' seems to lie in the assumption that it means something positive, and that if anything happens by chance, it must needs be something of an intrinsically irrational and preposterous sort. Now, chance means nothing of the kind. It is a purely negative and relative term, giving us no information about that of which it is predicated, except that it happens to be disconnected with something else,—not controlled, secured, or necessitated by other things in advance of its own actual presence. As this point is the most subtile one of the whole lecture, and at the same time the point on which all the rest hinges, I beg you to pay particular attention to it. What I say is that it tells us nothing about what a thing may be in itself to call it 'chance.' It may be a bad thing, it may be a good thing. It may be lucidity, transparency, fitness incarnate, matching the whole system of other things, when it has once befallen, in an unimaginably perfect way. All you mean by calling it 'chance' is that this is not guaranteed, that it may also fall out otherwise. For the system of other things has no positive hold on the chance-thing. Its origin is in a certain fashion negative: it escapes, and says, Hands off! coming, when it comes, as a free gift, or not at all.

This negativeness, however, and this opacity of the chance-thing when thus considered *ab extra,* or from the point of view of previous things or distant things, do not preclude its having any amount of positiveness and luminosity from within, and at its own place and moment. All that its chance-character asserts about it is that there is something in it really of its own, something that is not the unconditional property of the whole. If the whole wants this property, the whole must wait till it can get it, if it be a matter of chance. That the universe may actually be a sort of joint-stock society of this sort, in which the sharers have both limited liabilities and limited powers, is of course a simple and conceivable notion.

Nevertheless, many persons talk as if the minutest dose of disconnectedness of one part with another, the smallest modicum of independence, the faintest tremor of ambiguity about the future, for example, would ruin everything, and turn this goodly universe into a sort of insane sand-heap or nulliverse, no universe at all. Since future human volitions are as a matter of fact the only ambiguous things we are tempted to believe in, let us stop for a moment to make ourselves sure whether their independent and accidental character need be fraught with such direful consequences to the universe as these.

What is meant by saying that my choice of which way to walk home after the lecture is ambiguous and matter of chance as far as the present moment is concerned? It means that both Divinity Avenue and Oxford Street are called; but that only one, and that one *either* one, shall be chosen. Now, I ask you seriously to suppose that this ambiguity of my choice is real; and then to make the impossible hypothesis that the choice is made twice over, and each time falls on a different street. In other words, imagine that I first walk through Divinity Avenue, and then imagine that the powers governing the universe annihilate ten minutes of time with all that it contained, and set me back at the door of this hall just as I was before the choice was made. Imagine then that, everything else being the same, I now make a different choice and traverse Oxford Street. You, as passive spectators, look on and see the two alternative universes,—one of them with me walking through Divinity Avenue in it, the other with the same me walking through Oxford Street. Now, if you are determinists you believe one of these universes to have been from eternity impossible: you believe it to have been impossible because of the intrinsic irrationality or accidentality somewhere involved in it. But looking outwardly at these universes, can you say which is the impossible and accidental one, and which the rational and necessary one? I doubt if the most ironclad determinist among you could have the slightest glimmer of light on this point. In other words, either universe *after the fact* and once there would, to our means of observation and understanding, appear just as rational as the other. There would be absolutely no criterion by which we might judge one necessary and the other matter of chance. Suppose now we relieve the gods of their hypothetical task and assume my choice, once made, to be made forever. I go through Divinity Avenue for good and all. If, as good determinists, you now begin to affirm, what all good determinists punctually do affirm, that in the nature of things I *couldn't* have gone through Oxford Street,—had I done so it would have been chance, irra-

tionality, insanity, a horrid gap in nature,—I simply call your attention to this, that your affirmation is what the Germans call a *Machtspruch,* a mere conception fulminated as a dogma and based on no insight into details. Before my choice, either street seemed as natural to you as to me. Had I happened to take Oxford Street, Divinity Avenue would have figured in your philosophy as the gap in nature; and you would have so proclaimed it with the best deterministic conscience in the world.

But what a hollow outcry, then, is this against a chance which, if it were present to us, we could by no character whatever distinguish from a rational necessity! I have taken the most trivial of examples, but no possible example could lead to any different result. For what are the alternatives which, in point of fact, offer themselves to human volition? What are those futures that now seem matters of chance? Are they not one and all like the Divinity Avenue and Oxford Street of our example? Are they not all of them *kinds* of things already here and based in the existing frame of nature? Is any one ever tempted to produce an *absolute* accident, something utterly irrelevant to the rest of the world? Do not all the motives that assail us, all the futures that offer themselves to our choice, spring equally from the soil of the past; and would not either one of them, whether realized through chance or through necessity, the moment it was realized, seem to us to fit that past, and in the completest and most continuous manner to interdigitate with the phenomena already there?

The more one thinks of the matter, the more one wonders that so empty and gratuitous a hubbub as this outcry against chance should have found so great an echo in the hearts of men. It is a word which tells us absolutely nothing about what chances, or about the *modus operandi* of the chancing; and the use of it as a war-cry shows only a temper of intellectual absolutism, a demand that the world shall be a solid block, subject to one control,—which temper, which demand, the world may not be bound to gratify at all. In every outwardly verifiable and practical respect, a world in which the alternatives that now actually distract *your* choice were decided by pure chance would be by *me* absolutely undistinguished from the world in which I now live. I am, therefore, entirely willing to call it, so far as your choices go, a world of chance for me. To *yourselves,* it is true, those very acts of choice, which to me are so blind, opaque, and external, are the opposites of this, for you are within them and effect them. To you they appear as decisions; and decisions, for him who makes them, are altogether peculiar psychic facts. Self-luminous and self-justifying at the living moment at which they occur, they appeal to no outside moment to put its stamp upon them or make them continuous with the rest of nature. Themselves it is rather who seem to make nature continuous; and in their strange and intense function of granting consent to one possibility and withholding it from another, to transform an equivocal and double future into an inalterable and simple past.

But with the psychology of the matter we have no concern this evening. The quarrel which determinism has with chance fortunately has nothing to do with this or that psychological detail. It is a quarrel altogether metaphysical. Determinism denies the ambiguity of future volitions, because it affirms that nothing future can be ambiguous. But we have said enough to meet the issue. Indeterminate future volitions *do* mean chance. Let us not fear to shout it from the house-tops if need be; for we now know that the idea of chance is, at bottom, exactly the same thing as the idea of gift,—the one simply being a disparaging, and the other a eulogistic, name

for anything on which we have no effective *claim.* And whether the world be the better or the worse for having either chances or gifts in it will depend altogether on *what* these uncertain and unclaimable things turn out to be.

And this at last brings us within sight of our subject. We have seen what determinism means: we have seen that indeterminism is rightly described as meaning chance; and we have seen that chance, the very name of which we are urged to shrink from as from a metaphysical pestilence, means only the negative fact that no part of the world, however big, can claim to control absolutely the destinies of the whole. But although, in discussing the word 'chance,' I may at moments have seemed to be arguing for its real existence, I have not meant to do so yet. We have not yet ascertained whether this be a world of chance or no; at most, we have agreed that it seems so. And I now repeat what I said at the outset, that, from any strict theoretical point of view, the question is insoluble. To deepen our theoretic sense of the *difference* between a world with chances in it and a deterministic world is the most I can hope to do; and this I may now at last begin upon, after all our tedious clearing of the way.

I wish first of all to show you just what the notion that this is a deterministic world implies. The implications I call your attention to are all bound up with the fact that it is a world in which we constantly have to make what I shall, with your permission, call judgments of regret. Hardly an hour passes in which we do not wish that something might be otherwise; and happy indeed are those of us whose hearts have never echoed the wish of Omar Khayam—

"That we might clasp, ere closed, the book
    of fate,
And make the writer on a fairer leaf
Inscribe our names, or quite obliterate.

"Ah! Love, could you and I with fate con-
    spire
To mend this sorry scheme of things en-
    tire,
Would we not shatter it to bits, and then
Remould it nearer to the heart's desire?"

Now, it is undeniable that most of
these regrets are foolish, and quite on a
par in point of philosophic value with
the criticisms on the universe of that
friend of our infancy, the hero of the
fable The Atheist and the Acorn,—

"Fool! had that bough a pumpkin bore,
Thy whimsies would have worked no
    more," etc.

Even from the point of view of our own
ends, we should probably make a botch
of remodelling the universe. How much
more then from the point of view of ends
we cannot see! Wise men therefore regret as little as they can. But still some
regrets are pretty obstinate and hard to
stifle,—regrets for acts of wanton cruelty
or treachery, for example, whether performed by others or by ourselves.
Hardly any one can remain *entirely*
optimistic after reading the confession
of the murderer at Brockton the other
day: how, to get rid of the wife whose
continued existence bored him, he in-
veigled her into a desert spot, shot her
four times, and then, as she lay on the
ground and said to him, "You didn't do
it on purpose, did you, dear?" replied,
"No, I didn't do it on purpose," as he
raised a rock and smashed her skull.
Such an occurrence, with the mild sentence and self-satisfaction of the prisoner, is a field for a crop of regrets,
which one need not take up in detail.
We feel that, although a perfect mechanical fit to the rest of the universe, it
is a bad moral fit, and that something
else would really have been better in its
place.

But for the deterministic philosophy
the murder, the sentence, and the prisoner's optimism were all necessary from
eternity; and nothing else for a moment

had a ghost of a chance of being put into
their place. To admit such a chance, the
determinists tell us, would be to make
a suicide of reason; so we must steel our
hearts against the thought. And here our
plot thickens, for we see the first of those
difficult implications of determinism and
monism which it is my purpose to make
you feel. If this Brockton murder was
called for by the rest of the universe, if
it had to come at its preappointed hour,
and if nothing else would have been consistent with the sense of the whole, what
are we to think of the universe? Are we
stubbornly to stick to our judgment of
regret, and say, though it *couldn't* be,
yet it *would* have been a better universe
with something different from this
Brockton murder in it? That, of course,
seems the natural and spontaneous thing
for us to do; and yet it is nothing short
of deliberately espousing a kind of pessimism. The judgment of regret calls the
murder bad. Calling a thing bad means,
if it mean anything at all, that the thing
ought not to be, that something else
ought to be in its stead. Determinism, in
denying that anything else can be in its
stead, virtually defines the universe as
a place in which what ought to be is impossible,—in other words, as an organism whose constitution is afflicted with
an incurable taint, an irremediable flaw.
The pessimism of a Schopenhauer says
no more than this,—that the murder is
a symptom; and that it is a vicious
symptom because it belongs to a vicious
whole, which can express its nature no
otherwise than by bringing forth just
such a symptom as that at this particular spot. Regret for the murder must
transform itself, if we are determinists
and wise, into a larger regret. It is absurd to regret the murder alone. Other
things being what they are, *it* could not
be different. What we should regret is
that whole frame of things of which the
murder is one member. I see no escape
whatever from this pessimistic conclusion, if, being determinists, our judgment

of regret is to be allowed to stand at all. . . .

For the only consistent way of representing a pluralism and a world whose parts may affect one another through their conduct being either good or bad is the indeterministic way. What interest, zest, or excitement can there be in achieving the right way, unless we are enabled to feel that the wrong way is also a possible and a natural way,—nay, more, a menacing and an imminent way? And what sense can there be in condemning ourselves for taking the wrong way, unless we need have done nothing of the sort, unless the right way was open to us as well? I cannot understand the willingness to act, no matter how we feel, without the belief that acts are really good and bad. I cannot understand the belief that an act is bad, without regret at its happening. I cannot understand regret without the admission of real, genuine possibilities in the world. Only *then* is it other than a mockery to feel, after we have failed to do our best, that an irreparable opportunity is gone from the universe, the loss of which it must forever after mourn.

If you insist that this is all superstition, that possibility is in the eye of science and reason impossibility, and that if I act badly 't is that the universe was foredoomed to suffer this defect, you fall right back into the dilemma, the labyrinth, of pessimism and subjectivism, from out of whose toils we have just wound our way.

Now, we are of course free to fall back, if we please. For my own part, though, whatever difficulties may beset the philosophy of objective right and wrong, and the indeterminism it seems to imply, determinism, with its alternative of pessimism or romanticism, contains difficulties that are greater still. But you will remember that I expressly repu-

diated awhile ago the pretension to offer any arguments which could be coercive in a so-called scientific fashion in this matter. And I consequently find myself, at the end of this long talk, obliged to state my conclusions in an altogether personal way. This personal method of appeal seems to be among the very conditions of the problem; and the most any one can do is to confess as candidly as he can the grounds for the faith that is in him, and leave his example to work on others as it may.

Let me, then, without circumlocution say just this. The world is enigmatical enough in all conscience, whatever theory we may take up toward it. The indeterminism I defend, the free-will theory of popular sense based on the judgment of regret, represents that world as vulnerable, and liable to be injured by certain of its parts if they act wrong. And it represents their acting wrong as a matter of possibility or accident, neither inevitable nor yet to be infallibly warded off. In all this, it is a theory devoid either of transparency or of stability. It gives us a pluralistic, restless universe, in which no single point of view can ever take in the whole scene; and to a mind possessed of the love of unity at any cost, it will, no doubt, remain forever inacceptable. A friend with such a mind once told me that the thought of my universe made him sick, like the sight of the horrible motion of a mass of maggots in their carrion bed.

But while I freely admit that the pluralism and the restlessness are repugnant and irrational in a certain way, I find that every alternative to them is irrational in a deeper way. The indeterminism with its maggots, if you please to speak so about it, offends only the native absolutism of my intellect,—an absolutism which, after all, perhaps, deserves to be snubbed and kept in check. But the determinism with its necessary carrion, to continue the figure of speech, and with no possible maggots to eat the latter up, violates my sense of moral reality through and through. When, for example, I imagine such carrion as the Brockton murder, I cannot conceive it as an act by which the universe, as a whole, logically and necessarily expresses its nature without shrinking from complicity with such a whole. And I deliberately refuse to keep on terms of loyalty with the universe by saying blankly that the murder, since it does flow from the nature of the whole, is not carrion. There are *some* instinctive reactions which I, for one, will not tamper with. . . .

57. *Reality and Idealism* *

JOSIAH ROYCE (1855–1916)

Idealism has two aspects. It is, for the first, a kind of analysis of the world, an analysis which so far has no absolute character about it, but which undertakes, in a fashion that might be acceptable to any skeptic, to examine what you mean by all the things, whatever they are, that you believe in or experience. This idealistic analysis consists merely in a pointing out, by various devices, that the world of your knowledge, whatever it contains, is through and through such stuff as ideas are made of, that you never in your life believed in anything definable *but* ideas, that, as Berkeley put it, "this whole choir of heaven and furniture of earth" is nothing for any of us but a system of ideas which govern our belief and conduct. Such idealism has numerous statements, interpretations, embodiments: forms part of the most various systems and experiences, is consistent with Berkeley's theism, with Fichte's ethical absolutism, with Professor Huxley's agnostic empiricism, with Clifford's mind-stuff theory, with countless other theories that have used such idealism as a part of their scheme. In this aspect idealism is already a little puzzling to our natural consciousness, but it becomes quickly familiar, in fact almost commonplace, and seems after all to alter our practical faith or to solve our deeper problems very little.

The other aspect of idealism is the one which gives us our notion of the absolute Self. To it the first is only preparatory. This second aspect is the one which from Kant, until the present time, has formed the deeper problem of thought. Whenever the world has become more conscious of its significance, the work of human philosophy will be, not nearly ended (Heaven forbid an end!), but for the first time fairly begun. For then, in critically estimating our passions, we shall have some truer sense of whose passions they are.

I begin with the first and the less significant aspect of idealism. Our world, I say, whatever it may contain, is such stuff as ideas are made of. This prepara-

* Part of Lecture XI, *The Spirit of Modern Philosophy*. By kind permission of the publishers, Houghton Mifflin Co.

tory sort of idealism is the one that, as I just suggested, Berkeley made prominent, and, after a fashion familiar. I must state it in my own way, although one in vain seeks to attain novelty in illustrating so frequently described a view.

Here, then, is our so real world of the senses, full of light and warmth and sound. If anything could be solid and external, surely, one at first will say, it is this world. Hard facts, not mere ideas, meet us on every hand. Ideas any one can mould as he wishes. Not so facts. In idea socialists can dream out Utopias, disappointed lovers can imagine themselves successful, beggars can ride horses, wanderers can enjoy the fireside at home. In the realm of facts, society organizes itself as it must, rejected lovers stand for the time defeated, beggars are alone with their wishes, oceans roll drearily between home and the wanderer. Yet this world of fact is, after all, not entirely stubborn, not merely hard. The strenuous will can mould facts. We can form our world, in part, according to our ideas. Statesmen influence the social order, lovers woo afresh, wanderers find the way home. But thus to alter the world we must work, and just because the laborer is worthy of his hire, it is well that the real world should thus have such fixity of things as enables us to anticipate what facts will prove lasting, and to see of the travail of our souls when it is once done. This, then, is the presupposition of life, that we work in a real world, where house-walls do not melt away as in dreams, but stand firm against the winds of many winters, and can be felt as real. We do not wish to find facts wholly plastic; we want them to be stubborn, if only the stubbornness be not altogether unmerciful. Our will makes constantly a sort of agreement with the world, whereby, if the world will continually show some respect to the will, the will shall consent to be strenuous in its industry. Interfere with the reality of my world, and you therefore take the very life and heart out of my will.

The reality of the world, however, when thus defined in terms of its stubbornness, its firmness as against the will that has not conformed to its laws, its kindly rigidity in preserving for us the fruits of our labors,—such reality, I say, is still something wholly unanalyzed. In what does this stubbornness consist? Surely, many different sorts of reality, as it would seem, may be stubborn. Matter is stubborn when it stands in hard walls against us, or rises in vast mountain ranges before the path-finding explorer. But minds can be stubborn also. The lonely wanderer, who watches by the seashore the waves that roll between him and his home, talks of cruel facts, material barriers that, just because they *are* material, and not ideal, shall be the irresistible foes of his longing heart. "In wish," he says, "I am with my dear ones, but alas, wishes cannot cross oceans! Oceans are material facts, in the cold outer world. Would that the world of the heart were all!" But alas! to the rejected lover the world of the heart *is* all, and that is just his woe. Were the barrier between him and his beloved only made of those stubborn material facts, only of walls or of oceans, how lightly might his will erelong transcend them all! Matter stubborn! Outer nature cruelly the foe of ideas! Nay, it is just an idea that now opposes him,—just an idea, and that, too, in the mind of the maiden he loves. But in vain does he call this stubborn bit of disdain a merely ideal fact. No flint was ever more definite in preserving its identity and its edge than this disdain may be. Place me for a moment, then, in an external world that shall consist wholly of ideas,—the ideas, namely, of other people about me, a world of maidens who shall scorn me, of old friends who shall have learned to hate me, of angels who shall condemn me, of God who shall judge me. In what piercing north winds, amidst what fields of ice, in the labyrinths of what tangled forests, in the depths of what thick-walled dungeons, on the edges of what tremendous precipices, should I be more genuinely in the presence of stubborn and unyielding facts than in that conceived world of ideas! So, as one sees, I by no means deprive my world of stubborn reality, if I merely call it a world of ideas. On the contrary, as every teacher knows, the ideas of the people are often the most difficult of facts to influence. We were wrong, then, when we said that whilst matter was stubborn, ideas could be moulded at pleasure. Ideas are often the most implacable of facts. Even my own ideas, the facts of my own inner life, may cruelly decline to be plastic to my wish. The wicked will that refuses to be destroyed,—what rock has often more consistency for our senses than this will has for our inner consciousness! The king, in his soliloquy in "Hamlet,"—in what an unyielding world of hard facts does he not move! and yet they are now only inner facts. The fault is past; he is alone with his conscience:

What rests?
Try what repentance can. What can it not?
Yet what can it, when one cannot repent?
O wretched state! O bosom black as death!
O limëd soul, that, struggling to be free,
Art more engaged!

No, here are barriers worse than any material chains. The world of ideas has its own horrible dungeons and chasms. Let those who have refuted Bishop Berkeley's idealism by the wonder why he did not walk over every precipice or into every fire if these things existed only in his idea, let such, I say, first try some of the fires and the precipices of the inner life, ere they decide that dangers cease to be dangers as soon as they are called ideal, or even subjectively ideal in me.

Many sorts of reality, then, may be existent at the heart of any world of facts. But this bright and beautiful sense-world of ours,—what, amongst these many possible sorts of reality, does that embody? Are the stars and the oceans, the walls and the pictures, real as the maiden's heart is real,—embodying the ideas of somebody, but none the less stubbornly real for that? Or can we make something else of their reality? For, of course, that the stars and the oceans, the walls and the pictures have *some* sort of stubborn reality, just as the minds of our fellows have, our analysis so far does not for an instant think of denying. Our present question is, what sort of reality? Consider, then, in detail, certain aspects of the reality that seems to be exemplified in our sense-world. The sublimity of the sky, the life and majesty of the ocean, the interest of a picture,—to what sort of real facts do these belong? Evidently here we shall have no question. So far as the sense-world is beautiful, is majestic, is sublime, this beauty and dignity exist only for the appreciative observer. If they exist beyond him, they exist only for some other mind, or as the thought and embodied purpose of some universal soul of nature. A man who sees the same world, but who has no eye for the fairness of it, will find all the visible facts, but will catch nothing of their value. At once, then, the sublimity and beauty of the world are thus truths that one who pretends to insight ought to see, and they are truths which have no meaning except for such a beholder's mind, or except as embodying the thought of the mind of the world. So here, at least, is so much of the outer world that is ideal, just as the coin or the jewel or the bank-note or the bond has its value not alone in its physical presence, but in the idea that it symbolizes to a beholder's mind, or to the relatively universal thought of the commercial world. But let us look a little deeper. Surely, if the objects yonder are unideal and outer, odors and tastes and temperatures do not exist in these objects in just the way in which they exist in us. Part of the being of these properties, at least, if not all of it, is ideal and exists for us, or at best is once more the embodiment of the thought or purpose of some world-mind. About tastes you cannot dispute, because they are not only ideal but personal. For the benumbed tongue and palate of diseased bodily conditions, all things are tasteless. As for temperatures, a well known experiment will show how the same water may seem cold to one hand and warm to the other. But even so, colors and sounds are at least in part ideal. Their causes may have some other sort of reality; but colors themselves are not in the things, since they change with the light that falls on the things, vanish in the dark (whilst the things remained unchanged), and differ for different eyes. And as for sounds, both the pitch and the quality of tones depend for us upon certain interesting peculiarities of our hearing organs, and exist in nature only as voiceless sound-waves trembling through the air. All such sense qualities, then, are ideal. The world yonder may—yes, must —have attributes that give reasons why these qualities are thus felt by us; for so we assume. The world yonder may even be a mind that thus expresses its will to us. But these qualities need not, nay, cannot resemble the ideas that are produced in us, unless, indeed, that is because these qualities have placed as ideas in some world-mind. Sound-waves in the air are not like our musical sensations; nor is the symphony as we hear it and feel it any physical property of the strings and the wind instruments; nor are the ether-vibrations that the sun sends us like our ideas when we see the sun; nor yet is the flashing of moonlight on the water as we watch the waves a direct expression of the actual truths of fluid motion as the water embodies them.

Unless, then, the real physical world yonder is itself the embodiment of some world-spirit's ideas, which he conveys to us, unless it is real only as the maiden's heart is real, namely, as itself a conscious thought, then we have so far but one result: that real world (to repeat one of the commonplaces of modern popular science) is in itself, apart from somebody's eyes and tongue and ears and touch, neither colored nor tasteful, neither cool nor warm, neither light nor dark, neither musical nor silent. All these qualities belong to our ideas, being indeed none the less genuine facts for that, but being in so far ideal facts. We must see colors when we look, we must hear music when there is playing in our presence; but this *must* is a must that consists in a certain irresistible presence of an idea in us under certain conditions. *That* this idea must come is, indeed, a truth as unalterable, once more, as the king's settled remorse in Hamlet. But like this remorse, again, it exists as an ideal truth, objective, but through and through objective *for* somebody, and not *apart from* anybody. What this truth implies we have yet to see. So far it is only an ideal truth for the beholder, with just the bare possibility that behind it all there is the thought of a world-spirit. And, in fact, *so* far we must all go together if we reflect.

But now, at this point, the Berkeleyan idealist goes one step further. The real outside world that is still left unexplained and unanalyzed after its beauty, its warmth, its odors, its tastes, its colors, and its tones, have been relegated to the realm of ideal truths, what do you now *mean* by calling it real? No doubt it *is* known as somehow real, but *what* is this reality *known as* being? If you know that this world is still there and outer, as by hypothesis you know, you are bound to say *what* this outer character implies for your thought. And here you have trouble. Is the outer world, as it exists outside of your ideas, or of anybody's ideas, something having shape, filling space, possessing solidity, full of moving things? That would in the first place seem evident. The sound isn't outside of me, but the sound-waves, you say, are. The colors are ideal facts; but the ether-waves don't need a mind to know them. Warmth is ideal, but the physical fact called heat, this playing to and fro of molecules, is real, and is there apart from any mind. But once more, *is* this so evident? What do I *mean* by the shape of anything, or by the size of anything? Don't I mean just the idea of shape or of size that I am obliged to get under certain circumstances? What is the meaning of any property that I give to the real outer world? How can I express that property except in case I think it in terms of my ideas? As for the sound-waves and the ether-waves, what are they but things ideally conceived to explain the facts of nature? The conceptions have doubtless their truth, but it is an ideal truth. What I mean by saying that the things yonder have shape and size and trembling molecules, and that there is air with sound-waves, and ether with light-waves in it,—what I *mean* by all this is that experience forces upon me, directly or indirectly, a vast system of ideas, which may indeed be founded in truth beyond me, which in fact *must* be founded in such truth if my experience has any sense, but which, like my ideas of color and of warmth, are simply expressions of how the world's order must appear to me, and to anybody constituted like me. Above all, is this plain about space. The real things, I say, outside of me, fill space, and move about in it. But what do I mean by space? Only a vast system of ideas which experience and my own mind force upon me. Doubless these ideas have a validity. They have *this* validity, that I, at all events, when I look upon the world, am bound to see it in space, as much bound as the king in Hamlet was, when he looked within, to see himself as guilty and unrepentant. But just as his guilt was an idea,—a crushing, an irresistible, an overwhelming idea,—but still just an idea, so, too, the space in which I place my world is one great formal idea of mine. That is just why I can describe it to other people. "It has three dimensions," I say, "length, breadth, depth." I describe each. I form, I convey, I construct, an idea of it through them. I know space, as an idea, very well. I can compute all sorts of unseen truths about the relations of its parts. I am sure that you, too, share this idea. But, then, for all of us alike it is just an idea; and when we put our world into space, and call it real there, we simply think one idea into another idea, not voluntarily, to be sure, but inevitably, and yet without leaving the realm of ideas.

Thus, all the reality that *we* attribute to our world, in so far as *we* know and can tell what we mean thereby, becomes ideal. There is, in fact, a certain system of ideas, forced upon us by experience, which we have to use as the guide of our conduct. This system of ideas we can't change by our wish; it is for us as overwhelming a fact as guilt, or as the bearing of our fellows towards us, but we know it only *as* such a system of ideas. And we call it the world of matter. John Stuart Mill very well expressed the puzzle of the whole thing, as we have now reached the statement of this puzzle, when he called matter a mass of "permanent possibilities of experience" for each of us. Mill's definition has its faults, but is a very fair beginning. You know matter as something that either now gives you this idea or experience, or that would give you some other idea or experience under other circumstances. A fire, while it burns, is for you a permanent possibility of either getting the idea of an agreeable warmth, or of getting the idea of a bad burn, and you treat it accordingly. A precipice amongst mountains is a permanent possibility of your experiencing a fall, or of your getting a feeling of the exciting or of the sublime in mountain scenery. You have no experience just now of the tropics or of the poles, but both tropical and polar climates exist in your world as permanent possibilities of experience. When you call the sun 92,000,000 miles away, you mean that between you and the sun (that is, between your present experience and the possible experience of the sun's surface) there would inevitably lie the actually inaccessible, but still numerically conceivable series of experiences of distance expressed by the number of miles in question. In short, your whole attitude towards the real world may be summed up by saying: "I have experiences now which I seem bound to have, experiences of color, sound, and all the rest of my present ideas; and I am also bound by experience to believe that in case I did certain things (for instance, touched the wall, traveled to the tropics, visited Europe, studied physics), I then should get, in a determinate order, dependent wholly upon *what* I have done, certain other experiences (for instance, experiences of the wall's solidity, or of a tropical climate, or of the scenes of an European tour, or of the facts of physics)." And this acceptance of actual experience, this belief in possible experience, constitutes all that you mean by your faith in the outer world.

But, you say, Is not, then, all this faith of ours after all well founded? Isn't there really something yonder that corresponds in fact to this series of experiences in us? Yes, indeed, there no doubt is. But what if this, which so shall correspond without us to the ideas within us, what if this hard and fast reality should itself be a system of ideas, outside of our minds but not outside of every mind? As the maiden's disdain is outside the rejected lover's mind, unchangeable so far for him, but not on that account the less ideal, not the less a fact in a mind, as, to take afresh a former fashion of illustration, the price of a security or the objective existence of this lecture is an ideal fact, but real and external for the individual person,—even so why might not this world beyond us, this "permanent possibility of experience," be in essence itself a system of ideal experiences of some standard thought of which ours is only the copy? Nay, must it not be such a system in case it has any reality at all? For, after all, isn't this precisely what our analysis brings us to? Nothing whatever can I say about my world yonder that I do not express in terms of mind. *What* things are, extended, moving, colored, tuneful, majestic, beautiful, holy, *what* they are in any aspect of their nature, mathematical, logical, physical, sensuously pleasing, spiritually valuable, all this must mean for me only something that I have to express in the fashion of ideas. The more I am to know my world, the more of a mind I must have for the purpose. The closer I come to the truth about the things, the more ideas I get. Isn't it plain, then, that *if* my world yonder is anything knowable at all, it must be in and for itself essentially a mental world? Are my ideas to *resemble* in any way the world? Is the truth of my thought to consist in its *agreement* with reality? And am I thus capable, as common sense supposes, of *conforming* my ideas to things? Then reflect. What can, after all, so well agree with an idea as another idea? To what can things that go on in my mind conform unless it be to another mind? If the more my mind grows in mental clearness, the nearer it gets to the nature of reality, then surely the reality that my mind thus resembles must be in itself mental.

After all, then, would it deprive the world here about me of reality, nay, would it not rather save and assure the reality and the knowableness of my world of experience, if I said that this world, as it exists outside of my mind, and of any other human minds, exists in and for a standard, an universal mind, whose system of ideas simply constitutes the world? Even if I fail to prove that there is such a mind, do I not at least thus make plausible that, as I said, our world of common sense has no fact in it which we cannot interpret in terms of ideas, so that this world is throughout such stuff as ideas are made of? To say this, as you see, in no wise deprives our world of its due share of reality. If the standard mind knows now that its ideal fire has the quality of burning those who touch it, and if I in my finitude am bound to conform in my experiences to the thoughts of this standard mind, then in case I touch that fire I shall surely get the idea of a burn. The standard mind will be at least as hard and fast and real in its ideal consistency as is the maiden in her disdain for the rejected lover; and I, in presence of the ideal stars and the oceans, will see the genuine realities of fate as certainly as the lover hears his fate in the voice that expresses her will.

I need not now proceed further with an analysis that will be more or less familiar to many of you, especially after our foregoing historical lectures. What I have desired thus far is merely to give each of you, as it were, the sensation of being an idealist in this first and purely analytical sense of the word idealism. The sum and substance of it all is, you see, this: you know your world in fact as a system of ideas about things, such that from moment to moment you find this system forced upon you by experience. Even matter you know just as a mass of coherent ideas that you cannot help having. Space and time, as you think them, are surely ideas of yours. Now, what more natural than to say that *if* this be so, the real world beyond you must in itself be a system of somebody's ideas? If it is, then you can comprehend

what its existence means. If it isn't, then since all you can know of it is ideal, the real world must be utterly unknowable, a bare *x*. Minds I can understand, because I myself am a mind. An existence that has no mental attribute is wholly opaque to me. So far, however, from such a world of ideas, existent beyond me in another mind, seeming to coherent thought essentially *un*real, ideas and minds and their ways, are, on the contrary, the hardest and stubbornest facts that we can name. *If* the external world is in itself mental, then, be this reality a standard and universal thought, or a mass of little atomic minds constituting the various particles of matter, in any case one can comprehend what it is, and will have at the same time to submit to its stubborn authority as the lover accepts the reality of the maiden's moods. If the world *isn't* such an ideal thing, then indeed all our science, which is through and through concerned with our mental interpretations of things, can neither have objective validity, nor make satisfactory progress towards truth. For as science is concerned with ideas, the world beyond all ideas is a bare *x*.

III

But with this bare *x*, you will say, this analytical idealism after all leaves me, as with something that, in spite of all my analyses and interpretations, may after all be there beyond me as the real world, which my ideas are vainly striving to reach, but which eternally flees before me. So far, you will say, what idealism teaches is that the real world can only be interpreted by treating it as if it were somebody's thought. So regarded, the idealism of Berkeley and of other such thinkers is very suggestive; yet it doesn't tell us what the true world is, but only that *so much* of the true world as we ever get into our comprehension has to be conceived in ideal terms. Perhaps, however, whilst neither beauty, nor majesty, nor odor, nor warmth, nor tone, nor color, nor form, nor motion, nor space, nor time (all these being but ideas of ours), can be said to belong to the extra-mental world,—perhaps, after all, there does exist there yonder an extra-mental world, which has nothing to do, except by accident, with *any* mind, and which is through and through just extra-mental, something unknowable, inscrutable, the basis of experience, the source of ideas, but itself never experienced as it is in itself, never adequately represented by any idea in us. Perhaps it is there. Yes, you will say, *must* it not be there? Must not one accept our limitations once for all, and say, "What reality is, we can never hope to make clear to ourselves. That which has been made clear becomes an idea in us. But always there is the beyond, the mystery, the inscrutable, the real, the *x*. To be sure, perhaps we can't even know so much as that this *x* after all does exist. But then we feel bound to regard it as existent; or even if we doubt or deny it, may it not be there all the same?" In such doubt and darkness, then, this first form of idealism closes. If that were all there were to say, I should indeed have led you a long road in vain. Analyzing what the known world is for you, in case there is haply any world known to you at all, —this surely isn't proving that there is any real world, or that the real world can be known. Are we not just where we started?

No; there lies now just ahead of us the goal of a synthetic idealistic conception, which will not be content with this mere analysis of the colors and forms of things, and with the mere discovery that all these are for us nothing but ideas. In this second aspect, idealism grows bolder, and fears not the profoundest doubt that may have entered your mind as to whether there is any world at all, or as to whether it is in any fashion knowable. State in full the deepest problem, the hardest question about the world that your thought ever conceived. In this new form idealism offers you a suggestion that indeed will not wholly answer nor do away with every such problem, but that certainly will set the meaning of it in a new light. What this new light is, I must in conclusion seek to illustrate.

Note the point we have reached. *Either,* as you see, your real world yonder is through and through a world of ideas, an outer mind that you are more or less comprehending through your experience, *or else,* in so far as it is real and outer it is unknowable, an inscrutable *x,* an absolute mystery. The dilemma is perfect. There is no third alternative. Either a mind yonder, or else the unknowable; that is your choice. Philosophy loves such dilemmas, wherein all the mightiest interests of the spirit, all the deepest longings of human passion, are at stake, waiting as for the fall of a die. Philosophy loves such situations, I say, and loves, too, to keep its scrutiny as cool in the midst of them as if it were watching a game of chess, instead of the great world-game. Well, try the darker choice that the dilemma gives you. The world yonder shall be an *x,* an unknowable something, outer, problematic, foreign, opaque. And you,—you shall look upon it and believe in it. Yes, you shall for argument's sake first put on an air of resigned confidence, and say, "I do not only fancy it to be an extra-mental and unknowable something there, an impenetrable *x,* but I know it to be such. I can't help it. I didn't make it unknowable. I regret the fact. But there it is. I have to admit its existence. But I know that I shall never solve the problem of its nature." Ah, its nature is a *problem,* then. But what do you mean by this *"problem"*? Problems are, after a fashion, rather familiar things,—that is, in the world of ideas. There are problems soluble and problems insoluble in that world of ideas. It is a soluble problem if one asks what whole number is the square root of 64. The answer is 8. It is an insoluble problem if one asks me to find what whole number is the square root of 65. There is, namely, no such whole number. If one asks me to name the length of a straight line that shall be equal to the circumference of a circle of a known radius, that again, in the world of ideas, is an insoluble problem, because, as can be proved, the circumference of a circle is a length that cannot possibly be exactly expressed in terms of any statable number when the radius is of a stated length. So in the world of ideas, problems are definite questions which can be asked in knowable terms. Fair questions of this sort either may be fairly answered in our present state of knowledge, or else they could be answered if we knew a little or a good deal more, or finally they could not possibly be answered. But in the latter case, if they could not possibly be answered, they always must resemble the problem how to square the circle. They then always turn out, namely, to be absurdly stated questions, and it is their absurdity that makes these problems absolutely insoluble. Any fair question could be answered by one who knew enough. No fair question has an unknowable answer. But now, *if* your unknowable world out there is a thing of wholly, of absolutely problematic and inscrutable nature, is it so because you don't *yet* know enough about it, or because in its very nature and essence it is an absurd thing, an *x* that *would* answer a question, which actually it is nonsense to ask? Surely one must choose the former alternative. The real world may be unknown; it can't be essentially unknowable.

This subtlety is wearisome enough, I know, just here, but I shall not dwell long upon it. Plainly *if* the unknowable world out there is through and through in its nature a really inscrutable prob-

lem, this must mean that in nature it resembles such problems as, What is the whole number that is the square root of 65? Or, what two adjacent hills are there that have no valley between them? For in the world of thought such are the *only* insoluble problems. All others either may now be solved, or would be solved if we knew more than we now do. But, once more, *if* this unknowable is only just the real world as now unknown to us, but capable some time of becoming known, then remember that, as we have just seen, only a mind can ever become an object known to a mind. If I know you as external to me, it is only because you are minds. If I can come to know *any* truth, it is only in so far as this truth is essentially mental, is an idea, is a thought, that I can ever come to know it. Hence, if that so-called unknowable, that unknown outer world there, ever could, by any device, come within our ken, then it is already an ideal world. For just that is what our whole idealistic analysis has been proving. Only ideas are knowable. And nothing absolutely unknowable can exist. For the absolutely unknowable, the *x* pure and simple, the Kantian thing in itself, simply cannot be admitted. The notion of it is nonsense. The assertion of it is a contradiction. Round-squares, and sugar salt-lumps, and Snarks, and Boojums, and Jabberwocks, and Abracadabras; such, I insist, are the only unknowables there are. The unknown, that which our human and finite selfhood hasn't grasped, exists spread out before us in a boundless world of truth; but the unknowable is essentially, confessedly, *ipso facto* a fiction.

The nerve of our whole argument in the foregoing is now pretty fairly exposed. We have seen that the outer truth must be, if anything, a "possibility of experience." But we may now see that a *bare* "possibility" as such, is, like the unknowable, something meaningless.

That which, whenever I come to know it, turns out to be through and through an idea, an experience, must be in itself, before I know it, either somebody's idea, somebody's experience, or it must be nothing. What is a "possibility" of experience that is outside of me, and that is still nothing *for* any one else than myself? Isn't it a bare *x,* a nonsense phrase? Isn't it like an unseen color, an untasted taste, an unfelt feeling? In proving that the world is one of "possible" experience, we have proved that in so far as it is real it is one of actual experience.

Once more, then, to sum up here, *if,* however vast the world of the unknown, only the essentially knowable can exist, and *if* everything knowable is an idea, a mental somewhat, the content of some mind, then once for all we are the world of ideas. Your deepest doubt proves this. Only the nonsense of that inscrutable *x,* of that Abracadabra, of that Snark, the Unknowable of whose essence you make your real world, prevents you from seeing this.

To return, however, to our dilemma. *Either* idealism, we said, *or* the unknowable. What we have now said is that the absolutely unknowable is essentially an absurdity, a non-existent. For any fair and statable problem admits of an answer. *If* the world exists yonder, its essence is then already capable of being known by some mind. If capable of being known by a mind, this essence is then already essentially ideal and mental. A mind that knew the real world would, for instance, find it a something possessing qualities. But qualities are ideal existences, just as much as are the particular qualities called odors or tones or colors. A mind knowing the real world would again find in it relations, such as equality and inequality, attraction and repulsion, likeness and unlikeness. But such relations have no meaning except as objects of a mind. In brief, then, the

world as known would be found to be a world that had all the while been ideal and mental, even before it became known to the particular mind that we are to conceive as coming into connection with it. Thus, then, we are driven to the second alternative. The real world must be a mind, or else a group of minds.

IV

But with this result we come in presence of a final problem. All this, you say, depends upon my assurance that there is after all a real and therefore an essentially knowable and rational world yonder. Such a world would have to be in essence a mind, or a world of minds. But after all, how does one ever escape from the prison of the inner life? Am I not in all this merely wandering amidst the realm of my own ideas? *My* world, of course, isn't and can't be a mere *x,* an essentially unknowable thing, just because it *is my* world, and I have an idea of it. But then does not this mean that *my* world is, after all, forever just *my* world, so that I never get to any truth beyond myself? Isn't this result very disheartening? My world is thus a world of ideas, but alas! how do I then ever reach those ideas of the minds beyond me?

The answer is a simple, but in one sense a very problematic one. You, in one sense, namely, never *do* or can get beyond your own ideas, nor ought you to wish to do so, because in truth all those other minds that constitute your outer and real world are in essence one with your own self. This whole world of ideas is essentially *one* world, and so it is essentially the world of one self and *That art Thou.*

The truth and meaning of this deepest proposition of all idealism is now not at all remote from us. The considerations, however, upon which it depends are of the dryest possible sort, as commonplace as they are deep.

Whatever objects you may think about, whether they are objects directly known to you, or objects infinitely far removed, objects in the distant stars, or objects remote in time, or objects near and present,—such objects, then, as a number with fifty places of digits in it, or the mountains on the other side of the moon, or the day of your death, or the character of Cromwell, or the law of gravitation, or a name that you are just now trying to think of and have forgotten, or the meaning of some mood or feeling or idea now in your mind,—all such objects, I insist, stand in a certain constant and curious relation to your mind whenever you are thinking about them,—a relation that we often miss because it is so familiar. What is this relation? Such an object, while you think about it, needn't be, as popular thought often supposes it to be, the *cause* of your thoughts concerning it. Thus, when you think about Cromwell's character, Cromwell's character isn't just now *causing* any ideas in you,—isn't, so to speak, doing anything to you. Cromwell is dead, and after life's fitful fever his character is a very inactive thing. Not as the *cause,* but as the *object* of your thought is Cromwell present to you. Even so, if you choose now to think of the moment of your death, that moment is somewhere off there in the future, and you can make it your object, but it isn't now an active cause of your ideas. The moment of your death has no present physical existence at all, and just now causes nothing. So, too, with the mountains on the other side of the moon. When you make them the object of your thought, they remain indifferent to you. They do not affect you. You never saw them. But all the same you can think about them.

Yet this thinking *about* things is, after all, a very curious relation in which to stand to things. In order to think *about* a thing, it is *not* enough that I should

have an idea in me that merely resembles that thing. This last is a very important observation. I repeat, it is *not* enough that I should merely have an idea in me that resembles the thing whereof I think. I have, for instance, in me the idea of a pain. Another man has a pain just like mine. Say we both have toothache; or have both burned our fingertips in the same way. Now my idea of pain is just like the pain in him, but I am not on that account necessarily thinking about *his* pain, merely because what I am thinking about, namely my own pain, resembles his pain. No; to think about an object you must not merely have an idea that resembles the object, but you must *mean* to have your idea resemble that object. Stated in other form, to think of an object you must consciously aim at that object, you must pick out that object, you must already in some measure possess that object enough, namely, to identify it as what you mean. But how can you *mean,* how can you *aim at,* how can you *possess,* how can you *pick out,* how can you *identify* what is not already present in essence to your own hidden self? Here is surely a deep question. When you aim at yonder object, be it the mountains in the moon or the day of your death, you really say, "I, as my real self, as my larger self, as my complete consciousness, already in deepest truth possess that object, have it, own it, identify it. And that, and that alone, makes it possible for me in my transient, my individual, my momentary personality, to mean yonder object, to inquire about it, to be partly aware of it and partly ignorant of it." You can't mean what is utterly foreign to you. You mean an object, you assert about it, you talk about it, yes, you doubt or wonder about it, you admit your private and individual ignorance about it, only in so far as your larger self, your deeper personality, your total of normal consciousness already *has* that object. Your momentary and private wonder, ignorance, inquiry, or assertion, about the object, implies, asserts, presupposes, that your total self is in full and immediate possession of the object. This, in fact, is the very nature of that curious relation of a thought to an object which we are now considering. The self that is doubting or asserting, or that is even feeling its private ignorance about an object, and that still, even in consequence of all this, is *meaning*, is *aiming at* such object, is in essence identical with the self for which this object exists in its complete and consciously known truth.

So paradoxical seems this final assertion of idealism that I cannot hope in one moment to make it very plain to you. It is a difficult topic, about which I have elsewhere printed a very lengthy research,[1] wherewith I cannot here trouble you. But what I intend by thus saying that the self which thinks about an object, which really, even in the midst of the blindest ignorance and doubt concerning its object still means the object,—that this self is identical with the deeper self which possesses and truly knows the object,—what I intend hereby I can best illustrate by simple cases taken from your own experience. You are in doubt, say, about a name that you have forgotten, or about a thought that you just had, but that has now escaped you. As you hunt for the name or the lost idea, you are all the while sure that you mean just one particular name or idea and no other. But you don't yet know what name or idea this is. You try, and reject name after name. You query, "Was this what I was thinking of, or this?" But after searching you erelong find the name or the idea, and now at once you *recognize* it. "Oh, that," you say, "was what I meant

all along, only—I didn't know what I meant." Did not know? Yes, in one sense you knew all the while,—that is, your deeper self, your true consciousness knew. It was your momentary self that did not know. But when you found the long-sought name, recalled the lost idea, you recognized it at once, because it was all the while your own, because you, the true and larger self, who owned the name or the idea and were aware of what it was, now were seen to include the smaller and momentary self that sought the name or tried to recall the thought. Your deeper consciousness of the lost idea was all the while there. In fact, did you not presuppose this when you sought the lost idea? How can I mean a name, or an idea, unless I in truth am the self who knows the name, who possesses the idea? In hunting for the name or the lost idea, I am hunting for my own thought. Well, just so I know nothing about the far-off stars in detail, but in so far as I mean the far-off stars at all, as I speak of them, I am identical with that remote and deep thought of my own that already knows the stars. When I study the stars, I am trying to find out what I really mean by them. To be sure, only experience can tell me, but that is because only experience can bring me into relation with my larger self. The escape from the prison of the inner self is simply the fact that the inner self is through and through an appeal to a larger self. The self that inquires, either inquires without meaning, or if it has a meaning, this meaning exists in and for the larger self that knows.

Here is a suggestion of what I mean by Synthetic Idealism. No truth, I repeat, is more familiar. That I am always meaning to inquire into objects beyond me, what clearer fact could be mentioned? That only in case it is already I who, in deeper truth, in my real and hidden thought, *know* the lost object yonder, the object whose nature I seek

---

[1] See *The Religious Aspect of Philosophy* (Boston, 1885), ch. xi., "The Possibility of Error," pp. 384-435.

to comprehend, that only in this case I can truly *mean* the thing yonder,—this, as we must assert, is involved in the very idea of *meaning*. That is the logical analysis of it. You can mean what your deeper self knows; you cannot mean what your deeper self doesn't know. To be sure, the complete illustration of this most critical insight of idealism belongs elsewhere. Few see the familiar. Nothing is more common than for people to think that they mean objects that have nothing to do with themselves. Kant it was, who, despite his things in themselves, first showed us that nobody really means an object, really knows it, or doubts it, or aims at it, unless he does so by aiming at a truth that is present to his own larger self. Except for the unity of my true self, taught Kant, I have no objects. And so it makes no difference whether I know a thing or am in doubt about it. So long as I really *mean* it, that is enough. The self that *means* the object is identical with the larger self that possesses the object, just as when you seek the lost idea you are already in essence with the self that possesses the lost idea.

In this way I suggest to you the proof which a rigid analysis of the logic of our most commonplace thought would give for the doctrine that in the world there is but *one* Self, and that it is *his* world which we all alike are truly meaning, whether we talk of one another or of Cromwell's character or of the fixed stars or of the far-offs æons of the future. The relation of my thought to its object has, I insist, this curious character, that *unless* the thought and its object are parts of one larger thought, I can't even be *meaning* that object yonder, can't even be in error about it, can't even doubt its existence. You, for instance, are part of one larger self with me, or else I can't even be meaning to address you as outer beings. You are part of one larger self along with the most mysterious or most remote fact of nature, along with the moon, and all the hosts of

heaven, along with all truth and all beauty. Else could you not even intend to speak of such objects beyond you. For whatever you speak of you will find that your world is meant by you as just your world. Talk of the unknowable, and it forthwith becomes your unknowable, your problem, whose solution, unless the problem be a mere nonsense question, your larger self must own and be aware of. The deepest problem of life is, "What is this deeper self?" And the only answer is, *It is the self that knows in unity all truth*. This, I insist, is no hypothesis. It is actually the presupposition of your deepest doubt. And that is why I say: Everything finite is more or less obscure, dark, doubtful. Only the Infinite Self, the problem-solver, the complete thinker, the one who knows what we mean even when we are most confused and ignorant, the one who includes us, who has the world present to himself in unity, before whom all past and future truth, all distant and dark truth is clear in one eternal moment, to whom far and forgot is near, who thinks the whole of nature, and in whom are all things, the Logos, the world-possessor,— only his existence, I say, is perfectly sure.

V

Yet I must not state the outcome thus confidently without a little more analysis and exemplification. Let me put the whole matter in a slightly different way. When a man believes that he knows any truth about a fact beyond his present and momentary thought, what is the position, with reference to that fact, which he gives himself? We must first answer, He believes that one who really knew his, the thinker's, thought, and compared it with the fact yonder, would perceive the agreement between the two. Is this *all*, however, that the believer holds to be true of his own thought? No, not so, for he holds not only that his thought, as it is, agrees with *some* fact outside his present self (as my thought, for instance, of my toothache may agree with the fact yonder called my neighbor's toothache), but also that his thought agrees with the fact with which it *meant* to agree. To *mean* to agree, however, with a specific fact beyond my present self, involves such a relation to that fact that if I could somehow come directly into the presence of the fact itself, could somehow absorb it into my present consciousness, I should become immediately aware of it as the fact that I all along had meant. Our previous examples have been intended to bring clearly before us this curious and in fact unique character of the relation called *meaning* an object of our thought. To return, then, to our supposed believer: he believes that he *knows* some fact beyond his present consciousness. This involves, as we have now seen, the assertion that he believes himself to stand in such an actual relation to the fact yonder that were it in, instead of out of his present consciousness, he would recognize it both as the object *meant* by his present thought, and also as in agreement therewith; and it is all this which, as he believes, an immediate observer of his own thought and of the object—that is, an observer who should include our believer's present self, and the fact yonder, and who should reflect on their relations—would find as the real relation. Observe, however, that only by *reflection* would this higher observer find out that real relation. Nothing but Reflective Self-consciousness could discover it. To believe that you know anything beyond your present and momentary self, is, therefore, to believe that you do stand in such a relation to truth as only a larger and reflectively observant self, that included you and your object, could render intelligible. Or once more, so to believe is essentially to appeal confidently to a possible larger

self for approval. But now to say, I know a truth, and yet to say, This larger self to whom I appeal is appealed to only as to a possible self, that needn't be real, —all this involves just the absurdity against which our whole idealistic analysis has been directed in case of all the sorts of fact and truth in the world. To believe, is to say, I stand in a *real* relation to truth, a relation which transcends wholly my present momentary self; and this real relation is of such a curious nature that only a larger inclusive self which consciously reflected upon my meaning and consciously possessed the object that I mean, could know or grasp the reality of the relation. If, however, this *relation* is a real one, it must, like the colors, the sounds, and all the other things of which we spoke before be real *for* somebody. Bare possibilities are nothing. Really possible things are already in some sense real. If, then, my relation to the truth, this complex relation of meaning an object and conforming to it, when the object, although at this moment meant by me, is not now present to my momentary thought,—if this relation is genuine, and yet is such as only a possible larger self could render intelligible, then my possible larger self must be real in order that my momentary self should in fact possess the truth in question. Or, in briefest form, The relation of conforming one's thought to an outer object meant by this thought is a relation which only a Reflective Larger Self could grasp or find real. If the relation is real, the larger self is real, too.

So much, then, for the case when one *believes* that one has grasped a truth beyond the moment. But now for the case when one is actually in *error* about some object of his momentary and finite thought. Error is the actual failure to agree, not with any fact taken at random, but with just the fact that one had meant to agree with. Under what circumstances, then, is error possible? Only in case one's real thought, by virtue of its meaning, does transcend his own momentary and in so far ignorant self. As the true believer, meaning the truth that he believes, must be in real relation thereto, even so the blunderer, really meaning, as he does, the fact yonder, in order that he should be able even to blunder about it, must be, in so far, in the same real relation to truth as the true believer. His error lies in missing that conformity with the meant object at which he aimed. None the less, however, did he really mean and really aim; and, therefore, is he in error, because his real and larger self finds him to be so. True thinking and false thinking alike involve, then, the same fundamental conditions, in so far as both are carried on in moments; and in so far as, in both cases, the false moment and the true are such by virtue of being organic parts of a larger, critical, reflective, and so conscious self.

To sum up so far: Of no object do I speak either falsely or truly, unless I mean that object. Never do I mean an object, unless I stand in such relation thereto that were the object in this conscious moment, and immediately present to me, I should myself recognize it as completing and fulfilling my present and momentary meaning. The relation of meaning an object is thus one that only conscious Reflection can define, or observe, or constitute. No merely *foreign* observer, no external test, could decide upon what is meant at any moment. Therefore, when what is meant is outside of the moment which means, only a Self inclusive of the moment and its object could complete, and so confirm or refute, the opinion that the moment contains. Really to mean an object, then, whether in case of true opinion or in case of false opinion, involves the real possibility of such a reflective test of one's meaning from the point of view of a larger self.

But to say, My relation to the object is such that a reflective larger self, and *only* such a reflective and inclusive self, could see that I meant the object, is to assert a fact, a relation, an existent truth in the world, that either is a truth for nobody, or is a truth for an actual reflective self, inclusive of the moment, and critical of its meaning. Our whole idealistic analysis, however, from the beginning of this discussion, has been to the effect that facts must be facts for somebody, and can't be facts for nobody, and that *bare* possibilities are really impossible. Hence whoever believes, whether truly or falsely, about objects beyond the moment of his belief, is an organic part of a reflective and conscious larger self that has those objects immediately present to itself, and has them in organic relation with the erring or truthful momentary self that believes.

Belief, true and false, having been examined, the case of doubt follows at once. To doubt about objects beyond my momentary self is to admit the "possibility of error" as to such objects. Error would involve my inclusion in a larger self that has directly present to it the object meant by me as I doubt. Truth would involve the same inclusion. The inclusion itself, then, is, so far, no object of rational doubt. To doubt the inclusion would be merely to doubt whether I meant anything at all beyond the moment, and not to doubt as to my particular knowledge about the *nature* of some object beyond, when once the object had been supposed to be meant. Doubt presupposes then, whenever it is a definite doubt, the real possibility, and so, in the last analysis, the reality of the normal self-consciousness that possesses the object concerning which one doubts. But if, passing to the extreme of skepticism, and stating one's most despairing and most uncompromising doubt, one so far confines himself to the prison of the inner life as to doubt whether one ever does mean any object beyond the moment at all, there comes the final consideration that in doubting one's power to transcend the moment, one has already transcended the moment, just as we found in following Hegel's analysis. To say, It is impossible to mean any object beyond this moment of my thought, and the moment is for itself "the measure of all things," is at all events to give a meaning to the words *this moment*. And *this moment* means something only in opposition to *other* moments. Yes, even in saying *this moment*, I have already left this moment, and am meaning and speaking of a past moment. Moreover, to deny that one can mean an object "beyond the moment" is already to give a meaning to the phrase *beyond the moment*, and then to deny that anything is meant to fall within the scope of this meaning. In every case, then, one must transcend by one's meaning the moment to which one is confined by one's finitude.

Flee where we will, then, the net of the larger Self ensnares us. We are lost and imprisoned in the thickets of its tangled labyrinth. The moments are not at all in themselves, for as moments they have no meaning; they exist only in relation to the beyond. The larger Self alone is, and they are by reason of it, organic parts of it. They perish, but it remains; they have truth or error only in its overshadowing presence.

And now, as to the unity of this Self. Can there be many such organic selves, mutually separate unities of moments and of the objects that these moments mean? Nay, were there *many* such, would not their manifoldness be a truth? Their relations, would not these be real? Their distinct places in the world-order, would not these things be objects of possible true or false thoughts? If so, must not there be once more the inclusive real Self for whom these truths were true, these separate selves interrelated, and

their variety absorbed in the organism of its rational meaning?

There is, then, at last, but one Self, organically, reflectively, consciously inclusive of all the selves, and so of all truth. I have called this self, Logos, problem-solver, all-knower. Consider, then, last of all, his relation to problems. In the previous lecture we doubted many things; we questioned the whole seeming world of the outer order; we wondered as to space and time, as to nature and evolution, as to the beginning and the end of things. Now he who wonders is like him who doubts. Has his wonder any rationality about it? Does he *mean* anything by his doubt? Then the truth that he means, and about which he wonders, has its real constitution. As wonderer, he in the moment possesses not this solving truth; he appeals to the self who can solve. That self must possess the solution just as surely as the problem has a meaning. The real nature of space and time, the real beginning of things, where matter was at any point of time in the past, what is to become of the world's energy: these are matters of truth, and truth is necessarily present to the Self as in one all-comprehending self-completed moment, beyond which is naught, within which is the world.

The world, then, is such stuff as ideas are made of. Thought possesses all things. But the world isn't unreal. It extends infinitely beyond our private consciousness, because it is the world of an universal mind. What facts it is to contain only experience can inform us. There is no magic that can anticipate the work of science. Absolutely the *only* thing sure from the first about this world, however, is that it is intelligent, rational, orderly, essentially comprehensible, so that all its problems are somewhere solved, all its darkest mysteries are known to the supreme Self. This Self infinitely and reflectively transcends our consciousness, and therefore, since it includes us, it is at the very least a person, and more definitely conscious than we are; for what it possesses is self-reflecting knowledge, and what is knowledge aware of itself, but consciousness? Beyond the seeming wreck and chaos of our finite problems, its eternal insight dwells, therefore, in absolute and supreme majesty. Yet it is not far from every one of us. There is no least or most transient thought that flits through a child's mind, or that troubles with the faintest line of care a maiden's face, and that still does not contain and embody something of this divine Logos.

58. Natural Piety*

SAMUEL ALEXANDER (1859–1939)

I do not mean by natural piety exactly what Wordsworth [1] meant by it—the reverent joy in nature, by which he wished that his days might be bound to each other—though there is enough connection with his interpretation to justify me in using his phrase. The natural piety I am going to speak of is that of the scientific investigator, by which he accepts with loyalty the mysteries which he cannot explain in nature and has no right to try to explain. I may describe it as the habit of knowing when to stop in asking questions of nature. The limits to the right of asking questions are drawn differently for different purposes.

They are not the same in science as in ordinary intercourse between men in conversation. I may recall an incident in the life of Dr. Johnson. 'I was once present,' says Boswell, 'when a gentleman [perhaps it was Boswell himself] asked so many [questions], as "What did you do, sir?" "What did you say, sir?" that at last he grew enraged, and said, "I will not be put to the *question*. Don't you consider, sir, that these are not the manners of a gentleman? I will not be baited with *what* and *why*. What is this? What is that? Why is a cow's tail long? Why is a fox's tail bushy?" ' Boswell adds that the gentleman, who was a good deal out of countenance, said, 'Why, sir, you are so good, that I venture to trouble you.' JOHNSON.—'Sir, my being so *good* is no reason why you should be so *ill*.' The questions which Johnson regarded as typically offensive in conversation about the cow's and the fox's tail might quite legitimately be asked in science, and, I fancy, answered by a naturalist without any particular difficulty. There is a mental disease known as the questioning or metaphysical ma-

---

* From *The Hibbert Journal,* July, 1922. By kind permission of the editor, L. P. Jacks.

[1] In the fragment beginning 'My heart leaps up' and ending
'The Child is Father of the man:
And I could wish my days to be
 Bound each to each by natural piety.'
Wordsworth also used the phrase in *The Excursion,* Bk. III, line 266:
'Such acquiescence neither doth imply
In me, a meekly-bending spirit soothed
By natural piety; nor a lofty mind
By philosophic discipline prepared
For calm subjection to acknowledge law.'

nia, which cannot accept anything, even the most trivial, without demanding explanation. Why do I stand here where I stand? Why is a glass a glass, a chair a chair? How is it that men are only of the size they are? Why not as big as houses? etc. (I quote from William James). Now the very life of knowledge depends on asking questions. Is it not called enquiry? And its limits are not drawn by considerations of politeness or by shrinking from insanity. But it does recognize that, however far it may push its explanations, the world presents characters which must be accepted reverently as beyond explanation, though they do not pass understanding. And I call this habit of acceptance of nature by the name of natural piety, because simple-minded religion is accustomed to speak of events for which it can find no reason as the will of God.

I will illustrate my meaning from human matters, before passing on to the proper subject of nature. Familiar with the style of Shakespeare, we might with sufficient knowledge of his antecedents, his physiological inheritance, the influences upon him of the company in which he lived, the common speech of the time, and its literature, persuade ourselves that we can understand how he came to write as he did. But the distinctive flavour of it we could not with any amount of knowledge predict, as possibly we might predict with a style such as that of R. L. Stevenson, which carries with it the traces of its origin; we can but acknowledge it as a new creation and confine ourselves to enquiring into its conditions. The same thing may perhaps be said of the style of Plato, or of Pascal. The French Revolution introduced into political and social life a conception which, however hard to define, was new and gave a new direction to the political thought of Europe, inspiring even those who in the end overthrew the revolutionary régime. That a change was about to

occur could have been foreseen by those who considered the evils of the aristocratic polity of France and the direction of the thinking of political writers. But that the change would be the new idea of democracy could not have been foretold. A new feeling had arisen in men's minds of the claims of the common man. Even at the present moment, when the sanguine hopes which were entertained of a regenerated world which was to arise from the war seem to be swept away by the recrudescence of evil passions of domination, or terror, or selfishness, it can hardly be doubted that the world has suffered a political change, which we are too near the event to describe, which owes something to the ideals of the conquered as well as of the conquerors, a new flavour of political life, of which we can understand the conditions but can only feel the presence. We can tell how it has come about, but we do not explain why it should be what it is, and we hardly as yet realise what it is. Compare the teaching of Jesus with what we know of the Judaism of the first century of our era. If our authorities are to be trusted the difference appears to be far smaller than accounts for the immense consequences of the new teaching. That there was novelty, a new conception introduced into morality and the relations between man and God, it would be impossible to deny, and it provided the material when the organisation of Christianity by Paul came about. A religion had come into existence, not put forward by its founder as more than a reform of Judaism, and yet possessing a flavour of its own which was the mark of its originality. What may seem a mere difference of emphasis, a brighter flame of passion (I believe I am taking these phrases from Mr. Montefiore)—all these things, for which the historian can note the antecedents, were fused and welded into a new and distinctive idea. All great historical transformations might be used to supply further examples—the marvel which was born when men of Dorian birth adopted the civilisation and the arts of Egypt and Phoenicia; the limited idea of constitutional liberty for which the Great Rebellion in our own country was fought; the Reformation itself; and a hundred such great changes, of which once more we can understand with sufficient knowledge how they came to be, but not how they should have taken the particular colouring or flavour which actually they possessed.

In these critical changes, further, there is a constant feature. The new creation inherits the ancient ways out of which it grows, but it simplifies the old complexity. There was a chaos of conflicting forces; men's minds were groping confusedly in a tangle of divergent and intercrossing interests; there was a vast unrest; the old habits were lingering on though they had lost their convincingness and bred dissatisfaction; experiment after experiment upon the traditional lines had failed; yet the newer thoughts that were abroad had reached as yet no more than the condition of subterranean and indistinct rebellion. Suddenly, at the bidding of some great single mind, or oftener perhaps of some conspiration of many minds, stirred to their depths with obscure foreboding of the future birth of time, and finely if still vaguely touched to the fine issues, a light has arisen; the discordant elements fall into their places, and the complexity gives way to simplicity. The synthesis is no mere reconciliation; it is creative. So the historians have traced for us the birth of democratic freedom out of the turmoil of the eighteenth century, when once its complacence had broken down; or the preparation of the world to receive the Gentile gospel, when the dull universalising régime of the Roman Empire was fired with the deeper thinking of the Palestinian prophet. So, too, we may feel to-day that our minds are moving this way and that in a sheer confusion of old with new; the complexity and disorganisation of the world are more patent than its unification; and yet we doubt not, or at least we hope, that we have not passed through the ordeal in vain, and that some time and somehow the tangled skein of our present condition will be unravelled, and our conflicting ways may be found convergent towards a simpler and clearer ideal of national and international life. Hence it is, because the creative simplicity is conditioned by so immense a confusion and welter of interests, that it is sometimes more plainly revealed away from the place of its more immediate origin; that the smaller peoples may exhibit more definitely the principle for which larger and better organised nations have striven.

Nor is it only in political and industrial affairs that the creative simplicity emerges from the chaos of complexity. The same feature is even more palpable in science and all pursuit of knowledge. Simple and illuminating discoveries presuppose an immense labour, conducted upon older lines, of material which remains, till the new creation, incoordinated and blind. The new thought or theory reduces the old material to order, while it emancipates us from its confusion. The physical science of to-day uses a language singularly unlike that of the nineteenth century, which it half seems to forget; considered more closely, it is at once the continuance of that work and the discovery of a new and simpler world. Other sciences may not have reached this fulfilment so soon. In history I am told the vast accumulation of detailed investigations awaits as yet the constructive thought which is to give it coherence and simplicity. Philosophy exhibits at the moment all the signs of approaching creation, but is for the time a chaos of discordant doctrines, all of them containing their measure of truth, testifying the awakening of philosophy from its complacent dream, but none as yet completely binding experience into its desired unity. The extreme forms of idealism and realism, the traditional idealism and the antagonist ideas inspired by the revolt against intellect taken alone, or rather by the passion for seeing in the world the fulfilment of man's practical or aesthetic or religious ends; Bradley and Bergson, Croce and William James with his later followers, James Ward and Bertrand Russell; the 'discovery' of Time and the invasion of our ideas by the march of relativity, with its meaning and issues as yet half understood and certainly undecided; the breaking down of the older literary conception of philosophy and its return to its ancient unity and kinship with science, physical and biological; here is a picture of a world distraught by its own complex and abundant vitality. Yet the philosophic believer in philosophy never doubts the imminent birth of a more satisfying thought for which these labours have supplied the favouring marriage of unlikes feeling out towards their blending, and which once attained will set the mind free, as the older idealism has done for a century, to explore with a new guiding thread the vast provinces of special philosophical enquiry.

These features which have been traced in human affairs; new creations which lend an unexplained and strange flavour to existing institutions and remodel them; external habits and ways of life retained but their inward meaning transformed; immense complexities of elements, hitherto chaotic, now gathering themselves together and as it were flowering into some undreamed simplicity; these features are found in the nature of which man is but the latest stage. Nature is 'stratified', and if we apply to it our customary conceptions of growth

and development, we can regard it as a geological formation with a history. But the comparison is still inadequate; for new geological strata are but fresh deposits laid down upon the subjacent ones, not drawing from them their new life. Nature is rather a history of organic growth of species, in which the new type of organism is the outgrowth of the older type, and continues the earlier life into a form at once more complex and more highly simplified. As there is in the animal world or the plant world a hierarchy of forms, so in nature there is a hierarchy of qualities which are characteristics of various levels of development. There are, if I may borrow a metaphor used by Mr. Sellars of Michigan in his recent book [2] 'critical points' in the unfolding of nature when she gathers up her old resources for a new experiment and breeds a new quality of existence. The earliest of these qualities of being which is familiar to us is that of physical matter, whatever we are to suppose it is that materiality consists in. Other well-marked levels are those of chemical structure and behaviour, and life, which is the quality of things which behave physiologically.

I am not concerned to offer a complete enumeration of these levels of existence with their distinguishing qualities. The three qualities mentioned are but a selection. Every attempt at completeness raises questions of difficulty. Certain, however, it is now that mere physical materiality is a highly developed stage, late in the history of the world: that there are forms of submaterial being, and the line between the submaterial and the material is not for me to draw. Neither is it for me to say whether electrons are the lowest existence in the scale. Again, beyond life, some have maintained that mind is it-

---

[2] *Evolutionary Naturalism*, R. W. Sellars, Open Court, Chicago, 1922.

self a new quality which arises out of life, while others treat consciousness merely as a function of all life, and for them consciousness and life are one, and accordingly all the knowing on which we pride ourselves so much is in the end only a special form of vital behaviour. There is another debatable question. To me, colours and sounds and tastes and all the sensible characters of material things appear to be resident in things themselves; and coloured existence to be a critical point in nature. When a physical body is such that the light which it sends out to our eyes has a determinate wavelength, that body is red. To others, and they are the majority, the colour depends upon the possession by the percipient of eyes. These questions I need not raise in this place because they take us away from the central theme into historic problems which have occupied physics and philosophy from the days of Galileo and before. There is still another matter I leave open. Life is without doubt such a critical point in nature. Are the various gradations of life, first of all the difference of plants and animals as a whole, and next the marked differences of kinds among animals and plants themselves, to be regarded likewise? The differences which part a humble amoeba or hydra from the monkey, or even from the lizard or crab, are vast. Are they critical differences? All I need answer is that if they are not, at least the outgrowth of the higher from the lower forms of life helps us mightily to understand the outgrowth at the critical point of the higher level of quality from the lower. Further, if it is right to treat colours as real qualities, not dependent for existence on the physiological organs; which are but instruments in that case for apprehending, not for creating them; if this is so, the different kinds of colours—red, green, and the rest—are comparable to the species of animals or plants, and if they do not

mark a change of level they mark differences upon that level. All these matters of debate I leave aside, in order to insist on the vital feature of nature that she does exhibit critical changes of quality, which mark new syntheses, that we can but note. We may and must observe with care out of what previous conditions these new creations arise. We cannot tell why they should assume these qualities. We can but accept them as we find them, and this acceptance is natural piety.

These bodies with new qualities, these 'creative syntheses,' which arise at critical points from a lower level of existence, are therefore no mere mechanical resultants of their lower conditions. If they were they would have merely the quality of their antecedents or components, as the component pulls upon a body along the sides of a parallelogram are equivalent to a resultant pull along the diagonal. Even the chemical combination of sodium and sulphuric acid, though it leads to something new and its process is not purely mechanical, does but issue in a new chemical body, just as the pairing of two living beings may lead to a new variety, but still a variety of living being. They are, therefore, after the usage of the late George Henry Lewes, described as emergents by Mr. Lloyd Morgan, with whom I have for many years shared this conception of things, which he has expounded with a simplicity and lucidity beyond my powers in a chapter of his book, *Instinct and Experience,* and with particular force in the address with which he inaugurated the independent section of Psychology at the recent meeting of the British Association at Edinburgh (1921).

Without attempting to take in the whole field of nature, I will confine myself here to life, considered as an emergent from the realm of physico-chemical bodies. A living body is, according to this conception, a physico-chemical body of a certain degree and kind of complexity, whose actions may severally be viewed as physical or chemical, but taken in their integration, or entirety (to borrow a word of Lord Haldane's), have the quality of life. Life is therefore resoluble without remainder into physico-chemical processes; but it cannot be treated as *merely* physico-chemical. Certain of its functions may be referred to physical or chemical laws, but it is not these separable processes which constitute life. Life exists only when we have that particular collocation of such physico-chemical actions which we know as living. It is the special co-ordination which conditions the appearance or creation of the new quality of life. We might therefore be disposed to describe the living body indifferently as being a physico-chemical body which is *also* vital, or as being vital and *also* physico-chemical. In reality only the second designation is satisfactory. The first would imply that a certain grouping of such processes remains no more than physical and chemical, that life is not something new but a name for this integration, whereas it is a new quality conditioned by and equivalent to the particular complexity of integration. Given life, we can hope to resolve it into its physico-chemical equivalent. We can even hope to reproduce partially or wholly by artificial means the existence of life. It is well known, for instance, that certain foams or emulsions of oil have exhibited streaming movements like those of living protoplasm. But life has been already attained, and it is our clue to the invention of the necessary machinery. Given merely physical and chemical processes, we can only generate life when we have hit upon the requisite form of integration. Thus life is *also* physico-chemical, because in its separable activities it is comparable with other physico-chemical processes. But it is not *merely* physico-chemical, because

merely physico-chemical processes are not alive, and they do not give us life until the requisite complexity of integration is attained. So important is it to remember that besides elements there is the form of their combination, and that the form is as much a reality as the elements and gives them their significance; that it is not the patches of colour alone which make the picture, but their selection and arrangement which make the separate patches contribute to the expressiveness of the picture; that a melody is not merely the notes by which it is conveyed, but the choice and order which the musician has introduced into them; that in the choice and combination of the parts the whole receives a meaning which does not belong to the several components; and that while a combination of sounds is still a sound, and the blending of male and female elements in a human being is still human, there is still room at critical points for the combination to carry us into a new quality of being. Even where there is no such new quality of being, the change that is due to form may shadow forth these greater and more creative changes; as when, to revert to former illustrations, the choice of words generates the indescribable flavour of style, or, in music, to quote the often quoted words:

Consider it well: each tone in our scale in
    itself is nought;
  It is everywhere in the world—loud,
      soft, and all is said:
Give it to me to use! I mix it with two
    in my thought
  And, there! ye have heard and seen:
      consider and bow the head!

That attitude is an illustration of what I am calling natural piety.

It is here that we are brought face to face with the long-drawn-out dispute between the so-called mechanistic explanation of life and vitalism. The latest contribution to the controversy is to be found in the highly interesting work on 'the mechanism of life,' [3] by Mr. Johnstone, the professor of Oceanography at Liverpool. I do not mention his work in order to discuss his own explanation of life. He distinguishes the vital and the material mechanism in this way. All material mechanisms expend a part of the energy supplied to them not in doing work but in the form of heat which is no longer available for work; in the technical phrase they increase the sum of entropy or unavailing energy, and they represent a progression towards the condition of general dissipation of available energy. Living machines, on the contrary, delay or reverse the accumulation of entropy. It is beyond my competence to inquire into the correctness of this view. Rather I wish to direct your attention to the point that there is upon this doctrine such a 'mechanism' of life; because it suggests that the sharp distinction of the mechanical from the vital is unfounded, and that life may be a mechanism and yet have, as I have said, a new quality (though this view I am not attributing to Mr. Johnstone himself), and that while there is no new entity life, there is a new quality life, with which certain combinations of matter may be endowed. Vitalism supposed that there was an actual vital force, non-physical, which interfered with and directed the physical behaviour of the organism, and it has been reintroduced in our day by Mr. Hans Driesch under the guise of a presiding psychoid or entelechy, as he names it, a distinguishable principle, not resoluble into chemical or physical action. In this controversy a middle position is occupied by Mr. J. S. Haldane, who has called attention to a number of delicate adjustments performed by the organism which cannot be accounted for, he thinks, by the separate chemical proc-

esses of the body. Thus the respiratory actions under the guidance of the nervous centre are so delicate that they preserve the pressure of carbonic acid in the air in the lungs and therefore in the blood-vessels, and restore it to the normal when the amount of it has been disturbed even in the slightest degree, as by taking deeper breath and so diluting the carbonic acid. The arterial blood has, as he otherwise puts it, a normal faint alkalinity, and if this is disturbed, however slightly, by defect of carbonic acid, the pressure is restored. In the same way the blood has a normal salinity, which is kept constant in the face of the slightest changes by delicate reactions on the part of the kidneys. Mr. Haldane takes this delicacy of adjustment to mean that physiological action can only be understood by including in any function the organisation of the whole creature. Here we might seem to have a matter upon which only a physiologist has the right to speak. Still, a mere philosopher may be allowed to consider the wider issue raised. If this concept of organisation means only that vital action implies, and is not rightly described without it, a philosopher must declare Mr. Haldane right. If he means that vital action precludes the resolution of life without remainder into chemical and physical action, he is open to the charge that, in his zeal for this new fact of life, he is forgetting that the whole make-up of the organism is itself, as Mr. Lloyd Morgan has pointed out, a factor in the chemical and physical processes in question. The moral which I draw from his work is not his own, but precisely the statement made at the beginning, that that organisation which is alive is not merely physico-chemical, though completely resoluble into such terms, but has the new quality of life. No appeal is needed, so far as I can see, to a vital force or even an *élan vital*. It is enough to note the emergence of the

---

[3] *The Mechanism of Life,* London (Arnold), 1921. Cp. W. McDougall, *Body and Mind,* p. 245.

quality, and try to describe what is involved in its conditions. That task will be, I imagine, difficult enough, and Mr. Johnstone's own account [4] may be valued as an attempt towards performing it.

The emergence of life with this new collocation of conditions implies that life is continuous with chemical, physical and mechanical action. To be more explicit, the living body is also physical and chemical. It surrenders no claim to be considered a part of the physical world. But the new quality of life which it possesses is neither chemical nor mechanical, but something new. Thus the parts of the living body have colour but life is not coloured, and they are material but life itself is not material, but only the body which is alive is material. The lower conditions out of whose collocations life emerges supply a body as it were to a new soul. The specific characters which they possess are not continued into the new soul. The continuity which exists between life and the material does not mean that the material is carried over into life. There would not in that case be continuity between the living body as a new emergent and its predecessors; the living body would be nothing more than elaborate material mechanism, which would illustrate material action, but could not claim a position of privilege. The characters which *are* continued from the lower level into life are not the specific qualities of the lower level; they are rather those characters which all existence shares in common, such as existence in time and space, intensity, capacity of affecting other existences, all which belong to life as much as to matter.

From this it will be clear that when we draw a sharp contrast between life and mechanism, as too often we do, we are guilty of exaggeration if not of con-

fusion.[5] It is more to the purpose to indicate their differences after we have assured ourselves of a fundamental continuity or resemblance. What is salient in mechanical bodies is their general uniformity of response, the routine character of their behaviour. What is salient in life is its capacity of fine adjustment to varying conditions, a capacity such as no merely material body possesses, not even any machine made as yet by human design. This capacity of variation in its response may seem even to amount in certain cases to an originality which has led some to credit life with genuine freedom from determination by previous conditions, with indetermination, such as is supposed to appear in human beings as freewill—not in the ordinary sense in which we are undoubtedly free, as directing ourselves consciously to foreseen ends, but in the sense of making new departures without determining reasons. How, then, we may ask, if life is resoluble without remainder into mechanical, physical and chemical elements, can a living body be other than the automaton which Descartes declared it to be? (Descartes, observe in passing, would, if I am right, have been justified, if he had only realised that an automaton of sufficient complexity would cease to be a mere automaton). Now these questions are put because of confusing the determinate with the purely mechanical. All behaviour, it is safe to assert, is determinate, and its fine capacity of variation and spontaneity are determined by its delicately complex organisation. But not all determinate action is therefore mechanical. The mechanical is simple and its responses broadly constant; the vital is highly complex and its responses, though definite, may vary according to circum-

---

[4] *The Mechanism of Life,* chapter xi.

[5] Compare on this subject chapters vi, vii of Mr. R. F. A. Hoernlé's *Studies in Contemporary Metaphysics,* New York and London, 1920.

stances; and that is all. If one thing is appearing more clearly than another from recent science, it is that material action is not so much that from which vital action diverges, as a first approximation towards vital action. The idea of life tends in our day to be extended downwards towards more primitive kinds of existence. Not that material existence is to be regarded as a form of life, but that it exhibits features which correspond to life; so that the transition from matter to life is no longer the passage to something absolutely heterogeneous but the manifestation of a single principle operating under conditions of various complexity, and generating emergents with distinctive qualities, and yet retaining them all in one linked progression of affinity.

We are to combine in our thoughts this fundamental unity with the recognition of emergent qualities which can only be accepted but cannot be accounted for. One difficulty in the way of effecting this combination in our thought is the idea that if the world is a determinate growth, each new creation determined by its predecessors on a lower level, the history of the world must be capable of prediction, according to the famous assertion of Laplace. But this conclusion does not follow. Laplace's calculator might foresee that at a certain point a certain complexity might arise, whose actions were capable of measurement and would be those of living things. He could never affirm that this form of action would have the quality of life, unless he lived to see. He might predict ethereal waves but could not predict them to be light; still less that a material body would be material or when touched by light would be red, or even merely look red to a living body with eyes. All known forms of action could be predicted in their measurable characters, but never in their emergent ones. Not even God, if we suppose a God presiding over the birth of the world, in accordance with the conception of the crudest theism, could predict what these emergent qualities would be; he could only accept them like ourselves when the world he made had originated them.

I have chosen as illustrating the attitude of natural piety our acceptance of the emergence of these qualities. They remain for ever a mysterious fact. But they are after all only a part of the mystery which encompasses us and which we have no right to ask to penetrate. They are themselves related to simpler conditions, which it is the object of science to discover. Some persons have even supposed, following the precedent of the early Greek philosophers, and in particular of the chief Pythagorean speaker in Plato's great dialogue, the *Timaeus,* that all these features in the world are but specifications of some ultimate stuff of which the world is made. If this were true, it might be repugnant to the feelings of some, but natural piety would accept it, as it accepts the law of gravitation, or the law of the progression in the forms of life according to evolution, whatever the law of evolution may turn out to be; or as it would accept, if we are compelled to think so, that the four-dimensional space-time in which we live is bent in the neighborhood of matter. All science attempts to connect the variegated phenomena of the world by expressing them in terms of measurable motions. It seems to take the colour and richness from the world of secondary sensible qualities and expresses them in terms of primary qualities which in the end are terms of space and time. It does not, nor does it pretend to, remove the mystery of the secondary qualities, and in all its explanations it does but bring us in face of other mysteries which we must needs accept.

We are thus for ever in presence of miracles; and as old Nathan said, the greatest of all miracles is that the genuine miracles should be so familiar. And here I interpolate a remark, not altogether irrelevant to my subject, upon the uses of great men. The emergence of qualities is the familiar miracle, but great men, and in particular great men of science, are for ever enlarging our mysteries, simplifying them and extending their scope, as when they record the law of attraction, or the idea which lies at the basis of the notion of relativity. And thus with their fresher insight they keep for us our sense of piety to nature alive. Compared with other men they are like the springs of a river. Perhaps some of you may have shared with me the exquisite experience of seeing the springs of the Aberdeenshire Dee below the top of Brae Riach in the Grampians. There the clear water bubbles to the surface through mosses pink and yellow and green with all the varying shades of green; and as it gathers to the edge it falls in tiny trickles which unite with one another into rills, and these with like rills from other portions of the plateau, until in the end they combine to form the river which you see at the foot, already a considerable stream. The stream is discoloured in its course by the soil through which it flows or the products of human labour, and is put to the service of man before it reaches the sea. And as its springs are fed by the sea into which it falls, whose vapours are drawn up and fall in rain so that a continuous life is maintained between the ocean and the fresh waters on the heights, so it is that the thoughts of great men keep up for general mankind our communion with the circumambient mystery.

The mystery of facts, whether these facts are the individual facts of experience or the larger universal facts which are scientific laws, or such facts, more comprehensive still, as may be discovered by a prudent and scientific philosophy, is the last word of knowledge. The reverent temper which accepts them is the mood of natural piety.

59. *Process–Philosophy*[*]

ALFRED N. WHITEHEAD (1861–1947)

I. Matter and Process

The notion of empty space, the mere vehicle of spatial interconnections has been eliminated from recent science. The whole spatial universe is a field of force,

[*] From *Modes of Thought*, Lectures VII, VIII, and *Religion in the Making*, ch. IV, Section IV. By permission of The Macmillan Co. This selection has been prepared by Mr. Albert Lataner, formerly a member of Philosophy Department, The City College.

or in other words, a field of incessant activity. The mathematical formulae of physics express the mathematical relations realized in this activity.

The unexpected result has been the elimination of bits of matter, as the self-identical supports for physical properties. . . . Matter has been identified with energy, and energy is sheer activity; the passive substratum composed of self-identical enduring bits of matter has been abandoned, so far as concerns any fundamental description. Obviously this notion expresses an important derivative fact. But it has ceased to be the presupposed basis of theory. The modern point of view is expressed in terms of energy, activity, and the vibratory differentiations of space-time. Any local agitation shakes the whole universe. The distant effects are minute, but they are there. The concept of matter presupposed simple location. Each bit of matter was self-contained, localized in a region with a passive, static network of spatial relations, entwined in a uniform relational system from infinity to infinity and from eternity to eternity. But in the modern concept the group of agitations which we term matter is fused into its environment. There is no possibility of a detached, self-contained local existence. The environment enters into the nature of each thing. Some elements in the nature of a complete set of agitations may remain stable as those agitations are propelled through a changing environment. But such stability is only the case in a general, average way. This average fact is the reason why we find the same chair, the same rock, and the same planet, enduring for days, or for centuries, or for millions of years. In this average fact then time-factor takes the aspect of endurance, and change is a detail. The fundamental fact, according to the physics of the present day, is that the environment with its peculiarities seeps into the group-agitation which we call matter and the group-agitations extend their character to the environment. In truth, the notion of the self-contained particle of matter, self-sufficient within its local habitation, is an abstraction. Now an abstraction is nothing else than the omission of part of the truth. The abstraction is well-founded when the conclusions drawn from it are not vitiated by the omitted truth.

This general deduction from the modern doctrine of physics vitiates many conclusions drawn from the application of physics to other sciences, such as physiology, or even such as physics itself. For example, when geneticists conceive genes as the determinants of heredity. The analogy of the old concept of matter sometimes leads them to ignore the influence of the particular animal body in which they are functioning. They presuppose that a pellet of matter remains in all respects self-identical whatever be its changes of environment. So far as modern physics is concerned, any characteristic may, or may not, effect changes in the genes, changes which are as important in certain respects, though not in others. Thus no a priori argument as to the inheritance of characters can be drawn from the mere doctrine of genes. In fact recently physiologists have found that genes are modified in some respects by their environment. The presuppositions of the old common sense view survive, even when the view itself has been abandoned as a fundamental description.

II. Life

The doctrine that I am maintaining is that neither physical nature nor life can be understood unless we fuse them together as essential factors in the composition of "really real" things whose inter-connections and individual characters constitute the universe.

The first step in the argument must be to form some concept of what life can mean. Also we require that the deficiencies in our concept of physical nature should be supplied by its fusion with life. And we require that, on the other hand, the notion of life should involve the notion of physical nature.

Now as a first approximation the notion of life implies a certain absoluteness of self-enjoyment. This must mean a certain immediate individuality, which is a complex process of appropriating into a unity of existence the many data presented as relevant by the physical processes of nature. Life implies the absolute, individual self-enjoyment arising out of this process of appropriation. I have, in my recent writings, used the word "prehension" to express this process of appropriation. Also I have termed each individual act of immediate self-enjoyment an "occasion of experience." I hold that these unities of existence, these occasions of experience, are the really real things which in their collective unity compose the evolving universe, ever plunging into the creative advance.

This concept of self-enjoyment does not exhaust that aspect of process here termed "life." Process for its intelligibility involves the notion of a creative activity belonging to the very essence of each occasion. It is the process of eliciting into actual being factors in the universe which antecedently to that process exist only in the mode of unrealized potentialities. The process of self-creation is the transformation of the potential into the actual, and the fact of such transformation includes the immediacy of self-enjoyment.

Thus in conceiving the function of life in an occasion of experience, we must discriminate the actualized data presented by the antecedent world, the non-actualized potentialities which lie ready to promote their fusion into a new unity of experience, and the immediacy of self-enjoyment which belongs to the creative fusion of those data with those potentialities. This is the doctrine of the creative advance whereby it belongs to the essence of the universe, that it passes into a future. It is nonsense to conceive of nature as a static fact, even for an instant devoid of duration. There is no nature apart from transition, and there is no transition apart from temporal duration. This is the reason why the notion of an instant of time, conceived as a primary simple fact, is nonsense.

But even yet we have not exhausted the notion of creation which is essential to the understanding of nature. We must add yet another character to our description of life. This missing characteristic is "aim." By this term "aim" is meant the exclusion of the boundless wealth of alternative potentiality, and the inclusion of that definite factor of novelty which constitutes the selected way of entertaining those data in that process of unification. The aim is at that complex of feeling which is the enjoyment of those data in that way. "That way of enjoyment" is selected from the boundless wealth of alternatives. It has been aimed at for actualizations in that process.

Thus the characteristics of life are absolute self-enjoyment, creative activity, aim. Here "aim" evidently involves the entertainment of the purely ideal so as to be directive of the creative process. Also the enjoyment belongs to the process and is not a characteristic of any static result. The aim is at the enjoyment belonging to the process.

III. Mind

.... "Cogito, ergo sum" is wrongly translated, "I think, therefore I am." It is never bare thought or bare existence that we are aware of. I find myself as essentially a unity of emotions, enjoyments, hopes, fears, regrets, valuations of alternatives, decisions—all of them subjective reactions to the environment as active in my nature. My unity—which is Descartes' "I am"—is my process of shaping this welter of material into a consistent pattern of feeling. The individual enjoyment is what I am in my role of a natural activity, as I shape the activities of the environment into a new creation, which is myself at this moment; and yet, as being myself, it is a continuation of the antecedent world. If we stress the role of the environment, this process is causation. If we stress the role of my immediate pattern of active enjoyment, this process is self-creation. If we stress the role of the conceptual anticipation of the future whose existence is a necessity in the nature of the present, this process is the teleological aim at some ideal in the future. This aim, however, is not really beyond the present process. For the aim at the future is an enjoyment in the present. It thus effectively conditions the immediate self-creation of the new creature.

We can now again ask the final question as put forward at the close of the former lecture. Physical science has reduced nature to activity, and has discovered abstract mathematical formulae which are illustrated in these activities of Nature. But the fundamental question remains, How do we add content to the notion of bare activity? This question can only be answered by fusing life with nature.

In the first place, we must distinguish life from mentality. Mentality involves conceptual experience, and is only one variable ingredient in life. The sort of functioning here termed "conceptual experience" is the entertainment of possibilities for ideal realization in abstraction from any sheer physical realization. The most obvious example of conceptual experience is the entertainment of alternatives. Life lies below this grade of mentality. Life is the enjoyment of emotion, derived from the past and aimed at the future. It is the enjoyment of emotion which was then, which is now, and which will be then. This vector character is of the essence of such entertainment.

The emotion transcends the present in two ways. It issues from, and it issues towards. It is received, it is enjoyed, and it is passed along, from moment to moment. Each occasion is an activity of concern, in the Quaker sense of that

term. It is the conjunction of transcendence and immanence. The occasion is concerned, in the way of feeling and aim, with things that in their own essence lie beyond it; although these things in their present functions are factors in the concern of that occasion. Thus each occasion, although engaged in its own immediate self-realization, is concerned with the universe.

The process is always a process of modification by reason of the numberless avenues of supply, and by reason of the numberless modes of qualitative texture. The unity of emotion, which is the unity of the present occasion, is a patterned texture of qualities, always shifting as it is passed into the future. The creative activity aims at preservation of the components and at preservation of intensity. The modifications of pattern, the dismissal into elimination, are in obedience to this aim.

IV. Nature

A rough division can be made of six types of occurrences in nature. The first type is human existence, body and mind. The second type includes all sorts of animal life, insects, the vertebrates, and other genera. In fact all the various types of animal life other than human. The third type includes all vegetable life. The fourth type consists of the single living cells. The fifth type consists of all large scale inorganic aggregates, on a scale comparable to the size of animal bodies, or larger. The sixth type is composed of the happenings on an infinitesimal scale, disclosed by the minute analysis of modern physics.

Now all these functionings of Nature influence each other, require each other, and lead on to each other. The list has purposely been made roughly, without any scientific pretension. The sharp-cut scientific classifications are essential for scientific method. But they are dangerous for philosophy. Such classification hides the truth that the different modes of natural existence shade off into each other. There is the animal life with its central direction of a society of cells, there is the vegetable life with its organized republic of cells, there is the cell life with its organized republic of molecules, there is the large-scale inorganic society of molecules with its passive acceptance of necessities derived from spatial relations, there is the infra-molecular activity which has lost all trace of the passivity of inorganic nature on a larger scale.

In this survey some main conclusions stand out. One conclusion is the diverse modes of functioning which are produced by diverse modes of organization. The second conclusion is the aspect of continuity between these different modes. There are border-line cases, which bridge the gaps. Often the border-line cases are unstable, and pass quickly. But span of existence is merely relative to our habits of human life. For infra-molecular occurrence, a second is a vast period of time. A third conclusion is the difference in the aspect of nature according as we change the scale of observation. Each scale of observation presents us with average effects proper to that scale.

. . . . In so far as conceptual mentality does not intervene, the grand patterns pervading the environment are passed on with the inherited modes of adjustment. Here we find the patterns of activity studied by the physicists and chemists. Mentality is merely latent in all these occasions as thus studied. In the case of inorganic nature any sporadic flashes are inoperative so far as our powers of discernment are concerned. The lowest stages of effective mentality, controlled by the inheritance of physical pattern, involve the faint direction of emphasis by unconscious ideal aim. The various examples of the higher forms of life exhibit the variety of grades of effec-

tiveness of mentality. In the social habits of animals, there is evidence of flashes of mentality in the past which have degenerated into physical habits. Finally in the higher mammals and more particularly in mankind, we have clear evidence of mentality habitually effective. In our own experience, our knowledge consciously entertained and systematized can only mean such mentality, directly observed.

. . . . In these lectures I have not entered upon systematic metaphysical cosmology. The object of the lectures is to indicate those elements in our experience in terms of which such a cosmology should be constructed. The key notion from which such construction should start is that the energetic activity considered in physics is the emotional intensity entertained in life.

V. God

Unlimited possibility and abstract creativity can procure nothing. The limitation, and the basis arising from what is already actual, are both of them necessary and interconnected.

Thus the whole process itself, viewed at any stage as a definite limited fact which has issued from the creativity, requires a definite entity, already actual among the formative elements, as an antecedent ground for the entry of the ideal forms into the definite process of the temporal world.

But such a complete aboriginal actuality must differ from actuality in process of realization in respect to the blind occasions of perceptivity which issue from process and require process. These occasions build up the physical world which is essentially in transition.

God, who is the ground antecedent to transition, must include all possibilities of physical value conceptually, thereby holding the ideal forms apart in equal, conceptual realization of knowledge.

Thus, as concepts, they are grasped together in the synthesis of omniscience.

The limitation of God is his goodness. He gains his depth of actuality by his harmony of valuation. It is not true that God is in all respects infinite. If He were, He would be evil as well as good. Also this unlimited fusion of evil with good would mean mere nothingness. He is something decided and is thereby limited.

He is complete in the sense that his vision determines every possibility of value. Such a complete vision coordinates and adjusts every detail. Thus his knowledge of the relationships of particular modes of value is not added to, or disturbed, by the realization in the actual world of what is already conceptually realized in his ideal world. This ideal world of conceptual harmonization is merely a description of God himself. Thus the nature of God is the complete conceptual realization of the realm of ideal forms. The kingdom of heaven is God. But these forms are not realized by him in mere bare isolation, but as elements in the value of his conceptual experience. Also, the ideal forms are in God's vision as contributing to his complete experience, by reason of his conceptual realization of their possibilities as elements of value in any creature. Thus God is the one systematic, complete fact, which is the antecedent ground conditioning every creative act.

The depths of his existence lie beyond the vulgarities of praise or of power. He gives to suffering its swift insight into values which can issue from it. He is the ideal companion who transmutes what has been lost into a living fact within his own nature. He is the mirror which discloses to every creature its own greatness.

The kingdom of heaven is not the isolation of good from evil. It is the overcoming of evil by good. This transmutation of evil into good enters into the actual world by reason of the inclusion of the nature of God, which includes the ideal vision of each actual evil so met with a novel consequent as to issue in the restoration of goodness.

God has in his nature the knowledge of evil, of pain, and of degradation, but it is there as overcome with what is good. Every fact is what it is, a fact of pleasure, of joy, of pain, or of suffering. In its union with God that fact is not a total loss, but on its finer side is an element to be woven immortally into the rhythm of mortal things. Its very evil becomes a stepping stone in the all-embracing ideals of God.

Every event on its finer side introduces God into the world. Through it his ideal vision is given a base in actual fact to which He provides the ideal consequent, as a factor saving the world from the self-destruction of evil. The power by which God sustains the world is the power of himself as the ideal. He adds himself to the actual ground from which every creative act takes its rise. The world lives by its incarnation of God in itself.

He transcends the temporal world, because He is an actual fact in the nature of things. He is not there as derivative from the world; He is the actual fact from which the other formative elements cannot be torn apart.

But equally it stands in his nature that He is the realization of the ideal conceptual harmony by reason of which there is an actual process in the total universe—an evolving world which is actual because there is order.

The abstract forms are thus the link between God and the actual world. These forms are abstract and not real, because in themselves they represent no achievement of actual value. Actual fact always means fusion into one perceptivity. God is one such conceptual fusion, embracing the concept of all such possibilities graded in harmonious, relative subordination. Each actual occasion in the temporal world is another such fusion. The forms belong no more to God than to any one occasion. Apart from these forms, no rational description can be given either of God or of the actual world. Apart from God, there would be no actual world; and apart from the actual world with its creativity, there would be no rational explanation of the ideal vision which constitutes God.

Each actual occasion gives to the creativity which flows from it a definite character in two ways. In one way, as a fact, enjoying its complex of relationships with the rest of the world, it contributes a ground—partly good and partly bad—for the creativity to fuse with a novel consequent, which will be the outcome of its free urge. In another way, as transmuted in the nature of God, the ideal consequent as it stands in his vision is also added. Thus God in the world is the perpetual vision of the road which leads to the deeper realities.

60. Existentialism*

JEAN-PAUL SARTRE (1905–   )

What is meant by the term *existentialism?*

Most people who use the word would be rather embarrassed if they had to explain it, since, now that the word is all the rage, even the work of a musician or painter is being called existentialist. . . . It seems that for want of an advance-guard doctrine analogous to surrealism, the kind of people who are eager for scandal and flurry turn to this philosophy which in other respects does not at all serve their purposes in this sphere.

Actually, it is the least scandalous, the most austere of doctrines. It is intended strictly for specialists and philosophers. Yet it can be defined easily. What complicates matters is that there are two kinds of existentialist; first, those who are Christian, among whom I would include Jaspers and Gabriel Mar-

cel, both Catholic; and on the other hand the atheistic existentialists, among whom I class Heidegger, and then the French existentialists and myself. What they have in common is that they think that existence precedes essence, or, if you prefer, that subjectivity must be the starting point.

Just what does that mean? Let us consider some object that is manufactured, for example, a book or a paper-cutter: here is an object which has been made by an artisan whose inspiration came from a concept. He referred to the concept of what a paper-cutter is and likewise to a known method of production, which is part of the concept, something which is, by and large, a routine. Thus, the paper-cutter is at once an object produced in a certain way and, on the other hand, one having a specific use; and one can not postulate a man who produces a paper-cutter but does not know what it is used for. Therefore, let

* From *Existentialism*. By permission of publishers, Philosophical Library.

us say that, for the paper-cutter, essence —that is, the ensemble of both the production routines and the properties which enable it to be both produced and defined—precedes existence. Thus, the presence of the paper-cutter or book in front of me is determined. Therefore, we have here a technical view of the world whereby it can be said that production precedes existence.

When we conceive God as the Creator, He is generally thought of as a superior sort of artisan. Whatever doctrine we may be considering, whether one like that of Descartes or that of Leibnitz, we always grant that will more or less follows understanding or, at the very least, accompanies it, and that when God creates He knows exactly what He is creating. Thus, the concept of man in the mind of God is comparable to the concept of paper-cutter in the mind of the manufacturer, and, following certain techniques and a conception, God produces man, just as the artisan, following a definition and a technique, makes a paper-cutter. Thus, the individual man is the realisation of a certain concept in the divine intelligence.

In the eighteenth century, the atheism of the *philosophes* discarded the idea of God, but not so much for the notion that essence precedes existence. To a certain extent, this idea is found everywhere; we find it in Diderot, in Voltaire, and even in Kant. Man has a human nature; this human nature, which is the concept of the human, is found in all men, which means that each man is a particular example of a universal concept, man. In Kant, the result of this universality is that the wild-man, the natural man, as well as the bourgeois, are circumscribed by the same definition and have the same basic qualities. Thus, here too the essence of man precedes the historical existence that we find in nature.

Atheistic existentialism, which I rep-

resent, is more coherent. It states that if God does not exist, there is at least one being in whom existence precedes essence, a being who exists before he can be defined by any concept, and that this being is man, or, as Heidegger says, human reality. What is meant here by saying that existence precedes essence? It means that, first of all, man exists, turns up, appears on the scene, and, only afterwards, defines himself. If man, as the existentialist conceives him, is indefinable, it is because at first he is nothing. Only afterward will he be something, and he himself will have made what he will be. Thus, there is no human nature, since there is no God to conceive it. Not only is man what he conceives himself to be, but he is also only what he wills himself to be after this thrust toward existence.

Man is nothing else but what he makes of himself. Such is the first principle of existentialism. It is also what is called subjectivity, the name we are labeled with when charges are brought against us. But what do we mean by this, if not that man has a greater dignity than a stone or table? For we mean that man first exists, that is, that man first of all is the being who hurls himself toward a future and who is conscious of imagining himself as being in the future. Man is at the start a plan which is aware of itself, rather than a patch of moss, a piece of garbage, or a cauliflower; nothing exists prior to this plan; there is nothing in heaven; man will be what he will have planned to be. Not what he will want to be. Because by the word "will" we generally mean a conscious decision, which is subsequent to what we have already made of ourselves. I may want to belong to a political party, write a book, get married; but all that is only a manifestation of an earlier, more spontaneous choice that is called "will." But if existence really does precede essence, man is responsible for what he is.

Thus, existentialism's first move is to make every man aware of what he is and to make the full responsibility of his existence rest on him. And when we say that a man is responsible for himself, we do not only mean that he is responsible for his own individuality, but that he is responsible for all men.

The word subjectivism has two meanings, and our opponents play on the two. Subjectivism means, on the one hand, that an individual chooses and makes himself; and, on the other, that it is impossible for man to transcend human subjectivity. The second of these is the essential meaning of existentialism. When we say that man chooses his own self, we mean that every one of us does likewise; but we also mean by that that in making this choice he also chooses all men. In fact, in creating the man that we want to be, there is not a single one of our acts which does not at the same time create an image of man as we think he ought to be. To choose to be this or that is to affirm at the same time the value of what we choose, because we can never choose evil. We always choose the good, and nothing can be good for us without being good for all.

If, on the other hand, existence precedes essence, and if we grant that we exist and fashion our image at one and the same time, the image is valid for everybody and for our whole age. Thus, our responsibility is much greater than we might have supposed, because it involves all mankind. If I am a workingman and choose to join a Christian trade-union rather than be a communist, and if by being a member I want to show that the best thing for man is resignation, that the kingdom of man is not of this world, I am not only involving my own case—I want to be resigned for everyone. As a result, my action has involved all humanity. To take a more individual matter, if I want to marry, to have children; even if this marriage depends solely on my own circumstances or passion or wish, I am involving all humanity in monogamy and not merely myself. Therefore, I am responsible for myself and for everyone else. I am creating a certain image of man of my own choosing. In choosing myself, I choose man.

This helps us understand what the actual content is of such rather grandiloquent words as anguish, forlornness, despair. As you will see, it's all quite simple.

First, what is meant by anguish? The existentialists say at once that man is anguish. What that means is this: the man who involves himself and who realizes that he is not only the person he chooses to be, but also a law-maker who is, at the same time, choosing all mankind as well as himself, can not help escape the feeling of his total and deep responsibility. Of course, there are many people who are not anxious; but we claim that they are hiding their anxiety, that they are fleeing from it. Certainly, many people believe that when they do something, they themselves are the only ones involved, and when someone says to them, "What if everyone acted that way?" they shrug their shoulders and answer, "Everyone doesn't act that way." But really, one should always ask himself, "What would happen if everybody looked at things that way?" There is no escaping this disturbing thought except by a kind of double-dealing. A man who lies and makes excuses for himself by saying "not everybody does that," is someone with an uneasy conscience, because the act of lying implies that a universal value is conferred upon the lie.

Anguish is evident even when it conceals itself. This is the anguish that Kierkegaard called the anguish of Abraham. You know the story: an angel has ordered Abraham to sacrifice his son; if it really were an angel who has come and said, "You are Abraham, you shall sacrifice your son," everything would be all right. But everyone might first wonder, "Is it really an angel, and am I really Abraham? What proof do I have?" . . .

Now, I'm not being singled out as an Abraham, and yet at every moment I'm obliged to perform exemplary acts. For every man, everything happens as if all mankind had its eyes fixed on him and were guiding itself by what he does. And every man ought to say to himself, "Am I really the kind of man who has the right to act in such a way that humanity might guide itself by my actions?" And if he does not say that to himself, he is masking his anguish.

There is no question here of the kind of anguish which would lead to quietism, to inaction. It is a matter of a simple sort of anguish that anybody who has had responsibilities is familiar with. For example, when a military officer takes the responsibility for an attack and sends a certain number of men to death, he chooses to do so, and in the main he alone makes the choice. Doubtless, orders come from above, but they are too broad; he interprets them, and on this interpretation depend the lives of ten or fourteen or twenty men. In making a decision he can not help having a certain anguish. All leaders know this anguish. That doesn't keep them from acting; on the contrary, it is the very condition of their action. For it implies that they envisage a number of possibilities, and when they choose one, they realize that it has value only because it is chosen. We shall see that this kind of anguish, which is the kind that existentialism describes, is explained, in addition, by a direct responsibility to the other men whom it involves. It is not a curtain separating us from action, but is part of action itself.

When we speak of forlornness, a term Heidegger was fond of, we mean only that God does not exist and that we

have to face all the consequences of this. The existentialist is strongly opposed to a certain kind of secular ethics which would like to abolish God with the least possible expense. About 1880, some French teachers tried to set up a secular ethics which went something like this: God is a useless and costly hypothesis; we are discarding it; but, meanwhile, in order for there to be an ethics, a society, a civilization, it is essential that certain values be taken seriously and that they be considered as having an *a priori* existence. It must be obligatory, *a priori*, to be honest, not to lie, not to beat your wife, to have children, etc., etc. So we're going to try a little device which will make it possible to show that values exist all the same, inscribed in a heaven of ideas, though otherwise God does not exist. In other words—and this, I believe, is the tendency of everything called reformism in France—nothing will be changed if God does not exist. We shall find ourselves with the same norms of honesty, progress, and humanism, and we shall have made of God an outdated hypothesis which will peacefully die off by itself.

The existentialist, on the contrary, thinks it very distressing that God does not exist, because all possibility of finding values in a heaven of ideas disappears along with Him; there can no longer be an *a priori* Good, since there is no infinite and perfect consciousness to think it. Nowhere is it written that the Good exists, that we must be honest, that we must not lie; because the fact is we are on a plane where there are only men. Dostoievsky said, "If God didn't exist, everything would be possible." That is the very starting point of existentialism. Indeed, everything is permissible if God does not exist, and as a result man is forlorn, because neither within him nor without does he find anything to cling to. He can't start making excuses for himself.

If existence really does precede essence, there is no explaining things away by reference to a fixed and given human nature. In other words, there is no determinism, man is free, man is freedom. On the other hand, if God does not exist, we find no values or commands to turn to which legitimize our conduct. So, in the bright realm of values, we have no excuse behind us, no justification before us. We are alone, with no excuses.

That is the idea I shall try to convey when I say that man is condemned to be free. Condemned, because he did not create himself, yet, in other respects is free; because, once thrown into the world, he is responsible for everything he does. The existentialist does not believe in the power of passion. He will never agree that a sweeping passion is a ravaging torrent which fatally leads a man to certain acts and is therefore an excuse. He thinks that man is responsible for his passion.

The existentialist does not think that man is going to help himself by finding in the world some omen by which to orient himself. Because he thinks that man will interpret the omen to suit himself. Therefore, he thinks that man, with no support and no aid, is condemned every moment to invent man. Ponge, in a very fine article, has said, "Man is the future of man." That's exactly it. But if it is taken to mean that this future is recorded in heaven, that God sees it, then it is false, because it would really no longer be a future. If it is taken to mean that, whatever a man may be, there is a future to be forged, a virgin future before him, then this remark is sound. But then we are forlorn.

To give you an example which will enable you to understand forlornness better, I shall cite the case of one of my students who came to see me under the following circumstances: his father was on bad terms with his mother, and, moreover, was inclined to be a collabora-

tionist; his older brother had been killed in the German offensive of 1940, and the young man, with somewhat immature but generous feelings, wanted to avenge him. His mother lived alone with him, very much upset by the half-treason of her husband and the death of her older son; the boy was her only consolation.

The boy was faced with the choice of leaving for England and joining the Free French Forces—that is, leaving his mother behind—or remaining with his mother and helping her to carry on. He was fully aware that the woman lived only for him and that his going-off— and perhaps his death—would plunge her into despair. He was also aware that every act that he did for his mother's sake was a sure thing, in the sense that it was helping her to carry on, whereas every effort he made toward going off and fighting was an uncertain move which might run aground and prove completely useless; for example, on his way to England he might, while passing through Spain, be detained indefinitely in a Spanish camp; he might reach England or Algiers and be stuck in an office at a desk job. As a result, he was faced with two very different kinds of action: one, concrete, immediate, but concerning only one individual; the other concerned an incomparably vaster group, a national collectivity, but for that very reason was dubious, and might be interrupted en route. And, at the same time, he was wavering between two kinds of ethics. On the one hand, an ethics of sympathy, of personal devotion; on the other, a broader ethics, but one whose efficacy was more dubious. He had to choose between the two.

Who could help him choose? Christian doctrine? No. Christian doctrine says, "Be charitable, love your neighbor, take the more rugged path, etc., etc." But which is the more rugged path? Whom should he love as a brother? The fighting man or his mother? Which does the greater good, the vague act of fighting in a group, or the concrete one of helping a particular human being to go on living? Who can decide *a priori?* Nobody. No book of ethics can tell him. The Kantian ethics says, "Never treat any person as a means, but as an end." Very well, if I stay with my mother, I'll treat her as an end and not as a means; but by virtue of this very fact, I'm running the risk of treating the people around me who are fighting, as means; and, conversely, if I go to join those who are fighting, I'll be treating them as an end, and, by doing that, I run the risk of treating my mother as a means.

If values are vague, and if they are always too broad for the concrete and specific case that we are considering, the only thing left for us is to trust our instincts. That's what this young man tried to do; and when I saw him, he said, "In the end, feeling is what counts. I ought to choose whichever pushes me in one direction. If I feel that I love my mother enough to sacrifice everything else for her—my desire for vengeance, for action, for adventure—then I'll stay with her. If, on the contrary, I feel that my love for my mother isn't enough, I'll leave."

But how is the value of a feeling determined? What gives his feeling for his mother value? Precisely the fact that he remained with her. I may say that I like so-and-so well enough to sacrifice a certain amount of money for him, but I may say so only if I've done it. I may say "I love my mother well enough to remain with her" if I have remained with her. The only way to determine the value of this affection is, precisely, to perform an act which confirms and defines it. But, since I require this affection to justify my act, I find myself caught in a vicious circle....

As for despair, the term has a very simple meaning. It means that we shall confine ourselves to reckoning only with what depends upon our will, or on the ensemble of probabilities which make our action possible. When we want something, we always have to reckon with probabilities. I may be counting on the arrival of a friend. The friend is coming by rail or street-car; this supposes that the train will arrive on schedule, or that the street-car will not jump the track. I am left in the realm of possibility; but possibilities are to be reckoned with only to the point where my action comports with the ensemble of these possibilities, and no further. The moment the possibilities I am considering are not rigorously involved by my action, I ought to disengage myself from them, because no God, no scheme, can adapt the world and its possibilities to my will. When Descartes said, "Conquer yourself rather than the world," he meant essentially the same thing.

The Marxists to whom I have spoken reply, "You can rely on the support of others in your action, which obviously has certain limits because you're not going to live forever. That means: rely on both what others are doing elsewhere to help you, in China, in Russia, and what they will do later on, after your death, to carry on the action and lead it to its fulfillment, which will be the revolution. You even *have* to rely upon that, otherwise you're immoral." I reply at once that I will always rely on fellow-fighters insofar as these comrades are involved with me in a common struggle, in the unity of a party or a group in which I can more or less make my weight felt; that is, one whose ranks I am in as a fighter and whose movements I am aware of at every moment. In such a situation, relying on the unity and will of the party is exactly like counting on the fact that the train will arrive on time or that the car won't jump the track. But, given that man is free and that there is no human nature for me to depend on, I can not count on men whom

I do not know by relying on human goodness or man's concern for the good of society. I don't know what will become of the Russian revolution; I may make an example of it to the extent that at the present time it is apparent that the proletariat plays a part in Russia that it plays in no other nation. But I can't swear that this will inevitably lead to a triumph of the proletariat. I've got to limit myself to what I see.

Given that men are free, and that tomorrow they will freely decide what man will be, I can not be sure that, after my death, fellow-fighters will carry on my work to bring it to its maximum perfection. Tomorrow, after my death, some men may decide to set up Fascism, and the others may be cowardly and muddled enough to let them do it. Fascism will then be the human reality, so much the worse for us.

Actually, things will be as man will have decided they are to be. Does that mean that I should abandon myself to quietism? No. First, I should involve myself; then, act on the old saw, "Nothing ventured, nothing gained." Nor does it mean that I shouldn't belong to a party, but rather that I shall have no illusions and shall do what I can. For example, suppose I ask myself, "Will socialization, as such, ever come about?" I know nothing about it. All I know is that I'm going to do everything in my power to bring it about. Beyond that, I can't count on anything. Quietism is the attitude of people who say, "Let others do what I can't do." The doctrine I am presenting is the very opposite of quietism, since it declares, "There is no reality except in action." Moreover, it goes further, since it adds, "Man is nothing else than his plan; he exists only to the extent that he fulfills himself; he is therefore nothing else than the ensemble of his acts, nothing else than his life."

SUGGESTED FURTHER READINGS FOR CHAPTER EIGHT

Bergson, H., *Creative Evolution.*
Bradley, F. H., *Appearance and Reality.*
Dewey, J., *Experience and Nature.*
Leibniz, G. W., *Discourse on Metaphysics.*
Plato, *Timaeus.*
Royce, J., *The World and the Individual,* Vols. I and II.
Sheldon, W., *God and Polarity.*
Spinoza, B., *Ethics,* Part I.
Whitehead, A. N., *Process and Reality.*

Chapter Nine

WHAT IS PHILOSOPHY?

INTRODUCTION

W E have not attempted, in this book, to introduce the student to philosophy by defining the subject, because as a starting point such definitions are either not adequate or not illuminating. If couched in the common idiom so as to be intelligible to a beginner, the definition can scarcely be adequate. Suppose we had begun with one of the popular definitions such as: Philosophy is the search for wisdom, or for the truth, or for the good life. The inquiring student would want to know whether such a search is the exclusive prerogative of the philosopher, or whether the historian and the scientist are not also searching for wisdom and for the truth. He might also ask such embarrassing questions as: "What is wisdom?" and "What do you mean by the truth?" or "What is the good life?" The definition fails to differentiate the enterprise of the philosopher from that of other seekers for knowledge and the truth. But if the definition is to make this differentiation successfully it has to be more technical, in which case it will not enlighten the student since it is bound to contain ideas even less well known than that of philosophy itself. Of this kind are such definitions as: Philosophy is a study of the most fundamental categories such as reality, existence, causality, life, matter, and mind. Since these categories are themselves in need of explanation, they cannot usefully be employed to clarify the nature of philosophy. In fact, it is only by studying how these terms are used that one discovers what they mean. And philosophers do not all use them in the same way.

The student who has read the foregoing pages already knows something of what philosophy is about, by acquaintance with the thoughts of philosophers, both ancient and modern. With Plato and Kant he has studied the nature of right and wrong; with Hobbes and John Stuart Mill he has considered the relation of the individual to society and the state; he has read many interpretations of the meaning of art, science and religion, and their significance for human endeavor. Berkeley's and Hume's investigations into the nature of knowledge, its validity and limitations, have provided, we hope, plenty of food for thought. In one sense, by his acquaintance with, and reflection over, these and other problems of philosophy encountered in this book the student knows what philosophy is. The understanding acquired by this initial acquaintance with the subject would be deepened if we could provide some characterization of the problems of philosophy, which would fit not only those problems and types of philosophy treated here, but also those which we have had to omit due to lack of space. Such a characterization, acceptable to philosophers of all schools, is difficult to accomplish. In fact, it has never been accomplished; and as we shall see, there are reasons for doubting that it ever will be. For every school of philosophy has its own conception of what philosophy is, or ought to be.

I. The Platonic-Aristotelian Tradition

The goal of philosophy, for Plato, is the attainment of wisdom through a vision of the absolute ideas: *beauty, truth,* and *goodness.* Because of his notion that the body, with its passions and earthly desires, is a constant hindrance to the philosopher in the pursuit of his goal, Plato distinguishes sharply the life of contemplation (pure thought) from the active life (in which the body plays the leading role). But how is this vision of the Good to be achieved? How does the philosopher go about searching for wisdom? Plato's answer is that one must try to escape from the sensuous limitations of the body. Socrates even says (or Plato makes him say) that the true philosopher will not only accept death with equanimity, but welcome it as the final liberation of the soul from the body (*Phaedo*).

Some would argue that this is only *one* of Plato's answers. They think it possible to detach this other-worldliness from the rest of Plato's thought and to interpret the attainment of wisdom as a process of discovery and clarification of ideas by the methods of discussion and analysis as explained in the Introduction to Chapter One, and as illustrated in the selection from the *Republic.* An adequate treatment of Plato's theory of knowledge and wisdom, however, would soon become involved in his doctrine of *ideas,*—those forms or eternal archetypes which are, according to Plato, a necessary ingredient in all knowledge. These forms, or universals, have a life of their own, an ontological being which transcends the world of sensible experience. They are the realities of which the things we see and hear and touch are only images or imperfect copies. Human knowledge here and now is only a stepping stone to the apprehension of these absolute realities in and for themselves (*Symposium*). And the soul can only reach those pure and immutable forms, which shine by the light of The Good, if it turns its back on "the twilight of becoming and perishing" (*Republic,* VI). The interpreter of Plato would again be confronted by two distinct and separated realms—the temporal world of change in which our bodies move and the realm of absolute and timeless forms beckoning those who would become true philosophers, that is, lovers of wisdom.

Though Aristotle criticizes the ontological separation of the two realms, he too establishes a dichotomy between theoretical and practical knowledge, and subordinates the latter to the former:

> "It is right also that philosophy should be called knowledge of the truth. For the end of theoretical knowledge is truth, while that of practical knowledge is action (for even if they consider how things are, practical men do not study the eternal, but what is relative and in the present)." [1]

---

[1] Aristotle, *Metaphysics*, Book α.

According to Aristotle, philosophy had its origin when men began to wonder about the world and tried to explain its phenomena. They did this to escape from ignorance; and since their aim was knowledge, he says that the pursuit of philosophy was not for a utilitarian end. This is confirmed by the fact that it was only after most of the necessities of life had been secured that this knowledge began to be sought. A man who is hungry or who cannot find a place to live in peace will find it difficult to philosophize. Philosophy is not desired for any advantage other than that of knowledge itself,[2] and it is Aristotle's view that it alone exists for its own sake. The student will note—and James' essay, "Philosophy and Its Critics," makes this point clear—that in Aristotle's day, when philosophy was not separated from such sciences as physics and biology, the observations and speculations which constituted knowledge in these fields were considered as belonging to philosophy. Although Aristotle says that it is the function of the philosopher to investigate all things, he tends to think of philosophy as a fundamental science, in which man, using his own powers of thought, attempts to discern the nature of being, substance, unity, plurality, causality, change, and other such theoretical notions which are basic to the other sciences. In this investigation the extent of his knowledge is limited only by the powers of his own rational faculty.

The views of Plato and Aristotle on philosophy have had an incomparable influence on human thought for over two thousand years. Their conception of philosophy has shaped the dominant tradition of western thought and their influence continues to manifest itself in the work of contemporary philosophers. However, the traditional view of philosophy has not remained unchallenged. In the sections which follow we shall discuss, first, the pragmatic critique of the position that philosophy is an abstract and theoretical science (Sec. II); secondly, the Thomists' revision of the doctrine that philosophy is an autonomous discipline (Sec. III); and thirdly, the Logical Empiricists' rejection of the notion that the aim of philosophy is to construct a system of "philosophical" truths about a special subject matter (Sec. IV).

II. The Pragmatic Conception of Philosophy

The notion of philosophy as a theoretical science whose goal is the discovery of eternal truths and whose function is to satisfy a natural intellectual curiosity has been challenged by critics with different points of view and for a variety of reasons. It was to be expected that the steady progress of science side by side with the apparent stagnancy and unending conflicts in philosophy should sooner or later lead to a reconsideration of the goal and function of philosophy. This change in our conception of philosophy can be traced back to David Hume, who showed that there are good grounds for doubting the validity of any of the so-called eternal truths or laws of nature which philosophers had been discovering. Kant tried to circumvent Hume's arguments by developing what he called "critical philosophy." Idealistic philosophers subsequent to Kant took their cue from him and it was not until the end of the 19th century that the importance of Hume's arguments was fully realized,

---

[2] Contrast this with Francis Bacon's view that knowledge is power.

when his position was further developed by the positivists and the pragmatists.

Pragmatism, as originally conceived by Peirce, is a method of determining the *meaning* of ideas and of clarifying them. Even William James, who radically altered the doctrine by shifting the emphasis from logic to psychology, refers to it as a method of settling philosophical disputes. However, James expanded pragmatism until it embraced a theory of truth and metaphysics.

> "Grant an idea or belief to be true . . . , what concrete difference will its being true make in any one's actual life? What experiences will be different from those which would obtain if the belief were false? What, in short, is the truth's cash-value in experiential terms?"

In another place he says: "The true is only the expedient in the way of our thinking."

And again:

> "But if you follow the pragmatic method . . . you must bring out of each word its practical cash value, set it at work within the stream of your experience. It appears less as a solution then, than as a program for more work, and more particularly as an indication of the ways in which existing realities may be *changed. Theories thus become instruments, not answers to enigmas, in which we can rest.*" [3]

James is combatting the traditional conception by maintaining that philosophy is a practical venture, not a theoretical science. He has redefined "truth" so that it no longer signifies something independent of human thought which it is the goal of philosophy to discover. For him, the goal of philosophy is the transformation of existing realities.

Though the pragmatism of William James had many loose ends and vulnerable points which critics lost no time in attacking, it had a vitality which could not be argued away; there were many followers and pragmatism soon became a movement. The doctrine has been modified many times since its beginnings over forty years ago, each new exponent presenting his own version of its main themes. But one fundamental idea running through all versions is the stress on the intimate relation between theory and practice. The conception of philosophy as a theoretical enterprise which can be engaged in and understood without reference to the vicissitudes of time and place is constantly under attack by the pragmatists.

From the beginning of the century until his death in 1951, John Dewey developed the philosophy of pragmatism, eliminating many of its early weaknesses and enlarg-

---

[3] All quotations from William James, *Pragmatism,* 1907, italics in original. The view expressed by James in the above quotation has been compared with the following from Karl Marx:

> "The question whether objective truth can be attributed to human thinking is not a question of theory but is a practical question . . . The philosophers have only *interpreted* the world in various ways; the point however is to *change* it." (From Karl Marx, *Theses on Feuerbach,* 1845.)

There is, indeed, a striking similarity here; but there is also a difference. James was interested in clarifying ideas, moulding them to suit human purposes and to serve the end of human satisfaction. Under the fire of criticism he explained that in saying that truths should have *practical* consequences, he did not mean to restrict consequences to those which were physical, but to count mental effects as well. Thus, in saying that a philosophy, to be significant, must ensue in action, he at least sometimes included reflection as a mode of action. The *action* that Marx was interested in, on the other hand, was political and social action, directed toward specified goals; and he proposed to convert philosophy into an instrument for the attainment of these goals.

ing its scope. Freeing himself from the early identification by pragmatism of the *true* with the *useful* or the *personally satisfying,* which occasioned so much criticism of James' doctrines, Dewey arrived at a view much closer to the original pragmatism of Peirce, which is a theory of meaning. The consequences of this theory for the interpretation of philosophy are shown in the following quotation:

> "A first-rate test of the value of any philosophy which is offered us is this: Does it end in conclusions which, when they are referred back to ordinary life-experiences and their predicaments, render them more significant, more luminous to us, and make our dealings with them more fruitful?" [4]

Dewey's conception of philosophy is that it is one phase of the history of culture; and that philosophers, present as well as past, however much they may strive to attain objectivity and to discover ultimate truth, cannot help reflecting a certain climate of opinion—the cultural milieu of their times. Dewey considers it a mistake, in interpreting the history of philosophy, to *dwell* on the question of the truth of doctrines. The main questions for him are:

> "What are the cultural conditions, social, political, artistic, economic, which set the problems for the philosopher and influenced his thinking on them?"

and,

> "What alterations, if any, in the stream of culture were effected by the contributions of the philosopher?"

If this sounds more like a theory concerning the rôle of philosophy in the history of civilization than a conception of the nature of philosophy itself, Dewey's answer is that "there is no specifiable difference between philosophy and its rôle in the history of civilization. Discover and define some characteristic, some unique function in civilization, and you have defined philosophy itself."

It is worth noticing that here Dewey is not saying merely that philosophy is closely interrelated with other aspects of civilization and that its history cannot fruitfully be interpreted when treated in isolation from the cultural flux in which it arose. He is saying more. In the above quotation he is expressing the view that there is not one identifiable feature of civilization, called "philosophy," which can be distinguished from other characteristics of civilization—from which it would follow that, for Dewey, there are no problems of philosophy peculiarly its own.

Dewey is challenging not only the traditional conception of philosophy as theoretical knowledge; he is also challenging the *substantive* conception of philosophy [5] as a specialized discipline with a distinctive subject matter

III. *The Thomistic Conception of Philosophy*

Plato and Aristotle think of the philosopher as one who uses his reason to investigate the most sublime subjects. In this investigation, the conclusion is something to be discovered; the philosopher is not obliged to conform to dogmas of any sort. He is a servant of the truth and of nothing else. The idea that the results of philosophi-

---

[4] John Dewey, *Experience and Nature.*
[5] See Section IV of this Introduction.

cal thinking could be "corrected" by a higher authority, secular or otherwise, would have been strange and odious to them. But there are many today who hold such a view. In the chapter on the philosophy of politics we have referred to the subjugation of philosophy, as of all human thought, to the dictates of a political authority. We shall consider here the view of those who would subordinate philosophy to theology, by deciding in advance what conclusions may not be reached by philosophy.

The position of the neo-Thomists on the nature of philosophy is presented in this chapter by one of their most eloquent representatives, Jacques Maritain. The pervading influence of Aristotelianism on Thomistic thought is, of course, apparent and acknowledged. One need only recall that in medieval philosophy disputed philosophical questions were often decided simply by quoting "the philosopher's" (that is, Aristotle's) views on the subject. St. Thomas Aquinas, who in the 13th century constructed a great synthesis of philosophy and theology which remains to this day canonical doctrine, "actually transferred," in the words of Maritain, "the entire philosophy of Aristotle to the domain of Christian thought." [6]

Although Thomism has been grafted on the roots of Aristotle's philosophy, it develops characteristics quite out of harmony with Aristotle's views by the introduction of a modification in Aristotle's conception of philosophy as a free science. Without explicitly repudiating Aristotle's doctrine, Maritain writes: ". . . although philosophy is, of all human sciences, pre-eminently the free science, in the sense that it proceeds by means of premises and laws which depend on no science superior to itself, its freedom—that is, its freedom to err—is limited in so far as it is subject to theology, which controls it externally." [7] What is the meaning of the freedom here ascribed to philosophy? It means that the philosopher is free to investigate by the methods of rational inquiry, provided that his conclusions do not interfere with the established truths of theology. It is held that the latter, which are received by faith through revelation, cannot be contradicted by a truth of philosophy attained by reason, since both truths have a common source in God.[8] If, therefore, a philosophical proposition appears to conflict with a theological truth, it must be reïnterpreted (or "corrected") so as to resolve the conflict. In holding that the philosopher is compelled to accept these theological "truths" even when incomprehensible to his reason or incompatible with his philosophical conclusions, the Thomists are making a radical departure from the Platonic-Aristotelian view of philosophy as a disinterested search for truth and wisdom.

IV. The Positivistic Conception of Philosophy

With regard to the subject matter of philosophy, several positions can be taken. It can be said, and has been, first, that the subject matter of philosophy is the same

---

[6] Of course, he first "purged it from every trace of error." Jacques Maritain, *An Introduction to Philosophy*, p. 98.

[7] From the selection in this text. Maritain also explains that "the philosopher and the scientist are never entitled to deny the rights which theology possesses over philosophy and the sciences." (Also from the selection in the text.)

[8] Cf. the view of Thomas Aquinas, Selection 45, page 411.

as that of the sciences, or secondly, that the subject matter of philosophy is different from that of the sciences. A third position would be that philosophy has no special subject matter of its own—but that anything can be investigated philosophically. It is this last view, which may be called the adverbial conception of philosophy as opposed to the first two views, which are substantive, that we wish to consider now.

. This doctrine takes many forms. Indeed, the pragmatic conception found in the philosophy of Peirce is one of them. A similar view is expressed by Whitehead, when he says: "No one truth, thoroughly understood in all the infinitude of its bearings, is more or less philosophical than any other truth." But the most radical form of this doctrine concerning the nature of philosophy is to be found among the logical positivists, who are represented here by our selection from the work of one of the founders and leaders of this movement, Moritz Schlick. Others who have helped to develop and clarify the position known as logical positivism, or logical empiricism, are Ludwig Wittgenstein in England, and Rudolf Carnap and Hans Reichenbach in this country.

Philosophy, according to Schlick, is an activity of clarification of ideas by an analysis of meanings; it is not a theoretical science or super-science with a subject matter all its own. The problems of philosophy, on this view, turn out to be either the result of linguistic confusions, or problems of logic or science which have been misconstrued. Understandably, most philosophers have not taken kindly to these views; especially objectionable to them is the logical positivist's readiness to stigmatize many of the traditional problems of philosophy as nonsense or pseudo-problems and then dismiss them.

The idea of philosophy as a search for clarity is an admirable one which we believe should be welcomed by philosophers. But the logical positivists have not made sufficient application of their methods to the traditional problems of philosophy to introduce clarity where there is now confusion. A pseudo-problem is a misconception, resulting either from a confusion of language, or from scientific ignorance, or from some other source. Logical analysis should help to remove these misconceptions, thereby clarifying any real issues which remain. But it is a mistake to assume, as the logical positivists have sometimes done, that because there are confusions of thought, there are no real issues. Schlick does not make this mistake. He contends that "there are some 'philosophical' problems which prove to be real questions." However, his point about them is that they have "no special 'philosophical' character, but are simply scientific questions." Whether these questions are "simply scientific" or "really philosophical" hardly seems worthy of debate, because the issue will turn, in the end, on which definitions of *science* and *philosophy* we wish to adopt. What is important is that the methods of logical analysis can be (and have been) employed for the purpose of clarifying and reviving some of the ancient philosophical issues.

The taunt against philosophy that it is concerned with the same old insoluble problems is no longer valid. Progress in philosophy may be slower than in science; but there is progress. Sometimes such progress must wait for advances in logical and scientific techniques, which have proved useful in helping to solve many of the problems of philosophy. This has happened, for example, in those fields where concepts like infinity, continuity, space, time, and number have played a key rôle.

But the enterprise of philosophy cannot be evaluated solely in terms of solutions given to various problems. Since the content of human knowledge as achieved by the sciences at any period in history is bound to be fragmentary, and since man's intellectual curiosity outstrips his knowledge, he will construct hypotheses concerning the relations of the sciences, for example, biology and physics, psychology and medicine, the natural sciences and the social sciences; he will try to show the relevance of such knowledge as can be acquired, to human values and the ends of life; and he will try, by insight and analysis, to extend and deepen human understanding in fields as yet uncharted. Beginning at the last bastion conquered by the scientists, the philosopher will make his guesses at the riddle, perchance presenting the starting point in the creation of new sciences. This is what is known as speculative philosophy.

There has been considerable debate among philosophers concerning the value and significance of speculative philosophy. At its worst it has been an undisciplined wandering of the philosopher's fancy through worlds of his own creation which have little, if any, relevance to anything actual or even possible. But at its best speculative philosophy can push back our intellectual horizons, revealing unsuspected possibilities which lend new meanings to our old ideas. Some think the greatest value of speculative philosophy lies in the effects it can have on those who pursue it.[9] It would seem that one who had been enthralled by Socrates' discourses on love, virtue, and wisdom, or who had followed Spinoza and grasped his conception of *amor dei intellectualis,* could not help becoming a better man because of his experiences. At any rate, he would be less likely to fall a victim to the myopic philosophies of life and nature which are so often accepted as "truths of common sense" by practical men of affairs and scientific specialists.

But the speculative philosopher has one duty to his readers and to himself which he has not always fulfilled. He should acknowledge frankly the speculative character of his venture and not advance claims that he has by superior insight or special revelations obtained an exclusive preview of the Ultimate Truth.

There are, of course, other views of the nature of philosophy besides those presented here. For, as we have already mentioned, every type of philosophy has its own unique conception of philosophy. Naturalists,[10] for example, hold that the aim of philosophy is to understand and explain the nature of the world and of man by the methods of hypothesis, observation, and experimentation which have already proved so fruitful in the natural sciences. But a Bergsonian would say that one who thus restricts himself to the methods of science can never truly understand nature.[11] The philosopher, he believes, must strive for insights into reality which spring from sympathy and appreciation. Philosophy, according to this view, should be based primarily on feeling, rather than on reason or intellect. By others, Santayana for example, philosophy has been understood in another sense—as a personal expres-

---

[9] Cf. below, the selection from C. D. Broad.
[10] This includes pragmatists and positivists.
[11] Cf. the selection from Bergson in Chapter One.

sion of one's reactions to the world and of his reflections on the value of art, science, and religion in achieving whatever happiness is possible for man. Conceived in this sense, a philosophical system is an aesthetic creation and the categories of truth and falsehood are hardly applicable to it as a whole. Two such systems of philosophy may diverge and we may prefer one to another, without being compelled to reject either. They are not incompatible with one another any more than are different photographs of the same scene taken with different lenses and from different vantage points. Some of the so-called conflicts in philosophy don't need to be resolved because they are not really conflicts. Critics who ask: "Why can't philosophers agree?" might, in turn, be asked: "Why is agreement desirable in philosophy?" What such critics overlook is that while agreement is desirable concerning questions of fact, provided that such agreement has been reached as the result of free discussion and experimentation, in philosophy agreement might betoken nothing so much as a paucity of philosophical ideas. And where, in the past and in our own day, doctrinal uniformity has been achieved by the imposition of authority, philosophy has degenerated, becoming little more than textual exposition, and philosophers have produced few, if any, important ideas.

If the structure of the universe were revealed all at once and in all its aspects to all men in the same way, we might be expected to share a single all-inclusive philosophy. Or perhaps, since in such a world there would be no room for ignorance, there would also be no philosophy.[12] The variety of philosophical systems is due, in part, to the inexhaustibility of knowledge and to the necessarily partial viewpoint of any one philosopher or generation of philosophers. Such variety, far from signifying a sad state of affairs needing correction, as some are suggesting today, is only a natural and desirable consequence of the subtlety of nature, and of freedom of the mind and fertility of the imagination—the fountainhead of all genuine philosophy.

D. J. B.

---

[12] Cf. the selection from Whitehead, p. 558.

61. Philosophy and Its Critics*

WILLIAM JAMES (1842–1910)

The progress of society is due to the fact that individuals vary from the human average in all sorts of directions, and that the originality is often so attractive or useful that they are recognized by their tribe as leaders, and become objects of envy or admiration, and setters of new ideals.

Among the variations, every genera-

* From *Some Problems of Philosophy*, by kind permission of Longmans, Green and Co.

tion of men produces some individuals exceptionally preoccupied with theory. Such men find matter for puzzle and astonishment where no one else does. Their imagination invents explanations and combines them. They store up the learning of their time, utter prophecies and warnings, and are regarded as sages. Philosophy, etymologically meaning the love of wisdom, is the work of this class of minds, regarded with an indulgent relish, if not with admiration, even by those who do not understand them or believe much in the truth which they proclaim.

Philosophy, thus become a race-heritage, forms in its totality a monstrously unwieldy mass of learning. So taken, there is no reason why any special science like chemistry or astronomy should be excluded from it. By common consent, however, special sciences are to-day excluded, for reasons presently to be explained; and what remains is manageable enough to be taught under the name of philosophy by one man if his interests be broad enough.

If this were a German textbook I should first give my abstract definition of the topic, thus limited by usage, then proceed to display its *"Begriff, und Einteilung,"* and its *"Aufgabe und Methode."* But as such displays are usually unintelligible to beginners, and unnecessary after reading the book, it will conduce to brevity to omit that chapter altogether, useful though it might possibly be to more advanced readers as a summary of what is to follow.

I will tarry a moment, however, over the matter of definition. Limited by the omission of the special sciences, the name of philosophy has come more and more to denote ideas of universal scope exclusively. The principles of explanation that underlie all things without exception, the elements common to gods and men and animals and stones, the first *whence* and the last *whither* of the whole cosmic procession, the conditions of all knowing, and the most general rules of human action—these furnish the problems commonly deemed philosophic *par excellence;* and the philosopher is the man who finds the most to say about them. Philosophy is defined in the usual scholastic textbooks as "the knowledge of things in general by their ultimate causes, so far as natural reason can attain to such knowledge." This means that explanation of the universe at large, not description of its details, is what philosophy must aim at; and so it happens that a view of anything is termed philosophic just in proportion as it is broad and connected with other views, and as it uses principles not proximate, or intermediate, but ultimate and all-embracing, to justify itself. Any very sweeping view of the world is a philosophy in this sense, even though it may be a vague one. It is a *Weltanschauung,* an intellectualized attitude towards life. Professor Dewey well describes the constitution of all the philosophies that actually exist, when he says that philosophy expresses a certain attitude, purpose, and temper of conjoined intellect and will, rather than a discipline whose boundaries can be neatly marked off.[1]

To know the chief rival attitudes towards life, as the history of human thinking has developed them, and to have heard some of the reasons they can give for themselves, ought to be considered an essential part of liberal education. Philosophy, indeed, in one sense of the term is only a compendious name for the spirit in education which the word "college" stands for in America. Things can be taught in dry dogmatic ways or in a philosophic way. At a technical school a man may grow into a first-rate instrument for doing a certain job, but he may miss all the graciousness of

---

[1] Compare the article "Philosophy" in Baldwin's *Dictionary of Philosophy and Psychology.*

mind suggested by the term liberal culture. He may remain a cad and not a gentleman, intellectually pinned down to his one narrow subject, literal, unable to suppose anything different from what he has seen, without imagination, atmosphere, or mental perspective.

Philosophy, beginning in wonder, as Plato and Aristotle said, is able to fancy everything different from what it is. It sees the familiar as if it were strange, and the strange as if it were familiar. It can take things up and lay them down again. Its mind is full of air that plays round every subject. It rouses us from our native dogmatic slumber and breaks up our caked prejudices. Historically it has always been a sort of fecundation of four different human interests—science, poetry, religion, and logic—by one another. It has sought by hard reasoning for results emotionally valuable. To have some contact with it, to catch its influence, is thus good for both literary and scientific students. By its poetry it appeals to literary minds; but its logic stiffens them up and remedies their softness. By its logic it appeals to the scientific; but softens them by its other aspects, and saves them from too dry a technicality. Both types of student ought to get from philosophy a livelier spirit, more air, more mental background. "Hast any philosophy in thee, Shepherd?"—this question of Touchstone's is the one with which men should always meet one another. A man with no philosophy in him is the most inauspicious and unprofitable of all possible social mates.

I say nothing in all this of what may be called the gymnastic use of philosophic study, the purely intellectual power gained by defining the high and abstract concepts of the philosopher and discriminating between them.

In spite of the advantages thus enumerated, the study of philosophy has systematic enemies, and they were never as numerous as at the present day. The definite conquests of science and the apparent indefiniteness of philosophy's results partly account for this; to say nothing of man's native rudeness of mind, which maliciously enjoys deriding long words and abstractions. "Scholastic jargon," "mediaeval dialectics," are for many people synonyms of the word philosophy. With his obscure and uncertain speculations as to the intimate nature and causes of things, the philosopher is likened to a "blind man in a dark room looking for a black cat that is not there." His occupation is described as the art of "endlessly disputing without coming to any conclusion," or more contemptuously still as the *"systematische Missbrauch einer eben zu diesem Zwecke erfundenen Terminologie."* *

Only to a very limited degree is this sort of hostility reasonable. I will take up some of the current objections in successive order, since to reply to them will be a convenient way of entering into the interior of our subject.

Objection 1. Whereas the sciences make steady progress and yield applications of matchless utility, philosophy makes no progress and has no practical applications.

Reply. The opposition is unjustly founded, for the sciences are themselves branches of the tree of philosophy. As fast as questions got accurately answered, the answers were called "scientific," and what men call "philosophy" to-day is but the residuum of questions still unanswered. At this very moment we are seeing two sciences, psychology and general biology, drop off from the parent trunk and take independent root as specialties. The more general philosophy cannot as a rule follow the voluminous details of any special science.

A backward glance at the evolution of philosophy will reward us here. The ear-

---

* ["systematic misuse of a special terminology invented for this very purpose."]

liest philosophers in every land were encyclopædic sages, lovers of wisdom, sometimes with and sometimes without a dominantly ethical or religious interest. They were just men curious beyond immediate practical needs, and no particular problems, but rather the problematic generally, was their specialty. China, Persia, Egypt, India had such wise men, but those of Greece are the only sages who until very recently have influenced the course of western thinking. The earlier Greek philosophy lasted, roughly speaking, for about two hundred and fifty years, say from 600 B.C. onwards. Such men as Thales, Heraclitus, Pythagoras, Parmenides, Anaxagoras, Empedocles, Democritus were mathematicians, theologians, politicians, astronomers, and physicists. All the learning of their time, such as it was, was at their disposal. Plato and Aristotle continued their tradition, and the great mediæval philosophers only enlarged its field of application. If we turn to Saint Thomas Aquinas's great "Summa," written in the thirteenth century, we find opinions expressed about literally everything, from God down to matter, with angels, men, and demons taken in on the way. The relations of almost everything with everything else, of the creator with his creatures, of the knower with the known, of substances with forms, of mind with body, of sin with salvation, come successively up for treatment. A theology, a psychology, a system of duties and morals, are given in fullest detail, while physics and logic are established in their universal principles. The impression made on the reader is of almost superhuman intellectual resources. It is true that Saint Thomas's method of handling the mass of fact, or supposed fact, which he treated, was different from that to which we are accustomed. He deduced and proved everything, either from fixed principles of reason, or from holy Scripture. The properties and changes of

bodies, for example, were explained by the two principles of matter and form, as Aristotle had taught. Matter was the quantitative, determinable, passive element; form the qualitative, unifying, determining, and active principle. All activity was for an end. Things could act on each other only when in contact. The number of species of things was determinate, and their differences discrete, etc., etc.[2]

By the beginning of the seventeenth century, men were tired of the elaborate *a priori* methods of scholasticism. Suarez's treatises availed not to keep them in fashion. But the new philosophy of Descartes, which displaced the scholastic teaching, sweeping over Europe like wildfire, preserved the same encyclopædic character. We think of Descartes nowadays as the metaphysician who said "Cogito, ergo sum," separated mind from matter as two contrasted substances, and gave a renovated proof of God's existence. But his contemporaries thought of him much more as we think of Herbert Spencer in our day, as a great cosmic evolutionist who explained, by "the redistribution of matter and motion," and the laws of impact, the rotations of the heavens, the circulation of the blood, the refraction of light, apparatus of vision and of nervous action, the passions of the soul, and the connection of the mind and body.

Descartes died in 1650. With Locke's *Essay Concerning Human Understanding,* published in 1690, philosophy for the first time turned more exclusively to the problem of knowledge, and became "critical." This subjective tendency developed; and although the school of Leibnitz, who was the pattern of a universal sage, still kept up the more

[2] J. Rickaby's *General Metaphysics* (Longmans, Green and Co.) gives a popular account of the essentials of St. Thomas's philosophy of nature. Thomas J. Harper's *Metaphysics of the School* (Macmillan) goes into minute detail.

universal tradition—Leibnitz's follower Wolff published systematic treatises on everything, physical as well as moral—Hume, who succeeded Locke, woke Kant "from his dogmatic slumber," and since Kant's time the word "philosophy" has come to stand for mental and moral speculations far more than for physical theories. Until a comparatively recent time, philosophy was taught in our colleges under the name of "mental and moral philosophy," or "philosophy of the human mind," exclusively, to distinguish it from "natural philosophy."

But the older tradition is the better as well as the completer one. To know the actual peculiarities of the world we are born into is surely as important as to know what makes worlds anyhow abstractly possible. Yet this latter knowledge has been treated by many since Kant's time as the only knowledge worthy of being called philosophical. Common men feel the question "What is Nature like?" to be as meritorious as the Kantian question "How is Nature possible?" So philosophy, in order not to lose human respect, must take some notice of the actual constitution of reality. There are signs to-day of a return to the more objective tradition.[3]

Philosophy in the full sense is only *man thinking,* thinking about generalities rather than about particulars. But whether about generalities or particulars, man thinks always by the same methods. He observes, discriminates, generalizes, classifies, looks for causes, traces analogies, and makes hypotheses. Philosophy, taken as something distinct from science or from practical affairs, follows no method peculiar to itself. All our thinking to-day has evolved gradually out of primitive human thought, and the only really important changes that have come over its manner (as dis-

tinguished from the matters in which it believes) are a greater hesitancy in asserting its convictions, and the habit of seeking verification [4] for them whenever it can.

It will be instructive to trace very briefly the origins of our present habits of thought.

Auguste Comte, the founder of a philosophy which he called "positive," [5] said that human theory on any subject always took three forms in succession. In the theological stage of theorizing, phenomena are explained by spirits producing them; in the metaphysical stage, their essential feature is made into an abstract idea, and this is placed behind them as if it were an explanation; in the positive stage, phenomena are simply described as to their coexistences and successions. Their "laws" are formulated, but no explanation of their natures or existence is sought after. Thus a *"spiritus rector"* would be a theological—a "principle of attraction" a metaphysical—and "a law of the squares" would be a positive theory of the planetary movements.

Comte's account is too sharp and definite. Anthropology shows that the earliest attempts at human theorizing mixed the theological and metaphysical together. Common things needed no special explanation, remarkable things alone, odd things, especially deaths, calamities, diseases, called for it. What made things act was the mysterious energy in them, and the more awful they were the more of this *mana* they possessed. The great thing was to acquire *mana* oneself. "Sympathetic magic" is the collective name for what seems to have been the primitive philosophy here. You could act on anything by controlling anything else that either was associated with it or resembled it. If you wished to injure an

---

[3] For an excellent defence of it I refer my readers to Paulsen's *Introduction to Philosophy* (translated by Thilly), 1895, pp. 19–44.

[4] Compare G. H. Lewes, *Aristotle,* 1864, chap. iv.

[5] *Cours de philosophie positive,* 6 volumes, Paris, 1830–1842.

enemy, you should either make an image of him, or get some of his hair or other belongings, or get his name written. Injuring the substitute, you thus made him suffer correspondingly. If you wished the rain to come, you sprinkled the ground, if the wind, you whistled, etc. If you would have yams grow well in your garden, put a stone there that looks like a yam. Would you cure jaundice, give tumeric, that makes things look yellow; or give poppies for troubles of the head, because their seed vessels form a "head." This "doctrine of signatures" played a great part in early medicine. The various "-mancies" and "-mantics" come in here, in which witchcraft and incipient science are indistinguishably mixed. "Sympathetic" theorizing persists to the present day. "Thoughts are things" for a contemporary school—and on the whole a good school—of practical philosophy. Cultivate the thought of what you desire, affirm it, and it will bring all similar thoughts from elsewhere to reinforce it, so that finally your wish will be fulfilled.

Little by little, more positive ways of considering things began to prevail. Common elements in phenomena began to be singled out and to form the basis of generalizations. But these elements at first had necessarily to be the more dramatic or humanly interesting ones. The hot, the cold, the wet, the dry in things explained their behaviour. Some bodies were naturally warm, others cold. Motions were natural or violent. The heavens moved in circles because circular motion was the most perfect. The lever was explained by the greater quantity of perfection embodied in the movement of its longer arm. The sun went south in winter to escape the cold. Precious or beautiful things had exceptional properties. Peacock's flesh resisted putrefaction. The lodestone would drop the iron which it held if the superiorly powerful diamond was brought near, etc.

Such ideas sound to us grotesque, but imagine no tracks made for us by scientific ancestors, and what aspects would we single out from nature to understand things by? Not till the beginning of the seventeenth century did the more insipid kinds of regularity in things abstract men's attention away from the properties originally picked out. Few of us realize how short the career of what we know as "science" has been. Three hundred and fifty years ago hardly any one believed in the Copernican planetary theory. Optical combinations were not discovered. The circulation of the blood, the weight of air, the conduction of heat, the laws of motion were unknown; the common pump was inexplicable; there were no clocks; no thermometers; no general gravitation; the world was five thousand years old; spirits moved the planets; alchemy, magic, astrology, imposed on every one's belief. Modern science began only after 1600, with Kepler, Galileo, Descartes, Torricelli, Pascal, Harvey, Newton, Huygens, and Boyle. Five men telling one another in succession the discoveries which their lives had witnessed, could deliver the whole of it into our hands: Harvey might have told Newton, who might have told Voltaire; Voltaire might have told Dalton, who might have told Huxley, who might have told the readers of this book.

The men who began this work of emancipation were philosophers in the original sense of the word, universal sages. Galileo said that he had spent more years on philosophy than months on mathematics. Descartes was a universal philosopher in the fullest sense of the term. But the fertility of the newer conceptions made special departments of truth grow at such a rate that they became too unwieldy with details for the more universal minds to carry them, so the special sciences of mechanics, astronomy, and physics began to drop off from the parent stem.

No one could have foreseen in advance the extraordinary fertility of the more insipid mathematical aspects which these geniuses ferreted out. No one could have dreamed of the control over nature which the search for their concomitant variations would give. "Laws" describe these variations; and all our present laws of nature have as their model the proportionality of v to t, and of s to t^2 which Galileo first laid bare. Pascal's discovery of the proportionality of altitude to barometric height, Newton's of acceleration to distance, Boyle's of air-volume to pressure, Descartes' of sine to cosine in the refracted ray, were the first fruits of Galileo's discovery. There was no question of agencies, nothing animistic or sympathetic in this new way of taking nature. It was description only, of concomitant variations, after the particular quantities that varied had been successfully abstracted out. The result soon showed itself in a differentiation of human knowledge into two spheres, one called "Science," within which the more definite laws apply, the other "General Philosophy," in which they do not. The state of mind called positivistic is the result. "Down with philosophy!" is the cry of innumerable scientific minds. "Give us measurable facts only, phenomena, without the mind's additions, without entities or principles that pretend to explain." It is largely from this kind of mind that the objection that philosophy has made no progress, proceeds.

It is obvious enough that if every step forward which philosophy makes, every question to which an accurate answer is found, gets accredited to science the residuum of unanswered problems will alone remain to constitute the domain of philosophy, and will alone bear her name. In point of fact this is just what is happening. Philosophy has become a collective name for questions that have not yet been answered to the satisfaction of all by whom they have been asked. It does not follow, because some of these questions have waited two thousand years for an answer, that no answer will ever be forthcoming. Two thousand years probably measure but one paragraph in that great romance of adventure called the history of the intellect of man. The extraordinary progress of the last three hundred years is due to a rather sudden finding of the way in which a certain order of questions ought to be attacked, questions admitting of mathematical treatment. But to assume, therefore, that the only possible philosophy must be mechanical and mathematical, and to disparage all inquiry into the other sorts of questions, is to forget the extreme diversity of aspects under which reality undoubtedly exists. To the spiritual questions the proper avenues of philosophic approach will also undoubtedly be found. They have, to some extent, been found already. In some respects, indeed, "science" has made less progress than "philosophy"—its most general conceptions would astonish neither Aristotle nor Descartes, could they revisit our earth. The composition of things from elements, their evolution, the conservation of energy, the idea of a universal determinism, would seem to them commonplace enough—the little things, the microscopes, electric lights, telephones, and details of the sciences, would be to them the awe-inspiring things. But if they opened our books on metaphysics, or visited a philosophic lecture room, everything would sound strange. The whole idealistic or "critical" attitude of our time would be novel, and it would be long before they took it in.[6]

Objection 2. Philosophy is dogmatic, and pretends to settle things by pure

---

[6] The reader will find all that I have said, and much more, set forth in an excellent article by James Ward in *Mind,* vol. xv. No. 58: "The Progress of Philosophy."

reason, whereas the only fruitful mode of getting at truth is to appeal to concrete experience. Science collects, classifies, and analyzes facts, and thereby far outstrips philosophy.

Reply. This objection is historically valid. Too many philosophers have aimed at closed systems, established *a priori,* claiming infallibility, and to be accepted or rejected only as totals. The sciences on the other hand, using hypotheses only, but always seeking to verify them by experiment and observation, open a way for indefinite self-correction and increase. At the present day, it is getting more and more difficult for dogmatists claiming finality for their systems, to get a hearing in educated circles. Hypothesis and verification, the watchwords of science, have set the fashion too strongly in academic minds.

Since philosophers are only men thinking about things in the most comprehensive possible way, they can use any method whatsoever freely. Philosophy must, in any case, complete the sciences, and must incorporate their methods. One cannot see why, if such a policy should appear advisable, philosophy might not end by forswearing all dogmatism whatever, and become as hypothetical in her manners as the most empirical science of them all.

Objection 3. Philosophy is out of touch with real life, for which it substitutes abstractions. The real world is various, tangled, painful. Philosophers have almost without exception, treated it as noble, simple, and perfect, ignoring the complexity of fact, and indulging in a sort of optimism that exposes their systems to the contempt of common men, and to the satire of such writers as Vol-

taire and Schopenhauer. The great popular success of Schopenhauer is due to the fact that, first among philosophers, he spoke the concrete truth about the ills of life.

Reply. This objection also is historically valid, but no reason appears why philosophy should keep aloof from reality permanently. Her manners may change as she successfully develops. The thin and noble abstractions may give way to more solid and real constructions, when the materials and methods for making such constructions shall be more and more securely ascertained. In the end philosophers may get into as close contact as realistic novelists with the facts of life.

In conclusion. In its original acceptation, meaning the completest knowledge of the universe, philosophy must include the results of all the sciences, and cannot be contrasted with the latter. It simply aims at making of science what Herbert Spencer calls a "system of completely unified knowledge." [7] In the more modern sense, of something contrasted with the sciences, philosophy means "metaphysics." The older sense is the more worthy sense, and as the results of the sciences get more available for coordination, and the conditions for finding truth in different kinds of question get more methodically defined, we may hope that the term will revert to its original meaning. Science, metaphysics, and religion may then again form a single body of wisdom, and lend each other mutual support. At present this hope is far from its fulfilment.

----

[7] See the excellent chapter in Spencer's *First Principles* entitled "Philosophy Defined."

62. *What Is Speculative Philosophy?* *

C. D. BROAD (1887–   )

It is certainly held to be the function of a philosopher to discuss the nature of Reality as a whole, and to consider the position and prospects of men in it. In a sense Critical Philosophy presupposes a certain view on this question. It assumes that our minds are so far in accord with the rest of Reality that by using them carefully and critically we approach nearer to the truth. But it is still clearer that Speculative Philosophy presupposes a considerable amount of Critical Philosophy. Its business is to take over all aspects of human experience, to reflect upon them, and to try to think out a view of Reality as a whole which shall do justice to all of them. Now it is perfectly useless to take over the scientific, social, ethical, aesthetic, and religious experiences of mankind in their crude, unanalysed form. We do not know what they mean or what weight to attach to various parts of the whole mass till we have submitted them to a critical analytic investigation. Two results follow at once from this consideration. (i) We cannot admit the claim of any system of Speculative Philosophy to be the final truth. The best of them will be guesses at truth, and will be subject to modification as more facts are known, and as known facts become more and more fully analysed and criticized. (ii) We

must always admit the possibility that Critical Philosophy has not yet been carried far enough to make any attempt at Speculative Philosophy profitable.

There is another general point which it seems important to notice. I think that, in different forms, it plays a vital part in such different philosophies as those of Mr. Bradley and M. Bergson, and in the thought of most great theologians, whether Christian or non-Christian. This is the question how far the discursive form of cognition by means of general concepts can ever be completely adequate to the concrete Reality which it seeks to describe. Thought must always be "about" its objects; to speak metaphorically, it is a transcription of the whole of Reality into a medium which is itself one aspect of Reality. We are bound to think of Reality as a complex of terms having various qualities and standing in various relations; because, if we do not think of it on these lines, we cannot think of it at all. With Mr. Bradley's attempt to show that this scheme involves *internal* contradictions I do not agree. But I do see clearly that we have only to compare a tune, as heard, or an emotion, as felt, with any conceptual description which we can give them, to recognize how inadequate every conceptual description of Reality must be to Reality itself. When we can *both* be acquainted with something as a whole *and* can analyse and describe it conceptually, this difficulty is at its minimum.

---

* Part of an essay, "Critical and Speculative Philosophy," by C. D. Broad, in *Contemporary British Philosophy,* 1st series, ed. Muirhead, by permission of The Macmillan Co.

But we cannot be acquainted with Reality as a whole, as we can with a tune or an emotion, and therefore the difficulty is at a maximum in Speculative Philosophy. This limitation of the whole conceptual scheme is one which we must simply recognize once and for all and then ignore. We cannot avoid it in detail, and we cannot understand in outline any other kind of cognition. Since it is perfectly general, it applies equally to *every* system of Speculative Philosophy, and therefore gives us no ground for preferring one to another.

It has been held by many philosophers, e.g., Spinoza and Hegel in the past and Dr. McTaggart at present, that important results about the structure of Reality as a whole can be reached by deductive arguments from self-evident premises. The best general account of such a view will be found in Dr. McTaggart's *Nature of Existence*. I do not think that this view can be refuted; it *is* theoretically possible, so far as I can see. But I am completely sceptical about its practicability. I feel pretty certain that all known attempts to elaborate a system of Speculative Philosophy on these lines either contain logical fallacies, or introduce premises which are ambiguous and only become self-evident when so interpreted as to be trivial. And I have not the slightest expectation that future essays in this direction will be any more successful.

It seems to me that the main value of Speculative Philosophy lies, not in its conclusions, but in the collateral effects which it has, or ought to have, on the persons who pursue it. The speculative philosopher is forced to look at the world synoptically, and anyone who does not do this at some time in his life is bound to hold a very narrow and inadequate idea of Reality. This is a danger to which the natural scientist is peculiarly liable. The extraordinary success of physics and chemistry within their own sphere tempts men to think that the world is simply a physico-chemical system. These sciences, quite rightly for their own purposes, ignore the existence of minds; and scientists are liable to forget that somehow minds have grown up in a world of matter, and that it is by means of their activities that matter and its laws have become known. If a man referred to his brother or his cat as "an ingenious mechanism" we should know that he was either a fool or a physiologist. No one in practice treats himself or his fellowmen or his pet animals as machines, but scientists who have never made a study of Speculative Philosophy seem often to think it their duty to hold in theory what no one outside a lunatic asylum would accept in practice. If we remember that physics and chemistry are simply constructed to unify the correlations which we find among a selection of the sensa of three or four senses, the idea that these sciences give a complete account of the structure of all Reality becomes ludicrous. Thus our inability to explain the facts of life and mind in purely physico-chemical terms is not a paradox to be explained away, but is what might reasonably have been expected from the outset.

On the other hand, the man who starts from the side of mind is equally liable to fail to do justice to the facts. The properties with which physics and chemistry deal *are* very pervasive, and we *do* know them more accurately and thoroughly than we know anything else. And minds *are* very closely bound up with certain bits of matter, viz., our brains and nervous systems, and they *do* seem to have gradually developed in a world which once contained nothing but matter. The characteristic fault of Idealism is to be unable to see the trees for the wood, and the characteristic fault of Realism is to be unable to see the wood for the trees. The great merit of Idealism is that it really has tried to do justice to the social, ethical, aesthetic, and religious facts of the world. The great merit of Realism is that it really has tried to face in a patient and detailed way the problem of matter and of our perception of it. But neither of these activities is a substitute for the other and a genuine Speculative Philosophy must combine the detailed study of the lower categories with the due recognition of the higher categories, and must try to reconcile the pervasiveness of the former with the apparently growing importance of the latter.

There is one thing which Speculative Philosophy must take into most serious consideration, and that is the religious and mystical experiences of mankind. These form a vast mass of facts which obviously deserve at least as careful attention as the sensations of mankind. They are of course less uniform than our sensations; many people, of whom I am one, are practically without these experiences. But probably most people have them to some extent, and there is a considerable amount of agreement between these people of all nations and ages, who have them to a marked degree. Of course the theoretical interpretations which have been put upon them are very varied, and it is obvious that they depend largely on the traditions of the time, place, and society in which the experient lives. I have compared the experiences themselves with sensations; we might compare the common features in the interpretations which have been put upon them with our ordinary common-sense beliefs about matter; and elaborate systems of theology might be compared with big scientific theories, like the wave theory of light. Obviously there remains a further step to be taken, comparable with the philosophic criticism and interpretation of scientific theories about matter. It seems reasonable to suppose at the outset that the whole mass of mystical and religious experience brings us into contact with an aspect of Reality which is not revealed in ordinary sense-perception, and that any system of Speculative Philosophy which ignores it will be extremely one-sided. In fact it cannot safely be ignored. If we count all such experiences as purely delusive, we must explain how such a widespread and comparatively coherent mass of illusion arose. And, if we find it impossible to take this view, we must try to understand and criticize these experiences; to sift away those factors in them which are of merely local and temporary interest; and to see what the residuum has to tell us about the probable nature of Reality. The great practical difficulty here is that those who have the experiences most vividly are seldom well fitted for the task of philosophical criticism and construction; whilst those who are fitted for the latter task are not often mystics or persons of religious genius. It is alleged, and it may well be true, that the capacity for such experiences can be cultivated by a suitable mode of life and a suitable system of training and meditation. In so far as this can be done without detriment to the critical faculties it deserves the serious attention of philosophers; for theories which are built on experiences known only by description are always unsatisfactory.

63. The Aim of Philosophy*

ALFRED N. WHITEHEAD (1861–1947)

The task of a University is the creation of the future, so far as rational thought, and civilized modes of appreciation, can affect the issue. The future is big with every possibility of achievement and of tragedy.

Amid this scene of creative action, What is the special function of philosophy?

In order to answer this question, we must first decide what constitutes the philosophic character of any particular doctrine. What makes a doctrine philosophical? No one truth, thoroughly understood in all the infinitude of its bearings, is more or less philosophical than any other truth. The pursuit of philosophy is the one avocation denied to omniscience.

Philosophy is an attitude of mind towards doctrines ignorantly entertained. By the phrase "ignorantly entertained" I mean that the full meaning of the doctrine in respect to the infinitude of circumstances to which it is relevant, is not understood. The philosophic attitude is a resolute attempt to enlarge the understanding of the scope of application of every notion which enters into our current thought. The philosophic attempt takes every word, and every phrase, in the verbal expression of thought, and asks, What does it mean? It refuses to be satisfied by the conventional presup-

position that every sensible person knows the answer. As soon as you rest satisfied with primitive ideas, and with primitive propositions, you have ceased to be a philosopher.

Of course you have got to start somewhere for the purposes of discourse. But the philosopher, as he argues from his premises, has already marked down every word and phrase in them as topics for enquiry. No philosopher is satisfied with the concurrence of sensible people, whether they be his colleagues, or even his own previous self. He is always assaulting the boundaries of finitude.

The scientist is also enlarging knowledge. He starts with a group of primitive notions and of primitive relations between these notions, which defines the scope of his science. For example, Newtonian dynamics assumes Euclidean space, massive matter, motion, stresses and strains, and the more general notion of force. There are also the laws of motion, and a few other concepts added later. The sciences consisted in the deduction of consequences, presupposing the applicability of these ideas.

In respect to Newtonian Dynamics, the scientist and the philosopher face in opposite directions. The scientist asks for the consequences in the universe. The philosopher asks for the meaning of these ideas in terms of the welter of characterizations which infest the world.

It is evident that scientists and philosophers can help each other. For the

* Lecture 9 of *Modes of Thought*, by permission of The Macmillan Co.

scientist sometimes wants a new idea, and the philosopher is enlightened as to meanings by the study of the scientific consequences. Their usual mode of intercommunication is by sharing in the current habits of cultivated thought.

There is an insistent presupposition continually sterilizing philosophic thought. It is the belief, the very natural belief, that mankind has consciously entertained all the fundamental ideas which are applicable to its experience. Further it is held that human language, in single words or in phrases, explicitly expresses these ideas. I will term this presupposition, The Fallacy of the Perfect Dictionary.

It is here that the philosopher, as such, parts company with the scholar. The scholar investigates human thought and human achievement, armed with a dictionary. He is the main support of civilized thought. Apart from scholarship, you may be moral, religious, and delightful. But you are not wholly civilized. You will lack the power of delicate accuracy of expression.

It is obvious that the philosopher needs scholarship, just as he needs science. But both science and scholarship are subsidiary weapons for philosophy.

The Fallacy of the Perfect Dictionary divides philosophers into two schools, namely, the "Critical School" which repudiates speculative philosophy, and the "Speculative School" which includes it. The critical school confines itself to verbal analysis within the limits of the dictionary. The speculative school appeals to direct insight, and endeavours to indicate its meanings by further appeal to situations which promote such specific insights. It then enlarges the dictionary. The divergence between the schools is the quarrel between safety and adventure.

The strength of the critical school lies in the fact that the doctrine of evolution never entered, in any radical sense, into ancient scholarship. Thus there arises the presupposition of a fixed specification of the human mind; and the blue print of this specification is the dictionary.

I appeal to two great moments of philosophy. Socrates spent his life in analyzing the current presuppositions of the Athenian world. He explicitly recognized that his philosophy was an attitude in the face of ignorance. He was critical and yet constructive.

Harvard is justly proud of the great period of its philosophic department about thirty years ago. Josiah Royce, William James, Santayana, George Herbert Palmer, Münsterberg, constitute a group to be proud of. Among them Palmer's achievements centre chiefly in literature and in his brilliance as a lecturer. The group is a group of men individually great. But as a group they are greater still. It is a group of adventure, of speculation, of search for new ideas. To be a philosopher is to make some humble approach to the main characteristic of this group of men.

The use of philosophy is to maintain an active novelty of fundamental ideas illuminating the social system. It reverses the slow descent of accepted thought towards the inactive commonplace. If you like to phrase it so, philosophy is mystical. For mysticism is direct insight into depths as yet unspoken. But the purpose of philosophy is to rationalize mysticism: not by explaining it away, but by the introduction of novel verbal characterizations, rationally coördinated.

Philosophy is akin to poetry, and both of them seek to express that ultimate good sense which we term civilization. In each case there is reference to form beyond the direct meanings of words. Poetry allies itself to metre, philosophy to mathematic pattern.

64. The Value of Philosophy*

BERTRAND RUSSELL (1872–   )

Having now come to the end of our brief and very incomplete review of the problems of philosophy, it will be well to consider, in conclusion, what is the value of philosophy and why it ought to be studied. It is the more necessary to consider this question, in view of the fact that many men, under the influence of science or of practical affairs, are inclined to doubt whether philosophy is anything better than innocent but useless trifling, hair-splitting distinctions, and controversies on matters concerning which knowledge is impossible.

This view of philosophy appears to result, partly from a wrong conception of the ends of life, partly from a wrong conception of the kind of goods which philosophy strives to achieve. Physical science, through the medium of inventions, is useful to innumerable people who are wholly ignorant of it; thus the study of physical science is to be recommended, not only, or primarily, because of the effect on the student, but rather because of the effect on mankind in general. This utility does not belong to philosophy. If the study of philosophy has any value at all for others than students of philosophy, it must be only indirectly, through its effects upon the lives of those who study it. It is in these effects, therefore, if anywhere, that the

* The last chapter of *Problems of Philosophy* (Home University Library), by permission of Oxford University Press.

value of philosophy must be primarily sought.

But further, if we are not to fail in our endeavour to determine the value of philosophy, we must first free our minds from the prejudices of what are wrongly called "practical" men. The "practical" man, as this word is often used, is one who recognises only material needs, who realises that men must have food for the body, but is oblivious of the necessity of providing food for the mind. If all men were well off, if poverty and disease had been reduced to their lowest possible point, there would still remain much to be done to produce a valuable society; and even in the existing world the goods of the mind are at least as important as the goods of the body. It is exclusively among the goods of the mind that the value of philosophy is to be found; and only those who are not indifferent to these goods can be persuaded that the study of philosophy is not a waste of time.

Philosophy, like all other studies, aims primarily at knowledge. The knowledge it aims at is the kind of knowledge which gives unity and system to the body of the sciences, and the kind which results from a critical examination of the grounds of our convictions, prejudices, and beliefs. But it cannot be maintained that philosophy has had any very great measure of success in its attempts to provide definite answers to its questions. If you ask a mathematician, a mineralogist, a historian, or any other man of learning, what definite body of truths has been ascertained by his science, his answer will last as long as you are willing to listen. But if you put the same question to a philosopher, he will, if he is candid, have to confess that his study has not achieved positive results such as have been achieved by other sciences. It is true that this is partly accounted for by the fact that, as soon as definite knowledge concerning any subject becomes possible, this subject ceases to be called philosophy, and becomes a separate science. The whole study of the heavens, which now belongs to astronomy, was once included in philosophy; Newton's great work was called "the mathematical principles of natural philosophy." Similarly, the study of the human mind, which was, until very lately, a part of philosophy, has now been separated from philosophy and has become the science of psychology. Thus, to a great extent, the uncertainty of philosophy is more apparent than real: those questions which are already capable of definite answers are placed in the sciences, while those only to which, at present, no definite answer can be given, remain to form the residue which is called philosophy.

This is, however, only a part of the truth concerning the uncertainty of philosophy. There are many questions—and among them those that are of the profoundest interest to our spiritual life—which, so far as we can see, must remain insoluble to the human intellect unless its powers become of quite a different order from what they are now. Has the universe any unity of plan or purpose, or is it a fortuitous concourse of atoms? Is consciousness a permanent part of the universe, giving hope of indefinite growth in wisdom, or is it a transitory accident on a small planet on which life must ultimately become impossible? Are good and evil of importance to the uni-

verse or only to man? Such questions are asked by philosophy, and variously answered by various philosophers. But it would seem that, whether answers be otherwise discoverable or not, the answers suggested by philosophy are none of them demonstrably true. Yet, however slight may be the hope of discovering an answer, it is part of the business of philosophy to continue the consideration of such questions, to make us aware of their importance, to examine all the approaches to them, and to keep alive that speculative interest in the universe which is apt to be killed by confining ourselves to definitely ascertainable knowledge.

Many philosophers, it is true, have held that philosophy could establish the truth of certain answers to such fundamental questions. They have supposed that what is of most importance in religious beliefs could be proved by strict demonstration to be true. In order to judge of such attempts, it is necessary to take a survey of human knowledge, and to form an opinion as to its methods and its limitations.* On such a subject it would be unwise to pronounce dogmatically; but if the investigations of our previous chapters have not led us astray, we shall be compelled to renounce the hope of finding philosophical proofs of religious beliefs. We cannot, therefore, include as part of the value of philosophy any definite set of answers to such questions. Hence, once more, the value of philosophy must not depend upon any supposed body of definitely ascertainable knowledge to be acquired by those who study it.

The value of philosophy is, in fact, to be sought largely in its very uncertainty. The man who has no tincture of philosophy goes through life imprisoned in the prejudices derived from common sense, from the habitual beliefs of his age or

---

*[Cf. Chapters One and Five.]

his nation, and from convictions which have grown up in his mind without the co-operation or consent of his deliberate reason. To such a man the world tends to become definite, finite, obvious; common objects rouse no questions, and unfamiliar possibilities are contemptuously rejected. As soon as we begin to philosophise, on the contrary, we find, as we saw in our opening chapters, that even the most everyday things lead to problems to which only very incomplete answers can be given. Philosophy, though unable to tell us with certainty what is the true answer to the doubts which it raises, is able to suggest many possibilities which enlarge our thoughts and free them from the tyranny of custom. Thus, while diminishing our feeling of certainty as to what things are, it greatly increases our knowledge as to what they may be; it removes the somewhat arrogant dogmatism of those who have never travelled into the region of liberating doubt, and it keeps alive our sense of wonder by showing familiar things in an unfamiliar aspect.

Apart from its utility in showing unsuspected possibilities, philosophy has a value—perhaps its chief value—through the greatness of the objects which it contemplates, and the freedom from narrow and personal aims resulting from this contemplation. The life of the instinctive man is shut up within the circle of his private interests: family and friends may be included, but the outer world is not regarded except as it may help or hinder what comes within the circle of instinctive wishes. In such a life there is something feverish and confined, in comparison with which the philosophic life is calm and free. The private world of instinctive interests is a small one, set in the midst of a great and powerful world which must, sooner or later, lay our private world in ruins. Unless we can so enlarge our interests as to include the whole outer world, we remain like a garrison in a beleaguered fortress, knowing that the enemy prevents escape and that ultimate surrender is inevitable. In such a life there is no peace, but a constant strife between the insistence of desire and the powerlessness of will. In one way or another, if our life is to be great and free, we must escape this prison and this strife.

One way of escape is by philosophic contemplation. Philosophic contemplation does not, in its widest survey, divide the universe into two hostile camps—friends and foes, helpful and hostile, good and bad—it views the whole impartially. Philosophic contemplation, when it is unalloyed, does not aim at proving that the rest of the universe is akin to man. All acquisition of knowledge is an enlargement of the Self, but this enlargement is best attained when it is not directly sought. It is obtained when the desire for knowledge is alone operative, by a study which does not wish in advance that its objects should have this or that character, but adapts the Self to the characters which it finds in its objects. This enlargement of Self is not obtained when, taking the Self as it is, we try to show that the world is so similar to this Self that knowledge of it is possible without any admission of what seems alien. The desire to prove this is a form of self-assertion, and like all self-assertion, it is an obstacle to the growth of Self which it desires, and of which the Self knows that it is capable. Self-assertion, in philosophic speculation as elsewhere, views the world as a means to its own ends; thus it makes the world of less account than Self, and the Self sets bounds to the greatness of its goods. In contemplation, on the contrary, we start from the not-Self, and through its greatness the boundaries of Self are enlarged; through the infinity of the universe the mind which contemplates it achieves some share in infinity.

For this reason greatness of soul is not

fostered by those philosophies which assimilate the universe to Man. Knowledge is a form of union of Self and not-Self; like all union, it is impaired by dominion, and therefore by any attempt to force the universe into conformity with what we find in ourselves. There is a widespread philosophical tendency towards the view which tells us that man is the measure of all things, that truth is man-made, that space and time and the world of universals are properties of the mind, and that, if there be anything not created by the mind, it is unknowable and of no account for us. This view, if our previous discussions were correct, is untrue; but in addition to being untrue, it has the effect of robbing philosophic contemplation of all that gives it value, since it fetters contemplation to Self. What it calls knowledge is not a union with the not-Self, but a set of prejudices, habits, and desires, making an impenetrable veil between us and the world beyond. The man who finds pleasure in such a theory of knowledge is like the man who never leaves the domestic circle for fear his word might not be law.

The true philosophic contemplation, on the contrary, finds its satisfaction in every enlargement of the not-Self, in everything that magnifies the objects contemplated, and thereby the subject contemplating. Everything, in contemplation, that is personal or private, everything that depends upon habit, self-interest, or desire, distorts the object, and hence impairs the union which the intellect seeks. By thus making a barrier between subject and object, such personal and private things become a prison to the intellect. The free intellect will see as God might see, without a *here* and *now*, without hopes and fears, without the trammels of customary beliefs and traditional prejudices, calmly, dispassionately, in the sole and exclusive desire of knowledge—knowledge as impersonal, as purely contemplative, as it

is possible for man to attain. Hence also the free intellect will value more the abstract and universal knowledge into which the accidents of private history do not enter, than the knowledge brought by the senses, and dependent, as such knowledge must be, upon an exclusive and personal point of view and a body whose sense-organs distort as much as they reveal.

The mind which has become accustomed to the freedom and impartiality of philosophic contemplation will preserve something of the same freedom and impartiality in the world of action and emotion. It will view its purposes and desires as parts of the whole, with the absence of insistence that results from seeing them as infinitesimal fragments in a world of which all the rest is unaffected by any one man's deeds. The impartiality which, in contemplation, is the unalloyed desire for truth, is the very same quality of mind which, in action, is justice, and in emotion is that universal love which can be given to all, and not only to those who are judged useful or admirable. Thus contemplation enlarges not only the objects of our thoughts, but also the objects of our actions and our affections: it makes us citizens of the universe, not only of one walled city at war with all the rest. In this citizenship of the universe consists man's true freedom, and his liberation from the thraldom of narrow hopes and fears.

Thus, to sum up our discussion of the value of philosophy: Philosophy is to be studied, not for the sake of any definite answers to its questions, since no definite answers can, as a rule, be known to be true, but rather for the sake of the questions themselves; because these questions enlarge our conception of what is possible, enrich our intellectual imagination, and diminish the dogmatic assurance which closes the mind against speculation; but above all because, through the greatness of the universe which philosophy contemplates, the mind also is rendered great, and becomes capable of that union with the universe which constitutes its highest good.

65. *An Introduction to Philosophy**

JACQUES MARITAIN (1882–   )

Philosophy and Theology

Philosophy is the highest of the *human* sciences, that is, of the sciences which know things by the natural light of reason. But there is a science above it. For if there be a science which is a participation by man of the knowledge proper to God himself, obviously that science will be superior to the highest human science. Such a science, however, exists; it is *theology*.

The word *theology* means the science of God. The science or knowledge of God which we can attain naturally by the unassisted powers of reason, and which enables us to know God by means of creatures as the author of the natural order, is a philosophic science—the supreme department of metaphysics—and is known as *theodicy* or *natural theology*. The knowledge or science of God which is unattainable naturally by the unassisted powers of reason, and is possible only if God has informed men about himself by a revelation from which our reason, enlightened by faith, subsequently draws the implicit conclusions, is *supernatural theology* or simply *theology*. It is of this science that we are now speaking.

---

* Chapters VII and VIII, reprinted by permission of the publishers, Sheed and Ward.

Its object is something wholly inaccessible to the natural apprehension of any creature whatsoever, namely, God known in himself, in his own divine life, or in technical language *sub ratione Deitatis*, not, as in natural theology, God as the first cause of creatures and the author of the natural order. And all theological knowledge is knowledge in terms of God thus apprehended, whereas all metaphysical knowledge, including the metaphysical knowledge of God, is knowledge in terms of being in general.

The premises of theology are the truths formally revealed by God (*dogmas* or articles of faith), and its primary criterion of truth the authority of God who reveals it.

Its light is no longer the more natural light of reason, but the light of reason illuminated by faith, *virtual revelation* in the language of theology, that is to say, revelation in so far as it implicitly (virtually) contains whatever conclusions reason can draw from it.

Alike by the sublimity of its object, the certainty of its premises, and the excellence of its light, theology is above all merely human sciences. And although it is unable to perceive the truth of its premises, which the theologian believes, whereas the premises of philosophy are seen by the philosopher, it is nevertheless a science superior to philosophy.

Though, as St. Thomas points out, the argument from authority is the weakest of all, where human authority is concerned, the argument from the authority of God, the revealer, is more solid and powerful than any other.

And finally as the object of theology is he who is above all causes, it claims with a far better title than metaphysics the name of *wisdom*. It is wisdom *par excellence*.[1] What relations, then, must obtain between philosophy and theology?

As the superior science, theology *judges* philosophy in the same sense that philosophy judges the sciences.[2] It therefore exercises in respect of the latter a function of guidance or government, though a negative government, which consists in rejecting as false any philosophic affirmation which contradicts a theological truth. In this sense theology controls and exercises jurisdiction over the conclusions maintained by philosophers.

The *premisses* of philosophy, however, are independent of theology, being those primary truths which are self-evident to the understanding, whereas the premisses of theology are the truths revealed by God. The premisses of philosophy are self-supported and are not derived from those of theology. Similarly the light by which philosophy knows its object is independent of theology, since its light is the light of *reason*, which is its own guarantee.[3] For these reasons philosophy is not positively governed by theology,[4] nor has it any need of theology to defend its premisses (whereas it defends those of the other sciences). It develops its principles autonomously within its own sphere, though subject to the external control and negative regulation of theology.

It is therefore plain that philosophy and theology are entirely distinct, and that it would be as absurd for a philosopher to invoke the authority of revelation to prove a philosophical thesis as for a geometrician to attempt to prove a theorem by the aid of physics, for example, by weighing the figures he is comparing. But if philosophy and theology are entirely distinct, they are not therefore unrelated, and although philosophy is of all the human sciences pre-eminently the free science, in the sense that it proceeds by means of premisses and laws which depend on no science superior to itself, its freedom—

---

[1] Theology is theoretical wisdom, *par excellence* the wisdom which knows God by the intellect and its ideas, that is to say, by the normal processes of human knowledge. There is another wisdom of a still higher order which is a gift of the Holy Spirit, and enables us to know God experimentally and by means of charity. It enables us to judge of divine things instinctively, as the virtuous man judges of virtue (*per modum inclinationis*), not scientifically as the moralist judges of virtue (*per modum cognitionis*). *Cf.* St. Thomas, *Sum. Theol.* i, q. 1, a. 6, *ad* 3.

[2] The philosopher and the scientist are never entitled to deny the rights which theology possesses over philosophy and the sciences. They may, however, be justified in rejecting in a particular instance, not indeed the authority of the Church, but the judgment of an individual theologian, since the individual theologian does not necessarily speak as the mouthpiece of theology, and may therefore be mistaken.

[3] This light is its own evidence and in philosophy is sufficient of itself. But this does not prevent it serving also—in theology, however, not in philosophy—as the instrument of a superior light; neither, of course, does it imply that human reason is not subordinate in its very principles to the First Intellect.

[4] Theology can turn the investigations of philosophy in one direction rather than in another, in which case it may be said to regulate philosophy positively by accident (*per accidens*). But absolutely speaking theology can regulate philosophy only negatively, as has been explained above. Positively it does not regulate it either directly, by furnishing its proofs (as faith for apologetics), or indirectly, by classifying its divisions (as philosophy itself classifies the sciences).

that is, its freedom to err—is limited in so far as it is subject to theology, which controls it externally.

In the seventeenth century the Cartesian reform resulted in the severance of philosophy from theology,[5] the refusal to recognise the rightful control of theology and its function as a negative rule in respect of philosophy. This was tantamount to denying that theology is a science, or anything more than a mere practical discipline, and to claiming that philosophy, or human wisdom, is the absolutely sovereign science, which admits no other superior to itself. Thus, in spite of the religious beliefs of Descartes himself, Cartesianism introduced the principle of *rationalist* philosophy, which denies God the right to make known by revelation truths which exceed the natural scope of reason. For if God has indeed revealed truths of this kind, human reason enlightened by faith will inevitably employ them as premises from which to obtain further knowledge and thus form a science, theology. And if theology is a science, it must exercise in respect of philosophy the function of a negative rule, since the same proposition cannot be true in philosophy, false in theology.[6]

---

[5] It may, it is true, be replied that Descartes's intention was simply to emancipate philosophy from the authority of a particular theological system—Scholasticism—which he regarded as worthless, because it took its philosophic or metaphysical principles from Aristotle.

In reality, however, it was with theology itself that he broke, when he broke with Scholasticism, which is the traditional theology of the Church. And moreover his conception of science implied the denial of the scientific value of theology. In any case the result of his reform was the assertion of the absolute independence of philosophy in relation to theology. (*Cf.* Blondel, "Le Christianisme de Descartes." *Revue de Métaph. et de Morale,* 1896.)

[6] The theory of a double truth, by which the same thing may be true in philosophy, but false in theology, was invented by the mediaeval Averroists, who sought in this way to evade

On the other hand, philosophy renders to theology services of the greatest value where it is employed by the latter. For in fact theology employs in its demonstrations truths proved by philosophy. Philosophy thus becomes the instrument of theology, and it is in this respect and in so far as it serves theological argument that it is called *ancilla theologiae.* In itself, however, and when it is proving its own conclusions, it is not a bond-servant but free, subject only to the external control and negative ruling of theology.

As was shown above, philosophy is from the very nature of things obliged to employ as an instrument the evidence of the senses, and even, in a certain fashion, the conclusions of the special sciences. Theology, considered in itself as a science subordinate to the knowledge of God and the blessed, is not in this way obliged to make use of philosophy, but is absolutely independent.

In practice, however, on account of the nature of its possessor, that is to say, on account of the weakness of the human understanding, which can reason about the things of God only by analogy with creatures, it cannot be developed without the assistance of philosophy. But the theologian does not stand in the same relation to philosophy as the philosopher to the sciences.[7] We have seen

---

the censures of the Church. In various forms it has been revived in modern times by all who, like the modernists, wish to keep the name of Catholics while freely professing in philosophy opinions destructive of some particular dogmatic truth.

[7] This distinction between the relationship of theology to philosophy and that of philosophy to the special sciences derives from the fact that, since theology is a participation of the divine wisdom, the human subject is too weak for its unaided study and to draw conclusions from it is compelled to employ as premises conclusions established by an inferior discipline.

Since, however, philosophy is a human wisdom, at which reason can arrive, though with

above that the philosopher should employ the propositions or conclusions which he borrows from the sciences, not to establish his own conclusions (at any rate not conclusions for which metaphysical certainty is claimed), but merely to illustrate his principles, and therefore that the truth of a metaphysical system does not depend on the truth of the scientific material it employs. The theologian, on the contrary, makes use at every turn of philosophic propositions to prove his own conclusions. Therefore a system of theology could not possibly be true if the metaphysics which it employed were false. It is indeed an absolute necessity that the theologian should have at his disposal a true philosophy in conformity with the common sense of mankind.

Philosophy taken in itself normally precedes theology. Certain fundamental truths of the natural order are indeed what we may term the introductions to the faith (*praeambula fidei*). These truths, which are naturally known to all men by the light of common sense, are known and proved scientifically by philosophy. Theology, being the science of faith, presupposes the philosophical knowledge of these same truths.

Philosophy considered as the instrument of theology serves the latter, principally in three ways. In the first place theology employs philosophy to prove the truths which support the foundations of the faith in that department of theology which is termed apologetics, which shows, for example, how miracles prove the divine mission of the Church; secondarily to impart some notion of the mysteries of faith by the aid of analogies drawn from creatures—as for

instance when theology uses the philosophic conception of *verbum mentale,* the mental word,[8] to illustrate the dogma of the Trinity; and finally to refute the adversaries of the faith—as when theology shows by means of the philosophic theory of *quantity*[9] that the mystery of the Eucharist is in no way opposed to reason.

We must not forget that, if philosophy serves theology, it receives in return valuable assistance from the latter.

In the first place, so far as it is of its nature subject to the external control and negative ruling of theology, it is protected from a host of errors; and if its freedom to err is thus restricted, its freedom to attain truth is correspondingly safeguarded.[10]

In the second place, in so far as it is the instrument of theology, it is led to define more precisely and with more subtle refinements important concepts and theories which, left to itself, it would be in danger of neglecting. For example, it was under the influence of theology that Thomism elaborated the theory of *nature* and *personality,* and perfected the theory of the *habitus,* habits, etc.

Conclusion. Theology, or the science of God so far as He has been made known to us by revelation, is superior to philosophy. Philosophy is subject to it, neither in its premises nor in its method, but in its conclusions, over which theology exercises a control,

---

difficulty, by its unassisted natural power, the human mind should be able to draw from it certain conclusions (especially metaphysically certain conclusions) without employing as premises the conclusions of sciences to which it is superior in dignity and in certainty.

[8] A theory studied in psychology.

[9] An explanation given by cosmology.

[10] Unassisted reason can indeed avoid error on any particular point whatsoever within the sphere of philosophy, but in view of the weakness of human nature it is unable without the assistance of grace to avoid error on some point or other; that is to say, without a special grace or the negative control of revelation and theology it cannot achieve a perfect human wisdom. (*Cf.* St. Thomas, *Sum. Theol.,* i, q. 1, a. 1; *Sum. contra Gent.,* i, 4.)

thereby constituting itself a negative rule of philosophy.

Philosophy and Common Sense*

Before we know things with a scientific or perfect knowledge by reflecting upon them and by their causes, we know them imperfectly (*unscientific knowledge,* the knowledge of everyday life). We must remember that we are obliged not only to begin with this unscientific knowledge of everyday life; we must be content with it to the end, improving it more or less by study and reading, in that enormous number of cases where science in the strict sense is unattainable.

For, so far as the knowledge of secondary causes is concerned, no man can possibly attain, with the perfection required of the genuine scientist, universal knowledge; in other words, he cannot specialise in all branches of science, a contradiction in terms. He is fortunate, indeed, if he can make himself master of a single science. For all the others he must be satisfied with a knowledge which, however enriched and improved it may be in the case of what is known as a cultivated man, that is to say, a man well acquainted with the scientific knowledge of other people, is always inferior to science in the strict sense. But in the domain of first causes, the science of all things is within a man's grasp, for it is precisely the distinguishing character of the science called philosophy to know all things by their first causes,[1] and it is to the philosopher or the sage, the wise man, that we have the right to

* Chapter VIII.
[1] It is therefore obvious what a stupendous delusion is involved in the positivist view of philosophy. Were philosophy merely the co-ordination or systematisation of the sciences, its attainment would presuppose a perfect mastery of all the sciences, that is to say, specialisation in every science, which amounts to saying that philosophy is beyond the reach of man.

apply Leonardo da Vinci's aphorism: *facile cósa e farsi universale;* it is easy for a man to make himself universal.

Ordinary knowledge consists for the most part of mere opinions or beliefs, more or less well founded. But it implies a solid kernel of genuine *certainties* in which the philosopher recognises in the first place data of the senses (for example, that *bodies possess length, breadth, and height*), secondly, self-evident axioms (for example, *the whole is greater than the part, every event has a cause,* etc.), and thirdly, consequences immediately deducible from these axioms (proximate conclusions). These certainties which arise spontaneously in the mind when we first come to the use of reason are thus the work of nature in us, and may therefore be called an endowment of nature as proceeding from the natural perception, consent, instinct, or natural sense of the intellect. Since their source is human nature itself, they will be found in all men alike; in other words, they are common to all men. They may therefore be said to belong to the common perception, consent, or instinct, or to the *common sense* of mankind.

The great truths without which man's moral life is impossible—for example, knowledge of God's existence, the freedom of the will, etc.—belong to this domain of common sense, as consequences immediately deducible (proximate conclusions) from primary data apprehended by observation and first principles apprehended by the intellect. All men, unless spoiled by a faulty education or by some intellectual vice, possess a natural certainty of these truths. But those whose understanding has never been cultivated are not able to give any account or at least any satisfactory account of their convictions; that is to say, they cannot explain why they possess them.

These certainties of common sense,

conclusions of an implicit reasoning, are as well founded as the certainties of science. But their possessor has no knowledge, or an imperfect knowledge, of the grounds on which he bases them. They are therefore imperfect not in their value as truth but in the *mode* or condition under which they exist in the mind.

Of the self-evident truths (*the whole is greater than the part, every event has a cause,* etc.) which are the object of what is termed *the understanding of principles,* and whose certainty is superior to that of any conclusion of science, common sense possesses a knowledge whose mode is equally imperfect, because it is confused and implicit.

Common sense therefore may be regarded as the natural and primitive judgment of human reason, infallible, but imperfect in its mode.

The wholly spontaneous character of common sense, and its inability to give an account of its convictions, have led certain philosophers to regard it as a special faculty purely instinctive and unrelated to the intellect (the Scottish school, end of eighteenth and beginning of nineteenth century; Reid, Dugald Stewart, and in France, Jouffroy), or as a sentiment distinct from and superior to reason (the intuitive or sentimentalist school; for instance, Rousseau, Jacobi, and in our own time Bergson). But in that case it would necessarily be blind, for we possess no other light than that of the intellect or reason. The light of common sense is fundamentally the same light as that of science, that is to say, the natural light of the intellect. But in common sense this light does not return upon itself by critical reflection, and is not perfected by what we shall learn to know as a *scientific habit* (*habitus*).

We must now define the relations which obtain between philosophy and common sense.

Philosophy cannot, as the Scottish school maintained, be founded on the authority of common sense understood simply as the *common consent* or universal witness of mankind, or as an instinct which in fact compels our assent. For it is in fact founded on evidence, not on authority of any kind.

But if by common sense we understand only *the immediate apprehension of self-evident first principles,* which is one of its constituents, we may say with truth that it is the source of the whole of philosophy. For the premisses of philosophy are indeed the evident axioms which in virtue of its natural constitution implant in the mind its primary certainties.

It is important to be quite clear that, if philosophy finds its premisses already enunciated by common sense, it accepts them not because they are enunciated by common sense, or on the authority of common sense understood as the universal consent or common instinct of mankind, but entirely and solely on the authority of the *evidence.*

Finally, if we take into account the entire body of truths (premisses and conclusions) known by common sense with certainty but in an imperfect mode, we must conclude that philosophy is superior to common sense, as the perfect stage of anything (in this case the scientific stage of knowledge) is superior to the imperfect or rudimentary stage of the same thing (in this case the pre-scientific stage of the same knowledge, which is yet true and certain at both stages).

If in common sense we consider not the conclusions which it reaches but the premisses alone, it is still inferior to philosophy in respect of its *mode* of knowledge, but superior alike to philosophy and to all the sciences in respect of its *object* and of the *light* in which it knows. For, as we have said above, philosophy and all the sciences are ultimately founded on the natural evidence of first principles (to which philosophy returns —in criticism—to study them scientifically, whereas the other sciences are content to accept them from nature).

Philosophy studies scientifically the three categories of truths to which common sense bears instructive witness: (i) the truths of fact which represent the evidence of the senses; (ii) the self-evident first principles of the understanding, in as much as it clears up their meaning by critical reflection and defends them rationally; (iii) the consequences immediately deducible (proximate conclusions) from these first principles, inasmuch as it provides a rational proof of them. And, further, where common sense yields to the mere opinions of popular belief, philosophy continues to extend indefinitely the domain of scientific certainty. Thus philosophy *justifies* and continues common sense, as, for instance, the art of poetry justifies and continues the natural rhythms of language.

It is also the province of philosophy to decide what are the genuine certainties affirmed by common sense, and what is their true significance; a function which common sense is incapable of performing, for the very reason that it does not understand, or does not understand clearly, the grounds of its knowledge. In this sense philosophy *controls* common sense, as, for example, the art of poetry controls the natural rhythms of language.

Nevertheless, common sense has the right and duty to reject any philosophic teaching which denies a truth of which it possesses natural certainty, as the inferior has the right and duty to oppose a superior who acts in a manner evidently unjust. For as soon as a truth becomes known to us, by whatever channel, it is a sin not to accept it. Common sense may therefore *accidentally judge* philosophy.

It is related of Diogenes that when Zeno the Eleatic was arguing in his presence against the possibility of motion, his sole reply was to get up and walk. Similarly, when Descartes taught that motion is relative or "reciprocal," so that it makes no difference whether you say the moving object is moving towards the goal or the goal towards the moving object, the English philosopher Henry More retorted that when a man runs towards a goal panting and tiring himself, he has no doubt which of the two, the moving object or the goal, is in motion.

These protests of common sense based on the evidence of the senses were perfectly justified. It must, however, be added that they were insufficient—not indeed to confute the respective theses of Zeno and Descartes but to confute them as errors in philosophy. That would have demanded a philosophic refutation of the arguments adduced by these philosophers, and explanations showing why and at what point they went wrong.

It must be observed that though in itself and in order to establish its demonstrations philosophy does not depend upon the authority of common sense, understood as the universal consent or common instinct of mankind, nevertheless it is dependent upon it in a certain sense (*materially,* or in respect of the subject), in its origin as a human activity and in its development in the mind of philosophers. From this point of view philosophy may be compared to a building, and the great pre-scientific conclusions of common sense (the existence of God, the freedom of the will, etc.) to the scaffolding which nature has erected beforehand. Once the edifice has been completed it supports itself on its rockbed, the natural self-evidence of its first principles, and has no need of scaffolding. But without the scaffolding it could not have been built.

It is now evident how unreasonable

that philosophy is, which priding itself on its scientific knowledge of things despises common sense *a priori* and on principle, and cuts itself off from its natural convictions. Descartes (who in other respects and in his very conception of science concedes too much to common sense) began this divorce, on the one hand, by admitting as the only certain truths those scientifically established, thus denying the intrinsic value of the convictions of common sense, and on the other hand, by professing as part of his system several doctrines incompatible with those convictions. His disciple Malebranche, and above all the *critical* philosophers of the Kantian school, as also certain *modernist* philosophers, have carried this tendency to its extreme, until for some of these philosophers it is sufficient that a proposition should be acceptable to common sense for it to be questioned or denied by science, which would be contaminated by the "credulity" of the common herd, unless it taught the contrary of what mankind at large believes to be true.

Yet the greater the natural strength of a man's intelligence, the stronger should be his grasp of these natural certainties. He therefore who professes to condemn common sense shows not the strength but the weakness of his understanding.

It is now obvious that in its attitude to common sense, as in its solution of the majority of the great philosophic problems, Thomism keeps the golden mean between two opposing errors like a mountain summit between two valleys.

PHILOSOPHY OF ARISTOTLE AND ST. THOMAS

The convictions of common sense are valid, and science is untrue to itself if it rejects them. But the basis of philosophy is the natural witness of the intellect, not the authority of common sense.

SCOTTISH SCHOOL

Not only are the convictions of common sense valid, but the authority of common sense imposing itself as a blind instinct on the mind is the foundation on which philosophy should be based.

RATIONALIST, CRITICAL, AND MODERNIST SCHOOLS

Not only is the authority of common sense incapable of furnishing the basis of philosophy, but the convictions of common sense are destitute of any speculative value.

From all that has been said it is evident what an important part the certainties of common sense play as an introduction to philosophy. Those who are beginning the study of philosophy and about to acquaint themselves with the most recent problems, and even perhaps the most misleading systems, ought to repose an absolute trust in the convictions of common sense of which they find their minds already possessed, for they will help them to rise to a higher and more perfect knowledge, conclusions scientifically established.

Conclusion. Philosophy is not based upon the authority of common sense understood as the universal consent or common instinct of mankind; it is nevertheless derived from common sense considered as the understanding of self-evident first principles.

It is superior to common sense as the perfect or "scientific" stage of knowledge is superior to the imperfect or ordinary stage of the same knowledge. Nevertheless philosophy may be accidentally judged by common sense.

For the purposes of this present outline we need only add that philosophy is not constructed *a priori* on the basis of some particular fact selected by the philosopher (Descartes's *cogito*), or principle arbitrarily laid down by him (Spinoza's *substance,* Fichte's *pure ego,*

Schelling's *absolute,* Hegel's *idea*) whose consequences he ingeniously develops. Its formal principles are the first principles apprehended in the concept of being, whose cogency consists wholly in their evidence for the intellect, and on the other hand its matter is experience, and its facts the simplest and most obvious facts—the starting-point from which it rises to the causes and grounds which constitute the ultimate explanation. Not a whimsy spun out of his own brain, but the entire universe with its enormous multitude and variety of data must be the philosopher's teacher.

And he must always bear in mind that, if philosophy enables the human intellect to apprehend with absolute certainty the highest and most profound realities of the natural order, it cannot therefore claim to exhaust those realities by making them known to the utmost extent of their intelligibility. From this point of view science does not destroy the *mystery* of things, that in them which is still unknown and unfathomed, but on the contrary recognises and delimits it; even what it knows it never knows completely. The wise man knows all things, inasmuch as he knows them in their ultimate causes, but he does not know, is infinitely removed from knowing, everything about everything. Ignorance, however, is not the same as error. It is sufficient for the philosopher that he knows with certainty what it is his province to know and what it is of the first importance for us to know. Indeed, it is better not to know things which divert the mind from the highest knowledge, as Tacitus remarks: *nescire quaedam, magna pars sapientiae.*

66. The Future of Philosophy*

MORITZ SCHLICK (1882–1936)

The study of the history of philosophy is perhaps the most fascinating pursuit for anyone who is eager to understand the civilization and culture of the human race, for all of the different elements of human nature that help to build up the culture of a certain epoch or a nation mirror themselves in one way or another in the philosophy of that epoch or of that nation.

The history of philosophy can be studied from two distinct points of view.

* First appeared in "Publications in Philosophy," ed. by The College of the Pacific, 1932, by whose permission it is here reproduced.

The first point of view is that of the historian; the second one is that of the philosopher. They will each approach the study of the history of philosophy with different feelings. The historian will be excited to the greatest enthusiasm by the great works of the thinkers of all times, by the spectacle of the immense mental energy and imagination, zeal and unselfishness which they have devoted to their creations, and the historian will derive the highest enjoyment from all of these achievements. The philosopher, of course, when he studies the history of philosophy will also be delighted, and he cannot help being inspired by the wonderful display of genius throughout all the ages. But he will not be able to rejoice at the sight that philosophy presents to him with exactly the same feelings as the historian. He will not be able to enjoy the thoughts of ancient and modern times without being disturbed by feelings of an entirely different nature.

The philosopher cannot be satisfied to ask, as the historian would ask of all the systems of thought—are they beautiful, are they brilliant, are they historically important? and so on. The only question which will interest him is the question, "What truth is there in these systems?" And the moment he asks it he will be discouraged when he looks at the history of philosophy because, as you all know, there is so much contradiction between the various systems—so much quarreling and strife between the different opinions that have been advanced in different periods by different philosophers belonging to different nations—that it seems at first quite impossible to believe that there is anything like a steady advance in the history of philosophy as there seems to be in other pursuits of the human mind, for example, science or technique.

The question which we are going to ask tonight is "Will this chaos that has existed so far continue to exist in the future?" Will philosophers go on contradicting each other, ridiculing each other's opinions, or will there finally be some kind of universal agreement, a unity of philosophical belief in the world?

All of the great philosophers believed that with their own systems a new epoch of thinking had begun, that they, at last, had discovered the final truth. If they had not believed this they could hardly have accomplished anything. This was true of Descartes, for instance, when he introduced the method which made him "the father of modern philosophy," as he is usually called; of Spinoza when he tried to introduce the mathematical method into philosophy; or even of Kant when he said in the preface to his greatest work that from now on philosophy might begin to work as securely as only science had worked thus far. They all believed that they had been able to bring the chaos to an end and start something entirely new which would at last bring about a rise in the worth of philosophical opinions. But the historian cannot usually share such a belief; it may even seem ridiculous to him.

We want to ask the question, "What will be the future of philosophy?" entirely from the point of view of the philosopher. However, to answer the question we shall have to use the method of the historian because we shall not be able to say what the future of philosophy will be except in so far as our conclusions are derived from our knowledge of its past and its present.

The first effect of a historical consideration of philosophical opinions is that we feel sure we cannot have any confidence in any one system. If this is so—if we cannot be Cartesians, Spinozists, Kantians, and so forth—it seems that the only alternative is that we become skeptics, and we become inclined to believe that there can be no true system of philosophy because if there were any such system it seems that at least it must have been suspected and would have shown itself in some way. However, when we examine the history of philosophy honestly, it seems as if there were no traces of any discovery that might lead to unanimous philosophical opinion.

This skeptical inference, in fact, has been drawn by a good many historians, and even some philosophers have come to the conclusion that there is no such thing as philosophical advancement, and that philosophy itself is nothing but the history of philosophy. This view was advocated by more than one philosopher in the beginning of the century and it has been called "historicism." That philosophy consists only of its own history is a strange view to take, but it has been advocated and defended with apparently striking arguments. However, we shall not find ourselves compelled to take such a skeptical view.

We have thus far considered two possible alternatives that one may believe in. First, that the ultimate truth is really presented in some one system of philosophy and secondly, that there is no philosophy at all, but only a history of thought. I do not tonight propose to choose either of these two alternatives; but I should like to propose a third view which is neither skeptical nor based on the belief that there can be any system of philosophy as a system of ultimate truths. I intend to take an entirely different view of philosophy and it is, of course, my opinion that this view of philosophy will some time in the future be adopted by everybody. In fact, it would seem strange to me if philosophy, that noblest of intellectual pursuits, the tremendous human achievement that has so often been called the "queen of all sciences" were nothing at all but one great deception. Therefore it seems likely that a third view can be found by careful analysis and I believe that the view which I am going to advance here will do full justice to all the skeptical arguments against the possibility of a philosophical system and yet will not deprive philosophy of any of its nobility and grandeur.

Of course, the mere fact that thus far the great systems of philosophy have not been successful and have not been able to gain general acknowledgment is no sufficient reason why there should not be some philosophical system discovered in the future that would universally be regarded as the ultimate solution of the great problems. This might indeed be expected to happen if philosophy were a "science." For in science we continually find that unexpected satisfactory solutions for great problems are found, and when it is not possible to see clearly in any particular point on a scientific question we do not despair. We believe that future scientists will be more fortunate and discover what we have failed to discover. In this respect, however, the great difference between science and philosophy reveals itself. Science shows a gradual development. There is not the slightest doubt that science has advanced and continues to advance, although some people speak skeptically about science. It cannot be seriously doubted for an instant that we know very much more about nature, for example, than people living in former centuries knew. There is unquestionably some kind of advance shown in science, but if we are perfectly honest, a similar kind of advance cannot be discovered in philosophy.

The same great issues are discussed nowadays that were discussed in the time of Plato. When for a time it seemed as though a certain question were definitely settled, soon the same question comes up again and has to be discussed and reconsidered. It was characteristic of the work of the philosopher that he always had to begin at the beginning again. He never takes anything for granted. He feels that every solution to any philosophical problem is not certain or sure enough, and he feels that he must begin all over again in settling the problem. There is, then, this difference between science and philosophy which makes us very skeptical about any future advance of philosophy. Still we might believe that times may change, and that we might possibly find the true philosophical system. But this hope is in vain, for we can find reasons why philosophy has failed, and must fail, to produce lasting scientific results as science has done. If these reasons are good then we shall be justified in not trusting in any system of philosophy, and in believing that no such system will come forward in the future.

Let me say at once that these reasons do not lie in the difficulty of the problems with which philosophy deals; neither are they to be found in the weakness and incapacity of human understanding. If they lay there, it could easily be conceived that human understanding and reason might develop, that if we are not intelligent enough now our successors might be intelligent enough to develop a system. No, the real reason is to be found in a curious misunderstanding and misinterpretation of the nature of philosophy; it lies in the failure to distinguish between the scientific attitude and the philosophical attitude. It lies in the idea that the nature of philosophy and science are more or less the same, that they both consist of systems of true propositions about the world. In reality philosophy is never a system of propositions and therefore quite different from science. The proper understanding of the relationship between philosophy on one side and of the sciences on the other side is, I think, the best way of gaining insight into the nature of philosophy. We will therefore start with an investigation of this relationship and its historical development. This will furnish us the necessary facts in order to predict the future of philosophy. The future, of course, is always a matter of historical conjecture, because it can be calculated only from past and present experiences. So we ask now: what has the nature of philosophy been conceived to be in comparison with that of the sciences? and how has it developed in the course of history?

In its beginnings, as you perhaps know, philosophy was considered to be simply another name for the "search for truth"—it was identical with science.

Men who pursued the truth for its own sake were called philosophers, and there was no distinction made between men of science and philosophers.

A little change was brought about in this situation by Socrates. Socrates, one might say, despised science. He did not believe in all the speculations about astronomy and about the structure of the universe in which the early philosophers indulged. He believed one could never gain any certain knowledge about these matters and he restricted his investigations to the nature of human character. He was not a man of science, he had no faith in it, and yet we all acknowledge him to be one of the greatest philosophers who ever lived. It is not Socrates, however, who created the antagonism that we find to exist later on between science and philosophy. In fact, his successors combined very well the study of human nature with the science of the stars and of the universe.

Philosophy remained united with the various sciences until gradually the latter branched off from philosophy. In this way, perhaps, mathematics, astronomy, mechanics and medicine became independent one after the other and a difference between philosophy and science was created. Nevertheless some kind of unity or identity of the two persisted, we might say, almost to modern times, i. e. until the nineteenth century. I believe we can say truthfully that there are certain sciences—I am thinking particularly of physics—which were not completely separated from philosophy until the nineteenth century. Even now some university chairs for theoretical physics are officially labeled chairs of "natural philosophy."

It was in the nineteenth century also that the real antagonism began, with a certain feeling of unfriendliness developing on the part of the philosopher toward the scientist and the scientist toward the philosopher. This feeling arose when philosophy claimed to possess a nobler and better method of discovering truth than the scientific method of observation and experiment. In Germany at the beginning of the nineteenth century Schelling, Fichte, and Hegel believed that there was some kind of royal path leading to truth which was reserved for the philosopher, whereas the scientist walked the pathway of the vulgar and very tedious experimental method, which required so much merely mechanical technique. They thought that they could attain the same truth that the scientist was trying to find but could discover it in a much easier way by taking a short cut that was reserved for the very highest minds, only for the philosophical genius. About this, however, I will not speak because it may be regarded, I think, as having been superseded.

There is another view, however, which tried to distinguish between science and philosophy by saying that philosophy dealt with the most general truths that could be known about the world and that science dealt with the more particular truths. It is this last view of the nature of philosophy that I must discuss shortly tonight as it will help us to understand what will follow.

This opinion that philosophy is the science that deals with those most general truths which do not belong to the field of any special science is the most common view that you find in nearly all of the text books; it has been adopted by the majority of philosophical writers in our present day. It is generally believed that as, for example, chemistry concerns itself with the true propositions about the different chemical compounds and physics with the truth about physical behavior, so philosophy deals with the most general questions concerning the nature of matter. Similarly, as history investigates the various chains of single happenings which determine the fate of the human race, so philosophy (as "philosophy of history") is supposed to discover the general principles which govern all those happenings.

In this way, philosophy, conceived as the science dealing with the most general truths, is believed to give us what might be called a universal picture of the world, a general world view in which all the different truths of the special sciences find their places and are unified into one great picture—a goal which the special sciences themselves are thought incapable of reaching as they are not general enough and are concerned only with particular features and parts of the great whole.

This so-called "synoptic view" of philosophy, holding as it does that philosophy is also a science, only one of a more general character than the special sciences, has, it seems to me, led to terrible confusion. On the one hand it has given to the philosopher the character of the scientist. He sits in his library, he consults innumerable books, he works at his desk and studies various opinions of many philosophers as a historian would compare his different sources, or as a scientist would do while engaged in some particular pursuit in any special domain of knowledge; he has all the bearing of a scientist and really believes that he is using in some way the scientific method, only doing so on a more general scale. He regards philosophy as a more distinguished and much nobler science than the others, but not as essentially different from them.

On the other hand, with this picture of the philosopher in mind we find a very great contrast when we look at the results that have been really achieved by philosophical work carried on in this manner. There is all the outward appearance of the scientist in the philosopher's mode of work but there is no similarity of results. Scientific results go on developing, combining themselves with other achievements, and receiving general acknowledgment, but there is no such thing to be discovered in the work of the philosopher.

What are we to think of the situation? It has led to very curious and rather ridiculous results. When we open a text book on philosophy or when we view one of the large works of a present day philosopher we often find an immense amount of energy devoted to the task of finding out what philosophy is. We do not find this in any of the other sciences. Physicists or historians do not have to spend pages to find out what physics or history are. Even those who agree that philosophy in some way is the system of the most general truths explain this generality in rather different ways. I will not go into detail with respect to these varying definitions. Let me just mention that some say that philosophy is the "science of values" because they believe that the most general issues to which all questions finally lead have to do with value in some way or another. Others say that it is epistemology, i. e. the theory of knowledge, because the theory of knowledge is supposed to deal with the most general principles on which all particular truths rest. One of the consequences usually drawn by the adherents of the view we are discussing is that philosophy is either partly or entirely metaphysics. And metaphysics is supposed to be some kind of a structure built over and partly resting on the structure of science but towering into lofty heights which are far beyond the reach of all the sciences and of experience.

We see from all this that even those who adopt the definition of philosophy as the most general science cannot agree about its essential nature. This is certainly a little ridiculous and some future historian a few hundred or a thousand years from now will think it very curious that discussion about the nature of philosophy was taken so seriously in our days. There must be something wrong

when a discussion leads to such confusion. There are also very definite positive reasons why "generality" cannot be used as the characteristic that distinguishes philosophy from the "special" sciences, but I will not dwell upon them, but try to reach a positive conclusion in some shorter way.

When I spoke of Socrates a little while ago I pointed out that his thoughts were, in a certain sense, opposed to the natural sciences; his philosophy, therefore, was certainly not identical with the sciences, and it was not the "most general" one of them. It was rather a sort of Wisdom of Life. But the important feature which we should observe in Socrates, in order to understand his particular attitude as well as the nature of philosophy, is that this wisdom that dealt with human nature and human behavior consists essentially of a special method, different from the method of science and, therefore, not leading to any "scientific" results.

All of you have probably read some of Plato's Dialogues, wherein he pictures Socrates as giving and receiving questions and answers.[1] If you observe what was really done—or what Socrates tried to do—you discover that he did usually not arrive at certain definite truths which would appear at the end of the dialogue but the whole investigation was carried on for the primary purpose of making clear what was meant when certain questions were asked or when certain words were used. In one of the Platonic Dialogues, for instance, Socrates asks "What is Justice?"; he receives various answers to his question, and in turn he asks what was meant by these answers, why a particular word was used in this way or that way, and it usually turns out that his disciple or opponent is not at all clear about his own opinion. In short, Socrates' philos-

---

[1] [Cf. the selection from Plato's *Republic* in Chapter One.]

ophy consists of what we may call "The Pursuit of Meaning." He tried to clarify thought by analyzing the meaning of our expressions and the real sense of our propositions.

Here then we find a definite contrast between this philosophic method, which has for its object the discovery of meaning, and the method of the sciences, which have for their object the discovery of truth. In fact, before I go any farther, let me state shortly and clearly that I believe Science should be defined as the "pursuit of truth" and Philosophy as the "pursuit of meaning." Socrates has set the example of the true philosophic method for all times. But I shall have to explain this method from the modern point of view.

When we make a statement about anything we do this by pronouncing a sentence and the sentence stands for the proposition. This proposition is either true or false, but before we can know or decide whether it is true or false we must know what this proposition says. We must know the meaning of the proposition first. After we know its sense we may be able to find out whether it is true or not. These two things, of course, are inseparably connected. I cannot find out the truth without knowing the meaning, and if I know the meaning of the proposition I shall at least know the beginning of some path that will lead to the discovery of the truth or falsity of the proposition even if I am unable to find it at present. It is my opinion that the future of philosophy hinges on this distinction between the discovery of sense and the discovery of truth.

How do we decide what the sense of a proposition is, or what we mean by a sentence which is spoken, written, or printed? We try to present to ourselves the significance of the different words that we have learned to use, and then endeavor to find sense in the proposition. Sometimes we can do so and sometimes

we cannot; the latter case happens, unfortunately, most frequently with propositions which are supposed to be "philosophical." But how can we be quite sure that we really know and understand what we mean when we make an assertion? What is the ultimate criterion of its sense? The answer is this: We know the meaning of a proposition when we are able to indicate exactly the circumstances under which it would be true (or, what amounts to the same, the circumstances which would make it false). The description of these circumstances is absolutely the only way in which the meaning of a sentence can be made clear. After it has been made clear we can proceed to look for the actual circumstances in the world and decide whether they make our proposition true or false. There is no vital difference between the ways we decide about truth and falsity in science and in every-day life. Science develops in the same ways in which does knowledge in daily life. The method of verification is essentially the same; only the facts by which scientific statements are verified are usually more difficult to observe.

It seems evident that a scientist or a philosopher when he propounds a proposition must of necessity know what he is talking about before he proceeds to find out its truth. But it is very remarkable that oftentimes it has happened in the history of human thought that thinkers have tried to find out whether a certain proposition was true or false before being clear about the meaning of it, before really knowing what it was they were desirous of finding out. This has been the case sometimes even in scientific investigations, instances of which I will quote shortly. And it has, I am almost tempted to say, nearly always been the case in traditional philosophy. As I have stated, the scientist has two tasks. He must find out the truth of a proposition and he must also find out the meaning of it, or it must be found out for him, but usually he is able to find it for himself. In so far as the scientist does find out the hidden meaning of the propositions which he uses in his science he is a philosopher. All of the great scientists have given wonderful examples of this philosophical method. They have discovered the real significance of words which were used quite commonly in the beginning of science but of which nobody had ever given a perfectly clear and definite account. When Newton discovered the concept of "mass" he was at that time really a philosopher. The greatest example of this type of discovery in modern times is Einstein's analysis of the meaning of the word "simultaneity" as it is used in physics. Continually, something is happening "at the same time" in New York and San Francisco, and although people always thought they knew perfectly well what was meant by such a statement Einstein was the first one who made it really clear and did away with certain unjustified assumptions concerning time that had been made without anyone being aware of it. This was a real philosophical achievement—the discovery of meaning by a logical clarification of a proposition. I could give more instances, but perhaps these two will be sufficient. We see that meaning and truth are linked together by the process of verification; but the first is found by mere reflection about possible circumstances in the world, while the second is decided by really discovering the existence or nonexistence of those circumstances. The reflection in the first case is the philosophic method of which Socrates' dialectical proceeding has afforded us the simplest example.

From what I have said so far it might seem that philosophy would simply have to be defined as the science of meaning, as, for example, astronomy is the science of the heavenly bodies, or zoology the science of animals, and that philosophy would be a science just as other sciences, only its subject would be different, namely, "Meaning." This is the point of view taken in a very excellent book, *The Practice of Philosophy*, by Susanne K. Langer. The author has seen quite clearly that philosophy has to do with the pursuit of meaning, but she believes the pursuit of meaning can lead to a science, to "a set of true propositions"—for that is the correct interpretation of the term, science. Physics is nothing but a system of truths about physical bodies. Astronomy is a set of true propositions about the heavenly bodies, etc.

But philosophy is not a science in this sense. There can be no science of meaning, because there cannot be any set of true propositions about meaning. The reason for this is that in order to arrive at the meaning of a sentence or of a proposition we must go beyond propositions. For we cannot hope to explain the meaning of a proposition merely by presenting another proposition. When I ask somebody, "What is the meaning of this or that?" he must answer by a sentence that would try to describe the meaning. But he cannot ultimately succeed in this, for his answering sentence would be but another proposition and I would be perfectly justified in asking "What do you mean by this?" We would perhaps go on defining what he meant by using different words, and repeat his thought over and over again by using new sentences. I could always go on asking "But what does this new proposition mean?" You see, there would never be any end to this kind of inquiry, the meaning could never be clarified, if there were no other way of arriving at it than by a series of propositions.

An example will make the above clear, and I believe you will all understand it immediately. Whenever you come across a difficult word for which you desire to find the meaning you look it up in the Encyclopaedia Britannica. The definition of the word is given in various terms. If you don't happen to know them you look up these terms. However, this procedure can't go on indefinitely. Finally you will arrive at very simple terms for which you will not find any explanation in the encyclopedia. What are these terms? They are the terms which cannot be defined any more. You will admit that there are such terms. If I say, e. g., that the lamp shade is yellow, you might ask me to describe what I mean by yellow— and I could not do it. I should have to show you some color and say that this is yellow, but I should be perfectly unable to explain it to you by means of any sentences or words. If you had never seen yellow and I were not in a position to show you any yellow color it would be absolutely impossible for me to make clear what I meant when I uttered the word. And the blind man, of course, will never be able to understand what the word stands for.

All of our definitions must end by some demonstration, by some activity. There may be certain words at the meaning of which one may arrive by certain mental activities just as I can arrive at the signification of a word which denotes color by showing the color itself. It is impossible to define a color—it has to be shown. Reflection of some kind is necessary so that we may understand the use of certain words. We have to reflect, perhaps, about the way in which we learn these words, and there are also many ways of reflection which make it clear to us what we mean by various propositions. Think, for example, of the term "simultaneity" of events occurring in different places. To find what is really meant by the term we have to go into an analysis of the proposition and discover how the simultaneity of events occurring in different places is really determined, as was done by Einstein; we have to point to certain actual experiments and observations. This should lead to the

realization that philosophical activities can never be replaced and expressed by a set of propositions. The discovery of the meaning of any proposition must ultimately be achieved by some act, some immediate procedure, for instance, as the showing of yellow; it cannot be given in a proposition. Philosophy, the "pursuit of meaning," therefore cannot possibly consist of propositions; it cannot be a science. The pursuit of meaning consequently is nothing but a sort of mental activity.

Our conclusion is that philosophy was misunderstood when it was thought that philosophical results could be expressed in propositions, and that there could be a system of philosophy consisting of a system of propositions which would represent the answers to "philosophical" questions. There are no specific "philosophical" truths which would contain the solution of specific "philosophical" problems, but philosophy has the task of finding the meaning of all problems and their solutions. It must be defined as the activity of finding meaning.

Philosophy is an activity, not a science, but this activity, of course, is at work in every single science continually, because before the sciences can discover the truth of falsity of a proposition they have to get at the meaning first. And sometimes in the course of their work they are surprised to find, by the contradictory results at which they arrive, that they have been using words without a perfectly clear meaning, and then they will have to turn to the philosophical activity of clarification, and they cannot go on with the pursuit of truth before the pursuit of meaning has been successful. In this way philosophy is an extremely important factor within science and it very well deserves to bear the name of "The Queen of Sciences."

The Queen of Sciences is not itself a science. It is an activity which is needed by all scientists and pervades all their other activities. But all real problems are scientific questions, there are no others.

And what was the matter with those great questions that have been looked upon—or rather looked up to—as specific "philosophical problems" for so many centuries? Here we must distinguish two cases. In the first place, there are a great many questions which look like questions because they are formed according to a certain grammatical order but which nevertheless are not real questions, since it can easily be shown that the words, as they are put together, do not make logical sense.

If I should ask, for instance: "Is blue more identical than music?" you would see immediately that there is no meaning in this sentence, although it does not violate the rules of English grammar. The sentence is not a question at all, but just a series of words. Now, a careful analysis shows that this is the case with most so-called philosophical problems. They look like questions and it is very difficult to recognize them as nonsensical but logical analysis proves them none the less to be merely some kind of confusion of words. After this has been found out the question itself disappears and we are perfectly peaceful in our philosophical minds; we know that there can be no answers because there were no questions, the problems do not exist any longer.

In the second place, there are some "philosophical" problems which prove to be real questions. But of these it can always be shown by proper analysis that they are capable of being solved by the methods of science although we may not be able to apply these methods at present for merely technical reasons. We can at least say what would have to be done in order to answer the question even if we cannot actually do it with the means at our disposal. In other words: problems of this kind have no special "philosophical" character, but are simply sci-

entific questions. They are always answerable in principle, if not in practice, and the answer can be given only by scientific investigation.

Thus the fate of all "philosophical problems" is this: Some of them will disappear by being shown to be mistakes and misunderstandings of our language and the others will be found to be ordinary scientific questions in disguise. These remarks, I think, determine the whole future of philosophy.

Several great philosophers have recognized the essence of philosophical thinking with comparative clarity, although they have given no elaborate expression to it. Kant, e. g. used to say in his lectures that philosophy cannot be taught. However, if it were a science such as geology or astronomy, why then should it not be taught? It would then, in fact, be quite possible to teach it. Kant therefore had some kind of a suspicion that it was not a science when he stated "The only thing I can teach is philosophizing." By using the verb and rejecting the noun in this connection Kant indicated clearly, though almost involuntarily, the peculiar character of philosophy as an activity, thereby to a certain extent contradicting his books, in which he tries to build up philosophy after the manner of a scientific system.

A similar instance of the same insight is afforded by Leibniz. When he founded the Prussian Academy of Science in Berlin and sketched out the plans for its constitution, he assigned a place in it to all the sciences but Philosophy was not one of them. Leibniz found no place for philosophy in the system of the sciences because he was evidently aware that it is not a pursuit of a particular kind of truth, but an activity that must pervade every search for truth.

The view which I am advocating has at the present time been most clearly expressed by Ludwig Wittgenstein; he states his point in these sentences: "The object of philosophy is the logical clarification of thoughts. Philosophy is not a theory but an activity. The result of philosophy is not a number of 'philosophical propositions,' but to make propositions clear." This is exactly the view which I have been trying to explain here.

We can now understand historically why philosophy could be regarded as a very general science: it was misunderstood in this way because the "meaning" of propositions might seem to be something very "general," since in some way it forms the foundation of all discourse. We can also understand historically why in ancient times philosophy was identical with science: this was because at that time all the concepts which were used in the description of the world were extremely vague. The task of science was determined by the fact that there were no clear concepts. They had to be clarified by slow development, the chief endeavor of scientific investigation had to be directed towards this clarification, i. e. it had to be philosophical, no distinction could be made between science and philosophy.

At the present time we also find facts which prove the truth of our statements. In our day certain specific fields of study such as ethics and esthetics are called "philosophical" and are supposed to form part of philosophy. However, philosophy, being an activity, is a unit which cannot be divided into parts or independent disciplines. Why, then, are these pursuits called philosophy? Because they are only at the beginnings of the scientific stage; and I think this is true to a certain extent also of psychology. Ethics and esthetics certainly do not yet possess sufficiently clear concepts, most of their work is still devoted to clarifying them, and therefore it may justly be called philosophical. But in the future they will, of course, become part of the great system of the sciences.

It is my hope that the philosophers of the future will see that it is impossible

for them to adopt, even in outward appearance, the methods of the scientists. Most books on philosophy seem to be, I must confess, ridiculous when judged from the most elevated point of view. They have all the appearance of being extremely scientific books because they seem to use the scientific language. However, the finding of meaning cannot be done in the same way as the finding of truth. This difference will come out much more clearly in the future. There is a good deal of truth in the way in which Schopenhauer (although his own thinking seems to me to be very imperfect indeed) describes the contrast between the real philosopher and the academic scholar who regards philosophy as a subject of scientific pursuit. Schopenhauer had a very clear instinct when he spoke disparagingly of the "professorial philosophy of the professors of philosophy." His opinion was that one should not try to teach philosophy at all but only the history of philosophy and logic; and a good deal may be said in favor of this view.

I hope I have not been misunderstood as though I were advocating an actual separation of scientific and philosophical work. On the contrary, in most cases future philosophers will have to be scientists because it will be necessary for them to have a certain subject matter on which to work—and they will find cases of confused or vague meaning particularly in the foundations of the sciences. But, of course, clarification of meaning will be needed very badly also in a great many questions with which we are concerned in our ordinary human life. Some thinkers, and perhaps some of the strongest minds among them, may be especially gifted in this practical field. In such instances, the philosopher may not have to be a scientist—but in all cases he will have to be a man of deep understanding. In short he will have to be a wise man.

I am convinced that our view of the

nature of philosophy will be generally adopted in the future; and the consequence will be that it will no longer be attempted to teach philosophy as a system. We shall teach the special sciences and their history in the true philosophical spirit of searching for clarity and, by doing this, we shall develop the philosophical mind of future generations. This is all we can do, but it will be a great step in the mental progress of our race.

SUGGESTED FURTHER READINGS FOR CHAPTER NINE

Aristotle, *Metaphysics*, 980a-983b (Bk. A).

Blanshard, Brand; Ducasse, Curt J.; Hendel, Charles W.; Murphy, Arthur E.; and Otto, Max C., *Philosophy in American Education, Its Tasks and Opportunities*.

Cohen, M. R., "Vision and Technique in Philosophy," in *The Faith of a Liberal*, p. 365-391.

Dewey, John, *Intelligence in the Modern World*, Modern Library (ed. Ratner), Ch. I.

Edman, Irwin, *Four Ways of Philosophy*.

Plato, *Republic*, Bk. VI.

Spinoza, Benedict, *On the Improvement of the Understanding* (also see the selection in this text, Chapter Two).

Whitehead, Alfred N., *Adventures of Ideas*.

Wittgenstein, L., *Philosophical Investigations*.

INDEX

Index